JUNIOR ENGINEER

Computer Based Test (CBT)-II 2019

Chapter-Wise & Year-Wise
Solved Papers
(2014 & 2015)
(30 Sets)

Civil & Allied Engineering

CL MEDIA (P) LTD.

Edition : 2019

© **PUBLISHER**

No part of this book may be reproduced in a retrieval system or transmitted, in any form or by any means, electronics, mechanical, photocopying, recording, scanning and or without the written permission of the publisher.

ISBN : **978-93-89310-18-4**

Typeset by : *CL Media DTP Unit*

Administrative and Production Offices

Published by : **CL Media (P) Ltd.**

A-45, Mohan Cooperative Industrial Area, Near Mohan Estate Metro Station, New Delhi - 110044

Marketed by : **G.K. Publications (P) Ltd.**

A-45, Mohan Cooperative Industrial Area, Near Mohan Estate Metro Station, New Delhi - 110044

For product information :

Visit ***www.gkpublications.com*** or email to ***gkp@gkpublications.com***

Preface

Railway Recruitment Board (RRB) Junior Engineer Examination 2019 is a combined two-stage examination followed by Document Verification conducted by the respective RRBs for recruitment of Junior Engineer in Indian Railways (IR). In every two years, a large number of candidates appear for this exam, competing for a limited number of posts. Thus RRB(JE) is considered one of the most sought exams in India due to its low selection ratio and technical nature.

Unlike before, the RRB(JE) 2019 exam pattern and syllabus has been completely changed. The old pattern consisted of single stage examination wherein the candidates were allotted departments in Indian Railways after clearing the exam. But the revised pattern includes two stages – CBT-I and CBT-II followed by document verification, the candidate is required to qualify each stage in order to move on to the next stage. The prelims stage includes General Intelligence and Reasoning, Quantitative Aptitude, General Science and General Awareness. Here the CBT-I is common for all the branches. The second stage, CBT-II is of the objective type to test the technical ability of the respective engineering discipline. This book is for CBT-II, prepared as per the latest pattern and trend of the examination. This is solely a question bank so as to prepare students for the examination in a confident manner.

GK Publications has been the "publisher of choice" to students preparing for GATE, ESE and other technical test prep examinations in the country. GKP's RRB(JE) 2019 series provides a wide range of study material which is classified into guides and objective solved paper books to simplify the entire preparation. These books have been thoroughly updated as per the latest pattern and syllabus to provide everything you need to perfect your score.

GKP has also launched an android app to provide you with an update on all upcoming vacancies in the technical segment and it also has a lot of added content to aid your preparation.

We hope this little effort of ours will be helpful in achieving your dreams. If you have any suggestions for improvement of this book, you can write to us at gkp@gkpublications.com.

All the Best!

Team GKP

Contents

SYLLABUS

RECRUITMENT PROCESS

Only single online application *{common to all the notified posts in opted RRB - Junior Engineer (JE), Junior Engineer (Information Technology) [JE(IT)], Depot Material Superintendant (DMS) and Chemical & Metallurgical Assistant (CMA)}* *has to be submitted by the candidate through the link provided on the official website of RRBs.*

The entire recruitment process shall involve, 1st stage Computer Based Test (CBT), 2nd stage CBT, and Document Verification/Medical Examination as applicable. Selection is made strictly as per merit, on the basis of CBTs.

The date, time and venue for all the activities viz CBTs and DV or any other additional activity as applicable shall be fixed by the RRB and shall be intimated to the eligible candidates in due course. Request for postponement of any of the above activity or for change of venue, date and shift will not be entertained under any circumstances.

2nd Stage CBT

Short listing of Candidates for the 2nd Stage CBT exam shall be based on the normalized marks obtained by them in the 1st Stage CBT Exam. Total number of candidates to be shortlisted for 2nd Stage shall be 15 times the community wise total vacancy of Posts notified against the RRB as per their merit in 1st Stage CBT. However, Railways reserve the right to increase/decrease this limit in total or for any specific category(s) as required to ensure availability of adequate candidates for all the notified posts.

Duration   :   120 minutes *(160 Minutes for eligible PwBD candidates accompanied with Scribe)*

No. of Questions   :   150

Syllabus

The Questions will be of objective type with multiple choices and are likely to include questions pertaining to General Awareness, Physics and Chemistry, Basics of Computers and Applications, Basics of Environment and Pollution Control and Technical abilities for the post. The syllabus for General Awareness, Physics and Chemistry, Basics of Computers and Applications, Basics of Environment and Pollution Control is common for all notified posts under this CEN as detailed below:-

a) General Awareness

Knowledge of Current affairs, Indian geography, culture and history of India including freedom struggle, Indian Polity and constitution, Indian Economy, Environmental issues concerning India and the World, Sports, General scientific and technological developments etc.

b) Physics and Chemistry

Up to 10th standard CBSE syllabus.

c) Basics of Computers and Applications

Architecture of Computers; input and Output devices; Storage devices, Networking, Operating System like Windows, Unix, Linux; MS Office; Various data representation; Internet and Email; Websites & Web Browsers; Computer Virus.

d) Basics of Environment and Pollution Control:

Basics of Environment; Adverse effect of environmental pollution and control strategies; Air, water and Noise pollution, their effect and control; Waste Management, Global warming; Acid rain; Ozone depletion.

e) Technical Abilities:

The educational qualifications mentioned against each post shown in Annexure-A, have been grouped into different exam groups as below. Questions on the Technical abilities will be framed in the syllabus defined for various Exam Groups.

The section wise Number of questions and marks are as below :

Subjects	No. of Questions Stage-II	Marks for each Section Stage-II
General Awareness	15	15
Physics & Chemistry	15	15
Basics of Computers and Applications	10	10
Basics of Environment and Pollution		
Control	10	10
Technical Abilities	100	100
Total	150	150
Time in Minutes	120	

The section wise distribution given in the above table is only indicative and there may be some variations in the actual question papers.

Minimum percentage of marks for eligibility in various categories: UR -40%, OBC-30%, SC-30%, ST -25%. This percentage of marks for eligibility may be relaxed by 2% for PwBD candidates, in case of shortage of PwBD candidates against vacancies reserved for them.

Virtual calculator will be made available on the Computer Monitor during 2nd Stage CBT.

Discipline Mapping Tables:-

(I)

Sl. No.	Three years Diploma in Engineering or Bachelor's Degree in Engineering/Technology	Exam Group
1.	Mechanical Engineering Production Engineering Automobile Engineering Manufacturing Engineering Mechatronics Engineering Industrial Engineering Machining Engineering Tools and Machining Engineering Tools and Die Making Engineering Combination of any sub stream of basic streams of above disciplines	Mechanical and Allied Engineering
2.	Electrical Engineering Combination of any sub stream of basic streams of Electrical Engineering	Electrical and Allied Engineering
3.	Electronics Engineering Instrumentation and Control Engineering Communication Engineering Computer Science and Engineering Computer Engineering Computer Science Information Technology Combination of sub streams of basic streams of above disciplines.	Electronics and Allied Engineering

4.	Civil Engineering Combination of any sub stream of basic streams of Civil Engineering B.Sc., in Civil Engineering of 3years duration	Civil and Allied Engineering
5.	Printing Technology/Engineering	Printing Technology
(II)		
Sl. No.	**Educational Qualifications**	**Exam Group**
1.	B.Sc., Chemistry and Physics	CMA
(III)		
Sl. No.	**Educational Qualifications**	**Exam Group**
1.	BE/B.Tech., (Computer Science) BE/B.Tech., (Information Technology) PGDCA B.Sc. Computer Science BCA DOEACC "B" Level Course of 3 years duration or equivalent	Computer Science and Information Technology

Civil & Allied Engineering

1. Engineering Mechanics

Force (resolution of force, moment of force, force system, composition of forces), Equilibrium, Friction, Centroid and Center of gravity, Simple machines.

2. Building Construction

Building components (substructure, superstructure), type of structure (load bearing, framed and composite structures).

3. Building Materials

Masonry materials (stones, bricks, and mortars), Timber and miscellaneous materials (glass, plastic, fiber, aluminum steel, galvanized iron, bitumen, PVC, CPVC, and PPF).

4. Construction of Substructure

Job layout, earthwork, foundation (types, dewatering, coffer dams, bearing capacity).

5. Construction of Superstructure

Stone masonry, brick masonry, Hollow concrete block masonry, composite masonry, cavity wall, doors and windows, vertical communication (stairs, lifts, escalators), scaffolding and shoring.

6. Building Finishes

Floors (finishes, process of laying), walls (plastering, pointing, painting) and roofs (roofing materials including RCC).

7. Building Maintenance

Cracks (causes, type, repairs- grouting, guniting, epoxy etc.), settlement (causes and remedial measures), and re-baring techniques.

8. Building Drawing

Conventions (type of lines, symbols), planning of building (principles of planning for residential and public buildings, rules and byelaws), drawings (plan, elevation, section, site plan, location plan, foundation plan, working drawing), perspective drawing.

9. Concrete Technology

Properties of various types/grades of cement, properties of coarse and fine aggregates, properties of concrete (water cement ratio, properties of fresh and hardened concrete), Concrete mix design, testing of concrete, quality control of concrete (batching, formwork, transportation, placing, compaction, curing, waterproofing), extreme weather concreting and chemical admixtures, properties of special concrete (ready mix, RCC, pre-stressed, fiber reinforced, precast, high performance).

10. Surveying

Types of survey, chain and cross staff survey (principle, ranging, triangulation, chaining, errors, finding area), compass survey (principle, bearing of line, prismatic compass, traversing, local attraction, calculation of bearings, angles and local attraction) leveling (dumpy level, recording in level book, temporary adjustment, methods of reduction of levels, classification of leveling, tilting level, auto level, sources of errors, precautions and difficulties in leveling), contouring (contour interval, characteristics, method of locating, interpolation, establishing grade contours, uses of contour maps), area and volume measurements, plane table survey (principles, setting, method), theodolite survey (components, adjustments, measurements, traversing), Tacheometric survey, curves (types, setting out), advanced survey equipment, aerial survey and remote sensing.

11. Computer Aided Design

CAD Software (AutoCAD, Auto Civil, 3D Max etc.), CAD commands, generation of plan, elevation, section, site plan, area statement, 3D view.

12. Geo Technical Engineering

Application of Geo Technical Engineering in design of foundation, pavement, earth retaining structures, earthen dams etc., physical properties of soil, permeability of soil and seepage analysis, shear strength of soil, bearing capacity of soil, compaction and stabilization of soil, site investigation and sub soil exploration.

13. Hydraulics

Properties of fluid, hydrostatic pressure, measurement of liquid pressure in pipes, fundamentals of fluid flow, flow of liquid through pipes, flow through open channel, flow measuring devices, hydraulic machines.

14. Irrigation Engineering

Hydrology, investigation and reservoir planning, percolation tanks, diversion head works.

15. Mechanics of Structures

Stress and strain, shear force and bending moment, moment of inertia, stresses in beams, analysis of trusses, strain energy.

16. Theory of Structures

Direct and bending stresses, slope and deflection, fixed beam, continuous beam, moment distribution method, columns.

17. Design of Concrete Structures

Working Stress method, Limit State method, analysis and design of singly reinforced and doubly reinforced sections, shear, bond and development length, analysis and design of T Beam, slab, axially loaded column and footings.

18. Design of Steel Structures

Types of sections, grades of steel, strength characteristics, IS Code, Connections, Design of tension and compression members, steel roof truss, beams, column bases.

19. Transportation Engineering

Railway Engineering (alignment and gauges, permanent way, railway track geometrics, branching of tracks, stations and yards, track maintenance), Bridge engineering (site selection, investigation, component parts of bridge, permanent and temporary bridges, inspection and maintenance), Tunnel engineering (classification, shape and sizes, tunnel investigation and surveying, method of tunneling in various strata, precautions, equipment, explosives, lining and ventilation).

20. Highway Engineering

Road Engineering, investigation for road project, geometric design of highways, construction of road pavements and materials, traffic engineering, hill roads, drainage of roads, maintenance and repair of roads.

21. Environmental Engineering

Environmental pollution and control, public water supply, domestic sewage, solid waste management, environmental sanitation, and plumbing.

22. Advanced Construction Techniques and Equipment

Fibers and plastics, artificial timber, advanced concreting methods (under water concreting, ready mix concrete, tremix concreting, special concretes), formwork, pre-fabricated construction, soil reinforcing techniques, hoisting and conveying equipment, earth moving machinery (exaction and compaction equipment), concrete mixers, stone crushers, pile driving equipment, working of hot mix bitumen plant, bitumen paver, floor polishing machines.

23. Estimating and Costing

Types of estimates (approximate, detailed), mode of measurements and rate analysis.

24. Contracts and Accounts

Types of engineering contracts, Tender and tender documents, payment, specifications.

TECHNICAL ABILITIES (CIVIL)

SOIL MECHANICS

RRB JUNIOR ENGINEER

1. Sclerometer is used by

(*a*) Astronomers

(*b*) Civil Engineering Surveyors

(*c*) Doctors

(*d*) Metallurgists

[RRB JE 2014 GREEN SHIFT]

2. The relationship between Bulk density (γ), Dry density (γ_d) and water content (ω) for soil is :

(*a*) $\gamma = \gamma_d(1 + \omega)$

(*b*) $\gamma_d = \gamma(1 + \omega)$

(*c*) $\gamma = \dfrac{\gamma_d}{1 + \omega}$

(*d*) $\gamma = \gamma_d(1 - \omega)$

[RRB JE 2014 RED SHIFT]

3. If fineness Modulus of sand is 2.5, it is graded as:

(*a*) Medium sand

(*b*) Fine sand

(*c*) Coarse sand

(*d*) Very coarse sand

[RRB JE 2014 RED SHIFT]

4. Which one of the following diagrams represents the effective pressure distribution for a saturated soil mass of depth 'Z' submerged under water of height 'Z_1' above its top level (γ_{sat} = sat. density of soil, γ_w = unit wt. of water, γ' = submerged density of soil)

(*a*) 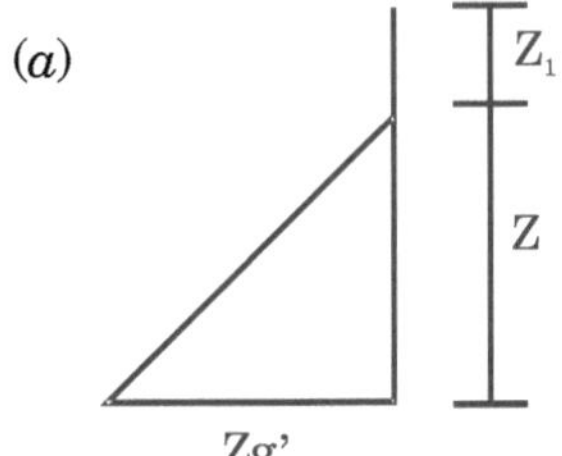

(*b*) 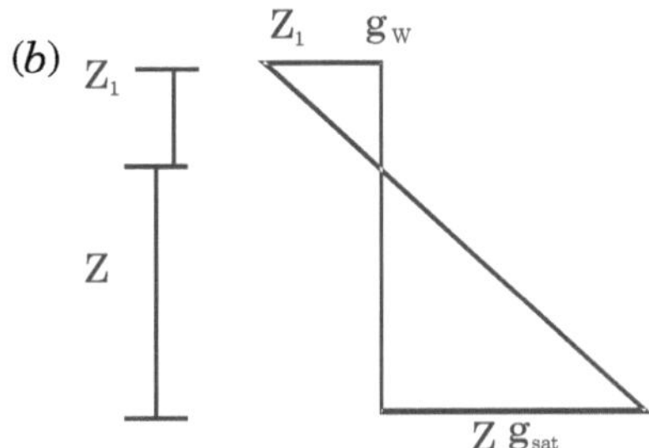

(*c*) 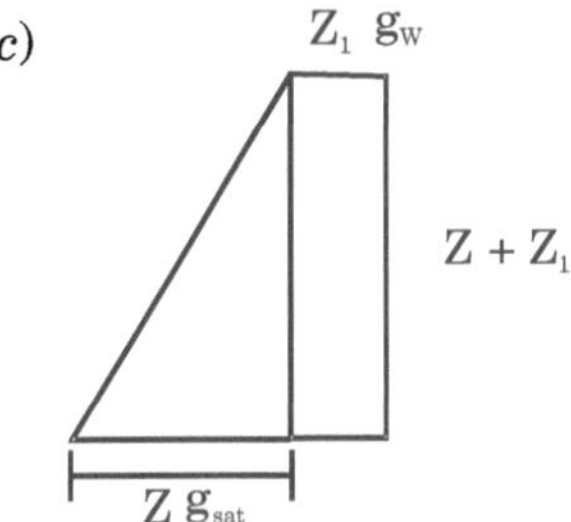

(*d*) 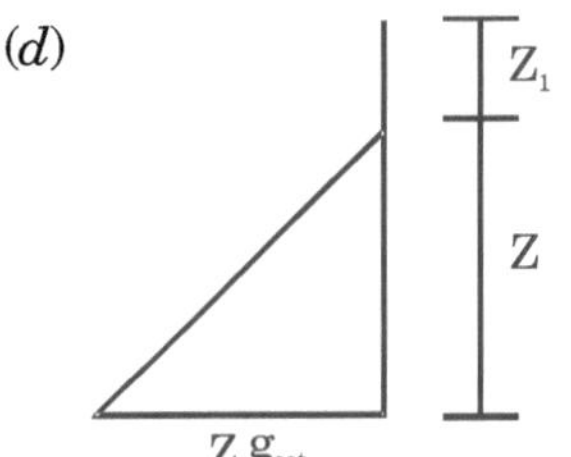

[RRB JE 2014 YELLOW SHIFT]

5. If the plasticity index of a soil mass is zero, the soil is

(*a*) Loess

(*b*) Clayey silt

(*c*) Silt

(*d*) Sand

[RRB JE 2015 26th AUG 1st SHIFT]

6. A fully saturated soil is said to be

(*a*) One phase system

(*b*) Two phase system with soil and air

(*c*) Two phase system with soil and water

(*d*) Three phase system

[RRB JE 2015 26th AUG 1st SHIFT]

7. Water content of soil can be

(*a*) Greater than 100%

(*b*) Less than 0%

(*c*) Only from 0% to 100%

(*d*) Never be greater than 100%

[RRB JE 2015 26th AUG 2nd SHIFT]

8. Voids ratio of a soil mass can

(*a*) Never be greater than unity

(*b*) Be zero

(*c*) Take any value greater than zero

(*d*) Take values between 0 and 1 only

[RRB JE 2015 26th AUG 2nd SHIFT]

9. Number of phases in soil mass is

(a) 3 (b) 2

(c) 1 (d) 4

[RRB JE 2015 26ᵗʰ AUG 3ʳᵈ SHIFT]

10. Which of the following soils has more plasticity index?

(a) Sand (b) Silt

(c) Clay (d) Gravel

[RRB JE 2015 26ᵗʰ AUG 3ʳᵈ SHIFT]

11. Relative density of a compacted dense sand is approximately equal to

(a) 0.95 (b) 0.95

(c) 0.50 (d) 1.10

[RRB JE 2015 27ᵗʰ AUG 1ˢᵗ SHIFT]

12. The ratio of volume of voids to the total volume of soil mass is called

(a) Air content

(b) Porosity

(c) Percentage air voids

(d) Voids ratio

[RRB JE 2015 27ᵗʰ AUG 1ˢᵗ SHIFT]

13. A pycnometer is used to determine

(a) Water content and voids ratio

(b) Specific gravity and dry density

(c) Water content and specific gravity

(d) voids ratio and dry density

[RRB JE 2015 27ᵗʰ AUG 2ⁿᵈ SHIFT]

14. Coarse grained soils are best compacted by a

(a) Drum roller

(b) Rubbed tyred roller

(c) Sheep's foot roller

(d) Vibratory roller

[RRB JE 2015 27ᵗʰ AUG 2ⁿᵈ SHIFT]

15. Inorganic with low compressibility is represented by

(a) MH (b) SL

(c) ML (d) CH

[RRB JE 2015 27ᵗʰ AUG 3ʳᵈ SHIFT]

16. Consistency as applied to cohesive soils is an indicator of its

(a) Density (b) Moisture content

(c) Shear strength (d) Porosity

[RRB JE 2015 28ᵗʰ AUG 1ˢᵗ SHIFT]

17. A soil having particles of nearly the same size is known as

(a) Well graded (b) Uniformly graded

(c) Poorly graded (d) Gap graded

[RRB JE 2015 28ᵗʰ AUG 1ˢᵗ SHIFT]

18. A well traded soil has a coefficient of curvature between

(a) 10 to 12 (b) 7 to 9

(c) 4 to 6 (d) 1 to 3

[RRB JE 2015 28ᵗʰ AUG 2ⁿᵈ SHIFT]

19. Consistency as applied to cohesive soils is an indicator of its

(a) Density (b) Moisture content

(c) Shear strength (d) Porosity

[RRB JE 2015 28ᵗʰ AUG 2ⁿᵈ SHIFT]

20. Liquid limit of a soil indicates its

(a) Compressibility

(b) Permeability

(c) Optimum moisture

(d) Shear strength

[RRB JE 2015 28ᵗʰ AUG 3ʳᵈ SHIFT]

21. The porosity of a soil sample having its void ratio equal to unity would be

(a) 33.34% (b) 50.0%

(c) 66.66% (d) 75.0%

[RRB JE 2015 28ᵗʰ AUG 3ʳᵈ SHIFT]

22. A clay sample has a void ratio 0.54 in dry state. The specific gravity of soil solids is 2.7. What is the shrinkage limit of the soil?

(a) 8.5% (b) 10.0%

(c) 17.0% (d) 20.0%

[RRB JE 2015 29ᵗʰ AUG 1ˢᵗ SHIFT]

23. Among the clay minerals, the one having the maximum swelling tendency is

(a) Kaolinite (b) Illite

(c) Montmorillonite (d) halloysite

[RRB JE 2015 29ᵗʰ AUG 1ˢᵗ SHIFT]

24. A soil has a liquid limit of 40% and plasticity index of 20%. The plastic limit of the soil will be

(a) 20% (b) 30%

(c) 40% (d) 60%

[RRB JE 2015 29ᵗʰ AUG 2ⁿᵈ SHIFT]

25. In a particular soil sample, laboratory analysis has yielded the following results:

A. Sand - 20%

B. Silt - 30%

C. Clay - 50%

Without using the textural

(a) Loam (b) Sandy soil

(c) Silty loam (d) Clay

[RRB JE 2015 29ᵗʰ AUG 2ⁿᵈ SHIFT]

26. The ratio between void ratio (e), degree of saturation (s), water content (w), and specific gravity of solids (G), is given by

(a) e + s = w + G   (b) e × s = w × G

(c) e/s = w/G   (d) (s + e)/w = (G + e)/s

[RRB JE 2015 29ᵗʰ AUG 3ʳᵈ SHIFT]

27. The coefficient of volume compressibility is

(a) directly proportional to the void ratio

(b) inversely proportional to the void ratio

(c) directly proportional to the coefficient of compressibility

(d) inversely proportional to the coefficient of compressibility

[RRB JE 2015 29ᵗʰ AUG 3ʳᵈ SHIFT]

28. Which one of the following parameters can be used to estimate the angle of friction of a sandy soil

(a) Particle size

(b) Roughness of particle

(c) Density Index

(d) Particle size distribution

[RRB JE 2015 30ᵗʰ AUG 3ʳᵈ SHIFT]

29. The coefficient of earth pressure at rest is given by; where μ = Poisson's ratio

(a) $\mu/(1 + \mu)$ (b) $(1 + \mu)/\mu$

(c) $\mu/(1 - \mu)$ (d) $(1 - \mu)/\mu$

[RRB JE 2015 30ᵗʰ AUG 3ʳᵈ SHIFT]

30. The dry density of which sample is expected to be highest

(a) Stiff clay   (b) Bentonite

(c) Organic clay   (d) Dense sand

[RRB JE 2015 16ᵗʰ SEP 3ʳᵈ SHIFT]

31. The liquid and plastic limit exist in

(a) Sandy soils   (b) Silty soils

(c) Gravel soils   (d) Clay soils

[RRB JE 2015 16ᵗʰ SEP 3ʳᵈ SHIFT]

32. The coarseness of the grains of a mineral is known as

(a) Fracture   (b) Texture

(c) Structure   (d) Lustre

[RRB JE 2015 16ᵗʰ SEP 3ʳᵈ SHIFT]

RRB SENIOR SECTION ENGINEER

1. Earthquakes cause damage when-

(a) Stress exceeds the strain of materials

(b) Stress exceeds the strength of materials

(c) Strain exceeds the strength of materials

(d) Strength exceeds the strain of materials

[RRB SSE 2014 GREEN SHIFT]

2. The property of a soil, which permits water to percolate through it, is called :

(a) Moisture content   (b) Capillarity

(c) Permeability   (d) None of these

[RRB SSE 2014 RED SHIFT]

3. The relationship between void ratio 'e' and porosity ratio 'n' for a given soil mass is :

(a) $n = \dfrac{1 + e}{1 - e}$ (b) $e = \dfrac{1 + n}{1 - e}$

(c) $e = n(1 + e)$ (d) $n = \dfrac{1 - e}{e}$

[RRB SSE 2014 RED SHIFT]

4. Shear failure of soils takes place when

(a) the angle of obliquity is maximum

(b) maximum cohesion is reached in cohesive soils

(c) ϕ reaches its maximum value in cohesionless soils

(d) residual strength of the soil is exhausted

[RRB SSE 2014 YELLOW SHIFT]

5. For a soil, the water content where further loss of moisture will not result in any more volume reduction is called as

(a) Liquid limit

(b) Shrinkage limit

(c) Natural moisture content

(b) Plastic limit

[RRB SSE 2015 1ˢᵗ SEP 1ˢᵗ SHIFT]

6. The degree of compaction for sand is usually defined in terms of

(a) Relative density

(b) Standard Proctor test

(c) Modified Proctor test

(d) Nuclear density meter

[RRB SSE 2015 1ˢᵗ SEP 1ˢᵗ SHIFT]

7. A clay has unconfined compressive strength of 240 kN/sq.m in undisturbed state. The clay was then remolded and the unconfined compressive strength was found to be 60 kN/sq.m. The sensitivity of this clay is

(a) 0.25   (b) 3.00

(c) 0.33   (d) 4.00

[RRB SSE 2015 1ˢᵗ SEP 1ˢᵗ SHIFT]

8. An earth retention and excavation support technique that retains soil, using steel sheet sections with interlocking edges is

(a) Retaining wall

(b) Anchored wall

(c) Sheet piling

(d) Interlocked end-bearing piling

[RRB SSE 2015 1ˢᵗ SEP 2ⁿᵈ SHIFT]

9. The property of soil mass pertaining to its susceptibility to decrease in volume under pressure is known as

(*a*) compatibility   (*b*) shrinkage

(*c*) compressibility   (*d*) expansion

[RRB SSE 2015 1ˢᵗ SEP 3ʳᵈ SHIFT]

10. A line which show the water content dry density relation for the compacted soil containing no air voids is known as

(*a*) Azimuth   (*b*) Zero-air voids line

(*c*) Proctor curve   (*d*) Constant density line

[RRB SSE 2015 2ⁿᵈ SEP 1ˢᵗ SHIFT]

11. The net loading intensity at which neither the soil fails in shear nor there is excessive settlement detrimental to the structure is called as

(*a*) Allowable bearing capacity

(*b*) Safe bearing capacity

(*c*) Ultimate bearing capacity

(*d*) Net safe bearing capacity

[RRB SSE 2015 2ⁿᵈ SEP 2ⁿᵈ SHIFT]

12. The liquid limit of a soil can be determined in the lab with

(*a*) Venturimeter

(*b*) Vane shear apparatus

(*c*) Proctor's apparatus

(*d*) Casagrande's apparatus

[RRB SSE 2015 2ⁿᵈ SEP 2ⁿᵈ SHIFT]

13. The minimum gross pressure intensity at the base of the foundation at which the soil fails in shear is called as

(*a*) Ultimate bearing capacity

(*b*) Net safe bearing capacity

(*c*) Allowable bearing capacity

(*d*) Safe bearing capacity

[RRB SSE 2015 2ⁿᵈ SEP 3ʳᵈ SHIFT]

14. The net loading intensity at which neither the soil fails in shear nor there is excessive settlement detrimental to the structure is called as

(*a*) Allowable bearing capacity

(*b*) Safe bearing capacity

(*c*) Ultimate bearing capacity

(*d*) Net safe bearing capacity

[RRB SSE 2015 2ⁿᵈ SEP 3ʳᵈ SHIFT]

15. If the sensitivity of a soil is between 4 and 8, then it will be called as

(*a*) Insensitive soil   (*b*) Less sensitive soil

(*c*) Less Sensitive soil   (*d*) Extra sensitive soil

[RRB SSE 2015 2ⁿᵈ SEP 3ʳᵈ SHIFT]

16. The property of a soil which allows it to be deformed rapidly, without rupture, with elastic rebound and without volume changes is called as

(*a*) Yielding   (*b*) Strain softening

(*c*) Strain hardening   (*d*) Plasticity

[RRB SSE 2015 3ʳᵈ SEP 1ˢᵗ SHIFT]

17. If the water table is likely to permanently remain at or below a depth of sum of the depth and width of the foundation beneath the ground level supporting the footing, then the water table correction used in the Bearing capacity equation is

(*a*) 1   (*b*) 0

(*c*) 0.5   (*d*) 0.75

[RRB SSE 2015 3ʳᵈ SEP 1ˢᵗ SHIFT]

18. The numerical difference between the plastic limit and shrinkage limit of a remoulded sample is called as:

(*a*) Plasticity index

(*b*) Shrinkage index

(*c*) Differential shrinkage

(*d*) Shrinkage ratio

[RRB SSE 2015 3ʳᵈ SEP 2ⁿᵈ SHIFT]

19. The process in which a stress applied to a soil causes densification as air is displaced from the pores between the soil grains is called as:

(*a*) Consolidation   (*b*) Liquefaction

(*c*) Compaction   (*d*) Settlement

[RRB SSE 2015 3ʳᵈ SEP 2ⁿᵈ SHIFT]

20. In general, consolidation of soil involves which of the following

(*a*) Expulsion of air

(*b*) Reduction in the shear stress of soil

(*c*) Application of static load

(*d*) Application of dynamic load

[RRB SSE 2015 3ʳᵈ SEP 3ʳᵈ SHIFT]

21. If a 6 m high retaining wall retains dry sand of unit weight 18 kN/cubm and if the coefficient of at-rest earth pressure is 0.5. Then the lateral earth pressure at a depth of 6 m will be

(*a*) 54   (*b*) 9

(*c*) 108   (*d*) 36

[RRB SSE 2015 3ʳᵈ SEP 3ʳᵈ SHIFT]

ANSWER KEY

RRB JUNIOR ENGINEER

1. (d)	**2.** (a)	**3.** (a)	**4.** (a)	**5.** (c)	**6.** (c)	**7.** (a)	**8.** (c)	**9.** (a)	**10.** (c)
11. (b)	**12.** (b)	**13.** (b)	**14.** (d)	**15.** (c)	**16.** (c)	**17.** (b)	**18.** (d)	**19.** (c)	**20.** (a)
21. (b)	**22.** (d)	**23.** (c)	**24.** (a)	**25.** (d)	**26.** (b)	**27.** (c)	**28.** (c)	**29.** (c)	**30.** (d)
31. (d)	**32.** (b)								

RRB SENIOR SECTION ENGINEER

1. (b)	**2.** (c)	**3.** (c)	**4.** (a)	**5.** (b)	**6.** (a)	**7.** (d)	**8.** (c)	**9.** (a)	**10.** (b)
11. (a)	**12.** (d)	**13.** (a)	**14.** (a)	**15.** (c)	**16.** (d)	**17.** (a)	**18.** (c)	**19.** (c)	**20.** (c)
21. (a)									

EXPLANATIONS

RRB JUNIOR ENGINEER

1. The **Sclerometer**, also known as the Turner-**Sclerometer** is an instrument **used** by metallurgists, material scientists and mineralogists to measure the scratch hardness of materials.

2. The expressions used are:

$$\rho = \frac{M - M_0}{V} \quad \text{and} \quad \rho_d = \frac{\rho}{1 + w}$$

   Bulk density, ρ (Mg/m³)

   Water content, w

   Dry density, ρ_d (Mg/m³)

3. Type of sandFineness modulus range

   Fine sand   2.2 – 2.6

   Medium sand   2.6 – 2.9

   Coarse sand   2.9 – 3.2

4.

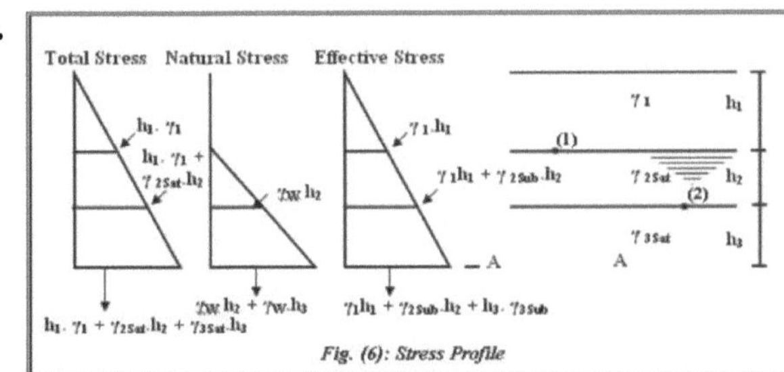

Fig. (6): Stress Profile

5. Soils having high plasticity index are considered **clay** and those having lower value are considered **silt**. In case of zero value, soil are considered to have little/no **clay** or **silt** and called non-plastic soil. A lower plasticity index of two soil is indicative to have high organic matter in soil.

6. Definition: A fully saturated soil is said to be two phase system with soil and water.

7. Water Contains shows us in what percentage water is present in whole soil sample. soils moisture content can range from 0 to **300 percent**. Water contain can't be greater than 100% cause it's impossible to get obtain marks greater than the total marks

9. Soils can be partially saturated (with both air and water present), or be fully saturated (no air content) or be perfectly dry (no water content). In a saturated soil or a dry soil, the **three**-phase system thus reduces to **two** phases only, as shown.

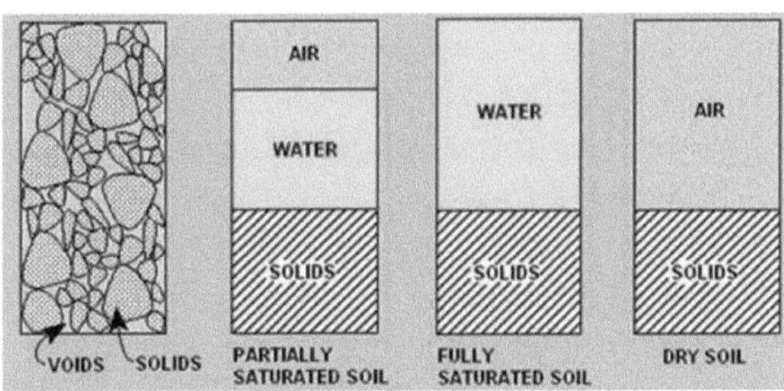

10. Clay has more plasticity index.

11. Relative density of a compacted dense sand is approximately equal to .95 .

12. **Porosity** or void fraction is a measure of the void (i.e. «empty») spaces in a material.In gas-liquid two-phase flow, the void fraction is **defined** as the fraction of the flow-channel volume that is occupied by the gas phase. **Porosity** of surface **soil** typically decreases as particle size increases.

13. A gas **pycnometer** is a laboratory device used for measuring the density—or, more accurately, the volume—of solids, be they regularly shaped, porous or non-porous, monolithic, powdered, granular or in some way comminuted, employing some method of gas displacement and the volume : pressure relationship known as Boyle's Law.

14. Tandem **vibratory rollers** compact freshly placed asphalt mats to specific densities using two, smooth steel drums that vibrate to consolidate the material.

15. Low compressibility is represented by ML

17. A soil having same particle size is called as uniformly graded.

18. The **uniformity coefficient** Cu is defined as the ratio of D60 by D10. So when Cu is greater than 4 to 6, it is understood as **a well graded soil** and when the Cu is less than 4, they are considered to be poorly **graded** or **uniformly graded. Uniformly graded** in the sense, the **soils have** got identical size of the particles.

19. Consistency as applied to cohesive soils is an indicator of its shear strength.

20. The **Atterberg limits** are a basic measure of the critical water contents of a fine-grained **soil: its shrinkage limit, plastic limit**, and **liquid limit**. Depending on **its** water content, a **soil** may appear in one of four states: solid, semi-solid, **plastic** and **liquid**.

21. n = e/(1 + e)
    n = 1/2 = 50%

22. Shrinkage limit = void Ratio/Specific gravity of soil solids = 0.54 × 100/2.7 = 20.0 %

23. **Montmorillonite** is a very soft phyllosilicate group of minerals that form when they precipitate from water solution as microscopic crystals, known as clay. It is named after Montmorillon in France.

24. **Plasticity Index** = Liquid Limit – Plastic Limit
    Plasticity Index = 40 – 20 = 20%

25. Clay

27. But **coefficient of volume compression** takes care of existing thickness of soil layer. Also, **coefficient of volume compression is directly proportional to coefficient of volume compressibility**.

28. Relative **density** or **density index** is the ratio of the difference between the void ratios of a cohesionless **soil** in its loosest state and existing natural state to the difference between its void ratio in the loosest and densest states.

29. When dealing with geotechnical problems often is required that the initial stress state in the **soil** has to be known. In order to define the initial state at **rest, the coefficient** K0, called **coefficient of earth pressure at rest**, has to be calculated.

Lateral Earth Pressure for at Rest Condition

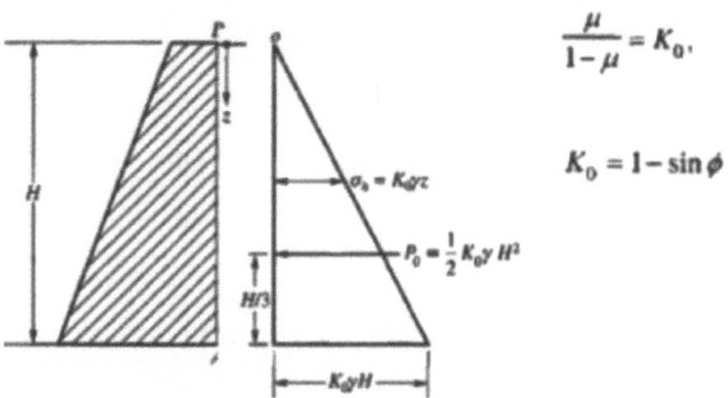

30. Dry density is to be expected of Dense sand.

31. The **Atterberg limits** are a basic measure of the critical water contents of a fine-grained soil: its shrinkage **limit, plastic limit**, and **liquid limit**. Depending on its water content, a soil may appear in one of four states: solid, semi-solid, **plastic** and **liquid**.

32. The coarseness of the grains of a mineral is known as texture.

RRB SENIOR SECTION ENGINEER

1. Earthquake cause damage when stress exceeds the strength of materials.

2. Soil permeability is the property of the soil to transmit water and air

3. **Void ratio** (e) is the **ratio of** volume **of voids to** the volume **of** solids. **Porosity** (n) is the **ratio of** volume **of voids to** the total volume **of** the soil.

$$\text{Void ratio (e)} = \frac{V_V}{V_S}$$

$$\text{Poroeity (h)} = \frac{V_V}{V_T}$$

$$V_T = V_V + V_S$$

$$n = \frac{V_V}{V_V + V_S} ; \frac{1}{n} = \frac{V_V + V_S}{V_V}$$

$$\frac{1}{n} = \frac{1 + V_S}{V_V}$$

$$\frac{1}{n} = 1 + \frac{1}{e}$$

$$\frac{1}{n} = e + \frac{1}{e} ; n = \frac{e}{1 + e}$$

5. For a soil, the water content where further loss of moisture will not result in any more volume reduction is called as Shrinkage limit.

6. The degree of compaction for sand is usually defined in terms of Relative Density.

7. Sensitivity of clay = 240/60 = 4

8. Sheet piles are sections of sheet materials with interlocking edges that are driven into the ground to provide earth retention and excavation support. Sheet piles are most commonly made of steel, but can also be formed of timber or reinforced concrete.

9. The property of soil mass pertaining to its susceptibility to decrease in volume under pressure is known as compatibility

10. A line which show the water content dry density relation for the compacted soil containing no air voids is known as Zero-air voids line.

11. The net loading intensity at which neither the soil fails in shear nor there is excessive settlement detrimental to the structure is called as Allowable bearing capacity.

12. To determine Liquid Limit of Soil Specimen , Casagrande Method is used. The liquid limit of a soil is the water content at which the soil behaves practically like a liquid, but has small shear strength. It flows to close the groove in just 25 blows in Casagrande's liquid limit device.

13. Ultimate bearing capacity is the theoretical maximum pressure which can be supported without failure; allowable bearing capacity is the ultimate bearing capacity divided by a factor of safety.

14. Ultimate bearing capacity or Gross bearing capacity : It is the least gross pressure which will cause shear failure of the supporting soil immediately below the footing.

    Net ultimate bearing capacity : It is the net pressure that can be applied to the footing by external loads that will just initiate failure in the underlying soil. It is equal to ultimate bearing capacity minus the stress due to the weight of the footing and any soil or surcharge directly above it.

    Safe bearing capacity: It is the bearing capacity after applying the factor of safety (FS)

15. Sensitivity of clays

Sensitivity	Classification
< 1	Insensitive
1-2	Slightly sensitive
2-4	Medium sensitive
4-8	Very sensitive
8-16	Slightly quick
16-32	Medium quick
32-64	Very quick
> 64	Extra quick

16. Plasticity is the ability of some fine-grained soils to lose and subsequently regain approximately 99% of their inherent shear resistance to sliding as they absorb or lose water.

17. Water table correction is 1.

18. The time dependent behaviour of composite prestressed concrete beams depends upon the presence of differential shrinkage and creep of the concretes of web and deck, in addition to other parameters, such as relaxation of steel, presence of untensioned steel, and compression steel etc.

19. In sedimentology, compaction refers to the process by which a sediment progressively loses its porosity due to the effects of loading. This forms part of the process of lithification.

20. Consolidation refers to the process by which soils change volume in response to a change in pressure. According to the "father of soil mechanics", Karl von Terzaghi, consolidation is "any process which involves a decrease in water content of saturated soil without replacement of water by air". In general it is the process in which reduction in volume takes place by expulsion of water under long-term static loads. It occurs when stress is applied to a soil that causes the soil particles to pack together more tightly. When this occurs in a soil that is saturated with water, water will be squeezed out of the soil. The magnitude of consolidation can be predicted by many different methods.

21. 54

BUILDING MATERIALS

RRB JUNIOR ENGINEER

1. A bond in a brick work when headers and stretchers are placed in alternate layers is called

(a) Header bond   (b) English bond

(c) Flemish bond   (d) Herring bone bond

[RRB JE 2014 GREEN SHIFT]

2. The outer protective layer of a tree is

(a) cambium layer   (b) pitch

(c) bark   (d) sap

[RRB JE 2014 GREEN SHIFT]

3. Which lime is most suitable for white washing?

(a) quick lime   (b) stone lime

(c) kankar lime   (d) shell lime

[RRB JE 2014 GREEN SHIFT]

4. A pigment generally used to impart white colour in a paint is

(a) graphite   (b) lead

(c) copper sulphate   (d) zinc

[RRB JE 2014 GREEN SHIFT]

5. The dimensions of a brick are 10 cm x4 cm x3 cm. What is the total surface area of this brick?

(a) 82 cm^2 (b) 164 cm^2

(c) 120 cm^2 (d) 180 cm^2

[RRB JE 2014 RED SHIFT]

6. Lime mortar is generally made with

(a) Quick lime   (b) Fat lime

(c) Hydraulic lime   (d) White lime

[RRB JE 2014 YELLOW SHIFT]

7. The invar tape is made of an alloy of

(a) Copper and steel   (b) Brass and nickel

(c) Brass and steel   (d) Nickel and steel

[RRB JE 2015 26th AUG 1st SHIFT]

8. Which of the following trees yields hard wood?

(a) Deodar   (b) Chir

(c) Shishum   (d) Pine

[RRB JE 2015 26th AUG 1st SHIFT]

9. The main ingredients of Portland cement are

(a) Lime and silica

(b) Lime and alumina

(c) Silica and alumina

(d) Lime and iron

[RRB JE 2015 26th AUG 2nd SHIFT]

10. Which of the following timbers is suitable for making sports goods?

(a) Mulberry   (b) Mahogany

(c) Sal   (d) Deodar

[RRB JE 2015 26th AUG 3rd SHIFT]

11. Seasoning of timber is required to

(a) Soften the timber

(b) Harden the timber

(c) Straighten the timber

(d) Remove sap from the timber

[RRB JE 2015 26th AUG 3rd SHIFT]

12. Plaster of pans is obtained by calcining

(a) Gypsum   (b) Bauxite

(c) Lime stone   (d) Ranker

[RRB JE 2015 27th AUG 2nd SHIFT]

13. Plywood is obtained from

(a) Bamboo

(b) Teak wood

(c) Structural timber

(d) Commonly available timber

[RRB JE 2015 27th AUG 2nd SHIFT]

14. In house water connection, a ferrule is provided, which is a

(a) small sized curved pipe made of a flexible material

(b) right angled sleeve made of brass or gun metal

(c) galvanised iron pipe of size less than 50 mm diameter

(d) flexible connection between the water main and the service pipe

[RRB JE 2015 27th AUG 2nd SHIFT]

15. First class timber has an average life of

(a) Less than one year   (b) 1 to 5 years

(c) 5 to 10 years   (d) More than 10 years

[RRB JE 2015 27th AUG 3rd SHIFT]

16. The strength of timber is maximum when load applied is

(a) Parallel to grain

(b) Perpendicular to grain

(c) Inclined at 45° to grain

(d) Inclined at 60° to grain

[RRB JE 2015 28ᵗʰ AUG 1ˢᵗ SHIFT]

17. Stainless steel resist corrosion due to

(a) Carbon   (b) Manganese

(c) Chromium   (d) Sulphur

[RRB JE 2015 28ᵗʰ AUG 2ⁿᵈ SHIFT]

18. What is the angle between two plane minors of an optical square?

(a) 30   (b) 60

(c) 45   (d) 90

[RRB JE 2015 28ᵗʰ AUG 3ʳᵈ SHIFT]

19. Theodolite is an instrument used for

(a) Tightening the capstan-headed nuts of level tube

(b) Measurement of horizontal angles only

(c) Measurement of vertical angles only

(d) Measurement of both horizontal and vertical angles

[RRB JE 2015 28ᵗʰ AUG 3ʳᵈ SHIFT]

20. Which of the following tape is least affected by temperature changes and is highly precise

(a) Linen tape   (b) Metallic tape

(c) Steel tape   (d) Invar tape

[RRB JE 2015 29ᵗʰ AUG 1ˢᵗ SHIFT]

21. For making spiral staircases, ideal material is

(a) pig iron   (b) cast iron

(c) wrought iron   (d) steel

[RRB JE 2015 29ᵗʰ AUG 3ʳᵈ SHIFT]

22. On the basis of durability test, Forest Research Institute of India, Dehradun, a tree is highly durable if its average life is more than

(a) 5 years   (b) 10 years

(c) 15 years   (d) 20 years

[RRB JE 2015 29ᵗʰ AUG 3ʳᵈ SHIFT]

23. In an optical square, the angle between the first incident ray and the last reflected ray is

(a) 60°   (b) 90°

(c) 120°   (d) 150°

[RRB JE 2015 30ᵗʰ AUG 3ʳᵈ SHIFT]

24. Which of the following is softwood?

(a) Deodar   (b) Teak

(c) Sal   (d) Mahogany

[RRB JE 2015 30ᵗʰ AUG 3ʳᵈ SHIFT]

25. Metallic tapes are made of

(a) Steel   (b) Invar

(c) Cloth and wires   (d) Nickel

[RRB JE 2015 16ᵗʰ SEP 3ʳᵈ SHIFT]

RRB SENIOR SECTION ENGINEER

1. English Bond, Flemish Bond, Dutch Bond pertain to-

(a) Masonry work

(b) Cement bonding

(c) Bonding between beams

(d) Bonding in foundation

[RRB SSE 2014 GREEN SHIFT]

2. King closers are related to

(a) doors and windows

(b) King post truss

(c) Queen Post truss

(d) Brick Masonry

[RRB SSE 2014 YELLOW SHIFT]

3. Seasoning of timber is required to

(a) Soften the timber

(b) Harden the timber

(c) Straighten the timber

(d) Remove sap from the timber

[RRB SSE 2014 YELLOW SHIFT]

4. Which of the following oxide is in the LOWEST % in ordinary portland cement?

(a) Iron oxide   (b) Magnesium oxide

(c) Soda+Potash   (d) Aluminium oxide

[RRB SSE 2015 1ˢᵗ SEP 1ˢᵗ SHIFT]

5. The minimum yield stress for a Fe415 is

(a) 415 MPa   (b) 395 MPa

(c) 500 MPa   (d) 550 MPa

[RRB SSE 2015 1ˢᵗ SEP 1ˢᵗ SHIFT]

6. The minimum time before striking the form for columns as per IS 456 is

(a) 14-day   (b) 7-day

(c) 3-day   (d) 16-24 h

[RRB SSE 2015 1ˢᵗ SEP 1ˢᵗ SHIFT]

7. A tight knot free from decay, which is solid across its face, and at least as hard as the surrounding wood.

(a) Punk knot   (b) Pith knot

(c) Loose knot   (d) Sound knot

[RRB SSE 2015 2ⁿᵈ SEP 1ˢᵗ SHIFT]

8. According to IS 1200, brickwork is usually measured in
(*a*) wall thickness   (*b*) cubic meter
(*c*) square meter   (*d*) linear meter
[RRB SSE 2015 2ⁿᵈ SEP 1ˢᵗ SHIFT]

9. Which of the following list of pile types is not a represented based on the functioning of the pile
(*a*) End-bearing pile   (*b*) Friction pile
(*c*) Anchor pile   (*d*) H-pile
[RRB SSE 2015 2ⁿᵈ SEP 1ˢᵗ SHIFT]

10. The mineral acidity in water is due to presence of
(*a*) dissolution of minerals
(*b*) dissolving of salts
(*c*) hydrolysis of multivalent cations
(*d*) addition mineral acids
[RRB SSE 2015 2ⁿᵈ SEP 2ⁿᵈ SHIFT]

11. A condition of timber during seasoning in which the different layers of wood are under stress by being under compression across the grain (usually due to rapid surface drying in the kiln).
(*a*) Case hardening   (*b*) Air seasoning
(*c*) Air drying   (*d*) Strain softening
[RRB SSE 2015 3ʳᵈ SEP 1ˢᵗ SHIFT]

12. Which of the following supplementary cementations materials have self-cementing properties?
(*a*) Class F fly ash
(*b*) Silica Fume
(*c*) Rice husk ash
(*d*) Ground-Granulated blast furnace slag
[RRB SSE 2015 3ʳᵈ SEP 2ⁿᵈ SHIFT]

13. A layer of wood formed during one year's growth in a timber is called as
(*a*) Bark   (*b*) All-heart
(*c*) Batch   (*d*) Annual ring
[RRB SSE 2015 3ʳᵈ SEP 3ʳᵈ SHIFT]

ANSWER KEY

RRB JUNIOR ENGINEER

1. (b)	**2.** (c)	**3.** (d)	**4.** (d)	**5.** (b)	**6.** (c)	**7.** (d)	**8.** (c)	**9.** (a)	**10.** (a)
11. (d)	**12.** (a)	**13.** (c)	**14.** (b)	**15.** (c)	**16.** (a)	**17.** (c)	**18.** (c)	**19.** (d)	**20.** (d)
21. (b)	**22.** (b)	**23.** (b)	**24.** (a)	**25.** (c)					

RRB SENIOR SECTION ENGINEER

1. (a)	**2.** (d)	**3.** (d)	**4.** (c)	**5.** (a)	**6.** (d)	**7.** (d)	**8.** (b)	**9.** (d)	**10.** (b)
11. (a)	**12.** (d)	**13.** (d)							

EXPLANATIONS

RRB JUNIOR ENGINEER

1. The most commonly used types of bonds in brick masonry are:
1. Stretcher bond
2. Header bond
3. English bond and
4. Flemish bond

Other Types of bonds are:
1. Facing bond
2. Dutch bond
3. English cross bond
4. Brick on edge bond
5. Raking bond
6. Zigzag bond
7. Garden wall bond

Fig. 1: Header Bond Isometric View

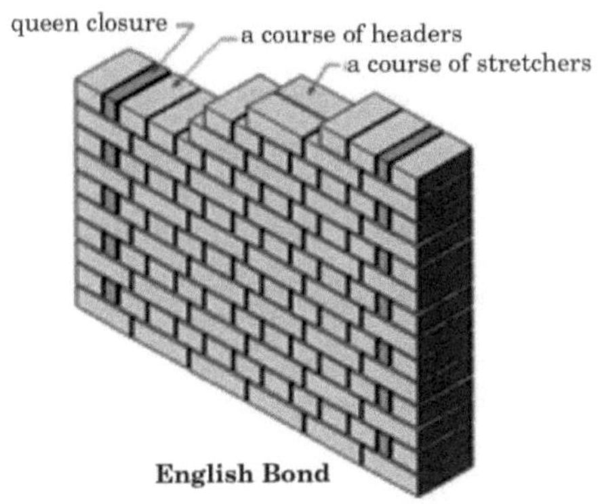

Fig. 2: English Bond – Isometric View

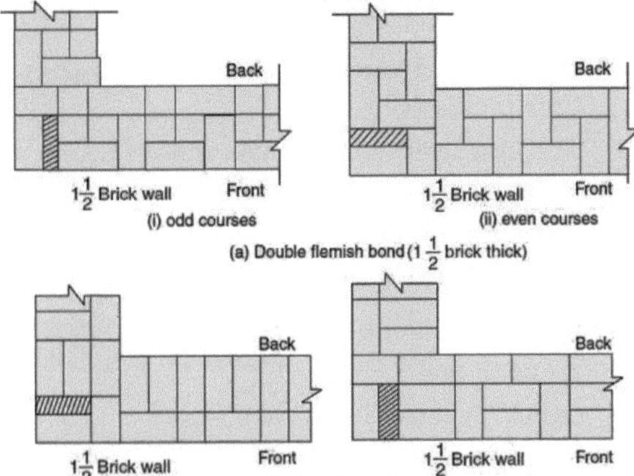

Fig. 3: Flemish Bond

English Bond

English bond in brick masonry has one course of stretcher only and a course of header above it, i.e. it has two alternating courses of stretchers and headers. Headers are laid centered on the stretchers in course below and each alternate row is vertically aligned.

To break the continuity of vertical joints, quoin closer is used in the beginning and end of a wall after first header. A quoin close is a brick cut lengthwise into two halves and used at corners in brick walls.

2. The inner bark, or **"phloem"**, is pipeline through which food is passed to the rest of the tree. It lives for only a short time, then dies and turns to cork to become part of the protective outer bark. The cambium cell layer is the growing part of the trunk.

3. Shell lime. Three different brands of kalsomine; the directions for use are visible when viewing image at full size.

Whitewash, or calcimine, kalsomine, calsomine, or lime paint is a type of paint made from **slaked** lime (calcium hydroxide,

$Ca(OH)_2$) and chalk calcium carbonate, $(CaCO_3)$, sometimes known as "whiting".

4. Photochemically inert rutile is used for protection of paints from degradation by light. Titanium oxide is the most widely used pigment. **Zinc** Oxide (ZnO) is a white synthetic inorganic pigment having refractive index 2.01.

5. Total surface area = 2(lb + bh + lh)
   = 2(10 x 4 + 4 x 3 + 10 x 3) = 164 cm^2

6. **Lime mortar** today is primarily used in the conservation of buildings originally built using **lime mortar**, but may be used as an alternative to ordinary portland cement. It is **made** principally of **lime(hydraulic**, or non **hydraulic)**, water and an aggregate such as sand.

7. Invar is a 36% **nickel** iron alloy which has the lowest thermal expansion among all metals and alloys in the range from room temperature up to approximately 230°C. The Invar alloy is **ductile** and easily **weldable**, and machinability is similar to **austenitic** stainless steel.

8. Shishum yields hard wood whereas others yield soft wood.

9. Materials that contain appropriate amounts of **calcium** compounds, **silica**, alumina and iron oxide are crushed and screened and placed in a rotating cement kiln. Ingredients used in this process are typically materials such as **limestone**, sandstone, marl, shale, iron, clay, and fly ash.

10. The main timber used for sports industry is Mulberry.

11. Seasoning of timber is carried out so that sap and moisture can be removed from the timber. Wood drying (also **seasoning lumber** or wood **seasoning**) reduces the moisture content of wood before its use. When the drying is done in a kiln, the product is known as kiln-dried **timber** or **lumber**, whereas air drying is the more traditional method.

12. Plaster of pans is obtained by calcining Gypsum.

13. Originally from the Asian region, it is now also manufactured in African and South American countries. Tropical plywood is superior to **softwood** plywood due to its density, strength, evenness of layers, and high quality. It is usually sold at a premium in many markets if manufactured with high standards.

14. A ferrule is any of a number of types of objects, generally used for fastening, joining, sealing or reinforcement. They are often narrow circular rings made from metal, or less commonly, plastic. Ferrules are also often referred to as eyelets or grommets within the manufacturing industry.

15. First class timber has an average life of 5 to 10 years.

16. The strength of timber is maximum when load applied is parallel to grain.

17. **Stainless steel** is known for its **corrosion** resistance in many environments in which carbon and low alloy tool steels would **corrode**. The **corrosion** resistance is a result of a very thin (about 5 nanometers) oxide layer on the **steel's** surface. The passive layer forms because of the chromium added to **stainless steel**.

18. The angle between two plane minors of an optical square is 45 degrees.

19. A theodolite is a precision optical instrument for measuring angles between designated visible points in the horizontal and vertical planes.

20. The alloy was named **invar**, from invariable, to reflect its low coefficient of expansion. **Invar** had several **advantages** over steel **tapes**.

21. Cast iron is an ideal material for making spiral structures.

22. The Forest Research Institute of India conducts durability tests on specimens of size 600 × 50 × 50 mm by burying them in the ground upto half their length and observing them over several years. On the basis of durability it classifies trees into the following three classes: 1. High durability: If the average life is more than 10 years. 2. Moderate durability: If the average life is 5-10 years. 3. Low durability: If the average life is less than 5 years.

23. According to the principle of reflecting surfaces, the **angle between the first incident ray and the last reflected ray** is twice the **angle between** the mirrors. In this case, the **angle between** the mirrors is fixed at 45°. So, the **angle between** the horizon sight and index sight will be 90⁰.

24. **Examples** of hardwood trees include alder, balsa, beech, hickory, mahogany, maple, oak, teak, and walnut. **Examples of softwood** trees are cedar, Douglas fir, juniper, pine, redwood, spruce, and yew. Most hardwoods have a higher density than most **softwoods**. Most **softwoods** have a lower density than most hardwoods.

25. A **metallic tape** is **made of** varnished strip of waterproof linen interwoven with small brass, copper or some other metal.

RRB SENIOR SECTION ENGINEER

1. Types of bonds in brick masonry wall construction are classified based on laying and bonding style of bricks in walls. The bonds in brick masonry is developed by the mortar filling between layers of bricks and in grooves when bricks are laid adjacent to each other and in layers in walls.

   Mostly used material for bonds in brick masonry is cement mortar. Lime mortar and mud mortar are also used.

   Types of Bonds in Brick Masonry Wall Construction :

   The most commonly used types of bonds in brick masonry are:

   Stretcher bond

   Header bond

   English bond and

   Flemish bond

   Other Types of bonds are:

   Facing bond

   Dutch bond

   English cross bond

   Brick on edge bond

   Raking bond

   Zigzag bond

   Garden wall bond

2. Beveled Closer. It is a form of king closer in which the whole length of the brick (i.e. stretcher face) is chamfered or beveled in **such** a way that half width is maintained at one end and full width is maintained at the other end.

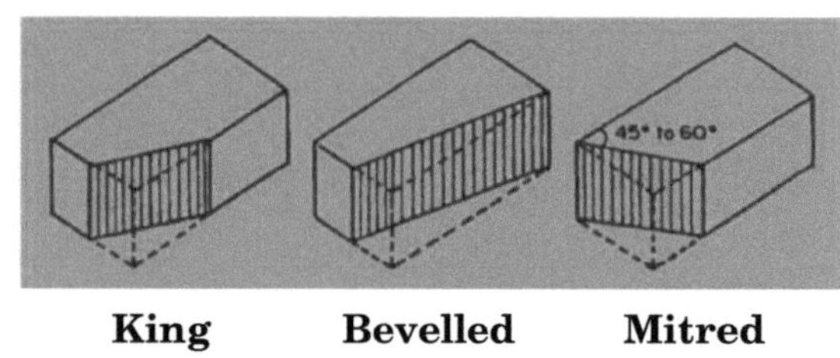

| **King Closer** | **Bevelled Closer** | **Mitred Closer** |

3. Wood drying (also wood **seasoning**) reduces the moisture content of wood before its use. When the drying is done in a kiln, the product is known as kiln-dried **timber** or **lumber**, whereas air drying is the more traditional method.

4. Soda and Potash oxide is in the LOWEST % in ordinary portland cement.

5. The minimum yield stress for a Fe415 is 415 MPa.

6. The minimum time before striking the form for columns as per IS 456 is 16-24 h.

7. Sound knot is a knot in lumber that is as hard as the surrounding wood and is so solid and free from decay that it will retain its place in the piece.

8. Brickwork is always measured in cubic metre.

9. H-Pile is not represented based on the functioning of the pile.

10. The mineral acidity in water is due to presence of dissolving of salts.

11. Wood is air-dried or dried in a purpose built oven (kiln). Usually the wood is sawed before drying, but sometimes the log is dried whole. **Case hardening** describes **lumber** or **timber** that has been dried too rapidly.

12. Ground-granulated blast-furnace slag is obtained by quenching molten iron slag from a blast furnace in water or steam, to produce a glassy, granular product that is then dried and ground into a fine powder.

13. Horizontal cross sections cut through the trunk of a tree can reveal growth rings, also referred to as tree rings or annual rings. Growth rings result from new growth in the vascular cambium, a layer of cells near the bark that botanists classify as a lateral meristem; this growth in diameter is known as secondary growth. Visible rings result from the change in growth speed through the seasons of the year; thus, critical for the title method, one ring generally marks the passage of one year in the life of the tree.

REINFORCED CEMENT CONCRETE

RRB JUNIOR ENGINEER

1. Excess silica in cement
   (a) increases the setting time
   (b) decreases the setting time
   (c) weakens the strength of the cement
   (d) does not affect the setting time
   [RRB JE 2014 GREEN SHIFT]

2. The word 'Brinell' is associated with
   (a) soil testing
   (b) tensile testing
   (c) hardness testing
   (d) testing of seasoning of wood
   [RRB JE 2014 GREEN SHIFT]

3. For plastering walls, cement mortar would be typically used in which ratio?
   (a) 1 : 2   (b) 1 : 4
   (c) 1 : 6   (d) 1 : 8
   [RRB JE 2014 GREEN SHIFT]

4. The grade M25 of concrete would approx, refer to the mix
   (a) 1 : 3 : 6   (b) 1 : 2 : 4
   (c) 1 : 1 : 2   (d) 1 : 4 : 8
   [RRB JE 2014 GREEN SHIFT]

5. Separation of water or sand or cement from a freshly mixed concrete is known as ;
   (a) Segregation   (b) Creeping
   (c) Bleeding   (d) Flooding
   [RRB JE 2014 RED SHIFT]

6. The BIS code which deals with steel structures is :
   (a) BIS : 456   (b) BIS : 800
   (c) BIS : 875   (d) BIS : 1893
   [RRB JE 2014 RED SHIFT]

7. The Modulus of Elasticity (E) of concrete as per IS 456:2000 is given by (notations are conventional)
   (a) $E = 1000 f_{ck}$ (b) $E = 5000 \sqrt{f_{ck}}$
   (c) $E = 5500 \sqrt{f_{ck}}$ (d) $E = 10000 \sqrt{f_{ck}}$
   [RRB JE 2014 YELLOW SHIFT]

8. In paints, linseed oil is used as
   (a) a solidifier
   (b) a driver
   (c) a vehicle
   (d) a water-proofing base
   [RRB JE 2014 YELLOW SHIFT]

9. In RCC beams, a the percentage area of tensile steel increases
   (a) Depth of neutral axis increases
   (b) Depth of neutral axis decreases
   (c) Depth of neutral axis does not change
   (d) Lever arm increases
   [RRB JE 2015 26ᵗʰ AUG 1ˢᵗ SHIFT]

10. When water is added to cement
   (a) Chemical reaction starts
   (b) Heat is absorbed
   (c) Heat is generated
   (d) Impurities are washed out
   [RRB JE 2015 26ᵗʰ AUG 1ˢᵗ SHIFT]

11. IS 800 : 2007 is based on
   (a) Elastic design method
   (b) Ultimate load method
   (c) Working stress method
   (d) Limit state method
   [RRB JE 2015 26ᵗʰ AUG 1ˢᵗ SHIFT]

12. The maximum percentage of moment redistribution allowed in RCC beams is
   (a) 10%
   (b) 20%
   (c) 30%
   (d) 40%
   [RRB JE 2015 26ᵗʰ AUG 2ⁿᵈ SHIFT]

13. Initial setting time is maximum for
   (a) Portland-Pozzolana cement
   (b) Portland-Slag cement
   (c) Low heat portland-pozzolana cement
   (d) High strength portland cement
   [RRB JE 2015 26ᵗʰ AUG 2ⁿᵈ SHIFT]

14. Cement concrete is a

(a) Elastic material

(b) Visco-elastic material

(c) Non elastic material

(d) Plastic material

[RRB JE 2015 26th AUG 3rd SHIFT]

15. A sample of cement is said to be sound when it does not contain free

(a) Lime   (b) Silica

(c) Iron oxide   (d) Alumina

[RRB JE 2015 27th AUG 1st SHIFT]

16. The tensile strength of concrete is approximately what percent of compressive strength of concrete

(a) 50%   (b) 20%

(c) 10%   (d) 5%

[RRB JE 2015 27th AUG 1st SHIFT]

17. For M20 grade of concrete, the maximum shear stress shall not exceed

(a) 1.6 N/mm^2 (b) 1.9 N/mm^2

(c) 2.8 N/mm^2 (d) 2.2 N/mm^2

[RRB JE 2015 27th AUG 2nd SHIFT]

18. Minimum grade of concrete to be used in reinforced concrete is

(a) M10   (b) M15

(c) M20   (d) M25

[RRB JE 2015 27th AUG 3rd SHIFT]

19. As per Indian Standard specifications, concrete is designated into

(a) 3 grades   (b) 5 grades

(c) 7 grades   (d) 10 grades

[RRB JE 2015 27th AUG 3rd SHIFT]

20. After storage, the strength of cement

(a) Decreases

(b) Increases

(c) Remains same

(d) May increase or decrease

[RRB JE 2015 27th AUG 3rd SHIFT]

21. Addition of pozzolana to ordinary portland cement increase

(a) Bleeding

(b) Shrinkage

(c) Permeability

(d) Heat of hydration

[RRB JE 2015 28th AUG 1st SHIFT]

22. How is the deflection in RC beams controlled as per IS:456?

(a) By using large aspect ratio

(b) By using small modular ratio

(c) By controlling span/depth ratio

(d) By moderating water-cement ratio

[RRB JE 2015 28th AUG 2nd SHIFT]

23. Which of the following cement has maximum percentage of C_3S

(a) Ordinary portland cement

(b) Low heat cement

(c) Sulphate resisting cement

(d) Rapid hardening cement

[RRB JE 2015 28th AUG 2nd SHIFT]

24. Which one of the following stresses is independent of yield stress as a permissible stress for steel member?

(a) Axial tensile stress

(b) Maximum shear stress

(c) Bearing stress

(d) Stress in slab base

[RRB JE 2015 28th AUG 3rd SHIFT]

25. Which one of the following does not react with concrete?

(a) Sewage water   (b) Sulphuric acid

(c) Vegetable oil   (d) Alcohol

[RRB JE 2015 28th AUG 3rd SHIFT]

26. The reinforced concrete beam curved in plane is designed for

(a) Bending moment and shear

(b) Bending moment and torsion

(c) Bending moment

(d) Bending moment shear and torsion

[RRB JE 2015 29th AUG 1st SHIFT]

27. As per IS specification, the maximum final setting time for ordinary portland cement should be

(a) 30 minutes   (b) 1 hour

(c) 6 hours   (d) 10 hours

[RRB JE 2015 29th AUG 1st SHIFT]

28. Bleeding of concrete is said to occur when

(a) Finer particles settle down at the bottom

(b) Coarser particles get separated

(c) Cement paste rises to the surface of concrete

(d) Finer particles collect in isolated pockets

[RRB JE 2015 29th AUG 1st SHIFT]

29. Permissible shear stress in concrete is a function of
   (a) Grade of concrete
   (b) Grade of steel
   (c) Percentage of steel reinforcement
   (d) Percentage of steel reinforcement and grade of concrete
   [RRB JE 2015 29th AUG 2nd SHIFT]

30. The setting and hardening of cement after addition of water is due to
   (a) The presence of gypsum
   (b) Binding action of water
   (c) Hydration of some of the constituent compounds of cement
   (d) Evaporation of water
   [RRB JE 2015 29th AUG 2nd SHIFT]

31. Grading of aggregate in a concrete mix is necessary to achieve
   (a) Adequate workability
   (b) Higher density
   (c) Reduction in voids
   (d) Better durability
   [RRB JE 2015 29th AUG 2nd SHIFT]

32. In the conventional pre-stressing, the diagonal tension in concrete
   (a) increases   (b) decreases
   (c) does not change   (d) may increase or decrease
   [RRB JE 2015 29th AUG 3rd SHIFT]

33. The percentage of gypsum added to the clinker during manufacturing
   (a) 0.2   (b) 0.25 to 0.35
   (c) 2.5 to 3.5   (d) 5 to 10
   [RRB JE 2015 30th AUG 3rd SHIFT]

RRB SENIOR SECTION ENGINEER

1. Strength of commonly used concrete, for constructing low rise residential buildings is:
   (a) 300 psi   (b) 8000 psi
   (c) 15000 psi   (d) 25000 psi
   [RRB SSE 2014 GREEN SHIFT]

2. The chemical reaction between cement and water is:
   (a) Hydration   (b) Chlorination
   (c) Calcination   (d) None of these
   [RRB SSE 2014 GREEN SHIFT]

3. In a singly Reinforced Beam, if the permissible stress in concrete reaches earlier than the permissible stress in steel, the Beam section is called :
   (a) Under Reinforced Section
   (b) Economic Section
   (c) Critical Section
   (d) Over Reinforced Section
   [RRB SSE 2014 RED SHIFT]

4. Batching in concrete refers to
   (a) Controlling the total quantity of each batch
   (b) Weighing accurately, the quantity of each material for a job before mixing
   (c) Controlling the quantity of each material into each batch
   (d) Adjusting the water to be added in each batch according to the moisture content of the materials being mixed in the batch
   [RRB SSE 2014 YELLOW SHIFT]

5. Gypsum is used as an admixture in cement grouts for
   (a) accelerating the setting time
   (b) retarding the setting time
   (c) increasing the plasticity
   (d) reducing the grout shrinkage
   [RRB SSE 2014 YELLOW SHIFT]

6. According to IS 456, the approximate estimated flexural strength (MPa) of concrete of grade M50 (fck = 50 MPa) would be
   (a) 4.9   (b) 5.5
   (c) 2.5   (d) 6.5
   [RRB SSE 2015 1st SEP 1st SHIFT]

7. Normally, when ordinary Portland cement hydrates,
   (a) Heat is absorbed
   (b) Heat evolves
   (c) Heat neither evolves nor is absorbed
   (d) Cement paste cools down below atmospheric temperature
   [RRB SSE 2015 1st SEP 1st SHIFT]

8. According to IS 456, under normal circumstances, the maximum cement content in kg/cum (including fly ash and slag) allowed is
   (a) 500   (b) 400
   (c) 450   (d) 600
   [RRB SSE 2015 1st SEP 2nd SHIFT]

9. The minimum time before striking the props to arches (less than 6 m) as per IS 456 is
   (a) 14-day   (b) 7-day
   (c) 3-day   (d) 16-24 h
   [RRB SSE 2015 1st SEP 2nd SHIFT]

10. According to IS 1200, the formwork shall be measured in

(*a*) Tonnage   (*b*) cubic m

(*c*) square meter   (*d*) Linear length

[RRB SSE 2015 1st SEP 2nd SHIFT]

11. The time elapsed between the moment water is added to the ordinary Portland cement and the time when the cement completely loses its plasticity and can resist certain definite pressure is termed as

(*a*) Initial setting time   (*b*) Final setting time

(*c*) Hydration time   (*d*) Gestation period

[RRB SSE 2015 1st SEP 2nd SHIFT]

12. Which of the following is not used in the design of concrete mixes as per the relevant Indian standard?

(*a*) Air content   (*b*) Water content

(*c*) Admixture content (*d*) Bulk density of cement

[RRB SSE 2015 1st SEP 3rd SHIFT]

13. The minimum time before striking the props to slabs (less than 4.5 m) as per IS 456 is

(*a*) 14-day   (*b*) 7-day

(*c*) 3-day   (*d*) 16-24 h

[RRB SSE 2015 1st SEP 3rd SHIFT]

14. According to IS 1200, granular sub-base used in pavement construction shall be measured as finished work in position in

(*a*) Tonnage

(*b*) Square m of plan area

(*c*) Cubic metres

(*d*) Thickness of the layer

[RRB SSE 2015 1st SEP 3rd SHIFT]

15. According to IS 456, nominal mix concrete can be used upto which of the following grade

(*a*) 10   (*b*) 15

(*c*) 20   (*d*) 25

[RRB SSE 2015 2nd SEP 1st SHIFT]

16. The batching tolerance for aggregates as per IS 456 is

(*a*) ±1%   (*b*) ±1.5%

(*c*) ±2%   (*d*) ±3%

[RRB SSE 2015 2nd SEP 1st SHIFT]

17. The excessive amount of expansion due to unsound cement is usually related to

(*a*) Magnesia   (*b*) Iron oxide

(*c*) Alkalies   (*d*) Water

[RRB SSE 2015 2nd SEP 1st SHIFT]

18. In the determination of total dissolved solids, the water sample is dried at the temperature of

(*a*) 150 ± 5°C   (*b*) 180°C

(*c*) 105 ± 5°C   (*d*) 550 ±5°C

[RRB SSE 2015 2nd SEP 1st SHIFT]

19. The batching tolerance for aggregates as per IS 456 is

(*a*) ±1%   (*b*) ±1.5%

(*c*) ±2%   (*d*) ±3%

[RRB SSE 2015 2nd SEP 2nd SHIFT]

20. According to IS 1200, reinforcing bars used in reinforced cement concrete shall be measured in

(*a*) meters   (*b*) cubic meter

(*c*) square meter   (*d*) litre

[RRB SSE 2015 2nd SEP 2nd SHIFT]

21. The rapid development of rigidity in a freshly mixed Portland cement paste, mortar, or concrete, usually happens with the evolution of considerable heat. This rigidity cannot be dispelled, nor can the plasticity be regained, by further mixing without addition of water. This is called as

(*a*) False set   (*b*) Flash set

(*c*) Rigidity index   (*d*) Set acceleration

[RRB SSE 2015 2nd SEP 2nd SHIFT]

22. The recommended slump of concrete for hand-placed pavements is

(*a*) 2-4 inches   (*b*) 3-4 inches

(*c*) 4-6 inches   (*d*) 1-3 inches

[RRB SSE 2015 2nd SEP 3rd SHIFT]

23. Which of the following is not a permanent adjustment in theodolite

(*a*) Adjustment of the orizontal plate level

(*b*) Adjustment of the telescope

(*c*) Adjustment of the vertical circle index

(*d*) Elimination of parallax

[RRB SSE 2015 2nd SEP 3rd SHIFT]

24. According to IS 1200, floor finishes shall be measured in

(*a*) running meter   (*b*) cubic meter

(*c*) square meter   (*d*) Thickness

[RRB SSE 2015 2nd SEP 3rd SHIFT]

25. According to IS 456, the modulus of elasticity of steel can be assumed as

(*a*) 200 kN/mm^2 (*b*) 225 kN/mm^2

(*c*) 250 kN/mm^2 (*d*) 300 kN/mm^2

[RRB SSE 2015 3rd SEP 1st SHIFT]

26. The recommended slump for pumped concrete is

(*a*) 1-2 inches   (*b*) 2-4 inch

(*c*) 3-4 inches   (*d*) 4-6 inches

[RRB SSE 2015 3ʳᵈ SEP 1ˢᵗ SHIFT]

27. According to IS 1200, the metal sheet roofing shall be described in terms of

(*a*) meter   (*b*) cubic meter

(*c*) square meter   (*d*) Thickness

[RRB SSE 2015 3ʳᵈ SEP 1ˢᵗ SHIFT]

28. Concrete in a member represented by a core test shall be considered acceptable, if the average equivalent cube strength of the cores is equal to at least X% of the corresponding cube strength. What is the value of X?

(*a*) 70   (*b*) 75

(*c*) 80   (*d*) 85

[RRB SSE 2015 3ʳᵈ SEP 2ⁿᵈ SHIFT]

29. According to IS 1200, during demolition and dismantling, the concrete and brick roofs and floors shall be measured in:

(*a*) meter

(*b*) cubic meter

(*c*) square metres

(*d*) thickness

[RRB SSE 2015 3ʳᵈ SEP 2ⁿᵈ SHIFT]

30. Which of the following is not applicable to pile foundations?

(*a*) Piles transfer load to stratum of adequate capacity

(*b*) Piles resist lateral loads

(*c*) Piles transfer through scour zone to bearing stratum

(*d*) Piles do not anchor structures subjected to hydrostatic uplift

[RRB SSE 2015 3ʳᵈ SEP 2ⁿᵈ SHIFT]

31. Normally, the consistency of cement is measured using:

(*a*) Le Chatelier's apparatus

(*b*) Blaine's permeameter

(*c*) Vicat apparatus

(*d*) Venturimeter

[RRB SSE 2015 3ʳᵈ SEP 2ⁿᵈ SHIFT]

32. According to IS 516, what is t a minimum number of specimen to be tested for estimating the compressive strength

(*a*) 2   (*b*) 3

(*c*) 4   (*d*) 5

[RRB SSE 2015 3ʳᵈ SEP 3ʳᵈ SHIFT]

33. In general, the coefficient of thermal expansion of concrete does not depend on which of the following factors

(*a*) Type of cement

(*b*) Type of aggregate

(*c*) The cement content

(*d*) The quality of water

[RRB SSE 2015 3ʳᵈ SEP 3ʳᵈ SHIFT]

34. Which of the following is not a non-destructive test used for concrete?

(*a*) Rebound hammer   (*b*) Pull-out

(*c*) Ultra-sonic   (*d*) Direct tensile test

[RRB SSE 2015 3ʳᵈ SEP 3ʳᵈ SHIFT]

ANSWER KEY

RRB JUNIOR ENGINEER

1. (a)	**2.** (c)	**3.** (b)	**4.** (c)	**5.** (c)	**6.** (b)	**7.** (b)	**8.** (c)	**9.** (a)	**10.** (c)
11. (d)	**12.** (c)	**13.** (c)	**14.** (b)	**15.** (a)	**16.** (c)	**17.** (a)	**18.** (c)	**19.** (c)	**20.** (a)
21. (b)	**22.** (c)	**23.** (d)	**24.** (d)	**25.** (d)	**26.** (d)	**27.** (d)	**28.** (c)	**29.** (d)	**30.** (c)
31. (c)	**32.** (b)	**33.** (c)							

RRB SENIOR SECTION ENGINEER

1. (b)	**2.** (a)	**3.** (d)	**4.** (b)	**5.** (b)	**6.** (a)	**7.** (b)	**8.** (c)	**9.** (a)	**10.** (c)
11. (b)	**12.** (d)	**13.** (b)	**14.** (c)	**15.** (c)	**16.** (c)	**17.** (a)	**18.** (b)	**19.** (d)	**20.** (a)
21. (b)	**22.** (b)	**23.** (d)	**24.** (c)	**25.** (a)	**26.** (d)	**27.** (d)	**28.** (d)	**29.** (b)	**30.** (d)
31. (c)	**32.** (b)	**33.** (d)	**34.** (d)						

EXPLANATIONS

RRB JUNIOR ENGINEER

1. **Silica** (SiO_2): It imparts strength to the **cement** due to the formation of dicalcium and tricalcium silicates. If **silica** is present in **excess** quantity, the strength of **cement** increases but at the same time, its setting time is prolonged.The major ingredient of **cement** is Lime.

2. The word 'Brinell' is associated with hardness.

3. For plastering walls, cement mortar would be typically used in 1 : 4 ratio.

4. The mixes of grades M10, M15, M20 and M25 correspond approximately to the mix proportions (1 : 3 : 6), (1 : 2 : 4), (1 : 1 . 5 : 3) and (1 : 1 : 2) respectively.

5. Bleeding in fresh concrete refers to the process where free water in the mix is pushed upward to the surface due to the settlement of heavier solid particles such as cement and water. Some bleeding is normal but excessive bleeding can be problematic.

6. BIS:800 deals with steel structures.

7. According to IS:456 the modulus of concrete is $5000 \sqrt{(fck)}$, MPa, where fck is the characteristic compressive strength of concrete.

   The mean modulus of elasticity of concrete at the appropriate age (E_{cj}) shall be either–

   (a) taken as equal to–

   (i) $\left(\rho^{1.5}\right) \times \left(0.043\sqrt{f_{cmi}}\right)$ (in megapascals) when $f_{cmi} \leq 40$ MPa; or

   (ii) $\left(\rho^{1.5}\right) \times \left(0.024\sqrt{f_{cmi}} + 0.12\right)$ (in megapascals) when $f_{cmi} > 40$ MPa

   consideration being given to the fact that this value has a range of $\pm 20\%$.

8. In paints, linseed oil is used as a vehicle. It is produced by heating raw linseed oil and then air is blown inside. It has quick and completely drying quality and a forms a film on the surface. It is often used as a pigment binder in oil paints, and in the paint industry to produce alkyd resins, drying oil finish or varnish in **wood** finishing.

10. When Portland **cement** is blended with **water**, **heat** will be **generated**. This **heat** is named the **heat** of hydration, and it is the product of the exothermic chemical reaction between **cement** and **water**. The two calcium silicates produce very analogous hydration reactions.

11. ISO 800:2007 is based on Limit state method.

12. The maximum percentage of moment redistribution allowed in RCC beam is 30%.

13. Low heat Portland-pozzolona cement has maximum initial settling time.

14. Cement concrete is viscoelastic material.

15. **Cement is sound when there is no lime in it.**

16. 10%

17. For M20 grade of concrete, the maximum shear stress shall not exceed 1.6 N/mm^2.

18. M20 is the minimum grade of the cement to be used.

19. Designated into 7 grades.

20. The strength of cement decreases after storage.

21. Addition of pozzolona increase shrinkage. **Pozzolana**, also known as **pozzolanic** ash (pulvis puteolanus in Latin), is a natural siliceous or siliceous and aluminous material which reacts with calcium hydroxide in the presence of water at room temperature (cf. **pozzolanic** reaction).

22. By controlling span/depth ratio

23. Manufacturing

   Rapid hardening cement is burnt at a higher temperature than that of the OPC under more controlled conditions.

   Strength

   The 3 days strength of rapid hardening cement is equivalent to the 7 days strength of OPC when the water-cement ratio for both the cement is taken to be same. The increased rate of strength is due to the fact that higher proportion of tricalcium silicate (C_3S) is contained in RHC along with finer grinding of the cement clinker. Though, the rate at which RHC gains strength is higher than the rate at which OPC gains strength, the ultimate strength is only a bit higher for RHC.

   Uses

   Rapid hardening cement is mostly used in construction of road where the traffic cannot be halted for long period of time. Besides, RHC is used where the formwork need to be removed early for reuse. It is also used on those circumstances where sufficient strength for further construction is wanted as quickly as practicable. These are also used in manufacturing precast slabs, posts, electric poles.

Advantages

As the curing period for rapid hardening cement is less, it turns out to be economical.

Shrinkage during curing and hardening of cement is less in case of RHC.

RHC are good at Sulphur resistance.

Good speed of construction can be achieved as the strength is gained in relatively shorter time.

Disadvantages

It is expensive than Ordinary Portland Cement.

24. Stress in slab base

25. Alcohol does not react with Concrete.

26. The reinforced concrete beam curved in plane is designed for Bending moment shear and torsion.

27. Maximum settling time is 10 hours.

28. **Bleeding** is one form of segregation, where water comes out to the surface of the **concrete**, being lowest specific gravity among all the ingredients of **concrete**. **Bleeding** can be easily identified in the field by the appearance of a thin layer of water in the top surface of freshly mixed **concrete**.

29. Permissible shear stress in concrete is a function of Percentage of Steel reinforcement and grade of concrete.

30. **The setting** of **cement** and **hardening of concrete. Cement hardens** when it comes into contact with **water**. This **hardening** is a process of crystallization. Crystals form (**after** a certain length of time which is known as the initial **set** time) and interlock with each other.

31. Some overfilling of the void space between the coarse particles by the sand fraction and between the sand particles by a **cement** paste is **necessary** for workability, placeability and durability of the **concrete**.

32. Decreases.

33. It is a fine powder, produced by heating limestone and clay minerals in a kiln to form clinker, grinding the clinker, and adding 2.5 to **3.5 percent** of gypsum.

RRB SENIOR SECTION ENGINEER

1. Industrial and commercial **buildings** will require higher than 4000 psi. Some **structures** also require an exceptional **strength** of 10,000 psi, but these cases are not too **common**. In every day **concrete** work, professionals usually go for a compression **strength** of 7,500 psi.

2. **Water** is the key ingredient, which when mixed with cement, forms a paste that binds the aggregate together. The water causes the hardening of concrete through a process called hydration. Hydration is a chemical reaction in which the major compounds in cement form chemical bonds with water molecules and become hydrates or hydration products.

3. Every singly reinforced beam should be designed as under-reinforced sections because this section gives enough warning before failure. Reinforced concrete beam sections in which the failure strain in concrete is reached earlier than the yield strain of steel is reached, are called over-reinforced sections.

4. A **concrete** plant, also known as a **batch** plant or **batching** plant or a **concrete batching** plant, is equipment that combines various ingredients to form **concrete**. Some of these inputs include water, air, admixtures, sand, aggregate (rocks, gravel, etc.), fly ash, silica fume, slag, and cement.

5. Gypsum is added to that settling time of concrete can be retarded.

6. 4.9 MPa

7. During hydration, heat evolves.

8. According to IS 456, under normal circumstances, the maximum cement content in kg/cum (including fly ash and slag) allowed is 450.

9. Minimum time is 14-day.

10. All concrete work are measured in m^2.

11. The time elapsed between the moment water is added to the ordinary Portland cement and the time when the cement completely loses its plasticity and can resist certain definite pressure is termed as final setting time.

12. Bulk density of cement is not used.

13. 7 days of time.

14. According to IS 1200, granular sub-base used in pavement construction shall be measured as finished work in position in cubic metres.

15. According to IS 456, nominal mix concrete can be used upto grade 20.

16. The batching tolerance for cement as per IS 456 is ±2%.

17. The excessive amount of expansion due to unsound cement is usually related to Magnesia

18. In the determination of total dissolved solids, the water sample is dried at the temperature of 180°C.

19. The batching tolerance for aggregates as per IS 456 is ±3%.

20. According to IS 1200, reinforcing bars used in reinforced cement concrete shall be measured in meters.

21. If inadequate amounts of gypsum are added to the cement, flash set can occur—a rapid development of rigidity in freshly mixed portland cement paste, mortar, or concrete. Further mixing can't dispel this rigidity, and a large amount of heat is produced in the process.

22. The recommended slump of concrete for hand placed pavements is 1-3 inches.

Very low	0-1 (0-25)	Very dry mixes used in paving machines with high-powered vibration
Low	1-2 (25-50)	Low-workability mixes used for foundations with light reinforcement; Pavements consolidated by hand-operated vibrators

Medium	2-4 (50-100)	Medium workability mixes; manually consolidated flat slabs. Normal reinforced concrete manually placed; heavily reinforced sections with mechanical vibration
High	4-7 (100-175)	High workability concrete for sections with congested reinforcement; May not respond well to vibration

23. **Elimination of Parallax: Elimination of parallax** may be done by focusing the eye piece for distinct vision of cross hairs and focusing the objective to bring the image of the object in the plane of cross hairs. This is not permanent adjustment in theodolite.

24. Floor finishes is always measured in square meter.

25. According to IS 456, the modulus of elasticity of steel can be assumed as $200kN/m^2$

26. The recommended slump for pumped concrete is 4-6 inches.

27. Metal sheet roofing is always described in thickness.

28. 85%

29. According to IS 1200, during demolition and dismantling, the concrete and brick roofs and floors shall be measured in m^3.

30. Piles do not anchor structures subjected to hydrostatic uplift.

31. The standard consistency of a cement paste is defined as that consistency which will permit the vicat plunger to penetrate to a point 5 to 7 mm from the bottom of thevicat mould.

32. According to IS 516, 3 specimen to be tested for estimating the compressive strength.

33. The coefficient of thermal expansion (CTE) in concrete is the measure of how concrete changes in volume in response to changes in temperature. CTE is defined as the change in unit length per degree of temperature change and isdependent on the type of aggregate in the concrete mix and the degree of saturation. It is independent of quality of water.

34. Direct tensile test is not a non-destructive test.

4
CHAPTER

SURVEYING

RRB JUNIOR ENGINEER

1. The branch of surveying in which only linear measurements are directly made in the field is

(*a*) land surveying

(*b*) chain surveying

(*c*) engineering survey

(*d*) topographical survey

[RRB JE 2014 GREEN SHIFT]

2. Contour lines drawn on a map, are the lines which pass through

(*a*) hills and depressions

(*b*) same elevation

(*c*) same latitude

(*d*) none of the above

[RRB JE 2014 GREEN SHIFT]

3. The reduced bearing of a line is N 87° W. Its whole circle bearing is :

(*a*) 273°　　　　　(*b*) 3°

(*c*) 93°　　　　　(*d*) 87"

[RRB JE 2014 RED SHIFT]

4. A 30m metric chain is found to be 0.1 m too short throughout the measurement. If the distance measured is recorded as 300m, then the actual distance measured will be

(*a*) 300.1 m　　　　(*b*) 301.0 m

(*c*) 299 m　　　　(*d*) 310 m

[RRB JE 2014 YELLOW SHIFT]

5. Which one of the following methods of levelling eliminates the error due to curvature and refraction ?

(*a*) Fly levelling

(*b*) Levelling by equalizing the distances of backsight and foresight

(*c*) Check levelling

(*d*) Precise levelling

[RRB JE 2014 YELLOW SHIFT]

6. Which of the following is not used in measuring perpendicular offsets?

(*a*) Line ranger　　(*b*) Steel tape

(*c*) Optical square　(*d*) Cross staff

[RRB JE 2015 26ᵗʰ AUG 1ˢᵗ SHIFT]

7. The spacing between two bars in medium size screen ranges from

(*a*) 20-50 mm　　　(*b*) 20-40 mm

(*c*) 10-20 mm　　　(*d*) 10-30 mm

[RRB JE 2015 26ᵗʰ AUG 1ˢᵗ SHIFT]

8. Which of the following instruments is generally used for base line measurements?

(*a*) Chain　　　　(*b*) Metallic tape

(*c*) Steel tape　　(*d*) Invar tape

[RRB JE 2015 26ᵗʰ AUG 2ⁿᵈ SHIFT]

9. The method of orienting a plane table with two inaccessible points is known as

(*a*) Intersection　(*b*) Resection

(*c*) Back sighting　(*d*) Two-point problem

[RRB JE 2015 26ᵗʰ AUG 3ʳᵈ SHIFT]

10. Direct method of contouring is

(*a*) A quick method

(*b*) Adopted for large surveys only

(*c*) Most accurate method

(*d*) Suitable for hilly terrains

[RRB JE 2015 26ᵗʰ AUG 3ʳᵈ SHIFT]

11. Benchmark is established by

(*a*) Hypsometry

(*b*) Barometric levelling

(*c*) Spirit levelling

(*d*) Trigonometrical levelling

[RRB JE 2015 27ᵗʰ AUG 1ˢᵗ SHIFT]

12. The type of surveying which requires least office work is

(*a*) Tacheometry

(*b*) Trigonometrical levelling

(*c*) Plane table surveying

(*d*) Theodolite surveying

[RRB JE 2015 27ᵗʰ AUG 1ˢᵗ SHIFT]

13. Intersection method of detailed plotting is most suitable for

(*a*) Forests　　　(*b*) Urban areas

(*c*) Hilly areas　(*d*) Plains

[RRB JE 2015 27ᵗʰ AUG 2ⁿᵈ SHIFT]

14. The instrument used for accurate centering in plane table survey is

(a) Spirit level   (b) Alidade

(c) Plumbing fork   (d) Through compass

[RRB JE 2015 27ᵗʰ AUG 3ʳᵈ SHIFT]

15. A series of closely spaced contour lines represents a

(a) Steep slope   (b) Gentle slope

(c) Uniform slope   (d) Plane surface

[RRB JE 2015 27ᵗʰ AUG 3ʳᵈ SHIFT]

16. The two point problem and three point problem are methods of

(a) Resection

(b) Orientation

(c) Traversing

(d) Resection and orientation

[RRB JE 2015 28ᵗʰ AUG 1ˢᵗ SHIFT]

17. Substense bar is an instrument used for

(a) Levelling

(b) Measurement of horizontal distances in plane areas

(c) Measurement of horizontal distances in undulated areas

(d) Measurement of angles

[RRB JE 2015 28ᵗʰ AUG 1ˢᵗ SHIFT]

18. The representative fraction 1/2500 means that the scale 1 cm is equal to

(a) 0.25 m   (b) 2.5 m

(c) 25 m   (d) 2.5 km

[RRB JE 2015 28ᵗʰ AUG 2ⁿᵈ SHIFT]

19. The needle of a magnetic compass is generally supported on a

(a) Bush bearing

(b) Ball bearing

(c) Needle bearing

(d) Jewel bearing

[RRB JE 2015 28ᵗʰ AUG 2ⁿᵈ SHIFT]

20. Ranging is the process of

(a) Fixing ranging rods on the extremities of the area

(b) Aligning the chain in a straight line between two extremities

(c) Taking offsets from a chain line

(d) Chaining over a range of mountains

[RRB JE 2015 28ᵗʰ AUG 3ʳᵈ SHIFT]

21. A series of closely spaced contour lines represents a

(a) Steep slope   (b) Gentle slope

(c) Uniform slope   (d) Plane slope

[RRB JE 2015 29ᵗʰ AUG 1ˢᵗ SHIFT]

22. For a well conditional triangle, no angle should be less than

(a) 20°   (b) 30°

(c) 45°   (d) 60°

[RRB JE 2015 29ᵗʰ AUG 2ⁿᵈ SHIFT]

23. What is the magnetic declination at a place if the magnetic bearing of the sun at noon is 184°?

(a) 4°W   (b) 4°E

(c) 176°W   (d) 176°E

[RRB JE 2015 29ᵗʰ AUG 2ⁿᵈ SHIFT]

24. The fundamental principle of surveying is to work from the

(a) whole to the part

(b) part to the whole

(c) lower level to higher level

(d) higher level to lower level

[RRB JE 2015 29ᵗʰ AUG 3ʳᵈ SHIFT]

25. The error in measured length due to sag of chain or tape is known as

(a) positive error

(b) negative error

(c) compensating error

(d) instrumental error

[RRB JE 2015 29ᵗʰ AUG 3ʳᵈ SHIFT]

26. In order to determine the natural features such as valleys, rivers, lakes etc. the surveying preferred is

(a) City surveying

(b) Location suiveying

(c) Cadastral surveying

(d) Topographical surveying

[RRB JE 2015 30ᵗʰ AUG 3ʳᵈ SHIFT]

27. Hydrographic survey deals with the mapping of

(a) Larger water bodies

(b) Rainfall data

(c) Wave movement

(d) Hilly areas

[RRB JE 2015 16ᵗʰ SEP 3ʳᵈ SHIFT]

RRB SENIOR SECTION ENGINEER

1. Consider following contours:

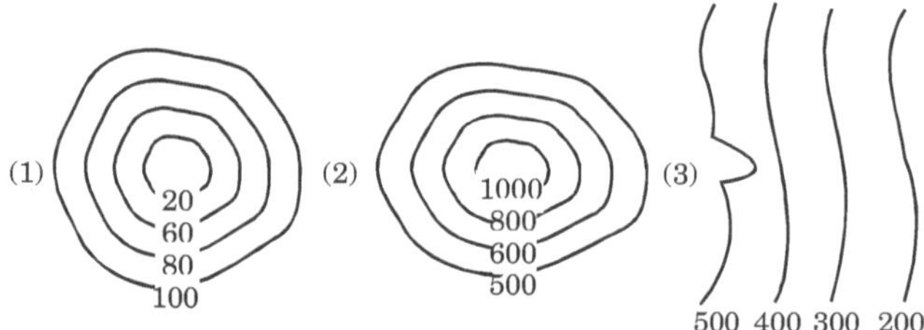

Match the following a) Hill b) Pond c) Slope

(a) 1-b, 2-a, 3-c (b) 1-a, 2-b, 3-c

(c) 1-a,2-c,3-c (d) 1-c, 2-b, 3-a

[RRB SSE 2014 GREEN SHIFT]

2. Chain surveying is well adopted for :

(a) Small areas in open ground

(b) Large areas with simple details

(c) Small areas with crowded details

(d) Large areas with difficult details

[RRB SSE 2014 RED SHIFT]

3. If whole Circle Bearing of a line is 120°, then its Reduced Bearing is :

(a) S 20°E (b) S 60°F

(c) N 120°E (d) N 60°E

[RRB SSE 2014 RED SHIFT]

4. The main principle of surveying is to work from:

(a) Part to whole

(b) Whole to part

(c) Higher Level to Lower Level

(d) Lower Level to Higher Level

[RRB SSE 2014 RED SHIFT]

5. In Surveying. Offsets are

(a) lateral measurements made with respect to main survey line

(b) perpendiculars erected from chain lines

(c) taken to avoid unnecessary walking between stations

(d) measurements which are not made at right angles to the chain line

[RRB SSE 2014 YELLOW SHIFT]

6. A contour line joins all the points having

(a) Equal elevation

(b) Zero elevation

(c) Similar reference points

(d) Equal vertical angles

[RRB SSE 2015 1ˢᵗ SEP 1ˢᵗ SHIFT]

7. In surveying, the horizontal angle which a line makes with the magnet meridian is called as

(a) Magnetic meridian

(b) Grid meridian

(c) Arbitrary meridian

(d) Grid bearing

[RRB SSE 2015 1ˢᵗ SEP 3ʳᵈ SHIFT]

8. Which of the following is not a method used for plane table surveying

(a) Radiation method

(b) Travelling method

(c) Intersection method

(d) Backscattering method

[RRB SSE 2015 2ⁿᵈ SEP 1ˢᵗ SHIFT]

9. The bearing of line in the direction of the progress of the survey is called as

(a) Forward bearing (b) Reverse bearing

(c) Backward bearing (d) Quadrilateral bearing

[RRB SSE 2015 2ⁿᵈ SEP 2ⁿᵈ SHIFT]

10. The reference points on which a day's work is closed and from where levelling is continued the next day are called as

(a) Temporary benchmarks

(b) Arbitrary benchmarks

(c) Permanent benchmarks

(d) GTS benchmarks

[RRB SSE 2015 2ⁿᵈ SEP 3ʳᵈ SHIFT]

11. The point at which both foresight and back sight are taken during the course of levelling is called as

(a) Intermediate site (b) Benchmark

(c) Station (d) Change point

[RRB SSE 2015 3ʳᵈ SEP 1ˢᵗ SHIFT]

12. Which of the following is not true for the direct and indirect methods of contouring?

(a) Direct method is most accurate but is slow

(b) Indirect method is less accurate but is faster

(c) Direct method is expensive

(d) Indirect method is relatively more expensive

[RRB SSE 2015 3ʳᵈ SEP 1ˢᵗ SHIFT]

13. The line joining the intersection of the cross hairs to the optical centre of the object glass and its continuation is called as:

(a) Line of collimation

(b) Telescopic axis

(c) Vertical axis

(d) Horizontal axis

[RRB SSE 2015 3ʳᵈ SEP 2ⁿᵈ SHIFT]

14. The imaginary surface connecting points to which water would rise in tightly cased wells from a given point in an aquifer is called as:

(a) Specific surface

(b) Phreatic surface

(c) Potentiometric surface

(d) Normal surface

[RRB SSE 2015 3rd SEP 2nd SHIFT]

15. In surveying, the triangles having angles smaller than 30 degree are called as

(a) Ideal triangles

(b) Well-conditioned triangles

(c) Ill-conditioned triangles

(d) Acute triangles

[RRB SSE 2015 3rd SEP 3rd SHIFT]

ANSWER KEY

RRB JUNIOR ENGINEER

1. (b)	**2.** (b)	**3.** (a)	**4.** (c)	**5.** (b)	**6.** (a)	**7.** (b)	**8.** (d)	**9.** (d)	**10.** (c)
11. (c)	**12.** (c)	**13.** (c)	**14.** (c)	**15.** (a)	**16.** (d)	**17.** (c)	**18.** (c)	**19.** (d)	**20.** (b)
21. (a)	**22.** (b)	**23.** (a)	**24.** (a)	**25.** (a)	**26.** (d)	**27.** (a)			

RRB SENIOR SECTION ENGINEER

1. (a)	**2.** (a)	**3.** (b)	**4.** (b)	**5.** (a)	**6.** (a)	**7.** (a)	**8.** (d)	**9.** (a)	**10.** (a)
11. (d)	**12.** (d)	**13.** (a)	**14.** (c)	**15.** (c)					

EXPLANATIONS

RRB JUNIOR ENGINEER

1. Chain survey is the simplest method of surveying. In this survey only measurements are taken in the field, and the rest work, such as plotting calculation etc. are done in the office. This is most suitable adapted to small plane areas with very few details. If carefully done, it gives quite accurate results. The necessary requirements for field work are chain, tape, ranging rod, arrows and sometime cross staff.

- It is a system of surveying in which sides of various triangles are measured directly in the field and NO angular measurements are taken.
- It is the simplest kind of Surveying
- It is adopted when Level of accuracy required is not high

2. In cartography, a **contour line** (often just called a "**contour**") joins points of equal elevation (height) above a given level, such as mean sea level. A **contour map** is a **map** illustrated with **contour lines**, for example a topographic **map**, which thus shows valleys and hills, and the steepness or gentleness of slopes.

3. Whole circle bearing is 273 degrees.

4. 30 m is actually 29.9 m. Therefore, 300 m measurement will be 299 m in actual.

5. Levelling by equalizing the distances of backsight and foresight eliminates the error due to curvature and refraction.

6. Line ranger is not used for Surveying purpose.

7. The spacing between two bars in medium size screen ranges from 20-40 mm.

8. Invar Tape is used for base line measurements. **INVAR TAPE**: **Invar tapes** are available in lengths of 20, 30 and 100 metres. **Invar tapes** are **used** whey high degree of accuracy and precision in linear **measurements** is required such as **measurement** of **base lines**. **Invar tapes** are made of alloys of nickel and steel and have very low coefficient of thermal expansion.

9. Resection is a method of **plane table surveying** in which location of **plane table** is unknown and it is determined by sighting it to known **points** or plotted **points**. It is also called method of orientation and it can be conducted by **two** field conditions as follows.

10. In the **direct method**, the **contour** to be plotted is actually traced on the ground. This **method** is slow and tedious and thus used for large scale maps, small **contour** interval and at high degree of precision.

11. A **spirit level** is an instrument consisting of a telescope with a crosshair and a tube **level** or bubble **level** used to indicate whether a surface is horizontal (**level**) or vertical (plumb).

12. **Plane Table Surveying** is a graphical method of **survey** in which the field observations and plotting are done simultaneously. •It is simple and cheaper than theodolite **survey**. It is most suitable for small scale maps.

13. Intersection method of detailed plotting is most suitable for hilly areas. It is most suitable method for inaccessible areas

14. **Plumbing fork** with a plumb bob is used in large scale surveying for Centring of plane table and for Transferring of ground point.

15. Closely spaced contour lines represent a steep slope.

16. The two point problem and three point problem are methods of Resection and Orientation.

17. SUBTENSE BAR

- The subtence bar is an instrument used for measuring the horizontal distance between the instrument station and a station where the subtence bar is to be set up.

- Substence method is an indirect method of distance determination.

- This method essentially consists of measurin the angle subtended by two ends of a horizontal rod of fixed length, called a subtense bar.

- In this method a staff or target rod is not necessary and the theodolite required is also of the ordinary transit type.

18. 25 m

19. The needle of magnetic compass is generally supported on a Jewel Bearing. A jewel bearing is a plain bearing in which a metal spindle turns in a jewel-lined pivot hole.

The hole is typically shaped like a torus and is slightly larger than the shaft diameter.

These are used in instruments where low friction, long life, and dimensional accuracy are important.

They are largely used in mechanical watches and galvanometers, compasses, turbine flow meters.

20. "**Ranging**" **is the process of**. Fixing ranging rods on the extremeties of the area. Aligning the chain in a straight line between two extremeties.

21. Steep slope: If contours are very closed to each other than the slope **is** called «**steep slope**».

22. Well condition triangle means the **angle** is acute and doesn›t **less than** 30degree. The **angle** between the **triangle must** be greater **than** 30 degree and**less than** 120 degree. Hence it is said to be **well conditioned triangle** .

23. Magnetic declination=184-180

24. According to whole to part principle whole area enclosed by main survey line & station. Then area divided into well conditioned triangles. This principle help to prevent accumulation error. If any error in the measurement of any sides of triangle not affect the whole work.

25. The error in measured length due to sag of chain or tape is known as positive error.

26. A **Topographic Survey** is a **survey** that gathers data about the elevation of points on a piece of land and presents them as contour lines on a plot. The purpose of a **topographic survey** is to collect **survey** data about the natural and man-made features of the land, as well as its elevations.

27. Hydrohraphic survey deals with the mapping of larger water bodies.

RRB SENIOR SECTION ENGINEER

1.

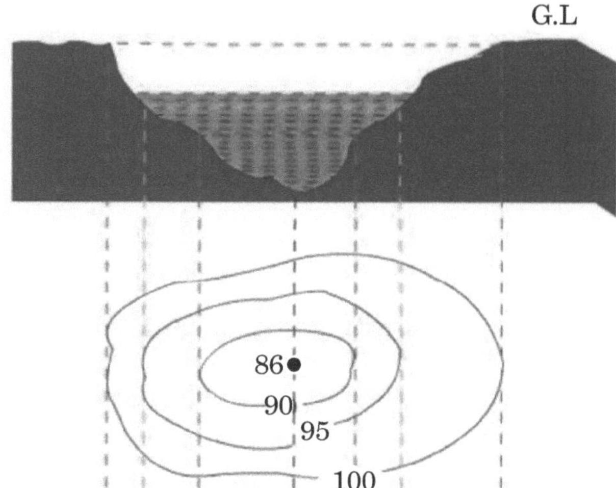

Pond and its contour

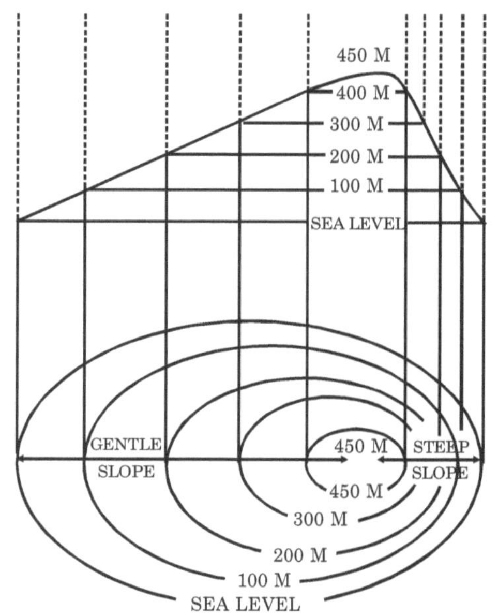

Hill and its contour

Concave Slope

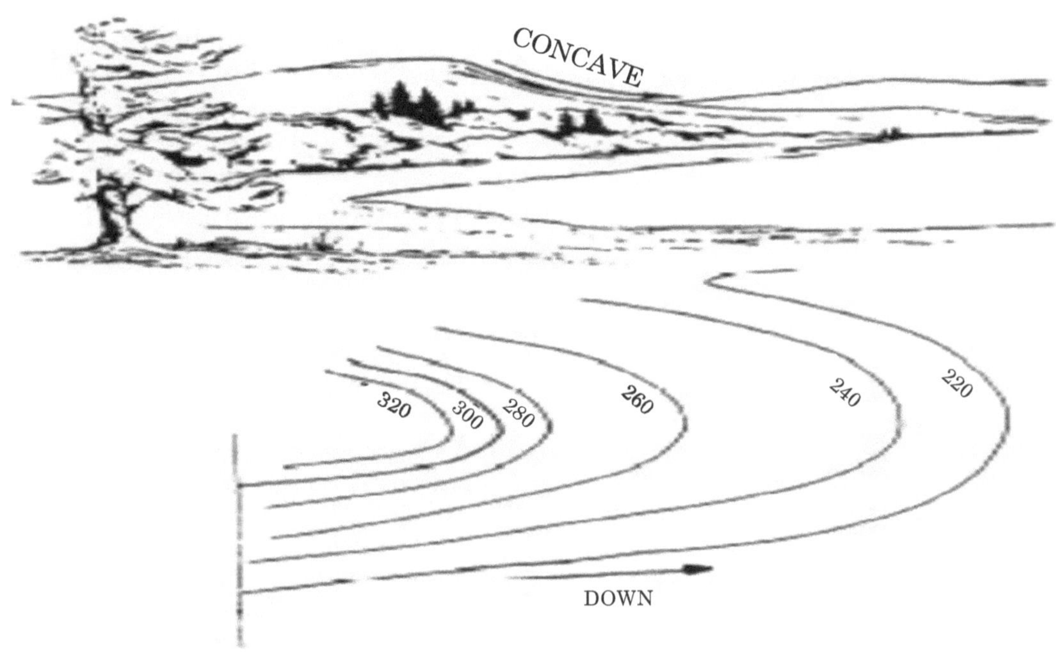

Slope and its contour

2. Well adopted for small areas in open ground.

3. This azimuth lies in 2nd quadrant (SE), If you take the angle starting from South and move towards East, this line will make 180° - 120° = 60° from South direction towards East, So the Bearing of this line will be S 60° E.

4. The fundamental principles upon which the surveying is being carried out are

- working from whole to part.
- after deciding the position of any point, its reference must be kept from at least two permanent objects or stations whose position have already been well defined.

The purpose of working from whole to part is

- to localise the errors and
- to control the accumulation of errors.

5. A short distance measured perpendicularly from a main **survey** line. Also called **offset** line. A line a short distance from and parallel to a main **survey** line.

6. It can take compressive loads only.

7. Defined by a horizontal angle between the line and a defined reference line called a meridian. True meridian is the north-south reference line through the earth's geographic poles. Magnetic meridian is a north-south reference line as defined by the earth's magnetic field.

8. Backscatter (or backscattering) is the reflection of waves, particles, or signals back to the direction from which they came. It is a diffuse reflection due to scattering, as opposed to specular reflection as from a mirror. Backscattering has important applications in astronomy, photography, and medical ultrasonography. The opposite effect is forward scatter, e.g. when a translucent material like a cloud diffuses sunlight, giving soft light.

9. The bearing of line in the direction of the progress of the survey is called as Forward bearing.

10. 1. **Permanent Benchmark:** These are the benchmarks established by state government agencies like PWD. They are established with reference to GTS benchmarks. They are usually on the corner of plinth of public buildings.

2. **Arbitrary Benchmark:** In many engineering projects the difference in elevations of neighbouring points is more important than their reduced level with respect to mean sea level. In such cases a relatively permanent point, like plinth of a building or corner of a culvert, are taken as benchmarks, their level assumed arbitrarily such as 100.0 m, 300.0 m, etc.

3. **Temporary Benchmark:** This type of benchmark is established at the end of the day's work, so that the next day work may be continued from that point. Such point should be on a permanent object so that next day it is easily identified.

11. • **Height of Instrument (HI):** The elevation of the line of sight with respect to assumed datum is known as HI. This is obtained by adding back sight to RL of B.M or change point.

    • **Change Point (CP):** The point on which both the foresight and back sight are taken during the operation of levelling is called change point.

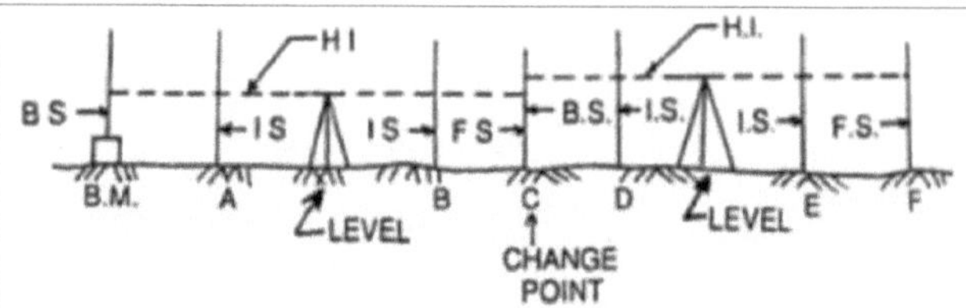

12. Indirect method is relatively more expensive.

13. Line of collimation: Line joining the intersection of the cross-hairs to the optical center of the objective and its continuation. It is also know as Line of sight.

    Line of sight: is defined as the intersection of the cross hairs and the optical centre of the objective lens.

14. A potentiometric surface is the imaginary plane where a given reservoir of fluid will "equalize out to" if allowed to flow. A potentiometric surface is based on hydraulic principles. For example, we know that two connected storage tanks with one full and one empty will gradually fill/drain to the same level.

15. A well conditioned triangle has no angle in it as less than 30 degree or greater than 120 degree. An equilateral triangle is the best-condition or ideal triangle. Hence ill conditioned triangles are those triangles in which atleast one angle is less than 30 degree or greater than 120 degree.

ENGINEERING DRAWING AND GRAPHICS

RRB JUNIOR ENGINEER

1. How many lines can be said to exist or be drawn in a three dimensional space, which are mutually perpendicular to each other?

(a) 2   (b) 3

(c) 4   (d) 8

[RRB JE 2014 GREEN SHIFT]

2. A third angle orthographic projection of an object' is given below. What is this object?

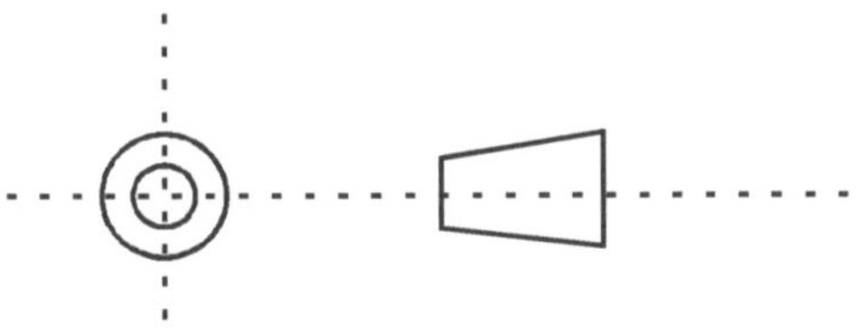

(a) Triangle   (b) Trapezium

(c) Cone   (d) Frustrum of a cone

[RRB JE 2014 GREEN SHIFT]

3. In an engineering drawing it is written scale 1 cm = 100 m. Which ratio does it correspond to?

(a) 1 : 100   (b) 1 : 1000

(c) 1: 10,000   (d) 1 : 1,00,000

[RRB JE 2014 GREEN SHIFT]

4. In machine drawing, a 'sectional view' cut portion is shown by

(a) diagonal hatching (b) dots

(c) cross marks   (d) red colour

[RRB JE 2014 GREEN SHIFT]

5. For complete description of a component, a machine drawing would require minimum how many orthographic projections?

(a) 1   (b) 2

(c) 3   (d) 4

[RRB JE 2014 GREEN SHIFT]

6. If an object lies in third quadrant, its position with respect to reference planes will be :

(a) Infront of V.P., Above H.P.

(b) Behind V.P., AboveH.P.

(c) Infront of V.P., Below H.P.

(d) Behind V.P., BelowH.P.

[RRB JE 2014 RED SHIFT]

7. If a thin rectangular plate of 60 mm × 30 mm is inclined at an angle of 60° to the Horizontal Plane, its top view may be :

(a) Square of 30 mm size

(b) Square of 60 mm size

(c) Rectangle of 60 mm × 45 mm size

(d) Rectangle of 45 mm × 30 mm size

[RRB JE 2014 RED SHIFT]

8. Projection of an object shown by three views is known as :

(a) Perspective

(b) Oblique

(c) Orthographic

(d) None of these

[RRB JE 2014 RED SHIFT]

9. If a point moves in a plane in such a way that the sum of its distances from two fixed point; is constant, the curve so traced is called :

(a) Parabola

(b) Ellipse

(c) Hyperbola

(d) All of these

[RRB JE 2014 RED SHIFT]

10. For Engineering Drawings, match the Col. X and Col. Y

Col. X (Type)	Col. Y (Use)
P. Large sized letters	1. Sub-Titles
Q. Medium sized letters	2. Dimensions
R. Small sized letters	3. Main Titles

(a) P-3, Q-1, R-2

(b) P-2, Q-1. R-3

(c) P-3, Q-2, R-1

(d) P-2, Q-3, R-1

[RRB JE 2014 YELLOW SHIFT]

11. For drawing engineering curves, which is correct option (e = eccentricity)

(a) For Ellipse, e > 1

(b) For Parabola, e < 1

(c) For Hyperbola, e = 1

(d) For Parabola, e = 1

[RRB JE 2014 YELLOW SHIFT]

12. Match Col. X (Line Type) with Col. Y (Application)

Col. X   **Col. Y**

P------------------   1. Centre lines

Q __ _ ___ _   2. Ground lines

R_______________   3. Hidden edges

S _\/_____\/____   4.   Long break lines

(a) P-2, Q-1, R-4, S-3   (b) P-3, Q-1, R-2, S-4

(c) P-4, Q-3, R-1, S-2   (d) P-2, Q-1- R-3, S-4

[RRB JE 2014 YELLOW SHIFT]

13. Which statement is NOT correct in respect of Engineering Drawings.

(a) Circular Features are Indicated by the centre lines

(b) A visible line has precedence over a hidden line

(c) The faces perpendicular to the direction of viewing are seen as edge views

(d) In Isometric projection, an Isometic scale is used.

[RRB JE 2014 YELLOW SHIFT]

14. An area of 64 square kilometre is represented by 256 square centimetre on a map. The R. F. of the scale is

(a) 1/4   (b) 1/50000

(c) 1/2   (d) 1/5000

[RRB JE 2015 26th AUG 1st SHIFT]

15. An involute profile is used in

(a) pulleys   (b) cams

(c) chains   (d) gears

[RRB JE 2015 26th AUG 1st SHIFT]

16. If a line is parallel to H.P. and inclined to V.P., its front view will be

(a) a line of smaller dimension

(b) a line of larger dimension

(c) a line of same dimension

(d) a point

[RRB JE 2015 26th AUG 1st SHIFT]

17. In multi-view projections, the xy line is known as

(a) horizontal line   (b) vertical line

(c) traces   (d) reference line

[RRB JE 2015 26th AUG 1st SHIFT]

18. Isometric drawings fall into the category of

(a) multi-view drawings

(b) oblique drawings

(c) axonometric drawings

(d) perspective drawings

[RRB JE 2015 26th AUG 1st SHIFT]

19. The R.F. of a scale is

(a) < 1   (b) = 1

(c) > 1   (d) any of these

[RRB JE 2015 26th AUG 2nd SHIFT]

20. Which of the following methods is not used for drawing elliptical curves?

(a) oblong method

(b) tangent method

(c) concentric circles method

(d) intersecting arc method

[RRB JE 2015 26th AUG 2nd SHIFT]

21. If a line is parallel to V.P. and inclined to H.P., its top view will be

(a) a point

(b) a line of larger dimension

(c) a line of smaller dimension

(d) a line of same dimension

[RRB JE 2015 26th AUG 2nd SHIFT]

22. In first - angle projection method, the relative positions of the observer, object and plane are

(a) Plane is placed between observer and object

(b) Observer is placed between object and plane

(c) Object is placed between observer and plane

(d) May be placed in any order

[RRB JE 2015 26th AUG 2nd SHIFT]

23. A square lamina is perpendicular to both the reference planes. Its top and front views will be

(a) the straight lines

(b) the squares

(c) a square and a straight line respectively

(d) a straight line and a square respectively

[RRB JE 2015 26th AUG 2nd SHIFT]

24. The diagonal scale is used to represent

(a) three consecutive units

(b) two consecutive units

(c) it diagonal of square

(d) diagonal of rectangle

[RRB JE 2015 26th AUG 3rd SHIFT]

25. If a line is parallel to H.P. and inclined to V.P., its true length will be seen in

(a) Front view

(b) Top view

(c) Side view

(d) Both front and top views

[RRB JE 2015 26th AUG 3rd SHIFT]

26. If both the front and top views of a plane are straight lines, it may be
(a) perpendicular to both horizontal and vertical planes
(b) parallel to horizontal plane and perpendicular to vertical plane
(c) perpendicular to horizontal plane and parallel to vertical plane
(d) parallel to both horizontal and vertical planes
[RRB JE 2015 26th AUG 3rd SHIFT]

27. For orthographic projections. BIS Recommends the following projections.
(a) Fourth-angle projection
(b) Third-angle projection
(c) First- angle projection
(d) Second-angle projection
[RRB JE 2015 26th AUG 3rd SHIFT]

28. A square lamina is perpendicular to the H.P. and inclined to V.P. Its
(a) V.T. will be perpendicular to the reference line
(b) H.T. will be parallel to the reference line
(c) V.T. will be parallel to the reference line
(d) V.T. will be inclined to the reference line
[RRB JE 2015 26th AUG 3rd SHIFT]

29. The meaning of R.F. is
(a) Reducing fraction
(b) Representative fraction
(c) Reduction factor
(d) Representative factor
[RRB JE 2015 27th AUG 1st SHIFT]

30. If a line is parallel to both H.P and V.P., its true length will be seen in
(a) Both front and top views
(b) only in side view
(c) only in front view
(d) only in top view
[RRB JE 2015 27th AUG 1st SHIFT]

31. Planes which are inclined to both the horizontal and vertical planes are known as
(a) auxiliary planes
(b) profile planes
(c) reference planes
(d) oblique planes
[RRB JE 2015 27th AUG 1st SHIFT]

32. In first - angle projection system, the light hand side view of an object is drawn
(a) right of the elevation
(b) above the elevation
(c) left of the elevation
(d) below the elevation
[RRB JE 2015 27th AUG 1st SHIFT]

33. A square lamina is perpendicular to the H.P. and parallel to V.P.. Its horizontal trace will be
(a) perpendicular to the reference line
(b) parallel to the reference line
(c) inclined to the reference line
(d) a point
[RRB JE 2015 27th AUG 1st SHIFT]

34. The diagonal scale is used to represent
(a) three consecutive units
(b) two consecutive units
(c) diagonal of square
(d) diagonal of rectangle
[RRB JE 2015 27th AUG 2nd SHIFT]

35. If a line is parallel to H.P. and inclined to V.P., its true length will be seen in
(a) Front view
(b) Top view
(c) Side view
(d) Both front and top views
[RRB JE 2015 27th AUG 2nd SHIFT]

36. If both the front an top views of a plane are straight lines, it may be
(a) perpendicular to both horizontal and vertical planes
(b) parallel to horizontal plane and perpendicular to vertical plane
(c) perpendicular to horizontal plane and parallel to vertical plane
(d) parallel to both horizontal and vertical planes
[RRB JE 2015 27th AUG 2nd SHIFT]

37. For orthographic projections, BIS recommends the following projections.
(a) Fourth-angle projection
(b) Third-angle projection
(c) First-angle projection
(d) Second-angle projection
[RRB JE 2015 27th AUG 2nd SHIFT]

38. A square lamina perpendicular to the H.P. and inclined to V P., Its
(a) V.T. will be perpendicular to the reference line
(b) H.T. will be parallel to the reference line
(c) V.T. will be parallel to the reference line
(d) V.T. will be inclined to the reference line
[RRB JE 2015 27th AUG 2nd SHIFT]

39. Angle is measured by
(a) plain scale
(b) comparative scale
(c) scale of chords
(d) diagonal scale
[RRB JE 2015 27th AUG 3rd SHIFT]

40. If a line is parallel to V.P. and inclined To H.P., its true length will be seen in
   (a) Side view
   (b) Top view
   (c) Both front and top views
   (d) Front view
   [RRB JE 2015 27ᵗʰ AUG 3ʳᵈ SHIFT]

41. If a circular plane is inclined at 60° with the H.P. and 30° with the V.P., its side view will be
   (a) a circle   (b) a straight line
   (c) an ellipse   (d) true shape
   [RRB JE 2015 27ᵗʰ AUG 3ʳᵈ SHIFT]

42. The exact value of R.F. on an isometric scale is
   (a) 0.815   (b) 0.8165
   (c) $(2/3)^{1/2}$ (d) 9/11
   [RRB JE 2015 27ᵗʰ AUG 3ʳᵈ SHIFT]

43. The eccentricity of an ellipse is
   (a) = 1   (b) < 1
   (c) > 1   (d) = 0
   [RRB JE 2015 27ᵗʰ AUG 3ʳᵈ SHIFT]

44. The distance between two stations is 20 kilometres. If the R.F. of the scale is 1/400000. Then the distance between the two stations on the map will be
   (a) 50 cm   (b) 5 cm
   (c) 5 cm   (d) 1 cm
   [RRB JE 2015 28ᵗʰ AUG 1ˢᵗ SHIFT]

45. If a line is perpendicular to V.P. and parallel to H.P., its front view will be
   (a) a point
   (b) a line of smaller dimension
   (c) a line of larger dimension
   (d) a line of same dimension
   [RRB JE 2015 28ᵗʰ AUG 1ˢᵗ SHIFT]

46. A circular plane with a 60 mni diameter is resting on a point of it circumference on the V.P. The surface of the plane is inclined at 45° to the V.P. and perpendicular to H.P.. Its front view will be
   (a) a straight line   (b) an ellipse
   (c) a circle   (d) a rectangle
   [RRB JE 2015 28ᵗʰ AUG 1ˢᵗ SHIFT]

47. The angle that isometric lines make with each other is
   (a) 90°   (b) 60°
   (c) 120°   (d) 45°
   [RRB JE 2015 28ᵗʰ AUG 1ˢᵗ SHIFT]

48. The eccentricity of a parabola is
   (a) = 1   (b) < 1
   (c) > 1   (d) = 0
   [RRB JE 2015 28ᵗʰ AUG 1ˢᵗ SHIFT]

49. The front view and top view of a line both line above the XY line. The line is located in:
   (a) First Quadrant   (b) S on Quadrant
   (c) Third Quadrant   (d) fourth Quadrant.
   [RRB JE 2015 28ᵗʰ AUG 2ⁿᵈ SHIFT]

50. If the nominal diameter of a bolt is "D", then the width of the hexagonal nut across flat surfaces is empirically given as:
   (a) D   (b) 1.5 × D
   (c) 1.5 × D + 3 mm,   (d) 1.5 × D + 5 mm.
   [RRB JE 2015 28ᵗʰ AUG 2ⁿᵈ SHIFT]

51. A vernier scale is good enough to read in .... after decimal.
   (a) One digit,   (b) Two digits,
   (c) Three digits,   (d) Four digits.
   [RRB JE 2015 28ᵗʰ AUG 2ⁿᵈ SHIFT]

52. A sectioning plane cuts a cone such that it is inclined to cone axis at an angle other than 90 and it cuts all its generators. The section so cut is.
   (a) Rectangular Hyperbola
   (b) A Parabola
   (c) A Hyperbola
   (d) An ellipse.
   [RRB JE 2015 28ᵗʰ AUG 2ⁿᵈ SHIFT]

53. An isometric projection is a:
   (a) 2D view   (b) 3D view
   (c) 2½D view   (d) perspective view.
   [RRB JE 2015 28ᵗʰ AUG 2ⁿᵈ SHIFT]

54. The term "plan" in orthographic projection refers to:
   (a) top view,   (b) front view,
   (c) side view,   (d) sectioned view.
   [RRB JE 2015 28ᵗʰ AUG 3ʳᵈ SHIFT]

55. A thread profile having included 55° angle is:
   (a) V thread,   (b) Acme thread,
   (c) Square thread,   (d) Whitworth thread.
   [RRB JE 2015 28ᵗʰ AUG 3ʳᵈ SHIFT]

56. The common map of "road network" is drawn to scale with RF:
   (a) Less than one,
   (b) Greater than one,
   (c) Equal to one,
   (d) RF is not relevant for such maps.
   [RRB JE 2015 28ᵗʰ AUG 3ʳᵈ SHIFT]

57. The eccentricity of a hyperbola is equal to:
   (a) less than **One,**
   (b) greater than **One,**
   (c) **One,**
   (d) There is no term as eccentricity for a parabola.
   [RRB JE 2015 28ᵗʰ AUG 3ʳᵈ SHIFT]

58. The angle between the vertical iso-axis and rest of the two iso-axix are:

(a) 15° each, (b) 90° each,

(c) 30° each, (d) 60° each.

[RRB JE 2015 28th AUG 3rd SHIFT]

59. A square shaped plane rests on HP with its plane lying on HP. Its front view would appear as a:

(a) square of reduced size

(b) square of equal size

(c) rhombus

(d) straight line

[RRB JE 2015 29th AUG 1st SHIFT]

60. A joint that facilitates rotation about axis but arrests displacement is a:

(a) cotter joint (b) knuckle joint

(c) spigot joint (d) socket joint

[RRB JE 2015 29th AUG 1st SHIFT]

61. A one metre distance is to be measured in decimetre, centimetre and millimetre units. Which type of scale do you suggest?

(a) plain scale

(b) comparative scale

(c) diagonal scale

(d) Either plain scale or diagonal scale will serve the purpose

[RRB JE 2015 29th AUG 1st SHIFT]

62. A circle rolls without slipping on a flat surface. The path traced by a point; lying on circle's periphery during its rolling is:

(a) Involute (b) Hyperbola

(c) Epicycloid (d) Cycloid

[RRB JE 2015 29th AUG 1st SHIFT]

63. Vertical edges of an object appear in its isometric view as:

(a) Vertical

(b) Inclined at 30° clockwise

(c) Inclined at 30° counter clockwise

(d) Inclined at 15°

[RRB JE 2015 29th AUG 1st SHIFT]

64. The "front view" and "top view" of a line are represented below and above the XY line respectively. The projections are drawn in:

(a) First angle

(b) Second angle

(c) Third angle

(d) It's an orthographic projection

[RRB JE 2015 29th AUG 2nd SHIFT]

65. Which of the following is not a type of bearing:

(a) Thrust bearing

(b) Journal Bearing

(c) Ball bearing

(d) Pulley.

[RRB JE 2015 29th AUG 2nd SHIFT]

66. Very small parts of a wrist watch are to be represented on drawings. Which type of scale do you suggest?

(a) Reducing scales (b) full size scales

(c) enlarging scales. (d) Scales with R.F. = 1 : 1

[RRB JE 2015 29th AUG 2nd SHIFT]

67. Major axis and Minor Axis are found in:

(a) Circle (b) Ellipse

(c) Cycloid (d) Involute.

[RRB JE 2015 29th AUG 2nd SHIFT]

68. The size of vertical and horizontal edges on an object appear in its isometric projection as

(a) shortened by 81% (b) shortened by 30%

(c) shortened by 19% (d) shortened by 29%

[RRB JE 2015 29th AUG 2nd SHIFT]

69. Top view of a triangular plane appears as line and its front view as triangle of original size. The plane is:

(a) perpendicular to HP and parallel to VP,

(b) perpendicular to VP and parallel to HP,

(c) Parallel to HP and VP both are perpendicular to PP,

(d) Inclined to HP and VP both.

[RRB JE 2015 29th AUG 3rd SHIFT]

70. The bolt shown in the following figure represents a:

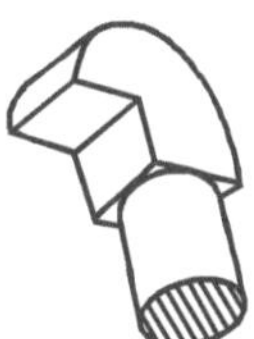

(a) Square bolt, (b) T-headed bolt,

(c) Hook bolt, (d) Eye bolt.

[RRB JE 2015 29th AUG 3rd SHIFT]

71. On a drawing 10 cm length represents an actual distance of 1 m. The R.F. of the scale is:

(a) 10 (b) 100

(c) $\dfrac{1}{10}$ (d) $\dfrac{1}{100}$

[RRB JE 2015 29th AUG 3rd SHIFT]

72. A string is wound over a circular disc. It is now unwound with its "free end" keeping it remain tight and tangent to the disc. The curve traced by the "free end" is

(a) Spiral (b) Involute

(c) Cycloid (d) Epicycloid

[RRB JE 2015 29th AUG 3rd SHIFT]

73. An isometric projection plane is one which is inclined to the three orthogonal planes at:

(a) 30°　　　　　　　　(b) 60°

(c) 15°　　　　　　　　(d) equally

[RRB JE 2015 29ᵗʰ AUG 3ʳᵈ SHIFT]

74. The projections of an "end point" of a "straight line" lie on XY. The "end point" is situated on:

(a) HP and VP both　　(b) VP

(c) HP　　　　　　　　(d) Neither HP not VP

[RRB JE 2015 30ᵗʰ AUG 3ʳᵈ SHIFT]

75. The "male" part of a "socket and spigot" joint is:

(a) Cotter　　　　　　(b) Socket

(c) Spigot　　　　　　(d) Eye bolt.

For the above question, User had specified 'ignore' during keys upload.

[RRB JE 2015 30ᵗʰ AUG 3ʳᵈ SHIFT]

76. A map showing "network of roads" has to display distances in units of "miles" and "kilometres" both. Which type of the following types of sea is suitable for this purpose?

(a) Plain scale

(b) diagonal scale

(c) Comparative scale

(d) Vernier scale

[RRB JE 2015 30ᵗʰ AUG 3ʳᵈ SHIFT]

77. What is common to:

circle, ellipse, parabola, hyperbola?

(a) Sphere　　　　　　(b) Cone

(c) Prism　　　　　　(d) Pyramid

[RRB JE 2015 30ᵗʰ AUG 3ʳᵈ SHIFT]

78. Isometric projections are commonly drawn with _____ iso-axes:

(a) One　　　　　　　(b) Four

(c) Two　　　　　　　(d) Three

[RRB JE 2015 30ᵗʰ AUG 3ʳᵈ SHIFT]

79. In a "first angle" orthographic projection, the distance of a point lying on the object being projected, from HP will be visible in:

(a) "Front view"

(b) "Top view"

(c) "Front view" and "side view"

(d) All the three views

[RRB JE 2015 16ᵗʰ SEP 3ʳᵈ SHIFT]

80. A "socket and spigot" joint:

(a) is a "rigid joint",

(b) permits only oscillation about the joint,

(c) permits only displacement about the joint,

(d) permits oscillation and displacement both.

[RRB JE 2015 16ᵗʰ SEP 3ʳᵈ SHIFT]

81. A scale is to read in "metre" and "decimetre". The fust "major division" of the scale shall be divided into:

(a) five equal parts,

(b) ten equal parts.

(c) twenty five equal parts.

(d) hundred equal parts.

[RRB JE 2015 16ᵗʰ SEP 3ʳᵈ SHIFT]

82. The eccentricity of an ellipse is:

(a) ratio of distances of a point, lying on the ellipse, from focus to directrix.

(b) ratio of distance of a point, lying on the ellipse, from directrix to focus.

(c) product of distances of a point, lying on the ellipse, from focus to directrix.

(d) sum of distances of a point, lying on the ellipse, from focus to directrix

[RRB JE 2015 16ᵗʰ SEP 3ʳᵈ SHIFT]

83. A circle is represented as a "top view", "front view" and "side view". If all these views are converted into isometric views then:

(a) All the three isometric view shall be same.

(b) Isometric views of "front view" and "side view" shall be same.

(c) "top view" and "front view" shall be same.

(d) Neither the "top view", "front view" or "side view" shall be the same.

[RRB JE 2015 16ᵗʰ SEP 3ʳᵈ SHIFT]

RRB SENIOR SECTION ENGINEER

1. In an orthogonal projection the axis of a cylinder or a cone is denoted by-

(a) A thin line

(b) A medium dashed line

(c) A sequence of long and short dashes

(d) Dashes of uniform lengths

[RRB SSE 2014 GREEN SHIFT]

2. Consider the following orthogonal projections of an object is and answer what could this object be:

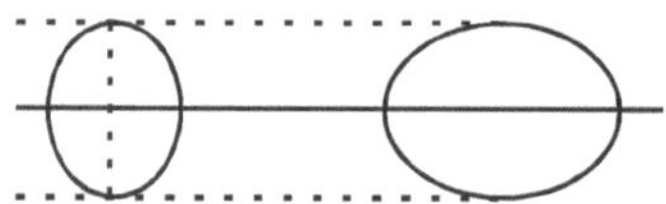

(a) Circle　　　　　　(b) Sphere

(c) Ellipse　　　　　　(d) Spheroid

[RRB SSE 2014 GREEN SHIFT]

3. Which of the following information is NOT contained in engineering drawings?

(a) Tolerances

(b) Material composition

(c) Surface finish

(d) All of these are included in engineering drawing

[RRB SSE 2014 GREEN SHIFT]

4. Consider the following orthogonal projections of an object.

This object is a-

(a) Tetrahedron   (b) Conical cylinder

(c) Prism   (d) Trapezium

[RRB SSE 2014 GREEN SHIFT]

5. A map mentions the scale 1 cm = l km.
The scale is in the ratio:

(a) $1 : 10^3$ (b) $1 : 10^4$

(c) $1 : 10^5$ (d) $1 : 10^6$

[RRB SSE 2014 GREEN SHIFT]

6. The length of a line measured with 20 m chain is found to be 400 m. If the actual length of the chain is 20.05 m, then the true length of the line is :

(a) 400.50 m   (b) 401.50 m

(c) 402.50 m   (d) 401.0 m

[RRB SSE 2014 RED SHIFT]

7. When an object is cut by a section plane parallel to horizontal plane and perpendicular to vertical plane, then the sectional view of the object is obtained in :

(a) Front view   (b) Left side view

(c) Right side view   (d) Top view

[RRB SSE 2014 RED SHIFT]

8. In Drawing, the surface roughness is represented by :

(a) Circles   (b) Squares

(c) Triangles   (d) Zig - Zag lines

[RRB SSE 2014 RED SHIFT]

9. The Height, Width and Depth of an object can be shown with a minimum of how many Orthographic projection views ?

(a) Six   (b) Three

(c) Two   (d) Four

[RRB SSE 2014 RED SHIFT]

10. A circle will appear, on an isometric drawing as a/an________.

(a) Parabola   (b) Ellipse

(c) Circle   (d) Cycloid

[RRB SSE 2014 RED SHIFT]

11. In an Engineering drawing, in double stroke Gothic lettering, which is correct.

(a) Letters are drawn thin

(b) The lettering template is used to draw the outline of letter

(c) This is not preferred for ink drawings

(d) This is having non-uniform line width

[RRB SSE 2014 YELLOW SHIFT]

12. Match Col. X (Category) and Col. Y (Recommended Scale) in reference to an Engineering drawing.

Col. X		Col. Y	
P	Enlarging Scale	1.	1:500
Q	Full Scale	2	10:1
R	Reducing Scale	3.	1:1
		4	1 : 20

(a) P–4, Q–1, R–2, P–3

(b) P – 2, Q – 3, R – 4, R – 1

(c) P –1, Q–3, R–2, P–4

(d) P–2, Q–1, R–4, Q–3

[RRB SSE 2014 YELLOW SHIFT]

13. If RF is $\dfrac{1}{60000}$ and distance to be shown on drawing is 7.5 km. what is the length of line on drawing ?

(a) 12.5 cm   (b) 8 cm

(c) 45 cm   (d) 10 cm

[RRB SSE 2014 YELLOW SHIFT]

14. A parabola can be constructed on a drawing by the methods EXCEPT

(a) Eccentricity Method

(b) Rectangle Method

(c) Parallelogram Method

(d) Asymptote Method

[RRB SSE 2014 YELLOW SHIFT]

15. Which of the Statements is NOT correct.

(a) Isometric scale is used to draw isometric projection

(b) Isometric scale is not used to draw isometric view

(c) A square is seen as rectangle in isometric

(d) A rectangle is seen as parallelogram in isometric

[RRB SSE 2014 YELLOW SHIFT]

16. A room of 2744 m³ volume is shown by a cube of 7 cm side. The R.F. of the scale is

(a) $\dfrac{1}{392}$ (b) $\dfrac{1}{3920}$

(c) $\dfrac{1}{20}$ (d) $\dfrac{1}{200}$

[RRB SSE 2015 1ˢᵗ SEP 1ˢᵗ SHIFT]

17. The curve traced out by a point lying on the circumference of the circle which rolls on a straight line is known as

(a) hypocycloid   (b) epicycloids

(c) circle   (d) cycloid

[RRB SSE 2015 1ˢᵗ SEP 1ˢᵗ SHIFT]

18. If the true and apparent inclinations of a line with H.P. are equal, the line is

(a) Parallel to vertical plane

(b) Parallel to horizontal plane

(c) Parallel to profile plane

(d) Inclined to both reference plane.

[RRB SSE 2015 1st SEP 1st SHIFT]

19. If a thin 60° set square is kept perpendicular to both the horizontal and vertical planes, its true shape is seen in

(a) horizontal plane   (b) auxiliary inclined plane

(c) profile plane   (d) vertical plane

[RRB SSE 2015 1st SEP 1st SHIFT]

20. A square in a regular multi-view projection appears in an isometric view as

(a) parallelogram   (b) rhombus

(c) box   (d) square

[RRB SSE 2015 1st SEP 1st SHIFT]

21. If the distance between the two stations is 200 kilometres and on a map it is shown by 5 cm. The R.F. of the scale will be

(a) $\dfrac{1}{40}$ (b) $\dfrac{1}{4000000}$

(c) $\dfrac{1}{2000}$ (d) $\dfrac{1}{200}$

[RRB SSE 2015 1st SEP 2nd SHIFT]

22. The curve traced out by a point on the circumference of a circle, which rolls without slipping along another larger diameter circle outside it

(a) epicycloid   (b) spiral

(c) hypocycloid   (d) involute

[RRB SSE 2015 1st SEP 2nd SHIFT]

23. If the true and apparent inclinations of a line with V.P. are equal, the line is

(a) Parallel to profile plane

(b) Parallel to vertical plane

(c) Parallel to horizontal plane

(d) Inclined to both reference planes

[RRB SSE 2015 1st SEP 2nd SHIFT]

24. A circular plane with 80 mm diameter has one of its ends of the diameter in the H.P. while the other end is in the V.P.. The plane is inclined at 30° to H.P. and 60° to V.P.. The shape of its projection on profile plane will be

(a) a circle of same diameter

(b) a circle of larger diameter

(c) a circle of smaller diameter

(d) straight line

[RRB SSE 2015 1st SEP 2nd SHIFT]

25. The type of projection in which the surfaces are equally foreshortened is

(a) cabinet   (b) isometric

(c) oblique   (d) orthographic

[RRB SSE 2015 1st SEP 2nd SHIFT]

26. A map of 12 cm × 10 cm represents an area of 75000 square Meter of a field. The R. F. Of the scale is

(a) $\dfrac{1}{625}$ (b) $\dfrac{1}{250}$

(c) $\dfrac{1}{2500}$ (d) $\dfrac{1}{6250000}$

[RRB SSE 2015 1st SEP 3rd SHIFT]

27. The curve traced by a point on straight line which rolls without slipping on a circle, is called

(a) hypocycloid   (b) involute

(c) epicycloids   (d) cycloid

[RRB SSE 2015 1st SEP 3rd SHIFT]

28. The point at which line intersects the V.P., if extended, is known as

(a) Auxiliary trace   (b) Horizontal trace

(c) Profile trace   (d) Vertical trace

[RRB SSE 2015 1st SEP 3rd SHIFT]

29. Projection of an object shown by three views is known as

(a) Oblique   (b) Perspective

(c) Orthographic   (d) Isometric

[RRB SSE 2015 1st SEP 3rd SHIFT]

30. In comparison to an isometric projection, the appearance of an isometric view is

(a) more accurate   (b) more realistic

(c) smaller   (d) larger

[RRB SSE 2015 1st SEP 3rd SHIFT]

31. A map of 10 cm × 10 cm represents an area of 40000 square Metre of a field. The R. F. Of the scale is

(a) 1/400   (b) 1/4000000

(c) 1/2000   (d) 1/200

[RRB SSE 2015 2nd SEP 1st SHIFT]

32. If a line rotates in a plane about one of its ends and at the same time, if a point moves along the line continuously in one direction then the curve traced out by the moving point is called

(a) epicycloid   (b) helix

(c) involute   (d) spiral

[RRB SSE 2015 2nd SEP 1st SHIFT]

33. The point at which line intersects the H.P., if extended, is known as

(a) Horizontal trace   (b) Profile trace

(c) Auxiliary trace   (d) Vertical tract

[RRB SSE 2015 2nd SEP 1st SHIFT]

34. Which of the following describes the theory of orthographic projection?

(a) Projectors parallel to each other and oblique to the plane of projection

(b) Projectors parallel to each other and perpendicular to the plane of projection

(c) Projectors parallel to each other and parallel to the plane of projection

(d) Projectors perpendicular to each other and parallel to the plane of projection

[RRB SSE 2015 2nd SEP 1st SHIFT]

35. In isometric projection, a circle appears as

(a) an ellipse   (b) an involute

(c) a cycloid   (d) a circle

[RRB SSE 2015 2nd SEP 1st SHIFT]

36. An area of 9 square kilometre is represented by 144 square centimetre on a map. The R. F. of the scale is

(a) 1/16   (b) 1/1600

(c) 1/2500   (d) 1/25000

[RRB SSE 2015 2nd SEP 2nd SHIFT]

37. When a pendulum oscillates, the curve traces out by a point moving along its string at a constant speed is known as

(a) circle   (b) spiral

(c) cycloid   (d) helix

[RRB SSE 2015 2nd SEP 2nd SHIFT]

38. If top view of a line is a point, its front view is

(a) Perpendicular to reference line and of true length

(b) Perpendicular to reference line and of apparent length

(c) Parallel to reference line and of true length

(d) Parallel to reference line and of apparent length

[RRB SSE 2015 2nd SEP 2nd SHIFT]

39. In an orthographic projection, the elevation obtained on a plane is

(a) horizontal   (b) auxiliary

(c) vertical   (d) profile

[RRB SSE 2015 2nd SEP 2nd SHIFT]

40. While making isometric projection, the ellipse is preferably drawn by

(a) concentric circles method

(b) four centre method

(c) parallelogram method

(d) oblong method

[RRB SSE 2015 2nd SEP 2nd SHIFT]

41. The orthographic projections of one of the "end points" of line are described as lying 20 mm below HP and 25 mm in front of VP. This point lies in:

(a) First Quadrant   (b) Second Quadrant

(c) Third Quadrant   (d) fourth Quadrant.

[RRB SSE 2015 2nd SEP 3rd SHIFT]

42. The object shown in following figure is a:

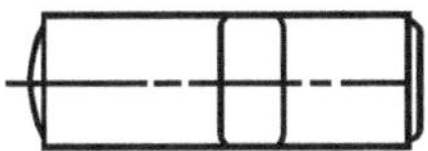

(a) Bolt   (b) Square Bolt

(c) Stud   (d) Post.

[RRB SSE 2015 2nd SEP 3rd SHIFT]

43. A scale is to be devised to read into Metre, Decimetre and Centimetre. Which type of the following scales is suited best for this purpose?

(a) Plain Scale

(b) Vernier Scale

(c) Diagonal Scale

(d) Diagonal scale or Vernier Scale.

[RRB SSE 2015 2nd SEP 3rd SHIFT]

44. Which of the following is not a "conic section":

(a) Circle   (b) Square

(c) Parabola   (d) Ellipse.

[RRB SSE 2015 2nd SEP 3rd SHIFT]

45. In an "isometric scale" the angle between a "line" and its "iso-equivalent line" is:

(a) 30°   (b) 45°

(c) 15°   (d) 60°

[RRB SSE 2015 2nd SEP 3rd SHIFT]

46. One end of a line rests on VP and the other on HP. It is inclined to VP and HP at 30° & 60° respectively. Its "true length" will be visible in:

(a) Plan

(b) Profile

(c) Elevation

(d) Its true length will not be visible in any of the orthographic views.

[RRB SSE 2015 3rd SEP 1st SHIFT]

47. The joint shown below represents a:

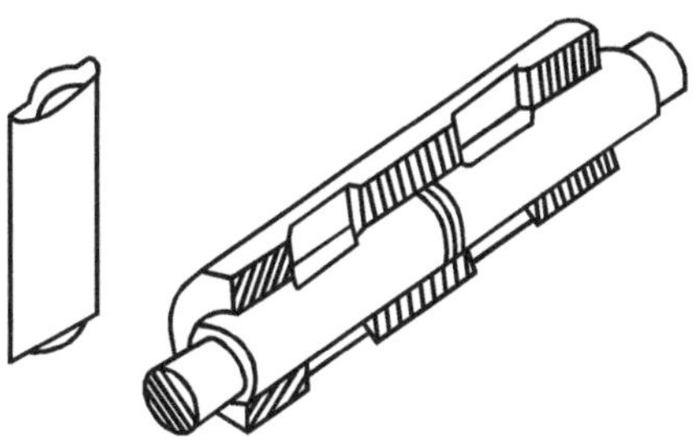

(a) Spigot joint,   (b) cotter joint,

(c) knuckle joint,   (d) keyed coupling.

[RRB SSE 2015 3rd SEP 1st SHIFT]

48. The most commonly used ten " "R.F." of a scale is:

(a) Reprographic Factor

(b) Refractive Factor,

(c) Representative Fraction,

(d) Reducing Fraction.

[RRB SSE 2015 3rd SEP 1st SHIFT]

49. The asymptote of a hyperbola is the one:

(a) which passes through its focus and is normal to its axis,

(b) it joins focus to its vertex,

(c) it joins focus to its centre

(d) will be tangent to it at infinity.

[RRB SSE 2015 3rd SEP 1st SHIFT]

50. When drawing "isometric view" of an object its horizontal edges are drawn along iso-axes which are inclined to horizontal at:

(a) 30°   (b) 90°

(c) 15°   (d) 75°

[RRB SSE 2015 3rd SEP 1st SHIFT]

51. One "end point" of a straight line lies in First Quadrant and the other in the Third Quadrant. The line passes through:

(a) Second Quadrant

(b) Fourth Quadrant

(c) Either Second or Fourth Quadrant

(d) It will not pass through either of these two quadrants.

[RRB SSE 2015 3rd SEP 2nd SHIFT]

52. Commonly used gear teeth profiles are________ in shape.

(a) Elliptical

(b) Cycloidal

(c) Involute

(d) either Involute or cycloidal

[RRB SSE 2015 3rd SEP 2nd SHIFT]

53. When a quantity represented in two different measuring unit systems is to be measured; which type of scale is used?

(a) diagonal scale

(b) comparative scale with different RF

(c) comparative scale with same RF

(d) vernier scale

[RRB SSE 2015 3rd SEP 2nd SHIFT]

54. The eccentricity of a parabola is equal to:

(a) less than One

(b) greater than One

(c) One

(d) There is no term as eccentricity for a parabola.

[RRB SSE 2015 3rd SEP 2nd SHIFT]

55. The "Isometric view" of a circle would appear as:

(a) a circle of reduced diameter

(b) Ellipse

(c) a circle of increased diameter

(d) a circle of equal diameter

[RRB SSE 2015 3rd SEP 2nd SHIFT]

56. The olane of a circle makes an anale of 45° with HP and VP each. Its plane will be inclined to the "profile plane" (PP) at:

(a) 90°

(b) 30°

(c) 60°

(d) its plane will be parallel to PP.

[RRB SSE 2015 3rd SEP 3rd SHIFT]

57. A rack is a gear in which:

(a) teeth are cut on a flat surface.

(b) teeth are cut on the periphery of a conical surface.

(c) Teeth are cut on the outside surface of a disc,

(d) teeth are cut on the inside of an annular surface.

[RRB SSE 2015 3rd SEP 3rd SHIFT]

58. Which of the following scales can be used interchangeably?

(a) comparative scales and diagonal scales.

(b) Diagonal scales and plain scales.

(c) vernier scale and comparative scale,

(d) diagonal scale and vernier scale.

[RRB SSE 2015 3rd SEP 3rd SHIFT]

59. An ant sitting on the "second's hand" of a clock moves at a constant speed away from the centre. The path traced by the ant is:

(a) Spiral.   (b) Involute.

(c) Epicycloid.   (d) Hypocycloid.

[RRB SSE 2015 3rd SEP 3rd SHIFT]

60. A square shaped plane is represented in orthographic view as Plan, Elevation and Side View. The isometric projections of all three views would appear to be:

(a) All three views will be identical,

(b) Isometric of Side view and Elevation will be identical but that of plan will be different,

(c) All three views will be different.

(d) Isometric of Plan and Elevation will be identical but that of side view will be different.

[RRB SSE 2015 3rd SEP 3rd SHIFT]

ANSWERS

RRB JUNIOR ENGINEER

1. (b)	**2.** (d)	**3.** (c)	**4.** (a)	**5.** (d)	**6.** (d)	**7.** (c)	**8.** (b)	**9.** (a)	**10.** (d)
11. (b)	**12.** (c)	**13.** (b)	**14.** (b)	**15.** (d)	**16.** (c)	**17.** (d)	**18.** (c)	**19.** (d)	**20.** (b)
21. (d)	**22.** (c)	**23.** (a)	**24.** (a)	**25.** (b)	**26.** (a)	**27.** (c)	**28.** (a)	**29.** (b)	**30.** (b)
31. (d)	**32.** (c)	**33.** (b)	**34.** (a)	**35.** (b)	**36.** (a)	**37.** (c)	**38.** (a)	**39.** (c)	**40.** (d)
41. (b)	**42.** (c)	**43.** (b)	**44.** (b)	**45.** (a)	**46.** (b)	**47.** (c)	**48.** (a)	**49.** (b)	**50.** (c)
51. (b)	**52.** (d)	**53.** (a)	**54.** (a)	**55.** (d)	**56.** (a)	**57.** (b)	**58.** (c)	**59.** (d)	**60.** (b)
61. (c)	**62.** (d)	**63.** (a)	**64.** (c)	**65.** (d)	**66.** (c)	**67.** (b)	**68.** (c)	**69.** (a)	**70.** (c)
71. (c)	**72.** (b)	**73.** (d)	**74.** (a)	**75.** (c)	**76.** (c)	**77.** (b)	**78.** (d)	**79.** (c)	**80.** (a)
81. (b)	**82.** (a)	**83.** (d)							

RRB SENIOR SECTION ENGINEER

1. (c)	**2.** (a)	**3.** (d)	**4.** (c)	**5.** (a)	**6.** (d)	**7.** (d)	**8.** (c)	**9.** (c)	**10.** (b)
11. (c)	**12.** (b)	**13.** (a)	**14.** (d)	**15.** (c)	**16.** (d)	**17.** (d)	**18.** (a)	**19.** (c)	**20.** (b)
21. (b)	**22.** (a)	**23.** (c)	**24.** (d)	**25.** (b)	**26.** (c)	**27.** (b)	**28.** (d)	**29.** (c)	**30.** (d)
31. (c)	**32.** (d)	**33.** (a)	**34.** (b)	**35.** (a)	**36.** (d)	**37.** (b)	**38.** (a)	**39.** (c)	**40.** (b)
41. (d)	**42.** (c)	**43.** (d)	**44.** (a)	**45.** (c)	**46.** (b)	**47.** (b)	**48.** (c)	**49.** (c)	**50.** (*)
51. (c)	**52.** (d)	**53.** (c)	**54.** (c)	**55.** (b)	**56.** (a)	**57.** (a)	**58.** (d)	**59.** (a)	**60.** (c)

EXPLANATIONS

RRB JUNIOR ENGINEER

1. Three lines are said to be exist in 3D space which are perpendicular to each other.

2.

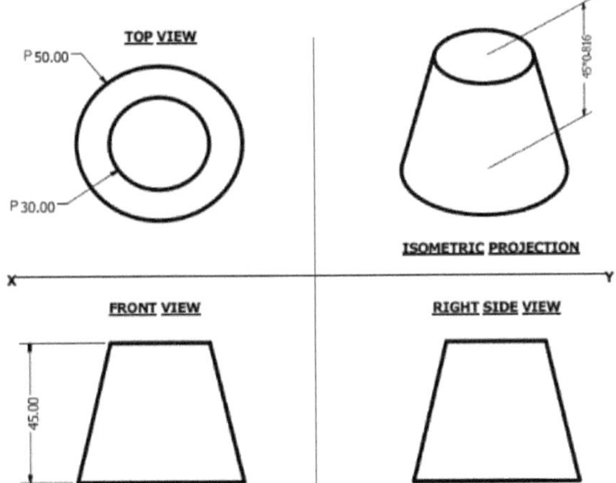

Figure: Third angle orthographic projection

3. Ratio $= 100/10^{-2} = 10000$

4. In machine drawing, a 'sectional view' cut portion is always shown by diagonal hatching.

5.

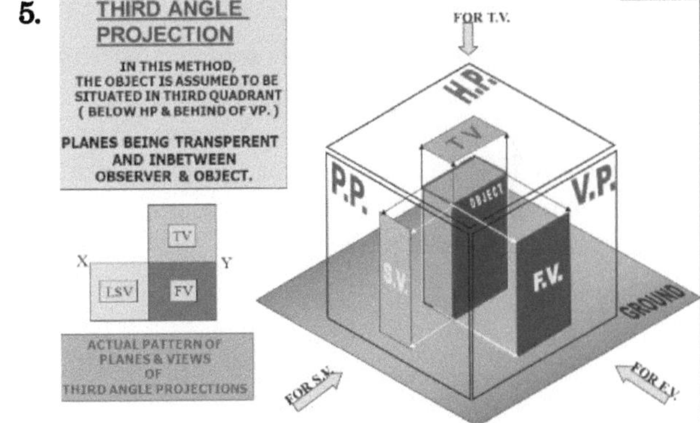

7. Orthographic projection, is a means of representing three-dimensional objects in two dimensions. It is a form of parallel projection, in which all the projection lines are orthogonal to the projection plane, resulting in every plane of the scene appearing in affine transformation on the viewing surface.

8. An ellipse is also defined as a curve traced by a point, moving in a plane such that the sum of its distances from two fixed points is always the same.

9. P-3, Q-1, R-2

10. A conic section is the curve described by a point which moves in a plane in such a manner that it's distance from a fixed point in the plane (a focus) is in a constant ratio to it's distance from a fixed line (a directrix) in the plane. This ratio is known as the eccentricity.

The curve is an ellipse, a parabola, or a hyperbola, according as its eccentricity is less than, equal to, or greater than unity (one).

Therefore the angle between the line of eccentricity and the axis will always be less than 45° for an ellipse, greater than 45° for a hyperbola and exactly 45° for a parabola.

11.

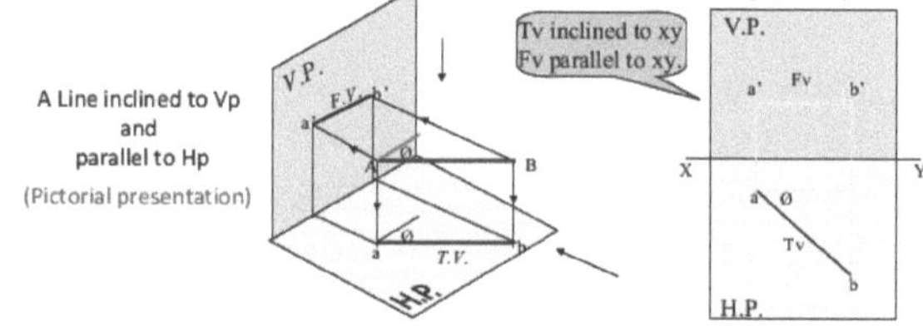

Types of Lines used in Engineering Graphics

TYPE	ILLUSTRATION	APPLICATION
A – Continuous Thick	———————	Visible Outlines
B – Continuous Thin	———————	Dimension Lines, Leader Lines, Extension Lines, Construction Lines of Adjacent Parts
C – Continuous Thin– Wavy	~~~~~	Irregular Boundary Lines, Short Break Lines
D – Short Dashes Medium	– – – – – – –	Hidden Outlines & Edges
E – Long Chain Thin	—— — —— — ——	Centre Lines, Locus Lines, Extreme Positions of The Movable Parts Situated In Front of The Cutting Plants And Pitch Circles
F – Long Chain Line Thick at Ends & Thin Elsewhere	—— —— — — ——	Cutting Plane Lines
G – Long Chain Thick	—— — — — ——	To Indicate Surfaces Which are to Receive Additional Treatment
H – Ruled Line & Short Zigzag Thin.	—— ⅄ — ⅄ —	Long Break Lines

14. $\text{R.F.} = \sqrt{\dfrac{256 \times 10^{-4}}{64 \times 10^{6}}} = \dfrac{1}{50000}$

15. Application: The involute has some properties that makes it extremely important to the gear industry: If two intermeshed gears have teeth with the profile-shape of involutes (rather than, for example, a traditional triangular shape), they form an involute gear system.

16.

17. x-y line is always shown as a reference line in multi-view projections.

18. Axonometric projection is a type of orthographic projection used for creating a pictorial drawing of an object, where the lines of sight are perpendicular to the plane of projection, and the object is rotated around one or more of its axes to reveal multiple sides.

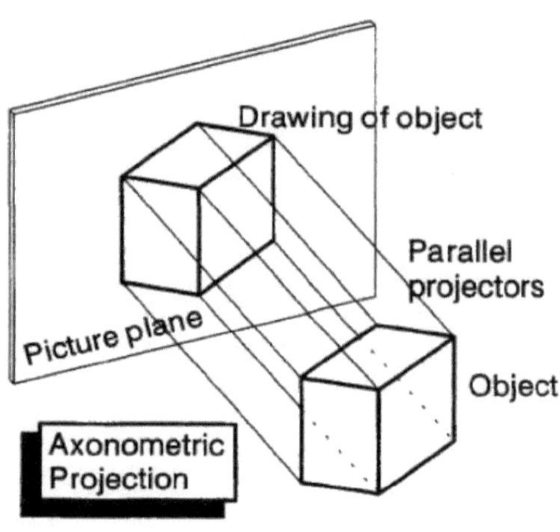

Axonometric projection

19. Representation factor can be unity, less than unity or greater than unty.

20. Tangent method is not used for drawing elliptical curves.

21.

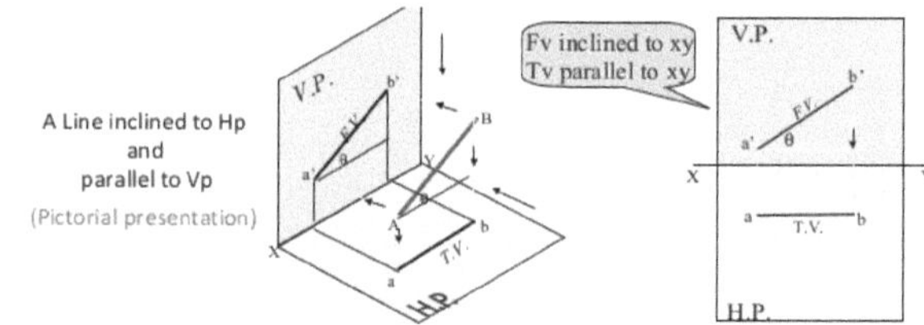

22. Object is placed between observer and plane.

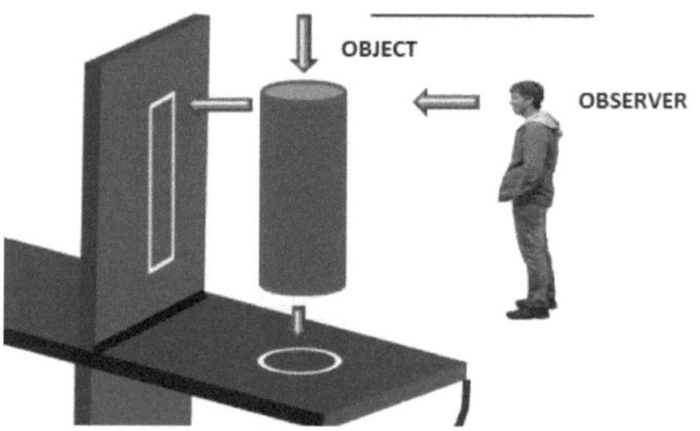

23. The straight lines will be visible in H.P. and V.P.

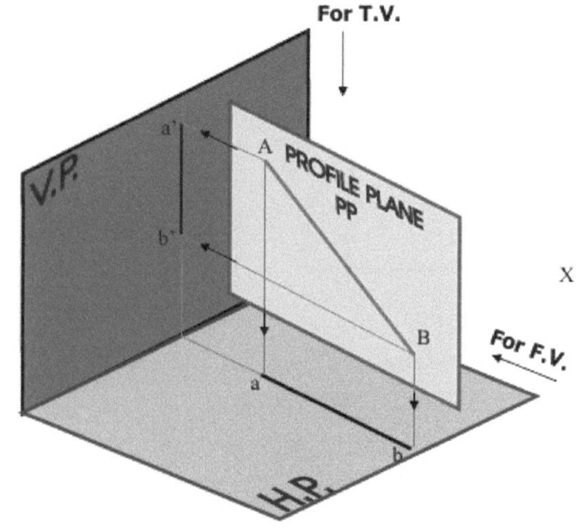

24. Diagonal scale is used in engineering to read lengths with higher accuarcy as it represents a unit into three different multiple in metres, centimeters and millimeters. Diagonal scale is an important part in Engineering drawings.

25. True length will be visible in Top view.

26. If both the front and top views of a plane are straight lines, it may be perpendicular to both horizontal and vertical planes.

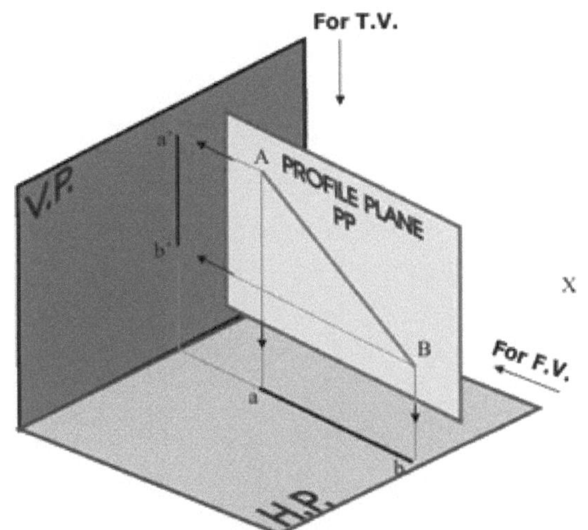

27. BIS recommends First angle projection. First Angle Projection is commonly used in all countries other than United States. The Indian Standard Institution (ISI) recommend the use of First Angle Projection method now in all the institutions

28. Vertical trace will be perpendicular to the reference line.

29. Definition of representative fraction. : a map scale in which figures representing units (as centimeters, inches, or feet) are expressed in the form of the fraction 1/x (as 1/250,000) or of the ratio 1:x to indicate that one unit on the map represents x units (as 250,000 centimeters) on the earth's surface.

30. True length will be visible in side view only

31. The plane which is perpendicular to both the reference planes(horizontal and vertical plane) is called profile plane or picture plane. The plane which is inclined to both the reference planes(horizontal and vertical plane) is called oblique plane.

32. The right-hand side view is projected on the plane placed at the left of the object.

33. Horizontal trace will be parallel to the reference line.

34. Diagonal scale is used in engineering to read lengths with higher accuarcy as it represents a unit into three different multiple in metres, centimeters and millimeters. Diagonal scale is an important part in Engineering drawings.

35. True length can be observed from the Top.

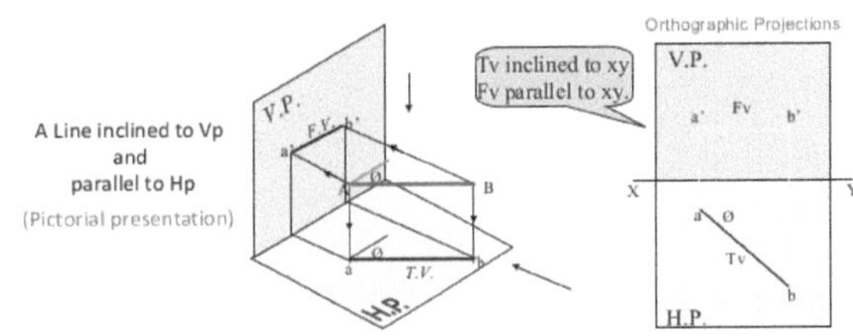

36. If both the front and top views of a plane are straight lines, it may be perpendicular to both horizontal and vertical planes.

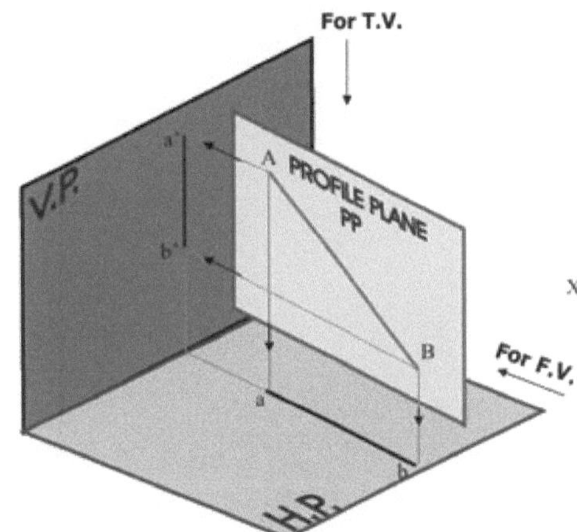

37. BIS recommends First angle projection. First Angle Projection is commonly used in all countries other than United States. The Indian Standard Institution (ISI) recommend the use of First Angle Projection method now in all the institutions

38. V.T. will be perpendicular to the reference line.

39. Scale of chords is used to measure angles when a protractor is not available, by comparing the angles subtended by chords of an arc at the centre of the arc.

40. True length will be seen in front view.

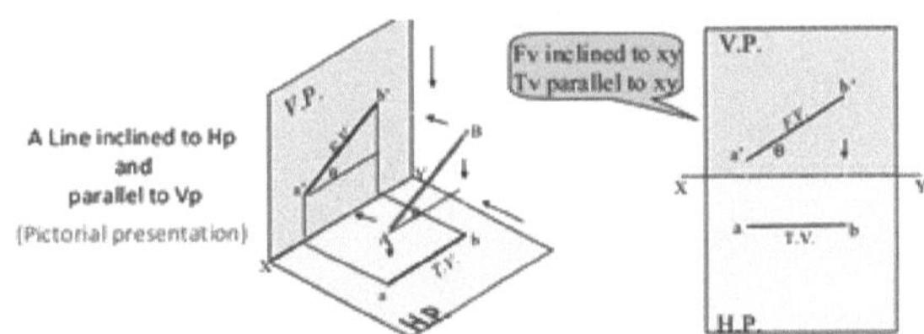

41. Its side view will be a plane.

42. $\sqrt{\dfrac{2}{3}}$

43. The eccentricity of a circle is zero. The eccentricity of an ellipse which is not a circle is greater than zero but less than 1. The eccentricity of a parabola is 1. The eccentricity of a hyperbola is greater than 1.

44. Distance between two stations

= 2000000/400000 = 5 cm

45.

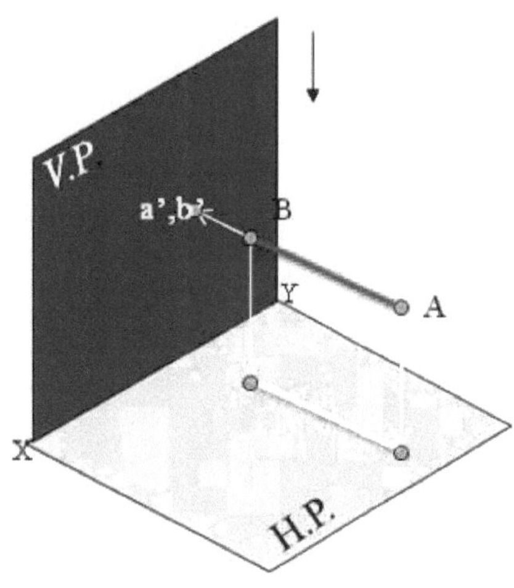

46. Front view will be an ellipse.

47. Isometric projection is a method for visually representing three-dimensional objects in two dimensions in technical and engineering drawings.

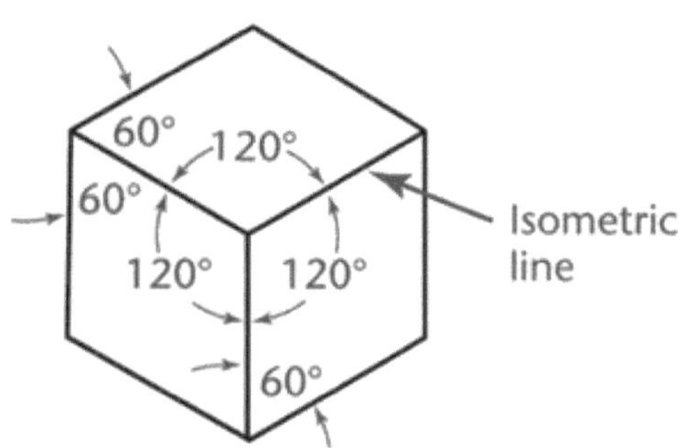

It is an axonometric projection in which the three coordinate axes appear equally foreshortened and the angle between any two of them is 120 degrees.

48. The eccentricity of a circle is zero. The eccentricity of an ellipse which is not a circle is greater than zero but less than 1. The eccentricity of a parabola is 1. The eccentricity of a hyperbola is greater than 1.

49.

2nd Quadrant	1st Quadrant
Above H.P.	Above H.P.
Behind V.P.	In Front of V.P.
3rd Quadrant	4th Quadrant
Below H.P.	Below H.P.
Behind V.P.	In Front of V.P.

50. 1.5 D + 3 mm

51. A vernier scale is good enough to read in two digits after decimal.

52.

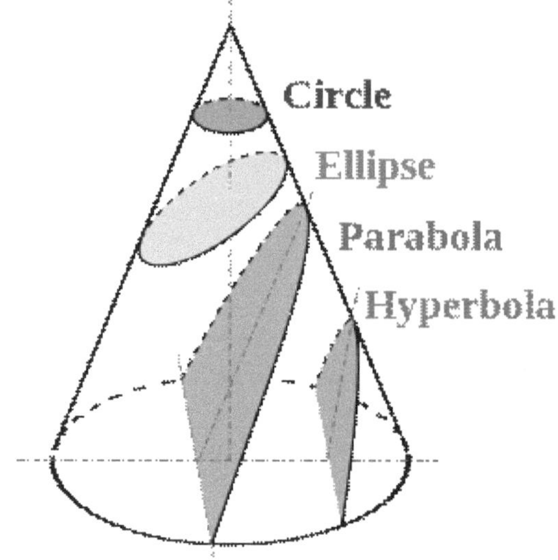

53. An isometric projection is a two dimensional view.

54. Plan view is a top view where as Front view is an elevation view.

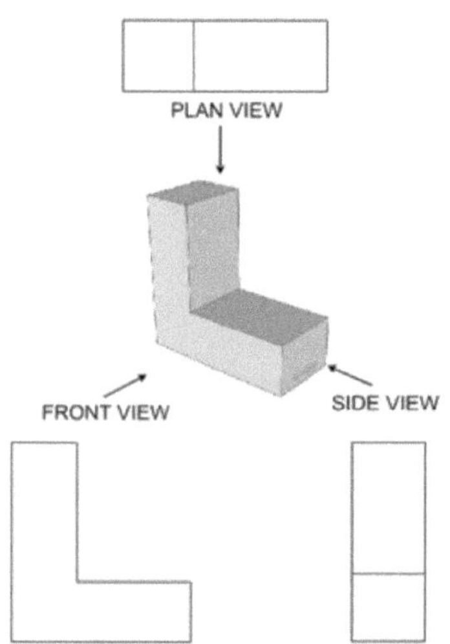

55. The form of a Whitworth thread is based on a fundamental triangle with an angle of 55 at each peak and valley.

56. Road Map factor is less than unity.

57. The eccentricity of a circle is zero. The eccentricity of an ellipse which is not a circle is greater than zero but less than 1. The eccentricity of a parabola is 1. The eccentricity of a hyperbola is greater than 1.

58. 30 degrees each

59. Plane would appear as a line.

60. A knuckle joint is a mechanical joint used to connect two rods which are under a tensile load, when there is a requirement of small amount of flexibility, or angular moment is necessary. There is always axial or linear line of action of load.

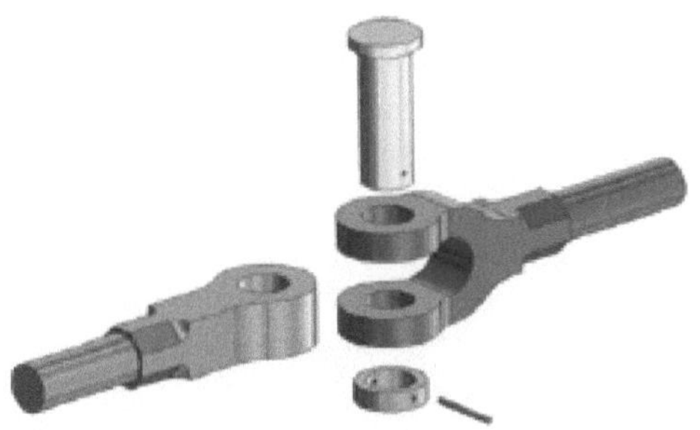

61. Diagonal scale is an engineering measuring instrument which is composed of a set of parallel straight lines which are obliquely crossed by another set of straight lines. Diagonal scales are used to measure small fractions of the unit of measurement.

62. A cycloid is the curve traced by a point on the rim of a circular wheel as the wheel rolls along a straight line without slipping. A cycloid is a specific form of trochoid and is an example of a roulette, a curve generated by a curve rolling on another curve.

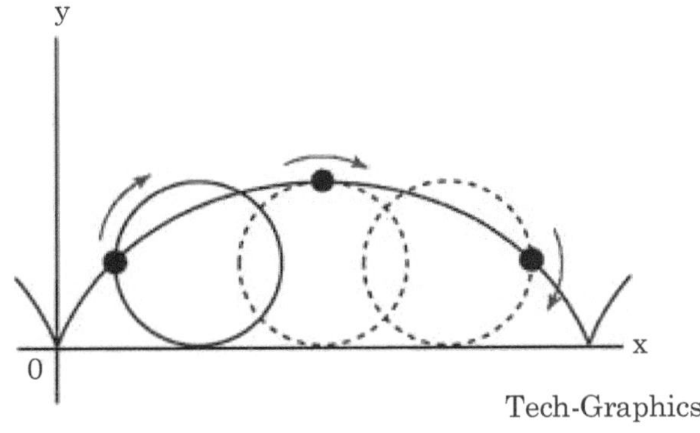

63. Vertical edges of an object appear in its isometric view as Vertical.

64.

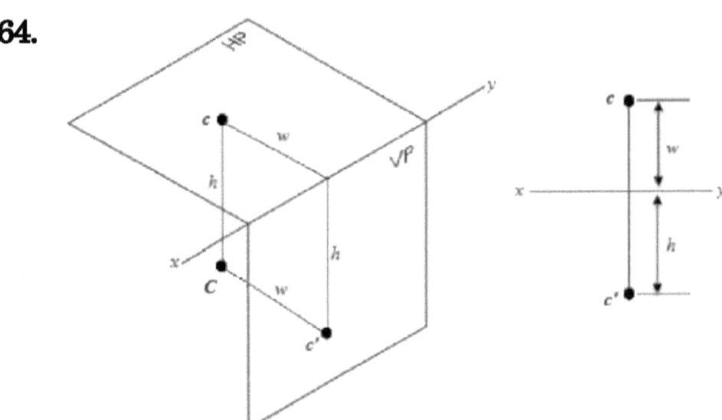

65. Pulley is not a bearing but a wheel with a grooved rim around which a cord passes, which acts to change the direction of a force applied to the cord and is used to raise heavy weights.

66. Enlarging scale having RF more than unity.

67. The ellipse changes shape as you change the length of the major or minor axis. The major and minor axes of an ellipse are diameters (lines through the center) of the ellipse. The major axis is the longest diameter and the minor axis the shortest. If they are equal in length then the ellipse is a circle.

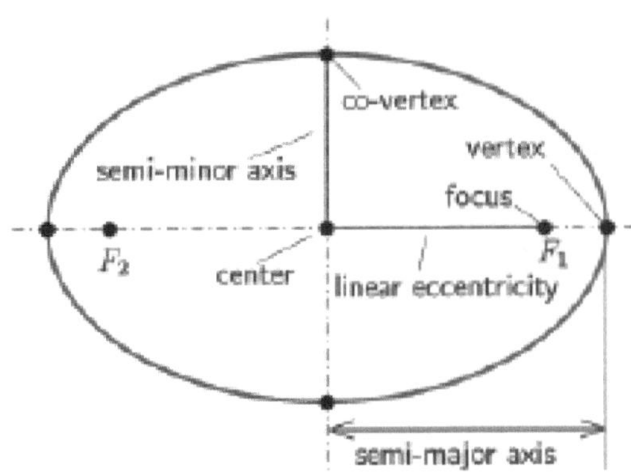

68. In isometric projection, object appears 19% less.

69. Perpendicular to HP and parallel to VP

70. Hook Bolt

71. R.F.=10 cm/100 cm=1/10

72. In the differential geometry of curves, an involute is a curve obtained from another given curve by one of two methods.

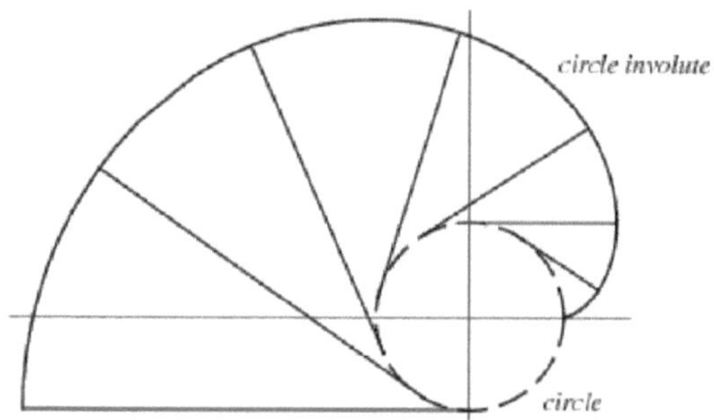

By attaching an imaginary taut string to the given curve and tracing its free end as it is wound onto that given curve; or in reverse, unwound.

73. An isometric projection plane is the one which is inclined to the three orthogonal planes equally.

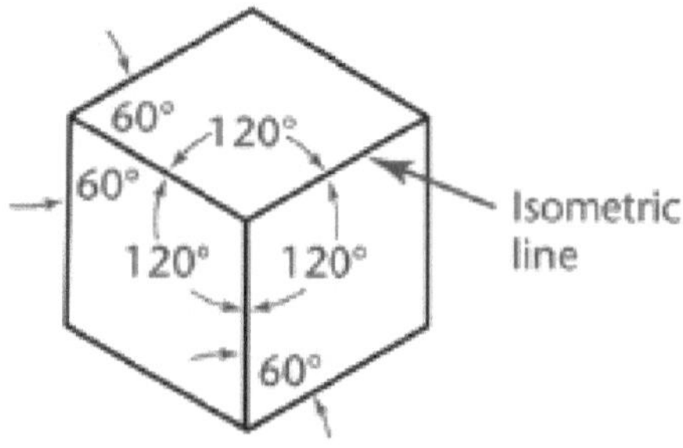

74. The end point should lie on reference axis i.e. xy axis in order to have end point representation in both V.P. and H.P.

75. A spigot end is the equivalent of a male end, and a socket end is the equivalent of a female end. A spigot end fits into a socket end. PVC pipe has spigot ends and must connect to socket connections on both ends.

76. A comparative scale is an ordinal or rank order scale that can also be referred to as a non metric scale.

77. All curves are attained by cutting cone at different angles.

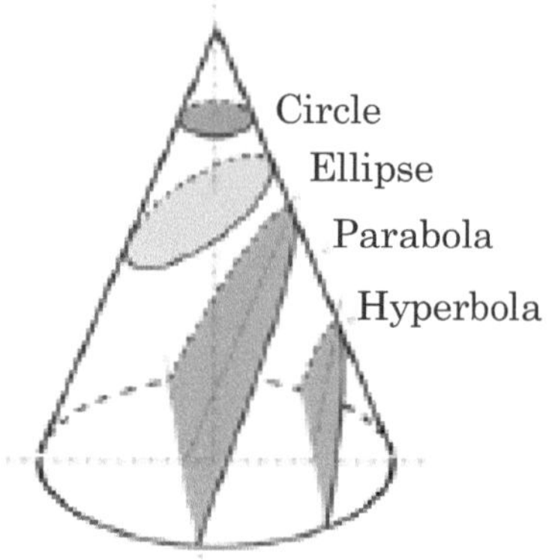

78. In isometric projections, three iso-axes are drawn at 120 degrees.

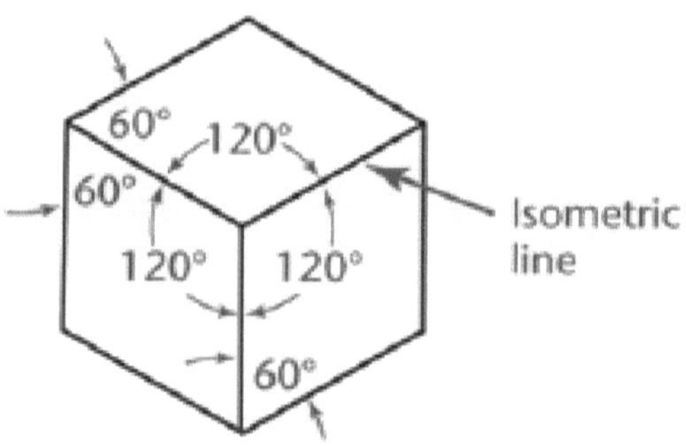

79. Front view and Side view.

80. Cotter Joint for Circular rods (Socket and spigot): Socket and spigot cotter joint is used to connect circular rods. One of the rods is formed into a socket by enlarging its end while the other rod, called spigot end is formed with enlarged diameter and an integral collar as shown in figure. The spigot is put inside the socket and the cotter is driven through the slots in socket and spigot ends. A pictorial view of socket and spigot cotter joint is shown in figure. While a sectional view of socket and spigot cotter joint is shown in figure. An exploded view of this joint is also shown here in figure.

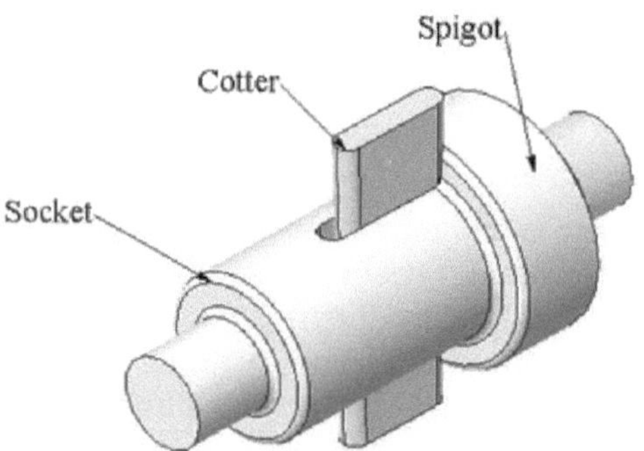

81. The first major division of the scale shall be divided into ten equal parts.

82. Any conic section can be defined as the locus of points whose distances to a point (the focus) and a line (the directrix) are in a constant ratio. That ratio is called the eccentricity, commonly denoted as e.

83. In isometric view, neither of the three views will be identical.

RRB SENIOR SECTION ENGINEER

1. Types of Lines used in Engineering Graphics

TYPE	ILLUSTRATION	APPLICATION
A – Continuous Thick		Visible Outlines
B – Continuous Thin		Dimension Lines, Leader Lines, Extension Lines, Construction Lines of Adjacent Parts
C – Continuous Thin – Wavy		Irregular Boundary Lines, Short Break Lines
D – Short Dashes Medium		Hidden Outlines & Edges
E – Long Chain Thin		Centre lines, Locus lines, Extreme Positions of The Movable Parts Situated in Front of The Cutting Plants and Pitch Circles
F – Long Chain Line Thick at Ends & Thin Elsewhere		Cutting Plane Lines
G – Long Chain Thick		To Indicate Surface Which are to Receive Additional Treatment
H – Ruled Line & Short Zigzag Think.		Long Break Lines

In an orthogonal projection the axis of a cylinder or a cone is denoted by a sequence of long and short dashes.

2. Circle

3. Engineering Drawings contain all information.

4. Triangular prism

Prism :

This is a polyhedron having two equal and similar faces called its ends or bases, aprallel to each other and joined by other faces, which are parallelograms. The imaginary line joining the centers of the bases is called the axis.

A right and regular prism has its axis perpendicular to the bases. All its faces are equal rectangles.

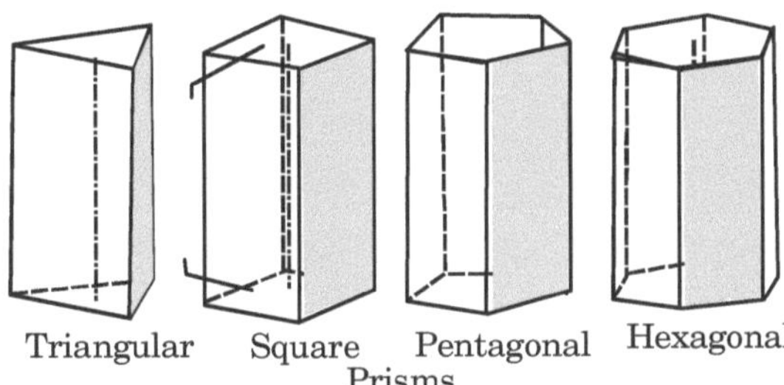

Triangular   Square   Pentagonal   Hexagonal
Prisms

5. Scale Ratio = $\left(\dfrac{1}{1000}\right)$

6. Error in chain = $(20.05 - 20) * \dfrac{100}{20} = .25\%$

Therefore error in line will also be .25%.

So 400 m line will be measured as 400 + .25% of 400 = 410 m

7. Top view will represent the sectional view of the object.

8.

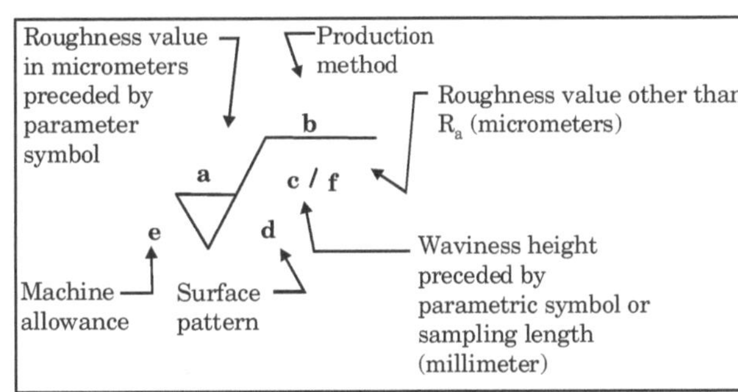

9. All three dimensions can be shown with at least two views of orthographic projections.

10. A circle will appear , on an isometric drawing as an Ellipse.

11. Not preferred for ink Drawings.

Double Stroke Vertical Gothic Lettering

Vertical letter drawn by double Stroke of panicle with uniform thickness between these strokes are called Double Stroke Vertical Gothic Lettering.

12.

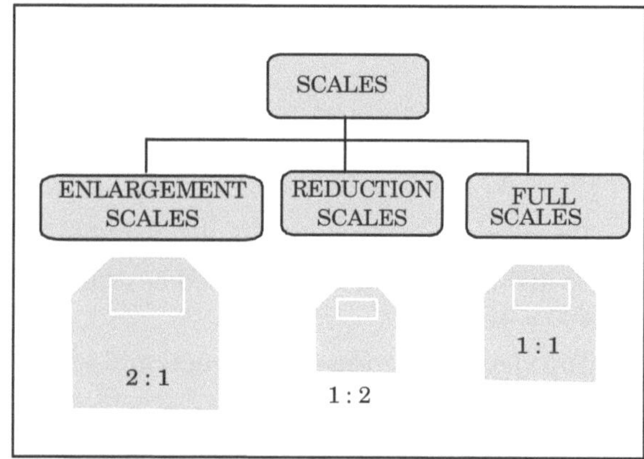

13. Length of line $= \left(\dfrac{7500}{60000}\right)$ m $= 12.5$ cm

14. A parabola can be constructed on a drawing by the methods except asymptote method.

15. A square is seen as rhombus in isometric view.

16. $\text{R.F} = \left(\dfrac{\text{Map volume}}{\text{Actual volume}}\right)^{\frac{1}{3}}$

$\quad\quad = \left(\dfrac{7 \times 7 \times 7 \times 10^{-6}}{2744}\right)^{\frac{1}{3}} = \dfrac{1}{200}$

17. A cycloid is the curve traced by a point on the rim of a circular wheel as the wheel rolls along a straight line without slipping. A cycloid is a specific form of trochoid and is an example of a roulette, a curve generated by a curve rolling on another curve.

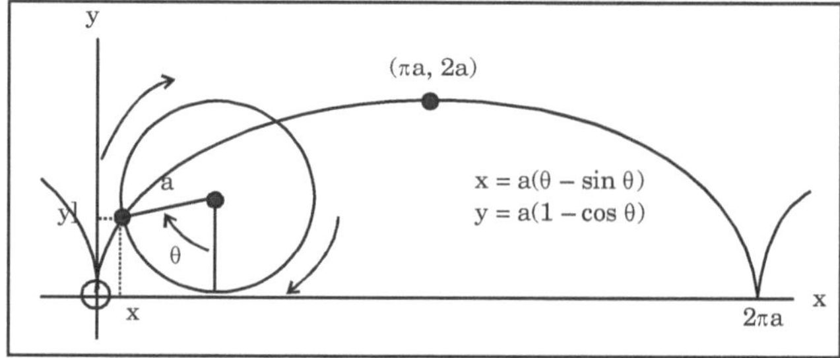

18. If the true and apparent inclinations of a line with H.P. are equal, the line is parallel to vertical plane

19. If a thin 60° set square is kept perpendicular to both the horizontal and vertical planes, its true shape is seen in profile plane.

20. A square in a regular multi-view projection appears in an isometric view as rhombus.

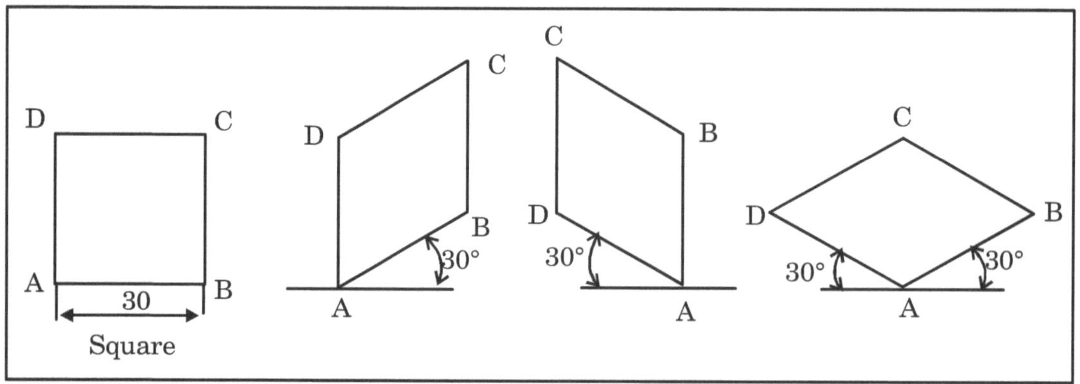

21. $\text{R.F} = \dfrac{\text{Map Scale}}{\text{Actual Scale}} = \dfrac{5 \times 10^{-2}}{200 \times 10^{3}} = \dfrac{1}{4000000}$

22. In geometry, an epicycloid or hypercycloid is a plane curve produced by tracing the path of a chosen point on the circumference of a circle-called an epicycle-which rolls without slipping around a fixed circle. It is a particular kind of roulette.

23. If the true and apparent inclinations of a line with V.P. are equal , the line is parallel to horizontal plane.

24.

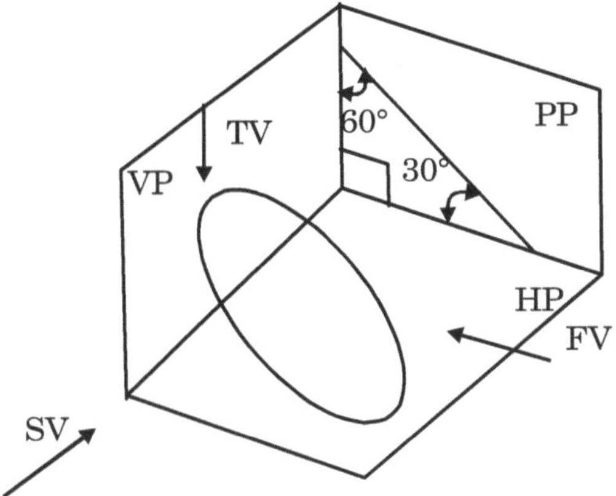

The final three views of the plane surface are shown below.

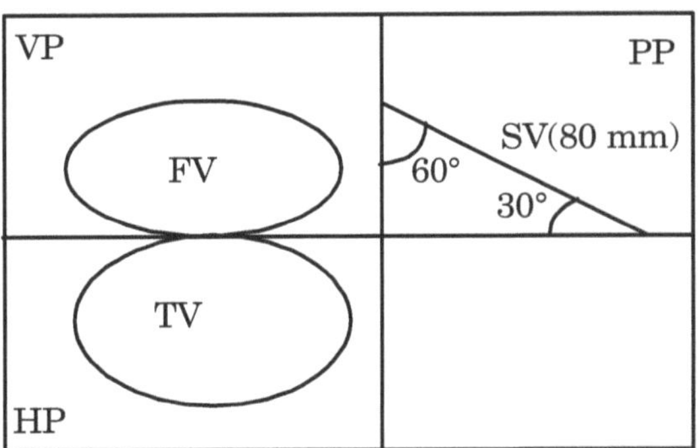

25. The type of projection in which the surfaces are equally foreshortened is isometric.

26. $\text{R.F} = \sqrt{\dfrac{\text{Map Area}}{\text{Aetual Area}}} = \sqrt{\dfrac{12 \times 10 \times 10^{-4}}{75000}} = \dfrac{1}{2500}$

27. INVOLUTE

Involute is a locus of a free end of string when it is wound round on a circular pole.

It is also a curve obtained from another given curve by attaching an imaginary taut string too the given curve and tracing its free end as it is wound to that given curve, or in reverse, unwound.

28. The trace, situated in the horizontal place, is called the horizontal trace, and the trace, situated in the vertical plane, is called the vertical trace.

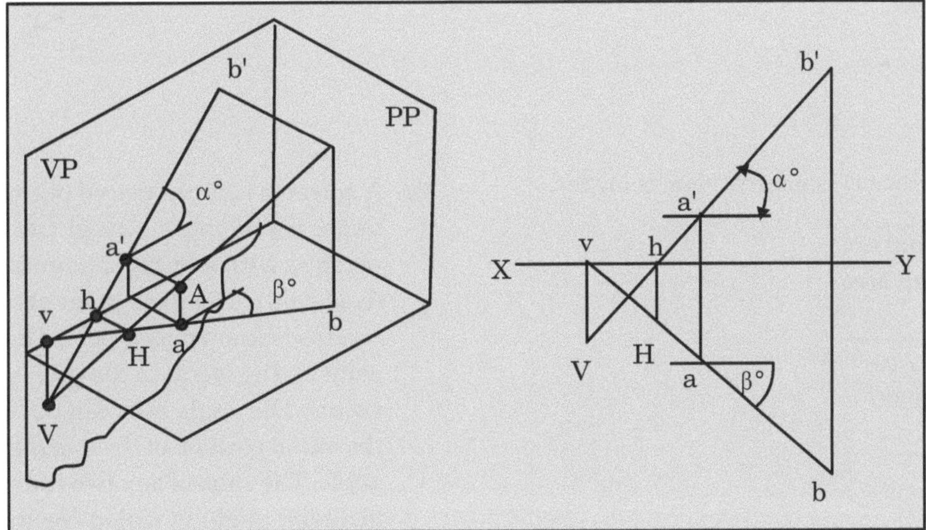

The point where the line or line produced meets the plane is called trace. Horizontal Trace: The point of intersection of the inclined line with the H.P. is called Horizontal Trace or simply H.T. Vertical Trace: The point of intersection of the inclined line with the V.P. is called Vertical Trace or simply V.T.

29. Orthographic projection, is a means of representing three-dimensional objects in two dimensions. It is a form of parallel projection, in which all the projection lines are orthogonal to the projection plane, resulting in every plane of the scene appearing in affine transformation on the viewing surface.

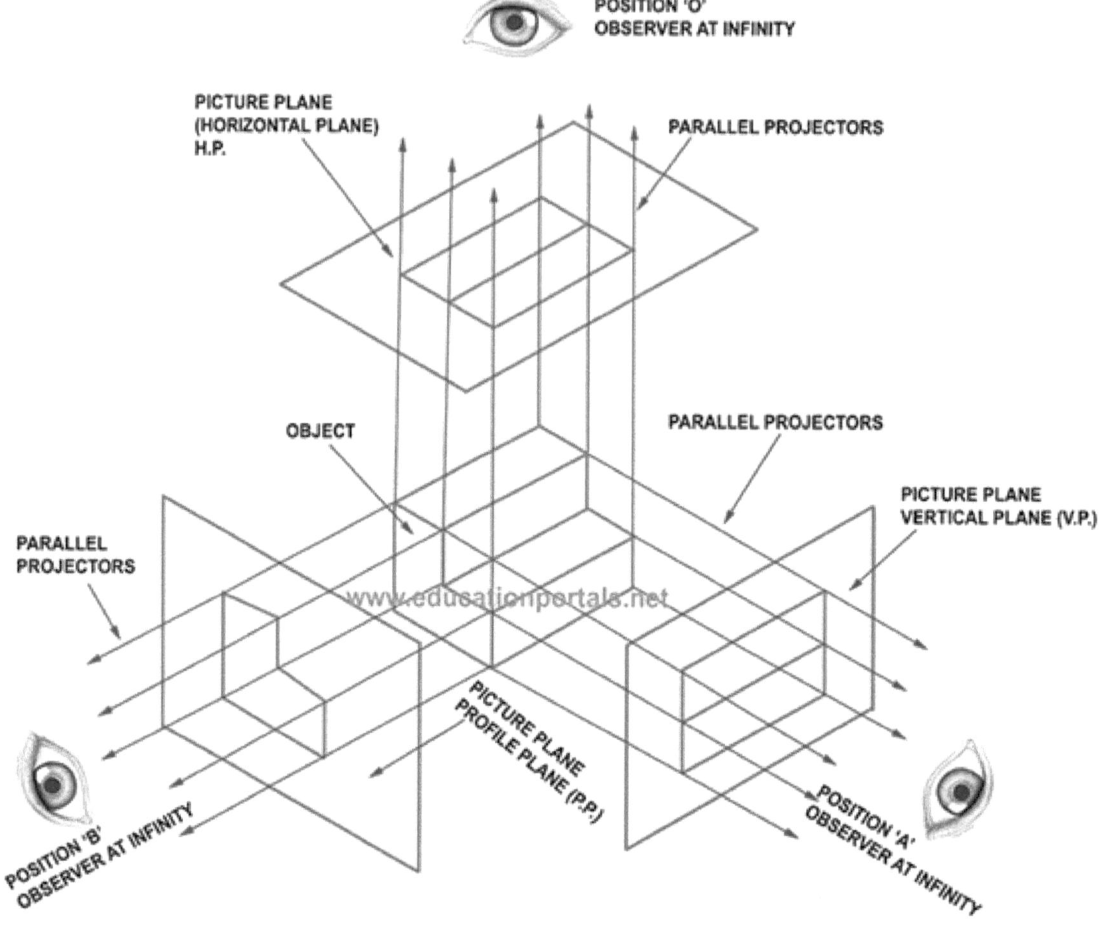

30. The appearance of isometric view is larger.

31.

$$\text{R.F} = \sqrt{\frac{\text{Actual area}}{\text{Map area}}}$$

$$= \sqrt{\frac{100 \times 10^{-4}}{40000}}$$

$$= \sqrt{\frac{1}{4 \times 10^6}}$$

$$= \frac{1}{2 \times 10^3}$$

32. A spiral is a curve traced out by a point moving uniformly along a straight line while the line revolves with a uniform angular velocity about a fixed point. The fixed point about which the line rotates is known as a pole. The line joining any point on the spiral to the pole is known as radius vector. The angle between the radius vector and the initial position of the line is known as vectorial angle. The ratio of any two radius vectors to their included angle is called constant of the curve. With this terminology the spiral curves are categorized as spiral of Arhimedes and logarithmic spiral.

33. The trace, situated in the horizontal plane, is called the horizontal trace, and the trace, situated in the vertical plane, is called the vertical trace.

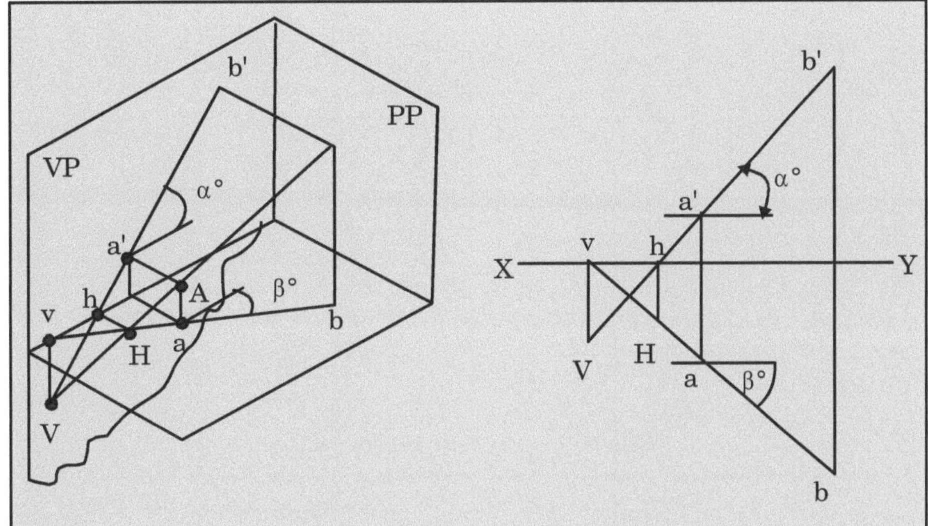

The point where the line or line produced meets the plane is called trace. Horizontal Trace: The point of intersection of the inclined line with the H.P. is called Horizontal Trace or simply H.T. Vertical Trace: The point of intersection of the inclined line with the V.P. is called Vertical Trace or simply V.T.

34. THEORY OF ORTHOGRAPHIC PROJECTION

A method to describe shape by the process of causing an image to be formed by rays of sight taken in a particular direction from an object too an picture plane.

- If the rays are perpendicular to the picture plane, the projection is known as Orthographic Projection.
- If the rays are at an angle to the plane, the projection is known as Oblique Projection.
- If the rays are taken to a particular station point, the projection is know as Perspective Projection.

35. A circle appears as an ellipse on the isometric drawing.

36. R.F $= \sqrt{\dfrac{\text{Actual area}}{\text{Map area}}}$

$$= \sqrt{\dfrac{9\text{km}^2}{144\text{cm}^2}}$$

$$= \sqrt{\dfrac{9 \times \left(10^3\right)^2}{144 \times \left(10^{-2}\right)^2}} = \dfrac{1}{25000}$$

37. Spiral curve will be traced.

38.

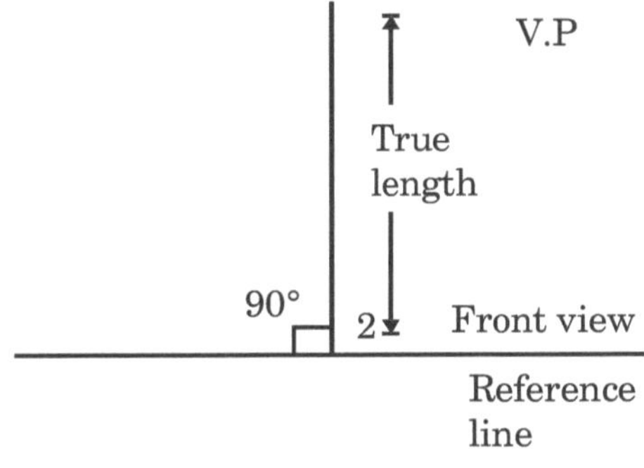

If top view of a line is a point, its front view is perpendicular to reference line and of true length.

39. When we Project the Elevation onto a Plane behind the object, This Plane is called the **Vertical Plane**. The Elevation is projected like a shadow. The Plan is projected onto a Plane underneath the object, at 90 degrees to the Vertical Plane, this Plane is called the **Horizontal Plane**. The Plan is projected like a shadow.

40.

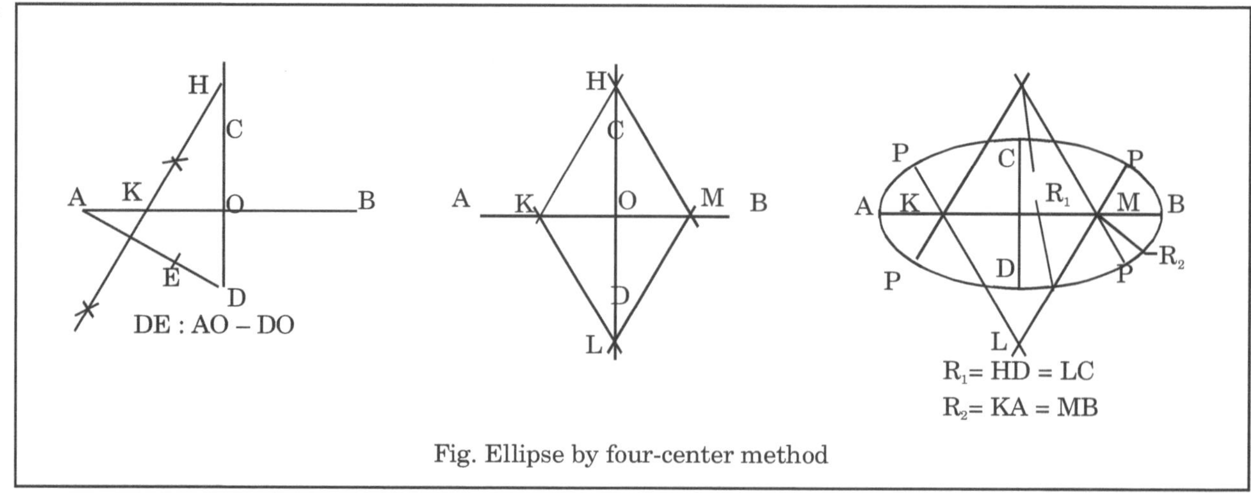

Fig. Ellipse by four-center method

ELLIPSE BY FOUR-CENTER METHOD

The four-center method is used for small ellipses. Given major axis, AB, and minor axis, CD, mutually perpendicular at their midpoint, O, as shown in figure 4-45, draw AD, connecting the end points of the two axes. With the dividers set to DO, measure DO along AO and reset the dividers on the remaining distance to O. With the difference of semiaxes thus set on the dividers, mark off DE equal to AO minus DO. Draw perpendicular bisector AE, and extend it to intersect the major axis at K and the minor axis extended at H. With the dividers, mark off OM equal to OK, and OL equal to OH. With H as a center and radius R_1 equal to HD, draw the bottom arc. With L as a center and the same radius as R_1, draw the top arc. With M as a center and the radius R_2 equal to MB draw the end arc. With K as a center and the same radius, R_2, draw the end arc. The four circular arcs thus drawn meet, in common points of tangency, P, at the ends of their radii in their lines of centers.

41.

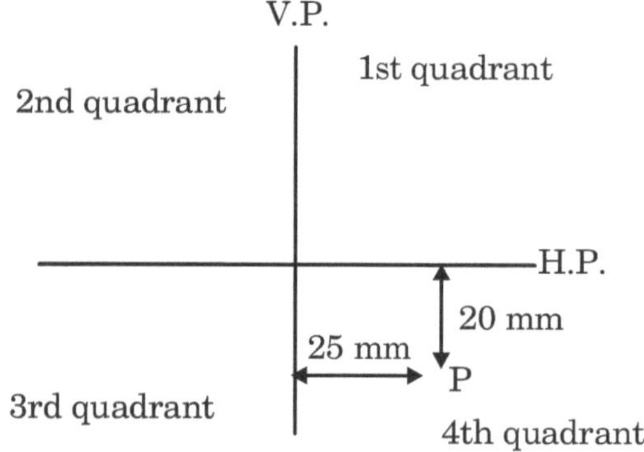

Point P lies in the fourth quadrant

42. A large headed piece of metal that pierces & projects from a surface is called as stud.

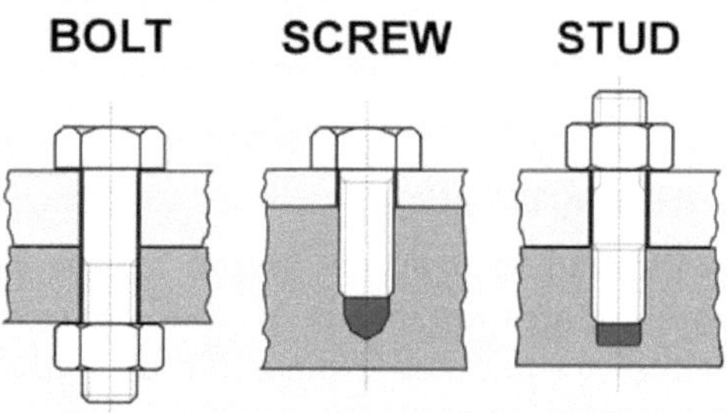

43. Diagonal scale is an engineering measuring instrument which is composed of a set of parallel straight lines which are obliquely crossed by another set of straight lines. Diagonal scales are used to measure small fractions of the unit of measurement.

A **vernier scale** is a visual aid to taking an accurate measurement reading between two graduation markings on a linear scale by using mechanical interpolation; thereby increasing resolution and reducing measurement uncertainty by using Vernieracuity to reduce human estimation error.

44. Conic sections are curves formed by intersecting a cone and a plane. These curves include circles, ellipses, parabolas and hyperbolas. Wolfram.

Table. Equations for Conic Sections				
	Circle	**Ellipse**	**Parabola**	**Hyperbola**
Equation (horizontal vertex)	$x^2 + y^2 = r^2$	$\dfrac{x^2}{a^2} + \dfrac{y}{b^2} = 1$	$4px = y^2$	$\dfrac{x^2}{a^2} - \dfrac{y^2}{b^2} = 1$
Equation (vertical vertex)	$x^2 + y^2 = r^2$	$\dfrac{y^2}{a^2} + \dfrac{x^2}{b^2} = 1$	$4py = x^2$	$\dfrac{y^2}{a^2} - \dfrac{x^2}{b^2} = 1$
Variables	r = circle radius	l = major radius $(=\dfrac{1}{2}$ length minor axis) l = minor radius $(=\dfrac{1}{2}$ length minor axis)	p = distance from vertex to focus (or directrix)	$a = \dfrac{1}{2}$ length major axis = $\dfrac{1}{2}$ length minor axis
Definition	Distance to the origin is constant	sum of distances to each focus is constant	distance to focus = distance to directrix	difference between distances to each focus constant

45. Angle between line & iso equivalent line is 15°

46.

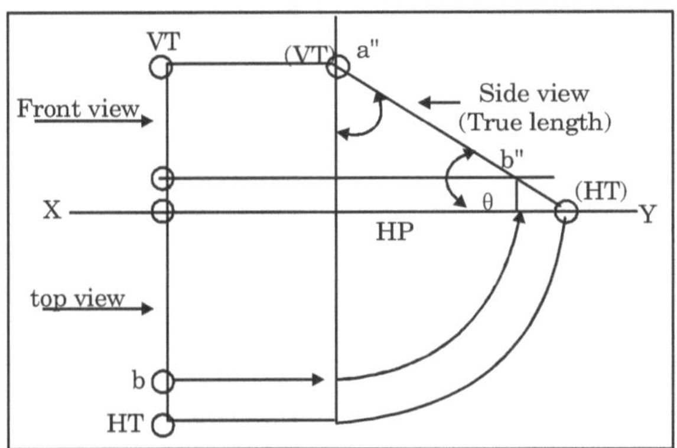

True length will be shown in Profile from Side view.

47. Cotter Joint

- A cotter joint is used to connect rigidly two co-axial rods or bars which are subjected to axial tensile or compressive forces. It is a temporary fattening.

- A cotter is a flat wedge shaped piece of rectangular cross section and its width is tapered (either on one side or on both sides) from one end to another for an easy adjustment.

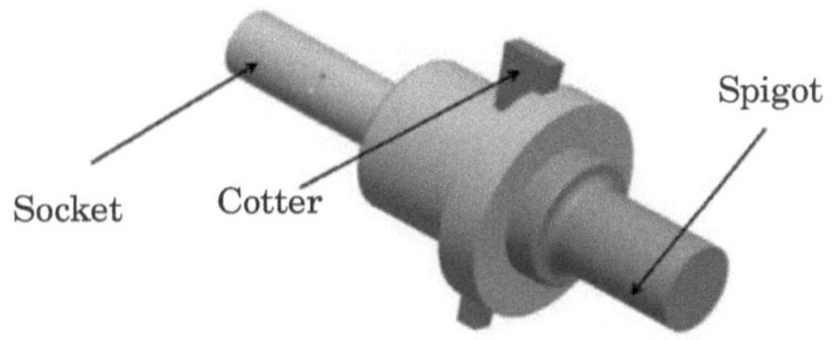

48. The Representative Fraction (R. F.); The scale is given as a fraction: $\dfrac{1}{10}$ or as a ratio: 1:10. What it means is that one unit measured on the map stands for ten of the same units on the ground. You can use any units that you are familiar with. So, you can say 1 centimeter represents 10 cm. On most maps, the Representative Fraction is given as a ratio, which is usually 1:50,000 on topographic maps. Note that the larger the Representative Fraction denominator, the smaller the scale and the less detail that can be shown. A scale of 1:25 000 will show more detail than a scale of 1:100000. The smaller the denominator of the Representative Fraction, the larger the scale and more detail can be shown for a given area.

49. Theorem 5.2 shows that any line l intersects a conic in at most two points. When l is line at infinity, this confirms that every conic restricts to an ellipse, a parabola, or a hyperbola in the Euclidean plane. Moreover, a coni intersects the line at infinity in only one point if and only if it is tangent to the line at infinity (by Theorem 5.2). Thus, a conic is a parabola if and only if it is tangent to the line at infinity (Figure 5.2).

We have seen that two points at infinity on the hyperbola in (14) lie on the asymptotes y = ± $\left(\dfrac{b}{a}\right)$ x (Figure 5.3). The asymptotes do not intersect the hyperbola in the Euclidean plane (since substituting $\pm\left(\dfrac{b}{a}\right)x$ for y makes the left

side of (14) zero). Thus each asymptote intersects the hyperbola at exactly one point of the projective plane, a point at infinity. It follows from Theorem 5.2 that the asysmptotes of a hyperbola are the tangents at the two points at infinity on the hyperbola.

50. 30°

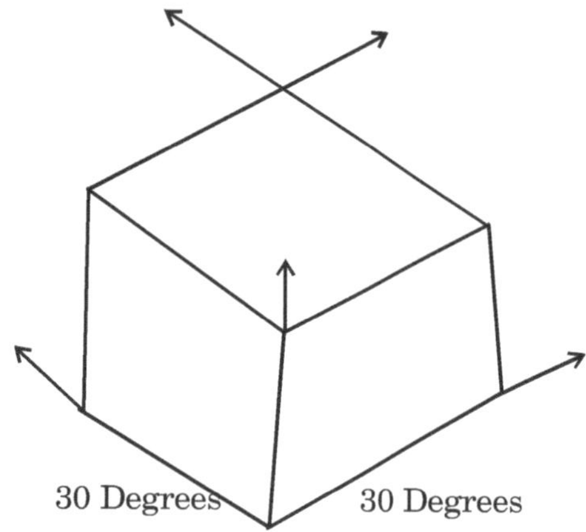

RRB SSE 3rd Sep Shift 2

51.

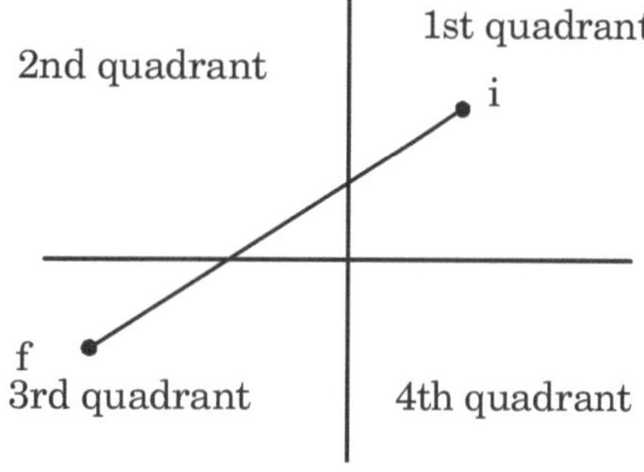

OR

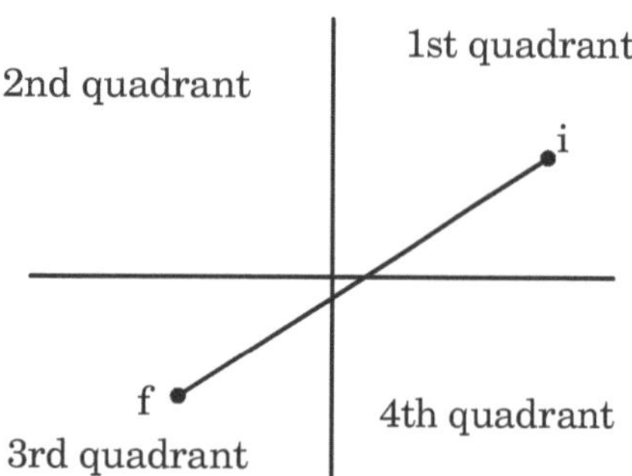

Line passing throuth   Line passing through
2nd quadrant   4th quadrant

52. Either Imolute or cycloidal

53. Comparative scales

(i) Comparative scale conists of two scales of the same R.F but graduated to read different unit, contructed separately or one above the other.

(ii) used to compare distances expressed in different systems of unit.

54.

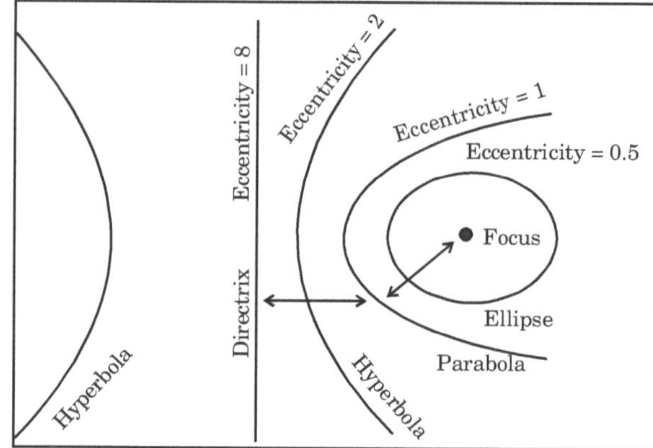

By placing a hyperbola on an $x-y$ graph (centered over the $x-$ axis and $y-$ axis), the equation of the curve is:

$$\frac{x^2}{a^2} - \frac{y^2}{b^2} = 1$$

Also:

One vertex is at (a, 0), and the other us at $(-a, 0)$

The asymptotes are the straight lines:

. $y = \left(\dfrac{b}{a}\right)x$

. $y = -\left(\dfrac{b}{a}\right)x$

(Note: the equation is similar to the equation of the ellipse:

$$\frac{x^2}{a^2} + \frac{y^2}{b^2} = 1, \text{ except for a " – " instead of a "+")}$$

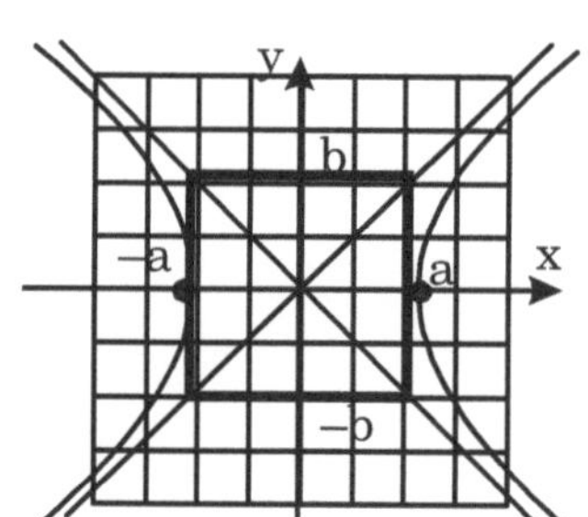

Eccentricity

Any branch of a hyperbola can also be defined as a curve where the distances of any point from:

.   a fixed point (the focus), and

.   a fixed straight line (the directrix) are always in the same ratio.

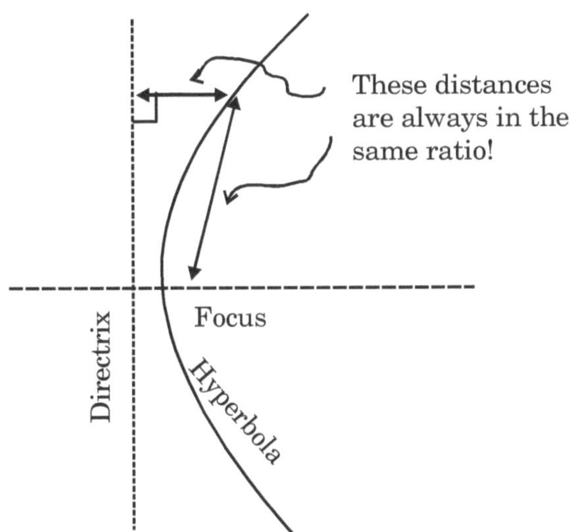

This ratio is called the eccentricity. and for a hyperbola it is always greater than 1.

The eccentricity (usually shown as the letter e) shows how "uncurvy" (varying from being a circle) the hyperbola is.

On this diagram:

•   P is a point on the curve,

•   F is the focus and

•   N is the point on the directrix so that PN is perpendicular to the directrix.

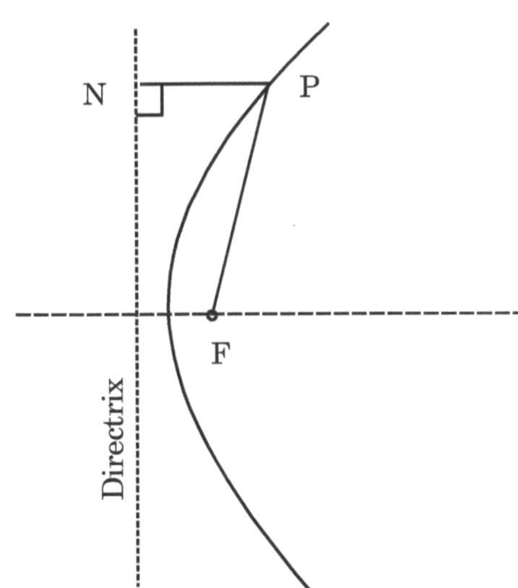

The eccentricity is the ratio PF/ PN, and has the formula:

$$e = \frac{\sqrt{\left(a^2 + b^2\right)}}{a}$$

Using "a" and "b" from the diagram above.

55. Equation

RRB SSE 3ʳᵈ Sep Shift 3

56.

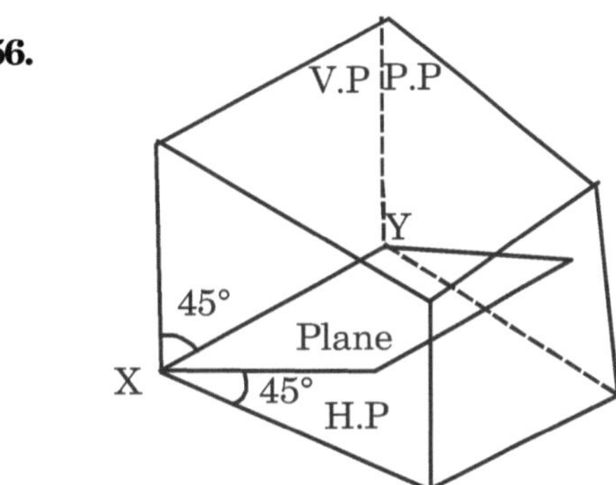

As we can observe plane makes angle 45° with H.P & V.P but it makes an angle of 90° with P.P.

57. Each side of the profile of the basiccrack is a straight line which is a special case of the involute curve when the base circle diameter is infinite.

58. Diagonal scale & vernier scale can be used interchangeably

59. Spiral path will be traced by Ant

60.

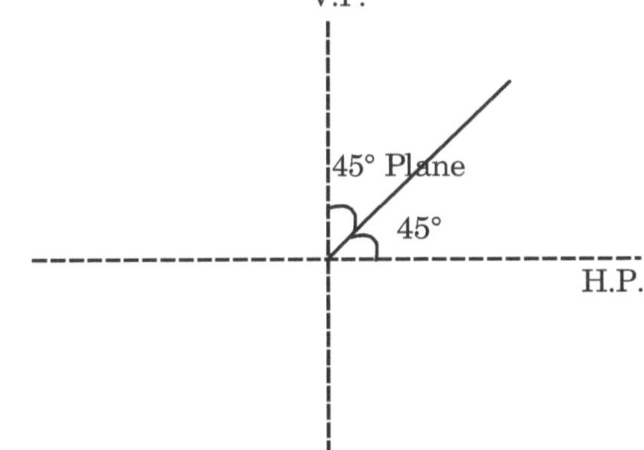

All three views will be different

6 STRENGTH OF MATERIAL

CHAPTER

RRB JUNIOR ENGINEER

1. The main purpose of providing foundation to a building is

(*a*) to provide a level base over which masonry may be laid

(*b*) to fix the super structure to the ground

(*c*) to distribute the weight of the structure on a sufficiently large area of the substratum

(*d*) to prevent uneven distribution of load of beams on the substratum

[RRB JE 2014 GREEN SHIFT]

2. A Simply supported beam of span L and flexural rigidity El, carries a unit point load at its centre. The strain energy in the beam due to bending is

(*a*) $\dfrac{L^3}{48EI}$

(*b*) $\dfrac{L^3}{192EI}$

(*c*) $\dfrac{L^3}{96EI}$

(*d*) $\dfrac{L^3}{16EI}$

[RRB JE 2014 YELLOW SHIFT]

3. In terms of bulk modulus (K) and modulus of rigidity (G), Poisson's ratio can be expressed as

(*a*) $\dfrac{3K - 4G}{6K - 4G}$

(*b*) $\dfrac{3K + 4G}{6K - 4G}$

(*c*) $\dfrac{3K - 2G}{6K + 2G}$

(*d*) $\dfrac{3K + 2G}{6K - 2G}$

[RRB JE 2014 YELLOW SHIFT]

4. The stress – strain curve for an ideally plastic material is (conventional symbols)

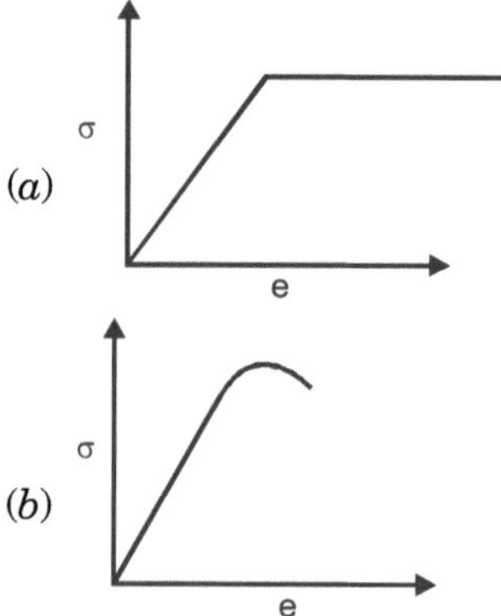

[RRB JE 2014 YELLOW SHIFT]

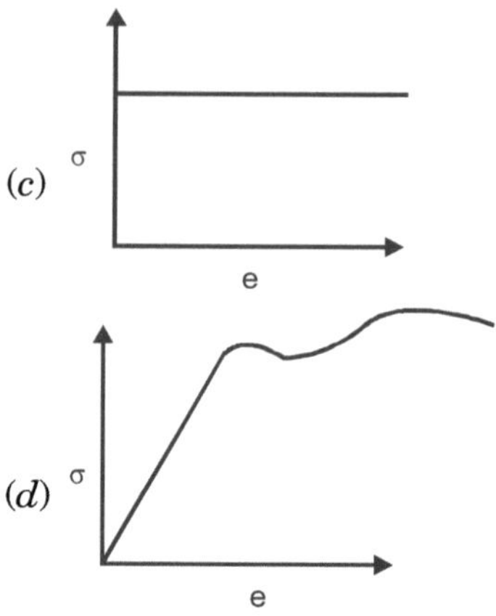

[RRB JE 2014 YELLOW SHIFT]

5. What is the force in the vertical member CD of the pin - jointed frame shown below ?

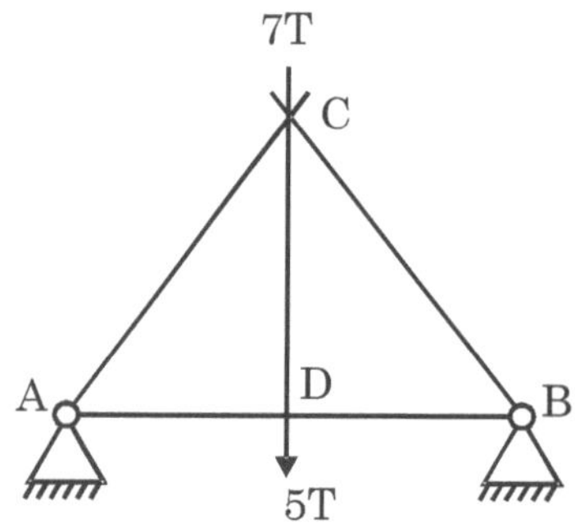

(*a*) 12T (Tension)

(*b*) 2T (Compression)

(*c*) 7T (Compression)

(*d*) 5T (Tension)

[RRB JE 2014 YELLOW SHIFT]

6. In a situation where torsion is dominant, which one of the following is the desirable section ?

(*a*) Angle Section

(*b*) Channel Section

(*c*) l-Section

(*d*) Box-Type Section

[RRB JE 2014 YELLOW SHIFT]

7. Lateral ties in RCC columns are provided to resist

(*a*) Bending moment

(*b*) Shear

(*c*) Buckling of longitudinal steel base

(*d*) Both Bending moment and Shear

[RRB JE 2014 YELLOW SHIFT]

8. In a Cantilever beam carrying gravity load, main reinforcement to resist Bending moment is provided
   - (*a*) above theNeutral Axis
   - (*b*) as vertical stirrups
   - (*c*) as a helical reinforcement
   - (*d*) below the Neutral Axis

   [RRB JE 2014 YELLOW SHIFT]

9. If a material has identical properties in all directions, it is said to be
   - (*a*) Homogeneous
   - (*b*) Isotropic
   - (*c*) Elastic
   - (*d*) Orthotropic

   [RRB JE 2015 26th AUG 1st SHIFT]

10. If the modulus of elasticity is zero, the material is said to be
    - (*a*) Rigid
    - (*b*) Elastic
    - (*c*) Flexible
    - (*d*) Plastic

    [RRB JE 2015 26th AUG 2nd SHIFT]

11. Bending compressive and tensile stresses respectively are calculated based on
    - (*a*) Net area and gross area
    - (*b*) Gross area and net area
    - (*c*) Net area in both cases
    - (*d*) Gross area in both cases

    [RRB JE 2015 26th AUG 2nd SHIFT]

12. Bolts are most suitable to carry
    - (*a*) Shear
    - (*b*) Bending
    - (*c*) Axial tension
    - (*d*) Shear and bending

    [RRB JE 2015 26th AUG 3rd SHIFT]

13. The unit of elastic modulus is the same as those of
    - (*a*) Stress, shear modulus and pressure
    - (*b*) Strain, shear modulus and force
    - (*c*) Shear modulus, stress and force
    - (*d*) Stress strain and pressure

    [RRB JE 2015 27th AUG 1st SHIFT]

14. Which one of the following is the mode of failure in a fillet weld material?
    - (*a*) Tension
    - (*b*) Shear
    - (*c*) Bearing
    - (*d*) Crushing

    [RRB JE 2015 27th AUG 1st SHIFT]

15. The stress below which a material has a high probability of not failing under reversal of stress is known as
    - (*a*) Tolerance limit
    - (*b*) Elastic limit
    - (*c*) Proportional limit
    - (*d*) Endurance limit

    [RRB JE 2015 27th AUG 2nd SHIFT]

16. Lacings are subjected to
    - (*a*) Transverse loading
    - (*b*) Axial loading plus bending
    - (*c*) Axial loading plus shear force
    - (*d*) Axial loading only

    [RRB JE 2015 27th AUG 2nd SHIFT]

17. The term nominal stress in stress-strain curve for mild steel implies
    - (*a*) Average stress
    - (*b*) Actual stress
    - (*c*) Yield stress
    - (*d*) Stress at necking

    [RRB JE 2015 27th AUG 3rd SHIFT]

18. Which one of following is a compression member?
    - (*a*) Purlin
    - (*b*) Boom
    - (*c*) Girt
    - (*d*) Tie

    [RRB JE 2015 27th AUG 3rd SHIFT]

19. In the case of pure bending, the beam will bend into an arc of a
    - (*a*) Circle
    - (*b*) Parabola
    - (*c*) Ellipse
    - (*d*) Hyperbola

    [RRB JE 2015 28th AUG 1st SHIFT]

20. Which one of the following is not a compression member?
    - (*a*) Strut
    - (*b*) Tie
    - (*c*) Rafter
    - (*d*) Boom

    [RRB JE 2015 28th AUG 1st SHIFT]

21. A prismatic beam has uniform
    - (*a*) Depth
    - (*b*) Width
    - (*c*) Strength
    - (*d*) C ross-section

    [RRB JE 2015 28th AUG 2nd SHIFT]

22. A steel beam supporting loads from the floor slab as well as from wall is termed as
    - (*a*) Stringer beam
    - (*b*) Lintel beam
    - (*c*) Spandrel beam
    - (*d*) Header beam

    [RRB JE 2015 28th AUG 2nd SHIFT]

23. Cup-and-cone type fracture occurs in the case of
    - (*a*) Cast iron
    - (*b*) Round specimen of ductile metals
    - (*c*) Tough steel
    - (*d*) Soft brass

    [RRB JE 2015 28th AUG 3rd SHIFT]

24. Deep beams are designed for
    - (*a*) Shear force only
    - (*b*) Bending moment only
    - (*c*) Both shear force and bending moment
    - (*d*) Bearing

    [RRB JE 2015 28th AUG 3rd SHIFT]

25. The type of stress induced in the foundation bolts fixing a column to its footing is

(a) Pure compression (b) Bearing

(c) Pure tension (d) Bending

[RRB JE 2015 29ᵗʰ AUG 1ˢᵗ SHIFT]

26. In which of the following case we avoid bolted connection

(a) Connection subjected to fire

(b) Connection subjected to frequent earthquake load

(c) Connection subjected to snow load

(d) Connection subjected to corrosion problem

[RRB JE 2015 29ᵗʰ AUG 2ⁿᵈ SHIFT]

27. The ratio of transverse strain to the longitudinal strain under an axial load is known as

(a) tangent modulus of elasticity

(b) bulk modulus of elasticity

(c) modulus of rigidity

(d) Poisson's ratio

[RRB JE 2015 29ᵗʰ AUG 3ʳᵈ SHIFT]

28. A channel section consists of

(a) two webs

(b) two flanges

(c) two webs and two flanges

(d) one web and two flanges

[RRB JE 2015 29ᵗʰ AUG 3ʳᵈ SHIFT]

29. If p is the pitch of the rivets and d is the aross diameter of rivets, the tearing efficiency of joints is equal to

(a) p/(p − d) (b) p/(p + d)

(c) (p − d)/p (d) (p + d)/p

[RRB JE 2015 30ᵗʰ AUG 3ʳᵈ SHIFT]

30. The ultimate strength of the steel used for pre-stressing is nearly

(a) 250 N/mm² (b) 415 N/mm²

(c) 500 N/mm² (d) 1500 N/mm²

[RRB JE 2015 30ᵗʰ AUG 3ʳᵈ SHIFT]

31. For rivet diameter upto 24 mm. the diameter of rivet hole is larger than the diameter of rivet by

(a) 1 mm (b) 1.5 mm

(c) 2 mm (d) 2.5 mm

[RRB JE 2015 30ᵗʰ AUG 3ʳᵈ SHIFT]

32. The structure made of rigid curved surfaces are known as

(a) Surface structure (b) Frame structure

(c) Shell structure (d) Space structure

[RRB JE 2015 16ᵗʰ SEP 3ʳᵈ SHIFT]

33. The failure of column depends upon

(a) Weight of column

(b) Length of column

(c) Slenderness ratio

(d) Cross sectional area of column

[RRB JE 2015 16ᵗʰ SEP 3ʳᵈ SHIFT]

RRB SENIOR SECTION ENGINEER

1. Stiffners are used in a Plate Girder to :

(a) Avoid buckling of web plate

(b) Reduce the shear stress

(c) Reduce the compressive stress

(d) Take the bearing stress

[RRB SSE 2014 RED SHIFT]

2. The distance between C.G. of compression and C.G. of Tension Flanges of a Plate Girder is known as :

(a) Clear depth (b) Effective depth

(c) Overall depth (d) None of these

[RRB SSE 2014 RED SHIFT]

3. In a three-hinged arch, the Bending Moment will be zero at:

(a) Right Hinge Only

(b) Left Hinge Only

(c) Both Right and Left Hinges

(d) All the three Hinges

[RRB SSE 2014 RED SHIFT]

4. Maximum defection of a fixed beam carrying a central load is one form of maximum deflection is equal to (other notations standard)

(a) $\dfrac{WL^3}{48EI}$ (b) $\dfrac{WL^3}{96EI}$

(c) $\dfrac{WL^3}{192EI}$ (d) $\dfrac{5}{384}\dfrac{WL^3}{EI}$

[RRB SSE 2014 YELLOW SHIFT]

5. In a thin-wall T-section, the shear centre C is located at the point shown in

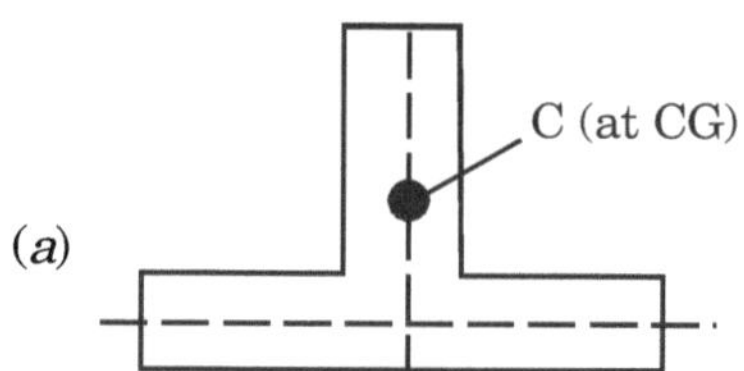

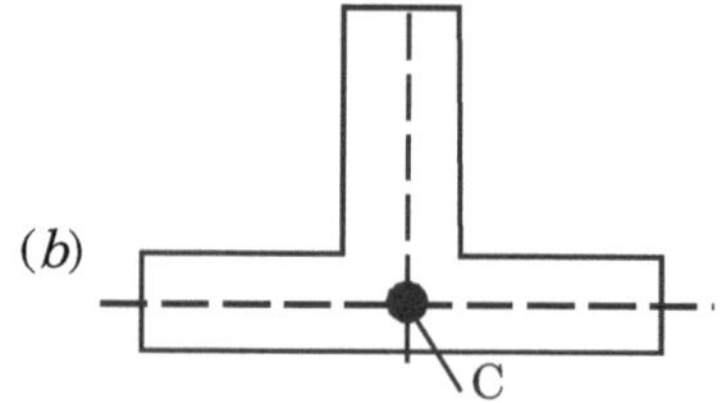

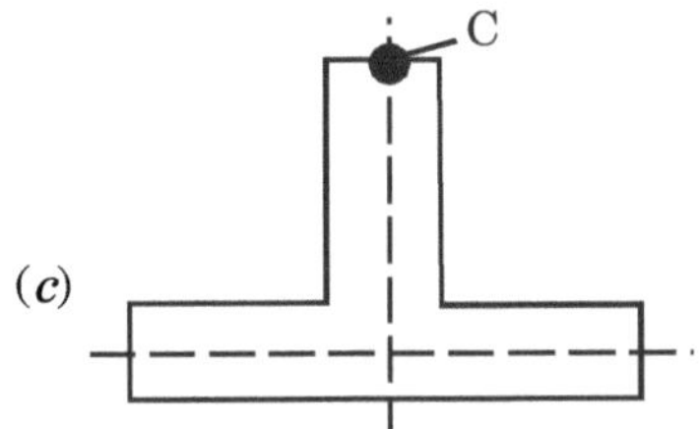

(c)

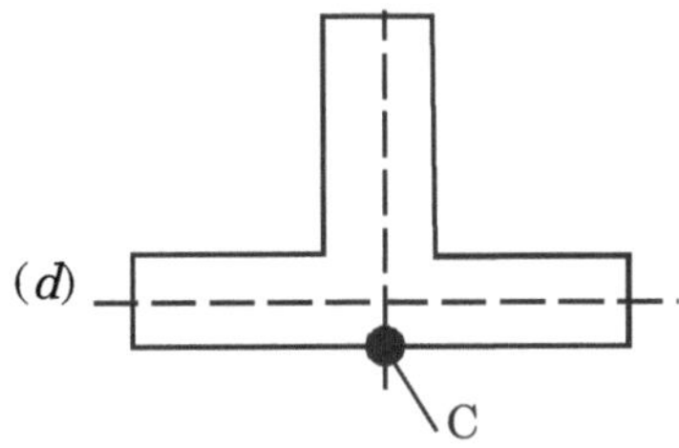

(d)

6. A simply supported beam is loaded as below

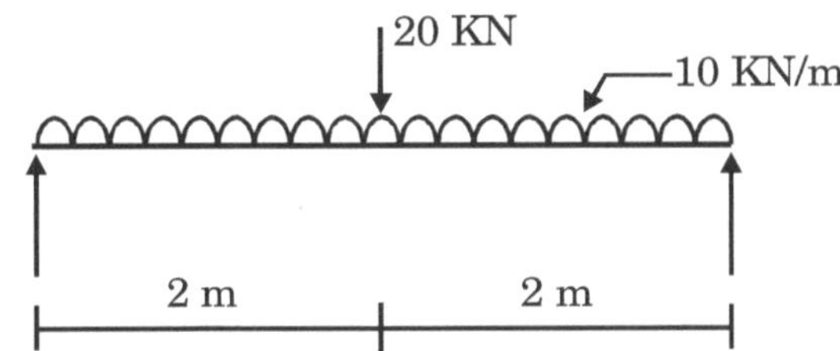

The corresponding Bending Moment Diagram is

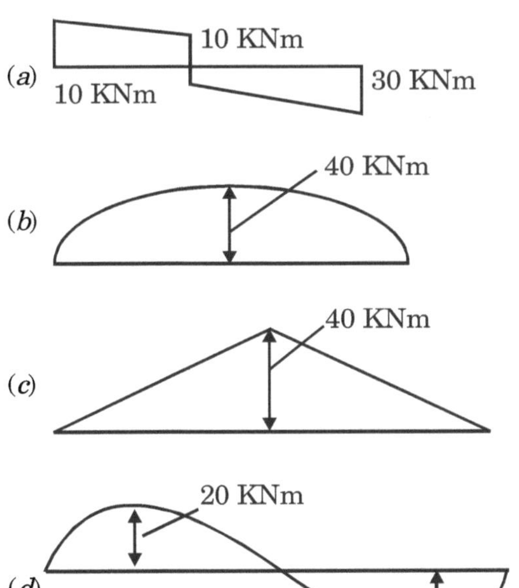

7. What is the radius of Mohr's circle in case of bi-axial state of stress ?

(a) Half the sum of the two principal stresses

(b) Half the difference of the two principal stresses

(c) Difference of the two principal stresses

(d) Sum of the two principal stresses

[RRB SSE 2014 YELLOW SHIFT]

8. What is the moment at A for a frame shown below:

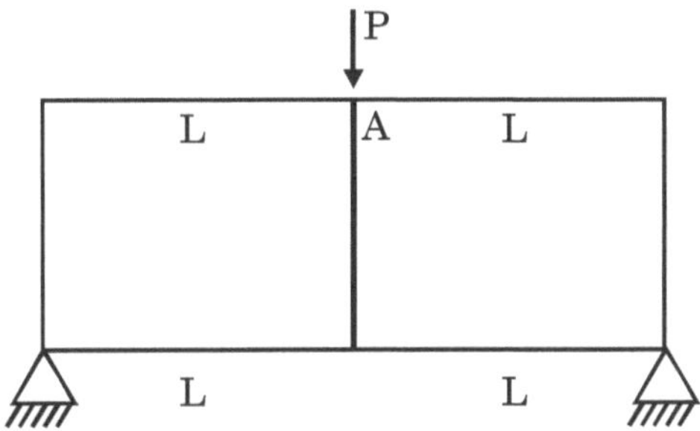

Each vertical member has very large Moment of Inertia

(a) $\dfrac{PL}{2}$ (b) $\dfrac{PL}{4}$

(c) $\dfrac{PL}{8}$ (d) $\dfrac{PL}{16}$

[RRB SSE 2014 YELLOW SHIFT]

9. A structure has two degree of indeterminacy. The number of plastic hinges that would be formed at complete collapse is

(a) 0   (b) 1

(c) 2   (d) 3

[RRB SSE 2014 YELLOW SHIFT]

10. A column is a structural member designed primarily to take which of the following type of load

(a) Torsional   (b) Tensile

(c) Compressive   (d) Shear

[RRB SSE 2015 1ˢᵗ SEP 1ˢᵗ SHIFT]

11. A roof member directly supporting the roof covering or rafter and roof battens is called as

(a) Truss   (b) Beam

(c) Strut   (d) Purlin

[RRB SSE 2015 1ˢᵗ SEP 3ʳᵈ SHIFT]

12. The centre-to-centre distance between individual fasteners in a line, in the direction of load/ stress is called as

(a) Camber   (b) Pitch

(c) Specific distance (d) Stress lag

[RRB SSE 2015 1ˢᵗ SEP 3ʳᵈ SHIFT]

13. In the design of steel structures, the ratio of the effective length of a member to the radius of gyration of the cross-section about the axis under consideration is called as

(a) Modulus of elasticity

(b) Slenderness ratio

(c) Stress ratio

(d) Aspect ratio

[RRB SSE 2015 2nd SEP 1st SHIFT]

14. The point where the bending moment is zero is called as

(a) Point of contraflexure

(b) Yield point

(c) Plastic hinge

(d) Limit of elasticity

[RRB SSE 2015 2nd SEP 1st SHIFT]

15. The area under the stress-strain plot (product of stress and strain) represents

(a) Hardness of the material

(b) Energy required to cause failure

(c) Rigidity of the material

(d) Flexibility of the material

[RRB SSE 2015 2nd SEP 2nd SHIFT]

16. The effective length of a h meter high column with one end fixed and other free is

(a) 2h　　　　　　　　　(b) 0.5h

(c) h　　　　　　　　　(d) h/1.414

[RRB SSE 2015 2nd SEP 2nd SHIFT]

17. If a material shows different properties in different directions, then it is called as

(a) Isotropic　　　　　(b) Homogeneous

(c) Anisotropic　　　　(d) Heterogeneous

[RRB SSE 2015 2nd SEP 2nd SHIFT]

18. The phenomenon of increase in stress with increase in strain beyond yielding is called as

(a) Plastic hinge formation

(b) Strain hardening

(c) Strain softening

(d) Yielding

[RRB SSE 2015 2nd SEP 2nd SHIFT]

19. Which of the following is not used in calculating the area between the base line and the boundary line

(a) Mid-ordinate rule　(b) Simpson's rule

(c) Trapezoidal rule　(d) Prismoidal formula

[RRB SSE 2015 2nd SEP 2nd SHIFT]

20. A non-yielding support has

(a) Zero slope at the end point (support point)

(b) No bending moment

(c) Can support any amount of vertical load

(d) Frictionless

[RRB SSE 2015 2nd SEP 3rd SHIFT]

21. If a material shows similar properties in different directions, then it is called as

(a) Isotropic　　　　　(b) Flomogeneous

(c) Anisotropic　　　　(d) Heterogeneou

[RRB SSE 2015 2nd SEP 3rd SHIFT]

22. An element used to retain or prevent the out-of-plane deformations of plates is referred as

(a) Strut　　　　　　　(b) Stiffener

(c) Purlin　　　　　　　(d) Raft

[RRB SSE 2015 2nd SEP 3rd SHIFT]

23. Regarding the idealization of support to a structural system, which of the following is false

(a) Roller supports are free to rotate and translate along the surface upon which the roller rests.

(b) A pinned support can resist both vertical and horizontal forces but not a moment

(c) Fixed supports can resist vertical and horizontal forces as well as a moment.

(d) Rigid supports can resist translation, but not the moments

[RRB SSE 2015 3rd SEP 1st SHIFT]

24. The load at which an element, a member or a structure as a whole, either collapses in service or buckles in a load test and develops excessive lateral (out of plane) deformation or instability is called as

(a) Buckling load　　　(b) Yielding load

(c) Eccentric load　　　(d) Failure load

[RRB SSE 2015 3rd SEP 1st SHIFT]

25. The stress below which a material regains its original size and shape when the load is removed is called as:

(a) Failure stress　　　(b) Shrinkage limit

(c) Plastic limit　　　　(d) Elastic limit

[RRB SSE 2015 3rd SEP 2nd SHIFT]

26. The behaviour shown by some materials by virtue of which, as the shear stress reduces continuously with the development in the plastic strain is called as:

(a) Yielding

(b) Strain softening

(c) Strain hardening

(d) Plasticity

[RRB SSE 2015 3rd SEP 2nd SHIFT]

27. The time period for which a structure or a structural element is required to perform its function without damage is called as

(*a*) Loading period

(*b*) Design life

(*c*) Life cycle that structure

(*d*) Serviceability duration

[RRB SSE 2015 3ʳᵈ SEP 3ʳᵈ SHIFT]

28. Which of the following is not applicable to limit state method?

(*a*) The stresses are obtained from design loads and compared with design strengths

(*b*) The method follows linear stress-strain behaviour of both the materials i.e. steel and concrete

(*c*) The ultimate stresses of the materials are used as allowable stresses

(*d*) Partial safety factors are used

[RRB SSE 2015 3ʳᵈ SEP 3ʳᵈ SHIFT]

29. Which of the following does not fall under tensioning devices used for prestressed concrete?

(*a*) Chemical   (*b*) Thermal

(*c*) Hydraulic   (*d*) Rotating

[RRB SSE 2015 3ʳᵈ SEP 3ʳᵈ SHIFT]

ANSWER KEY

RRB JUNIOR ENGINEER

1. (c)	**2.** (c)	**3.** (c)	**4.** (c)	**5.** (d)	**6.** (d)	**7.** (c)	**8.** (a)	**9.** (b)	**10.** (d)
11. (b)	**12.** (c)	**13.** (a)	**14.** (b)	**15.** (d)	**16.** (d)	**17.** (a)	**18.** (b)	**19.** (a)	**20.** (b)
21. (d)	**22.** (c)	**23.** (b)	**24.** (b)	**25.** (c)	**26.** (b)	**27.** (d)	**28.** (d)	**29.** (c)	**30.** (c)
31. (b)	**32.** (c)	**33.** (c)							

RRB SENIOR SECTION ENGINEER

1. (a)	**2.** (b)	**3.** (d)	**4.** (c)	**5.** (b)	**6.** (d)	**7.** (b)	**8.** (a)	**9.** (d)	**10.** (c)
11. (d)	**12.** (b)	**13.** (b)	**14.** (a)	**15.** (b)	**16.** (a)	**17.** (c)	**18.** (b)	**19.** (d)	**20.** (a)
21. (a)	**22.** (b)	**23.** (d)	**24.** (a)	**25.** (d)	**26.** (b)	**27.** (b)	**28.** (b)	**29.** (d)	

EXPLANATIONS

RRB JUNIOR ENGINEER

1. To distribute the weight of the structure.

2. For simply supported beam carrying a point load 'P' at the centre

$$\text{Strain energy } U = \int_0^{\frac{L}{2}} \frac{M^2}{2EI} dx; \quad M = \frac{P}{2}x;$$

$$\therefore U = \int_0^{\frac{L}{2}} \frac{P^2 x^2 dx}{2 \times 4EI} = \left[\frac{2P^2 x^3}{2 \times 4EI \times 3} \right]_0^{\frac{L}{2}}$$

$$\text{At } P = I, \ U = \frac{L^3}{96\,EI}$$

3. $B = \dfrac{E}{3(1-2v)}, \ B = \dfrac{GE}{3(3G-E)}$

$v = \dfrac{E}{2G} - 1, \ v = \dfrac{3B-2G}{6B+2G}, \ v = \dfrac{1}{2} - \dfrac{E}{6B}$

4. In ideal plastic material, stress remains constant and deformation is continuous in nature.

5. By using the concept of zero force members, Forces in member AD and BD are equal. Where as, Force in member CD will be equal to 5T.

7. **Lateral ties in rcc column are provided to resist** buckling of longitudinal. **Lateral ties in rcc column are provided to resist** buckling of longitudinal steel bars .

8. Main reinforcement is done above the neutral axis.

9. **Homogeneous material-** A **material** of uniform composition throughout that cannot be mechanically separated into different **materials**. Examples of "**homogeneous materials**" are certain types of plastics, ceramics, glass, metals, alloys, paper, board, resins, and coatings.

Isotropic material means a material having identical values of a property in all directions. **Glass** and **metals** are examples of isotropic materials.

10. If the modulus of elasticity is zero the material is said to be plastic.

12. Bolts used in column are suitable to carry axial tension.

13. The unit of Elastic modulus, stress, shear modulus and pressure is N/m².

14. Shear is the mode of failure in a fillet weld material.

15. Endurance limit (Se) is the stress level below which a specimen can withstand cyclic stress indefinitely without exhibiting **fatigue** failure.

16. Lacings are subjected to axial loading only.

17. Average stress

18. Boom is a compression member.

19. In case of pure bending, radius of curvature will exist and it corresponds to circle.

20. Tie is not a compression member.

21. Prismatic beam is simply a **beam** in which there **is** a **uniform** cross section throughout. I.e - A piece of 2x4 would be considered a **prismatic beam** as it **has** a constant width and height the entire length of the wood.

22. In concrete or steel construction, an exterior beamextending from column to column usually carrying an exterior wall load is known as a spandrel beam. Thespandrels over doorways in perpendicular work are generally richly decorated.

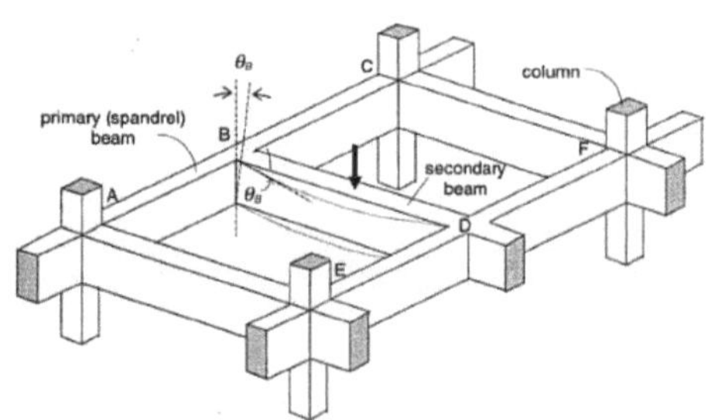

23. Cup and **Cone Fracture.** The majority of engineering metals experience moderately ductile failure. In uniaxial tension this failure mode has a characteristic appearance known as **cup** and **cone fracture. Cup** and **cone fracture occurs** as a stepwise process.

24. A **beam**, whether **deep** or conventional, is always **designed** for bending moment, apart from checks for safety in shear, deflections and cracking. A **beam** is said to be**deep** when the ratio of its effective span to overall depth is less than 2 for simply supported **beams**, or 2.5 for continuous **beams**.

25. Pure tension is the type of loading which is encountered in the foundation of bolts while fixing a column to its footing.

27. Poisson's ratio is the **ratio** of transverse contraction strain to longitudinal extension strain in the direction of stretching force. Tensile deformation is considered positive and compressive deformation is considered negative.

28. The structural **channel**, also known as a C-beam or Parallel Flange **Channel** (PFC), is a type of (usually structural steel) beam, used primarily in building construction and civil engineering.

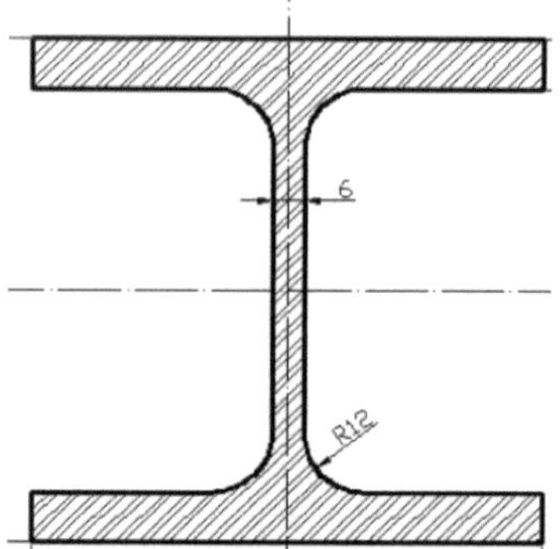

It is distinguished from I-beam or H-beam or W-beam type steel cross **sections** in that those have flanges on both sides of the web.

29. If p is the pitch of the rivets and d is the aross diameter of rivets, the tearing efficiency of joints is equal to (p-d)/p

30. The ultimate strength of the steel used for prestressing is nearly 500 N/mm².

32. The structure made of rigid curved surface or conical form are known as shell structure.

33. The failure of column depends on slenderness ration. Failure can be due to buckling, compression or bending.

RRB SENIOR SECTION ENGINEER

1. Stiffeners are secondary **plates** or sections which are attached to beam webs or flanges to stiffen them against out of plane deformations.

2. The distance between c.g. of compression and c.g. of tension flanges of a plate girder, is known as effective depth.

3.

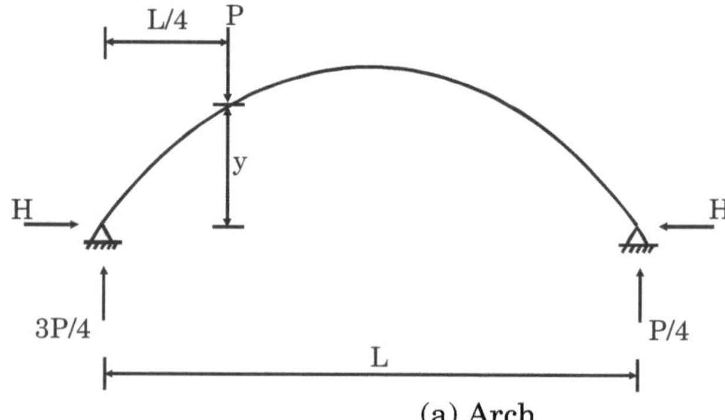

(a) Arch

4. The centre point deflection of fixed beam carrying central load is one-fourth of the centre point deflection of simply supported carrying same load

$$\therefore \delta_{max} = \frac{1}{4}\left(\frac{WL^3}{48EI}\right) = \frac{Wl^3}{192EI}$$

5.

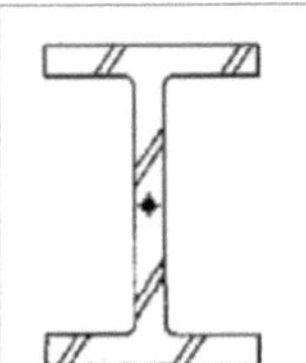 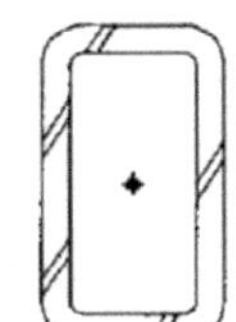 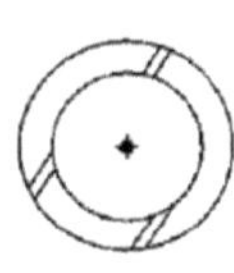

(a) doubly symmetric shapes,
shear center and centroid coincide

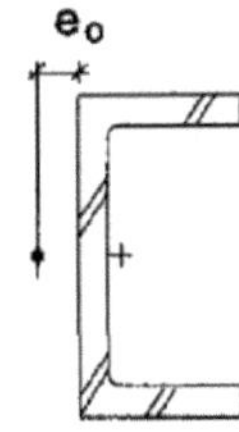 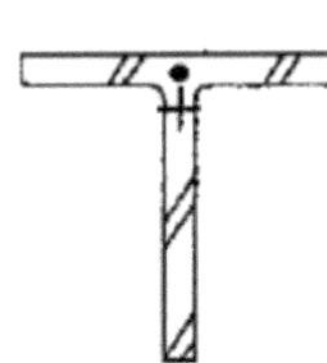

(b) singly symmetric shapes

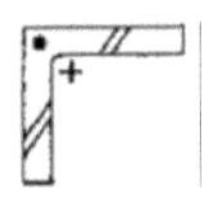 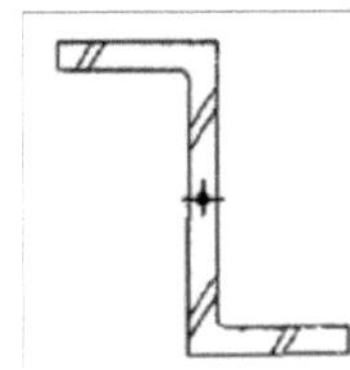

(c) unsymmetric shapes

+ centroid   • shear center

6.

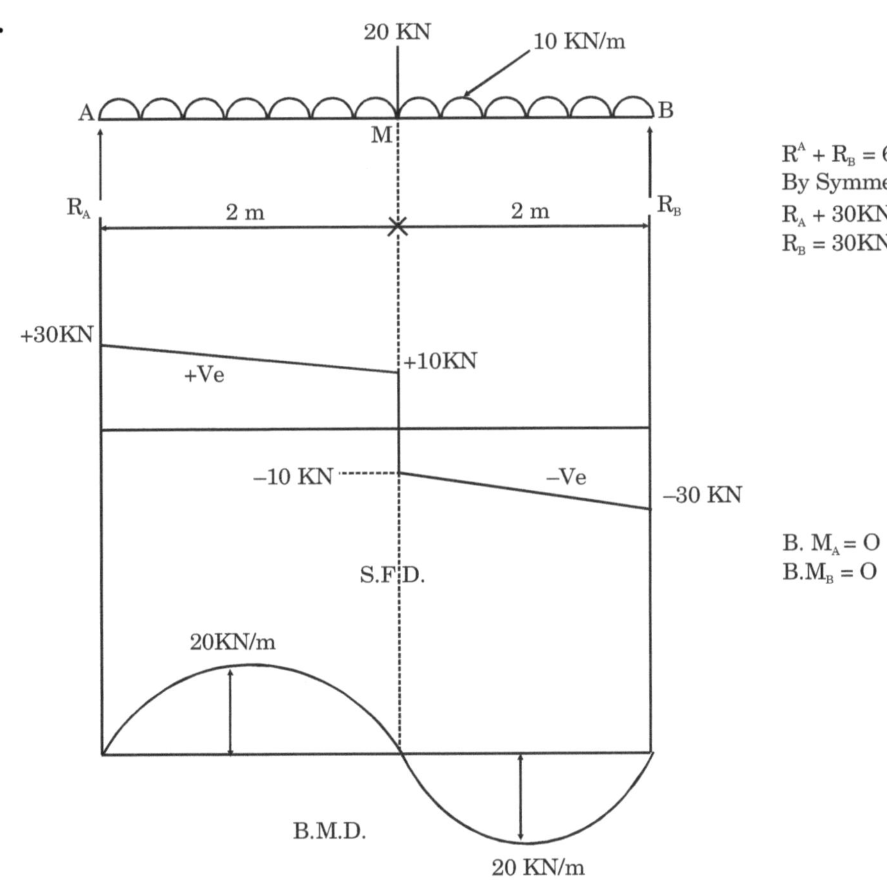

$R_A + R_B = 60$
By Symmetry
$R_A + 30$KN
$R_B = 30$KN

B. $M_A = O$
B.$M_B = O$

7.

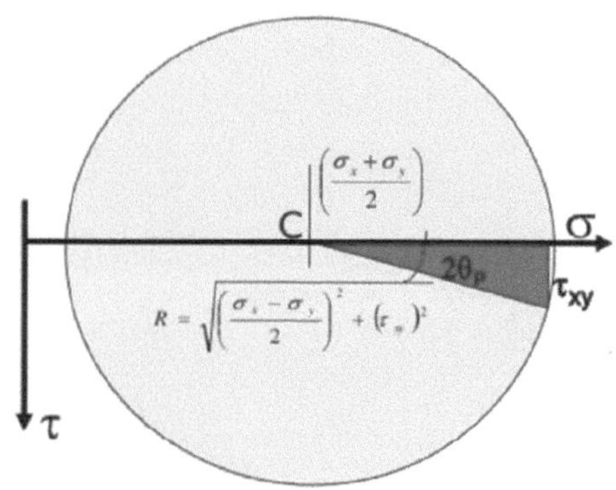

Mohr Circle

The radius of the Mohr circle is the magnitude R.

$$R = \sqrt{\left(\frac{\sigma_x - \sigma_y}{2}\right)^2 + \left(\tau_{xy}\right)^2}$$

The center of the Mohr circle is the magnitude

$$\sigma_{AVER} = \frac{\left(\sigma_x + \sigma_y\right)}{2}$$

$$(\sigma_{x1} - \sigma_{AVER})^2 + (\tau_{x1\,y1})^2 = \left(\frac{\sigma_x - \sigma_y}{2}\right) + (\tau_{xy})^2$$

9. Number of plastic hinges=Degree of indeterminacy + 1...........for complete collapse

Therefore, Number of plastic hinges = 2 + 1 = 3

10.

> ### Definition of Columns
>
> A vertical sub-structural element, installed in-situ by ground improvement techniques (replacement, displacement, and/or mixture with chemical agents), that carries the load of the super-structure or earth structure with surrounding soil and transmits it

11. In architecture, structural engineering or building, a purlin is any longitudinal, horizontal, structural member in a roof except a type of framing with what is called a crown plate.

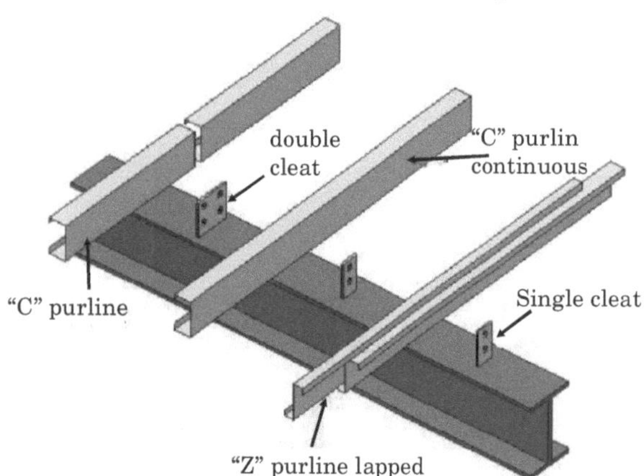

In traditional timber framing there are three basic types of purlin: purlin plate, principal purlin and common purlin.

12. The centre-to-centre distance between individual fasteners in a line, in the direction of load/ stress is called as Pitch.

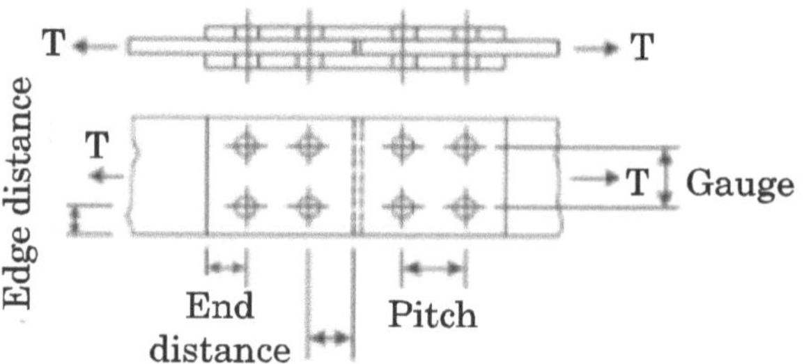

End distance
(a) Double-cover butt joint

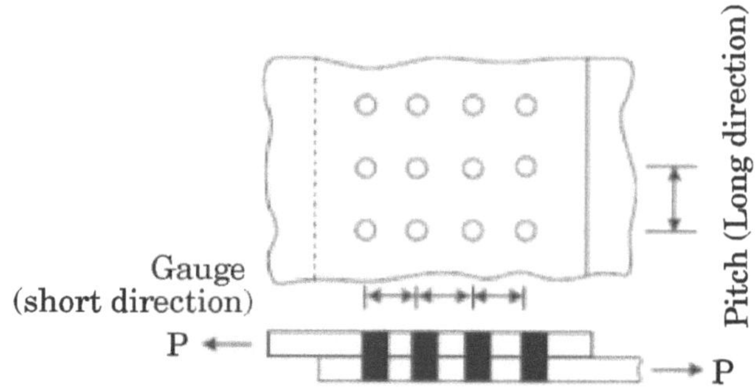

(b) Lap joint with wide plates
Fig. Spacing of bolt holes

13. Slenderness ratio is the ratio of the effective length of a column (L_e) and the least <u>radius of gyration</u> (r) about the axis under consideration. It is given by the symbol "ë" (lambda).

Slenderness ratio (λ)

$$= \frac{\text{Effective length}}{\text{Least radius of gyration}} = \frac{Le}{r}$$

Effective slenderness ratio of the section about the minor axis of cross-section = L_e/r_y.

Effective slenderness ratio of the section about the major axis of cross section = L_e/r_x.

Significance:

As slenderness ratio increases, permissible stress or critical stress reduces. Consequently, load carrying capacity also reduces.

- Radius of gyration will be least along major axis of cross section.

  Example: For a rectangular column along y-axis.

- For a given area, Tubular section will have maximum radius of gyration.

- H-Section is more efficient than I-Section.

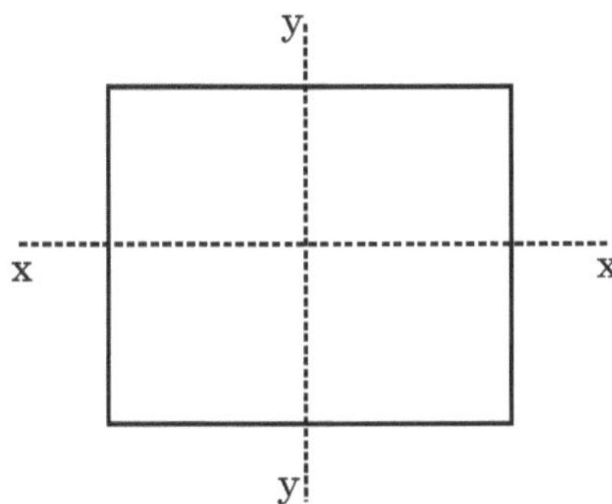

$I_y = I_{min}$ (Column buckles about y-axis)

14. In a bending beam, a **point** is known as a **point of contraflexure** if it is a location at which no bending occurs. In a bending moment diagram, it is the **point** at which the bending moment curve intersects with the zero line. In other words, where the bending moment changes its sign from negative to positive or vice versa.

15. The **area under stress-strain curve** represents the energy required or stored in the material before its failure.

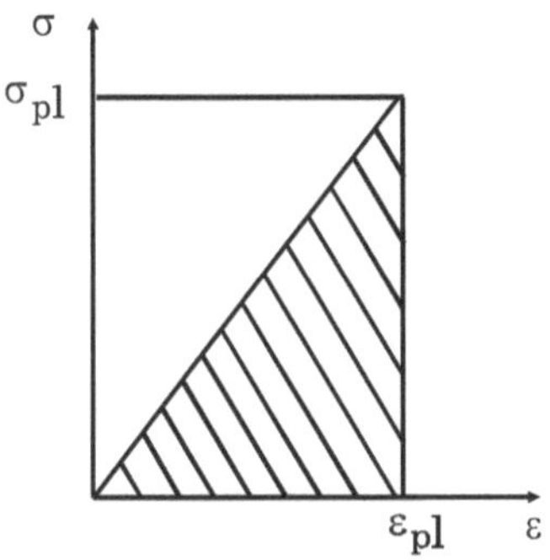

Modulus of Resilience

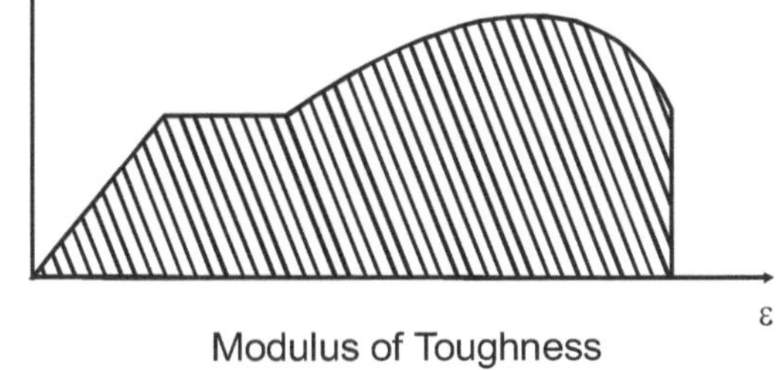

Modulus of Toughness

This energy is called Modulus of toughness or simply toughness.

16.

Both ends pinned   Both ends fixed

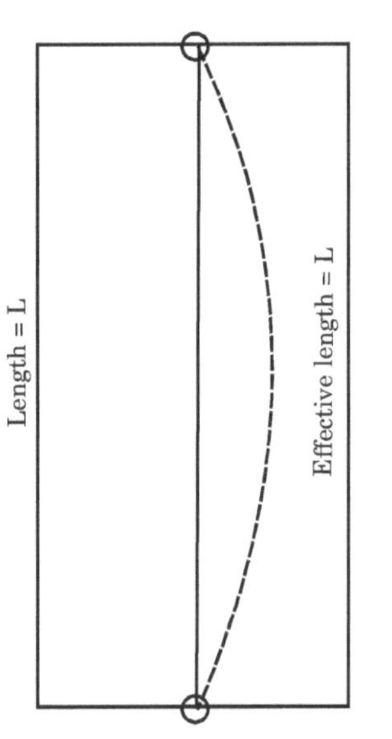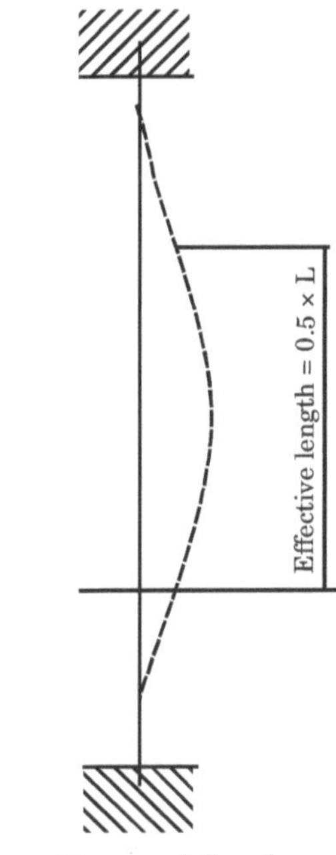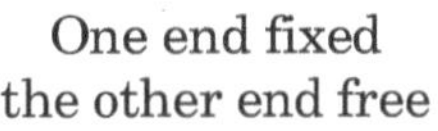

One end fixed the other end pinned

One end fixed the other end free

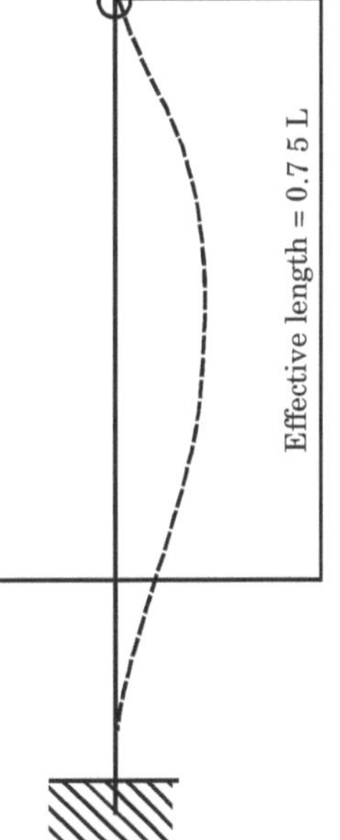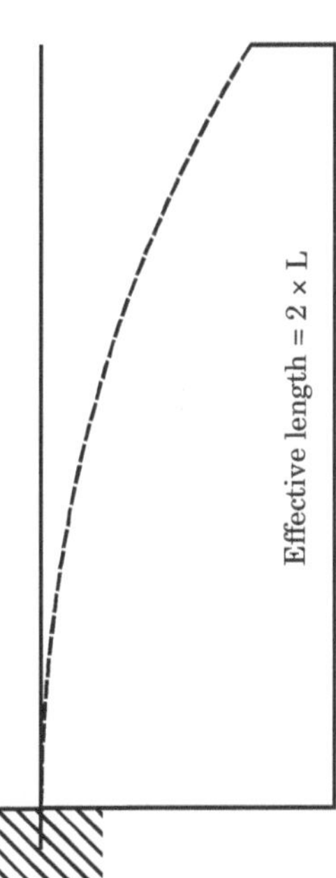

17. Anisotropy is the property of being directionally dependent, which implies different properties in different directions, as opposed to isotropy. It can be defined as a difference, when measured along different axes, in a material's physical or mechanical properties (absorbance, refractive index, conductivity, tensile strength, etc.) An example of anisotropy is light coming through a polarizer.

18. **Work hardening**, also known as **strain hardening**, is the strengthening of a metal or polymer by plastic deformation. This strengthening occurs because of dislocation movements and dislocation generation within the crystal structure of the material.

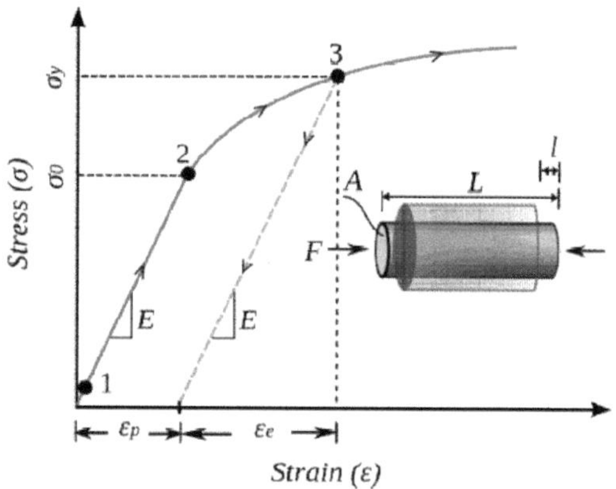

19. Prismoidal formula is not used.

20. The deflection is zero at non-yielding supports, the slope is zero at the free end and at the point of maximum positive moment and the bending moment is zero at roller and hinge supports.

21. Isotropy comes from the Greek words *isos* (equal) and *tropos*(way) and means uniform in all directions. Isotropic materials like glass exhibit the same material properties in all directions, whereas anisotropic materials like graphite exhibit different material properties depending on the direction.

22. Stiffener is an element used to retain or prevent the out-of-plane deformations of plates.

23. Rigid supports resist translation in all directions as well as rotation . That is why option d is not correct.

24. The load at which an element, a member or a structure as a whole, either collapses in service or buckles in a load test and develops excessive lateral (out of plane) deformation or instability is called as Buckling load.

25. Elastic limit,maximum stress or force per unit area within a solid material that can arise before the onset of permanent deformation. The proportional limit is the end point ofwhat is called linearly elastic behaviour.

26. Strain softening is referred to as a behaviour where. the shear resistance (or shear stress) reduces with continuous development of plastic shear'strains.

27. The design life of a component or product is the period of time during which the item is expected by its designers to work within its specified parameters; in other words, the life expectancy of the item. It is the length of time between placement into service of a single item and that item's onset of wearout.

28. Limit state design (LSD), also known as load and resistance factor design (LRFD), refers to a design method used in structural engineering. A limit state is a condition of a structure beyond which it no longer fulfills the relevant design criteria.

29. Tensioning Devices

   The various types devices used for tensioning steel are grouped under four principal categories, viz.

   1. Mechanical devices: The mechanical devices generally used include weights with or without lever transmission, geared transmission in conjunction with pulley blocks, screw jacks with or without gear devices and wire-winding machines. These devices are employed mainly for prestressing structural concrete components produced on a mass scale in factory.

   2. Hydraulic devices: These are simplest means for producing large prestressing force, extensively used as tensioning devices.

   3. Electrical devices: The wires are electrically heated and anchored before placing concrete in the mould. This method is often referred to as thermo-prestressing and used for tensioning of steel wires and deformed bars.

   4. Chemical devices: Expanding cements are used and the degree of expansion is controlled by varying the curing condition. Since the expansive action of cement 90 while setting is restrained, it induces tensile forces in tendons and compressive stresses in concrete.

FLUID MECHANICS AND HYDRAULIC MACHINERY

RRB JUNIOR ENGINEER

1. Fluid is a substance which offers no resistance to change of

(a) Volume   (b) Pressure

(c) Shape   (d) Flow

[RRB JE 2015 26th AUG 1st SHIFT]

2. Pascal-second is the unit of

(a) Pressure

(b) Kinematic viscosity

(c) Dynamic viscosity

(d) Surface tension

[RRB JE 2015 26th AUG 1st SHIFT]

3. The liquid used in manometers should have

(a) Low density

(b) High density

(c) Low surface tension

(d) High surface tension

[RRB JE 2015 26th AUG 2nd SHIFT]

4. Poise can also be expressed as

(a) Dyne-cm/s^2 (b) Dyne-cm/s

(c) Dyne-s/cm   (d) Dyne-s/cm^3

[RRB JE 2015 26th AUG 3rd SHIFT]

5. Spherical shape of droplets of mercury is due to

(a) High density   (b) High surface tension

(c) High adhesion   (d) Water

[RRB JE 2015 26th AUG 3rd SHIFT]

6. Which of the following is used to measure the discharge?

(a) Current meter

(b) Venturimeter

(c) Pitot tube

(d) Hotwire anemometer

[RRB JE 2015 26th AUG 3rd SHIFT]

7. Water hammer pressure is relieved by

(a) penstock   (b) draft tube

(c) turbine   (d) surge tank

[RRB JE 2015 27th AUG 1st SHIFT]

8. The eddy viscosity for turbulent flow is

(a) A function of temperature only

(b) A physical property of the fluid

(c) Dependent or the flow

(d) Independent of the flow

[RRB JE 2015 27th AUG 1st SHIFT]

9. The flow profile of a fluid depends upon

(a) Velocity of the fluid only

(b) The diameter of the tube only

(c) The Reynold number

(d) The surface roughness

[RRB JE 2015 27th AUG 2nd SHIFT]

10. Which of the following device is not used to measure the rate of flow

(a) Venturimeter   (b) Pitot tube

(c) Orificemeter   (d) Rotameter

[RRB JE 2015 27th AUG 2nd SHIFT]

11. Absolute pressure in flow system

(a) is always above local atmospheric pressure

(b) is equal to a vacuum pressure

(c) May be above, below or equal to the local atmospheric pressure

(d) is also called negative pressure

[RRB JE 2015 27th AUG 3rd SHIFT]

12. Equation of continuity is based on the principle of conservation of

(a) Mass

(b) Energy

(c) Momentum

(d) Time

[RRB JE 2015 27th AUG 3rd SHIFT]

13. Milk mixes with water due to

(a) Very good cohesion

(b) Very good adhesion

(c) Very good surface tension

(d) Very good vapour pressure

[RRB JE 2015 28th AUG 1st SHIFT]

14. An ideal fluid

(*a*) obey's Newton's law of viscosity

(*b*) is both incompressible and non-viscous

(*c*) is non viscous

(*d*) Frictionless and compressible

[RRB JE 2015 28ᵗʰ AUG 1ˢᵗ SHIFT]

15. The dimensions of dynamic viscosity μ are

(*a*) $ML^{-1}T^{-2}$ (*b*) $ML^{-1}T^{-1}$

(*c*) MLT^{-2} (*d*) $M^{\circ}L^{\circ}T^{\circ}$

[RRB JE 2015 28ᵗʰ AUG 2ⁿᵈ SHIFT]

16. A barometer is used to measure

(*a*) Very low pressure

(*b*) Very High pressure

(*c*) Pressure difference between two points

(*d*) Atmospheric pressure

[RRB JE 2015 28ᵗʰ AUG 2ⁿᵈ SHIFT]

17. The function of sluice valve provided in pipe line is

(*a*) to reduce the chances of pollution reaching into the pipe

(*b*) to reduce the pressure on pipes

(*c*) to regulate the flow of water through the pipes

(*d*) to allow the air to enter the pipe

[RRB JE 2015 28ᵗʰ AUG 2ⁿᵈ SHIFT]

18. The capillary depression in mercury is on account of

(*a*) Adhesion being larger than the viscosity

(*b*) Surface tension being larger than the viscosity

(*c*) Cohesion being greater than the adhesion

(*d*) Vapour pressure being small

[RRB JE 2015 28ᵗʰ AUG 3ʳᵈ SHIFT]

19. An aeroplane works on

(*a*) Archimedes principle

(*b*) Pascal's law

(*c*) Bernoulli's principle

(*d*) Stoke's law

[RRB JE 2015 28ᵗʰ AUG 3ʳᵈ SHIFT]

20. The capillary rise at 20°C in clean glass tube of 1 mm diameter, containing water is

(*a*) 15 mm

(*b*) 50 mm

(*c*) 20 mm

(*d*) 30 mm

[RRB JE 2015 29ᵗʰ AUG 1ˢᵗ SHIFT]

21. Newton's law of viscosity depends upon the

(*a*) Stress and strain in the fluid

(*b*) Shear stress, pressure and velocity

(*c*) Shear stress and rate of strain

(*d*) Viscosity and shear stress

[RRB JE 2015 29ᵗʰ AUG 1ˢᵗ SHIFT]

22. Which one of the following is defined as force per unit length

(*a*) Surface tension

(*b*) Compressibility

(*c*) Capillarity

(*d*) Viscosity

[RRB JE 2015 29ᵗʰ AUG 1ˢᵗ SHIFT]

23. The specific gravity of water is taken as

(*a*) 0.001   (*b*) 0.01

(*c*) 0.1   (*d*) 1

[RRB JE 2015 29ᵗʰ AUG 2ⁿᵈ SHIFT]

24. Falling drops of water become spheres due to the property of

(*a*) Surface tension of water

(*b*) Compressibility of water

(*c*) Capillarity of water

(*d*) Viscosity of water

[RRB JE 2015 29ᵗʰ AUG 2ⁿᵈ SHIFT]

25. The liquid used in manometer should have

(*a*) Low density

(*b*) High density

(*c*) Low surface tension

(*d*) High surface tension

[RRB JE 2015 29ᵗʰ AUG 2ⁿᵈ SHIFT]

26. If the dynamic viscosity of a fluid is 0.5 poise and specific gravity is 0.5, then kinematic viscosity of that fluid in stokes is

(*a*) 0.25

(*b*) 0.50

(*c*) 1.0

(*d*) 2.0

[RRB JE 2015 29ᵗʰ AUG 3ʳᵈ SHIFT]

27. The variation in the volume of a liquid with the variation of pressure is called its

(*a*) surface tension

(*b*) compressibility

(*c*) capillarity

(*d*) viscosity

[RRB JE 2015 29ᵗʰ AUG 3ʳᵈ SHIFT]

28. The intensity of pressure developed by surface tension of 0.075 N/m in a droplet of water of 0.075 mm diameter is

(a) 0.8 N/cm^2 (b) 0.6 N/cm^2

(c) 0.4 N/cm^2 (d) 400 N/cm^2

[RRB JE 2015 30th AUG 3rd SHIFT]

29. The point at which the resultant pressure on an immersed surface acts, is known as

(a) Centre of gravity

(b) Centre of depth

(c) Centre of pressure

(d) Centre of immersed surface

[RRB JE 2015 30th AUG 3rd SHIFT]

30. Mercury is considered as a superior barometric fluid chiefly due to its

(a) Negligible small vapour pressure

(b) High specific heat

(c) High specific gravity

(d) Convex meniscus

[RRB JE 2015 16th SEP 3rd SHIFT]

31. Bourdon gauge measures

(a) Absolute pressure

(b) Gauge pressure

(c) Local atmospheric pressure

(d) Standard atmospheric pressure

[RRB JE 2015 16th SEP 3rd SHIFT]

RRB SENIOR SECTION ENGINEER

1. A fluid flow in which the density of the fluid changes significantly during flow is called as

(a) Incompressible   (b) Uniform

(c) Compressible   (d) Non-linear

[RRB SSE 2015 1st SEP 1st SHIFT]

2. The property, which characterizes the resistance which a fluid offers to applied shear force is called as

(a) Relative density   (b) Elasticity

(c) Fluidity   (d) Viscosity

[RRB SSE 2015 1st SEP 1st SHIFT]

3. Capillarity of liquid in small-diameter tubes is due to molecular attraction. In case of Mercury, the following occurs in terms of capillarity

(a) Capillary rise

(b) Capillary depression

(c) Capillary flattening

(d) Compressibility

[RRB SSE 2015 2nd SEP 1st SHIFT]

4. If a substance resists shear stress by elastic deformation, then the substance is

(a) Fluid   (b) Liquid

(c) Solid   (d) Gas

[RRB SSE 2015 3rd SEP 1st SHIFT]

5. The piezometric head in a stationary and static liquid

(a) remains constant only on the horizontal plane

(b) increases non-linearly with depth below the surface

(c) increases linearly with depth below the surface

(d) remains constant at all the points in the fluid

[RRB SSE 2015 3rd SEP 1st SHIFT]

6. In general, surface tension

(a) remains unaffected by temperature up to critical temperature

(b) remains unaffected by temperature

(c) increases with increase in temperature

(d) decreases with increase of temperature

[RRB SSE 2015 3rd SEP 2nd SHIFT]

7. A liquid undergoing a rigid body rotation in a container is said to have

(a) Forced vortex motion

(b) Circulation

(c) Free vortex motion

(d) Translation

[RRB SSE 2015 3rd SEP 3rd SHIFT]

8. Cavitation is primarily associated with which of the following fluid properties

(a) Specific gravity   (b) Surface tension

(c) Viscosity   (d) Vapour pressure

[RRB SSE 2015 3rd SEP 3rd SHIFT]

9. When a particle is suspended in water, two forces are acting on it, which are

(a) gravity and drag force

(b) gravity and buoyant force

(c) buoyant and drag force

(d) viscous and buoyant force

[RRB SSE 2015 3rd SEP 3rd SHIFT]

ANSWER KEY

RRB JUNIOR ENGINEER

1. (c)	**2.** (c)	**3.** (b)	**4.** (d)	**5.** (b)	**6.** (b)	**7.** (d)	**8.** (c)	**9.** (c)	**10.** (b)
11. (c)	**12.** (a)	**13.** (b)	**14.** (a)	**15.** (b)	**16.** (d)	**17.** (c)	**18.** (c)	**19.** (c)	**20.** (d)
21. (c)	**22.** (a)	**23.** (d)	**24.** (a)	**25.** (b)	**26.** (c)	**27.** (b)	**28.** (c)	**29.** (c)	**30.** (a)
31. (b)									

RRB SENIOR SECTION ENGINEER

1. (c)	**2.** (d)	**3.** (b)	**4.** (c)	**5.** (d)	**6.** (d)	**7.** (a)	**8.** (d)	**9.** (b)

EXPLANATIONS

RRB JUNIOR ENGINEER

1. Fluid is a substance which offers no resistance to change of shape.

2. The **poise** is the unit of <u>dynamic viscosity</u> (absolute viscosity) in the <u>centimetre–gram–second system of units</u>. The analogous unit in the <u>International System of Units</u> is the <u>pascal-second</u> (Pa·s).

   Pressure has the unit of Pa. Surface tension has the unit of Pa-m.

3. The most commonly used liquid as **manometric** fluid are mercury, water, alcohol and kerosenes etc. Most of the case, for gauge pressure measurements, mercury is widely used as **manometric** fluid because it has **non-**evaporating quality under normal conditions, sharp meniscus and stable density.

4. The poise is the unit of dynamic viscosity (absolute viscosity) in the centimetre–gram–**second** system of units. The analogous unit in the International. System of Units is the **pascal-second** (Pa·s). Its c.g.s. unit is Dyne-s/cm².

5. Its due to high surface tension.

6. A **venturimeter** is a device used to measure the fluid flow through pipes. This flow measurement device is based on the principle of Bernoulli's equation. A **venturi meter** is device used to measure the flow rate of the fluid.

7. **Surge Tank** vs Air Valves in **Water Hammer** reduction. **Surge tanks** are one of the oldest of **surge** alleviation methods. ...**Surge tanks** inject **water** into a pipeline where a **surge** event causes low pressure, or allow **water** out of a pipeline where a **surge** event causes in high pressure. They're mostly closed systems.

8. The **turbulent** transfer of momentum by **eddies** giving rise to an internal fluid friction, in a manner analogous to the action of molecular **viscosity** in laminar **flow**, but taking place on a much larger scale.

9. Flow can be laminar , turbulent or transition depending on the magnitude of Reynolds Number.

10. Pitot probe, is a **flow** measurement device used to measure **fluid flow velocity**.

11. Absolute pressure may be less than or more than atmospheric pressure.

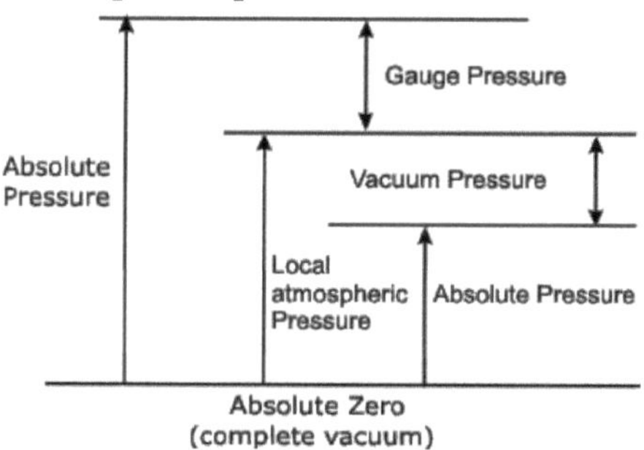

12. The **law of conservation of mass** or **principle of mass conservation** states that for any system closed to all transfers of **matter** and energy, the **mass** of the system must remain constant over time, as system's **mass** cannot change, so quantity cannot be added nor removed. Hence, the quantity of **mass** is conserved over time

13. Milk mixes with water due to adhesion.

14. Consider a hypothetical **fluid** having a zero viscosity (= 0). Such a **fluid** is called **an ideal fluid** and the resulting motion is called as **ideal** or inviscid flow. In **an ideal** flow, there is no existence of shear force because of vanishing viscosity.

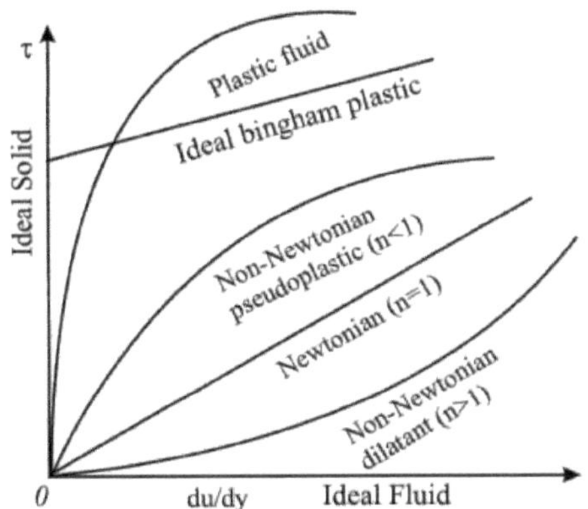

15. The **dynamic viscosity** has **the dimension** ML^{-1}T^{-1} and the unit of kg/m.s (or, N.s/m^2 or Pa.s). A common unit of **dynamic viscosity** is poise which is equivalent to 0.1 Pa.s. Many a times, the ratio of **dynamic viscosity** to density appears frequently and this ratio is given by the name **kinematic viscosity** .

16. A barometer is a scientific instrument used in meteorology to measure atmospheric pressure. Pressure tendency can forecast **short** term changes in the weather. Many measurements of air pressure are used within surface weather analysis to help find surface troughs, high pressure systems and frontal boundaries.

17. **Gate valve** or **Sluice valve** is used to strictly start or stop the water flow ... **pipeline** stem is vertical and for vertical running **pipeline** stem is horizontal. The valves are placed in valve chambers **provided** with caps or hand wheels for **operation**.

18.

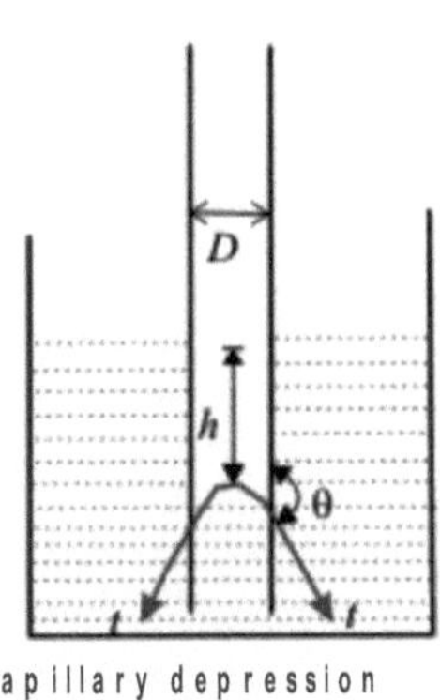

Figure: Phenomenon of Capillarity

19. According to a **principle** of aerodynamics called Bernoulli›s law, fast-moving air is at lower pressure than slow-moving air, so the pressure above the wing is lower than the pressure below, and this creates the lift that powers the **plane** upward.

20. $h = \dfrac{4\sigma\cos\theta}{\rho g d}$

$h = \dfrac{4 \times 0.0725 \times \cos\theta}{1000 \times 9.81 \times 10^{-3}}$

h = 0.02956 m = 29.56 mm

For water and glass, Contact Angle (θ) = 0° and Surface tension is 0.0725 N/m

For mercury and glass, Contact Angle (θ) = 128° and Surface tension is 0.52 N/m

Contact Angle

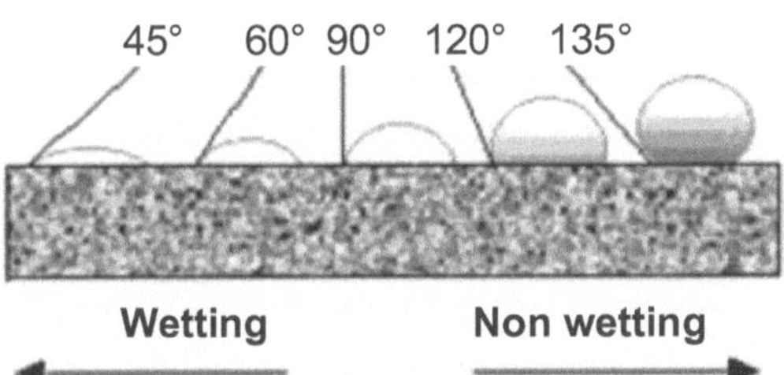

21. **Newton's law of viscosity** and states that the shear stress between adjacent fluid layers is proportional to the negative value of the velocity gradient between the two layers.

22. Surface tension, represented by the symbol ³ (alternatively Ã or T), is measured in force per **unit length**. Its **SI unit** is **newton** per **meter** but the **cgs** unit of dyne per **centimeter** is also used.

23. In that case **specific gravity of Water** is 1.

24. Falling drops of water become spheres due to the property of surface tension. Surface tension is the elastic tendency of a fluid surface which makes it acquire the least surface area possible. Surface tension allows insects, usually denser than water, to float and stride on a water surface.

25. The most commonly used liquid as **manometric** fluid are mercury, water, alcohol and kerosenes etc. Most of the case, for gauge pressure measurements, mercury is widely used as **manometric** fluid because it has **non-**evaporating quality under normal conditions, sharp meniscus and stable density.

26. The **relationship between** these two properties is quite straightforward. **Dynamic viscosity** (also known as **absolute viscosity**) is the measurement of the fluid's internal resistance to flow while **kinematic viscosity** refers to the ratio of **dynamic viscosity** to density.

$$\text{Kinematic viscosity} = \dfrac{\text{Dynamic viscosity}}{\text{Density}}$$

$$= \dfrac{0.5 \times 10^3}{500} = \dfrac{500}{500} = 1$$

27. Compressibility is a measure of the relative volume change of a fluid or solid as a response to a pressure change. where V is volume and p is pressure.

29. The center of pressure is the point where the total sum of a pressure field acts on a body, causing a force to act through that point. The total force vector acting at the center of pressure is the value of the integrated vectorial pressure field.

30. Negligible small vapour pressure.

31. **Bourdon** tubes **measure gauge** pressure, relative to ambient atmospheric pressure, as opposed to absolute pressure; vacuum is sensed as a reverse motion.

RRB SENIOR SECTION ENGINEER

1. A fluid flow in which the density of the fluid changes significantly during flow in is called as compressible flow.

2. Viscosity is a measure of a fluid's resistance to flow. It describes the internal friction of a moving fluid. A fluid with large viscosity resists motion because its molecular makeup gives it a lot of internal friction. A fluid with low viscosity flows easily because its molecular makeup results in very little friction when it is in motion.

3. **Capillarity**

   - The interplay of the forces of cohesion and adhesion explains the phenomenon of capillarity. When a liquid is in contact with a solid, if the forces of adhesion between the molecules of the liquid and the solid are greater than the forces of cohesion among the liquid molecules themselves the liquid molecules crowd towards the solid surface. The area of contact between the liquid and solid increases and the liquid thus wets the solid surface.

   - The reverse phenomenon takes place when the force of cohesion is greater than the force of adhesion. These adhesion and cohesion properties result in the phenomenon of capillarity by which a liquid either rises or falls in a tube dipped into the liquid depending upon whether the force of adhesion is more than that of cohesion or not (Fig.)

   - The angle θ as shown in Fig., is the area wetting contact angle made by the interface with the solid surface.

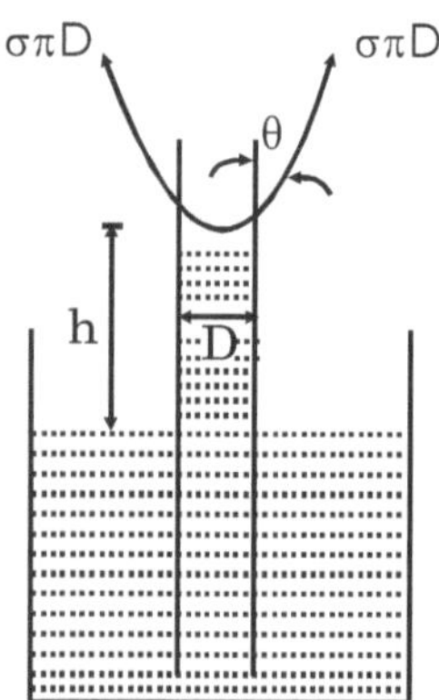
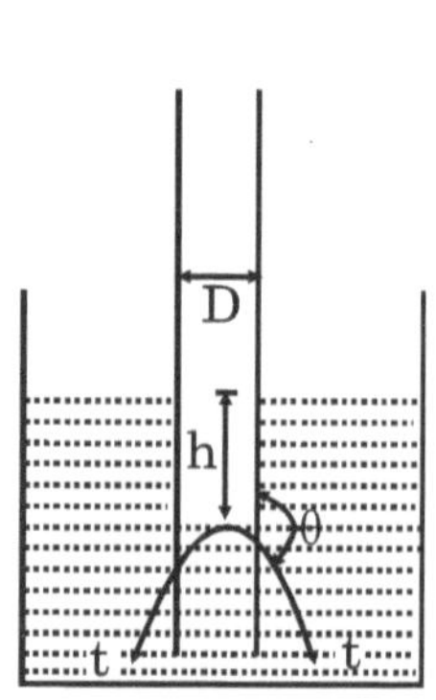

Capillary rise
Adhesion > cohesion
Liquid wets the
surface

Capillary depression
Adhesion < cohesion
Liquid stays away
from the surface

- For pure water in contact with air in a clean glass tube, the capillary rise takes place with θ = 0. Mercury causes capillary depression with an angle of contact of about 130° in a clean glass in contact with air. Since h varies inversely with D as found from Eq. $\left(h = \dfrac{4\sigma\cos\theta}{\rho g D}\right)$, an appreciable capillary rise or depression is observed in tubes of small diameter only.

4. Solid

   1. More Compact Structure

   2. Attractive Forces between the molecules are larger therefore more closely packed

   3. Solids can resist tangential stresses in static condition

   4. Whenever a solid is subjected to shear stress

      a. It undergoes a definite deformation á or breaks

      b. α is proportional to shear stress upto some limiting condition

   5. Solid may regain partly or fully its original shape when the tangential stress is removed.

Fluid:-

1. Less Compact Structure

2. Attractive Forces between the molecules are smaller therefore more loosely packed

3. Fluids cannot resist tangential stresses in static condition.

4. Whenever a fluid is subjected to shear stress

   a. No fixed deformation

   b. Continious deformation takes place until the shear stress is applied

5. A fluid can never regain its original shape, once it has been distorted by the shear stress

5. The piezometric head in a stationary and static liquid remains constant at all the points in the fluid. Hydraulic head or piezometric head is a specific measurement of liquid pressure above a geodetic datum. It is usually measured as a liquid surface elevation, expressed in units of length, at the entrance (or bottom) of a piezometer.

6. In general, surface tension decreases when temperature increases because cohesive forces decrease with an increase of molecular thermal activity. The influence of the surrounding environment is due to the adhesive action liquid molecules have at the interface.

7. When a liquid in a container is rotated about its vertical axis at constant angular velocity, after sometime the liquid will move like a solid together with the container. Since every liquid particle moves with the same angular velocity: no shear stresses exit in the liquid. This type of motion is also known as forced vortex motion.

8. Vapour Pressure: The pressure exerted by the vapour of a liquid/solid on the liquid/solid when in thermodynamic equilibrium. Vapour pressure is constant at a given fluid/solid temperature.

Cavitation: One of the mechanism by which fluid machinery, etc. get worn out. Let me explain it a bit.

Vapour Bubble Formation & Vapour Pressure

Imagine water & water vapour in a closed cup/beaker, etc. Observe the fluid-vapour interface carefully.

If the fluid pressure is more than vapour's, more fluid molecules would escape into vapour form. On the contrary, if the fluid pressure is less than vapour's, the vapour molecules would want to form a bubble inside the bulk fluid. This is the basic concept behind cavitation.

Cavitation Process & Vapour Pressure

1. Take a venturi tube/orifice. When water passes through the venturi contraction, its velocity increases (as per mass continuity equation), thereby decreasing the water pressure (as per Bernoulli equation)

2. If the water pressure drops below the vapour pressure at that temperature, vapour bubbles are formed.

3. When the fluid decelerates again after passing through the venturi tube, the pressure increases, forcing the water vapour bubbles to collapse.

4. Now, when these bubbles collapse near any surface (like pump impeller blade, etc.) it generates a shockwave (somewhat like ripples in a pond when a bubble on the surface bursts)

5. Repeated formation & collapse of such vapour bubbles sends shockwaves repeatedly that collide with the impeller or any other nearby surface. Thus, the impeller is stressed in a cyclic manner.

6. This gives rise to fatigue loading of the impeller, resulting in severe wear of the fluid machine's parts.

7. Wear of the blades isn't a pretty thing for good operation of your machine. It can lead to dynamic shaft unbalance, leading to dangerous operation of the pump, bearings, etc.

9. When a particle is suspended in water, two forces are acting on it, which are gravity and buoyant force.

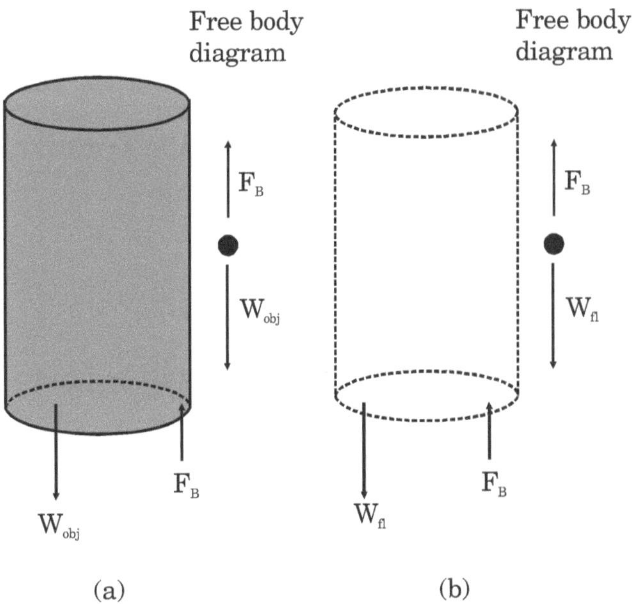

8
CHAPTER

PROJECT MANAGEMENT, CPM & PERT

RRB JUNIOR ENGINEER

1. Gantt chart provides information about
  (a) Break even point analysis
  (b) Production schedule
  (c) Material handling layout
  (d) Determining selling price
[RRB JE 2015 26ᵗʰ AUG 1ˢᵗ SHIFT]

2. In a bar chart the vertical axis represents
  (a) Time
  (b) Types of activities
  (c) Number of labours
  (d) Various activities of the project
[RRB JE 2015 26ᵗʰ AUG 2ⁿᵈ SHIFT]

3. The most likely time (m) is 'mode' of the
  (a) Normal distribution
  (b) Beta distribution
  (c) Binomial distribution
  (d) Poisson distribution
[RRB JE 2015 26ᵗʰ AUG 3ʳᵈ SHIFT]

4. A critical path has
  (a) Zero float
  (b) Minimum float
  (c) Maximum float
  (d) Infinite float
[RRB JE 2015 27ᵗʰ AUG 1ˢᵗ SHIFT]

5. Gantt charts indicate
  (a) Comparison of actual progress with the scheduled progress
  (b) Balance of work to be done
  (c) Progressive cost of project
  (d) Inventory costs
[RRB JE 2015 27ᵗʰ AUG 3ʳᵈ SHIFT]

6. The probability distribution taken to represent the completion time in PERT analysis is
  (a) Gamma distribution
  (b) Normal distribution
  (c) Beta distribution
  (d) Log normal distribution
[RRB JE 2015 28ᵗʰ AUG 1ˢᵗ SHIFT]

7. Critical path
  (a) is always longest
  (b) is always shortest
  (c) May be longest
  (d) May be shortest
[RRB JE 2015 28ᵗʰ AUG 1ˢᵗ SHIFT]

8. CPM is the
  (a) time oriented technique
  (b) event oriented technique
  (c) activity oriented technique
  (d) target oriented technique
[RRB JE 2015 28ᵗʰ AUG 2ⁿᵈ SHIFT]

9. Economic saving of time results by crashing
  (a) Cheapest critical activity
  (b) Cheapest non critical activity
  (c) Costliest critical activity
  (d) Costliest non critical activity
[RRB JE 2015 28ᵗʰ AUG 3ʳᵈ SHIFT]

10. The process of inspiring the subordinates to do a work or achieve an objective is called as
  (a) Management (b) Supervision
  (c) Motivation (d) Communication
[RRB JE 2015 29ᵗʰ AUG 1ˢᵗ SHIFT]

11. Slack represents the difference between the
  (a) Earliest completion time and latest allowable time
  (b) Latest allowable time and earliest completion time
  (c) Earliest completion time and normal expected time
  (d) Latest allowable time and normal allowable time
[RRB JE 2015 29ᵗʰ AUG 2ⁿᵈ SHIFT]

12. Which of the following is not a PERT event
  (a) Site investigation started
  (b) Sessional work completed
  (c) Bus starts from Jaipur
  (d) Class is being attended
[RRB JE 2015 29ᵗʰ AUG 3ʳᵈ SHIFT]

13. In a CPM network the activity is non critical if
  (a) EST = LST & EFT = LFT
  (b) EST < LST & EFT < LFT
  (c) EST > LST & EFT > LFT
  (d) EST < LST & EFT > LFT
                    [RRB JE 2015 30th AUG 3rd SHIFT]

14. The cost associated with defective products produced is called, cost of ____?
  (a) Internal failure
  (b) External failure
  (c) Cost of prevention
  (d) Cost of appraisal
                    [RRB JE 2015 16th SEP 3rd SHIFT]

15. Simo charts are used for
  (a) Inspection of part
  (b) Operator movements
  (c) Work done at one place
  (d) Simulation of models
                    [RRB JE 2015 16th SEP 3rd SHIFT]

RRB SENIOR SECTION ENGINEER

1. Which of the following software is generally used for managing large number of activities of a civil engineering project?
  (a) MS Eng   (b) MS Project
  (c) SQL Projects   (d) d Base Project
                    [RRB SSE 2014 GREEN SHIFT]

2. Free float is the amount of time that a task in a project network can be delayed without causing a delay to the
  (a) Subsequent tasks
  (b) Milestone completion date
  (c) Project completion date
  (d) Subsequent project
                    [RRB SSE 2015 2nd SEP 1st SHIFT]

3. Total float is the amount of time that a task in a project network can be delayed without causing a delay to the
  (a) Subsequent tasks
  (b) Milestone completion late
  (c) Project completion date
  (d) Subsequent project
                    [RRB SSE 2015 2nd SEP 2nd SHIFT]

4. A term referring to the shortest possible time for which an activity can be schedule
  (a) Crash duration   (b) Expansion
  (c) Slack   (d) Flexibility
                    [RRB SSE 2015 2nd SEP 3rd SHIFT]

ANSWER KEY

RRB JUNIOR ENGINEER

1. (b)   **2.** (d)   **3.** (b)   **4.** (a)   **5.** (a)   **6.** (c)   **7.** (a)   **8.** (c)   **9.** (a)   **10.** (c)

11. (a)   **12.** (d)   **13.** (b)   **14.** (a)   **15.** (b)

RRB SENIOR SECTION ENGINEER

1. (b)   **2.** (a)   **3.** (c)   **4.** (a)

EXPLANATIONS

RRB JUNIOR ENGINEER

1. Gantt chart provides information about production schedule.

2. **Bar charts represent** a **project** work item or **activity** as a time scaled bar.

3. The most likely time is the mode of Beta Distribution.

4. Slack, or **float**, refers to the amount of days or hours that various related tasks can be delayed without pushing the project back. The **critical path**, by definition, **has** no slack. But other tasks not on the **critical path** may **have** built-in **float**.

5. A **Gantt chart** is a visual representation of a project schedule.

6. The **PERT distribution** produces a bell-shaped curve that is nearly normal. It is essentially a **Beta Distribution** that has been extended to the maximum and minimum and given strict definitions for the mean and variance (a technique called "reparameterization").

7. In project management, a **critical path** is the sequence of project network activities which add up to the longest overall duration, regardless if that longest duration has float or not. This determines the shortest time possible to complete the project. There can be ‹total float› (unused time) within the **critical path**.

8. The critical path method (**CPM**) is a step-by-step project management technique for process planning that defines critical and non-critical tasks with the goal of preventing time-frame problems and process bottlenecks.

9. By crashing cheapest critical activity.

10. The process of inspiring the subordinates to do a work or achieve an objective is called as motivation.

11. Slack represents the difference between the earliest completion time and latest allowable time.

12. Class is being attended is not an PERT event.

13. In a CPM network the activity is non critical if EST < LST & EFT < LFT

14. Refective products produced is called as internal failure.

Internal failure costs

Internal failure costs are incurred to remedy defects discovered before the product or service is delivered to the customer. These costs occur when the results of work fail to reach design quality standards and are detected before they are transferred to the customer. They could include:

Waste—performance of unnecessary work or holding of stock as a result of errors, poor organization, or communication

Scrap—defective product or material that cannot be repaired, used, or sold

Rework or rectification—correction of defective material or errors

Failure analysis—activity required to establish the causes of internal product or service failure

External failure costs

External failure costs are incurred to remedy defects discovered by customers. These costs occur when products or services that fail to reach design quality standards are not detected until after transfer to the customer. They could include:

Repairs and servicing—of both returned products and those in the field

Warranty claims—failed products that are replaced or services that are re-performed under a guarantee

Complaints—all work and costs associated with handling and servicing customers' complaints

Returns—handling and investigation of rejected or recalled products, including transport costs

15. **SIMO** (Simultaneous-Motion Cycle) **Chart**: Meaning, Method to Improve and Construction! "**SIMO**" stands for simultaneous-Motion Cycle **chart**. It is one of micro motion study devised by Gilbreth and it presents graphically the separable steps of each pertinent limb of the operator under study.

S.No.	Left hand description	Therblig	Time	Therblig	Right hand
1.	Searching and lifting	SH,H	0.2		
2.			0.4	U	Opening the vice
3.	Clamping workpiece	PP	0.8	PP	clamping work piece in the vice piece in the vice.
4.			1.0	TL	Take the file
5.	Do the hand filling operation.	U	2.0	U	Do the hand filing Operation.
6.			2.2	TL	Taking the micrometer
7.	Check the dimension	I	3.0	I	Check the dimension
8.			3.2	U	Open the vice
9.	Remove the work piece	TL		3.4	

RRB SENIOR SECTION ENGINEER

1. MS project is the software used for managing large number of activities in a civil engineering project.

2. In **project management, float** or **slack** is the amount of time that a task in a project network can be delayed without causing a delay to: subsequent tasks (**"free float"**) project completion date (**"total float"**).

3. *Total float* is associated with the path. If a project network chart/diagram has 4 non-critical paths then that project would have 4 *total float* values. The *total float* of a path is the combined *free float* values of all activities in a path. Project completion date is also called as total float.

4. Project **crashing** is a method for shortening the project duration by reducing the time of one (or more) of the critical project activities to less than its normal activity time. Crash duration is the shortest possible time for which an activity can be scheduled.

NON-TECHNICAL
General Science

CHAPTER 1

PHYSICS

RRB JUNIOR ENGINEER

1. As the speed of charged particle increases in a cyclotron, (choose True (T) or False (F))

   (a) the particle moves to a larger circle

   (b) there is relativistic change in the mass of the particle

   (c) frequency of the cyclotron has to be adjusted

   (a) F, F, F
   (b) T, T, T
   (c) T, F, T
   (d) T, T, F

   [RRB JE 2014 GREEN SHIFT]

2. The formula $R = \dfrac{R_1 R_2}{R_1 + R_2}$ represents

   (a) series connection

   (b) parallel connection

   (c) bridge connection

   (d) linear connection

   [RRB JE 2014 GREEN SHIFT]

3. The earth conductor provides a path to ground for

   (a) circuit current
   (b) leakage current

   (c) over current
   (d) high voltage

   [RRB JE 2014 GREEN SHIFT]

4. If the mass of sun, earth and distance between them is respectively M, m and r; work done by the sun's gravity on earth for one revolution round the sun is

   (a) zero
   (b) $\dfrac{GMm}{r^2}$

   (c) $\dfrac{GMm}{r} 2\pi$
   (d) $\dfrac{GMm}{r^2} 2\pi$

   [RRB JE 2014 GREEN SHIFT]

5. The choke of a tube light works on the principle of

   (a) bi-metallic
   (b) capacitance

   (c) inductance
   (d) ionization

   [RRB JE 2014 GREEN SHIFT]

6. In the figure below, what is the acceleration of body with mass m_2, given g is the acceleration due to gravity (assume pulley and surfaces are smooth)

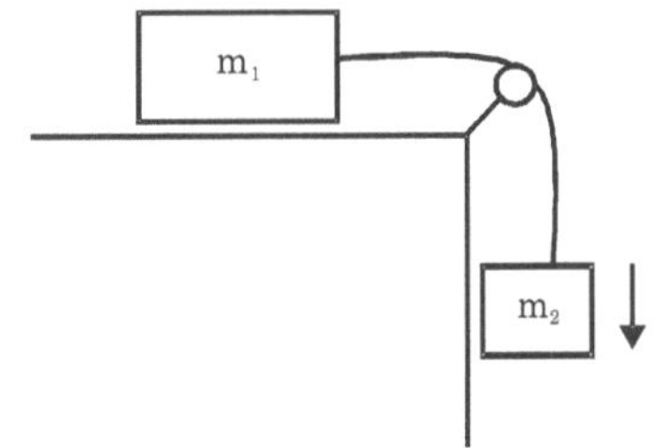

   (a) g
   (b) $\dfrac{m_1 + m_2}{m_1} g$

   (c) $\dfrac{m_1 + m_2}{m_2} g$
   (d) $\dfrac{m_2}{m_1 + m_2} \cdot g$

   [RRB JE 2014 GREEN SHIFT]

7. Which of the following statements is correct?

   (a) Speed of light in vacuum is 3×10^8 m/s

   (b) Speed of light is different for different colours

   (c) Speed of light is different in different media

   (d) All of the above

   [RRB JE 2014 GREEN SHIFT]

8. In Heisenberg's Uncertainity principle, the uncertainity of momentum and position of a particle can be

   (a) reduced using smaller wavelength of probing light

   (b) reduced using larger wavelength of probing light

   (c) reduced using high energy probe particles accelerated by cyclotron

   (d) can't be reduced as it is fundamentally inherent

   [RRB JE 2014 GREEN SHIFT]

9. The speed of sound in air is approximately equal to :

   (a) 3×10^8 m/sec
   (b) 330 m/sec

   (c) 5000 m/sec
   (d) 1500 m/sec

   [RRB JE 2014 RED SHIFT]

10. 'When a body is wholly or partially, immersed in a fluid, it experiences an upthrust equal to the weight of the fluid displaced'. This is known as:

    (a) Pascal's principle

    (b) Archimedes principle

    (c) Stoke's law

    (d) Newton's Laws of Motion

    [RRB JE 2014 RED SHIFT]

11. Which one of the following is not a scalar quantity?

    (a) Volume   (b) Mass

    (c) Force   (d) Length

    [RRB JE 2014 RED SHIFT]

12. The resultant of two forces P and Q acting at an angle 0, is given by :

    (a) $\sqrt{P^2 + Q^2 + 2PQ \tan \theta}$

    (b) $\sqrt{P^2 + Q^2 + 2PQ \sin \theta}$

    (c) $\sqrt{P^2 + Q^2 + 2PQ \cos \theta}$

    (d) $P + Q + 2PQ \tan \theta$

    [RRB JE 2014 RED SHIFT]

13. A cyclotron is a :

    (a) Bunch of Gamma Rays

    (b) High Frequency Oscillator

    (c) Particle Accelerator

    (d) None of these

    [RRB JE 2014 RED SHIFT]

14. The nucleus of an atom generally, contains :

    (a) Protons and Neutrons

    (b) Protons and Electrons

    (c) Electrons and Neutrons

    (d) Only Neutrons

    [RRB JE 2014 RED SHIFT]

15. A bullet is fired vertically upwards with a velocity of 196 m/sec. What is the maximum height reached by the bullet ? (Assuming g = 9.8 m/sec²)

    (a) 1960 m   (b) 196 m

    (c) 980 m   (d) 490 m

    [RRB JE 2014 RED SHIFT]

16. Water has its maximum density at :

    (a) 0°C   (b) 100°C

    (c) 50°C   (d) 4°C

    [RRB JE 2014 RED SHIFT]

17. A conductor of axial length 30 cms carries a current of 100 A and lies at right angle to a magnetic field of strength 0.4 tesla. What is the force exerted on it ?

    (a) 10N   (b) 12 N

    (c) 1.2 N   (d) 0

    [RRB JE 2014 RED SHIFT]

18. Ampere second is the unit of:

    (a) Charge   (b) Power

    (c) Voltage   (d) Energy

    [RRB JE 2014 RED SHIFT]

19. Power Loss in a resistor is given by :

    (a) $P = V^2 R$ (b) $P = \dfrac{V}{I}$

    (c) $P = \dfrac{I^2}{R}$ (d) $P = \dfrac{V^2}{R}$

    [RRB JE 2014 RED SHIFT]

20. A capacitor stores 1 coulomb at 10 volts. Its capacitance is (f = farad) :

    (a) 1 f   (b) 10 f

    (c) 0.1 f   (d) 0.01 f

    [RRB JE 2014 RED SHIFT]

21. Bulbs in street lighting are all connected in

    (a) parallel   (b) series

    (c) series parallel   (d) end of end

    [RRB JE 2014 YELLOW SHIFT]

22. The electric field strength of a charge

    (a) increases with distance

    (b) decreases with cube of distance

    (c) decreases with distance

    (d) decreases with square of distance

    [RRB JE 2014 YELLOW SHIFT]

23. With conventional symbols, the Lens formula is given by

    (a) $\dfrac{1}{v} - \dfrac{1}{u} = \dfrac{1}{f}$ (b) $\dfrac{1}{u} - \dfrac{1}{v} = \dfrac{1}{f}$

    (c) $\dfrac{1}{v} + \dfrac{1}{u} = \dfrac{1}{f}$ (d) $u + v = f$

    [RRB JE 2014 YELLOW SHIFT]

24. A magnifying glass comprises a simple

    (a) Convex lens

    (b) Convex mirror

    (c) Concave lens

    (d) Concave mirror

    [RRB JE 2014 YELLOW SHIFT]

25. The atomic number of an element is determined by

    (a) the number of electrons in one atom

    (b) the number of neutrons in one atom

    (c) the valency of the element

    (d) the number of protons in one atom

    [RRB JE 2014 YELLOW SHIFT]

26. An object of weight 49 N is accelerated across a level surface at 0.20 m/s². The net force acting on the object is (g = 9.8 m/s²)

    (a) 9.8 N   (b) 1.0 N

    (c) 5.0 N   (d) 0.5 N.

    [RRB JE 2015 26ᵗʰ AUG 1ˢᵗ SHIFT]

27. The weight of an object on the surface of Earth is 60 N. On the surface of Moon, its weight will be

(a) 10 N   (b) 30 N

(c) 60 N   (d) 360 N

[RRB JE 2015 26th AUG 1st SHIFT]

28. Shyam pushes a box 10 m on a horizontal surface by applying a 30 N force parallel to the surface. The work done is

(a) 3 J   (b) 30 J

(c) 300 J   (d) 0.3 J

[RRB JE 2015 26th AUG 1st SHIFT]

29. A sound wave passes a point of observation. At this point, the time interval between two successive crests is 0.02 s. Which of the following statements about the wave is correct?

(a) The wavelength is 50 m

(b) The wavelength is 0.02 m

(c) The velocity of propagation is 50 m/s

(d) The frequency is 50 Hz

[RRB JE 2015 26th AUG 1st SHIFT]

30. A ray is incident on a plane mirror. As the angle of incidence is increased, the angle between the incident and reflected rays ultimately approaches the value

(a) 90°   (b) 180°

(c) 45°   (d) zero

[RRB JE 2015 26th AUG 1st SHIFT]

31. Two resistors of 3 Ω and 6 Ω are connected in parallel. This combination in turn is connected in series with a 2 Ω resistor and a 6 V battery. The current in the 2 Ω resistor is

(a) 3.7 A   (b) 5.4 A

(c) 1.5 A   (d) 3.0 A

[RRB JE 2015 26th AUG 1st SHIFT]

32. At the airport, a suitcase was offloaded from a trolley and lay there till someone came and pushed it away. Which one of Newton's Laws of motion explains this?

(a) Newton's first law of motion

(b) Newton's second law of motion

(c) Newton's third law of motion

(d) Partially the second and partially the third law

[RRB JE 2015 26th AUG 1st SHIFT]

33. Eclipse happens because light

(a) travels in waves

(b) travels in straight lines

(c) travels with great speed

(d) rays are static

[RRB JE 2015 26th AUG 1st SHIFT]

34. A magnet attracts filings made of

(a) Only Iron   (b) Iron and Steel

(c) Brass and Iron   (d) Brass, Iron and Steel

[RRB JE 2015 26th AUG 1st SHIFT]

35. The viscosity of a gas

(a) Decreases with increase in temperature

(b) Increases with increase in temperature

(c) is independent of temperature

(d) is independent of pressure for very high pressure intensities

[RRB JE 2015 26th AUG 2nd SHIFT]

36. In an internal focussing type of telescope, the lens provided is

(a) Concave   (b) Convex

(c) Plano-convex   (d) Plano-concave

[RRB JE 2015 26th AUG 2nd SHIFT]

37. A 5 kg mass at rest on a frictionless table is acted upon by a constant force of 12 N. The distance travelled by it in 2s is

(a) 1.2 m   (b) 2.4 m

(c) 4.8 m   (d) 9.6 m

[RRB JE 2015 26th AUG 2nd SHIFT]

38. The gravitational force between two bodies kept at a distance d is proportional to

(a) $1/d$ (b) d

(c) $1/d^2$ (d) d^2

[RRB JE 2015 26th AUG 2nd SHIFT]

39. An object of 10 kg is raised through a height of 2 m. The work done is (g = 9.8 m/s²)

(a) 196 J   (b) 98 J

(c) 19.6 J   (d) 4.9 J.

[RRB JE 2015 26th AUG 2nd SHIFT]

40. Which of the following statements about sound and light waves is correct?

(a) Both sound and light waves are transverse

(b) Both sound and light waves are longitudinal

(c) Sound wave is transverse but light wave is longitudinal

(d) Sound wave is longitudinal but light wave is transverse

[RRB JE 2015 26th AUG 2nd SHIFT]

41. A beam of light is incident on a surface of a rectangular glass slab ($\mu = 1.52$). If the velocity of the beam before it enters the slab is 3×10^8 m/s, its velocity after emerging from the slab is

(a) 1.97×10^8 m/s   (b) 3×10^8 m/s

(c) 4.56×10^8 m/s   (d) 1.5×10^8 m/s

[RRB JE 2015 26th AUG 2nd SHIFT]

42. Three resistors, each with resistance r, are in series in a circuit. They are replaced by one equivalent resistor of resistance R. Which of the following statements is correct?

(a) R is smaller than r

(b) The voltage across R equals the voltage across r

(c) The current through R equals the current through r

(d) The power dissipated in R equals the power dissipated in r

[RRB JE 2015 26ᵗʰ AUG 2ⁿᵈ SHIFT]

43. The frequency range of audibility of a healthy person with perfect hearing is

(a) 200 to 10000 Hz

(b) 2000 to 5000 Hz

(c) 20 to 20.000 Hz

(d) 20 to 2000 Hz

[RRB JE 2015 26ᵗʰ AUG 3ʳᵈ SHIFT]

44. A truck of mass 1000 kg moving at a speed of 20 m/s is braked suddenly with a braking force of 5000 N. The distance travelled by the truck before stopping is

(a) 20 m   (b) 30 m

(c) 40 m   (d) 80 m

[RRB JE 2015 26ᵗʰ AUG 3ʳᵈ SHIFT]

45. A cubical box (each side 10 cm) of weight 19.6 N is placed on a table. The pressure exerted by the box on the table is

(a) $19.6 \ N/m^2$ (b) $1.96 \times 10^3 \ N/m^2$

(c) $1.96 \ N/m^2$ (d) $0.98 \times 10^3 \ N/m^2$

[RRB JE 2015 26ᵗʰ AUG 3ʳᵈ SHIFT]

46. Rohan does 150 J of work in 5 s. The power delivered by him is

(a) 30 W   (b) 15 W

(c) 150 W   (d) 750 W

[RRB JE 2015 26ᵗʰ AUG 3ʳᵈ SHIFT]

47. For a sound wave, the amplitude is

(a) the distance between two consecutive crests

(b) the distance between two consecutive troughs

(c) the height difference between a crest and a trough

(d) one-half the height difference between a crest and a trough.

[RRB JE 2015 26ᵗʰ AUG 3ʳᵈ SHIFT]

48. An object and a screen are separated by 25 cm. When a convex lens is placed between them at a distance of 5 cm from the object, a sharp image is formed on the screen. The focal length of the lens is

(a) 20 cm   (b) 6.67 cm

(c) 4.0 cm   (d) 2.0 cm.

[RRB JE 2015 26ᵗʰ AUG 3ʳᵈ SHIFT]

49. Two conducting wires A (resistance R_A) and B (resistance R_B) are made of same material and have the same length. If the diameter of wire B is twice that of wire A. the ratio R_A / R_B is

(a) 4   (b) 1/4

(c) 1/2   (d) 1

[RRB JE 2015 26ᵗʰ AUG 3ʳᵈ SHIFT]

50. We are able to walk on the ground because of

(a) Friction

(b) Gravitation

(c) Rotation

(d) Combination of gravity and Rotation

[RRB JE 2015 26ᵗʰ AUG 3ʳᵈ SHIFT]

51. Scissors belong to the category of simple machines called levers. It is a first class lever because

(a) Fulcrum (fixed point) is between load and effort

(b) Load is between Fulcrum and effort

(c) Effort is between fulcrum and load

(d) It does not have a fulcrum

[RRB JE 2015 26ᵗʰ AUG 3ʳᵈ SHIFT]

52. As I was folding my blanket of synthetic fibers, there were sparks due to generation of

(a) Frictional electricity

(b) Current electricity

(c) Flow of electric field

(d) Flow of potential

[RRB JE 2015 26ᵗʰ AUG 3ʳᵈ SHIFT]

53. A 0.5 kg ball is accelerated from rest to 12 m/s in 0.30 s. The force applied on the ball during its motion is

(a) 20 N   (b) 6.0 N

(c) 40 N   (d) 3.6 N

[RRB JE 2015 27ᵗʰ AUG 1ˢᵗ SHIFT]

54. The acceleration due to gravity near the surface of Earth (radius R) is proportional to

(a) R   (b) 1/R

(c) R^2 (d) $1/R^2$

[RRB JE 2015 27ᵗʰ AUG 1ˢᵗ SHIFT]

55. A ball of mass 10 kg is moving with a velocity 5 m/s. The kinetic energy of the ball is

(a) 50 J   (b) 125 J

(d) 250 J   (d) 25 J

[RRB JE 2015 27ᵗʰ AUG 1ˢᵗ SHIFT]

56. The end of a string is vibrated up and down once every 1.5 s and waves propagate at 6 m/s along the string. The wavelength of the waves is

(a) 4.0 m   (b) 9.0 m

(c) 0.25 m   (d) 1.5 m.

[RRB JE 2015 27th AUG 1st SHIFT]

57. An object is placed somewhere between the focus and centre of curvature of a concave mirror. Which of the following best describes the image formed?

(a) Real, inverted and magnification greater than one

(b) Real, inverted and magnification less than one

(c) Virtual, upright and magnification greater than one

(d) Virtual, upright and magnification less than one.

[RRB JE 2015 27th AUG 1st SHIFT]

58. Two 1.5 V batteries in series power a transistor radio. The batteries hold a total charge of 270 C. If the radio has a resistance of 100 Ω, the batteries will last

(a) 5.0 hours   (b) 2.5 hours

(c) 1.25 hours   (d) 33 hours

[RRB JE 2015 27th AUG 1st SHIFT]

59. If you were to measure the strength of a current which instrument would you look for ?

(a) Voltmeter   (b) Thermometer

(c) Ammeter   (d) Barometer

[RRB JE 2015 27th AUG 1st SHIFT]

60. A bicycle pump works on the principle:

(a) When volume decreases, pressure increases

(b) When volume increases, pressure increases

(c) Air pressure at one point becomes zero

(d) At one point volume and pressure become equal

[RRB JE 2015 27th AUG 1st SHIFT]

61. A force gives a certain mass an acceleration a. If the force is doubled and the mass is reduced to half of its original valued the acceleration becomes

(a) a   (b) 2a

(c) 4a   (d) 6a

[RRB JE 2015 27th AUG 2nd SHIFT]

62. Let F1 and F2 be the force between two bodies separated by a distance d and 2d respectively. Then F2/F1 is

(a) 2   (b) 1/2

(c) 4   (d) 1/4.

[RRB JE 2015 27th AUG 2nd SHIFT]

63. The time taken to perform 320 J of work at a rate of 64 W is

(a) 0.2 s   (b) 5 s

(c) 10 s   (d) 64 s.

[RRB JE 2015 27th AUG 2nd SHIFT]

64. Radha uses a source A of frequency f and Meera uses another source B of frequency 2f to produce sound waves in a school science laboratory. Let λA and λB represent the wavelength of waves produced by the sources A and B respectively. Then λB / λA is

(a) 1   (b) 2

(c) 0.5   (d) 4.

[RRB JE 2015 27th AUG 2nd SHIFT]

65. An object is placed at a distance less than one focal length from a thin convex lens. Which of the following best describes the image formed?

(a) Erect, virtual and enlarged

(b) Erect, virtual and diminished

(c) Inverted, real and enlarged

(d) Inverted, real and diminished.

[RRB JE 2015 27th AUG 2nd SHIFT]

66. When two identical resistors are connected in series across a battery, the power dissipated is 10 W. If these resistors are connected in parallel across the same battery, the total power dissipated will be

(a) 10 W   (b) 20 W

(c) 40 W   (d) 80 W

[RRB JE 2015 27th AUG 2nd SHIFT]

67. A force acting on a body of mass 1.5 kg. accelerates it from rest to a velocity of 4 m/s. The change in the momentum of the body is

(a) 1.5 kg m/s   (b) 3.0 kg m/s

(c) 4.5 kg m/s   (d) 6.0 kg m/s

[RRB JE 2015 27th AUG 3rd SHIFT]

68. Let g be the acceleration due to gravity on the surface of Earth. The acceleration due to gravity on the surface of Moon is

(a) 6 g   (b) g/6

(c) g   (d) g/3

[RRB JE 2015 27th AUG 3rd SHIFT]

69. The quantity of work equal to one joule is also equivalent to one

(a) watt x second   (b) watt/second

(c) watt/second^2 (d) watt

[RRB JE 2015 27th AUG 3rd SHIFT]

70. A source A of frequency f and another source of frequency $2f$ are used to produce sound waves in a science laboratory. Let v_A and v_B represent the velocity of waves produced by the sources A and B. respectively. Then v_A/v_B is

(a) 1 (b) 2

(c) 0.5 (d) 4

[RRB JE 2015 27ᵗʰ AUG 3ʳᵈ SHIFT]

71. The size of image formed by a convex lens (focal length f) is equal to the size of the object. The object is placed at a distance

(a) between f and $2f$

(b) greater than $2f$

(c) $2f$

(d) less than f

[RRB JE 2015 27ᵗʰ AUG 3ʳᵈ SHIFT]

72. A 1 m long metal wire of radius 1 cm has a resistance of 1.6×10^{-4} Ω. The resistivity of the metal is

(a) 5.0×10^{-8} Ω m

(b) 1.0×10^{-8} Ω m

(c) 1.6×10^{-8} Ω m

(d) 3.2×10^{-8} Ω m

[RRB JE 2015 27ᵗʰ AUG 3ʳᵈ SHIFT]

73. What is not true about, "what forces can do"?

(a) Speed up and slow down

(b) Turn and change shape

(c) Push and pull

(d) Turn but not change direction

[RRB JE 2015 27ᵗʰ AUG 3ʳᵈ SHIFT]

74. What is **not** true regarding your image, when you see yourself in the plane minor?

(a) Image is of the same size as you

(b) It is at the same distance behind the mirror as you are infront of it

(c) The face, hands and legs are in the same direction in the mirror as yours

(d) Your image is laterally inverted in the mirror

[RRB JE 2015 27ᵗʰ AUG 3ʳᵈ SHIFT]

75. A force of 20 N accelerates a body from rest to a velocity of 3 m/s in 10 s. The magnitude of change in momentum of the body in one second is

(a) 2 kg m/s (b) 20 kg m/s

(c) 60 kg m/s (d) 6 kg m/s

[RRB JE 2015 28ᵗʰ AUG 1ˢᵗ SHIFT]

76. The mass of an object is 24 kg on the surface of Earth. It's mass on the surface of Moon will be

(a) 24 kg (b) 4 kg

(c) 2.4 kg (d) 0.24 kg

[RRB JE 2015 28ᵗʰ AUG 1ˢᵗ SHIFT]

77. A 5 kg box is raised through a height. Its potential energy increases by 49 J. The height is

($g = 9.8$ m/s²)

(a) 9.8 m (b) 5.0 m

(c) 1.0 m (d) 0.5 m

[RRB JE 2015 28ᵗʰ AUG 1ˢᵗ SHIFT]

78. Smita uses a tuning fork of frequency 512 Hz to produce sound in the science laboratory of her school. The velocity of sound in the laboratory is 344 m/s. The distance between two consecutive crests of the sound waves produced is

(a) 1.34 m (b) 0.67 m

(c) 6.7 m (d) 1.49 m

[RRB JE 2015 28ᵗʰ AUG 1ˢᵗ SHIFT]

79. A concave lens forms an image of a real object. This image is necessarily

(a) enlarged, erect and real

(b) enlarged, erect and virtual

(c) diminished, inverted and virtual

(d) diminished, erect and virtual

[RRB JE 2015 28ᵗʰ AUG 1ˢᵗ SHIFT]

80. A wire has a radius of 0.50 mm and carries a current of 0.5 A. The resistivity of the material of wire is 1.1×10^{-6} ohm-m. The potential difference per unit length along the wire is

(a) 0.70 V/m (b) 1.4 V/m

(c) 2.2 V/m (d) 0.90 V/m.

[RRB JE 2015 28ᵗʰ AUG 1ˢᵗ SHIFT]

81. Which of the following is the best conductor of heat

(a) mercury (b) water

(c) leather (d) benzene

[RRB JE 2015 28ᵗʰ AUG 1ˢᵗ SHIFT]

82. Due to contraction of eyeball, a long sighted eye can see only

(a) farther objects which is corrected using convex lens

(b) farther objects which is corrected using concave lens

(c) nearer objects which is corrected using convex lens

(d) nearer objects which is corrected using concave lens

[RRB JE 2015 28ᵗʰ AUG 1ˢᵗ SHIFT]

83. A radioactive substance has a half life of four months. Three-fourth of the substance would decay in

(a) 3 months (b) 4 months

(c) 8 months (d) 12 months

[RRB JE 2015 28ᵗʰ AUG 1ˢᵗ SHIFT]

84. Which of the following is a unit of momentum?

(a) N m

(b) kg m s^{-1}

(c) kg m s^{-2}

(d) kg m^{-2}

[RRB JE 2015 28th AUG 2nd SHIFT]

85. A ball is thrown vertically upward with a velocity of 19.6 m/s. The maximum height it attains is (g = 9.8 m/s^2)

(a) 4.9 m

(b) 9.8 m

(c) 19.6m

(d) 39.2 m

[RRB JE 2015 28th AUG 2nd SHIFT]

86. A 10 kg box is placed at a height h above the ground. The potential energy of the box is 980 J. The value of h is (g = 9.8 m/s^2)

(a) 10 m

(b) 20 m

(c) 98 m

(d) 49 m.

[RRB JE 2015 28th AUG 2nd SHIFT]

87. A source produces sound waves under water. Waves travel through water and some of it is transmitted into air. Which of the following statements about the frequency f and wavelength λ is correct as sound passes from water to air?

(a) f and λ remain unchanged

(b) f increases but λ decreases

(c) f remains unchanged but λ increases

(d) f remains unchanged but λ decreases.

[RRB JE 2015 28th AUG 2nd SHIFT]

88. A light ray from air enters and passes through a glass slab. Which of the following statements is true about its speed after it emerges from the block?

(a) Speed is same as that before it entered glass slab

(b) Speed is same as that in glass slab

(c) Speed is less than when in glass slab

(d) Speed is less than before it entered glass slab.

[RRB JE 2015 28th AUG 2nd SHIFT]

89. An object of mass m at rest is acted upon by a force. When the velocity-time graph of the object is plotted (with velocity on y-axis and time on x-axis), we get a straight line passing through origin and inclined to x-axis. If the force (on x-axis) versus time (on x-axis) graph is plotted, the graph is a straight line

(a) passing through origin and inclined to x-axis

(b) passing through origin and coinciding with x-axis

(c) parallel to x-axis

(d) parallel to y-axis.

[RRB JE 2015 28th AUG 3rd SHIFT]

90. The acceleration due to gravity, g, is

(a) independent of the mass of the earth

(b) inversely proportional to the radius of the earth

(c) proportional to the mass of the earth and inversely proportional to the square of the radius of the earth

(d) same at the poles and the equator.

[RRB JE 2015 28th AUG 3rd SHIFT]

91. Rohan (mass 40 kg) and Sohan (mass 60 kg) climb the stairs of their school building to reach the first floor in 40 s and 60 s, respectively. Let P_1 and P_2 be the power delivered in this task by Rohan and Sohan, respectively. Which one the following is correct?

(a) $P_1 = P_2$

(b) $P_2 > P_2$

(c) $P_1 < P_2$

(d) $P_1 = 2P_1$.

[RRB JE 2015 28th AUG 3rd SHIFT]

92. The loudness or softness of a sound is determined basically by its

(a) amplitude

(b) frequency

(c) speed

(d) speed and frequency both

[RRB JE 2015 28th AUG 3rd SHIFT]

93. A ray of light travelling in air is incident on a glass slab. Part of it is reflected and part is refracted. Let i, r and s be the angle of incidence, angle of reflection and angle of refraction. Which one of the following is correct?

(a) i = r = s

(b) i ≠ r ≠ s

(c) i = r and s < i

(d) i = r and s > i

[RRB JE 2015 28th AUG 3rd SHIFT]

94. A conducting wire has length l and area of cross-section A. The resistivity of its material is ρ and its resistance is R. It is connected in series with another wire of the same dimensions but of a resistivity 2 ρ The net resistance of the combination is

(a) R

(b) 2 R

(c) 3 R

(d) 2R/3

[RRB JE 2015 28th AUG 3rd SHIFT]

95. An object of mass m at rest is acted upon by a force. The velocity-time graph (velocity on y-axis and time on x-axis) is found be a straight line passing through origin and inclined to x-axis with a slope c. The force acting on the object is

(a) 0

(b) m/c

(c) m c

(d) 2m c.

[RRB JE 2015 29th AUG 1st SHIFT]

96. The SI unit of gravitational constant. G, is

(a) $N\ m^2\ kg^{-2}$ (b) $N\ m^{-2}\ kg^{-2}$

(c) $N\ kg^2\ m^{-2}$ (d) $m^2\ kg^{-1}\ s^{-2}$

[RRB JE 2015 29th AUG 1st SHIFT]

97. A force acting on an object of mass m changes its velocity during its course of motion, which of the following cases, the work done by the force is maximum?

(a) When velocity of the object changes from 0 to v m/s

(b) When velocity of the object changes from v m/s to 2 v m/s

(c) When velocity of the object changes from 2 v m/s to 3 v m/s

(d) When velocity of the object changes from 3 v m/s to 4 v/m s

[RRB JE 2015 29th AUG 1st SHIFT]

98. In a longitudinal sound wave, the particles of the medium move

(a) about their position of rest in a direction parallel to the direction of propagation of disturbance

(b) about their position of rest in a direction perpendicular to the direction of propagation of disturbance

(c) from one place to another in a direction parallel to the direction of propagation of disturbance

(d) From one place to other in a direction perpendicular to the direction of propagation of disturbance

[RRB JE 2015 29th AUG 1st SHIFT]

99. Rays of light are evident on a concave mirror parallel to the principal axis. After reflection, they meet at

(a) Infinity

(b) the centre of curvature

(c) at focus

(d) At a point half way to the focus

[RRB JE 2015 29th AUG 1st SHIFT]

100. A conducting wire of length l and resistance R is cut into two equal parts, which are then connected in parallel. The resistance of the combination is

(a) R/2 (b) R/4

(c) R (d) 2 R

[RRB JE 2015 29th AUG 1st SHIFT]

101. A ball is rolled on a floor. Moving in straight line, it stops after some time due to frictional force exerted by the floor. Which of the following statements about acceleration and force during the motion of the ball is correct?

(a) Both acceleration and force are positive

(b) Both acceleration and force are negative

(c) Acceleration is positive but force is negative

(d) Acceleration is negative but force is positive.

[RRB JE 2015 29th AUG 2nd SHIFT]

102. Let g be the acceleration due to gravity at a place on earth (mass M and radius R). The ratio g/G at the place is given by (G - Universal gravitational constant)

(a) M/R (b) M/R^2

(c) MR (d) MR^2.

[RRB JE 2015 29th AUG 2nd SHIFT]

103. A ball of mass m is raised to height h and then dropped to the ground. When the ball has fallen half of the height, the velocity of the ball is (neglecting air resistance), where g is the acceleration due to gravity.

(a) $\sqrt{gh}$ (b) $\sqrt{2gh}$

(c) $\sqrt{\dfrac{gh}{2}}$ (d) $2\sqrt{gh}$

[RRB JE 2015 29th AUG 2nd SHIFT]

104. Three tuning forks (of different frequencies) are used to produce sound in a science Laboratory. Which of the following statements is correct?

(a) The wavelength of sound produced by the tuning fork of highest frequency is smallest

(b) The wavelength of sound produced by the tuning fork of highest frequency is largest

(c) The velocities of sound produced by the three tuning forks are different

(d) The pitch of sound produced by the timing fork of lowest frequency is highest.

[RRB JE 2015 29th AUG 2nd SHIFT]

105. An image of an object is seen in a plane mirror. The image is

(a) real and inverted

(b) real and erect

(c) virtual and inverted

(d) virtual and erect

[RRB JE 2015 29th AUG 2nd SHIFT]

106. A current of 1 A flows towards right in a conductor. The number of electrons passing per second through any cross section of the conductor and their direction is about

(a) 6×10^{18} towards right

(b) 6×10^{18} towards left

(c) 6×10^{16} towards right

(d) 6×10^{16} towards left.

[RRB JE 2015 29th AUG 2nd SHIFT]

107. A bullet of mass m kg is fired horizontally with a velocity v m/s from a gun of mass 100 m kg. The recoil velocity of the gun is

(a) v m/s   (b) $-v$ m/s

(c) $(v/100)$ m/s   (d) $-(v/100)$ m/s.

[RRB JE 2015 29th AUG 3rd SHIFT]

108. Let g m/s^2 be the acceleration due to gravity at a place. If mass and radius of the earth are reduced to half of its value, the weight of 1 kg object will become

(a) $0.5\,g$N   (b) $1\,g$N

(c) $2\,g$N   (d) $4\,g$N

[RRB JE 2015 29th AUG 3rd SHIFT]

109. The kinetic energy of an object of mass m is twice the kinetic energy of object B of mass 2 m. Let v_A and v_B represent represent the velocity of object A and B, respectively. Then v_A/v_B is

(a) 1/2   (b) 1

(c) 2   (d) 4.

[RRB JE 2015 29th AUG 3rd SHIFT]

110. When a sound wave travels in a medium, it creates

(a) compressions and rarefactions alternatively

(b) compressions only

(c) rarefactions only

(d) few successive regions of compressions and then few successive regions of rarefactions.

[RRB JE 2015 29th AUG 3rd SHIFT]

111. An object is placed before a convex mirror. The image is

(a) real

(b) virtual

(c) may be real or virtual depending upon distance of the object from the mirror.

(d) magnified.

[RRB JE 2015 29th AUG 3rd SHIFT]

112. A current of 0.1 A flows towards left in a conductor. The number of electrons passing per second through any cross section of the conductor and their direction is about

(a) 6×10^{17} towards right

(b) 6×10^{17} towards left

(c) 6×10^{18} towards right

(d) 6×10^{18} towards left.

[RRB JE 2015 29th AUG 3rd SHIFT]

113. Bats can fly during the night because they produce

(a) Ultrasonic waves

(b) Sound waves

(c) Ultra violet waves

(d) Infra-red waves

[RRB JE 2015 29th AUG 3rd SHIFT]

114. An object A of mass m moving with velocity v collides with a second object B of the same mass lying at rest. Dining the collision, object A transfers its total kinetic energy to object B and comes to rest. After collision, the velocity of object B is

(a) v (b) $v/2$

(c) $2\,v$ (d) zero.

[RRB JE 2015 30th AUG 3rd SHIFT]

115. A particular place is at a height h above the surface of the earth (radius R). The acceleration due to gravity at that place is proportional to

(a) $(R + h)$ (b) $(R + h)^{-2}$

(c) $(R - h)$ (d) $(R - h)^{-2}$

[RRB JE 2015 30th AUG 3rd SHIFT]

116. A ball of mass m is raised to height h and then dropped to the ground. At what height, kinetic energy of the ball is thrice its potential energy? Neglect air resistance.

(a) $\dfrac{3h}{4}$ (b) $\dfrac{h}{2}$

(c) $\dfrac{h}{4}$ (d) Zero.

[RRB JE 2015 30th AUG 3rd SHIFT]

117. In a transverse wave, the particles of the medium move

(a) about their position of rest in a direction parallel to the direction of propagation of disturbance

(b) about their position of rest in a direction perpendicular to the direction of propagation of disturbance

(c) from one place to another in a direction parallel to the direction of propagation of disturbance

(d) from one place to another in a direction perpendicular to the direction of propagation of disturbance.

[RRB JE 2015 30th AUG 3rd SHIFT]

118. An object is place in front of a convex mirror at a distance less than the value of its focal length.

Which of the following best describes the image formed?

(a) real inverted and magnification greater than one

(b) real, inverted and magnification less than one

(c) virtual, erect and magnification greater than one

(d) virtual, erect and magnification less than one

[RRB JE 2015 30ᵗʰ AUG 3ʳᵈ SHIFT]

119. A conducing wire has length l and area of cross-section A. The resistivity of its material is ρ and its resistance is R. It is connected in parallel with another wire of the same dimensions but of a resistivity 2ρ. The net resistance of the combination s

(a) R   (b) 2 R

(c) 3 R   (d) $\dfrac{2R}{3}$

[RRB JE 2015 30ᵗʰ AUG 3ʳᵈ SHIFT]

120. A bullet of mass m kg is fired horizontally with a velocity v m/s from a pistol of mass M kg. The recoil velocity of the pistol is

(a) $(m/M)\,v$ m/s   (b) $-(m/M)\,v$ m/s

(c) v m/s   (d) $-(M/m)\,v$ m/s.

[RRB JE 2015 16ᵗʰ SEP 3ʳᵈ SHIFT]

121. The acceleration due to gravity, g

(a) decreases as we go up the earth

(b) increases as we go up the earth

(c) Increases as we go down the earth

(d) Is less at poles than at equator.

[RRB JE 2015 16ᵗʰ SEP 3ʳᵈ SHIFT]

122. A ball of mass m is raised to height h and then dropped to the ground. When the ball reaches the ground, the velocity of the ball is (neglecting air resistance), where g is the acceleration due to gravity.

(a) $\sqrt{gh}$ (b) $\sqrt{2gh}$

(c) $\sqrt{\dfrac{gh}{2}}$ (d) $2\sqrt{gh}$

[RRB JE 2015 16ᵗʰ SEP 3ʳᵈ SHIFT]

123. The pitch of a sound is basically determined by its

(a) amplitude   (b) frequency

(c) speed   (d) speed and amplitude.

[RRB JE 2015 16ᵗʰ SEP 3ʳᵈ SHIFT]

124. A ray of light travelling in a glass slab is incident on the surface separating glass from air. Part of it is reflected and part is refracted. Let i, r and s be the angle of incidence, angle of reflection and angle of refraction. Which one of the following is correct?

(a) i = r = s

(b) $i \neq r \neq s$

(c) i = r and s < i

(d) i = r and s > i

[RRB JE 2015 16ᵗʰ SEP 3ʳᵈ SHIFT]

125. A conducting wire of length l and resistance R is cut into four equal parts. The four parts are then connected in parallel. The resistance of the combination is

(a) R/4   (b) R/8

(c) R/16   (d) 4R

[RRB JE 2015 16ᵗʰ SEP 3ʳᵈ SHIFT]

126. The filament of incandescent bulbs is made of

(a) Nichrome   (b) Copper

(c) Iron   (d) Tungsten

[RRB JE 2015 16ᵗʰ SEP 3ʳᵈ SHIFT]

127. What does the voltmeter measure?

(a) Strength of current

(b) Potential difference between two points

(c) Resistance

(d) Energy consumed

[RRB JE 2015 16ᵗʰ SEP 3ʳᵈ SHIFT]

128. We see an identical image of the object in the mirror because of

(a) Reflection   (b) Refraction

(c) Dispersion   (d) Diffraction

[RRB JE 2015 16ᵗʰ SEP 3ʳᵈ SHIFT]

RRB SENIOR SECTION ENGINEER

1. In a classical blood pressure measuring instrument in which the doctor observes the rise and fall of mercury, the hand air pump is attached to a-
(a) Isobar (b) Transducer
(c) Manometer (d) Mercury column
[RRB SSE 2014 GREEN SHIFT]

2. Conservation of energy corresponds to which law of thermodynamics?
(a) Zeroth law (b) First law
(c) Second law (d) Third law
[RRB SSE 2014 GREEN SHIFT]

3. In our house when we switch on heavy load appliances, we notice that there is slight dip in the glow of the bulb that was already switched on. This is due to-
(a) Heavy current drawn by heavy load
(b) Additional resistance added to the circuit
(c) Resistance of electrical wiring
(d) Resistance of part of the circuit decreasing from infinity to a positive value
[RRB SSE 2014 GREEN SHIFT]

4. What is the boiling point of water in Kelvin Seale?
(a) 100 K (b) 273 K
(c) 373 K (d) 300 K
[RRB SSE 2014 GREEN SHIFT]

5. Acid rain is caused by:
(a) CO & CO_2 (b) SO_2 & O_2
(c) SO_2 & NO_2 (d) NO_2 & O_2
[RRB SSE 2014 GREEN SHIFT]

6. Which planet has hot turbulent atmosphere dominated by carbon-di-oxide?
(a) Venus (b) Mars
(c) Jupiter (d) Neptune
[RRB SSE 2014 GREEN SHIFT]

7. A tunic fork when sounded together with another tuning fork of known frequency of 240 Hz, emits 2 beats. On loading the tuning fork of known frequency the number of heats heard are one per second. The frequency of the tuning fork is:
(a) 241Hz (b) 242 Hz
(c) 239 Hz (d) 238 Hz
[RRB SSE 2014 GREEN SHIFT]

8. Tachymeter (or Tacheometer is an instrument for measuring-
(a) rpm
(b) Torque
(c) Rotational kinetic energy
(d) Distances
[RRB SSE 2014 GREEN SHIFT]

9. Which of the following is NOT used for measurement of temperature?
(a) Thermocouples (b) Thermostats
(c) Pyrometers (d) All are used
[RRB SSE 2014 GREEN SHIFT]

10. Aluminium is commonly used as conductor material in transmission lines compared to copper because:
(a) It is more conductive
(b) Its tensile strength is more
(c) It is costlier
(d) It is cheaper and lighter
[RRB SSE 2014 RED SHIFT]

11. Find the distance of object from a concave mirror of focal length 10 cm so that the size of its real image is four times the size of the object.
(a) 7.5 cm (b) 5 cm
(c) 2.5 cm (d) 12.5 cm
[RRB SSE 2014 RED SHIFT]

12. A barometer measures :
(a) Absolute pressure
(b) Atmospheric pressure
(c) Gauge pressure
(d) Vacuum **[RRB SSE 2014 RED SHIFT]**

13. Which one of the following has the dimensions of pressure ?
(a) MLT^{-2} (b) $ML^{-1}T^{-2}$
(c) $ML^{-2}T^{-2}$ (d) $ML^{-1}T^{-1}$
[RRB SSE 2014 RED SHIFT]

14. The refractive index of water is $\dfrac{4}{3}$. What is the speed of light in water ?
(a) 2.25×10^8 m/sec (b) 4×10^8 m/sec
(c) 1.5×10^8 m/sec (d) 2.67×10^8 m/sec
[RRB SSE 2014 RED SHIFT]

15. If the electron in hydrogen orbit jumps from third orbit to second orbit then the wavelength (λ o f the emitted radiation is given by : (where R = Rydberg constant)
(a) $\lambda = \dfrac{R}{6}$ (b) $\lambda = \dfrac{R}{5}$
(c) $\lambda = \dfrac{36}{5R}$ (d) $\lambda = \dfrac{5R}{36}$
[RRB SSE 2014 RED SHIFT]

16. Which of the following is used as a moderator in nuclear reactors ?
(a) Hard water (b) Mineral water
(c) Deionized water (d) Heavy water
[RRB SSE 2014 RED SHIFT]

17. A particle moves along a circular path with constant speed. What is the nature of its acceleration ?

(a) It is zero

(b) It is Uniform

(c) Its direction changes

(d Its magnitude changes

[RRB SSE 2014 YELLOW SHIFT]

18. A body is at rest on the surface of the earth. Which of the following Statements is correct ?

(a) No force is acting on the body

(b) Only weight of the body acts on it

(c) Net downward force is equal to net upward force

(d) None of these is correct

[RRB SSE 2014 YELLOW SHIFT]

19. The Specific Heat of the gas in an isothermal process is

(a) Zero   (b) Infinite

(c) Negative   (d) Remains constant

[RRB SSE 2014 YELLOW SHIFT]

20. In a Simple Harmonic Oscillator, at the mean position

(a) Kinetic Energy is minimum, Potential Energy is maximum

(b) Both Kinetic and Potential Energies are maximum

(c) Kinetic Energy is maximum. Potential Energy is minimum

(d) Both Kinetic and Potential Energies are minimum

[RRB SSE 2014 YELLOW SHIFT]

21. Mirage is a phenomenon due to

(a) Reflection of light

(b) Refraction of light

(c) Total Internal reflection of light

(d Diffraction of light

[RRB SSE 2014 YELLOW SHIFT]

22. Which of the following cannot be speed-time (v-t graph of a body in motion ?

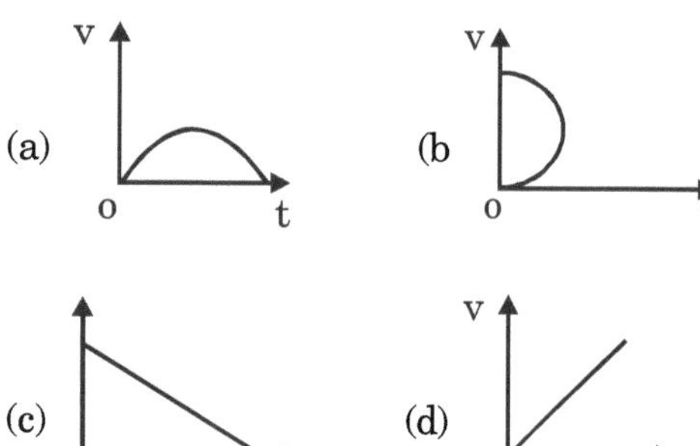

[RRB SSE 2014 YELLOW SHIFT]

23. Which one of the following is correct ?

The specific volume of water when heated from 0°C

(a) first increases and then decreases

(b) first decreases and then increases

(c) increases steadily

(d) decreases steadily

[RRB SSE 2014 YELLOW SHIFT]

24. Two blocks which are at different states are brought into contact with each other and allowed to reach a final state of thermal equilibrium The final temperature attained is specified by the

(a) Zeroth Law of Thermodynamics

(b) First Law of Thermodynamics

(c) 2nd Law of Thermodynamics

(d) 3rd Law of Thermodynamics

[RRB SSE 2014 YELLOW SHIFT]

25. A composite wall consists of two layers of different materials having conductivities K_1 and K_2. For equal thickness of the two layers, the equivalent thermal conductivity of the slab will be

(a) $K_1 + K_2$ (b) $K_1 K_2$

(c) $\dfrac{2K_1 + K_2}{K_1 + K_2}$ (d) $\dfrac{K_1 + K_2}{K_1 K_2}$

[RRB SSE 2014 YELLOW SHIFT]

26. Soft iron is used in the manufacture of electromagnets because of its

(a) high saturation magnetisation only

(b) low retentively only

(c) low coercive field only

(d) high saturation magnetisation, low retentively and low coercive field

[RRB SSE 2014 YELLOW SHIFT]

27. Which of the following is piezo-electric material?

(a) Quartz   (b) Silica Sand

(c) Corundum   (d) Polystyrene

[RRB SSE 2014 YELLOW SHIFT]

28. If two conductors carry current in the same direction

(a) Conductors attract each other

(b) Conductors are in resonance

(c) Conductors repel each other

(d) Voltage between two conductors increases

[RRB SSE 2014 YELLOW SHIFT]

29. The true length of a line is known to be 200 m When this is measured with a 20 m tape, the length is 200.8 m. The correct length of the 20 m tape is

(a) 19.92 m   (b) 19 98 m

(c) 20.04 m   (d) 20.08 m

[RRB SSE 2014 YELLOW SHIFT]

30. Mohan hits a cricket ball which hits the glass of a window of a nearby building. The ball does not break the glass. It reverses its direction and falls on the ground. Which of the following statements is correct?

(a) The force exerted by the ball on the glass is less than the force exerted by the glass on the ball

(b) The force exerted by the ball on the glass is more than the force exerted by the glass on the ball

(c) The force exerted by the ball on the glass is equal to the force exerted by the glass on the ball

(d) The force exerted by the ball on the glass may be less or more than the force exerted by the glass on the ball, depending upon the toughness of the glass.

[RRB SSE 2015 1ˢᵗ SEP 1ˢᵗ SHIFT]

31. Let g be the acceleration due to gravity at the surface earth (radius R. Then the acceleration due to gravity g (hat a height h above the surface of the earth is given by

(a) $g(h) = g (1 - h/R)$

(b) $g(h) = g (1 - 2h/R)$

(c) $g(h) = g (1 + h/R)$

(d) $g(h) = g (1 + 2h/R)$

[RRB SSE 2015 1ˢᵗ SEP 1ˢᵗ SHIFT]

32. The work done by a variable force of the form F = k x is equal to

(a) kx^2

(b) kx

(c) $2k x^2$

(d) equal to the area under the F versus x curve.

[RRB SSE 2015 1ˢᵗ SEP 1ˢᵗ SHIFT]

33. An object in simple harmonic motion is at its maximum displacement. Which of the following quantities is at a maximum?

(a) acceleration   (b) velocity

(c) frequency   (d) kinetic energy.

[RRB SSE 2015 1ˢᵗ SEP 1ˢᵗ SHIFT]

34. In case of total internal reflection occurring glass-air interface,

(a) light from air strikes the glass with an incident angle less than the critical angle

(b) light from air strikes the glass with an incident angle more than the critical angle

(c) no light is reflected

(d) no light is refracted.

[RRB SSE 2015 1ˢᵗ SEP 1ˢᵗ SHIFT]

35. The quantity, electromotive force (emf), is dimensionally equivalent to

(a) coulomb/ohm   (b) joule/coulomb

(c) joule x metre   (d) joule x coulomb

[RRB SSE 2015 1ˢᵗ SEP 1ˢᵗ SHIFT]

36. Rainbows show that different colours have different wavelengths? Which one has the shortest wavelength?

(a) Violet   (b) Blue

(c) Red   (d) Orange

[RRB SSE 2015 1ˢᵗ SEP 1ˢᵗ SHIFT]

37. Which law governs the movement of manmade satellites in space?

(a) Harley's law

(b) Newton's Laws of Motion

(c) Hubble's laws

(d) Kepler's laws

[RRB SSE 2015 1ˢᵗ SEP 1ˢᵗ SHIFT]

38. In comparison to the measurement on the surface of the Earth, those on top of Mt. Everest demonstrate

(a) decrease in eight with mass remaining the same

(b) increase the mass with weight remaining the same

(c) decrease in both mass and weight

(d) increase in both mass and weight

[RRB SSE 2015 1ˢᵗ SEP 1ˢᵗ SHIFT]

39. Radhey slides a box at a constant speed up a frictionless slope. During the motion, he pulls the rope attached to the box keeping it parallel to the slope. The tension in the rope is

(a) less than the weight of the box

(b) equal to the weight of the box

(c) more than the weight of the box

(d) more than the tension would be if the box were stationary.

[RRB SSE 2015 1ˢᵗ SEP 2ⁿᵈ SHIFT]

40. Let g be the acceleration due to gravity at the surface of earth (radius R.Then the acceleration due to gravity g (dat a depth d below the surface of the eart is given by

(a) $g(d) = g (1-d/R)$ (b) $g(d) = g(1- 2d/R)$

(c) $g(d) = g (1+ d/R)$ (d) $g(d) = g (1 + 2d/R)$

[RRB SSE 2015 1ˢᵗ SEP 2ⁿᵈ SHIFT]

41. An organ pipe open at both ends is made to go into resonance at a frequency f_o . When one end of the pipe is closed, it is found that it goes into resonance at a frequency f_c. If both the resonances are first harmonics, which of the following relations between f_o and f_c is correct ?

(a) $f_o = f_c$ (b) $f_o = \dfrac{1}{2}f_c$

(c) $f_o = 2f_c$ (d) $f_o = \dfrac{2}{3}f_c$

[RRB SSE 2015 1ˢᵗ SEP 2ⁿᵈ SHIFT]

42. Two identical thin lenses of same focal lengths f are placed in contact so that their optic axes coincide. The focal length of the combination is

(a) f   (b) f/2

(c) 2f   (d) 4f

[RRB SSE 2015 1ˢᵗ SEP 2ⁿᵈ SHIFT]

43. During the rainy season, lightning is seen first and the thunder is heard afterwards because

(a) Speed of light is higher than that of sound

(b) Both travel first in lithosphere and then in the hydrosphere

(c) Both travel in hydrosphere and then lithosphere

(d) Speed of sound is higher than that of light

[RRB SSE 2015 1ˢᵗ SEP 2ⁿᵈ SHIFT]

44. When a wooden ball weighing 500 gms is shot upward vertically through a mechanical device, it would gain

(a) Force   (b) Momentum

(c) Speed   (d) Inertia

[RRB SSE 2015 1ˢᵗ SEP 2ⁿᵈ SHIFT]

45. Which is the gas used inside a electric bulb ?

(a) Oxygen   (b) Hydrogen

(c) Inert Gas   (d) Nitrogen

[RRB SSE 2015 1ˢᵗ SEP 2ⁿᵈ SHIFT]

46. Alka is standing in a lift. The force exerted by the floor of the lift on the Alka's foot is more than the weight of Alka if the lift is

(a) moving upward with increasing speed

(b) moving upward with decreasing speed

(c) moving downward with increasing speed

(d) moving upward with constant speed.

[RRB SSE 2015 1ˢᵗ SEP 3ʳᵈ SHIFT]

47. For an orbiting satellite, in magnitude

(a) the kinetic energy is equal to the potential energy

(b) the kinetic energy is twice the potential energy

(c) the kinetic energy is half the potential energy

(d) the kinetic energy is one-fourth the potential energy .

[RRB SSE 2015 1ˢᵗ SEP 3ʳᵈ SHIFT]

48. An object of mass m_1 collides with a stationary object of mass m_2. The collision is elastic. There is complete transfer of kinetic energy if

(a) $m_1 = m_2$

(b) $m_1 >> m_2$

(c) $m_1 << m_2$

(d) the masses stick together.

[RRB SSE 2015 1ˢᵗ SEP 3ʳᵈ SHIFT]

49. Which one of the following represents a standing wave?

(a) $y(x,t) = 4.7 \sin(5x - 0.4t)$

(b) $y(x,t) = 8.2 \sin(2x - t)$

(c) $y(x,t) = 5.6 \cos 0.5(t - x/2.4)$

(d) $y(x,t) = 4 \cos(3x\sin(11t))$.

[RRB SSE 2015 1ˢᵗ SEP 3ʳᵈ SHIFT]

50. Two identical thin convex lenses of same power P are placed in contact so that their optic axes coincide. The net power of combination is

(a) P   (b) 2 P

(c) P/2   (d) P/4

[RRB SSE 2015 1ˢᵗ SEP 3ʳᵈ SHIFT]

51. Which one of following is not a force?

(a) Electric Force   (b) Gravity

(c) Friction   (d) Electromotive force.

[RRB SSE 2015 1ˢᵗ SEP 3ʳᵈ SHIFT]

52. A seasoned cricketer draws in his hands backward in act of catching a ball. It hurts the hands less because this

(a) makes the momentum change less

(b) makes the kinetic energy change less

(c) makes the time interval for stopping more

(d) increases the impulse of the collision.

[RRB SSE 2015 2ⁿᵈ SEP 1ˢᵗ SHIFT]

53. For a geostationary satellite, the time period is

    (a) 6 h   (b) 12 h

    (c) 18 h   (d) 24 h.

[RRB SSE 2015 2nd SEP 1st SHIFT]

54. Radha and Mohan move identical boxes equal distances in a horizontal direction. Radha slides the box on a surface that is frictionless. Mohan lifts the box, carries it that distance and sets it down again.

    (a) Radha does more work than Mohan

    (b) Radha does less work than Mohan

    (c) Neither Radha nor Mohan do any work

    (d) The amount of work done by each depends on the time taken.

[RRB SSE 2015 2nd SEP 1st SHIFT]

55. Following equations represent four travelling waves. Which one has the maximum speed?

    (a) $y = 3.2 \sin(5x - 2t)$

    (b) $y = 4.3 \sin(1.5x - 3.1t)$

    (c) $y = 2.1 \sin(7x - 8t)$

    (d) $y = 1.5 \sin(25x - 1.25t)$.

[RRB SSE 2015 2nd SEP 1st SHIFT]

56. Four identical thin convex lenses of same power P are placed in contact so that their optic axes coincide. The net power of the combination is

    a. P/4   (b) P

    (c) 2 P   (d) 4 P.

[RRB SSE 2015 2nd SEP 1st SHIFT]

57. Consider the electric field between two parallel plates of a charged capacitor. The electric field is

    (a) strongest in magnitude near the positive plate

    (b) strongest in magnitude near the negative plate

    (c) strongest in magnitude midway between the plat

    (d) constant throughout the space between the plates.

[RRB SSE 2015 2nd SEP 1st SHIFT]

58. A body is floating in a liquid which has a density equal to that of the body. .What will happen if the body is slightly pressed down and released?

    (a) Sink to the bottom and rise up again slowly.

    (b) Come back to the same position immediately

    (c) Come back to the same position slowly.

    (d) it will start shaking

[RRB SSE 2015 2nd SEP 1st SHIFT]

59. Which instrument is used both as a measuring device and for predictive purposes?

    (a) Barometer   (b) Thermometer

    (c) Voltmeter   (d) Lactometer

[RRB SSE 2015 2nd SEP 1st SHIFT]

60. What is the effect of the rotation of the earth on the direction of movement of ships?

    (a) Ships slow down when they move from the Poles towards the Equator.

    (b) Ships travelling west are more affected by the speed and direction of winds and ocean currents

    (c) Ships move faster when they travel from the Equator Poleward due to gravity

    (d) Ships slow down when moving eastward, as gravity seemed to fade away a little.

[RRB SSE 2015 2nd SEP 1st SHIFT]

61. An object is moving with constant velocity. The net force acting on the object is given by

    (a) $F = mg$ (b) $F = 0$

    (c) $F = mv$ (d) $F = v^2/2m$

[RRB SSE 2015 2nd SEP 2nd SHIFT]

62. An object of mass 1.6 kg is taken to the surface of a planet of radius 4×10^6 m. There the weight of the object is found to b 66.7 N. The mass of the planet is ($G = 6.67 \times 10^{-11}$ N m^2/kg^2)

    (a) 1.6×10^{25} kg   (b) 8.0×10^{24} kg

    (c) 1.0×10^{25} kg   (d) 2.0×10^{25} kg

[RRB SSE 2015 2nd SEP 2nd SHIFT]

63. Govind pushes a cart 5 m on a level surface by applying a 49 N force horizontally. If a frictional force of 26 N acts on the cart, the net work done is

    (a) 115 J   (b) 375 J

    (c) 130 J   (d) 245 J.

[RRB SSE 2015 2nd SEP 2nd SHIFT]

64. A periodic SHM is given by $y = 6\sin(7\pi t)$ m, where t is in seconds. The period of the system is

    (a) 3 m   (b) 2 Hz

    (c) 2 s   (d) 0.5 s.

[RRB SSE 2015 2nd SEP 2nd SHIFT]

65. If atmospheric refraction did not occur, which of the following statements about apparent time of sunrise and sunset is correct?

    (a) Sunrise would be late and sunset earlier.

    (b) Sunrise would be earlie and sunset later.

    (c) Both would be earlier

    (d) Both would be later

[RRB SSE 2015 2nd SEP 2nd SHIFT]

66. Consider a conductor of area of cross-section A, length l and volume V. When a current I flows through it, heat is produced at a rate given by I^2 R . If j is the current density and ρ the resistivity, the rate at which heat is produced per unit volume of the conductor is

(a) j/ρ (b) $j^2\rho$

(c) Vj   (d) V^2/ρ

[RRB SSE 2015 2ⁿᵈ SEP 2ⁿᵈ SHIFT]

67. Why does one get a sinking feeling when going down a elevator?

(a) Weightlessness on our body.

(b) Speed is more than gravity

(c) Our body I no support.

(d) Our muscles become slow.

[RRB SSE 2015 2ⁿᵈ SEP 2ⁿᵈ SHIFT]

68. What causes the light of street lamp to look as if it has dark and light patches?

(a) Infraction   (b) Diffraction

(c) Refraction   (d) Infusion.

[RRB SSE 2015 2ⁿᵈ SEP 2ⁿᵈ SHIFT]

69. A lift weighing 1.96×10^4 N is supported by a steel cable. When the lift is moving up with an acceleration of 2.2 m/s², the tension in the cable is (G = 9.8 m/s²)

(a) 2.40×10^4 N   (b) 1.52×10^4 N

(c) 2.35×10^5 N   (d) 1.49×10^5 N.

[RRB SSE 2015 2ⁿᵈ SEP 3ʳᵈ SHIFT]

70. The escape speed from the surface of the Earth is 11.2 km/s. The mass of the moon is 1/81 that of the Earth and its radius is 1/4 that of the Earth. The escape speed for an object on the surface of the moon is

(a) 50.4 km/s   (b) 25.2 km/s

(c) 2.5 km/s   (d) 5.0 km/s.

[RRB SSE 2015 2ⁿᵈ SEP 3ʳᵈ SHIFT]

71. A 1 kg ball has zero kinetic and potential energy. Shashi drops the ball into a 15 m deep well. The sum of its kinetic and potential energy, just before it hits the bottom is (g = 9.8 m/s²)

(a) 0   (b) 294 J

(c) -147 J   (d) 147 J.

[RRB SSE 2015 2ⁿᵈ SEP 3ʳᵈ SHIFT]

72. The motion of an object is described by the equation x = 0.70 cos (π t/4   m, where t is in seconds. The frequency of the motion is

(a) (1/4) Hz   (b) (1/8) Hz

(c) 4 Hz   (d) 8 Hz.

[RRB SSE 2015 2ⁿᵈ SEP 3ʳᵈ SHIFT]

73. The wavelength of a monochromatic source is 460 nm in vacuum. Waves from the same source pass through a medium where the velocity of light is 2.1×10^8 m/s. The wavelength of the source in the medium is (c = 3×10^8 m/s)

(a) 657 nm   (b) 460 nm

(c) 161 nn   (d) 322 nm.

[RRB SSE 2015 2ⁿᵈ SEP 3ʳᵈ SHIFT]

74. Two resistors of 2 Ω and 3 Ω are connected in series between two points A and B. A third resistor of 5 Ω is also connected between the same points.. When points A and B are connected to terminals of a battery, power dissipated in the 5 Ω resistor is 10 W. The power dissipated in 2 Ω resistor is

(a) 1W   (b) 2W

(c) 3 W   (d) 4 W.

[RRB SSE 2015 2ⁿᵈ SEP 3ʳᵈ SHIFT]

75. A block of wood floats in water with 4/5th part under water. If it floats in another liquid 9/10th part floats under it. What will be the relative density of the second liquid?

(a) 0.89 g/ml   (b) 0.87 g/ml

(c) 0.90 g/ml   (d) 1.0 g/ml

[RRB SSE 2015 2ⁿᵈ SEP 3ʳᵈ SHIFT]

76. Which one is an example of the effect of Refraction in our everyday life?

(a) Halos are formed around street lights during foggy nights

(b) Moon appears blue on some days and bright orange on others

(c) Mirrors reflect distorted images and enlarge reflection .

(d) Colours of rainbow appear on rainy days in water pools on the road.

[RRB SSE 2015 2ⁿᵈ SEP 3ʳᵈ SHIFT]

77. Heat is the agent that transforms one state of water into another. What is the calorie of heat required to convert 1 gram of ice at 0 degrees centigrade to steam at 100 degrees centigrade?

(a) 660 calories   (b) 36 calories

(c) 40 calories   (d) 720 calories

[RRB SSE 2015 2ⁿᵈ SEP 3ʳᵈ SHIFT]

78. P and Q are two points at same distance from the Centre of a short electric dipole on axial line and equatorial line respectively. V1 and V2 are the resultant electric potential due to the dipole at P and Q . The only correct condition for V_1 and V_2 for this situation is

(a) $V_1 = 2V_2$ (b) $V_2 = 2V_1$

(c) $V_1 = 0; V_2 \neq 0$ (d) $V_2 = 0 \; V_1 \neq 0$

[RRB SSE 2015 3ʳᵈ SEP 1ˢᵗ SHIFT]

79. Kirchhoff's junction rule and loop rule for an electrical network are respectively based on

(a) Conservation of energy, Conservation of charge

(b) Conservation of charge, conservation of momentum

(c) Conservation of energy, conservation of momentum

(d) Conservation of charge, conservation of energy

[RRB SSE 2015 3ʳᵈ SEP 1ˢᵗ SHIFT]

80. Which one of the following is the correct statement for a photon of blue and red light of electromagnetic spectrum?

(a) Blue light and red light have equal energy and equal momentum.

(b) Blue light has higher momentum than red light

(c) Red light has higher momentum than blue light.

(d) Red light has higher energy than blue light

[RRB SSE 2015 3ʳᵈ SEP 1ˢᵗ SHIFT]

81. A double convex lens of focal length f is cut into two exactly similar parts in two different ways, once along the vertical line and second time along the horizontal line. The focal length of each part after cutting in two cases respectively will be

(a) $\dfrac{f}{2}; \dfrac{f}{2}$ (b) $\dfrac{f}{2}; f$

(c) $2f; \dfrac{f}{2}$ (d) $2f; f$

[RRB SSE 2015 3ʳᵈ SEP 1ˢᵗ SHIFT]

82. N_S and N_P represent the number of turns, E_S and E_P represent e.m.f and I_S and I_P represent current for the secondary coil and primary coil of an ideal transformer respectively. The completely correct relation between these quantities is

(a) $\dfrac{N_s}{N_P} = \dfrac{E_s}{E_P} = \dfrac{I_S}{I_P}$ (b) $\dfrac{N_s}{N_P} = \dfrac{E_P}{E_S} = \dfrac{I_P}{I_S}$

(c) $\dfrac{N_s}{N_P} = \dfrac{E_s}{E_P} = \dfrac{I_P}{I_S}$ (d) $\dfrac{N_s}{N_P} = \dfrac{E_P}{E_s} = \dfrac{I_s}{I_P}$

[RRB SSE 2015 3ʳᵈ SEP 1ˢᵗ SHIFT]

83. While conducting an experiment on photo - electric effect, the incident radiations of yellow light are replaced with radiations of violet light, keeping the same intensity. This will result in

(a) increase in photo electric current without any change in the kinetic energy of emitted electrons

(b) Decrease in kinetic energy of the emitted electrons without any change in the photo electric current.

(c) Increase in kinetic energy of the emitted electrons without any change in photoelectric current

(d) Decrease in photo electric current and increase in kinetic energy of the emitted electrons

[RRB SSE 2015 3ʳᵈ SEP 1ˢᵗ SHIFT]

84. In which one of the following scales of temperature are both freezing and boiling points of water higher than the others?

(a) Reaumur scale (b) Kelvin scale

(c) Fahrenheit scale (d) Centigrade scale

[RRB SSE 2015 3ʳᵈ SEP 1ˢᵗ SHIFT]

85. The unit of heat is calorie. 1 calorie yields the amount of heat required for raising the temperature of 1 gram of water by 1 degree centigrade from

(a) 14.5 degree centigrade to 15.5. degree centigrade

(b) 15.5 degree centigrade to 16.5 degre centigrade

(c) 16.5 degree centigrade to 17.5 degree centigrade

(d) 17.5 degree centigrade to 18.5 degree centigrade

[RRB SSE 2015 3ʳᵈ SEP 1ˢᵗ SHIFT]

86. Which one of the following types of lenses is used for correcting the defect of focus in the eye called astigmatism?

(a) Prismatic Lens (b) Concave Lens

(c) Convex Lens (d) Cylindrical lens

[RRB SSE 2015 3ʳᵈ SEP 2ⁿᵈ SHIFT]

87. Four equal and similar point electric charges are kept at four corners of a square.

If E and V represent the resultant electric field and electric potential respectively at the Centre of the square, which are of the following is correct for this arrangement?

(a) $E \neq 0 ; V \neq 0$ (b) $E = 0 ; V = 0$

(c) $E = 0; V \neq 0$ (d) $E \neq 0 ; V = 0$

[RRB SSE 2015 3ʳᵈ SEP 2ⁿᵈ SHIFT]

88. Identify the only wrong statement from the following for Binding Energy of a nucleus.

(a) It is the energy released when free nucleons combine together to form the nucleus.

(b) It is the energy required to split up the nucleus into its constituent nucleons.

(c) It is equal to the difference of rest mass energies of all the nucleons and the rest mass energy of the nucleus.

(d) It is equal to sum of rest mass energies of all the nucleons.

[RRB SSE 2015 3ʳᵈ SEP 2ⁿᵈ SHIFT]

89. You have four convex lens A, B, C and D of focal length f_1, f_2, f_3 and f_4 respectively such that $f_2 < f_1 < f_4 < f_3$. Which of the two lenses should be used to design an astronomical telescope having maximum magnifying power?

(a) A and B

(b) B and D

(c) C and B

(d) A and D

[RRB SSE 2015 3rd SEP 2nd SHIFT]

90. Out of an ammeter, a milli ammeter, a voltmeter and a milli voltmeter, which pair of the instruments have maximum and minimum resistance respectively?

(a) Voltmeter ; Milli ammeter

(b) Voltmeter; Ammeter

(c) Milli voltmeter ; Ammeter

(d) Milli voltmeter; Milli ammeter

[RRB SSE 2015 3rd SEP 2nd SHIFT]

91. When a ray of light enters for air into glass, its:

(a) Speed decrease, frequency remains the same and wave-length decreases.

(b) Speed decreases, frequency and wavelength remains the same

(c) Speed increases, frequency and wavelength remains the same

(d) Speed increases, frequency increases and wavelength remains the same.

[RRB SSE 2015 3rd SEP 2nd SHIFT]

92. The material used for making permanent magnets should have:

(a) Low retentively, Low permeability, High coactivity

(b) High retentively, Low permeability, Low coactivity

(c) High permeability, Low retentivity, Low coactivity

(d) High retentively, High permeability, High coactivity

[RRB SSE 2015 3rd SEP 2nd SHIFT]

93. When a body is moving along a circular path with constant speed

(a) Work done on it is zero.

(b) Force acting on it is zero.

(c) Its velocity remains constant

(d) Its acceleration is zero

[RRB SSE 2015 3rd SEP 3rd SHIFT]

94. According to Bohr's theory of hydrogen atom, the spectral lines corresponding to transitions from higher energy levels to energy level n = 2 belong to

(a) P fund series

(b) Lyman series

(c) Panchen series

(d) Balmer series

[RRB SSE 2015 3rd SEP 3rd SHIFT]

95. The working of an optical fibre is bases on

(a) Dispersion of light

(b) Total internal reflection

(c) Polarisation of light

(d) Diffraction of light

[RRB SSE 2015 3rd SEP 3rd SHIFT]

96. Fleming's Right Hand Rule is used for the determination of direction of

(a) Force acting on a current carrying conductor kept in a magnetic field

(b) Motion of a current carrying conductor kept in on electric field.

(c) Current induced in a conductor Due to its motion in a magnetic field

(d) Deflection of a charged particle moving a magnetic field

[RRB SSE 2015 3rd SEP 3rd SHIFT]

97. Which one of the following statements is correct?

(a) Resistance of semiconductor material increases with rise in temperature

(b) Internal resistance of a cell depends on the distance between its electrodes.

(c) An alloy of tin and lead is used to make the element of an electric heater

(d) Drift Velocity of electrons in a metal does not depend upon mass of the electron.

[RRB SSE 2015 3rd SEP 3rd SHIFT]

98. A and B are two points at same distance from the centre of a short electric dipole on axial line and equatorial line respectively. E_1 and E_2 are respectively the resultant electric fields due to the dipole at these points. Identify the only correct condition between E_1 and E_2 from the following for this situation

(a) $E_1 = 4 E_2$

(b) $E_2 = 4 E_1$

(c) $E_1 = E_2$

(d) $E_1 = 2E_2$

[RRB SSE 2015 3rd SEP 3rd SHIFT]

ANSWERS

RRB JUNIOR ENGINEER

1. (b)	2. (b)	3. (b)	4. (a)	5. (c)	6. (d)	7. (d)	8. (d)	9. (b)	10. (b)
11. (c)	12. (c)	13. (c)	14. (a)	15. (a)	16. (b)	17. (d)	18. (a)	19. (d)	20. (c)
21. (a)	22. (d)	23. (a)	24. (a)	25. (d)	26. (b)	27. (a)	28. (c)	29. (d)	30. (b)
31. (c)	32. (a)	33. (b)	34. (b)	35. (b)	36. (a)	37. (c)	38. (c)	39. (a)	40. (d)
41. (b)	42. (c)	43. (c)	44. (c)	45. (b)	46. (a)	47. (d)	48. (b)	49. (a)	50. (a)
51. (a)	52. (a)	53. (a)	54. (d)	55. (b)	56. (b)	57. (a)	58. (b)	59. (c)	60. (a)
61. (c)	62. (d)	63. (b)	64. (c)	65. (a)	66. (c)	67. (d)	68. (b)	69. (a)	70. (a)
71. (c)	72. (a)	73. (d)	74. (c)	75. (b)	76. (a)	77. (c)	78. (b)	79. (d)	80. (a)
81. (a)	82. (c)	83. (c)	84. (b)	85. (c)	86. (a)	87. (d)	88. (a)	89. (c)	90. (c)
91. (a)	92. (a)	93. (c)	94. (c)	95. (c)	96. (a)	97. (d)	98. (a)	99. (c)	100. (b)
101. (b)	102. (b)	103. (a)	104. (a)	105. (d)	106. (b)	107. (d)	108. (c)	109. (c)	110. (a)
111. (b)	112. (a)	113. (a)	114. (a)	115. (b)	116. (c)	117. (b)	118. (d)	119. (d)	120. (b)
121. (d)	122. (d)	123. (b)	124. (d)	125. (c)	126. (d)	127. (b)	128. (a)		

RRB SENIOR SECTION ENGINEER

1. (c)	2. (b)	3. (a)	4. (c)	5. (c)	6. (*)	7. (*)	8. (d)	9. (d)	10. (b)
11. (d)	12. (b)	13. (b)	14. (a)	15. (d)	16. (d)	17. (c)	18. (c)	19. (b)	20. (c)
21. (c)	22. (b)	23. (b)	24. (b)	25. (c)	26. (d)	27. (a)	28. (a)	29. (a)	30. (c)
31. (b)	32. (d)	33. (a)	34. (d)	35. (b)	36. (a)	37. (d)	38. (a)	39. (a)	40. (a)
41. (c)	42. (b)	43. (a)	44. (d)	45. (c)	46. (a)	47. (c)	48. (a)	49. (d)	50. (b)
51. (d)	52. (c)	53. (d)	54. (c)	55. (b)	56. (d)	57. (d)	58. (b)	59. (a)	60. (d)
61. (b)	62. (c)	63. (a)	64. (c)	65. (a)	66. (b)	67. (a)	68. (b)	69. (a)	70. (c)
71. (a)	72. (b)	73. (d)	74. (d)	75. (a)	76. (d)	77. (d)	78. (d)	79. (d)	80. (b)
81. (d)	82. (c)	83. (c)	84. (b)	85. (a)	86. (d)	87. (c)	88. (d)	89. (c)	90. (b)
91. (a)	92. (d)	93. (a)	94. (d)	95. (b)	96. (c)	97. (b)	98. (d)		

EXPLANATIONS

RRB JUNIOR ENGINEER

1. All 3 points are true about charged particle in cyclotron whose speed increases. Particle moves to a larger circle, its relativistic mass changes because of speed change and frequency of cyclotron has to be adjusted.

2. When two resistances are in parallel, the formula gives the value of combined resistance of the circuit.

3. Earth conductor allows path for the leakage current in the body of the equipment or tool to ground.

4. Work done is zero because force is always perpendicular to the direction of movement of the earth. Also another way to look at this is earth returns to the same point after one revolution so work done must be zero as there are no latent energy forms involved.

5. Choke works on inductance principle. The function of choke is to provide high voltage enough for ionization to take place in a tube light and after establishment and sustenance of ionization, limit the voltage across the tube. That is the reason why a tube fuses when the choke is shorted.

6. Force = m.a Here $m = m_1 + m_2$ But force applied is m_2g. Therefore acceleration = F/m.

7. All the statements are correct. Speed of light changes in different media and it is different for different colours in media other than vacuum.

8. The uncertainty of position and momentum of particle in Heisenberg's Uncertainly principle cannot be reduced because it is inherent.

10. Archimedes' principle states that the upward buoyant force that is exerted on a body immersed in a fluid, whether fully or partially submerged, is equal to the weight of the fluid that the body displaces and acts in the upward direction at the center of mass of the displaced fluid.

11. Force is a vector quantity. F = m.a and the direction of acceleration will determine the direction of force.

12. Whenever two vector quantities are added, their resultant vector is given by this formula.

$$\sqrt{P^2 + Q^2 + 2PQ\cos\theta}$$

13. A cyclotron accelerates charged particles outwards from the center along a spiral path. The particles are held to a spiral trajectory by a static magnetic field and accelerated by a rapidly varying (radio frequency) electric field.

14. Both protons and neutrons are found in the nucleus and are together called nucleons. However, electrons revolve in orbits outside of the nucleus.

15. $v^2 - u^2 = 2as$
$\Rightarrow 0 - (196)^2 = -2 \times 9.8 \times S$
$S = 1960$

16. Water had maximum density at 4 degrees Celsius. It is $1g/cm^3$. And ice is lighter than water.

17. Since the current and magnetic field are perpendicular to each other, their vector multiplication would be zero. So no net force would be applied.

18. Ampere is the unit of current which is rate of flow of charge. So Ampere second is unit of charge.

19. Power loss is given by I^2R or V^2R.

20. Capacitance = Charge/Voltage, so here capacitance = 1/10 = 0.1 f

21. In street lighting all bulbs are connected in parallel because all bulbs should get the entire voltage across to be able to provide bright light.

22. Electric field strength is inversely proportional to square of distance. So decreases accordingly with distance.

23. The lens equation can be used to calculate the image distance for either real or virtual images and for either positive or negative lenses. Here 'f' is focus and 'v' is distance of image from lens while 'u' is distance of object from lens.

$$\frac{1}{u} + \frac{1}{v} = \frac{1}{f}$$

24. Magnifying glass is just a convex lens where image created is larger than object.

25. Atomic number is always determined by the number of protons, since electrons can increase or decrease depending on ionization. And neutrons are not charged particles, so they add to atomic mass but can't be used for atomic number.

26.

$$M = \frac{F}{g} = \frac{49}{98} = 5kg$$

Net force = m × a = 5 × 0.2 = 1N

27. Since moon's mass is 1/6th of earth, therefore weight of the body would reduce to 1/6th.

28. Work done = Force applied x Displacement. Therefore here it is 30 x 10 = 300

29. The wave does one cycle in 0.02 seconds.

Therefore frequency $= \dfrac{1}{0.02} = 50\text{Hz}.$

30. The angle between incident ray and reflected ray is double of the angle of incidence. Therefore as the angle of incidence approaches 90 degree, it will approach 180 degrees.

31. $R_1 = 3$, $R_2 = 6$, $R_3 = 2$

$$R_1 \text{ parallel } = \dfrac{3 \times 6}{3 + 6} = 2$$

Total R = 2 + 2 = 4

$$\therefore \text{Current } = \dfrac{V}{I} = \dfrac{6}{4} = 1.5\text{A}$$

32. It is explained by Newton's first law of motion. An object at rest stays at rest and an object in motion stays in motion with the same speed and in the same direction unless acted upon by an unbalanced force. It is also called Law of Inertia.

33. Eclipse happens because path of light is obstructed by another heavenly body, and since light travels in straight line, it cannot cross the opaque obstacle.

34. Both iron and steel are magnetic, and so filings made of these get attracted by a magnet.

35. Increasing the temperature of a gas causes the gas molecules to collide more often. This increases the gas viscosity because the transfer of momentum between stationary and moving molecules is what causes gas viscosity. For a liquid, when it is heated, the viscosity decreases, which is the opposite effect as in gases.

36. An internal focus lens (sometimes known as IF) is a photographic lens design in which focus is shifted by moving the inner lens group or groups only, without any rotation or shifting of the front lens element. In such a telescope, concave lens is used.

37. M = 5, F = 12

$\therefore a = 2.4$

$$D = \dfrac{1}{2}\,at^2 = \dfrac{1}{2} \times 2.4 \times 2^2 = 4.8 \text{ m}$$

38. Gravitational force is directly proportional to masses of both the bodies and inversely proportional to the square distance between their cores.

39. Work done = Force x distance. And force = Mass x acceleration. So work done = 10 x 9.8 x 2 = 196J

40. A transverse wave is a moving wave that consists of oscillations occurring perpendicular (right angled) to the direction of energy transfer (or the propagation of the wave). So light waves are transverse like all electromagnetic waves. But sound waves are longitudinal because oscillations occur in the direction of energy transfer.

41. Once the light has come out of the slab it will again travel with its original speed.

42. Since the resistors are connected in series, the same current flows through them. Now when they are replaced by an equivalent resistor, same current will flow through it as well.

43. Human beings can't hear frequencies below 20 Hz unlike elephants, and above 20000 Hz unlike dogs and bats etc.

44. M = 1000, F = 5000

$$\therefore a = \dfrac{F}{M} = 5\text{m}/\text{s}^2$$

$v^2 - u^2 = 2as$

or $20^2 = 2 \times 5 \times S$

or $S = 40\text{m}$

45. Pressure $= \dfrac{\text{Force}}{\text{Area}} = \dfrac{19.6}{9(0.1)^2} = 1.96 \times 10^3 \text{ N/m}^2$

46. Power = Energy / Time . Here Power $= \dfrac{150}{5}$

$= 30$ W

47. Amplitude for longitudinal waves is one half the height difference between crest and trough so that is average height of either a crest or a trough.

48. $\dfrac{1}{u} + \dfrac{1}{v} = \dfrac{1}{f}$

$\Rightarrow \dfrac{1}{5} - \dfrac{1}{20} = \dfrac{1}{f}$ or f = 6.67

49. Resistance is inversely proportional to cross sectional area, directly proportional to length and depends on resistivity of material. Here Diameter of B is twice, so cross sectional area is 4 times. So $R_A = R_B$.

50. Friction helps our ankles apply force and on the ground and the opposite force helps us to walk.

51. Scissors is a first class lever because the fulcrum is between the load (object being cut) and effort (applied by our hands)

52. Blankets or other woolen materials when rubbed create static or frictional electricity due to movement of electrons.

53. $F = m.a$, here 'a' $= \dfrac{v}{t} = \dfrac{12}{0.3} = 40$

$\therefore F = 0.5 \times 40 = 20N$

54. Gravitational force is inversely proportional to distance squared. So close to surface of earth, acceleration also is inversely proportional to distance squared.

55. Kinetic energy $= \frac{1}{2}mv^2 = \frac{1}{2} \times 10 \times 5^2 = 125$ J.

56. wavelength = velocity/frequency. Here frequency

$= \dfrac{1}{1.5}$, So wavelength = 9m

57. When object is at focus the image is formed at infinity. At centre of curvature, image is also formed there, because centre of curvature is basically centre of circle from where if a ray hits the mirror, it will return to its original position. So when object is placed between focus and centre, image will be beyond the centre. So it will be real, larger than object and inverted.

58. $I = \dfrac{V}{R} = \dfrac{1.5 + 1.5}{100}$

Charge = time $\times$ I

$\therefore 270 = \dfrac{3}{100} \times t$

or t = 9000 seconds = 2.5 hours

59. Ammeter is used to measure current in circuits.

60. In a bicycle pump when we compress air in the pump, its pressure increases and it gets filled in the bicycle tube.

61. $F_2 = 2F_1$ and $m_2 = m\dfrac{1}{2}$. So $a_2 = a_1 \times 2 / \frac{1}{2} = 4a$

62. Gravitational force is inversely proportional to distance squared. So when distance doubles force becomes $\frac{1}{4}$.

63. power $= \dfrac{\text{Energy}}{\text{Time}}$, so here time $= \dfrac{320}{64} = 5s$.

64. velocity of wave = wavelength x frequency. When frequency is doubled, wavelength will become half since velocity is same.

65. When object is placed at focus, its light becomes parallel after passing through the lens. So image is formed at infinity. However if it is placed before the focus, its image will remain erect, virtual but enlarged, with a maxima going towards infinity.

66. Power dissipated $= V^2/R$. Here when resistors are in series, resistance = 2R. When in parallel, resistance is $\dfrac{R}{2}$. Since resistance reduces by multiple of 4, power will increase by multiple of 4.

67. Momentum = mass x velocity. Here m= 1.5, velocity = 4 finally, and 0 initially. So momentum change = 4x 1.5 = 6 kgm/s.

68. Force due to gravity is proportional to masses of the bodies. And that divided by mass gives acceleration due to gravity. Since moon's mass is $\dfrac{1}{6}$ of earth, acceleration due to gravity $= \dfrac{g}{6}$.

69. Power x time gives energy spent or work done. So joule = watt x second.

70. Velocity of sound waves remains same even if waves are of different frequencies.

71. $\dfrac{1}{u} + \dfrac{1}{v} = \dfrac{1}{f}$

$\Rightarrow \dfrac{1}{u} + \dfrac{1}{v} = \dfrac{1}{f}$

or $\dfrac{2}{u} = \dfrac{1}{f}$

$\Rightarrow u = 2f$

72. $\rho\dfrac{l}{A} = R$

$\therefore \rho = \dfrac{1.6 \times 10^{-4}}{1} \times \pi (0.01)^2$

$= 5 \times 10^{-8}\,\Omega m$

73. Forces can do all activities mentioned here: push, pull, speed up, slow down, turn and change shape, change direction etc.

74. When we see ourselves in the mirror, our left side is seen as the right side of the image. So if I have a pen in my left hand, my image will have a pen in its right hand.

75. $F = m \cdot a$, $P = m \cdot v$, where P is momentum

so $\dfrac{P}{F} = \dfrac{v}{a}$

or $P = \dfrac{F.v}{a}$, and $\dfrac{v}{a} = $ time

so in 1 second, $P = 20 \times 1 = 20$ kg m/s

76. Mass of a body does not change basis location. So it will remain same.

77. Energy = force x distance. And force = mass x acceleration due to gravity. So 49 = 5 x 9.8 x height. So height = 1 m.

78. speed of wave = 344 m/s. frequency = 512 Hz. So

$$\text{wavelength } = \frac{344}{512} = 0.67 \text{ m.}$$

79. All images formed by concave lens are erect, virtual and smaller in size than the object.

80. $r = 5 \times 10^{-4}$m, $I = 0.5$A, $\rho = 1.1 \times 10^{-6}$ ohm-in

$\therefore$ Resistance per unit length

$$= \frac{\rho \times l}{Area} = \frac{1 \times 10^{-6} \times 1}{3.14 \times \left(5 \times 10^{-4}\right)^2} \simeq 1.4$$

So, V = I. R

$= 0.5 \times 1.4 = 0.7$

81. Mercury is a metal and hence very good conductor of heat. All others are insulators. Water becomes a good conductor where salts are dissolved in it.

83. Half life is 4 months. So in 4 months 50% of it will decrease. So in another 4 months remaining 50% will also half and become 75% reduction.

84. Momentum = mass x velocity. So kgm/s is a unit.

85. $v^2 - u^2 = 2as$

or $- (19.6)^2 = 2 \times (- 9.8) \times 5$

or $S = 19.6$m

86. Potential energy = mgh. Here 980 = 10 x 9.8 x h, so h = 10 m.

87. As speed of sound is more in water than air, and frequency does not depend on medium, so frequency remains same but wavelength increases. Since speed= frequency x wavelength.

88. As light ray has emerged from the glass slab, its speed will remain as same before it entered the glass slab.

89. In graph 1, velocity is increasing at a uniform rate. So acceleration is constant. That means force is also constant. Thus its graph when plotted will be a straight line parallel to x-axis.

90. $g = \dfrac{G.M_e}{R_e^{\,2}}$. Hence it is proportional to the mass of earth but inversely proportional to the square of the radius of the earth.

91. Power = potential energy gained / time. PE = mgh. Since time taken are same and mass of Rohan is 40 and Sohan is 60 so power delivered are same as time of climbing is also in same ratio.

92. Intensity of any wave is determined by its amplitude. So loudness of sound, which is basically intensity of sound also depends on amplitude.

93. Angle of reflection is always equal to angle of incidence. However, angle of refraction is less than angle of incidence if light travels from higher speed medium to lesser speed medium.

94. Resistance is directly proportional to resistivity. So resistance of 2nd wire is 2R. When both resistances are connected in series, total resistance = R+2R = 3R.

95. Force = mass x acceleration. Here acceleration is slope of the velocity time graph, so it is c. Therefore force = m.c

96. $g = \dfrac{GM}{R^2}$, So SI unit of G is Mm^2kg^{-2}

97. Change in kinetic energy

$$= \frac{1}{2}mv_2^2 - \frac{1}{2}mv_1^2$$

For option a : change $= \dfrac{1}{2}mv^2 - 0$

For option b : change

$$= \frac{1}{2}m\left[2v^2 - v^2 \right] = \frac{1}{2}.m\ 3v^2$$

For option c : change

$$= \frac{1}{2}m\left[\left(3v\right)^2 - \left(2v\right)^2 \right] = \frac{1}{2}.m.5v^2$$

For option d : change

$$= \frac{1}{2}m\left[\left(4v\right)^2 - \left(3v\right)^2 \right] = \frac{1}{2}.m.7v^2$$

So maximum work done is corresponds to maximum change in energy

98. Sound waves are longitudinal because oscillations occur in the direction of energy transfer. Thus particles move about their position of rest in a direction parallel to the direction of wave movement.

99. For concave mirror, parallel rays always move at the focus. And rays from the focus always move parallely after reflection. Thus they are used in places like car headlights etc.

100. When wire is cut, resistances of each part become R/2. When two same resistance are connected in parallel, the overall resistance of the circuit becomes half. So here it becomes $\dfrac{R}{4}$.

101. acceleration would always be in the direction of force. Here ball stops, means acceleration is negative to the direction of motion. So force is also in the same direction.

102. $g = \dfrac{GM}{R^2}$, So we get $\dfrac{g}{G} = \dfrac{M}{R^2}$

103. Potential energy at highest point = mgh. At half the height $PE = \dfrac{mgh}{2}$. It would be equal to the Kinetic energy of the ball, which is ½ mv². So mv² = mgh, or $v = (gh)^{\frac{1}{2}}$

104. Tuning forks produce sound waves in the laboratory which have a frequency which is multiple of the resonant frequency of the fork. So the highest frequency fork will produce the highest frequency wave. Since speed of sound is constant in a medium and speed = frequency x wavelength, so highest frequency wave will have lowest wavelength.

105. Image in a plane mirror is always erect, virtual and of the same size.

106. 1 Ampere current roughly equals a charge of 6×10^{18} coulomb per second passing through the medium. Since electrons are negatively charged, if current is towards right, means electrons are moving towards left.

107. From conservation of momentum, we get momentum gained by bullet = negative of momentum gained by gun. So mv = 100m x recoil velocity. So recoil velocity $= -\dfrac{v}{100}\dfrac{m}{s}$.

108. weight $= mg = \dfrac{GM_m}{R^2}$. Since M is halved and R is halved, new weight will become 1.g.2 or 2g N.

109. $KE = \dfrac{1}{2}mv^2$. Here $m_B = 2m_A$ and $KE_A = 2\,KE_B$, so putting in formula we get, $v_A = 2v_B$

110. When any wave travels, it has crests and troughs alternatively that are the highest and lowest intensity points. Similarly when sound waves travel they create compressions, which have the highest pressure and rarefactions, which have the lowest pressure alternatively.

111. Convex mirrors and plane mirrors always produce virtual images of finite objects because the reflected light rays never actually meet, but can only meet behind the mirror and produce virtual image.

112. 1 Ampere current roughly equals a charge of 6 x 10^{18} coulomb per second passing through the medium. Since electrons are negatively charged, if current is towards right, means electrons are moving towards left. Here current = 0.1 A, so electrons = 6×10^{17}

113. Bats emit ultrasonic waves, which are reflected by objects and reach the bats and help them identify objects or animals in the way and find their paths accordingly.

114. Complete transfer of kinetic energy happens only if both objects are of equal mass and it is elastic collision. In that mass the moving object stops and the stationary object starts moving at that speed.

115. Gravitational force and hence acceleration due to gravity is inversely proportional to distance squared. Here distance from earth's core of the object is R+h. So g is proportional to $(R+h)^{-2}$

116. As ball drops, its potential energy is getting converted to kinetic energy. At h/4, its potential energy = ¼ of original, and thus kinetic energy equals ¾ of original.

117. A transverse wave is a moving wave that consists of oscillations occurring perpendicular (right angled) to the direction of energy transfer (or the propagation of the wave). For example light waves are transverse like all electromagnetic waves.

118. When object is placed in front of convex mirror at less than focal length, the rays of light from it will be very divergent and won't meet. So image will be virtual and erect but diminished in size.

119. Resistance of 2nd wire is 2R since resistance is directly proportional to resistivity. So when R and 2R are connected in parallel, resistance $\dfrac{2R}{3}$

120. From conservation of momentum, we get momentum gained by bullet = negative of momentum gained by pistol. So mv = M x recoil velocity. So recoil velocity $= -\dfrac{vm}{M}\dfrac{m}{s}$.

121. Acceleration due to gravity is inversely proportional to distance squared of the bodies. As the height of object increases, it gets farther from earth's core so 'g' decreases.

122. When ball drops, potential energy is getting converted to Kinetic energy. PE was initially mgh and finally became 0. KE was initially 0. So final KE = ½ mv² = mgh . So v = (gh) ½

123. The sensation of a frequency is commonly referred to as the pitch of a sound. A high pitch sound corresponds to a high frequency sound wave and a low pitch sound corresponds to a low frequency sound wave.

124. Angle of reflection is always equal to angle of incidence. However, angle of refraction is more than angle of incidence if light travels from lower speed medium to higher speed medium.

125. When wire is cut, resistances of each part become $\dfrac{R}{4}$. When 4 same resistance are connected in parallel, the overall resistance of the circuit becomes ¼ . So here it becomes $\dfrac{R}{4}$ divided by 4 = $\dfrac{R}{16}$.

126. Tungsten is used to create the filament of incandescent bulbs because it does not melt or wear out at very high temperatures and it is very ductile so can be made into long thin wires to be coiled into a filament.

127. Voltmeter and Ammeter are 2 of the most widely used laboratory devices in electrical applications. Voltmeter measures the potential difference between two points and has a very high internal resistance.

128. Reflection of light from the mirror surface helps us see an identical image of the object.

RRB SENIOR SECTION ENGINEER

1. Manometer is an instrument in which doctor observes the rise and fall of mercury.

2. First law also known as law of conservation of energy, states that energy can neither the created not be destroyed in an Isolated system.

Second law of thermodynamics states hot the entropy of an isolated system always increase.

Third law of thermodynamics states that entropy of a system approaches a confound value as the temperature approaches absolute zero.

∴ Option (b) is correct.

3. Heavy current drawn by heavy load because it has low resistance and takes more power.

4. Boiling point of water is 373K.

5. Acid rain is caused by chemical reaction when compounds like sulphur dioxide and nitrogen oxides are released into air, these substance rize very high into atmosphere, where they mix and react with water, oxygen and other chemicals to form acid rain.

∴ Option (c) is correct.

6. Planet Venus has hot-turbulent atmosphere dominated by CO_2.

7. The frequency of tuning fork is
= 240 − 2 = 238 Hz

8. Tachymeter can measure rpm.

∴ Option (a) is correct.

9. All devices are used to measure temperature.

10. Copper has highest conductivity but low tensile strength compare to aluminium as copper is must costly so it is no used for transmission line.

11. $\dfrac{1}{u} + \dfrac{1}{4u} = \dfrac{1}{f}$

$\dfrac{5u}{4u^2} = \dfrac{1}{10}$

∴ u = 12.5 cm.

12. A barometer is an instrument used to measure atmospheric pressure.

∴ Option (b) is correct

13. $Pressure = \dfrac{Force}{Area} = \dfrac{mass \times acceleration}{Area}$

$\dfrac{M^1 \times L^1\, T^{-2}}{L^2}$

$M^1\, L^1\, T^{-2}$

∴ Option (b) is correct

14. $Refractive\ index = \dfrac{C}{V}$

$\therefore \dfrac{4}{3} = \dfrac{3 \times 10^8}{V}$

$\therefore V = \dfrac{9 \times 10^8}{4} = 2.25 \times 10^8 \text{ m/s}$

∴ Option (a) is correct

15. Emitted radiation

$\lambda = 4R\left[\dfrac{1}{4^2} - \dfrac{1}{6^2}\right] = 4R\left[\dfrac{1}{16} - \dfrac{1}{36}\right]$

$= 4R\left[\dfrac{36 - 16}{16 \times 36}\right] = 4R\left[\dfrac{20}{16 \times 36}\right]$

$\lambda = \dfrac{5R}{36}$

∴ Option (d) is correct

16. Heavy water is used as moderator in nuclear reactor. Because it is heavier than water but has same chemical prpoerties.

∴ Option (d) is correct

17. When a particle moves along a circular path with constant speed, its direction changes and if direction or speed changes acceleration comes into role.

∴ Option (c) is correct

18. According to Newton third low, if body is at rest on the surface of the earth, net downward force is equal to net upward force. Hence there is no unbalanced force to make allied move and so it is at rest

∴ Option (c) is correct

19. Specific heat for a substance is the amount of thermal energy that must be supplied (or removed) to (or from) unit mass of a substance to bring in its change in temperature by a unit degree.

And specific heat of gas in an isothermal process is infinite

∴ Option (b) is correct

20. In S.H.M, at mean position, kinetic energy is maximum ⇒ potential energy is minimum

∴ Option (c) is correct

21. Mirage is naturally occurring phenomena in which light rays tend to produce a displaced image of distant objects by total internal reflection of light

∴ Option (c) is correct

22. The curve given in option (b) is not possible for any motion because at same time it has 2 velocisations.

23. The specific volume of water when heated from 0°c first decreases and then increase because water at 4°C is dimension.

∴ Option (b) is correct

24. 1st law of thermodynamics states that energy is conserved. So heat energy transferred from are body will be absorbed by the other.

25. Two layers have different conductivity K_1 and K_2

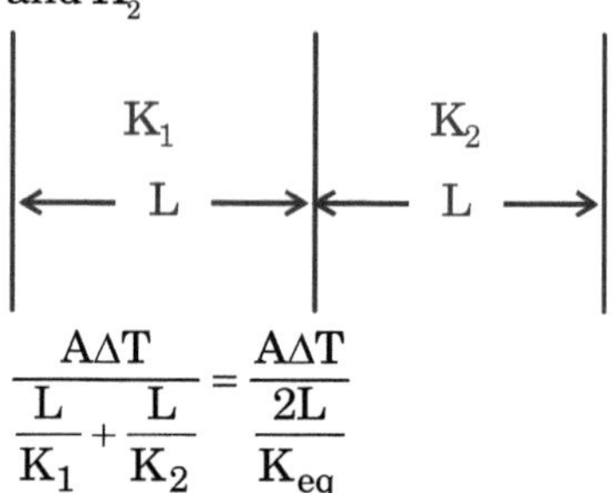

$$\frac{A\Delta T}{\dfrac{L}{K_1} + \dfrac{L}{K_2}} = \frac{A\Delta T}{\dfrac{2L}{K_{eq}}}$$

$$K_{eq} = \frac{2K_1 K_2}{K_1 + K_2}$$

∴ Option (c) is correct

26. Soft iron is used in manufacture of electromagnetic because of its high saturation limit and retentivity and coercive force is low.

27. Quartz is a piezo-electric material applied when pressure it generates collect rating.

28. If two conductors carry current in same direction they attract each other while two conductors carrying current in opposite direction repel each other.

∴ Option (a) is correct

29. $\dfrac{\text{correct length of tape}}{\text{Designated length of tape}}$

$$= \frac{\text{correct length of line}}{\substack{\text{length of line observed} \\ \text{with the tape}}}$$

$$\frac{\text{correct length tape}}{20} = \frac{200}{200.8}$$

∴ Correct length of tape $= \dfrac{200 \times 20}{200.8} = 19.92\text{m}$

∴ Option (a) is correct

30. Equals & opposite force

31. $mg_1 = \dfrac{GmM}{R^2}$, M is mass of earth & 'm' is mass of anybody

$$mg_2 = \frac{GmM}{(R+h)^2}$$

$$\Rightarrow \frac{g_1}{g_2} = \frac{(R+h)^2}{R^2}$$

or $g_2 = g\left(\dfrac{R^2}{R^2 + h^2 + 2h}\right) \simeq g\left(\dfrac{1}{1 + \dfrac{2h}{R} + h^2}\right)$

$$\simeq g\left(1 - \frac{2h}{R}\right) \text{ for small 'h'}$$

32. Work done by variable force is equal to sum of all infinitesimal work done in infinitesimal displacements. Here it would be integration of area under the curve F versus x.

33. At maximum displacement, velocity is zero but acceleration is maximum, which brings the object towards the equilibrium position.

34. Total internal reflection is a special case of refraction where the incident ray can't travel to the next medium but gets reflected internally. So no light is refracted at glass-air interface.

35. emf is dimensionally equivalent to joule/coulomb, because charge into potential difference leads to energy change.

36. Violet has the shortest wavelength and it is refracted the most.

37. In astronomy, Kepler's laws of planetary motion are three scientific laws describing the motion of planets around the Sun. The orbit of a planet is an ellipse with the Sun at one of the two foci. The same laws govern the movement of satellites in space.

38. Those on top of mount Everest show decrease in acceleration due to gravity due to the earth because of increased distance from the earth's core. So even though mass remains same, weight decreases. g(Everest) = g(1-2 x height of Everest/ Radius of earth)

39. Radhey has to take the box up an incline, and not directly vertical. So to reach a height H, he has to travel longer than H. Even though potential energy gained by box is equivalent to that when height increases by H. So force applied (Which is tension in the rope) would be less than the weight of the box.

40. $mg_1 = \dfrac{GmM}{R^2}$, M is mass of earth & 'm' is m a s s of anybody

$$mg_2 = \dfrac{GmM.(R-d)^3}{(R-d)^2.R^3}$$

$$\dfrac{g_1}{g_2} = \dfrac{R^3(R-d)^2}{(R-d)^3.R^2} = \dfrac{R}{R-d}$$

or $g_2 = g_1\left(1 - \dfrac{d}{R}\right)$

41. An open pipe has double the resonance frequency of the same length pipe closed at one end, because the wavelength is half.

42. Power can be directly added for this lenses so focal length can be added reciprocally. Here power doubles so focal length is halved when two lenses are put together.

43. Since speed of light is higher than sound, the sound and light are produced at the same time during thunderstorms but light reaches us faster.

44. When ball is shot up, speed decrease, and momentum also thus decreases. There is constant gravitational force acting on it. So only increase is in Inertia.

45. Electric bulbs use inert gases so that they are stable at higher temperatures.

46. If the lift is accelerating upwards, the force exerted by the floor of the life on Alka's foot would be more than Alka's weight because her weight would become W=m(g+a), where m is Alka's mass, g is acceleration due to gravity and a is acceleration.

47. The total energy of a satellite is just the sum of its gravitational potential and kinetic energies. The centripetal force on a satellite in a circular orbit is provided by gravity. Here 2 x Kinetic Energy + Potential energy = 0. Therefore magnitude of potential energy is twice of kinetic energy.

48. Complete transfer of kinetic energy happens only if both objects are of equal mass and it is elastic collision. In that mass the moving object stops and the stationary object starts moving at that speed.

49. Only in this case the wave's frequency is not dependent on the value 'x' but on time. Therefore, it depicts a standing wave with find amplitude of different values of 'x'.

50. Power can be directly added for lenses but focal length can be added reciprocally. Here power doubles when two lenses are put together.

51. Electromotive force actually is a measure of potential difference and not force.

52. This is a practical case of decreasing deceleration to decrease the force applied. Since Force applied is directly proportional to acceleration of a body, here the player reduces force on hand by drawing hands backwards to decelerate the ball to zero speed.

53. Geostationary satellites are always overhead a particular point of earth, that is they are stationary relative to the earth. So they have to keep a time period of 24 hours to match the earth's time period of rotation.

54. Since Radha slides the box on a frictionless surface force applied by her would be zero. Since work done is vector multiplication of force and displacement, it is zero here. Similarly when Mohan moves the box, there is no net energy gained by the box, therefore no net work is done on the box. Mohan lifted the box and put it down so that cancels net work. When Mohan carried the box horizontally, it is on a frictionless surface that he is walking, so no net energy expended.

55. All waves are sign functions, so net velocity would be zero. But in option B, magnitude of wave is 4.3 units which is the highest so it is travelling the longest distances, hence speed would be maximum.

56. Power of lenses can directly be added. So net power is 4P.

57. Electric field between the plates of capacitor is constant throughout the space between the plates in a straight line. This leads to constant drop in potential.

58. The body will float in the liquid fully submersed just below the surface. Now when pressed slightly and released, it will return to the same position which is the equilibrium position.

59. Barometer measures atmospheric pressure, and is also used to predict weather, because pressure differences lead to movement of air.

60. When ships move eastward, they slow down because earth's rotation from west to east results in gravity seeming to fade away a little due to centrifugal force.

61. Net force leads to acceleration. $F = m.a$. But here since velocity is constant means no acceleration, so $F = 0$.

62. Weight $= G\dfrac{m_1 m_2}{r^2}$

$$66.7 = 6.67 \times 10^{-11} \times \dfrac{1.6 \times m_2}{(4 \times 10^6)^2}$$

$$\Rightarrow m_2 = \dfrac{66.7 \times 16 \times 10^{12}}{6.67 \times 10^{-11} \times 1.6} = 10^{25}\,\text{kg}$$

63. Net work done = Net force x Displacement
$= (49 - 26) \times 5 = 23 \times 5 = 115\ \text{J}$

64. Since the SHM is a sin function, its period is 2 seconds, because in 2 seconds it will traverse the entire cycle completely.

65. If atmospheric refraction did not occur, rays travelling from the sun would reach people on earth slightly later, as due to refraction the angle of rays changes when it enters the atmosphere and reaches us faster. The reverse would happen at sunset. So sunrise would be late and sunset earlier (only fraction of record).

66. $j = \dfrac{I}{A}, P = R\dfrac{A}{l}$

$$\dfrac{\text{Heat}}{V} = \dfrac{I^2 R}{V} = \dfrac{J^2 A^2 . Pl}{A.A.l} = j^2 P$$

67. When going down an elevator, one feels weightlessness because of the free fall. Only gravitational force is acting on the body. So one starts feeling sick, as it is an unusual state for the body.

68. Because of the phenomenon of Diffraction through the air, light from street lamp looks as if it has light and dark patches.

69. Tension $= \dfrac{w \times (g + a)}{g} = \dfrac{1.96 \times 10^4 \times 12}{9.8}$

$= 2.40 \times 10^4 \text{N}$

70. $F = G\dfrac{m_1 m_2}{r^2}$

$$\Rightarrow \dfrac{F_1}{F_2} = \dfrac{Gm_1 m_2}{R^2} \times \dfrac{r^2}{Gm_1 m_2}$$

$$\Rightarrow \dfrac{F_1}{F_2} = \dfrac{V_1}{V_2} = \dfrac{81}{16}$$

$$\Rightarrow v_2 = \dfrac{11.2 \times 16}{81} = 2.2$$

Only option 'c' is close

71. Since no external force is applied on the ball, its potential energy is getting converted to kinetic energy. But no energy is gained. So net energy is 0.

72. This cosine function wave will complete one cycle in 8 seconds, therefore its period is 8 and frequency is 1/8 Hz.

73. $w_1 f_1 = v_1$
$w_2 f_2 = v_2$
But $f_1 = f_2$

$\therefore \dfrac{w_2}{w_1} = \dfrac{v_2}{v_1}$

or $w_2 = \dfrac{2.1 \times 10^8}{3 \times 10^8} \times 460\ \text{nm}$

$= 322\ \text{nm}$

74. Power dissipated in resistor is equal to $I^2 R$. Since both the two sets of resistors have same value of 5 ohm, therefore same current will flow through them when connected in parallel. So 10W power would be dissipated in 2 and 3 ohm resistor combined. 4W in 2 ohm and 6W in 3 ohm.

75. $d_w = \dfrac{4}{5}$

$d_l = \dfrac{4}{5} \times \dfrac{10}{9} = 0.89\ \text{g/ml}$

76. Rainbow colours appear because of the phenomenon of refraction of light through water pools on road.

77. Heat required to convert ice to steam needs heat for ice at 0° to water at 0°. Then from water at 0°. to water at 100°. Then water at 100° to steam at 100°. The total for 1 gm of ice is 720 calories.

78. $V_2 = 0$ always since equidistant from both ends of the dipole but V_1 is not zero as potential changes in between the ends of the dipole.

79. Kirchoff's junction rule states that current coming at a point would be equal to current leaving, so it is based on conservation of charge. Loop rule is based on conservation of energy because when you travel a complete loop, there should not be a change in potential.

80. Blue light has higher frequency and higher energy. Momentum = mc and $E=mc^2$. Since E/momentum = c, which is fixed light speed therefore blue light has higher momentum also.

81. Power can be directly added but focal length can be added reciprocally. So when lens is cut vertically its power will halve and focal length will double. When cut horizontally, there will be no change of focal length.

82. In transformers number of turns is directly proportional to e.m.f but e.m.f. is inversely proportional to current flow, to conserve energy.

83. Since the violet light has more energy per photon than yellow light, it will also release the same number of electrons (because intensity is same, so photon count will remain same) but provide them with extra kinetic energy.

84. Kelvin scale has 0 at -273 degree Celsius. Therefore freezing point of water is 273K and boiling point is 373K.

85. This is the standard definition of calorie.

86. Astigmatism is a type of refractive error in which the eye does not focus light evenly on the retina. This results in distorted or blurred vision at all distances. Thus cylindrical lenses are used to correct this defect of focus.

87. Electric field at the centre of the rectangle would be zero because of equal charges being equidistant. However there will be an electric potential created because of the charges. Hence potential won't be zero.

88. Only option D is incorrect as all other represent the Binding energy of the nucleus.

89. For maximum magnifying power of astronomical telescope, we should use the lenses which have the highest and the lowest focal lengths. Hence C and B.

90. Voltmeter has the maximum resistance since it should not let current flow otherwise that would disturb its reading. Ideal voltmeter has infinite resistance. Ammeter has minimum resistance since it should not obstruct current.

91. When light enters from air into glass its speed decreases. Since frequency can't change so wavelength also decreases. This phenomenon is called refraction.

92. Materials to be made into magnets must have high retentivity, so that they can remain magnets when external magnetic field is removed. High permeability is needed so that entire material is magnetized and coactivity also helps.

93. Force is continuously getting applied in circular motion but its direction keeps changing. Also speed remains constant but velocity will differ because of direction. And there is acceleration because of the force. However net work done is zero because force and displacement are always perpendicular.

95. Total internal reflection is a case of refraction when light falls on an angle that the refracted ray is not able to leave the originating medium. Optical fibre works on this principle, where minimum loss of signal in form of light takes place.

96. Fleming's Right-hand Rule (for generators) shows the direction of induced current when a conductor attached to a circuit moves in a magnetic field. The right hand is held with the thumb, index finger and middle finger mutually perpendicular to each other (at right angles)

97. Internal resistance of a cell depends on the distance between its electrodes and its electrolytic solution.

98. This comes from the electric field formula of a short electric dipole.

CHEMISTRY

RRB JUNIOR ENGINEER

1. Hadrons and Baryons are
   (a) Industrial chemicals
   (b) Types of subatomic particles
   (c) Alkalies
   (d) Cyclotrons
   [RRB JE 2014 GREEN SHIFT]

2. Which of the following is a heterogeneous mixture?
   (a) Brass
   (b) Sugar solution in water
   (c) Air
   (d) Milk
   [RRB JE 2014 GREEN SHIFT]

3. A class of compounds which are used as fragrances when molecular weight is low and are naturally occurring fats when molecular weight is high in the series, is called
   (a) amino acids   (b) aromatic compounds
   (c) esters   (d) organic acids
   [RRB JE 2014 GREEN SHIFT]

4. Disinfection of drinking water is done to remove:
   (a) Odour   (b) Bacterias
   (c) Turbidity   (d) Colour
   [RRB JE 2014 RED SHIFT]

5. Global warming is caused by :
   (a) N_2 (b) CO_2
   (c) Ozone   (d) None of these
   [RRB JE 2014 RED SHIFT]

6. What is the General formula of Alkanes ?
   (a) C_nH_{2n+2} (b) C_nH_{2n}
   (c) C_nH_{2n-2} (d) C_nH_{2n+4}
   [RRB JE 2014 RED SHIFT]

7. The pollutant responsible for ozone holes is :
   (a) CO_2 (b) CO
   (c) SO_2 (d) CFC
   [RRB JE 2014 RED SHIFT]

8. Ammonia is prepared commercially by the :
   (a) Oswald process   (b) Hall process
   (c) Contact process   (d) Haber process
   [RRB JE 2014 RED SHIFT]

9. The elements which have same mass number but different atomic numbers are know as :
   (a) Isotones   (b) Isobars
   (c) Isotopes   (d) Halogens
   [RRB JE 2014 RED SHIFT]

10. Which one of the following is not a Noble Gas ?
   (a) Helium   (b) Bromine
   (c) Argon   (d) Neon
   [RRB JE 2014 RED SHIFT]

11. Major contributing activity towards Global Warming by Greenhouse gases
   (a) Agriculture   (b) Deforestation
   (c) Energy   (d) lndustry
   [RRB JE 2014 YELLOW SHIFT]

12. Electrostatic Precipitators are devices for
   (a) Particulate Emission Control
   (b) Water Pollution Control
   (c) Noise Pollution Control
   (d) Energy Pollution Control
   [RRB JE 2014 YELLOW SHIFT]

13. Biochemical Oxygen Demand (BOD) is a measure of
   (a) Oxygen utilized during oxidation of organic matters
   (b) Suspended particles in water
   (c) Suspended particles in air
   (d) Noise level in air
   [RRB JE 2014 YELLOW SHIFT]

14. Biodegradable pollutants are
   (a) quickly degraded by natural means
   (b) can not be degraded
   (c) can be degraded by burning only
   (d) disposed in flowing water only
   [RRB JE 2014 YELLOW SHIFT]

15. The state in which molecular attractions are very strong is
   (a) Solid   (b) Liquid
   (c) Gas   (d) Vapour
   [RRB JE 2014 YELLOW SHIFT]

16. Which of the following acids is present in sour milk?
    (a) Glycolic Acid   (b) Lactic Acid
    (c) Citrus Acid   (d) Tartaric Acid
    [RRB JE 2014 YELLOW SHIFT]

17. Elements belonging to the same group have similar chemical properties because
    (a) they are all metallic elements
    (b) they have similar electronic configuration
    (c) atomic number increases on moving down the group
    (d) None of these
    [RRB JE 2014 YELLOW SHIFT]

18. Which of the following alloys contains Tin ?
    (a) Brass   (b) Solder
    (c) Duralumin   (d) steel
    [RRB JE 2014 YELLOW SHIFT]

19. The number of atoms in a body centred unit cell is
    (a) 1   (b) 2
    (c) 3   (d) 4
    [RRB JE 2015 26th AUG 1st SHIFT]

20. What is the value of $\underline{\mathbf{X}}$ in the following equation?
    $$MnO_2 + X\ HCl \longrightarrow MnCl_2 + 2\ H_2O + Cl_2$$
    (a) 2   (b) 3
    (c) 4   (d) 5
    [RRB JE 2015 26th AUG 1st SHIFT]

21. Which of the following element is lustrous in nature?
    (a) Carbon   (b) Iodine
    (c) Sulphur   (d) Nitrogen
    [RRB JE 2015 26th AUG 1st SHIFT]

22. In Modern Periodic Table, the electronegativity of elements
    (a) Increases down the group
    (b) Increases in moving from left to right
    (c) Decreases in moving from left to right in a period
    (d) Does not follow any regular trend in a group or a period
    [RRB JE 2015 26th AUG 1st SHIFT]

23. A trivalent metal "M" was made to react with nitrogen to yield 0.5 mole of metal nitride. Which of the following is a correct statement about the product of this reaction? There reaction product contains
    (a) 3.0165×10^{23} molecules of oxide of formula M_3N
    (b) 3.0165×10^{23} molecules of oxide of formula M_3N
    (c) $3.0165 \times 10^{11.5}$ molecules of oxide of formula M_3N
    (d) $3.0165 \times 10^{11.5}$ molecules of oxide of formula MN
    [RRB JE 2015 26th AUG 1st SHIFT]

24. How many C-H bonds are there in a molecule of ethanoic acid?
    (a) 6   (b) 5
    (c) 4   (d) 3
    [RRB JE 2015 26th AUG 1st SHIFT]

25. 49 mL of 0.1 M sodium hydroxide solution is added to 50 mL of 0.1 M solution of nitric acid. Approximate pH of the resulting solution will be
    (a) 3   (b) 7
    (c) 8   (d) 13
    [RRB JE 2015 26th AUG 1st SHIFT]

26. Bleaching powder is manufactured through a reaction between
    (a) Flaked lime and chlorine
    (b) Quicklime and chlorine
    (c) Washing soda and ammonia
    (d) Baking soda and iodine
    [RRB JE 2015 26th AUG 1st SHIFT]

27. It is possible to make LPG available in a cylinder because of its
    (a) Inflammability   (b) Dispersibility
    (c) Compressibility   (d) Diffusability
    [RRB JE 2015 26th AUG 1st SHIFT]

28. According to the law of constant proportions, what lass of oxygen would be present in a sample of carbon dioxide gas containing 3 grams of carbon?
    (a) 3 g   (b) 6 g
    (c) 8 g   (d) 12 g
    [RRB JE 2015 26th AUG 2nd SHIFT]

29. Which of the following is a process of galvanization?
    (a) Mixing of a metal with another metal by melting
    (b) Coating the surface of a metal with Zinc
    (c) Coating the surface of a metal with its oxide
    (d) Painting a metal
    [RRB JE 2015 26th AUG 2nd SHIFT]

30. Which element has the least number of valence electrons?
    (a) Chlorine   (b) Sodium
    (c) Fluorine   (d) Oxygen
    [RRB JE 2015 26th AUG 2nd SHIFT]

31. For the reaction, $2\,Na + H_2 \longrightarrow 2NaH$, which of the following statements are correct?

(i)   Na is oxidized

(ii) H_2 is oxidized

(iii) H_2 acts as an oxidizing agent

(iv) Na acts as an oxidizing agent

(a) (i & iii)   (b) (i & ii)

(c) (ii & iii)   (d) (ii & iv)

[RRB JE 2015 26th AUG 2nd SHIFT]

32. Which of the following compounds would react with sodium hydrogen carbonate to produce carbon dioxide gas?

(a) CH_3CH_2OH (b) CH_3CH_3

(c) $CH_2 = CH_2$ (d) CH_3COOH

[RRB JE 2015 26th AUG 2nd SHIFT]

33. In which of the following reactions does NH_3 act both as an acid and a base?

(a) $NH_3 + H_2O \longrightarrow NH_4^+ + OH$

(b) $2NH_3 \longrightarrow NH_2^- + NH_4^+$

(c) $NH_3 + HCl \longrightarrow NH_4^+ + Cl^-$

(d) $NH_3 + NaOH \longrightarrow NaNH_2 + H_2O$

[RRB JE 2015 26th AUG 2nd SHIFT]

34. Where would you place vinegar if you were to show its pH on a scale showing pH from 1 to 8 to?

(a) Left of 7   (b) Right of 7

(c) On 7   (d) On 8

[RRB JE 2015 26th AUG 2nd SHIFT]

35. For its complete combustion, one mole of an alkane required 3.5 mole of oxygen gas at the same temperature and pressure. What is the name of alkane?

(a) Methane   (b) Ethane

(c) Propane   (d) Butane

[RRB JE 2015 26th AUG 3rd SHIFT]

36. Which one of the following is a molecule of an element?

(a) Cl_2 (b) H_2S

(c) $NaCl$ (d) CO_2

[RRB JE 2015 26th AUG 3rd SHIFT]

37. Rancidity of oils and fats can be controlled by controlling the process of

(a) Decomposition   (b) Neutralization

(c) Reduction   (d) Oxidation

[RRB JE 2015 26th AUG 3rd SHIFT]

38. All element **X** contains only one electron in its outermost shell. Which of the following statements are correct about X ?

(i)   It forms an acidic oxide.

(ii) It forms a basic oxide.

(iii) It is a good conductor of electricity.

(iv) It has a dull and non lustrous surface.

(a) (i) & (iii)   (b) (ii) & (iii)

(c) (i) & (iv)   (d) (iii) & (iv)

[RRB JE 2015 26th AUG 3rd SHIFT]

39. Which one of the following can act as an olfactory indicator?

(a) Phenolphthalein

(b) Methyl orange

(c) Vanilla essence

(d) Litmus solution

[RRB JE 2015 26th AUG 3rd SHIFT]

40. Which one of the following elements is the most metallic in nature?

(a) Na   (b) Al

(c) Li   (d) B

[RRB JE 2015 26th AUG 3rd SHIFT]

41. You can make soap at home from vegetable oil and

(a) Caustic Potash

(b) Ammonium Hydroxide

(c) Caustic Soda

(d) Sodium Chloride

[RRB JE 2015 26th AUG 3rd SHIFT]

42. Students were asked to present a "balanced equation" regarding Photosynthesis. Which is the correct equation?

(a) $6CO_2 + H_2O \rightarrow C_6H_{12}O_6 + O_2$

(b) $6CO_2 + 6H_2O \rightarrow C_6H_{12}O_6 + 6O_2$

(c) $CO_2 + 6H_2O \rightarrow C_6H_{12}O_6 + O_2$

(d) $CO_2 + H_2O \rightarrow C_6H_{12}O_6 + O_2$

[RRB JE 2015 26th AUG 3rd SHIFT]

43. Which out of the F, Br, Ca and Mg which are important elements because their salts are useful to humans may be grouped as halogens?

(a) F and Br   (b) F and Ca

(c) Br and Mg   (d) Ca and Br

[RRB JE 2015 26th AUG 3rd SHIFT]

44. What is the value of **X** in the following equation; $4NH_3 + XO_2 \longrightarrow 4NO + 6H_2O$

(a) 2   (b) 3

(c) 4   (d) 5

[RRB JE 2015 27th AUG 1st SHIFT]

45. During the electrolytic refining of copper using copper sulphate as an electrolyte

(a) Impure copper is made the anode

(b) Impure copper is made the cathode

(c) (ii) only

(d) (iii)only

[RRB JE 2015 27th AUG 1st SHIFT]

46. The electronic configuration of an element is 2, 1. To which of the following elements will it be similar?

   (a) 2,1   (b) 2,8,4

   (c) 2,7   (d) 2,8,7

[RRB JE 2015 27th AUG 1st SHIFT]

47. A solution containing 80 grams of sodium hydroxide (molecular mass = 40) completely neutralizes another solution containing 98 grams of an acid **"A"** (molecular mass = 98). The charge on the anion part of **"A"** is

   (a) −1   (b) −2

   (c) −3   (d) −4

[RRB JE 2015 27th AUG 1st SHIFT]

48. Which of the following is a saponification reaction?

   (a) $CH_3COOH + NaOH \longrightarrow CH_3COONa + H_2O$

   (b) $2CH_3COOH + 2\,Na \longrightarrow 2CH_3COONa + H_2$

   (c) $2CH_3CH_2OH + Na \longrightarrow 2CH_3COONa + H_2$

   (d) $CH_3COOCH_3 + NaOH \longrightarrow CH_3COONa + CH_3OH$

[RRB JE 2015 27th AUG 1st SHIFT]

49. Which of the following is a molecule of an element?

   (a) Neon (g)

   (b) Chlorine (g)

   (c) Sulphur dioxide (g)

   (d) Water (I)

[RRB JE 2015 27th AUG 1st SHIFT]

50. Which of the following chemical equation represents the reaction of roasting process?

   (a) $ZnCO_3 \rightarrow ZnO + CO_2$

   (b) $ZnO + C \rightarrow Zn + CO$

   (c) $2CuS + O_2 \rightarrow 2CuO + 2SO_2$

   (d) $Cu + O_2 \rightarrow 2CuO$

[RRB JE 2015 27th AUG 2nd SHIFT]

51. The charges on aluminum and sulphate ions are +3 and −2 respectively. The correct molecular formula of aluminum sulphate is

   (a) $AlSO_4$ (b) $Al_3(SO_4)_2$

   (c) $Al_2(SO_4)_3$ (d) $Al_2(SO_4)_3$

[RRB JE 2015 27th AUG 2nd SHIFT]

52. Corrosion of iron is

   (a) Protection of its surface from atmospheric gases

   (b) A physical change

   (c) a process of oxidation

   (d) a process of Reduction

[RRB JE 2015 27th AUG 2nd SHIFT]

53. Which one of the following set of elements is written in increasing order of their atomic radii?

   (a) K Na Li   (b) Br F Cl

   (c) O F Cl   (d) O N P

[RRB JE 2015 27th AUG 2nd SHIFT]

54. Which one of the following is an amphoteric oxide?

   (a) Na_2O (b) SO_3

   (c) Ag_2O (d) ZnO

[RRB JE 2015 27th AUG 2nd SHIFT]

55. Which reaction of an alcohol would produce a sweet smelling compound?

   (a) Esterification   (b) Addition

   (c) Decomposition   (d) Dehydration

[RRB JE 2015 27th AUG 2nd SHIFT]

56. The decreasing order of reactivity of four metals is in the order: Zn > Fe > Cu > Ag. In view of the order of reactivity, which of the following reaction is feasible?

   (a) $CuSO_4 + 2Ag \rightarrow Ag_2SO_4 + 2Ag$

   (b) $ZnCl_2 + Cu \rightarrow CuCl_2 + Zn$

   (c) $2AgNO_3 + Cu \rightarrow Cu(NO_3)_2 + 2Ag$

   (d) $FeSO_4 + Cu \rightarrow CuSO_4 + Fe$

[RRB JE 2015 27th AUG 3rd SHIFT]

57. Sodium sulphate dissociates in water as follows:

$$Na_2SO_4 = 2Na^+ + SO_4^{2-}$$

What is the total number of ions present in the solution containing one mole of dissolved sodium sulphate in water?

   (a) 6.023×10^{23} (b) 12.046×10^{46}

   (c) 18.069×10^{69} (d) 18.069×10^{23}

[RRB JE 2015 27th AUG 3rd SHIFT]

58. Which of the following is an endothermic process?

Dissolution of

   (a) NH_4CI in water

   (b) NaOH in water

   (b) Quick lime in water

   (c) Sulphuric acid in water

[RRB JE 2015 27th AUG 3rd SHIFT]

59. An organic compound **X**. molecular mass = 46, undergoes dehydration reaction to yield the compound **Y**, the first member of olefin homologous series. What is the compound **X**?

   (a) Aldehyde   (b) Alcohol

   (c) Ester   (d) Carboxylic acid

[RRB JE 2015 27th AUG 3rd SHIFT]

60. The values of pH of four different solutions of salts W, X, Y, & Z respectively in water are 6.2, 6.5, 6.8 and 7.5 respectively. Which of them is a basic salt?

(a) W   (b) X

(c) Y   (d) Z

[RRB JE 2015 27th AUG 3rd SHIFT]

61. Which one of the following set of elements has the same number of valence electrons?

(a) Li Be Mg   (b) B Al Si

(c) Li Na K   (d) Li Na Mg

[RRB JE 2015 27th AUG 3rd SHIFT]

62. How can you know that vinegar is an acid?

(a) It will turn blue litmus red

(b) It will turn red litmus blue

(c) Phenolphthalein turns pink when added to vinegar

(d) Its pH will be more than 7

[RRB JE 2015 27th AUG 3rd SHIFT]

63. Alcohols are studied in Organic Chemistry because there are

(a) Hydrocarbons   (b) Silicon compounds

(c) Ring compounds   (d) Made C, O, N

[RRB JE 2015 27th AUG 3rd SHIFT]

64. Which salt of Calcium is Plaster of Paris?

(a) Calcium Sulphate

(b) Calcium Oxide

(c) Calcium Carbonate

(d) Calcium Hydroxide

[RRB JE 2015 27th AUG 3rd SHIFT]

65. A substance "A" reacts win another substance "B" to yield a substance "C" and a gas "D". The gas "D" which when passed through lime water turns it milky. The substances "A" and "B" are

(a) A) = HCl & B) = Na_2CO_3

(b) A) = $NaHCO_3$ & Bl = H_2O

(c) A) = Na_2CO_3 & B) = H_2O

(d) A) = CH_3COOH & B) = NaOH

[RRB JE 2015 28th AUG 1st SHIFT]

66. Which of the following represents a double displacement reaction?

(a) $Zn + 2HCl \rightarrow ZnCl_2 + H_2$

(b) $Cu + AgNO_3 \rightarrow Cu(NO_3)_2 + 2Ag$

(c) $K_2SO_4 + BaCl_2 \rightarrow BaSO_4 + 2KCl$

(d) $CH_4 + 2O_2 \rightarrow O2 + 2H_2O$

[RRB JE 2015 28th AUG 1st SHIFT]

67. Which of the following set of conditions are the most favourable for corrosion of metals?

(i) Dry air

(ii) Humid air

(iii) Presence of acidic gases

(a) (ii) only   (b) (iii) only

(c) (i) & (iii)   (d) (ii) & (iii)

[RRB JE 2015 28th AUG 1st SHIFT]

68. A trivalent metal "M" was made to react with oxygen to yield 0.25 mole of metal oxide. Which of the following is a correct statement about the product of this reaction? The reaction product contains

(a) 1.506×10^{23} molecules of oxide of formula M_2O_3.

(b) 1.506×10^{23} molecules of oxide of formula M_3O_2.

(c) 1.506×105.75 molecules of oxide of formula M_3O_2.

(d) 1.506×105.75 molecules of oxide of formula M_2O_3.

[RRB JE 2015 28th AUG 1st SHIFT]

69. In Modern Periodic Table, there are

(a) 18 Groups and 09 periods

(b) 18 Groups and 07 periods

(c) 07 Groups and 18 period

(d) 08 Groups and 06 periods

[RRB JE 2015 28th AUG 1st SHIFT]

70. Which of the following would immediately decolorize bromine dissolved in Carbon disulphide?

(a) Ethane   (b) Pentane

(c) Benzene   (d) Propene

[RRB JE 2015 28th AUG 1st SHIFT]

71. In an atom the order of filling up of the orbitals is governed by

(a) Aufbau principle

(b) Heisenberg's uncertainty principle

(c) Hund's rule

(d) Pauli's exclusion principle

[RRB JE 2015 28th AUG 1st SHIFT]

72. Which among the following is a displacement reaction?

(a) $CaCO_3 \rightarrow CaO + CO_2$

(b) $2H_2 + O_2 \rightarrow 2H_2O$

(c) $Pb + CuCl_2 \rightarrow PbCl_2 + Cu$

(d) $C_2H_4 + H_2 \rightarrow C_2H_6$

[RRB JE 2015 28th AUG 2nd SHIFT]

73. A metal forms an amphoteric oxide on reaction with oxygen. The metal is

(a) Al   (b) Na

(c) Cu   (d) Fe

[RRB JE 2015 28th AUG 2nd SHIFT]

74. A hydrocarbon contains one carbon-carbon single bond, one carbon-carbon double bond and one carbon-carbon triple bond. What is its molecular formula?

(a) C_4H_4

(b) C_4H_6

(c) C_4H_8

(d) C_4H_{10}

[RRB JE 2015 28th AUG 2nd SHIFT]

75. Which of the following are correct for the reaction $H_2SO_4 + 2NaOH \rightarrow Na_2SO_4 + 2H_2O$ it is

(i) an endothermic reaction

(ii) an exothermic reaction

(iii) a neutralization reaction

(iv) a combination reaction

(a) (i) & (iii)

(b) (ii) & (iii)

(c) (ii) & (iv)

(d) (iii) & (iv)

[RRB JE 2015 28th AUG 2nd SHIFT]

76. The electronic configuration of an element is 2,7. In which group of the moden periodic table is this element placed?

(a) 7

(b) 9

(c) 15

(d) 1

[RRB JE 2015 28th AUG 2nd SHIFT]

77. What are the type of bonds present in $CuSO_4.5H_2O$

(a) Electro valent and covalent

(b) Electrovalent and co-ordinate

(c) Electrovalent. covalent, co-ordinate and hydrogen bond

(d) Covalent and co-ordinate covalent

[RRB JE 2015 28th AUG 2nd SHIFT]

78. Match List-I with List-II and select the correct answer using the codes given the Lists

List-I		List-II	
A.	Blue vitriol	1.	Sodium bicarbaonate
B.	Epsom salt	2.	Sodium hydroxide
C.	Baking soda	3.	Magnesium sulphate
D.	Caustic soda	4.	Copper sulphate

(a) A-3 B-4 C-2 D-1

(b) A-4 B-3 C-2 D-1

(c) A-3 B-4 C-1 D-2

(d) A-4 B-3 C-1 D-2

[RRB JE 2015 28th AUG 2nd SHIFT]

79. Which one of the following changes will decrease the vapour pressure of water contained in a sealed tube?

(a) Increasing the quantity of water

(b) decreasing the quantity of water

(c) Decreasing the temperature of water

(d) Decreasing the volume of the vessel

[RRB JE 2015 28th AUG 3rd SHIFT]

80. Which of the following reaction represents the process of calcination?

(a) $Cu_2S + O_2 \rightarrow Cu_2O + SO_2$

(b) $ZnCO_3(s) \rightarrow ZnO(s) + CO_2$

(c) $ZnO(s) + C(s) \rightarrow Zn(s) + CO(g)$

(d) $2ZnS + 3O_2 \rightarrow 2ZnO + 2SO_2(g)$

[RRB JE 2015 28th AUG 3rd SHIFT]

81. Which of the following has only covalent bonds between the atoms?

(a) KCl

(b) HCHO

(c) Na

(d) MgO

[RRB JE 2015 28th AUG 3rd SHIFT]

82. An acid reacts with a base to form salt and water. What type of reaction is this?

(a) Combination

(b) Decomposition

(c) Displacement

(d) Double displacement

[RRB JE 2015 28th AUG 3rd SHIFT]

83. An acid produces a gas 'X' on reaction with metal carbonates and hydrogen carbonates separately. What is 'X' in these reactions?

(a) Carbon dioxide

(b) Carbon monoxide

(c) Sulphur dioxide

(d) Hydrogen

[RRB JE 2015 28th AUG 3rd SHIFT]

84. Which one of the following statements is correct about Mendeleev's periodic table of elements?

(a) It has 18 groups.

(b) It had some gaps for the new elements to be discovered later.

(c) It has the elements arranged in order of their increasing atomic numbers.

(d) The table initially contained 112 elements.

[RRB JE 2015 28th AUG 3rd SHIFT]

85. H_2O is liquid, H_2S is a gas because

(a) Oxygen forms stronger hydrogen bond than sulphur.

(b) Oxygen is less electromagnetic than that of sulphur.

(c) Atomic radius of oxygen is less than that of sulphur.

(d) Atomic radius of oxygen is greater than that of sulphur.

[RRB JE 2015 28th AUG 3rd SHIFT]

86. In reaction between HCl and O_2 is given by

$$4HCl + O_2 \rightarrow 2H_2O + 2Cl_2$$

The equivalent weight of HCl equal to

(a) Its molecular weight

(b) Half of its molecular weight

(c) Twice of its molecular weight

(d) Four times of its molecular weight

[RRB JE 2015 28th AUG 3rd SHIFT]

87. Which has the highest electron affinity

(a) F (b) Cl

(c) Br (d) I

[RRB JE 2015 28th AUG 3rd SHIFT]

88. A student heats a beaker containing water continuously and measures the temperature as a function of time. She found that the temperature of water increases with time. After sometime, it becomes constant in spite of heat being supplied. The temperature remains constant up to a certain stage. The value of the constant temperature of water is

(a) 25°C (b) 45°c

(c) 85°c (d) 100°c

[RRB JE 2015 29th AUG 1st SHIFT]

89. Which one of the following is correct regarding the electrolytic refining of impure copper?

(a) Impure copper is taken as the cathode.

(b) Pure copper is deposited at the anode.

(c) Pure copper is deposited at the cathode.

(d) Impurities are settled as the cathode mud.

[RRB JE 2015 29th AUG 1st SHIFT]

90. On heating with an alkaline solution of $KMnO_4$, ethanol produces

(a) Ethanoic acid (b) Ethanol

(c) Methanol (d) Methanoic acid

[RRB JE 2015 29th AUG 1st SHIFT]

91. A triatomic oxide of an element 'X' reacts with hydrochloric acid to produce the solution of a diatomic salt and water. Winch of the following is correct about the formula of the oxide and its chemical nature?

(a) The formula is XO and it is acidic in nature.

(b) The formula is XO and it is basic in nature.

(c) The formula is X_2O and it is acidic in nature.

(d) The formula is X_2O and it is basic in nature.

[RRB JE 2015 29th AUG 1st SHIFT]

92. Lime water turns milky on passing through it. On passing excess of carbon dioxide gas, milkiness disappears. It is due to the formation of

(a) $CaCO_3$ (b) $CaHCO_3$

(c) $Ca(HCO_3)_2$ (d) $Ca(OH)_2$

[RRB JE 2015 29th AUG 1st SHIFT]

93. Eka-aluminium predicted by Mendeleev was found to have properties similar to

(a) Scandium (b) gallium

(c) Germanium (d) Thallium

[RRB JE 2015 29th AUG 1st SHIFT]

94. Which one of the following was used as a chemical weapon in the First World War

(a) Carbon mono-oxide

(b) Hydrogen cyanide

(c) Mustard gas

(d) Water gas

[RRB JE 2015 29th AUG 1st SHIFT]

95. Which of the following is used in making ointment for curing skin disease?

(a) $ZnCO_3$ (b) $ZnSO_4$

(c) ZnO (d) ZnS

[RRB JE 2015 29th AUG 1st SHIFT]

96. The characteristic odour of garlic is due to

(a) A chloro compound

(b) A sulphur compound

(c) A fluorine compound

(d) Acetic acid

[RRB JE 2015 29th AUG 1st SHIFT]

97. The oxide of an element 'A' can react separately with an acid and a base to produce salt and water.

(a) The element 'A' is metallic and the oxide is amphoteric.

(b) The element 'A' is metallic and the oxide is basic.

(c) The element 'A' is non metallic and the oxide is acidic.

(d) The element 'A' is non metallic and the oxide is amphoteric.

[RRB JE 2015 29th AUG 2nd SHIFT]

98. Which one of the following sets of conditions favours the liquefaction of gases?

(a) Low pressure and low temperature

(b) High pressure and high temperature

(c) High pressure and low temperature

(d) Low pressure and high temperature

[RRB JE 2015 29th AUG 2nd SHIFT]

99. What is the value of the coefficient 'A' in the following chemical equation?

$$2Al + 'A'\,HCl \rightarrow 2AlCl_3 + 3H_2$$

(a) 3 (b) 4

(c) 5 (d) 6

[RRB JE 2015 29th AUG 2nd SHIFT]

100. On hydration, a hydrocarbon 'X' produces a compound 'Y' with molecular formula C_2H_6O. 'X' forms a dibromo compound with bromine. The compound 'Y' produces a carboxylic acid on oxidation with acidified $K_2Cr_2O_7$. The hydrocarbon 'X' is

(a) Ethene　　　　　(b) Ethane

(c) Propane　　　　(d) Propene

[RRB JE 2015 29th AUG 2nd SHIFT]

101. Which one of the following is the greatest in atomic size?

(a) Aluminum　　　(b) Magnesium

(c) Sodium　　　　(d) potassium

[RRB JE 2015 29th AUG 2nd SHIFT]

102. An acid solution is completely neutralized by a base. The pH of the salt solution so produced is

(a) 14　　　　　　(b) 7

(c) 5　　　　　　 (d) 0

[RRB JE 2015 29th AUG 2nd SHIFT]

103. The catalyst used in the manufacture of the sulphuric acid by contact process is

(a) Al_2O_3　　　　(b) Cr_2O_3

(c) V_2O_5　　　　(d) MnO_2

[RRB JE 2015 29th AUG 2nd SHIFT]

104. Which one of the following pairs of materials serves as electrodes in chargeable batteries commonly used in devices such as torch lights, electric shavers etc?

(a) Nickel and cadmium

(b) Zinc and carbon

(c) lead peroxide and lead

(d) Iron and cadmium

[RRB JE 2015 29th AUG 2nd SHIFT]

105. Which one of the following is correct concerning the reaction?

$$2H_2S + SO_2 \rightarrow 2H_2O + 3S$$

(a) H_2S is reduced

(b) H_2S is oxidized

(c) SO_2 is a reducing agent

(d) H_2S is an oxidizing agent

[RRB JE 2015 29th AUG 3rd SHIFT]

106. Conversion of a solid directly to a gaseous state is known as

(a) Sublimation　　(b) Evaporation

(c) Diffusion　　　(d) Liquefaction

[RRB JE 2015 29th AUG 3rd SHIFT]

107. The solution of a substance 'A' turns red litmus blue. Which one of the following is the most appropriate pH range in which the substance 'A' will be found?

(a) 0 – less than 6　　(b) 6 – less than 12

(c) 7 – less than 13　(d) 7 – less than 14

[RRB JE 2015 29th AUG 3rd SHIFT]

108. Which one of the following sets of elements is arranged in correct order of their increasing electro negativity?

(a) S O N P　　　　(b) S P Si Al

(c) I Br Cl F　　　(d) Mg Na K Ca

[RRB JE 2015 29th AUG 3rd SHIFT]

109. Which one of the following is the molecular formula of n-hexyne?

(a) C_6H_{14}　　　　(b) C_6H_{12}

(c) C_6H_{10}　　　　(d) C_6H_8

[RRB JE 2015 29th AUG 3rd SHIFT]

110. Malleability is the property of metals

(a) to be drawn into wires

(b) to be converted into sheets

(c) to conduct electricity

(d) to conduct heat

[RRB JE 2015 29th AUG 3rd SHIFT]

111. Which one of the following sequence of the chemical elements is correct in terms of the descending order of atomic radius

(a) B - C - N - O　　(b) C - B - O - N

(c) N - O - B - C　　(d) O - N - C - B

[RRB JE 2015 29th AUG 3rd SHIFT]

112. Which one of the following is known a salt peter?

(a) NaCl　　　　　(b) KNO_3

(c) Na_2CO_3　　　(d) $NaHCO_3$

[RRB JE 2015 29th AUG 3rd SHIFT]

113. In which among the following molecules is the distance between two adjacent carbon atoms largest

(a) Benzene　　　　(b) Ethane

(c) Ethene　　　　(d) Ethyene

[RRB JE 2015 29th AUG 3rd SHIFT]

114. The number of moles of water in 90 grams of water is

(a) 1　　　　　　(b) 3

(c) 5　　　　　　(d) 7

[RRB JE 2015 30th AUG 3rd SHIFT]

115. The reactions which involve an exchange of ions between the reactants are known as

(a) Combination   (b) Decomposition

(c) Displacement   (d) Double displacement

[RRB JE 2015 30ᵗʰ AUG 3ʳᵈ SHIFT]

116. Which gas is produced when an acid reacts with sodium carbonate?

(a) Hydrogen   (b) Chlorine

(c) Sulphur dioxide   (d) Carbon dioxide

[RRB JE 2015 30ᵗʰ AUG 3ʳᵈ SHIFT]

117. The ability of an element to exhibit different forms having different physical properties but same chemical properties is known as

(a) Allotropy   (b) Sonorousity

(c) Malleability   (d) Conductivity

[RRB JE 2015 30ᵗʰ AUG 3ʳᵈ SHIFT]

118. A molecule of benzene has

(a) 09 single bond and 03 double bonds

(b) 12 single bonds and 03 double bonds

(c) 09 single bonds and 06 double bonds

(d) 12 single bonds and 06 double bonds

[RRB JE 2015 30ᵗʰ AUG 3ʳᵈ SHIFT]

119. The maximum number of electrons that can be accommodated in M shell of an atom is

(a) 2   (b) 8

(c) 18   (d) 32

[RRB JE 2015 30ᵗʰ AUG 3ʳᵈ SHIFT]

120. Which of the following gases will have the highest rate of diffusion

(a) O_2 (b) CO_2

(c) NH_3 (d) N_2

[RRB JE 2015 30ᵗʰ AUG 3ʳᵈ SHIFT]

121. Which one of the following is not a strong electrolyte

(a) $NaCl$ (b) KNO_3

(c) NH_4OH (d) $FeSO_4$

[RRB JE 2015 30ᵗʰ AUG 3ʳᵈ SHIFT]

122. Which of the following is not a colloid

(a) Chlorophyll   (b) Smoke

(c) Ruby glass   (d) Milk

[RRB JE 2015 30ᵗʰ AUG 3ʳᵈ SHIFT]

123. The number of water molecules present in 36 grams of water is

(a) 3.023×10^{23} (b) 6.046×10^{23}

(c) 3.023×10^{46} (d) 6.046×10^{46}

[RRB JE 2015 16ᵗʰ SEP 3ʳᵈ SHIFT]

124. A substance is said to be oxidised if it

(a) gains oxygen   (b) loses oxygen

(c) gains hydrogen   (d) gains electrons

[RRB JE 2015 16ᵗʰ SEP 3ʳᵈ SHIFT]

125. An aqueous solution of a substance turns red litmus blue. The substance is

(a) Acetic acid

(b) Copper sulphate

(c) Sodium carbonate

(d) Sodium chloride

[RRB JE 2015 16ᵗʰ SEP 3ʳᵈ SHIFT]

126. Which one of the following element is **NOT** lustrous?

(a) Copper   (b) Aluminium

(c) Iodine   (d) Sulphur

[RRB JE 2015 16ᵗʰ SEP 3ʳᵈ SHIFT]

127. A molecule of propyne has

(a) 06 single bonds and 01 double bond

(b) 05 single bonds and 01 triple bond

(c) 08 single bonds

(d) 04 single bonds and 02 double bonds

[RRB JE 2015 16ᵗʰ SEP 3ʳᵈ SHIFT]

128. In a modern periodic table, the metallic character of elements

(i) increases as we move from left to right in a period.

(ii) decreases as we move from left to right in a period.

(iii) decreases as we move from top to bottom in a group.

(iv) increases as we move from top to bottom in a group.

(a) (i) & (iii)   (b) (ii) & (iii)

(c) (i) & (iv)   (d) (ii) & (iv)

[RRB JE 2015 16ᵗʰ SEP 3ʳᵈ SHIFT]

129. The pH of water is

(a) 5   (b) 6

(c) 7   (d) 8

[RRB JE 2015 16ᵗʰ SEP 3ʳᵈ SHIFT]

130. Thin foils of which metal are used for packaging food?

(a) Aluminium   (b) Zinc

(c) Nickel   (d) Copper

[RRB JE 2015 16ᵗʰ SEP 3ʳᵈ SHIFT]

131. The nucleus of an atom contains

(a) Only protons   (b) Only neutrons

(c) Only electrons   (d) Protons and neutrons

[RRB JE 2015 16ᵗʰ SEP 3ʳᵈ SHIFT]

RRB SENIOR SECTION ENGINEER

1. What is the common property between $LiAlH_4$, Sodium amalgam and $NaBH_4$?

(a) They are used in removing slag from molten metals

(b) They are used in manufacturing esters

(c) They are reducing agents

(d) They are coated on welding electrodes

[RRB SSE 2014 GREEN SHIFT]

2. Soaps are manufactured by:

(a) Reaction of alkalies with glycerol

(b) Reaction of fats with soluble hydroxides

(c) Reaction of calcium and magnesium ions with dilute sulphuric acid

(d) Reaction of dodecyl benzene with H_2SO_4 and then NaOH

[RRB SSE 2014 GREEN SHIFT]

3. Chemical bonding which results in formation of molecules from atoms is basically-

(a) Nuclear force　　(b) Short range forces

(c) Electrostatic force　(d) Gravitational force

[RRB SSE 2014 GREEN SHIFT]

4. Glycerol can be represented by chemical formula:

(a) C_2HSO_2　　　　(b) C_3H_7OH

(c) C_3H_5OH　　　　(d) $C_3H_8O_3$

[RRB SSE 2014 GREEN SHIFT]

5. The most ideal disinfectant used for drinking water is :

(a) Alum　　　　(b) Chlorine

(c) Lime　　　　(d) Nitrogen

[RRB SSE 2014 GREEN SHIFT]

6. Which one of the following is generally added to Table Salt to make it flow freely in rainy season ?

(a) $Ca_3(PO_4)_2$　　　(b) Na_3PO_4

(c) KCI　　　　(d) KI

[RRB SSE 2014 RED SHIFT]

7. Valence electrons in the element A are 3 and that in element B are 6. Most probable compound formed from A and B is :

(a) A_2B　　　　(b) AB_2

(c) A_2B_3　　　　(d) A_3B_2

[RRB SSE 2014 RED SHIFT]

8. Atoms of the elements belonging to the same group of periodic table will have :

(a) Same number of protons

(b) Same number of neutrons

(c) Same number of electrons

(d) Same number of electrons in the valence shell

[RRB SSE 2014 RED SHIFT]

9. Avogadro's number, N_A means

(a) number of protons in nucleus of an atom

(b) number of atoms in one gram atom of an element

(c) sum of the number of protons and the neutrons in the nucleus of an atom

(d) number of protons or electrons in one gram of Sodium

[RRB SSE 2014 YELLOW SHIFT]

10. Isotopes of the same element have

(a) Same number of neutrons

(b) Same atomic mass

(c) Same number of protons

(d) Different atomic number

[RRB SSE 2014 YELLOW SHIFT]

11. In a reaction between Zinc and Iodine. Zinc Iodide is formed. What is being oxidised ?

(a) Zinc ions　　　　(b) Iodide ions

(c) Zinc Atom　　　　(d) Iodine

[RRB SSE 2014 YELLOW SHIFT]

12. Which of the following halogens is the best oxidising agent ?

(a) F_2　　　　　　(b) Cl_2

(c) Br_2　　　　　(d) l_2

[RRB SSE 2014 YELLOW SHIFT]

13. Nitrogen is used to fill electric bulbs because it

(a) is lighter than air

(b) makes the bulb to give more light

(c) does not support combustion

(d) is non-toxic

[RRB SSE 2014 YELLOW SHIFT]

14. Froth floatation process for the concentration of Ores is an illustration of the practical application of

(a) Adsorption　　　(b) Absorption

(c) Coagulation　　　(d) Sedimentation

[RRB SSE 2014 YELLOW SHIFT]

15. The presence of nitrogen in the products of combustion ensures that

(a) Complete combustion of fuel takes place

(b) Incomplete combustion of fuel takes place

(c) dry products of combustion are analysed

(d) air is used for the combustion

[RRB SSE 2014 YELLOW SHIFT]

16. To reduce air pollution due to smoke. ________ are used in thermal power plants.

(a) repeaters

(b) superheaters

(c) induced draft fans

(d) Electrostatic precipitators

[RRB SSE 2014 YELLOW SHIFT]

17. The solubility product (Ksp) of silver iodate in water at 20°C is $4 \times 10^{-8} \text{mol}^2 \text{ L}^{-2}$. What is the concentration of silver ions, Ag^+ (aq) in a solution of silver iodate in water at 20°C ?
 (a) $2 \times 10^{-8} \text{ mol L}^{-1}$
 (b) $4 \times 10^{-8} \text{ mol L}^{-1}$
 (c) $2 \times 10^{-4} \text{ mol L}^{-1}$
 (d) $16 \times 10^{-16} \text{mol L}^{-1}$
[RRB SSE 2015 1ˢᵗ SEP 1ˢᵗ SHIFT]

18. Which of the following pair of compounds will react together under suitable conditions to form 1- ethoxypropane as the major product?
 (a) $C_2H_5ONa + CH_3CH(I) CH_3$
 (b) $C_2H_5COONa + C_2H_5OH$
 (c) $CH_3COCl + CH_3CH_2CH_2OH$
 (d) $C_2H_5ONa + CH_3CH_2CH_2I$
[RRB SSE 2015 1ˢᵗ SEP 1ˢᵗ SHIFT]

19. Which one of the allowing compounds includes a transition element with zero oxidation state?
 (a) $[\text{Fe} <H_2O)_6]^{3+}$
 (b) $[\text{Ni} (CO)_4]$
 (c) $[\text{Cu} (H_2O)_6]^{2+} SO_4^{2-}$
 (d) $[\text{Fe} (H_2O)_6] SO_4$
[RRB SSE 2015 1ˢᵗ SEP 1ˢᵗ SHIFT]

20. If 0.005 moles each of the following substances are separately dissolved in 100 grams of water, the solution of which substance will have the highest boiling point?
 (a) Magnesium chloride
 (b) Aluminium chloride
 (c) Sodium chloride
 (d) Glucose
[RRB SSE 2015 1ˢᵗ SEP 1ˢᵗ SHIFT]

21. Which of the following represents nucleophilic add -on reaction?
 (a) $CH_3CHO + NH_2NH_2 \rightarrow CH_3CH=NNH_2 + H_2O$
 (b) $CH_3CH = CHCH_3 + HBr \rightarrow CH_3CH_2 - CH (Br) CH_3$
 (c) $C_6H_5CHO + NaHSO_3 \rightarrow C_6H_5CH(OH) Na$
 (d) $CH_3CHO + 3I_2 \rightarrow CHI_3$
[RRB SSE 2015 1ˢᵗ SEP 1ˢᵗ SHIFT]

22. In which of the following, nitrogen has an oxidation number -1?
 (a) NH_2OH
 (b) HNO_3
 (c) HNO_2
 (d) NO
[RRB SSE 2015 1ˢᵗ SEP 1ˢᵗ SHIFT]

23. The solubility product (Ksp) of $PbCO_3$ at 20°C is $7.84 \times 10^{-14} \text{ mol}^2 \text{ L}^{-2}$. What is its solubility in water at 20°C?
 (a) $2.80 \times 10^{-7} \text{ mol L}^{-1}$
 (b) $3.92 \times 10^{-14} \text{ mol L}^{-1}$
 (c) $3.92 \times 10^{-7} \text{ mol L}^{-1}$
 (d) $2.80 \times 10^{-14} \text{ mol L}^{-1}$
[RRB SSE 2015 1ˢᵗ SEP 2ⁿᵈ SHIFT]

24. Which of the following is the most acidic in nature?
 (a) Phenol
 (b) 2-Nitrophenol
 (c) 3- Nitrophenol
 (d) 2,4- Dinitrophenol
[RRB SSE 2015 1ˢᵗ SEP 2ⁿᵈ SHIFT]

25. What is the coordination number of zinc in the complex ion $[\text{Zn} (OH)_4 (H_2O)_2]^{2-}$?
 (a) 6
 (b) 4
 (c) 2
 (d) 0
[RRB SSE 2015 1ˢᵗ SEP 2ⁿᵈ SHIFT]

26. Addition of 5 grams of solute $\underline{A}$ (molecular mass=100) to 100 grams of solvent $\underline{B}$ causes the same elevation of boiling point as the addition of 10 grams of solute $\underline{C}$ to 200 grams of the same solvent $\underline{B}$. What is the molecular mass of the solute C?
 (a) 200
 (b) 50
 (c) 150
 (d) 100
[RRB SSE 2015 1ˢᵗ SEP 2ⁿᵈ SHIFT]

27. Which of the following pair of molecules of the compounds will react together in presence of sodium hydroxide solution under suitable conditions to produce a mixture of four compounds?
 (a) $CH_3CH_2CHO + CH_3CH_2CHO$
 (b) $CH_3CHO + CH_3CHO$
 (c) $CH_3CHO + CH_3CH_2CHO$
 (d) $CH_3CHO + C_6H_5CHO$
[RRB SSE 2015 1ˢᵗ SEP 2ⁿᵈ SHIFT]

28. The correct statement concerning the molecule of ammonia is
 (a) It is a V- shaped molecule.
 (b) The H-N-H bond angle are less than 109°-28′.
 (c) The repulsion between pair and bond pairs of electrons is less than that bond pair- bond pair.
 (d) Its shape is tetrahedral with lone pairs in two positions.
[RRB SSE 2015 1ˢᵗ SEP 2ⁿᵈ SHIFT]

29. In an industrial area, a sample of 10 litres of air was found to contain ml of sulphur dioxide gas. The concentration of sulphur dioxide gas in air in ppm is
 (a) 300
 (b) 400
 (c) 500
 (d) 600
[RRB SSE 2015 1ˢᵗ SEP 3ʳᵈ SHIFT]

30. For the reaction $2NO, (g) \rightleftharpoons N_2O_4(g) + 60kJ$, an increase in temperature will
 (a) favour the decomposition of N_2O_4
 (b) favour the formation of N_2O_4
 (c) result in the formation of a different reaction product
 (d) stop the reaction.
[RRB SSE 2015 1ˢᵗ SEP 3ʳᵈ SHIFT]

31. Which one of the following is a correct order of increasing electro negativity of elements?

(a) N>P>0>F   (b) F>0>N >P

(c) F>N>P>0   (d) 0>P>N>F

[RRB SSE 2015 1st SEP 3rd SHIFT]

32. The major product formed by treating n- butyl chloride with boiling solution of potassium hydroxide in ethanol is

(a) 2- Butene   (b) 1- Butene

(c) n- Butanol   (d) Isobutanol

[RRB SSE 2015 1st SEP 3rd SHIFT]

33. Which one of the following aldehydes will not undergo aldol condensation when treated with an aqueous solution of sodium hydroxide?

(a) $C_6H_5CH_2CHO$ (b) CH_3CH_2CHO

(c) CH_3CHO (d) HCHO

[RRB SSE 2015 1st SEP 3rd SHIFT]

34. Which one of the following electronic configuration represents a transition element in its ground state?

(a) $3d^3\,4s^2$ (b) $2p^63s^1$

(c) $2s^22p^6$ (d) $3d^{10}\,4s^2$

[RRB SSE 2015 1st SEP 3rd SHIFT]

35. What is the modality of the solution which contains 11.70 grams of sodium chloride dissolved in 2.0 Kg of water?

(a) 5.85   (b) 0.1

(c) 0.2   (d) 0.001

[RRB SSE 2015 2nd SEP 1st SHIFT]

36. For the reaction $N_2(g) + 3H_2(g) \rightleftharpoons 2\,NH_3\,(g)$, the units of Kp are

(a) Atm   (b) Atm2

(c) Atm^{-1} (d) Atm^{-2}

[RRB SSE 2015 2nd SEP 1st SHIFT]

37. The general electronic configuration of elements placed in a group in the modern periodic table is $ns^2\,np^4$. In which group of the periodic table are the elements placed?

(a) 16   (b) 15

(c) 14   (d) 13

[RRB SSE 2015 2nd SEP 1st SHIFT]

38. The primary alcohol C_4H_7OH is oxidized using acidified $K_2O_2O_7$. The molecular formula of the possible product is

(a) G_4H_6O (b) C_4H_8O

(c) $C_4H_6O_2$ (d) $C_4H_8O_2$

[RRB SSE 2015 2nd SEP 1st SHIFT]

39. Which one of the following aldehydes will undergo Cannizarro's reaction when treated with concentrated solution of potassium hydroxide in water?

(a) Ethanal

(b) 2-(p- Hydroxyphenyl) ethanal

(c) 2,2-Dimethyl- 2- phenylethanal

(d) 2- Phenylethanal

[RRB SSE 2015 2nd SEP 1st SHIFT]

40. Given below are the electronic configurations of transition element. Which one of these elements is paramagnetic in nature?

(a) $3d^5\,4s^2$ (b) $3d^74s^2$

(c) $3d^8\,4s^2$ (d) $3d^14s^2$

[RRB SSE 2015 2nd SEP 1st SHIFT]

41. When we move from top to bottom in a group of periodic tables. Three will be variation in the properties of the elements. If we move from top to bottom group 17.

(a) Electrons gravity will increase

(b) Stability of hydroxides will increase

(c) Ionic radii will increase

(d) Ionization enthalpy will increase

[RRB SSE 2015 2nd SEP 2nd SHIFT]

42. If Rydberg constant is 1.0968×10^7 m^{-1}, the wavelength of light emitted when a hydrogen atom changes from n=5 to the n =3 state, will be

(a) 1.2821×10^{-5}m   (b) 1.2821×10^{-6}m

(c) 2.430×10^{-5}m   (d) 3.2821×10^{-6}m

[RRB SSE 2015 2nd SEP 2nd SHIFT]

43. Combustion of methane taken place in air. The number of moles of methane required to produce 66.0 g of $CO_2(g)$ will be

(a) 1.0 mol   (b) 1.5 mol

(c) 2.5 mol   (d) 3.0 mol

[RRB SSE 2015 2nd SEP 2nd SHIFT]

44. A solution is prepared by mixing 50 mL of 0.20M NaCl, 25 mL of 0.10M NaOH and 25mL of 0.30m HCI. The concentration of hydrogen ions (H+ion) In solution thus obtained will be

(a) 0.5 M

(b) 0.02 M

(c) 0.10 M

(d) 0.05 M

[RRB SSE 2015 2nd SEP 2nd SHIFT]

45. A flux is often added to remove impurities from an ore in a blast furnace. In the reaction, $CaO + SIO_2 \rightarrow CaSIO_3$, the slag and the flux are respectively

(a) $CaSiO_3$ and CaO

(b) CaO and SiO_2

(c) $CaSiO_3$ and SiO_2

(d) SiO_2 and $CaSiO_3$

[RRB SSE 2015 2nd SEP 2nd SHIFT]

46. You are given following compounds.

C_6H_5OH , C_3H_5OH, $HCOOH$ AND CH_3COOH

The correct order of decreasing acidity of these compounds will be,

(a) $HCOOH{>}CH_3COOH {>}C_6H_5OH{>}C_2H_5OH$

(b) $CH_3COOH{>} HCOOH{>} C_2H_5OH > C_6H_5OH$

(c) $CH_3COOH {>}C_2H_5OH{>}HCOOH > C_6H_5OH$

(d) $C_6H_5OH {>}C_2H_5OH {>}HCOOH > CH_3COOH$

[RRB SSE 2015 2nd SEP 2nd SHIFT]

47. If Avogadro constant is 6.02×10^{23} mol^{-1}, then mass of one C_2H_4 molecule (in gram) will be

(a) 5.02×10^{-23} g /molecule

(b) 4.65×10^{-23} g/molecule

(c) 2.38×10^{-23} g/molecule

(d) 6.02×10^{-23} g /molecule

[RRB SSE 2015 2nd SEP 3rd SHIFT]

48. Properties of certain elements resembles with the elements placed diagonally in the periodic table. Lithium will show liagonal relationship with

(a) Boron   (b) Beryllium

(c) Magnesium   (d) Aluminum

[RRB SSE 2015 2nd SEP 3rd SHIFT]

49. Which one of the following reactions is not a disproportionate reaction?

(a) $2H_2O_2 (aq) \rightarrow 2H_2O (I) + O_2(g)$

(b) $P_4(s) +30H'(aq) \rightarrow PH_3(g) +3H_2PO_2^-$

(c) $S_8(s) + 12OH{-}(aq) \rightarrow 4S^2(aq) + 2S_2O_3^2 \ aq)$ $+6H_2O(I)$

(d) $2F_2(g) + 20H{-}(aq) \rightarrow 2F (aq) +OF_2(g) +H_2O(l)$

[RRB SSE 2015 2nd SEP 3rd SHIFT]

50. You are given the species :

^-OH, F^-, H^+ and BCI_3

Identify the pair of acids from the following options:

(a) ^-OH and BCI_3 (b) F^- and ^-OH

(c) H^+ and BCI_3 (d) F^- andBCI_3

[RRB SSE 2015 2nd SEP 3rd SHIFT]

51. Which one of the following elements is extracted commercially by the electrolysis of an aqueous solution of one of its compounds?

(a) Sodium   (b) Aluminum

(c) Bromine   (d) Chlorine

[RRB SSE 2015 2nd SEP 3rd SHIFT]

52. Number of structural isomers for C_4H_8 would be

(a) 2   (b) 3

(c) 4   (d) 5

[RRB SSE 2015 2nd SEP 3rd SHIFT]

53. The molecules of elements and compounds exist in different structures .The molecule which is linear, is

(a) NO_2 (b) SO_2

(c) CO_2 (d) CIO_2

[RRB SSE 2015 3rd SEP 1st SHIFT]

54. The correct order of first ionization enthalpy of the elements of oxygen family in the periodic table is

(a) $O{>} S > Se$ (b) $S > O > Se$

(c) $S > Se > O$ (d) $Se > O > S$

[RRB SSE 2015 3rd SEP 1st SHIFT]

55. In a volumetric analysis, $KMnO_4$ reacts with oxalic acid according to the following equation,

$2MnO_4^- + 5C_2O_4^{2-} + 16 H+ \rightarrow 2Mn^2 +10CO_2 +8H_2O$

According to the above equation, 20mL of 0.1M $KMnO_4$ will be equivalent to

(a) 120 mL of $0.25M H_2C_2O_4$

(b) 150mL of $0.10M H_2C_2O_4$

(c) 50mL of $0.10 M H_2C_2O_4$

(d) 50 mL of $0.2 M H_2C_2O_4$

[RRB SSE 2015 3rd SEP 1st SHIFT]

56. Consider the following compounds:

$CH_3CH_2{=}CCH_3$ $CH_3CH_2CH_2CH_3$
    I   II

$CH_3CH{=}CH_2$ $CH_3C{=}CH$
    III   IV

Which reagent will ou use to distinguish compound IV from the rest of compounds?

(a) Bra/CCU

(b) Ammonia Cal $AgNO_3$

(c) Cold Alkal ine $KMnO_4$

(d) Br_2/Acetie acid

[RRB SSE 2015 3rd SEP 1st SHIFT]

57. The largest gland in the body, the liver, is not responsible for one function mentioned below. The liver

(a) protects the gallbladder

(b) removes certain wastes from the body

(c) stores glycogen

(d) produces bile

[RRB SSE 2015 3rd SEP 1st SHIFT]

58. In plants, which hormones can promote growth of plant parts?

(a) Cytokinin

(b) Only Auxin

(c) Only gibberellin

(d) Both auxin and gibberellin

[RRB SSE 2015 3rd SEP 1st SHIFT]

59. Neon has three natural isotopes with mass number 20, 21 and 22. The relative abundance of the isotopes is 90.51%, 0.27% and 9.22% respectively. The average atomic mass of neon will be:

(a) 22.0 u   (b) 21.179 u

(c) 22.800u   (d) 20.187 u

[RRB SSE 2015 3rd SEP 2nd SHIFT]

60. Four successive members of 3d block (of periodic table) are Vanadium (z = 23), Chromium (z = 24), manganese (z = 25) and iron (z = 26). Which one of these is expected to have the highest third ionization enthalpy?

(a) Vanadium (V)   (b) Chromium (Cr)

(c) Manganese (Mn)   (d) Iron (Fe)

[RRB SSE 2015 3ʳᵈ SEP 2ⁿᵈ SHIFT]

61. Which one of the following equations in an example of both, displacement reaction and redox reaction?

(a) $2FeSO_4(s) \xrightarrow{heat} Fe_2O_3(s)+SO_2(g)+SO_3(g)$

(b) $Fe(s)+CuSO_4(aq) \longrightarrow FeSO_4(aq)+Cu(s)$

(c) $AgCI(s) \xrightarrow{Sunlight} 2Ag(s)+Cl_2(g)$

(d) $2KCIO_3 \xrightarrow{\Delta} 2KCl(s)+3O_2(g)$

[RRB SSE 2015 3ʳᵈ SEP 2ⁿᵈ SHIFT]

62. A 0.10 M NaOH situation is prepared for an analytical laboratory work. pH of the solution will be:

(a) 10.0   (b) 12.0

(c) 11.5   (d) 13.0

[RRB SSE 2015 3ʳᵈ SEP 2ⁿᵈ SHIFT]

63. Activity of the metals is decided on he basis of their electrode potentials. Electrode potential of a few metals a provided below.

$E^0_{Na+/Na} = -2.71V$
$E^0_{mg^{2+}/m6} = -2.37V$
$E^0_{Cu^{2+}/CU} = +0.34V$
$E^0_{Fe^{2+}/Fe} = -0.44V$
$E^0_{Cr^{3+}/Cr} = -0.74V$

The correct order of reducing power of the metals will be:

(a) Cu < Fe < Cr < Mg < Na

(b) Na < Cu < Mg < Fe < Cr

(c) Na < Mg < Na < Cr < Cu

(d) Fe < Mg < Na < Cr < Cu

[RRB SSE 2015 3ʳᵈ SEP 2ⁿᵈ SHIFT]

64. The IUPAC name of the Compound $CH_3CH_2CH=C-CH_3$ is

$|$

CH_2CH_3

(a) 4- ethyl -2- pentene

(b) 3- methyl -3- hexene

(c) 2-ethyl -2- pentene

(d) 3-methyl -2- pentene

[RRB SSE 2015 3ʳᵈ SEP 2ⁿᵈ SHIFT]

65. You are provided a few homonuclear, diatomic molecules (as =given below). Identify the one which is paramagnetic in nature .

(a) H_2 (b) C_2

(c) B_2 (d) N_2

[RRB SSE 2015 3ʳᵈ SEP 3ⁿᵈ SHIFT]

66. Halogens have tendency to accept electrons and therefore work as oxidizing agent. The correct increasing order of oxidizing power of the halogens is

(a) $F_2 < CI_2 < Br_2 < I_2$ (b) $Br_2 < I_2 < F_2 < CI_2$

(c) $I_2 < F2 < CI_2 < Br_2$ (d) $I_2 < Br_2 < CI_2 < F_2$

[RRB SSE 2015 3ʳᵈ SEP 3ⁿᵈ SHIFT]

67. Which one of the following reaction is r A an ex<; pie of redox reaction?

(a) $3Mg + N_2 \rightarrow Mg_3N_2$

(b) $CuSO_4+ 4NH_3 \rightarrow PbSO_4 + Cu$

(c) $I_2 + 3CI_2 \rightarrow 2ICI_3$

(d) $CUSO_4 + 4NH_3 \rightarrow [CU(NH_3)SO_4$

[RRB SSE 2015 3ʳᵈ SEP 3ⁿᵈ SHIFT]

68. Following solution are prepared by mixing different volumes of NaOH and HCl of diffident concentrations, pH of which one of them will be equal to 1?

(a) $100mL \dfrac{M}{10} HCL + 100\ mL \dfrac{M}{10} NaOH$

(b) $75mL \dfrac{M}{5} HCL + 25\ mL \dfrac{M}{5} NaOH$

(c) $55mL \dfrac{M}{10} - HCL + 45\ mL \dfrac{M}{10} NaOH$

(d) $60mL \dfrac{M}{10} HCL + 40\ mL \dfrac{M}{10} NaOH$

[RRB SSE 2015 3ʳᵈ SEP 3ⁿᵈ SHIFT]

69. For obtaining a metal from its ore various metallurgy processes are adopted. Froth flotation process is metallurgy of

(a) Oxide ores   (b) Chloride ores

(c) sulphide ores   (d) Carbonate ores

[RRB SSE 2015 3ʳᵈ SEP 3ⁿᵈ SHIFT]

70. Which one of the following is most viscous?

(a) CH_3OH

(b) CH_2OH

$|$

$CHOH$

$|$

CH_2OH

(c) CH_2OH

$|$

CH_2OH

(d) CH_3CH_2OH

[RRB SSE 2015 3ʳᵈ SEP 3ⁿᵈ SHIFT]

ANSWERS

RRB JUNIOR ENGINEER

1. (b)	**2.** (d)	**3.** (c)	**4.** (b)	**5.** (b)	**6.** (a)	**7.** (d)	**8.** (d)	**9.** (b)	**10.** (b)
11. (c)	**12.** (a)	**13.** (a)	**14.** (a)	**15.** (a)	**16.** (b)	**17.** (b)	**18.** (b)	**19.** (b)	**20.** (c)
21. (b)	**22.** (b)	**23.** (a)	**24.** (d)	**25.** (a)	**26.** (a)	**27.** (c)	**28.** (c)	**29.** (b)	**30.** (b)
31. (a)	**32.** (d)	**33.** (b)	**34.** (a)	**35.** (b)	**36.** (a)	**37.** (d)	**38.** (b)	**39.** (c)	**40.** (a)
41. (c)	**42.** (b)	**43.** (a)	**44.** (d)	**45.** (a)	**46.** (a)	**47.** (b)	**48.** (d)	**49.** (b)	**50.** (c)
51. (d)	**52.** (c)	**53.** (d)	**54.** (d)	**55.** (a)	**56.** (c)	**57.** (d)	**58.** (a)	**59.** (b)	**60.** (d)
61. (c)	**62.** (a)	**63.** (a)	**64.** (a)	**65.** (a)	**66.** (c)	**67.** (d)	**68.** (a)	**69.** (b)	**70.** (d)
71. (a)	**72.** (c)	**73.** (a)	**74.** (a)	**75.** (b)	**76.** (a)	**77.** (c)	**78.** (d)	**79.** (c)	**80.** (b)
81. (b)	**82.** (d)	**83.** (a)	**84.** (b)	**85.** (a)	**86.** (a)	**87.** (b)	**88.** (d)	**89.** (c)	**90.** (a)
91. (d)	**92.** (c)	**93.** (b)	**94.** (c)	**95.** (a)	**96.** (b)	**97.** (a)	**98.** (c)	**99.** (d)	**100.** (a)
101. (d)	**102.** (b)	**103.** (c)	**104.** (a)	**105.** (b)	**106.** (a)	**107.** (d)	**108.** (c)	**109.** (c)	**110.** (b)
111. (a)	**112.** (b)	**113.** (b)	**114.** (c)	**115.** (d)	**116.** (d)	**117.** (a)	**118.** (a)	**119.** (c)	**120.** (c)
121. (c)	**122.** (a)	**123.** (b)	**124.** (a)	**125.** (c)	**126.** (d)	**127.** (b)	**128.** (d)	**129.** (c)	**130.** (a)
131. (d)									

RRB SENIOR SECTION ENGINEER

1. (a)	**2.** (b)	**3.** (c)	**4.** (d)	**5.** (b)	**6.** (a)	**7.** (b)	**8.** (d)	**9.** (b)	**10.** (c)
11. (a)	**12.** (a)	**13.** (c)	**14.** (a)	**15.** (d)	**16.** (d)	**17.** (c)	**18.** (d)	**19.** (b)	**20.** (b)
21. (a)	**22.** (a)	**23.** (a)	**24.** (d)	**25.** (a)	**26.** (d)	**27.** (c)	**28.** (b)	**29.** (c)	**30.** (a)
31. (b)	**32.** (a)	**33.** (d)	**34.** (a)	**35.** (b)	**36.** (d)	**37.** (a)	**38.** (c)	**39.** (c)	**40.** (a)
41. (c)	**42.** (b)	**43.** (b)	**44.** (d)	**45.** (c)	**46.** (a)	**47.** (b)	**48.** (c)	**49.** (d)	**50.** (c)
51. (d)	**52.** (c)	**53.** (c)	**54.** (a)	**55.** (c)	**56.** (b)	**57.** (d)	**58.** (b)	**59.** (d)	**60.** (c)
61. (b)	**62.** (d)	**63.** (a)	**64.** (b)	**65.** (c)	**66.** (d)	**67.** (d)	**68.** (b)	**69.** (c)	**70.** (b)

EXPLANATIONS

RRB JUNIOR ENGINEER

1. Hadrons and Baryons are types of subatomic particles. Baryons are heavy subatomic particles that are made up of three quarks.

2. Milk is an example of a heterogeneous mixture. Mixtures can be separated into two (or more) individual substances by physical means. Our glass of ice water is a mixture because we can easily separate the ice from the liquid water by filtration.

3. A class of compounds which are used as fragrances when molecular weight is low and are naturally occurring fats when molecular weight is high in the series, is called esters.

4. Disinfection of drinking water is done to remove Bacteria. Water disinfection means the removal, deactivation or killing of pathogenic microorganisms.

   Microorganisms are destroyed or deactivated, resulting in termination of growth and reproduction. When microorganisms are not removed from drinking water, drinking water usage will cause people to fall ill.

5. CO_2 causes green house effect trading to global warming.

6. The alkanes comprise a series of compounds that are composed of carbon and hydrogen atoms with single covalent bonds. This group of compounds comprises a homologous series with a general molecular formula of C_nH_{2n+2}.

7. Chlorofluorocarbons (CFCs) and other halogenated ozone depleting substances (ODS) are mainly responsible for man-made chemical ozone depletion. The total amount of effective halogens (chlorine and bromine) in the stratosphere can be calculated and are known as the equivalent effective stratospheric chlorine (EESC).

8. The Haber Process combines nitrogen from the air with hydrogen derived mainly from natural gas (methane) into ammonia. The reaction is reversible and the production of ammonia is exothermic. The catalyst is actually slightly more complicated than pure iron.

9. Atoms of chemical elements having same atomic mass but a different atomic number are called Isobars. The sum of the number of protons and neutrons together form the atomic mass.

10. Among the given options, Bromine is not a Noble Gas.The six noble gases that occur naturally are helium (He), neon (Ne), argon (Ar), krypton (Kr), xenon (Xe), and the radioactive radon (Rn).

11. A greenhouse gas is a gas that absorbs and emits radiant energy within the thermal infrared range. Increasing greenhouse gas emissions cause the greenhouse effect.

12. Electrostatic Precipitators are devices for particulate emission control.

13. Biochemical Oxygen Demand (BOD, also called Biological Oxygen Demand) is the amount of dissolved oxygen needed (i.e. demanded) by aerobic biological organisms to break down organic material present in a given water sample at certain temperature over a specific time period. The BOD value is most commonly expressed in milligrams of oxygen consumed per litre of sample during 5 days of incubation at 20 °C. Biochemical Oxygen Demand (BOD) is a measure of Oxygen utilized during oxidation of organic matters.

14. Biodegradable pollutants are quickly degraded by natural means. Biodegradable pollutants: Such pollutants are quickly degraded by microbes (bacteria and fungi) in nature e.g. sewage, ... Examples of such pollutants are: DDT, mercury, lead, arsenic, some pesticides, radioactive substances, glass, plastic, aluminium pieces, etc.

15. Solid has the highest molecular attractions hence is dense and compact.

16. Lactic Acid is formed from lactose. It sours milk

17. Elements belonging to the same group have similar chemical properties because they have similar electronic configuration.

18. Among the given options, Solder alloy contains Tin. Soldering filler materials are available in many different alloys for differing applications. In electronics assembly, the eutectic alloy of 63% tin and 37% lead (or 60/40, which is almost identical in melting point) has been the alloy of choice.

19. The number of atoms in a body centred unit cell is 2.

20. From the given equation the value of X is 4.
    $$MnO_2 + X\ HCL \rightarrow MnCl_2 + 2H_2O + Cl_2$$

21. Iodine is a chemical element with symbol I and atomic number 53. The heaviest of the stable halogens, it exists as a lustrous, purple-black metallic solid at standard conditions that sublimes readily to form a violet gas.Iodine is the fourth halogen, being a member of group 17 in the periodic table, below fluorine, chlorine, and bromine; it is the heaviest stable member of its group

22. Electronegativity is the tendency of an atom to attract a shared pair of electrons. The higher its electronegativity, the more an element attracts electrons. In general, electronegativity increases on passing from left to right along a period, and decreases on descending a group. Hence, fluorine is the most electronegative of the elements, while caesium is the least.

23. A trivalent metal "M" was made to react with nitrogen to yield 0.5 mole of metal nitride. There reaction product contains 3.0165×10^{23} molecules of oxide of formula M_3N is the correct statement.

24. 3 C-H bonds are there in a molecule of ethanoic acid.

25. 49 mL of 0.1 M sodium hydroxide solution is added to 50 mL of 0.1 M solution of nitric acid.Approximate pH of the resulting solution will be 3.

26. A Bleaching powder is manufactured through a reaction between Slaked lime and chlorine.

27. It is possible to make LPG available in a cylinder because of its Compressibility

28. According to the law of constant proportions, 8 g of oxygen would be present in a sample of carbon dioxide gas containing 3 grams of Carbon.

29. Galvanization or galvanizing is the process of applying a protective zinc coating to steel or iron, to prevent rusting. The most common method is hot-dip galvanizing, in which the parts are submerged in a bath of molten zinc

30. Among the given options, Sodium has the least number of valence electrons.

31. For the reaction, $2Na + H_2 \longrightarrow 2NaH$, Na is oxidized and H_2 acts as an oxidizing agent is the correct statement.

32. CH3COOH react with sodium hydrogen carbonate to produce carbon dioxide gas.

33. Among the given options, the NH_3 act both as an acid and a base of $2NH_3 \longrightarrow NH_2^- + NH_4^+$ ·

34. Where would you place vinegar if you were to show its pH on a scale showing pH from 1 to 8 to left of 7.

35. For its complete combustion, one mole of an alkane required 3.5 mole of oxygen gas at the same temperature and pressure. The name of alkane is Ethane.

36. Chlorine is a chemical element with symbol Cl and atomic number 17. It is an extremely reactive element and a strong oxidising agent: among the elements, it has the highest electron affinity and the third-highest electronegativity, behind only oxygen and fluorine.

37. Rancidity of oils and fats can be controlled by controlling the process of Oxidation.

38. All element X contains only one electron in its outermost shell. The correct statement about X are It forms a basic oxide and It is a good conductor of electricity.

39. Vanilla essence act as an olfactory indicator.Vanilla essence is extracted from vanilla beans and is used to flavor several desserts and dishes. It is the extract that is made from vanilla beans which are soaked in alcohol. It is widely used as a flavoring and vanilla ice cream is the most common flavor. It is used for both commercial and domestic purposes. After saffron, vanilla is the most expensive spice used.

40. Among the given options Na is the most metallic in nature.Sodium is a chemical element with symbol Na and atomic number 11. It is a soft, silvery-white, highly reactive metal.

41. You can make soap at home from vegetable oil and Caustic Soda.

42. Among the given options, the correct equation is $6CO_2 + 6H_2O\ C_6H_{12}O_6 + 6O_2$.

43. Among the given options, F and Br are important.

44. The value of X in the following equation is 5.

$$4NH_3 + XO_2 \rightarrow 4NO + 6H_2O$$

45. During the electrolytic refining of copper using copper sulphate as an electrolyte Impure copper is made at the anode

46. The electronic configuration of an element is 2,1. To 2, 1 given in the option a elements will be having similar electronic configuration .

47. A solution containing 80 grams of sodium hydroxide (molecular mass = 40) completely neutralizes another solution containing 98 grams of an acid "A" (molecular mass = 98). The charge on the anion part of "A" is –2.

48. Option D reaction is an example for saponification reaction.

$$CH_3COOCH_3 + NaOH \rightarrow CH_3COONa + CH_3OH$$

49. Chlorine is a chemical element with symbol Cl and atomic number 17. The second lightest of the halogens, it appears between fluorine and bromine in the periodic table and its properties are mostly intermediate between them. Chlorine is a yellow-green gas at room temperature. It is also a molecule of an element.

50. Chemical equation given in the option c, represents the reaction of roasting process.

$$2CuS + O_2 \rightarrow CuO + 2SO_2$$

51. The charges on aluminum and sulphate ions are +3 and −2 respectively. The correct molecular formula of aluminum sulphate is $Al_2(SO_4)_3$.

52. Corrosion of iron is a process of oxidation. The rusting of iron is an electrochemical process that begins with the transfer of electrons from iron to oxygen.

53. The following set of elements is written in increasing order of their atomic radii are O> N > P.

54. Zinc oxide is an inorganic compound with the formula ZnO. ZnO is a white powder that is insoluble in water, and it is widely used as an additive in numerous materials and products including rubbers. ZnO is an amphoteric oxide.

55. When a carboxylic acid is treated with an alcohol and an acid catalyst, an ester is formed (along with water). This reaction is called the Fischer esterification. Which reaction of an alcohol would produce a sweet smelling compound called esterification.

56. Among the given options, In view of the order of reactivity, the following reaction is feasible. That is $2AgNO_3 + Cu \rightarrow Cu(NO_3)_2 + 2Ag$.

57. Total number of ions present in the solution containing one mole of dissolved sodium sulphate in water is 18.069×10^{23}.

58. NH_4Cl in water is an endothermic process. The term endothermic process describes the process or reaction in which the system absorbs Energy from its surroundings, usually in the form of heat.

59. Among the given options, the compound X is Alcohol.

60. Among the given options, the basic salt is Z.

61. Among the given options, Li Na K has the same number of valence electrons.

62. Vinegar is an acid because it will turn blue litmus red.

63. Alcohols are studied in Organic Chemistry because these are Hydrocarbons.Organic compounds are classified according to functional groups, alcohols, carboxylic acids, amines, etc.

64. Calcium sulfate (or calcium sulphate) is the inorganic compound with the formula $CaSO_4$ and related hydrates. In the form of ã-anhydrite (the anhydrous form), it is used as a desiccant. One particular hydrate is better known as plaster of Paris, and another occurs naturally as the mineral gypsum.

65. A substance "A" reacts win another substance "B" to yield a substance "C" and a gas "D". The gas "D" which when passed through lime water turns it milky. The substances "A" and "B" are (A = HCl) & (B = Na_2CO_3).

66. Given below reaction in the option c represents a double displacement reaction.

$$K_2SO_4 + BaCl_2 \rightarrow BaSO_4 + 2KCl$$

67. Humid air and Presence of acidic gases set of conditions are the most favourable for corrosion of metals.

68. A trivalent metal "M" was made to react with oxygen to yield 0.25 mole of metal oxide. The reaction product contains 1.506×10^{23} molecules of oxide of formula M_2O_3.

69. In Modern Periodic Table, there are 18 Groups and 07 periods.

70. Propene would immediately decolorize bromine dissolved in Carbon disulphide.

71. In an atom the order of filling up of the orbitals is governed by Aufbau principle.

72. Reaction given in the option C is an example for displacement reaction.

73. A metal forms an amphoteric oxide on reaction with oxygen. The metal is Al.

74. A hydrocarbon contains one carbon-carbon single bond, one carbon-carbon double bond and one carbon-carbon triple bond. C4H4 is its molecular formula.

75. Reaction is an exothermic reaction and a neutralization reaction.

76. The electronic configuration of an element is 2,7. This element is placed in 7th group of modern periodic table.

77. The type of bonds present in CuSO4. 5H2O are electrovalent. covalent, coordinate and hydrogen bond.

78. Among the given options, option d is correctly matched, A-4 B-3 C-1 D-2 Baking soda is a familiar household product that also goes by the names sodium bicarbonate, bicarbonate of soda and sodium hydrogen carbonate.Sodium hydroxide, also known as lye and *caustic soda*, is an inorganic compound with the formula NaOH.Magnesium sulfate is an inorganic salt with the formula MgSO„ " where 0d"xd"7. It is often encountered as the heptahydrate sulfate mineral epsomite, commonly called Epsom salt. Th

79. Decreasing the temperature of water will decrease the vapour pressure of water contained in a sealed tube.

80. Among the given options, reaction given in the option below,represents the process of calcination.

$$ZnCO_3(s) \rightarrow ZnO(s) + CO_2$$

81. HCHO has only covalent bonds between the atoms. Formaldehyde (HCHO) is the most important carcinogen in outdoor air among the 187 hazardous air pollutants (HAPs) identified by the U.S. Environmental Protection Agency (EPA), not including ozone and particulate matter.

82. An acid reacts with a base to form salt and water is called the double displacement reaction.

83. An acid produces a gas 'X' on reaction with metal carbonates and hydrogen carbonates separately. The 'X' in these reactions is carbon dioxide.

84. The correct statement regarding the Mendeleev's periodic table of elements is that it had some gaps for the new elements to be discovered later.

85. H_2O is liquid H2S is a gas because oxygen forms stronger hydrogen bond than sulphur.

86. In reaction between HCl and O_2 is given by
$$4HCl + O_2 \rightarrow 2H_2O + 2Cl_2$$

The equivalent weight of HCL equal to its molecular weight.

87. Among the given options, Cl has the highest electron affinity. Chlorine has the highest electron affinity instead of Flourine though Fluorine has the highest electronegativity in the periodic table.

88. A student heats a beaker containing water continuously and measures the temperature as a function of time. She found that the temperature of water increases with time. After sometime, it becomes constant in spite of heat being supplied. The temperature remains constant up to a certain stage. The value of the constant temperature of water is 100°c.

89. Among the given options, Pure copper is deposited at the cathode is correct statement regarding of the electrolytic refining of impure copper.

90. On heating with an alkaline solution of KMnO4, ethanol produces Ethanoic acid.

91. From the given options, The formula is X_2O and it is basic in nature is correct about the formula of the oxide and its chemical nature.

92. Lime water turns milky on passing through it. On passing excess of carbon dioxide gas, milkiness disappears. It is due to the formation of $Ca(HCO_3)_2$.

93. Eka-aluminium predicted by Mendeleev was found to have properties similar to gallium.

94. Mustard agent was first used effectively in World War I by the German army against British and Canadian soldiers near Ypres, Belgium, in 1917. Mustard agent is a persistent weapon that remains on the ground for days and weeks, and it continues to cause ill effects. If mustard agent contaminates a soldier's clothing and equipment, then the other soldiers that he comes into contact with are also poisoned.

95. $ZnCO_3$ is used in making ointment for curing skin disease.Calamine, also known as calamine lotion, is a medication used to treat mild itchiness. Calamine is a combination of zinc oxide and 0.5% ferric oxide (Fe_2O_3).

96. The characteristic odour of garlic is due to sulphur compound.

97. The oxide of an element 'A' can react separately with an acid and a base to produce salt and water. The element 'A' is metallic and the oxide is amphoteric.

98. High pressure and low temperature favours the liquefaction of gases. Liquefaction of gases is the process by which substances in their gaseous state are converted to the liquid state. When pressure on a gas is increased, its molecules get closer together, and its temperature is reduced, which removes enough energy to make it change from the gaseous to the liquid state.

99. From the given chemical equation the value of the coefficient 'A' is 6.

$$2Al + 'A'\,HCl \rightarrow 2AlCl_3 + 3H_2$$

100. On hydration, a hydrocarbon 'X' produces a compound 'Y' with molecular formula C_2H_6O. 'X' forms a dibromo compound with bromine. The compound 'Y' produces a carboxylic acid on oxidation with acidified $K_2Cr_2O_7$. The hydrocarbon 'X' is Ethene.

101. Among the given options, the greatest in atomic size is potassium.

102. An acid solution is completely neutralized by a base. The pH of the salt solution so produced is 7.

103. The catalyst used in the manufacture of the sulphuric acid by contact process is V_2O_5.

104. Nickel and cadmium serves as electrodes in rechargeable batteries commonly used in devices such as torch lights, electric shavers etc.

105. Among the given options, H_2S is oxidized is correct concerning the reaction.

106. Freezing and melting are two common phase transitions, or changes in the states of matter to or from solid, liquid, gas, or plasma. Sublimation is another one of these phase transitions; except in this case, we have a solid turning directly into a gas. As a sublimating material changes from a solid to a gas, it never passes through the liquid state.

107. The solution of a substance 'A' turns red litmus blue. the most appropriate pH range in the substance 'A' will be 7 – less than 14.

108. Among the given options, the sets of elements are arranged in correct order of their increasing electronegativity is I >Br >Cl >F.

109. Among the given options, C_6H_{10} is the molecular formula of n-hexyne.

110. Malleability is a substance's ability to deform under pressure (compressive stress). If malleable, a material may be flattened into thin sheets by hammering or rolling. Malleable materials can be flattened into metal leaf. The property usually applies to the family groups 1 to 12 on the modern periodic table of elements.

111. Among the given options, the descending order of atomic radius is B - C - N - O.

112. Potassium nitrate is a chemical compound with the chemical formula KNO_3. It is an ionic salt of potassium ions K^+ and nitrate ions NO_3, and is therefore an alkali metal nitrate. It occurs in nature as a mineral, niter. It is a source of nitrogen, from which it derives its name. Potassium nitrate is one of several nitrogen-containing compounds collectively referred to as saltpeter or saltpetre.

113. Ethane molecules is the distance between two adjacent carbon atoms largest The name ethane is derived from the IUPAC nomenclature of organic chemistry. "Eth-" is derived from the German for potable alcohol (ethanol) and "-ane" refers to the presence of a single bond between the carbon atoms.

114. The number of moles of water in 90 grams of water is 5.

115. The reactions which involve an exchange of ions between the reactants are known as double displacement.

116. Carbon dioxide is produced when an acid reacts with sodium carbonate.

117. The ability of an element to exhibit different forms having different physical properties but same chemical properties is known as Allotropy.

118. A molecule of benzene has 09 single bond and 03 double bonds. Benzene is an important organic chemical compound with the chemical formula C_6H_6. The benzene molecule is composed of six carbon atoms joined in a ring with one hydrogen atom attached to each. Benzene is a natural constituent of crude oil and is one of the elementary petrochemicals.

119. The maximum number of electrons that can be accommodated in M shell of an atom is 18.

120. Among the given gases, NH3 will have the highest rate of diffusion.

121. Among the given options, NH4OH is not a strong electrolyte

122. Among the given options, Chlorophyll is not a colloid. Chlorophyll (also chlorophyl) is any of several related green pigments found in cyanobacteria and the chloroplasts of algae and plants. Its name is derived from the Greek words chloros ("green") and phyllon ("leaf").

123. The number of water molecules present in 36 grams of water is 6.046×10^{23}.

124. A substance is said to be oxidised if it gains oxygen or searches singular positive ion state .

125. An aqueous solution of a substance turns red litmus blue. The substance is sodium carbonate.

126. Sulfur or sulphur is a chemical element with symbol S and atomic number 16. It is abundant, multivalent, and nonmetallic. Under normal conditions, sulfur atoms form cyclic octatomic molecules with a chemical formula S_8. Elemental sulfur is a bright yellow crystalline solid at room temperature Sulphur is NOT lustre.

127. A molecule of propyne has 05 single bonds and 01 triple bond.

128. In a modem periodic table, the metallic character of elements decreases as we move from left to right in a period. increases as we move from top to bottom in a group.

129. The pH of pure water is 7. In general, water with a pH lower than 7 is considered acidic, and with a pH greater than 7 is considered basic.

130. Thin foils of Aluminium metal are used for packaging food.Food is the main source of aluminium. Drinking water contains more aluminium than solid food. however, aluminium in food may be absorbed more than aluminium from water.

131. The nucleus of an atom contains Protons and neutrons.

RRB SENIOR SECTION ENGINEER

1. In organic chemistry we normally learn about two important reducing reagents, sodium borohydride ($NaBH_4$) and lithium aluminum hydride ($LiAlH_4$ or LAH). We learn that $NaBH_4$ is a "weak reducing agent" and can only take aldehydes and ketones to alcohols easily. $NaBH_4$ can handle esters, but it is very slow at converting them and thus not preferable.

2. Fats and oils are composed of triglycerides; three molecules of fatty acids attach to a single molecule of glycerol. The alkaline solution, which is often called lye (although the term "lye soap" refers almost exclusively to soaps made with sodium hydroxide), brings about a chemical reaction known as saponification.

3. A chemical bond is a lasting attraction between atoms, ions or molecules that enables the formation of chemical compounds. The bond may result from the electrostatic force of attraction between oppositely charged ions as in ionic bonds or through the sharing of electrons as in covalent bonds.

4. The glycerol chemical formula is $C_3H_8O_3$ and its extended formula is $CH_2OH\text{-}CHOH\text{-}CH_2OH$. The IUPAC name for glycerol is 1, 2, 3- Trihydroxypropane or 1, 2, 3- Propanetriol.

5. The most ideal disinfectant used for drinking water is Chlorine. Chlorine is one of the most commonly used disinfectants for water disinfection.

6. $Ca_3(PO_4)_2$ is generally added to Table Salt to make it flow freely in rainy season.

7. Valence electrons in the element A are 3 and that in element B are 6. Most probable compound formed from A and B is A_2B_3.

8. Atoms of the elements belonging to the same group of periodic table will have Same number of electrons in the valence shell.

9. In chemistry and physics, the Avogadro constant, named after scientist Amedeo Avogadro, is the number of constituent particles, usually atoms or molecules, that are contained in the amount of substance given by one mole.

10. The atoms of a chemical element can exist in different types. These are called isotopes. They have the same number of protons (and electrons), but different numbers of neutrons. Different isotopes of the same element have different masses.

11. Zinc powder is added to a solution of iodine in ethanol. An exothermic redox reaction occurs, forming zinc iodide, which can be obtained by evaporating the solvent. In reaction between Zinc and Iodine. Zinc Iodide is formed. Zinc atom is being oxidised.

12. Fluorine is such a powerful oxidising agent that you can't reasonably do solution reactions with it.

13. Filling a bulb with an inert gas such as argon or nitrogen slows down the evaporation of the tungsten filament compared to operating it in a vacuum. This allows for greater temperatures and therefore greater efficacy with less reduction in filament life.

14. Froth floatation process for the concentration of Ores is an illustration of the practical application of Adsorption.

15. The presence of nitrogen in the products of combustion ensures that air is used for the combustion.

16. The equipment installed in power plants to reduce air pollution due to smoke is electrostatic precipitators.

17. The solubility product (Ksp) of silver iodate in water at 20°C is $4 \times 10{-}8$ mol^2 L^{-2}. The concentration of silver ions, Ag+(aq) in a solution is $2 \times 10{-}4$ mol L^{-1}.

18. $C_2H_5ONa + CH_3CH_2CH_2I$ pair of compounds will react together under suitable conditions to form 1- ethoxypropane as the major product.

19. Among the given compounds, $[Ni(CO)_4]$ includes a transition element with zero oxidation state.

20. If 0.005 moles each of the following substances are separately dissolved in 100 grams of water, the solution of Aluminium chloride substance will have the highest boiling point.

21. $CH_3CHO + NH_2NH_2$ $CH_3CH=NNH_2 + H_2O$ represents nucleophilic add -on reaction.

22. In NH_2OH, nitrogen has an oxidation number -1.

23. The solubility product (Ksp) of $PbCO_3$ at 20°C is $7.84 \times 10{-}14$ mol^2 L^{-2}. The solubility product (Ksp) of $PbCO_3$ in water at 20°C is $2.80 \times 10{-}7$ mol L^{-1}.

24. Among the given options, 2,4- Dinitrophenol is the most acidic in nature. 2,4-Dinitrophenol (2,4-DNP or simply DNP) is an organic compound with the formula $HOC_6H_3(NO_2)_2$. It is a yellow, crystalline solid that has a sweet, musty odor. It sublimes, is volatile with steam, and is soluble in most organic solvents as well as aqueous alkaline solutions.

25. 6 is the coordination number of zine in the complex ion [Zn (OH)4 (H2O)$_2$]$^{2-}$.

26. Addition of 5 grams of solute A (molecular mass=100) to 100 grams of solvent B causes the same elevation of boiling point as the addition of 10 grams of solute C to 200 grams of the same solvent B. The molecular mass of the solute C is 100.

27. Among the given pairs, $CH_3CHO + CH_3CH_2CHO$ pair of molecules of the compounds will react together in presence of sodium hydroxide solution under suitable conditions to produce a mixture of four compounds.

28. Among the given options, Ammonia molecule has a trigonal pyramidal shape as predicted by the valence shell electron pair repulsion theory (VSEPR theory) with an experimentally determined bond angle of 106.7°. The central nitrogen atom has five outer electrons with an additional electron from each hydrogen atom.

29. In an industrial area, a sample of 10 litres of air was found to contain ml of sulphur dioxide gas. The concentration of sulphur dioxide gas in air in ppm is 500.

30. For the reaction 2NO, (g) N_2O_4 (g) + 60kJ, an increase in temperature will favour the decomposition of N_2O_4.

31. The correct order of increasing electro negativity of elements is F>0>N >P.

32. The major product formed by treating n- butyl chloride with boiling solution of potassium hydroxide in ethanol is 2- Butene.

33. Among the given options, HCHO will not undergo aldol condensation when treated with an aqueous solution of sodium hydroxide.

34. $3d^3\ 4s^2$ electronic configuration represents a transition element in its ground state.

35. 0.1is the modality of the solution which contains 11.70 grams of sodium chloride dissolved in 2.0 Kg of water.

36. For the reaction N_2 (g) + $3H_2$ (g) $2NH_3$ (g), the units of Kp are Atm−2.

37. The general electronic configuration of elements placed in a group in the modern periodic table is ns^2np^4. This configuration of elements can be placed in 16th group of the periodic table.

38. The primary alcohol C_4H_7OH is oxidized using acidified $K_2O_2O_7$. The molecular formula of the possible product is $C_4H_6O_2$.

39. 2,2-Dimethyl- 2- phenylethanal will undergo Cannizarro's reaction when treated with concentrated solution of potassium hydroxide in water.

40. The electronic configuration of transition element $3d^5\ 4s^2$ is paramagnetic in nature.

41. When we move from top to bottom in a group of periodic tables. Three will be variation in the properties of the elements. If we move from top to bottom group 17 we will find Ionic radii will increase.

42. If Rydberg constant is $1.0968 \times 10^7 m^{-1}$, the wavelength of light emitted when a hydrogen atom changes from n=5 to the n =3 state, will be $1.2821 \times 10^{-6} m$.

43. Combustion of methane taken place in air. The number of moles of methane required to produce 66.0 g of CO_2(g) will be 1.5 mol.

44. A solution is prepared by mixing 50 mL of 0.20M NaCl, 25 mL of 0.10M NaOH and 25 mL of 0.30m HCL. The concentration of hydrogen ions (H+ion) in solution thus obtained will be 0.05 M.

45. A flux is often added to remove impurities from an ore in a blast furnace. In the reaction, CaO + SIO$_2$,' $CaSIO_3$, the slag and the flux are respectively $CaSIO_3$ and SiO_2.

46. The correct order of decreasing acidity of these compounds will be $HCOOH > CH_3COOH > C_6H_5OH > C_2H_5OH$.

47. If Avogadro constant is $6.02 \times 10^{23}\ mol^{-1}$, then mass of one C_2H_4 molecule (in gram) will be 4.65×10^{-23} g/molecule.

48. Properties of certain elements resembles with the elements placed diagonally in the periodic table. Lithium will show diagonal relationship with Magnesium.

49. Among the given options, $2F_2$(g) + 20H-(aq) 2F(aq)+OF$_2$(g)+H$_2$O(l) is not a disproportionate reaction.

50. H+ and BCI$_3$ are the pair of acids from the given options.

51. Chlorine is extracted commercially by the electrolysis of an aqueous solution of one of its compounds.

52. Number of structural isomers for C_4H_8 would be 4.

53. The molecules of elements and compounds exist in different structures .The molecule which is linear, is CO_2.

54. The correct order of first ionization enthalpy of the elements of oxygen family in the periodic table is 0> S > Se.

55. According to the equation given in the question, 20 mL of 0.1M $KMnO_4$ will be equivalent to 50 mL of 0.10 M $H_2C_2O_4$.

56. Ammoniacal $AgNO_3$ will be used to distinguish compound IV from the rest of compounds.

57. The largest gland in the body, the liver, is not responsible for one function mentioned below. The liver produces bile. The liver's main job is to filter the blood coming from the digestive tract, before passing it to the rest of the body. The liver also detoxifies chemicals and metabolizes drugs. As it does so, the liver secretes bile that ends up back in the intestines.

58. In plants, only Auxin hormones can promote growth of plant parts.Auxins promote stem elongation, inhibit growth of lateral buds (maintains apical dominance). They are produced in the stem, buds, and root tips. Example: Indole Acetic Acid (IA). Auxin is a plant hormone produced in the stem tip that promotes cell elongation.

59. Neon has three natural isotopes with mass number 20, 21 and 22. The relative abundance of the isotopes is 90.51%, 0.27% and 9.22% respectively. The average atomic mass of neon will be 20.187u.

60. Four successive members of 3d block (of periodic table) are Vanadium (z = 23), Chromium (z = 24), manganese (z = 25) and iron (z = 26). Among these, Manganese (Mn) is expected to have the highest third ionization enthalpy.

61. Second reaction in the given options, is an example of both, displacement reaction and redox reaction.

62. A 0.10 M NaOH situation is prepared for an analytical laboratory work. pH of the solution will be 13.0.

63. The correct order of reducing power of the metals will be Cu < Fe < Cr < Mg < Na.

64. The IUPAC name of the Compound $CH_3CH_2CH = C-CH_3$ is 3- methyl -3- hexene.

65. Among the given options, B2 is paramagnetic in nature.

66. Halogens have tendency to accept electrons and therefore work as oxidizing agent. The correct increasing order of oxidizing power of the halogens is $I2 < Br_2 < CI_2 < F_2$.

67. Among the given options, 4th reaction is an example for redox reaction.

68. Among the given options, pH of the Second option will be equal to 1.

69. For obtaining a metal from its ore various metallurgy processes are adopted. Froth flotation process is metallurgy of sulphide ores.

70. Among the given options, Second option is most viscous.

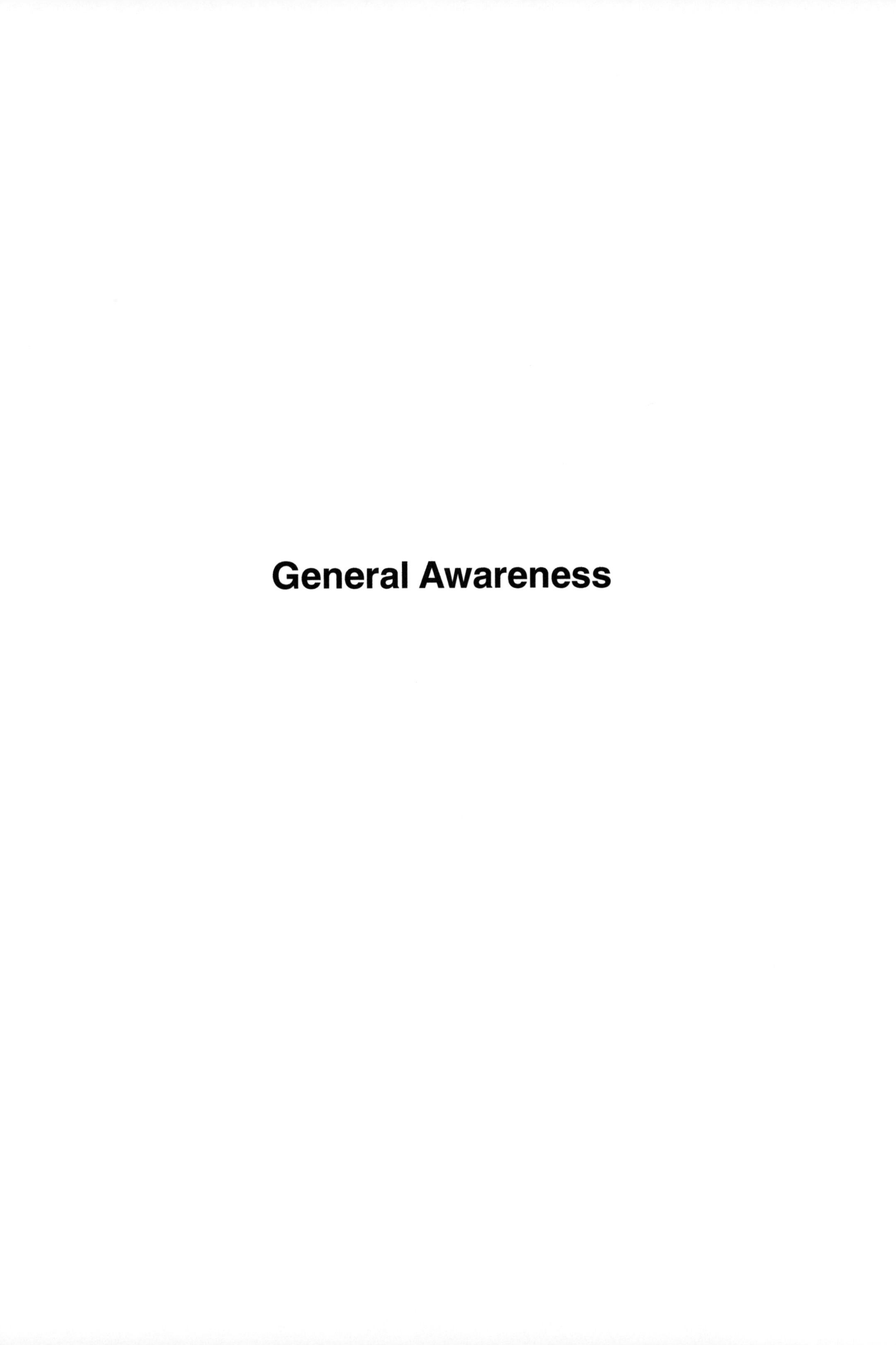# General Awareness

RRB JUNIOR ENGINEER

1. Ashoka in the 13th year of his coronation, appointed a special type of officer who surveyed the land, kept land records and carried out justice. These officers were called

(a) Amatyas   (b) Samahartas

(c) Rajukas   (d) Chalukyas

[RRB JE 2014 GREEN SHIFT]

2. Who built the Jagannatha temple of Puri?

(a) Anantavarmana Chodaganga

(b) Narsimahavarmana

(c) Aadiyavarmana

(d) Parmeshwaravarmana

[RRB JE 2014 GREEN SHIFT]

3. Section 66 A has been in media controversy recently. The section pertains to

(a) Communal Harmony

(b) Sexual Aggression

(c) Company's Act

(d) Information Technology

[RRB JE 2014 GREEN SHIFT]

4. In which of the following movement did Gandhiji make the first use of Hunger Strike as a weapon?

(a) Ahmedabad strike, 1918

(b) Rowlatt Satyagraha, 1919

(c) Swadeshi Movement, 1905

(d) Champaran Satyagraha, 1917

[RRB JE 2014 RED SHIFT]

5. The famous Chinese pilgrim 'Hieun Tsang' visited India during the reign of:

(a) Harshavardhan   (b) Chandragupta II

(c) Ashoka   (d) Kanishka

[RRB JE 2014 RED SHIFT]

6. Jama Masjid at Delhi was built by :

(a) Akbar   (b) Jahangir

(c) Shah Jahan   (d) Aurangzeb

[RRB JE 2014 RED SHIFT]

7. The 'Quit India Movement' was launched in the year :

(a) 1920 A.D.   (b) 1930 A.D.

(c) 1942 A.D.   (d) 1946 A.D.

[RRB JE 2014 RED SHIFT]

8. Who wrote 'Indica' ?

(a) Kautilya   (b) Kalidasa

(c) Shudraka   (d) Megasthenes

[RRB JE 2014 RED SHIFT]

9. 'Giddha' is a folk dance of :

(a) Punjab   (b) Uttar Pradesh

(c) Assam   (d) Maharashtra

[RRB JE 2014 RED SHIFT]

10. "The Servants of India Society' was founded by :

(a) Jyotiba Phule   (b) G.K. Gokhale

(c) B.G. Tilak   (d) B.R. Ambedkar

[RRB JE 2014 RED SHIFT]

11. Goutam Buddha delivered his first sermons at :

(a) Kusinagar   (b) Sarnath

(c) Pataliputra   (d) Vaishali

[RRB JE 2014 RED SHIFT]

12. The Governor General of India at the time of foundation of Indian National Congress was ?

(a) Lord Chelmsford   (b) Lord Dalhousie

(c) Lord Dufferin   (d) Lord Canning

[RRB JE 2014 YELLOW SHIFT]

13. Who was the advocate at the famous trials of three INA Soldiers ?

(a) Bhulabhai Desai

(b) Asaf Ali

(c) Subhash Chandra Bose

(d) C. Rajagopalachari

[RRB JE 2014 YELLOW SHIFT]

14. Match Column A (Dance type) and Column B (State).

Column A	Column B
P. Bihu	1. Gujarat
Q. Garba	2. UP
R. Tamasha	3. Assam
S. Nautanki	4. Maharashtra

(a) P-4, Q-1, R-2, S-3   (b) P-3, Q-1, R-4, S-2

(c) P-3, Q-1, R-2, S-4   (d) P-1, Q-4, R-2, S-3

[RRB JE 2014 YELLOW SHIFT]

15. The first capital of British Colonial India as

(a) Delhi   (b) Mumbai

(c) Kolkata   (d) Madras

[RRB JE 2015 26th AUG 1st SHIFT]

16. What was unexpected at the end of the battle of Waterloo?

A. Duke of Wellington lost

B. Napoleon Bonaparte won

C. Duke of wellington won

D. Napoleon Bonaparte lost

The correct response would be

(a) A   (b) B

(c) B and C   (d) C and D

[RRB JE 2015 26th AUG 1st SHIFT]

17. Who founded the Indian National congress?

(a) Allan Octavian Hume

(b) Womesh Chandra Banerji

(c) Gopal Krishna Gokhale

(d) Rash Behari Bose

[RRB JE 2015 26th AUG 1st SHIFT]

18. What is meant by secularism?

Having

(a) an elected person as head of state

(b) a culture of equal treatment to all without discrimination

(c) a government of the people, by the people and for the people

(d) the freedom to preach, practice and profess any religion

[RRB JE 2015 26th AUG 1st SHIFT]

19. Who discovered the sea route to India?

(a) Vasco da Gama

(b) Magellan

(c) Diaz

(d) Christopher Columbus

[RRB JE 2015 26th AUG 2nd SHIFT]

20. In the medieval times, Bedouins were

(a) Early Romans

(b) Greek Emperors

(c) Wandering Arab camel herdsmen

(d) Tribal horse riders

[RRB JE 2015 26th AUG 2nd SHIFT]

21. The term used for armed rebellion against a constituted authority is

(a) Insurgency   (b) Terrorism

(c) Naxalism   (d) Coup

[RRB JE 2015 26th AUG 2nd SHIFT]

22. The treaty of Versailles was signed in the summer of 1919 with

(a) Germany   (b) Austria

(c) Turkey   (d) Hungary

[RRB JE 2015 26th AUG 2nd SHIFT]

23. Pablo Picasso's creation 'Guernica' was based on consequences of

(a) Spanish civil war

(b) Sudanese civil war

(c) Second world war

(d) American war of independence

[RRB JE 2015 26th AUG 3rd SHIFT]

24. Three national leaders were together called Lal Bal Pal. Which name in the options is wrong?

(a) Bal Gangadhar Tilak

(b) Bipin Chandra Pal

(c) Lala Lajpat Rai

(d) Lai Bahadur Shastri

[RRB JE 2015 26th AUG 3rd SHIFT]

25. Who was the last Governor General in the two century rule of the British in India?

(a) Lord Clive

(b) Sir Warren Hastings

(c) Lord Mountbatten

(d) Lord Cornwallis

[RRB JE 2015 26th AUG 3rd SHIFT]

26. Of the Slav population scattered in Eastern Europe, those who began the Pan Slav movement to have one state were

(a) Serbians   (b) Bulgarians

(c) Romanians   (d) Polish

[RRB JE 2015 27th AUG 1st SHIFT]

27. Who built the Pyramids?

(a) Pharaohs   (b) Chinese

(c) Confucians   (d) Romans

[RRB JE 2015 27th AUG 1st SHIFT]

28. The king of Mauryan Empire who in 322 BC uprooted Greeks from Punjab and Nandas from the Gangetic plane was

(a) Chadragupta   (b) Bindusar

(c) Ashok   (d) Mahapadmananda

[RRB JE 2015 27th AUG 1st SHIFT]

29. Who founded the Ramakrishna Mission?

(a) Ramakrislma Paramahama

(b) Saradamani

(c) Swami Vivekananda

(d) Rani Rashmoni

[RRB JE 2015 27ᵗʰ AUG 2ⁿᵈ SHIFT]

30. After First World War political movement named fascism arose. Out of the following statements which one is not true of fascism

(a) Dictatorship introduced in Italy by Mussolini is called fascism

(b) German version of fascism is referred to as Nazism

(c) Fascists were not hostile to democracy and socialism

(d) Adolf Hitler was a fascist

[RRB JE 2015 27ᵗʰ AUG 2ⁿᵈ SHIFT]

31. Which Mughal emperor proclaimed Deen-e-Ilahi or Divine Faith?

(a) Babar   (b) Humayun

(c) Shahjahan   (d) Akbar

[RRB JE 2015 27ᵗʰ AUG 2ⁿᵈ SHIFT]

32. Who wrote our national song, 'Vande Mataram'?

(a) Bankim Chandra Chatteijee

(b) Rabindra Nath Tagore

(c) Sumitra Nandan Pant

(d) Mohan Das Karam Chand Gandhi

[RRB JE 2015 27ᵗʰ AUG 3ʳᵈ SHIFT]

33. Which out of the following is not correct?

(a) The Dutch invaded Indonesia

(b) The Japanese occupied Singapore during World War II

(c) India was colonized by the British for almost two centuries

(d) Palestinian territory was never part of Israel

[RRB JE 2015 27ᵗʰ AUG 3ʳᵈ SHIFT]

34. What was the name of the founder of Buddhism, before he renounced the world?

(a) Gautama   (b) Siddhartha

(c) Partha   (d) Mahaveera

[RRB JE 2015 27ᵗʰ AUG 3ʳᵈ SHIFT]

35. Which of the following became the greatest landmark in history of mankind as it ushered in an era of liberty, equality and fraternity?

(a) Spanish Revolution in 1936

(b) Russian Revolution in 1971

(c) Serbian Revolution in 1804

(d) French Revolution in 1789

[RRB JE 2015 27ᵗʰ AUG 3ʳᵈ SHIFT]

36. Match **List 1** with **List 2** and select the correct answer from the codes given below in the list

List 1 (State)	List 2 (Emblem)
A. Chera	1. Bow
B. Chola	2. Tiger
C. Pandya	3. Fish

(a) A-2, B-2, C-3

(b) A-3, B-2, C-1

(c) A-3, B-1, C-2

(d) A-2, B-1, C-3

[RRB JE 2015 28ᵗʰ AUG 1ˢᵗ SHIFT]

37. The medieval ruler who was the first to establish a ministry of agriculture (Diwan-i-Kohi) was

(a) Alauddin Khilji

(b) Mohammad Bin Tughlaq

(c) Sher Shah

(d) Akbar

[RRB JE 2015 28ᵗʰ AUG 1ˢᵗ SHIFT]

38. When did Queen Victoria declared the taking over the Indian Administration under British crown

(a) 1 November, 1858

(b) 31 December, 1857

(c) 6 January, 1958

(d) 17 November, 1859

[RRB JE 2015 28ᵗʰ AUG 1ˢᵗ SHIFT]

39. The first Census in India during the British period was held during the tenure of

(a) Lord Dufferin   (b) Lord Lytton

(c) Lord Mayo   (d) Lord Ripon

[RRB JE 2015 28ᵗʰ AUG 1ˢᵗ SHIFT]

40. Which one of the following animals was not represented on seals and terracota art of the Harappan culture

(a) Cow   (b) Elephant

(c) Rhinoceros   (d) Tiger

[RRB JE 2015 28ᵗʰ AUG 2ⁿᵈ SHIFT]

41. A "Forgotten Empire", written by the renowned historian Robert Sewell is about which of the following Empires

(a) Mauryan Empire   (b) Kushan Empire

(c) Vijaynagar Empire (d) Mughal Empire

[RRB JE 2015 28ᵗʰ AUG 2ⁿᵈ SHIFT]

42. During whose Victoroyship did the High Court came presidential cities of Calcutta. Madras and Bombay

(a) Warren Hastings

(b) Lord Cornwallis

(c) John Lawrence

(d) Lord Dalhousie

[RRB JE 2015 28ᵗʰ AUG 2ⁿᵈ SHIFT]

43. Who had estimated National income in India first

(a) Dadabhai Naoroji

(b) R.C Dutt

(c) M.G Ranade

(d) W.Hunter

[RRB JE 2015 28ᵗʰ AUG 2ⁿᵈ SHIFT]

44. Consider the following statements and select the difference between Chaitya and Vihara

(a) Chaitya is a place of worship whereas Vihara is a living place for Buddhist saints

(b) Vihara is a place of worship whereas Chaitya is a living place for Buddhist saints

(c) Chaitya and Vihara both can be used as a living place

(d) There is not much difference between the two

[RRB JE 2015 28ᵗʰ AUG 3ʳᵈ SHIFT]

45. The world famous Takht-i-Taus (the Peacock Throne) was kept in which of the following Mughal buildings?

(a) The Diwan-i-Khas at Fatehpur Sikri

(b) Agra Fort

(c) The Rang Mahal at the Red Fort at Delhi

(d) The Diwan-i-Aam at the Red Fort at Delhi

[RRB JE 2015 28ᵗʰ AUG 3ʳᵈ SHIFT]

46. With reference to the colonial rule in India, consider the following events

1. Morley-Minto Reforms Act

2. Transfer of capital from Calcutta to Delhi

3. First World War

4. Lucknow Pact

The correct chronological order of these events is

(a) 2-1-3-4   (b) 1-2-3-4

(c) 2-1-4-3   (d) 1-2-4-3

[RRB JE 2015 28ᵗʰ AUG 3ʳᵈ SHIFT]

47. Match List 1 with List 2 and select the correct answer from the codes given below in the list

List 1 (King)	**List 2 (Kingdom)**
A. Pradyota	1. Magadha
B. Udayana	2. Vatsa
C. Prasenjita	3. Avanthi
D. Ajatsatru	4. Kosala

(a) A-1, B-4, C-2, D-3

(b) A-2, B-3, C-1, D-4

(c) A-3, B-2, C-4, D-1

(d) A-4, B-1, C-3, D-2

[RRB JE 2015 29ᵗʰ AUG 1ˢᵗ SHIFT]

48. Who among the following was the first Bhakti saint to use Hindi for propagation of his message?

(a) Dadu   (b) Kabir

(c) Ramananda   (d) Tulsidas

[RRB JE 2015 29ᵗʰ AUG 1ˢᵗ SHIFT]

49. Who was the first Indian native ruler to accept the system of Subsidiary Alliance?

(a) Scindia of Gwalior

(b) Nizam of Hyderabad

(c) Dalip Singh of Punjab

(d) Gaikwad of Baroda

[RRB JE 2015 29ᵗʰ AUG 1ˢᵗ SHIFT]

50. With which of the following centres of learning, Chanakya, the famous teacher of Chandragupta Maurya was associated?

(a) Takshashila   (b) Nalanda

(c) Vikramsila   (d) Vaishali

[RRB JE 2015 29ᵗʰ AUG 2ⁿᵈ SHIFT]

51. The famous battle of Takkolam of South India was fought between

(a) Cholas and North Chalukyas

(b) Cholas and Rashtrakutas

(c) Cholas and Hoyasals

(d) Cholas and Pandyas

[RRB JE 2015 29ᵗʰ AUG 2ⁿᵈ SHIFT]

52. Which Congress President negotiated with both Cripps Mission and Lord Waved?

(a) Abul Kalam Azad

(b) Jawahar Lal Nehru

(c) JB Kriplani

(d) C. Rajgopalachari

[RRB JE 2015 29ᵗʰ AUG 2ⁿᵈ SHIFT]

53. Which one of the following propounded that 'destiny determines everything, man is powerless'

(a) Jains   (b) Buddhists

(c) Ajivakas   (d) Mimansakas

[RRB JE 2015 29th AUG 3rd SHIFT]

54. Arrange the following battles of the Mughal period in Chronological order-

1. Battle of Ghagara   2. Battle of Khanwa
3. Battle of Chausa   4. Battle of Samugarh

Select the answer from the following codes

(a) 2-1-3-4   (b) 1-3-2-4

(c) 3-2-1-4   (d) 2-3-1-4

[RRB JE 2015 29th AUG 3rd SHIFT]

55. During the period of Indian freedom struggle, who amongst the following started the Central Hindu School

(a) Annie Besant   (b) Bhikaji Cama

(c) MG Ranade   (d) Madan Mohan Malviya

[RRB JE 2015 29th AUG 3rd SHIFT]

56. What is the correct chronological order in which the following states of the Indian union were created or granted full statehood?

1. Andhra Pradesh   2. Maharashtra
3. Nagaland   4. Haryana

Select the correct answer using the code given below-

(a) 1, 2, 3, 4   (b) 2, 1, 3, 4

(c) 1, 2, 4, 3   (d) 2, 1, 4, 3

[RRB JE 2015 29th AUG 3rd SHIFT]

57. Consider the following foreign visitors to India:

1. Alberuni   2. Fahein
3. Hieun Tsang   4. Megasthenese

The correct chronological order in which these persons visited India is

(a) 4-3-1-2   (b) 2-4-3-1

(c) 4-2-3-1   (d) 1-2-4-3

[RRB JE 2015 30th AUG 3rd SHIFT]

58. Who was the last ruler of Tuglaq dynasty of the Delhi Sultanate?

(a) Firoz Shah Tuglaq

(b) Giyasuddin Tuglaq II

(c) Mahmud Shah Tuglaq

(d) Nasrat Shah

[RRB JE 2015 30th AUG 3rd SHIFT]

59. Which of the following pairs is not correctly matched?

(a) Poorna Swaraj Resolution: 1929

(b) Martyrdom of Sardar Bhagat Singh: 1931

(c) Formation of Congress Socialist Party: 1938

(d) Shimla Conference: 1945

[RRB JE 2015 30th AUG 3rd SHIFT]

60. Who founded the "Arya Samaj"?

(a) Ram Mohan Roy

(b) Swami Dayanand Saraswati

(c) Swami Vivekananda

(d) Ishwar Chandra Vidyasagar

[RRB JE 2015 16th SEP 3rd SHIFT]

61. Where in the ancient world, dead bodies were preserved as mummies?

(a) Babylon   (b) Greece

(c) Egypt   (d) China

[RRB JE 2015 16th SEP 3rd SHIFT]

62. Ramakrishna Missions were established in many countries and many parts of India by

(a) Ramakrishna Paramahansa

(b) Ma Sarada mai

(c) Raja Ram Mohan Roy

(d) Swami Vivekananda

[RRB JE 2015 16th SEP 3rd SHIFT]

RRB SENIOR SECTION ENGINEER

1. "Khalsa" was founded by-

(a) Guru Gobind Singh

(b) Guru Ramdas

(c) Guru Nanak

(d) Guru Arjun Dev

[RRB SSE 2014 GREEN SHIFT]

2. "Mahabharata" the epic was written by-

(a) Vyasa   (b) Kalidasa

(c) Tulsidasa   (d) Valmiki

[RRB SSE 2014 GREEN SHIFT]

3. The famous queen Chand Bibi who fought against Akbar, defended the city of -

(a) Berar   (b) Ahmad nagar

(c) Golconda   (d) Mysore

[RRB SSE 2014 GREEN SHIFT]

4. Arya samaj was founded by-

(a) Raja Ram Mohan

(b) Gopal Krishna Gokhale

(c) Swami Dayanand Saraswati

(d) Anne Besant

[RRB SSE 2014 GREEN SHIFT]

5. India's first war of Independence (related to Meerut mutiny) was in:

(a) 1835   (b) 1857

(c) 1892   (d) 1905

[RRB SSE 2014 GREEN SHIFT]

6. French power declined in India after the battle of-

(a) Plassey　　　　　(b) Buxar

(c) Talikota　　　　(d) Wandiwash

[RRB SSE 2014 GREEN SHIFT]

7. The first Indian railway train journey between Bombay and Thane was in the year-

(a) 1857　　　　　(b) 1853

(c) 1818　　　　　(d) 1854

[RRB SSE 2014 GREEN SHIFT]

8. With which one of the following movements is the slogan "Do or Die" associated ?

(a) Swadeshi Movement

(b) Non-CooperationMovement

(c) Civil Disobedience Movement

(d) Quit India Movement

[RRB SSE 2014 RED SHIFT]

9. Which one of the following places was associated with the beginning of Vinoba Bhave Bhoodan Movement ?

(a) Dandi　　　　　(b) Kheda

(c) Pochampalli　　(d) Champaran

[RRB SSE 2014 RED SHIFT]

10. Identify the Mughal Emperor who gave permission to East India Company to establish their factory at Surat :

(a) Akbar　　　　　(b) Jahangir

(c) Shahjahan　　　(d) Aurangzeb

[RRB SSE 2014 RED SHIFT]

11. The ruler of which of the following States was removed from power by the British on the pretext of Misgovernance ?

(a) Awadh　　　　　(b) Jhansi

(c) Satara　　　　　(d) Nagpur

[RRB SSE 2014 RED SHIFT]

12. Palitana Temples are located near :

(a) Bhavnagar, Gujarat

(b) Ujjain, Madhva Pradesh

(c) Nasik, Maharashtra

(d) Varanasi, Uttar Pradesh

[RRB SSE 2014 RED SHIFT]

13. Kunwar Singh, a prominent leader of Uprising of 1857, belonged to :

(a) Punjab　　　　　(b) Rajasthan

(c) Madhya Pradesh　(d) Bihar

14. Where was the First Session of Indian National Congress held in 1885 A.D. ?

(a) Delhi　　　　　(b) Calcutta

(c) Bombay　　　　(d) Surat

[RRB SSE 2014 RED SHIFT]

15. The 1929 session of Indian National Congress is of significance in the history of the Freedom Movement because the

(a) attainment of Self-Government was declared as the objective of the Congress

(b) attainment of Poorna Swaraj was adopted as the goal of the Congress

(c) Non-Cooperation Movement was launched

(d) decision to participate in the Round Table Conference in London was taken

[RRB SSE 2014 YELLOW SHIFT]

16. The movement that came to an abrupt end due to the Chauri Chaura incident was the

(a) Wahabi Movement

(b) Home Rule Movement

(c) Non-Cooperation Movement

(d) Civil Disobedience Movement

[RRB SSE 2014 YELLOW SHIFT]

17. Match the following:

P) C.R. Das　　　　　1. Bardoli Satyagraha

Q) Vallabh Bhai Patel　2. Swarajist

R) Abdul Ghaffar Khan　3. Khilafatist

S) Maulana Azad　　　4. Khudai Khidmatgar

(a) P-2, Q-1, R-4, S-3

(b) P-2. Q-4, R-1. S-3

(c) P-4.Q-1.R-3. S-2

(d) P-2, Q-1. R-3, S-4

[RRB SSE 2014 YELLOW SHIFT]

18. Consider the following pairs :

1. Garba : Gujarat

2. Mohiniattam: Odisha

3. Yakshagana: Karnataka

Which of the pairs given above is/are correctly matched ?

(a) 1 only　　　　　(b) 2 and 3 only

(c) 1 and 3 only　　(d) 1, 2 and 3

[RRB SSE 2014 YELLOW SHIFT]

19. Devdas and Parinita are Principal literary works by

(a) Rabindra Nath Tagore

(b) Sarat Chandra Chatterjee

(c) Satyajit Ray

(d) Munshi　Premchand

[RRB SSE 2014 YELLOW SHIFT]

20. What are the most common themes in the drawing found in the stone age Bhimbetka caves?

(a) Cutting logs, making fire, cooking, farming

(b) Hunting scenes, women and men, making fire

(c) Celebrations, Hunting , weaving, making fire

(d) Making tools, farming, hunting , making iron

[RRB SSE 2015 1ˢᵗ SEP 1ˢᵗ SHIFT]

21. Why is the Gupta period is considered the Golden age of Ancient India ?

(a) Increase of population, the expansion of textile and iron industry.

(b) Growth of towns and more ports were constructed.

(c) Growth of guilds, towns, trade routes and advanced agriculture.

(d) More people travelled by road and ship.

[RRB SSE 2015 1ˢᵗ SEP 1ˢᵗ SHIFT]

22. Which movement did both the Indian National Army, the Royal Indian Navy support?

(a) Non Cooperation

(b) Khilafat

(c) Home Rule Movement

(d) August Kranti

[RRB SSE 2015 1ˢᵗ SEP 1ˢᵗ SHIFT]

23. What are the main historical sources found in the Bhimbetka area ?

(a) Rock shelter and paintings

(b) Remains of the palace of the Pandavas

(c) Rock features shaped like Bhim

(d) Carvings of hunting scenes on the wall

[RRB SSE 2015 1ˢᵗ SEP 2ⁿᵈ SHIFT]

24. In which period of Ancient India were Guilds, new methods in agriculture, towns and trade routes found ?

(a) Mauryan   (b) Kushan Period

(c) Rastrakutas.   (d) Gupta Period

[RRB SSE 2015 1ˢᵗ SEP 2ⁿᵈ SHIFT]

25. Why was the Civil Disobedience movement successful in India?

(a) More women in the movement against British for Swaraj.

(b) British keenness to hand over power after World War 2.

(c) Support to people of the Indian National Army and the Royal Indian Navy

(d) Conviction of Congress not to seek support of the opposition parties.

[RRB SSE 2015 1ˢᵗ SEP 2ⁿᵈ SHIFT]

26. Where is rock art found in Central India?

(a) Ujjain   (b) Chanderi

(c) Lakhudiyar   (d) Bhimbetka

[RRB SSE 2015 1ˢᵗ SEP 3ʳᵈ SHIFT]

27. What were the advantages that the Gupta period had because of which it is considered the Golden age of Ancient India?

(a) Many Gold mines and access to the coastal trading area of Eastern India.

(b) Near Iron ore areas of Central India and South Bihar and the Byzantine trade route

(c) Fertile agricultural land and growth of revenue from religious towns.

(d) Increase in population and more artisans who would produce cloth for trade.

[RRB SSE 2015 1ˢᵗ SEP 3ʳᵈ SHIFT]

28. "In the democracy which I have envisaged, a democracy established by non-violence, there will be equal freedom for all. Everybody will be his own master. It is to join a struggle for such democracy that I invite you today." Mahatma Gandhi

For starting which movement were the above lines spoken ?

(a) Quit India

(b) Home rule

(c) Non Cooperation Movement

(d) Khilafat

[RRB SSE 2015 1ˢᵗ SEP 3ʳᵈ SHIFT]

29. Paintings of which animal is most common in Rock painitings ?

(a) bison, tiger, rhinoceros, wild boar, elephants, monkeys,

(b) Domesticated cattle, dogs, cows and Goats.

(c) Lions, butterflies, worms and snakes

(d) Rats, Bison, Deer

[RRB SSE 2015 2ⁿᵈ SEP 1ˢᵗ SHIFT]

30. Which town was the capital of the Guptas?

(a) Khajuraho   (b) Patna

(c) Ujjain   (d) Prayag

[RRB SSE 2015 2ⁿᵈ SEP 1ˢᵗ SHIFT]

31. When all the leaders were arrested, what was the source of news on how to follow up the Quit India Movement?

(a) Newspapers like The Hindu

(b) Congress Radio on 42.34 metres

(c) Pamphlets and Handouts

(d) Congress workers campaigns

[RRB SSE 2015 2ⁿᵈ SEP 1ˢᵗ SHIFT]

32. Why is the period 1928 to 1956, considered the Golden period of Indian Hockey?

(a) All the players were from the State of Punjab and Haryana.

(b) India defeated Pakistan in all these matches

(c) India had players with the same name for the 5 players

(d) India won 6 Gold medals each consecutive year in the Olympics.

[RRB SSE 2015 2ⁿᵈ SEP 1ˢᵗ SHIFT]

33. Which art form is common in the Eddakal caves, Bhimbetka,and Lakhudiyar caves.

(a) Depiction of farming in paintings

(b) Use of ochre and limestone for art

(c) Stone Age rock art evidence

(d) Depiction of hunting scenes.

[RRB SSE 2015 2ⁿᵈ SEP 2ⁿᵈ SHIFT]

34. Which Gupta ruler does the historian Vincent Smith call' The Napoleon of India?

(a) Samudragupta

(b) Chandrgupta I

(c) Chandragupta II

(d) Skanda Gupta

[RRB SSE 2015 2ⁿᵈ SEP 2ⁿᵈ SHIFT]

35. From which city was the Quit India movement launched and when ?

(a) 1940 Kolkatta

(b) 1952 Delhi

(c) 1931 Madras (Chennai)

(d) 1942 Mumbai

[RRB SSE 2015 2ⁿᵈ SEP 2ⁿᵈ SHIFT]

36. In which art form are the bison, giraffe, elephants and onkey most commonly animals painted ?

(a) Cave Murals

(b) Rock Art

(c) Minatures of Kangra

(d) Folk art of Chattisgarh.

[RRB SSE 2015 2ⁿᵈ SEP 3ʳᵈ SHIFT]

37. Which aspect under the Gupta had the most the organised and innovative structure ?

(a) Administration   (b) Army

(c) Industry   (d) Trade

[RRB SSE 2015 2ⁿᵈ SEP 3ʳᵈ SHIFT]

38. In which National Movement when all the top leaders of the Congress were arrested guided by radio broadcasts too?

(a) Home rule Agitation

(b) Non- Cooperation

(c) Khilafat Movement

(d) Quit India Movement

[RRB SSE 2015 2ⁿᵈ SEP 3ʳᵈ SHIFT]

39. To which period would rock engravings with geometrical designs like triangle, circle, square sun and flower belong?

(a) Megalithic at the end of Neolithic

(b) Paleolithic period to Chalcolithic.

(c) End of Iron Age and beginning of Bronze age

(d) End of Neolithic beginning of Iron Age

[RRB SSE 2015 3ʳᵈ SEP 1ˢᵗ SHIFT]

40. Which Gupta ruler does the historian Vincent Smith call' The Napoleon of India '?

(a) Samudragupta   (b) Chandrgupta 1

(c) Chandragupta II   (d) Skanda Gupta

[RRB SSE 2015 3ʳᵈ SEP 1ˢᵗ SHIFT]

41. In which Movement was the slogan 'Do or Die' given and there were mass arrests

(a) Home rule

(b) Non Cooperation

(c) Quit India Movement

(d) Khilafat

[RRB SSE 2015 3ʳᵈ SEP 1ˢᵗ SHIFT]

42. Which of these are not significant development of the Bronze age?

(a) Irrigated Farming

(b) Large empires

(c) Town development

(d) Cuneiform

[RRB SSE 2015 3ʳᵈ SEP 2ⁿᵈ SHIFT]

43. What were the causes of frequent occurrence of famines in India in the 19th century?

(a) Migration of farmers to cities

(b) Decrease in cultivated area

(c) Cultivation of commercial crops

(d) Increase in temperature, decrease in rainfall

[RRB SSE 2015 3ʳᵈ SEP 2ⁿᵈ SHIFT]

44. What is the main common tenets of Jainism and Buddhism ?

(a) Right knowledge is necessary.

(b) Ahimsa will lead to no rebirth

(c) Teacher is supreme master

(d) Suffering can be ended by conquering desire.

[RRB SSE 2015 3ʳᵈ SEP 3ʳᵈ SHIFT]

45. Who was the first Moghul ruler to support the transition of Sanskrit works into Persian?

    (a) Jehangir   (b) Akbar

    (c) Babur   (d) Humayun

[RRB SSE 2015 3ʳᵈ SEP 3ʳᵈ SHIFT]

46. Why is the Battle of Salbai 1782 significant in the establishment of British power in India?

    (a) The Marathas made a 20 year peace with the British and helped suppress Mysore.

    (b) The British were able to establish the Presidencies in Bombay, Calcutta and Madras

    (c) The Marathas were able to expand their territories and conquer Mysore

    (d) The British were able to trade with the interior of India and conquer Oudh.

[RRB SSE 2015 3ʳᵈ SEP 3ʳᵈ SHIFT]

ANSWER KEY

RRB JUNIOR ENGINEER

1. (b)	**2.** (a)	**3.** (d)	**4.** (a)	**5.** (b)	**6.** (c)	**7.** (c)	**8.** (d)	**9.** (a)	**10.** (b)
11. (b)	**12.** (c)	**13.** (a)	**14.** (b)	**15.** (c)	**16.** (d)	**17.** (a)	**18.** (d)	**19.** (a)	**20.** (c)
21. (a)	**22.** (a)	**23.** (a)	**24.** (d)	**25.** (c)	**26.** (a)	**27.** (a)	**28.** (a)	**29.** (c)	**30.** (c)
31. (d)	**32.** (a)	**33.** (d)	**34.** (b)	**35.** (d)	**36.** (a)	**37.** (b)	**38.** (a)	**39.** (c)	**40.** (a)
41. (c)	**42.** (c)	**43.** (a)	**44.** (a)	**45.** (d)	**46.** (b)	**47.** (c)	**48.** (c)	**49.** (b)	**50.** (a)
51. (b)	**52.** (a)	**53.** (c)	**54.** (a)	**55.** (a)	**56.** (a)	**57.** (c)	**58.** (c)	**59.** (c)	**60.** (b)
61. (c)	**62.** (d)								

RRB SENIOR SECTION ENGINEER

1. (a)	**2.** (a)	**3.** (b)	**4.** (c)	**5.** (b)	**6.** (d)	**7.** (b)	**8.** (d)	**9.** (c)	**10.** (b)
11. (a)	**12.** (a)	**13.** (d)	**14.** (c)	**15.** (b)	**16.** (c)	**17.** (a)	**18.** (c)	**19.** (b)	**20.** (b)
21. (c)	**22.** (d)	**23.** (a)	**24.** (a)	**25.** (c)	**26.** (d)	**27.** (b)	**28.** (a)	**29.** (a)	**30.** (d)
31. (b)	**32.** (d)	**33.** (c)	**34.** (a)	**35.** (d)	**36.** (b)	**37.** (a)	**38.** (d)	**39.** (d)	**40.** (a)
41. (c)	**42.** (c)	**43.** (c)	**44.** (d)	**45.** (b)	**46.** (a)				

EXPLANATIONS

RRB JUNIOR ENGINEER

1. Ashoka in the 13th year of his coronation, appointed a special type of officer who surveyed the land, kept land records and carried out justice. These officers were called Samahartas.

2. Shree Jagannath Temple of Puri is an important Hindu temple dedicated to Lord Jagannath, a form of lord Vishnu, located on the eastern coast of India, at Puri in the state of Odisha. Anantavarmana Chodaganga built the Jagannath temple of Puri.

3. Section 66 A has been in media controversy recently. The section pertains to information Technology.

4. During the Ahmedabad strike, 1918, Gandhiji made the first use of Hunger Strike as a weapon

5. The famous Chinese pilgrim 'Hieun Tsang' visited India during the reign of: Chandragupta II.

6. Mughal Emperor Shah Jahan built the Jama Masjid between 1644 and 1656. It was constructed by more than 5000 workers. It was originally called Masjid-i-Jahan Numa, meaning 'mosque commanding view of the world'.

7. The Quit India Movement, or the India August Movement, was a movement launched at the Bombay session of the All-India Congress Committee by Mahatma Gandhi on 8 August 1942, during World War II, demanding an end to British Rule of India.

8. Indika (Greek: Indica) is an account of Mauryan India by Megasthenes. The original book is now lost, but its fragments have survived in later Greek and Latin works. The earliest of these works are those by Diodorus Siculus, Strabo (Geographica), Pliny, and Arrian (Indica).

9. Giddha is a popular folk dance of women in Punjab region of India and Pakistan. The dance is often considered derived from the ancient dance known as the ring dance and is just as energetic as bhangra; at the same time it manages to creatively display feminine grace, elegance and flexibility.

10. The Servants of India Society was formed in Pune, Maharashtra, on June 12, 1905 by Gopal Krishna Gokhale, who left the Deccan Education Society to form this association.

11. The sermon Buddha gave to the five monks was his first sermon, called the Dhammacakkappavattana Sutta. It was given on the full-moon day of Asalha Puja. Buddha subsequently also spent his first rainy season at Sarnath at the Mulagandhakuti.

12. Lord Dufferin was Governor General of India at the time of foundation of Indian National Congress. He served as Viceroy and Governor-General of India from 13 December 1884 – 10 December 1888. Indian National Congress founded on 28 December 1885 by A.O Hume.

13. Bhulabhai Desai was an Indian independence activist and acclaimed lawyer. He is well-remembered for his defence of the three Indian National Army soldiers accused of treason during World War II, and for attempting to negotiate a secret power-sharing agreement with Liaquat Ali Khan of the Muslim League.

14. Bihu is the chief festival in the Assam state of India.Garba is a form of dance which originated in the state of Gujarat in India.Tamasha is a traditional form of Marathi theatre, often with singing and dancing, widely performed by local or travelling theatre groups within the state of Maharashtra, India. Nautanki is one of the most popular folk operatic theater performance forms of South Asia, particularly in northern India.

15. Kolkata, is the capital of the Indian state of West Bengal and is located in eastern India on the east bank of the River Hooghly. The city was a colonial city developed by the British East India Company and then by the British Empire. Kolkata was the capital of the British Indian empire until 1911 when the capital was relocated to Delhi

16. The Battle of Waterloo was fought 18 June 1815, near Waterloo in present-day Belgium, then part of the United Kingdom of the Netherlands. A French army under the command of Emperor Napoleon Bonaparte was defeated by two of the armies of the Seventh Coalition: a British-led Allied army under the command of the Duke of Wellington, and a Prussian army under the command of Gebhard Leberecht von Blücher, Prince of Wahlstatt.

17. Allan Octavian Hume founded the Indian National Congress,a political party that was later to lead in the Indian independence movement. This led in 1885 to the first session of the Indian National Congress held in Bombay

18. Secularism is having the freedom to preach, practice and profess any religion.One manifestation of secularism is asserting the right to be free from religious rule and teachings, or, in a state declared to be neutral on matters of belief, from the imposition by government of religion or religious practices upon its people. Another manifestation of secularism is the view that public activities and decisions, especially political ones, should be uninfluenced by religious beliefs or practices.

19. Da Gama's discovery of the sea route to India was significant and opened the way for an age of global imperialism and for the Portuguese to establish a long-lasting colonial empire in Asia. Traveling the ocean route allowed the Portuguese to avoid sailing across the highly disputed Mediterranean and traversing the dangerous Arabian Peninsula.

20. The Bedouin are a grouping of nomadic Arab people who have historically inhabited the desert regions in North Africa, the Arabian Peninsula, Iraq and the Levant. They are traditionally divided into tribes, or clans and share a common culture of herding camels and goats.

21. The term used for armed rebellion against a constituted authority is insurgency. An insurgency is a rebellion against authority (for example, an authority recognized as such by the United Nations) when those taking part in the rebellion are not recognized as belligerents (lawful combatants).

22. The treaty of Versailles was signed in the summer of 1919 with Germany.

23. Pablo Picasso's creation 'Guernica' was based on consequences of Spanish civil war.

24. Among the given options, the name Lai Bahadur Shastri is wrong.Lal Bal Pal (Lala Lajpat Rai, Bal Gangadhar Tilak, and Bipin Chandra Pal) were a triumvirate of assertive nationalists in British-ruled India in the early 20th century, from 1905 to 1918.

25. The last Governor General in the two century rule of the British in India is Lord Mountbatten.

26. Of the Slav population scattered in Eastern Europe, those who began the Pan Slav movement to have one state were Serbians.

27. Pharaohs built by the Pyramids. All three of Giza's famed pyramids and their elaborate burial complexes were built during a frenetic period of construction, from roughly 2550 to 2490 B.C. The pyramids were built by Pharaohs Khufu (tallest), Khafre (background), and Menkaure (front).

28. The king of Mauryan Empire who in 322 BC uprooted Greeks from Punjab and Nandas from the Gangetic plane was Chandragupta.

29. Ramakrishna Mission is a Hindu religious and spiritual organisation which forms the core of a worldwide spiritual movement known as the Ramakrishna Movement or the Vedanta Movement.The mission is named after and inspired by the Indian saint Ramakrishna Paramahamsa and founded by Ramakrishna's chief disciple Swami Vivekananda on 1 May 1897.

30. After First World War political movement called fascism arose. Fascists were not hostile to democracy and socialism statement not true of fascism.

31. Akbar promulgated Din-i-Ilahi, a syncretic creed derived mainly from Islam and Hinduism as well as some parts of Zoroastrianism and Christianity. A simple, monotheistic cult, tolerant in outlook, it centered on Akbar as a prophet, for which he drew the ire of the ulema and orthodox Muslims.

32. Bonkim Chondra Chattopadhyay or Bankim Chandra Chatterjee was an Indian writer, poet and journalist. He was the composer of Vande Mataram, originally in Sanskrit stotra personifying India as a mother goddess and inspiring the activists during the Indian Independence Movement.

33. Among the given options, Palestinian territory was never part of Israel because Palestinian territories and occupied Palestinian territories (OPT or oPt) are terms often used to describe the West Bank(including East Jerusalem) and the Gaza Strip, which are occupied or otherwise under the control of Israel.

34. The name of the founder of Buddhism,before he renounced the world is Siddhartha.Gautama was born as a Kshatriya.

35. The French Revolution was a period of far-reaching social and political upheaval in France and its colonies that lasted from 1789 until 1799. It was partially carried forward by Napoleon during the later expansion of the French Empire.

36. The correct answers for the matchings given in the list are A-2, B-2, C-3

37. The medieval ruler who was the first to establish a ministry of agriculture (Diwan-i-Kohi) was Mohammad Bin Tughlaq.

38. Queen Victoria declared the taking over the Indian Administration under British crown 1 November, 1858.

39. The first Census in India during the British period was held during the tenure of Lord Mayo.

40. Among the given animals, Cow was not represented on seals and terracota art of the Harappan culture. A large number of animal have been depicted on seals and terracota art of the Harappan culture. These include tiger, lion, sheep, goat, buffalo, elephant, the rhinoceros, etc.

41. A "Forgotten Empire", written by the renowned historian Robert Sewell is about which of Vijaynagar Empire.

42. Dining John Lawrence Viceroyship, the High Court came at the presidential cities of Calcutta. Madras and Bombay.

43. Dadabhai Naoroji for the first time had estimated National income in India.

44. The difference between Chaitya and Vihara is that Chaitya is a place of worship whereas Vihara is a living place for Buddhist saints.

45. The world famous Takht-i-Taus (the Peacock Throne) was kept in the Diwan-i-Aam at the Red Fort at Delhi.

46. With reference to the colonial rule in India,the correct chronological order of these events is Morley-Minto Reforms Act>Transfer of capital from Calcutta to Delhi>First World War>Lucknow Pact.

47. The correct Match of King and Kingdom is Pradyota- Avanthi, Udayana-Vatsa, Prasenjit- Kosala, Ajatashatru- Magadha.

48. Ramananda was the first Bhakti saint to use Hindi for propagation of his message . Ramananda was an influential social reformer of Northern India. His championed the pursuit of knowledge and direct devotional spirituality, and did not discriminate based on birth family, gender or religion.

49. A subsidiary alliance, in South Asian history, describes a tributary alliance between a Native state and either French India, or later the British East India Company. The pioneer of the subsidiary alliance system was French Governor Joseph François Dupleix, who in the late 1740s established treaties with the Nizam of Hyderabad, and Carnatic.

50. Taxila had great influence on hindu culture and the Sanskrit language. It is perhaps best known for its association with Chanakya, also known as Kautilya, the strategist who guided Chandragupta Maurya and assisted in the founding of the Mauryan empire. Chanakya's Arthashastra (The knowledge of Economics) is said to have been composed in Taxila.

51. The Battle of Takkolam was a military engagement between Rajaditya, son of the Chola king Parantaka I and a confederacy of Western Gangas, Banas and Vaidumbas led by the Rashtrakuta king Krishna III at Thakkolam in the present-day Vellore District of Tamil Nadu, India. The battle fought in 949 resulted in the defeat of the Cholas and the death of Rajaditya on the battlefield.

52. The Congress President Abul Kalam Azad negotiated with both Cripps Mission and Lord Wavell.

53. Ajivikas is propounded that destiny determines everything, man is powerless.

54. Among the given options the Chronological order is-Battle of Khanwa, Battle of Ghaghra, Battle of Chausa, Battle of Samugarh.

55. During the period of Indian freedom struggle, Annie Besant started Central Hindu School. Annie Besant was the first woman president of INC .In 1916 Besant launched the All India Home Rule League along with Lokmanya Tilak.

56. Among the given options, the chronological order of the Indian union were created or granted full statehood is Andhra Pradesh, Maharashtra, Nagaland, Haryana

57. The correct chronological order of persons visited India is Megasthenes>Fa Hien>Hiuen Tsang>Alberuni

58. The last ruler of Tughlaq dynasty of the Delhi Sultanate is Mahmud Shah Tughlaq.The Tughlaq dynasty was a Muslim dynasty of Turko-Indian origin which ruled over the Delhi sultanate in medieval India. Its reign started in 1320 in Delhi when Ghazi Malik assumed the throne under the title of Ghiyath al-Din Tughluq. The dynasty ended in 1413.

59. Among the given pairs, Formation of Congress Socialist Party: 1938 is not correctly Matched. The Congress Socialist Party was a socialist caucus within the Indian National Congress. It was founded in 1934 by Congress members who rejected what they saw as the anti-rational mysticism of Mohandas Karamchand Gandhi as well as the sectarian attitude of the Communist Party of India towards the Congress.

60. The Arya samaj was founded by the sannyasi (ascetic) Swami Dayanand Saraswati on 10 April 1875. Members of the Arya Samaj believe in one God and reject the worship of idols.Jawaharlal Nehru, the first prime minister of India in his book, The Discovery of India credits Arya Samaj in introducing proselytization in Hinduism.

61. In the ancient world, dead bodies were preserved as mummies in Egypt.

62. Ramakrishna Missions were established in many countries and many parts of India by Swami Vivekananda.

RRB SENIOR SECTION ENGINEER

1. The Khalsa tradition was initiated in 1699 by the last living Guru of Sikhism, Guru Gobind Singh. Its formation was a key event in the history of Sikhism. The founding of Khalsa is celebrated by Sikhs during the festival of Vaisakhi.

2. "Mahabharata" the epic was written by Vyasa. It is one of the two major Sanskrit epics of ancient India, the other being the Ramayana. The title may be translated as "the great tale of the Bharata dynasty".

3. Chand Bibi, was an Indian Muslim regent and warrior. She acted as the Regent of Bijapur and Regent of Ahmednagar. Chand Bibi is best known for defending Ahmednagar against the Mughal forces of Emperor Akbar in 1595.

4. Arya Samaj is an Indian Hindu reform movement that promotes values and practices based on the belief in the infallible authority of the Vedas. The samaj was founded by the sannyasi Dayanand Saraswati on 10 April 1875. Members of the Arya Samaj believe in one God and reject the worship of idols.

5. India's first war of Independence (related to Meerut mutiny) was in 1857. First War of Independence, Indian Mutiny, also called Sepoy Mutiny, widespread but unsuccessful rebellion against British rule in India in 1857–58. Begun in Meerut by Indian troops (sepoys) in the service of the British East India Company, it spread to Delhi, Agra, Kanpur, and Lucknow.

6. French power declined in India after the battle of Wandiwash.It was a confrontation between the French, under the comte de Lally, and the British, under Sir Eyre Coote. It was the decisive battle in the Anglo-French struggle in southern India during the Seven Years' War (1756–63).

7. The first Indian railway train journey between Bombay and Thane was in the year 1853. The country's first passenger train, which ran between Bombay's Bori Bunder station and Thane on 16 April 1853, was dedicated by Lord Dalhousie.

8. Quit India Movement is associated with the slogan "Do or Die".The Quit India speech is a speech made by Mahatma Gandhi on 8 August 1942, on the eve of the Quit India movement. He called for determined, but passive resistance that signified the certitude that Gandhi foresaw for the movement, best described by his call to Do or Die.

9. The Bhoodan Movement or Land Gift Movement, was a voluntary land reform movement in India, started by Acharya Vinoba Bhave in 1951 at Pochampally village in Telangana which is now known as Bhoodan Pochampally.

10. Mughal Emperor , Jahangir gave permission to FUist India Company to establish their factory at Surat.

11. The ruler of Awadh was removed from power by the British on the pretext of misgovernance.

12. The Palitana temples of Jainism are located on Shatrunjaya hill by the city of Palitana in Bhavnagar district, Gujarat, India. The city of the same name, known previously as Padliptapur, has been dubbed "City of Temples". Shatrunjaya means a "place of victory against inner enemies" or "which conquers inner enemies".

13. Kunwar Singh was a notable leader during the Indian Rebellion of 1857. He belonged to a royal house of Jagdispur, currently a part of Bhojpur district, Bihar, India. At the age of 80, he led a select band of armed soldiers against the troops under the command of the British East India Company.

14. The 72 delegates were attended the first Session of the Indian National Congress, held in Bombay in 1885.

15. The 1929 session of Indian National Congress is of significance in the history of the Freedom Movement because the attainment of Poorna Swaraj was adopted as the goal of the Congress.

16. The movement that came to an abrupt end due to the Chauri Chaura incident was the Non-Cooperation Movement.

17. Vallabh Bhai Patel is associated with Bardoli Satyagraha of 1928; Chittaranjan Das is the founder-leader of the Swaraj (Independence) Party in Bengal during British occupation in India. Abdul Ghaffar Khan founded the Khudai Khidmatgar ("Servants of God") movement in 1929. Abul Kalam Azad became the leader of the Khilafat Movement, during which he came into close contact with the Indian leader Mahatma Gandhi.

18. Garba is a form of dance which originated in the state of Gujarat in India. The name is derived from the Sanskrit term Garbha and Deep. Mohiniyattam, also spelled Mohiniattam, is one of two classical dances of India that developed and remains popular in the state of Kerala. The other classical dance form from Kerala is Kathakali. Yakshagana is a traditional theatre form that combines dance, music, dialogue, costume, make-up, and stage techniques with a unique style and form. This theatre style is mainly found in all parts of karnataka

19. Devdas and Parinita are Principal literary works by Sarat Chandra Chattopadhyay.

20. Cutting logs, making fire, cooking, farming are the most common themes in the drawing found in the stone age Bhimbetka caves.

21. Gupta period is considered the Golden age of Ancient India because more people travelled by road and ship.Gupta Empire was an ancient Indian empire, existing from the mid-to-late 3rd century CE to 590 CE.

22. August Kranti movement got the support from both the Indian National Army, the Royal Indian Navy.

23. Rock shelter and paintings are the main historical sources found in the Bhimbetka area.

24. During the period of Mauryan, Guilds, new methods in agriculture, towns and trade routes were found.

25. Civil Disobedience movement successful in India because of support to people of the Indian National Army and the Royal Indian Navy.

26. Bhimbetka rock shelters are an archaeological site in central India that spans the prehistoric paleolithic and mesolithic periods, as well as the historic period.

27. Near Iron ore areas of Central India and South Bihar and the Byzantine trade route were the advantages that the Gupta period had because of which it is considered the Golden age of Ancient India.

28. For stating the quit India movement, Mahatma Gandhi said that "In the democracy which I have envisaged, a democracy established by non-violence, there will be equal freedom for all. Everybody will be his own master. It is to join a struggle for such democracy that I invite you today".

29. Paintings of bison, tiger, rhinoceros, wild boar, elephants, and monkeys, animals are most common in Rock paintings.

30. Gupta Empire was an ancient Indian empire, existing from the mid-to-late 3rd century CE to 590 CE. Prayag was the capital of the Guptas.

31. When all the leaders were arrested, Congress Radio on 42.34 metres was the source of news on how to follow up the Quit India Movement.

32. India won 6 Gold medals each consecutive year in the Olympics from the period 1928 to 1956, is considered the Golden period of Indian Hockey.

33. Stone Age rock art evidence is common in the Eddakal caves, Bhimbetka,and Lakhudiyar caves.

34. The historian, Vincent Smith called the Samudragupta 'The Napoleon of India'

35. On 8 August 1942 at the All-India Congress Committee session in Bombay, Mohandas Karamchand Gandhi launched the 'Quit India' movement. The next day, Gandhi, Nehru and many other leaders of the Indian National Congress were arrested by the British Government.

36. The most commonly animals painted at rock art are the bison, giraffe, elephants and monkey.

37. Administration under the Gupta had the most the organised and innovative structure.

38. During the Quit India Movement all the top leaders of the Congress were arrested guided by radio broadcasts too.

39. rock engravings with geometrical designs like triangle, circle, square sun and flower belong to end of Neolithic beginning of Iron Age.

40. Samudragupta (335-375 AD) of the Gupta dynasty is known as the Napoleon of India. Historian A V Smith called him so because of his great military conquests known from the 'Prayag Prashati' written by his courtier and poet Harisena, who also describes him as the hero of a hundred battles.

41. On 7 to 8 August 1942, the All India Congress Committee met in Bombay and ratified the 'Quit India' resolution. Gandhi called for 'Do or Die'. The arrest of Gandhi and the Congress leaders led to mass demonstrations throughout India. Thousands were killed and injured in the wake of the 'Quit India' movement.

42. Town development is not not significant development of the Bronze age.The Bronze Age is a historical period characterized by the use of bronze, and in some areas proto-writing, and other early features of urban civilization.

43. The causes of frequent occurrence of famines in India in the 19th century was cultivation of commercial crops.

44. Suffering can be ended by conquering desire is the main common tenets of Jainism and Buddhism.

45. Akbar was the first Mughal ruler to support the transition of Sanskrit works into Persian. He popularly known as Akbar I, also as Akbar the Great, was the third Mughal emperor, who reigned from 1556 to 1605. Akbar succeeded his father, Humayun, under a regent, Bairam Khan, who helped the young emperor expand and consolidate Mughal domains in India.

46. The Treaty of Salbai was signed on May 17, 1782, by representatives of the Maratha Empire and the British East India Company after long negotiations to settle the outcome of the First Anglo-Maratha War.

POLITY

RRB JUNIOR ENGINEER

1. An individual who is not a member of either house of the parliament can be appointed as a member of the Council of Ministers, but he has to become the member of the either house in
(a) 3 months   (b) 6 months
(c) one year   (d) 2 years
[RRB JE 2014 GREEN SHIFT]

2. The term 'Republic' used in the preamble of the Constitution of India implies
(a) That the head of the state is hereditary
(b) That the head of the state is a constitutional ruler
(c) That the head of the state is an elected representative
(d) None of the above
[RRB JE 2014 GREEN SHIFT]

3. In India, what is the minimum permissible age for employment in a factory?
(a) 14 years   (b) 16 years
(c) 18 years   (d) 21 years
[RRB JE 2014 GREEN SHIFT]

4. Who is the speaker of present Lok Sabha ? (As on 01.11.2014)
(a) Smt. Sumitra Mahajan
(b) Smt. Sushma Swaraj
(c) Smt. Meira Kumar
(d) None of these
[RRB JE 2014 RED SHIFT]

5. The Fundamental Duties of the Indian citizens are incorporated in the following Article of our constitution ?
(a) Article 21 A   (b) Article 51 A
(c) Article 370 A   (d) Article 1. A
[RRB JE 2014 RED SHIFT]

6. To be eligible for elected as President, a candidate must be :
(a) Over 25 years of age
(b) Over 30 years of age
(c) Over 35 years of age
(d) Over 60 years of age
[RRB JE 2014 RED SHIFT]

7. The Consolidated Fund of India is a fund in which
(a) All taxes except Income Tax collected by the Union as well as State Governments are deposited
(b) All money received by or on behalf of the Government of India is deposited
(c) The Union as well as state Governments make equal contribution to this fund
(d) Savings of Union and State Governments are deposited
[RRB JE 2014 YELLOW SHIFT]

8. Which part of the Indian Constitution reflects the mind and ideals of the farmers?
(a) Preamble
(b) Fundamental Rights
(c) Directive Principles
(d) Emergency Provisions
[RRB JE 2014 YELLOW SHIFT]

9. How long can a Presidential Ordinance remain in force ?
(a) One year
(b) Two months
(c) Till the President revokes it
(d) Six months
[RRB JE 2014 YELLOW SHIFT]

10. A freedom not granted to citizens by the Indian Constitution is
(a) to reside and settle in any part of India
(b) move freely throughout Indian territory
(c) assemble peacefully even with arms
(d) form associations and Unions
[RRB JE 2015 26th AUG 1st SHIFT]

11. Which out of the following is incorrect regarding Lok Sabha?
(a) 530 members are elected from states
(b) 20 members are elected from Union Territories
(c) 2 members from Anglo Indian community are elected by the community
(d) 2 members of Anglo Indian community are nominated by the President if there is no member from the Anglo Indian community
[RRB JE 2015 26th AUG 2nd SHIFT]

12. Which democratic country has an unwritten constitution?

(a) United States   (b) England

(c) India   (d) Canada and America

[RRB JE 2015 26th AUG 2nd SHIFT]

13. Who presides over the present Lok Sabha when parliament session is on?

(a) President, Pranab Mukherji

(b) Vice President, Hamid Ansari

(c) Prime Minister, Narendra Modi

(d) Speaker, Sumitra Mahajan

[RRB JE 2015 26th AUG 3rd SHIFT]

14. The Indian constitution was written on 26/11/1949 and came into force on

(a) Same day   (b) 26.01.1950

(c) 15.08.1950   (d) 26.01.1952

[RRB JE 2015 26th AUG 3rd SHIFT]

15. A few children between ages 8 and 14 were rescued from a factory where they worked under inhuman conditions. Which fundamental right of the constitution made this possible?

(a) Right to Education

(b) Right to Freedom of Speech

(c) Right against exploitation

(d) Right to Freedom of Religion

[RRB JE 2015 26th AUG 3rd SHIFT]

16. The term 'collegium system' was recently seen in the newspapers. With which field is this term associated?

(a) Education   (b) Judiciary

(c) Politics   (d) Constitution

[RRB JE 2015 27th AUG 1st SHIFT]

17. Which one out of the values of the Indian constitution means 'having complete freedom and being the supreme authority'?

(a) Socialism   (b) Secularism

(c) Sovereignty   (d) Liberty

[RRB JE 2015 27th AUG 1st SHIFT]

18. There are two forms of government, presidential and parliamentary. Which type of government do India, US and England have?

(a) India – Parliamentary, England – Parliamentary, US – Parliamentary

(b) India – Presidential, England – Parliamentary, US – Presidential

(c) India – Parliamentary, England – Parliamentary, US – Presidential

(d) All three countries have Presidential form

[RRB JE 2015 27th AUG 1st SHIFT]

19. Of which political party is Mamata Banerjee the leader?

(a) Bahujan Samaj Party

(b) Trinamool Congress

(c) Forward Block

(d) Communist Party (Marxist)

[RRB JE 2015 27th AUG 2nd SHIFT]

20. To abide by the Constitution and respect its ideals and institutions is a

(a) Fundamental Right

(b) Fundamental duty

(c) Human Right

(d) Natural desire

[RRB JE 2015 27th AUG 2nd SHIFT]

21. What does Universal Adult Franchise mean?

(a) All adults who have completed 21 years of age have the right to participate in the electoral process

(b) Candidate aspiring to be member of legislative assembly should at least be 25 years old

(c) A girl cannot many ill she attains age of 18 and boy till he is 21

(d) Any citizen of India 18 years of age or above can vote irrespective of race, caste, religion, sex, place of birth

[RRB JE 2015 27th AUG 2nd SHIFT]

22. The majority of Members of Parliament of the present Lok Sabha are from

(a) Bharatiya Janta party

(b) Aam Aadmi party

(c) Congress

(d) Bahujan Samaj party

[RRB JE 2015 27th AUG 3rd SHIFT]

23. One of the India's past presidents was active as a scientist of repute till his death recently. Select his name,

(a) Rajendra Prasad

(b) Sarvapalli Radhakrishnan

(c) A P J Abdul Kalam

(d) Pranab Mukherji

[RRB JE 2015 27th AUG 3rd SHIFT]

24. Dr. Baba Saheb Bhimrao Ambedkar, is regarded as the architect of Indian constitution because, he

(a) Designed the cover page of the document

(b) Was elected the president of Constituent Assembly

(c) Was the chairman of the Drafting committee

(d) a and b

[RRB JE 2015 27th AUG 3rd SHIFT]

25. The President of India can declare Emergency under Article 352 on the advice of:

(a) Prime Minister

(b) Council of Ministers

(c) Governor

(d) Cabinet

[RRB JE 2015 27th AUG 3rd SHIFT]

26. Which one of the following Constitutional Amendments state that the total number of ministers, including the prime minister in the council of ministers shall not exceed 15% of the total number of members of the house of the people

(a) 90th   (b) 91st

(c) 92nd   (d) 93rd

[RRB JE 2015 28th AUG 1st SHIFT]

27. The indian legistature was made bi-cameral for the first time by

(a) Indian Council Act 1892

(b) Indian Council Act 1909

(c) The Government of India Act 1919

(d) The Government of India Act 1935

[RRB JE 2015 28th AUG 2nd SHIFT]

28. Recommendations to the president of india on the specific Union state fiscal relations are made by the-

(a) Finance Minister

(b) Reserve Bank of india

(c) Planning commission

(d) Finance Commission

[RRB JE 2015 28th AUG 2nd SHIFT]

29. The 99th constitution Amendment Act was in news recently. It is related to

(a) National Judicial appointments commission

(b) Right to work

(c) Reservation of women in police services

(d) Police action in Naxal-prone areas.

[RRB JE 2015 28th AUG 2nd SHIFT]

30. For distribution of powers between the union and the states, the constitution of india introduce three lists. Which two of the following Articles govern the distribution of power;

(a) Articles 3 and 4

(b) Articles 56 and 57

(c) Articles 41 and 142

(d) Articles 245 and 246

[RRB JE 2015 28th AUG 3rd SHIFT]

31. Which of the following can a court issue for enforcement of Fundamental Rights?

(a) A decree   (b) An ordinance

(c) A Writ   (d) A notification

[RRB JE 2015 28th AUG 3rd SHIFT]

32. LOK SABHA on MAY 7 cleared a bill to lower the age of Juveniles from 18 years to

(a) 16 years   (b) 5 years

(c) 14 years   (d) 17 years

[RRB JE 2015 28th AUG 3rd SHIFT]

33. The schedule of the Constitution of India which contains specific provisions for the administration and control of scheduled areas in several states?

(a) Third   (b) Fifth

(c) Seventh   (d) Ninth

[RRB JE 2015 29th AUG 1st SHIFT]

34. Who among the following Prime Ministers resigned before facing a vote of no-confidence in the Lok Sabha?

(a) Chandra Sekhar

(b) Morarji Desai

(c) Chaudhary Charan Singh

(d) V.P. Singh

[RRB JE 2015 29th AUG 1st SHIFT]

35. Which Amendment to the Constitution inserted a new Article 21 A providing rights to education in the Constitution?

(a) 86th Amendment

(b) 87th Amendment

(c) 88th Amendment

(d) 89th Amendment

[RRB JE 2015 29th AUG 2nd SHIFT]

36. Which one of the following subjects comes under the common jurisdiction of the Supreme Court and the high court?

(a) Mutual disputes among state

(b) Dispute between centre and states

(c) Protection of the fundamental right

(d) protection from the violation of the constitution.

[RRB JE 2015 29th AUG 2nd SHIFT]

37. "Equal pay for equal work" has been insured in the Indian constitution as one of the

(a) Fundamental rights

(b) Directive principles of state policy

(c) Fundamental duties

(d) Economic rights

[RRB JE 2015 29th AUG 3rd SHIFT]

38. If the finance minister fails to get the Annual Budget passed in the Lok Sabha, the Prime Minister is expected to

(a) Compel the Finance Minister to resign

(b) Submit the resignation of his /her cabinet

(c) Refer it to the joint session of both the Houses of Parliament

(d) Form another cabinet with different members

[RRB JE 2015 30ᵗʰ AUG 3ʳᵈ SHIFT]

39. The right to property was removed from the list of fundamental Rights enlisted in the constitution of the India through which one of the Following Amendments?

(a) 42nd Amendment

(b) 44th Amendment

(c) 46th Amendment

(d) 47th Amendment

[RRB JE 2015 30ᵗʰ AUG 3ʳᵈ SHIFT]

RRB SENIOR SECTION ENGINEER

1. By which constitutional amendment did the Parliament acquire the right to amend Fundamental Rights?

(a) 23ʳᵈ

(b) 24ᵗʰ

(c) 25ᵗʰ

(d) 26ᵗʰ

[RRB SSE 2014 GREEN SHIFT]

2. How many Fundamental Rights are guaranteed by the Constitution of India?

(a) 7

(b) 3

(c) 5

(d) 6

[RRB SSE 2014 GREEN SHIFT]

3. An interpretation of the Indian Constitution is based on the spirit of the-

(a) Fundamental rights

(b) Fundamental duties

(c) Preamble

(d) Directive principles

[RRB SSE 2014 GREEN SHIFT]

4. To be eligible for membership of the Lok Sabha, a person should be at least:

(a) 18 years of age

(b) 30 years of age

(c) 35 years of age

(d) 25 years of age

[RRB SSE 2014 RED SHIFT]

5. Who is the Chairman of Rajya Sabha ? (As on 01.11.2014)

(a) Sumitra Mahajan

(b) Hamid Ansari

(c) Arun Jaitley

(d) Thambi Durai

[RRB SSE 2014 RED SHIFT]

6. Who of the following is regarded as the architect of the Indian Constitution ?

(a) Pandit Nehru

(b) B.R. Ambedkar

(c) Mahatma Gandhi

(P) Rajendra Prasad

[RRB SSE 2014 RED SHIFT]

7. What was the overall voting percentage in the recently held General Elections for 16th Lok Sabha ?

(a) About 60%

(b) About 55%

(c) About 66%

(d) About 78%

[RRB SSE 2014 RED SHIFT]

8. Money can be spent out of the Consolidated Fund of India

(a) with the approval of the President

(b) with the approval of the Parliament

(c) with the approval of the CAG

(d) with the approval of the above authorities

[RRB SSE 2014 YELLOW SHIFT]

9. Which of the following is not a condition for becoming a Citizen of India ?

(a) Birth

(b) Descent

(c) Acquiring property

(d) Naturalisation

[RRB SSE 2014 YELLOW SHIFT]

10. The Oath of Office is conducted to the President of India by

(a) The Speaker of Lok Sabha

(b) The Chief Justice ofIndia

(c) The Vice-President of India

(d) The Prime-Minister of India

[RRB SSE 2014 YELLOW SHIFT]

11. Which one is a part of the Directive Principle of State Policy ?

(a) Right to equality before law

(b) Right to adult franchise

(c) Organisation of Trade Unions and workers rights

(d) Organisation of Village Panchayats

[RRB SSE 2015 1ˢᵗ SEP 1ˢᵗ SHIFT]

12. The implement of which one of the following does not need any legislation?

(a) Fundament Rights and Duties

(b) Directive principles of State Policy.

(c) Promotion of community welfare

(d) Suggestion to States for citizen welfare.

[RRB SSE 2015 1ˢᵗ SEP 1ˢᵗ SHIFT]

13. Which special area related to children is included in the Directive Principles of State Policy in India

 (a) Early child ood care and education

 (b) Compulsory education for all

 (c) Education upto age of 14

 (d) Free education for Economically weaker sections

[RRB SSE 2015 1ˢᵗ SEP 2ⁿᵈ SHIFT]

14. Which amendment added Fundamental Duties to the Indian Constitution?

 (a) 37th Amendment act in 1975

 (b) 41 Amendment act in 1976

 (c) 38th Amendment act in 1975

 (d) 42nd Amendment Act in 1976

[RRB SSE 2015 1ˢᵗ SEP 2ⁿᵈ SHIFT]

15. Which aspect would need regulation if there is more Foreign Direct Investment in horticulture?

 (a) Consumption of water and rights of farmers to water

 (b) Soil conservation , and renewal using natural processes

 (c) Subsidy to farmers, for spending time away from their farms

 (d) Education of farmers on advantages of growing other crops

[RRB SSE 2015 1ˢᵗ SEP 3ʳᵈ SHIFT]

16. In a survey during 2009-2010 reveals that none of the female worker were found engaged as 'carpenters', 'blacksmiths', 'cobblers', 'masons' or 'tractor drivers' and hence no wage rate was reported for these occupations during the year 2009–10

 Which aspect of the Constitution could stand violated in this situation.

 (a) Right to Education (b) Right to equal wages

 (c) Right to Equality (d) Right to work

[RRB SSE 2015 1ˢᵗ SEP 3ʳᵈ SHIFT]

17. Which one is a fundamental Duty ?

 (a) Setting all border and international disputes peacefully

 (b) Establishing facilities' for the development of agriculture.

 (c) Setting up cottage industries in rural areas for self employment.

 (d) Safeguarding the sovereignty, integrity and unity of India .

[RRB SSE 2015 1ˢᵗ SEP 3ʳᵈ SHIFT]

18. Which Directive Principle of State Policy has become enforceable by a law ?

 (a) Care of Cultural Heritage

 (b) Prohibition of intoxicating drinks

 (c) Care of Natural Heritage

 (d) Equal pay for equal work

[RRB SSE 2015 2ⁿᵈ SEP 1ˢᵗ SHIFT]

19. What is the special feature of the Fundamental Rights ?

 (a) All the rights are for the individual citizen and not for the State

 (b) Some are positive and others are negative statements.

 (c) Rights are only for the Indian citizens living in India .

 (d) Rights can be changed by the law of the land.

[RRB SSE 2015 2ⁿᵈ SEP 1ˢᵗ SHIFT]

20. What is the relationship between Fundamental Rights and Duties and the Directive Principles of State Policy?

 (a) Directive Principles must agree with Fundamental Rights

 (b) Each State can choose which Directive Principles of State policy

 (c) More importance of Fundamental Rights

 (d) Freedom of the individual cannot be affected

[RRB SSE 2015 2ⁿᵈ SEP 2ⁿᵈ SHIFT]

21. As a part of which Right can any citizen choose to settle in any part of the country?

 (a) Right to Freedom

 (b) Right to Constitutional Remedies

 (c) Right to Equality

 (d) Right to Property.

[RRB SSE 2015 2ⁿᵈ SEP 2ⁿᵈ SHIFT]

22. Which of the Directive Principles of State Policy are based on Gaudhian ideals?

 (a) Free legal aid

 (b) Right to education

 (c) No cow slaughter

 (d) Equal wages for men and women

[RRB SSE 2015 2ⁿᵈ SEP 3ʳᵈ SHIFT]

23. Which of these situations would be all wed in the Right to Free Speech?

 (a) Send emails questioning the decision to set up Nuclear Plant.

 (b) Calling on a community to boycott another community or people.

 (c) Scolding children in school for not doing their homework.

 (d) Make a film which shows obscenity and sex.

[RRB SSE 2015 2ⁿᵈ SEP 3ʳᵈ SHIFT]

24. Where in the constitution has it been stated that the Judiciary must be separated from the Executive ?

(a) Directive principles of State Policy

(b) Fundamental Rights

(c) Preamble of the Constitution

(d) Schedules

[RRB SSE 2015 3ʳᵈ SEP 1ˢᵗ SHIFT]

25. Which State institution can truly be considered to be the one in which people's voice matters?

(a) Gram Panchayat

(b) Zilla Parishad

(c) Nyaya Panchayat

(d) Gram Sabha

[RRB SSE 2015 3ʳᵈ SEP 2ⁿᵈ SHIFT]

26. For which type of question in Parliament is a written reply required?

(a) Unstarred question

(b) Starred question

(c) Short notice questions

(d) Questions for private members

[RRB SSE 2015 3ʳᵈ SEP 2ⁿᵈ SHIFT]

27. What is the reason why compulsory voting cannot be insisted in a democracy?

(a) The right of free speech

(b) The right to dissent

(c) Equality of all citizens

(d) Right to work where one wants.

[RRB SSE 2015 3ʳᵈ SEP 3ʳᵈ SHIFT]

28. Who is allowed to introduce a Money bill In Parliament in India?

(a) Member   (b) Minister

(c) Speaker   (d) Opposition Leader

[RRB SSE 2015 3ʳᵈ SEP 3ʳᵈ SHIFT]

ANSWER KEY

RRB JUNIOR ENGINEER

1. (b)	**2.** (c)	**3.** (a)	**4.** (a)	**5.** (b)	**6.** (c)	**7.** (b)	**8.** (a)	**9.** (d)	**10.** (c)
11. (c)	**12.** (b)	**13.** (d)	**14.** (b)	**15.** (c)	**16.** (b)	**17.** (c)	**18.** (c)	**19.** (b)	**20.** (b)
21. (d)	**22.** (a)	**23.** (c)	**24.** (c)	**25.** (d)	**26.** (b)	**27.** (c)	**28.** (d)	**29.** (a)	**30.** (d)
31. (c)	**32.** (a)	**33.** (b)	**34.** (c)	**35.** (a)	**36.** (c)	**37.** (b)	**38.** (b)	**39.** (b)	

RRB SENIOR SECTION ENGINEER

1. (b)	**2.** (d)	**3.** (c)	**4.** (d)	**5.** (b)	**6.** (b)	**7.** (c)	**8.** (b)	**9.** (c)	**10.** (b)
11. (d)	**12.** (a)	**13.** (a)	**14.** (d)	**15.** (a)	**16.** (c)	**17.** (d)	**18.** (d)	**19.** (b)	**20.** (c)
21. (c)	**22.** (c)	**23.** (a)	**24.** (a)	**25.** (d)	**26.** (a)	**27.** (b)	**28.** (b)		

EXPLANATIONS

RRB JUNIOR ENGINEER

1. An individual who is not a member of either house of the parliament can be appointed as , a member of the Council of Ministers, but he has to become the member of the either house in 6 months.

2. The term 'Republic' used in the preamble of the Constitution of India implies that the head of the state is an elected representative.

3. In India, 14 years is the minimum permissible age for employment in a factory.

4. As on 01.11.2014, Smt. Sumitra Mahajan is the speaker of present Lok Sabha.She belongs to Bharatiya Janata Party. In 2014, she got elected to the Lok Sabha for the eighth time, one of three members of the 16th Lok Sabha to do so, and is currently the longest-serving woman member.

5. The Fundamental Duties of the Indian citizens are incorporated under the Article 51 A of the Indian Constitution.

6. Article 58 of the constitution sets the principal qualifications one must meet to be eligible to the office of the president. A President must be a citizen of India, must be having 35 years of age or above and qualified to become a member of the Lok Sabha.

7. All money received by or on behalf of the Government of India is deposited Consolidated Fund of India. This fund was constituted under Article 266 (1) of the Constitution of India.

8. Preamble of the Indian Constitution reflects the mind and ideals of the framers. The preamble to the Constitution of India is a brief introductory statement that sets out guiding people and principles of the document, and it indicates the source from which the ordinary document derives its authority, meaning, the people.

9. President can issue ordinance when one of the houses of the Parliament is not in session. The maximum validity of an ordinance is 6 months and 6 weeks. Ordinances must be approved by Parliament within six weeks of reassembling or they shall cease to operate. They also cease to operate in case resolutions disapproving the Ordinance are passed by both Houses.

10. A freedom not granted to citizens by the Indian Constitution is assemble peacefully even with arms. Article 19 (1) (b) provides that all citizens have the right to assemble peaceably and without arms.

11. Regarding Lok Sabha 2 members from Anglo Indian community are elected by the community is incorrect statement.

12. England has an unwritten constitution. Unlike most modern states, Britain does not have a codified constitution but an unwritten one formed of Acts of Parliament, court judgments and conventions. Professor Robert Blackburn explains this system, including Magna Carta's place within it, and asks whether the UK should now have a written constitution.

13. The current speaker is Sumitra Mahajan of the Bharatiya Janata Party, who is presiding over the 16th Lok Sabha. She is the second woman to hold the office, after her immediate predecessor Meira Kumar.

14. Indian constitution was adopted by the Constituent Assembly of India on 26 November 1949, and became effective on 26 January 1950. The constitution replaced the Government of India Act, 1935 as the country's fundamental governing document, and the Dominion of India became the republic of India.

15. The right against exploitation, given in Articles 23 and 24, provides for two provisions, namely the abolition of trafficking in human beings and *Begar* (forced labour), and abolition of employment of children below the age of 14 years in dangerous jobs like factories, mines, etc. Child labour is considered a gross violation of the spirit and provisions of the constitution.

16. The Supreme Court of India's collegium system, which appoints judges to the nation's constitutional courts, has its genesis in, and continued basis resting on, three of its own judgments which are collectively known as the Three Judges Cases..

17. Sovereignty of the Indian constitution means 'having complete freedom and being the supreme authority'.

18. There are two forms of government, presidential and parliamentary. The type of government do India, US and England have: India – Parliamentary, England –Parliamentary, US – Presidential

19. The All India Trinamool Congress is an Indian political party based in West Bengal. Founded on 1 January 1998, the party is led by its founder and current Chief Minister of West Bengal Mamata Banerjee.

20. The Fundamental Duties of citizens were added to the Constitution by the 42nd Amendment in 1976, upon the recommendations of the Swaran Singh Committee that was constituted by the government earlier that year. Originally ten in number, the Fundamental Duties were increased to eleven by the 86th Amendment in 2002, which added a duty on every parent or guardian to ensure that their child or ward was provided opportunities for education between the ages of six and fourteen years.

21. Universal Adult Franchise mean Any citizen of India 18 years of age or above can vote irrespective of race, caste, religion, sex, place of birth.

22. Members of the 16th Lok Sabha were elected during the 2014 Indian general election. The elections were conducted in 9 phases from 7 April 2014 to 12 May 2014 by the Election Commission of India. The Bharatiya Janata Party (of the NDA) achieved an absolute majority with 282 seats out of 543, 166 more than previous 15th Lok Sabha. Its PM candidate Narendra Modi took office on 26 May 2014 as the 14th prime minister of independent India.

23. Avul Pakir Jainulabdeen Abdul Kalam was an Indian scientist. Kalam was elected as the 11th President of India in 2002 with the support of both the ruling Bharatiya Janata Party and the then-opposition Indian National Congress. He was a recipient of several prestigious awards, including the Bharat Ratna, India's highest civilian honour who served as the 11th President of India from 2002 to 2007.

24. Bhimrao Ramji Ambedkar popularly known as Babasaheb, was campaigned against social discrimination towards Untouchables (Dalits). He was Independent India's first law minister, the principal architect of the Constitution of India and a founding father of the Republic of India.He was appointed Chairman of the Constitution Drafting Committee, and was appointed by the Assembly to write India's new Constitution.

25. The President of India can declare emergency under Article 352 on the advice of Cabinet. National emergency can be declared on the basis of external aggression or armed rebellion in the whole of India or a part of its territory.

26. 91st Constitutional Amendments state that the total number of ministers, including the prime minister in the council of ministers shall not exceed 15% of the total number of members of the house of the people.

27. The indian legislature was made bicameral for the first time by the Government of India Act 1919.

28. Recommendations to the president of india on the specific Union state fiscal relations are made by the Finance Commission.

29. The 99th constitution Amendment Act was in news recently. It is related to National Judicial appointments commission.

30. For distribution of powers between the union and the states, the constitution of india introduce three lists. Articles 245 and 246 govern the distribution of power;

31. Court can issue writ for enforcement of Fundamental Rights. A writ is a formal written order issued by a body with administrative or judicial jurisdiction, this body is generally a court for enforcement of any of the fundamental rights conferred by part III of Indian Constitution under article 32 the Constitution of India empowers the supreme Court to Issue writs.

32. Lok Sabha on May 7, 2015 cleared a bill to lower the age of Juveniles from 18 years to 16 years.

33. The Fifth schedule of the Constitution of India contains specific provisions for the administration and control of scheduled areas in several states.

34. During Chaudhary Charan Singh term as Prime Minister, Lok Sabha never met. The day before the Lok Sabha was due to meet for the first time the Indian National Congress withdrew their support from his Bharatiya Lok Dal Government. Chaudhary Charan Singh resigned and fresh elections were held six months later

35. The Constitution 86th Amendment Act, 2002 enshrined right to education as a fundamental right in part-III of the constitution. A new article 21A was inserted below the Article 21 which made Right to Education a Fundamental Right for children in the range of 6-14 years.

36. All people, irrespective of race, religion, caste or sex, have been given the right to petition directly the Supreme Court or the High Courts for the enforcement of their fundamental rights. However, in case of fundamental rights violation, the Supreme Court of India can be approached directly for ultimate justice per Article 32.

37. The Directive Principles of State Policy (DPSP) are the guidelines or principles given to the federal institutes governing the state of India, to be kept in citation while framing laws and policies. These provisions, contained in Part IV (Article 36-51) of the Constitution of India, are not enforceable by any court.

38. If the finance minister fails to get the Annual Budget passed in the Lok Sabha, the Prime Minister is expected to submit the resignation of his /her cabinet.

39. The right to property was removed from the list of fundamental Rights enlisted in the constitution of the India through 44th Amendment.

RRB SENIOR SECTION ENGINEER

1. By 24th constitutional amendment, Parliament acquires the right to amend Fundamental Rights. The 24th Amendment was enacted by the Congress government headed by Indira Gandhi, to abrogate the Supreme Court ruling in Golaknath v. State of Punjab. It enables Parliament to dilute Fundamental Rights through Amendments of the Constitution, and empowers it to amend any provision of the Constitution.

2. The Constitution of India guarantees six fundamental rights to Indian citizens as follows: (i) right to equality, (ii) right to freedom, (iii) right against exploitation, (iv) right to freedom of religion, (v) cultural and educational rights, and (vi) right to constitutional remedies.

3. As Constitution is the conscience of our Nation India that is Bharat so is the Preamble as the conscience of our Constitution. Our Constitution's spirit is the Preamble, which is the Backbone of our Constitution.

4. A person must satisfy all following conditions to be qualified to become a Member of Parliament of the Lok Sabha; Must be a citizen of India. Must not be less than 25 years of age. Must be a voter for any parliamentary constituency in India.

5. As on 01.11.2014, Hamid Ansari is the Chairman of Rajya Sabha.Mohammad Hamid Ansari is an Indian politician who served as Vice-President of India from 2007 to 2017. He has also served as an Indian ambassador and is ex-chairman of Rajya Sabha. Ansari was the first person to be re-elected as Indian VP after Sarvepalli Radhakrishnan in 1957.

6. Bhimrao Ramji Ambedkar, popularly known as Babasaheb, was an Indian jurist, economist, politician and social reformer who inspired the Dalit Buddhist movement and campaigned against social discrimination towards Untouchables, while also supporting the rights of women and labour. He is regarded as the architect of the Indian Constitution.

7. About 66% was the overall voting percentage in the recently held General Elections for 16th Lok Sabha.

8. Money can be spent out of the Consolidated Fund of India with the approval of the Parliament.Article 266 of the Constitution of India requires revenues received by the Government of India to be paid to the Consolidated Fund of India.

9. Acquiring property is not a condition for becoming a Citizen of India.Indian citizenship can be acquired by birth, descent, registration and naturalization.

10. The Oath of Office is conducted to the President of India by the Chief Justice of India and in his absence for any reason,the oath then is administered by the senior most judge of the supreme court of India. Honourable Chief justice of India (CJI) administers the oath of office to the president of India.

11. The State shall take steps to organise village panchayats and endow them with such powers and authority as may be necessary to enable them to function as units of self-government mentioned under the Article 40 of the Directive Principle of State Policy.

12. For the implementation of Fundamental Rights and Duties do not require any legislation.

13. The special areas related to children included in the Directive Principles of State Policy in India are early childhood care and education.

14. 42nd Amendment Act in 1976 added Fundamental Duties to the Indian Constitution.The 42nd amendment to Constitution of India, officially known as The Constitution (Forty-second amendment) Act, 1976, was enacted during the Emergency (25 June 1975 – 21 March 1977) by the Indian National Congress government headed by Indira Gandhi.

15. Consumption of water and rights of farmers to water aspect would need regulation if there is more Foreign Direct Investment in horticulture.

16. Right to Equality aspect of the Constitution could stand violated in the given situation.

17. Among the given options, Safeguarding the sovereignty, integrity and unity of India is the Fundamental Duty.

18. The founding fathers of the Constitution had set certain goals in the directive principles of state policy, but they are not enforceable in a court of law. Equal pay for equal work of the Directive Principle of State Policy has become enforceable by a law.

19. The special features of the Fundamental Rights are there are some are positive and others are negative statements.

20. The relationships between Fundamental Rights and Duties and the Directive Principles of State Policy are that in the Constitution of India Fundamental Rights are given more importance.

21. Right to Equality can be chosen by any citizen choose to settle in any part of the country.

22. To prohibit the slaughter of cows, calves and other milch and draught cattle and to improve their breeds mentioned under the Article 48.

23. Send emails questioning the decision to set up Nuclear Plant would be allowed in the Right to Free Speech.

24. Under the article 50 of Constitution of India, the State shall take steps to separate the judiciary from the executive in the public services of the State. Article 50 of Constitution of India is a directive principle of state policy. Therefore the Constitution is directing the legislature to maintain judicial independence.

25. Gram Sabha institution can truly be considered to be the one in which people's voice matters.A gram panchayat is the only grassroots-level of panchayati raj formalised local self-governance system in India at the village or small-town level, and has a sarpanch as its elected head.

26. For unstarred question in Parliament is a written reply required.

27. The right to dissent is the reason why compulsory voting cannot be insisted in a democracy.

28. Minister is allowed to introduce a Money bill in Parliament in India.Procedure for a Money Bill: Money Bills can be introduced only in Lok Sabha (the directly elected 'people's house' of the Indian Parliament). Money bills passed by the Lok Sabha are sent to the Rajya Sabha (the upper house of parliament, elected by the state and territorial legislatures or appointed by the president).

GEOGRAPHY AND ENVIRONMENTAL SCIENCE

RRB JUNIOR ENGINEER

1. Hirakud dam has been built on the river
(a) Cauvery   (b) Mahanadi
(c) Krishna   (d) Yamuna
[RRB JE 2014 GREEN SHIFT]

2. With reference to water pollution, BOD means
(a) Biochemical Oxygen Dilution
(b) Biochemical Oxygen Demand
(c) Bio Organic Dissolutes
(d) Basic Organic Dissolutes
[RRB JE 2014 GREEN SHIFT]

3. Approx, percentage of oxygen in Earth's atmosphere is
(a) 17%   (b) 21%
(c) 25%   (d) 33%
[RRB JE 2014 GREEN SHIFT]

4. Lunar Eclipse occurs only on a
(a) First quarter day   (b) New moon day
(c) Full moon day   (d) Last quarter day
[RRB JE 2014 GREEN SHIFT]

5. Mirages generally occur in
(a) mountains   (b) forests
(c) deserts   (d) sea
[RRB JE 2014 GREEN SHIFT]

6. In October 2014 a cyclone hit Vishakhapatnam. The name of the cyclone was
(a) Katrina   (b) Hudhud
(c) Laila   (d) Helen
[RRB JE 2014 GREEN SHIFT]

7. Which National Park is known for the 'Asiatic Lions' ?
(a) Corbett National Park
(b) Kanha National Park
(c) Bandipur National Park
(d) Gir National Park
[RRB JE 2014 RED SHIFT]

8. The Indian Standard Time (I.S.T.) is ahead of Greenwich Mean Time (G.M.T.) by :
(a) 6 hours
(b) 5 hours
(c) 6 hours 30 minutes
(d) 5 hours 30 minutes
[RRB JE 2014 RED SHIFT]

9. Red rot is a plant disease which affects :
(a) Wheat   (b) Rice
(c) Sugarcane   (d) Cotton
[RRB JE 2014 RED SHIFT]

10. Which one of the following is also known as Red Planet ?
(a) Mercury   (b) Venus
(c) Earth   (d) Mars
[RRB JE 2014 RED SHIFT]

11. Galena is an ore of :
(a) Lead   (b) Copper
(c) Aluminium   (d) Iron
[RRB JE 2014 RED SHIFT]

12. Identify the city which faced large scale destructions due to 'Hudhud' cyclone recently ?
(a) Chennai   (b) Vishakhapatnam
(c) Kolkata   (d) Hyderabad
[RRB JE 2014 RED SHIFT]

13. The most effective farming method for returning minerals to the soil is
(a) Contour ploughing
(b) Terracing
(c) Crop rotation
(d) Furrowing
[RRB JE 2014 YELLOW SHIFT]

14. Winter rains in North-Western India are caused by
(a) Western Disturbances
(b) South West Monsoon
(c) South Easterly Disturbances
(d) Easterly Disturbances
[RRB JE 2014 YELLOW SHIFT]

15. Kaziranga National Park is in
(a) Uttar Pradesh   (b) Tamil Nadu
(c) Assam   (d) Kerala
[RRB JE 2014 YELLOW SHIFT]

16. UNDP has aim

(a) to provide technical assistance to stimulate economic and social development

(b) to promote International Trade

(c) to promote cooperation on Environmental Problems

(d) to help establish Child Health and Welfare Services

[RRB JE 2014 YELLOW SHIFT]

17. What are plate tectonics?

(a) Movement of plates supporting the continents

(b) Volcanic eruptions

(c) Term for erosion of land in the Himalayan region

(d) Mountain formation due to collision of plates

[RRB JE 2015 26th AUG 1st SHIFT]

18. What Saraswati river is to the Triveni Sangam or confluence of rivers at Allahabad _______ is to confluence of rivers at Coorg.

Mark the option which can fill the blank in the statement.

(a) Shujyothi   (b) Krishna

(c) Godavari   (d) Meghna

[RRB JE 2015 26th AUG 1st SHIFT]

19. What is likely to happen if the supply of coffee goes up?

(a) The demand for tea goes up

(b) The price of coffee goes down

(c) There is no change in the demand for tea

(d) Demand for tea escalates and price of coffee diminishes

[RRB JE 2015 26th AUG 1st SHIFT]

20. One of the following is not a 'social insect'

(a) Ant   (b) Beetle

(c) Termite   (d) Wasp

[RRB JE 2015 26th AUG 1st SHIFT]

21. Who coined the phrase 'Survival of the fittest' to mean Natural Selection?

(a) Charles Darwin   (b) Bertrand Russell

(c) JBS Haldane   (d) Herbert Spencer

[RRB JE 2015 26th AUG 1st SHIFT]

22. The major cause of top soil being lost due to soil erosion is

(a) Westerly winds

(b) Thermal inversion

(c) Deforestation

(d) Cattle grazing

[RRB JE 2015 26th AUG 2nd SHIFT]

23. Is Virus a living being?

(a) Yes, because it has DNA

(b) No, because it does not possess the machinery to duplicate itself

(c) Yes, because it can divide to reproduce when inside a living being

(d) No, because its coat is made of Protein

[RRB JE 2015 26th AUG 2nd SHIFT]

24. What does a plant do with the sugar it makes?

(a) Uses it up completely to get energy for its survival

(b) Stores it in its roots

(c) Converts it into starch

(d) Stores it for herbivores to feed upon

[RRB JE 2015 26th AUG 2nd SHIFT]

25. Which out of the following is in all cases a hereditary disorder

(a) Thallasemia   (b) Diabetes mellitus

(c) Tuberculosis   (d) Anaemia

[RRB JE 2015 26th AUG 2nd SHIFT]

26. In the geography class students were confused regarding the difference between climate and weather. Four of the students gave four answers. Which one is the correct difference?

(a) Climate is the sum total of variation in weather in an area whereas weather is the state of atmosphere over an area.

(b) Climate and weather are synonymous

(c) Climate is the sum total of weather conditions over a large area for a long period of time and weather is the state of atmosphere over an area at any point of time.

(d) Climate is the duration of seasons in a large area and weather refers to seasonal changes in a small area.

[RRB JE 2015 26th AUG 2nd SHIFT]

27. A gel is a

(a) Suspension of a solid in a liquid

(b) Suspension of tiny liquid droplets in another liquid

(c) Gas trapped in a viscous liquid

(d) Gas trapped in a semi-solid

[RRB JE 2015 26th AUG 2nd SHIFT]

28. Some salts we use in the kitchen for cooking are given below but one is erroneously mentioned. Identify it

(a) Sodium chloride

(b) Sodium bi carbonate

(c) Calcium Phosphate

(d) Monosodium glutamate

[RRB JE 2015 26th AUG 2nd SHIFT]

29. When mother was heating the oven to a certain temperature for baking a cake, the daughter wanted to know the difference between heat and temperature. In mother's response which one statement was incorrect?

(a) Heat is a form of energy and temperature measures how hot something is

(b) Heat is measured in Joules and temperature in degree Celsius (°C)

(c) Heat and temperature both flow between temperatures

(d) When heat energy flows, temperature increases or decreases

[RRB JE 2015 26th AUG 2nd SHIFT]

30. Read the poem written by a child.

Plants will always grow

Wind will always blow

Solar cells will give electrical energy

Waves forever will make energy

About what did a child write in the above poem?

(a) Renewable energy resources

(b) Non renewable energy resources

(c) Energy resources of all kinds

(d) Principle of conservation of energy

[RRB JE 2015 26th AUG 2nd SHIFT]

31. The colour of an object is the colour it reflects. So a red boot ____ Identify the wrong statement among the ones written below.

(a) looks red in white light as it reflects red and absorbs all other colours

(b) red in red light as it reflects red light falling on it

(c) looks black in green light which it absorbs

(d) red in green light when there is no red light

[RRB JE 2015 26th AUG 2nd SHIFT]

32. One long river of our country which flows through the North-East is

(a) Ganges   (b) Brahmaputra

(c) Narmada   (d) Kaveri

[RRB JE 2015 26th AUG 3rd SHIFT]

33. Whose saying 'Earth has enough for man's need but not enough for man's greed' is often being quoted by speakers on Environment?

(a) Independent India's first Prime Minister

(b) The second President of India

(c) The Environmentalist, Madhav Gadgil

(d) The father of our nation

[RRB JE 2015 27th AUG 1st SHIFT]

34. The artificial satellites cannot be used for

(a) Relaying Radio, TV and Telephone signals

(b) Weather forecasting

(c) Monitoring atmospheric pollution

(d) Exploring solar system

[RRB JE 2015 27th AUG 1st SHIFT]

35. Which method will you use to separate yoghurt (Curd) from water contained in it?

(a) Distillation   (b) Crystallisation

(c) Filtration   (d) Decantation

[RRB JE 2015 27th AUG 1st SHIFT]

36. Out of two bottles of pickle, one old and one freshly made, the old one can be detected by its smell and taste caused by

(a) Oxidation of oil in the pickle making it rancid

(b) Invasion of bacteria causing putrefaction

(c) Reduction in volume of oil in the pickle

(d) Fermentation by yeast

[RRB JE 2015 27th AUG 1st SHIFT]

37. Hair dyes may contain the base

(a) Sodium Hydroxide

(b) Ammonium Hydroxide

(c) Calcium Hydroxide

(d) Potassium Hydroxide

[RRB JE 2015 27th AUG 1st SHIFT]

38. What is not true of the Thar Desert?

(a) Has arid and semiarid weather conditions throughout the year

(b) The flora is mainly cacti and thorny bushes

(c) Water is available in sinduates and streams which are always there even without rainfall

(d) Rainfall is scanty

[RRB JE 2015 27th AUG 1st SHIFT]

39. What is a hotspot?

(a) A region of high endemic biodiversity

(b) A geographical area with very high exotic biodiversity

(c) A region of scanty rainfall

(d) An area of constant high temperature

[RRB JE 2015 27th AUG 1st SHIFT]

40. Decibel is the unit of

(a) Speed of light

(b) Intensity of heat

(c) Intensity of sound

(d) Quantum of mass

[RRB JE 2015 27th AUG 2nd SHIFT]

41. One early morning, with no traffic on roads, Rahul while cycling down from Red Fort to his residence noted the distance covered and the total time taken to reach home. What can he calculate from this data?

(a) Velocity   (b) Speed

(c) Acceleration   (d) Displacement

[RRB JE 2015 27th AUG 2nd SHIFT]

42. Which pair out of the following is radioactive as available abundantly?

(a) Lead & Mercury

(b) Radium & Uranium

(c) Sodium & Potassium

(d) Carbon & Silicon

[RRB JE 2015 27th AUG 2nd SHIFT]

43. Sun's energy does not get converted into

(a) biomass

(b) wind power

(c) nuclear energy

(d) energy from oceanic waves

[RRB JE 2015 27th AUG 2nd SHIFT]

44. The unit for measurement of energy is

(a) Pascal   (b) Joule

(c) Calorie   (d) Horse power

[RRB JE 2015 27th AUG 2nd SHIFT]

45. Energy experts predict that many countries will face severe electricity blackouts very soon because

(a) Demand would surpass supply

(b) World's natural oil supply is fixed

(c) Electrical supply is fist being eroded by terrorists in many pans of the world

(d) Greater demand for energy and extreme depletion of oil and natural gas

[RRB JE 2015 27th AUG 2nd SHIFT]

46. Which is the correct difference between topography and landscape

(a) Topography is natural, landscape is the handiwork of humans

(b) Topography is of diverse kinds, landscaping is not

(c) Landscape is determined by nature, topography by humans

(d) Himalayas and Thar desert are pair of landscape of India, sea beach is topographical

[RRB JE 2015 27th AUG 2nd SHIFT]

47. Wires in our homes are made of metal because metals are

(a) good conductors of electricity

(b) cheap and wires are long

(c) easily available

(d) conveniently covered by insulators

[RRB JE 2015 27th AUG 3rd SHIFT]

48. Summer solstice falls on 20th or 21st on this day

(a) Day and night are equal

(b) Day is the longest of all days in the year

(c) Night is longest of all night in the year

(d) The temperature is usually the highest in the year

[RRB JE 2015 27th AUG 3rd SHIFT]

49. Through which one of the following continent, do the equator, the tropic of cancer and the tropic of capricorn pass through

(a) Africa   (b) South America

(c) North America   (d) Australia

[RRB JE 2015 28th AUG 1st SHIFT]

50. Shivasundaram Falls are located in the course of the river

(a) Krishna   (b) Godavari

(c) Kaveri   (d) Mahanadi

[RRB JE 2015 28th AUG 1st SHIFT]

51. When one state of India is surrounded by Bangladesh from three sides

(a) Mizoram   (b) Meghalaya

(c) Tripura   (d) West Bengal

[RRB JE 2015 28th AUG 1st SHIFT]

52. The torque on a rectangular coil placed in uniform magnetic field is large when the

(a) number of turns is large

(b) number of turns is less

(c) plane of the coil is perpendicular to the magnetic field

(d) area of the coil is small

[RRB JE 2015 28th AUG 1st SHIFT]

53. The Eastern and Western Ghats meet at the

(a) Cardamom Hills   (b) Annamalai Hills

(c) Nilgiri Hills   (d) Palani Hills

54. Match **List 1** with **List 2** and select the correct answer from the codes given below in the list

List 1 (State)	List 2 (Emblem)
A. Zoji La Pass	1. Sikkim
B. Bara Lacha Pass	2. Uttarakhand
C. Jelep La Pass	3. Himachal Pradesh
D. Niti Pass	4. Jammu and Kashmir

(a) A-4 B-1 C-2 D-3   (b) A-2 B-3 C-4 D-1

(c) A-4 B-3 C-1 D-2   (d) A-2 B-1 C-4 D-3

[RRB JE 2015 28th AUG 2nd SHIFT]

55. The Karakoram highway connects which of the following pair of countries
  (a) India-Nepal   (b) India-China
  (c) India-Pakistan   (d) China-Pakistan
[RRB JE 2015 28ᵗʰ AUG 2ⁿᵈ SHIFT]

56. On raising the temperature of the medium, velocity of light
  (a) increases
  (b) decreases
  (c) remains the same
  (d) suddenly decreases
[RRB JE 2015 28ᵗʰ AUG 2ⁿᵈ SHIFT]

57. Which of the following is a paramagnetic
  (a) nickel   (b) cobalt
  (c) chromium   (d) copper
[RRB JE 2015 28ᵗʰ AUG 2ⁿᵈ SHIFT]

58. If the length of a simple pendulum increases by 4%, then its time period will be
  (a) increased by 3%
  (b) increased by 4%
  (c) increased by 2%
  (d) increased by 8%
[RRB JE 2015 28ᵗʰ AUG 2ⁿᵈ SHIFT]

59. Match the Dams and the States in which they are situated

List-1 (Dam)	List-2 (State)
A. Tungabhadra	1. Kerala
B. Lower bhawani	2. Andhra Pradesh
C. Idukki	3. Tamil Nadu
D. Nagarjuna Sagar	4. Karnataka

  (a) A-3, B-2, C-4, D-1   (b) A-2, B-4, C-3, D-1
  (c) A-4, B-3, C-1, D-2   (d) A-1, B-4, C-2, D-3
[RRB JE 2015 28ᵗʰ AUG 2ⁿᵈ SHIFT]

60. The latitudes that pass through Sikkim also pass through
  (a) Rajasthan
  (b) Jammu and Kashmir
  (c) Himachal Pradesh
  (d) Punjab
[RRB JE 2015 28ᵗʰ AUG 3ʳᵈ SHIFT]

61. River Indus originates from
  (a) Hindukush Range
  (b) Himalayan Range
  (c) Karakoram Range
  (d) Kailash Range
[RRB JE 2015 28ᵗʰ AUG 3ʳᵈ SHIFT]

62. If a ship moves from fresh water into sea water, it will
  (a) sink completely
  (b) sink a little bit
  (c) rise a little higher
  (d) remain unaffected
[RRB JE 2015 28ᵗʰ AUG 3ʳᵈ SHIFT]

63. The focal length of a convex lens is
  (a) same for all the colours
  (b) shorter for blue light than for red
  (c) shorter for red light than for blue
  (d) maximum for yellow light
[RRB JE 2015 28ᵗʰ AUG 3ʳᵈ SHIFT]

64. Which of the following is not correctly matched
  (a) Decibel-unit of sound
  (b) Horse power-Unit of power
  (c) Nautical mile-unit of distance
  (d) Celcius-unit of heat
[RRB JE 2015 28ᵗʰ AUG 3ʳᵈ SHIFT]

65. If a small raindrop falls through air,
  (a) Its velocity goes on decreasing
  (b) Its velocity goes on increasing
  (c) Its value goes on increasing for some time and then becomes constant
  (d) It falls with constant speed for some time and then its velocity increases

For the above question, User had specified 'ignore' during keys upload.
[RRB JE 2015 29ᵗʰ AUG 1ˢᵗ SHIFT]

66. Neap tides occur during which of the following phases of moon
  (a) First quarter only
  (b) First and Third quarter
  (c) Second and third quarter
  (d) Fourth quarter
[RRB JE 2015 29ᵗʰ AUG 1ˢᵗ SHIFT]

67. If a moving body doubles its velocity, then its kinetic energy becomes
  (a) double   (b) four times
  (c) same   (d) three times
[RRB JE 2015 29ᵗʰ AUG 1ˢᵗ SHIFT]

68. The blackboard seems black because it
  (a) reflects every colour
  (b) does not reflect any colour
  (c) absorbs black colour
  (d) reflects black colour
[RRB JE 2015 29ᵗʰ AUG 1ˢᵗ SHIFT]

69. The magnetic lines of force produced through a bar magnet
    (a) cross inside the magnetic body
    (b) only cross across the neutral point of the magnet
    (c) only cross across the north pole and south pole
    (d) does not cross anywhere in the magnet
    [RRB JE 2015 29th AUG 1st SHIFT]

70. Because of which one of the following reason, clouds do not precipitate in deserts?
    (a) Low Pressure
    (b) Low Humidity
    (c) High wind velocity
    (d) High temperature
    [RRB JE 2015 29th AUG 2nd SHIFT]

71. The atmospheric layer which reflects radio waves is called
    (a) Exosphere
    (b) Stratosphere
    (c) Ionosphere
    (d) Thermosphere
    [RRB JE 2015 29th AUG 2nd SHIFT]

72. In the interior of Earth,
    (a) temperature falls with increasing depth
    (b) pressure falls with increasing depth
    (c) temperature rises with increasing depth
    (d) both temperature and pressure fall with increasing depth
    [RRB JE 2015 29th AUG 2nd SHIFT]

73. If an object is placed at the centre of curvature of a concave mirror, the position of image is
    (a) at the principal focus
    (b) between the principal focus and the centre of curvature
    (c) at centre of curvature
    (d) beyond centre of curvature
    [RRB JE 2015 29th AUG 2nd SHIFT]

74. In which of the following, speed of sound is maximum
    (a) air at 0°C
    (b) air at 100°C
    (c) in the water
    (d) in the wood
    [RRB JE 2015 29th AUG 2nd SHIFT]

75. Microwave oven consumes less power due to
    (a) small frequency of radiation
    (b) short wavelength of radiation
    (c) large frequency as well as wavelength of radiation
    (d) small frequency as well as wavelength of radiation
    [RRB JE 2015 29th AUG 2nd SHIFT]

76. The difference in the duration of day and night increases as one moves from
    (a) West to East
    (b) East and West of Prime Meridian
    (c) Poles to Equator
    (d) Equator to Poles
    [RRB JE 2015 29th AUG 3rd SHIFT]

77. An endoscope, used by doctors for examine the inside of patient's stomach, works on the principle of
    (a) Reflection of light
    (b) Dispersion of light
    (c) Refraction of light
    (d) Total internal reflection of fight
    [RRB JE 2015 29th AUG 3rd SHIFT]

78. The coil in a heater is made up of
    (a) Chromium
    (b) Nichrome
    (c) Tungsten
    (d) Nickel
    [RRB JE 2015 29th AUG 3rd SHIFT]

79. When a body moves in a simple harmonic motion, then the phase difference (in degrees) between velocity and acceleration is
    (a) 90
    (b) 180
    (c) 0
    (d) 270
    [RRB JE 2015 29th AUG 3rd SHIFT]

80. Match List 1 with List 2 and select the correct answer from the codes given below in the list

List 1 (Towns)	List 2 (Rivers)
A. Jabalpur	1. Ravi
B. Paris	2. Narmada
C. London	3. Siene
D. Lahore	4. Thames

    (a) A-2, B-3, C-4, D-1
    (b) A-3, B-2, C-1, D-4
    (c) A-1, B-4, C-3, D-2
    (d) A-4, B-1, C-2, D-3
    [RRB JE 2015 30th AUG 3rd SHIFT]

81. Which one of the following sequence correctly represents the percentage of given salt in sea water in decreasing order
    (a) Magnesium Chloride-Sodium Chloride-Magnesium Sulphate-Calcium Sulphate
    (b) Magnesium Sulphate-Magnesium Chloride-Calcium Sulphate-Sodium Chloride
    (c) Sodium Chloride-Magnesium Chloride-Magnesium Sulphate-Calcium Sulphate
    (d) Sodium chloride-Magnesium Sulphate-Magnesium Chloride-Calcium Sulphate
    [RRB JE 2015 30th AUG 3rd SHIFT]

82. The large states of India in order of area are

(a) Rajasthan, Madhya Pradesh, Maharashtra

(b) Madhya Pradesh, Rajasthan, Maharashtra

(c) Maharashtra, Rajasthan, Madhya Pradesh

(d) Madhya Pradesh, Maharashtra, Rajasthan

[RRB JE 2015 30ᵗʰ AUG 3ʳᵈ SHIFT]

83. The best and poorest conductor of heat are respectively

(a) silver and lead

(b) copper and aluminium

(c) silver and gold

(d) copper and gold

[RRB JE 2015 30ᵗʰ AUG 3ʳᵈ SHIFT]

84. The ratio of transverse deformation to longitudinal deformation is called

(a) Poisson Ratio   (b) Bulk modulus

(c) Young's modulus   (d) Modulus of rigidity

[RRB JE 2015 30ᵗʰ AUG 3ʳᵈ SHIFT]

85. Burning of dry leaves is not permitted because it produces Carbon dioxide which is

(a) a greenhouse gas and causes global warming

(b) a gas responsible for ozone hole

(c) poisonous and kills living things

(d) a gas that irritates the eyes

[RRB JE 2015 16ᵗʰ SEP 3ʳᵈ SHIFT]

86. Which concept was given by India to the world?

(a) Concept of Zero

(b) Pythagoras theorem

(c) Invention of the wheel

(d) Scientific naming of living things

[RRB JE 2015 16ᵗʰ SEP 3ʳᵈ SHIFT]

87. Over which states of India does the Thar Desert spread?

(a) Madhya Pradesh and Gujarat

(b) Gujarat and Rajasthan

(c) Rajasthan and Uttar Pradesh

(d) Uttar Pradesh and Madhya Pradesh

[RRB JE 2015 16ᵗʰ SEP 3ʳᵈ SHIFT]

88. Development that meets the needs of the present without compromising ability of future generations to meet their own needs is

(a) Sustainable development

(b) Social development

(c) Economic development

(d) Regional development

[RRB JE 2015 16ᵗʰ SEP 3ʳᵈ SHIFT]

RRB SENIOR SECTION ENGINEER

1. Approximate quantity of CO_2 in the atmosphere in PPM (parts per million) is:

(a) 2   (b) 20

(c) 200   (d) 400

[RRB SSE 2014 GREEN SHIFT]

2. Average Albedo (overall) of the Earth is:

(a) 5×10^6 candela/day

(b) 5×10^7 candela/day

(c) 30 to 35%

(d) 60 to 65%

[RRB SSE 2014 GREEN SHIFT]

3. The illumination of a beam of light due to scattering on collision with particles suspended in a fluid, is called:

(a) Raman effect   (b) Tyndall effect

(c) Snell's effect   (d) Huygens effect

[RRB SSE 2014 GREEN SHIFT]

4. Intensity of earthquake is measured in -

(a) Barometer scale   (b) Pyrometer scale

(c) Tachometer scale   (d) Richter scale

[RRB SSE 2014 GREEN SHIFT]

5. Several nations are following a protocol which binds them to reduce emission targets. This protocol was adopted in:

(a) Kyoto, Japan   (b) Geneva, Switzerland

(c) New York, USA   (d) Paris, France

[RRB SSE 2014 GREEN SHIFT]

6. Which of these rocks would have alumina as their main component?

(a) Siliceous   (b) Argillaceous

(c) Calcareous   (d) Igneous

[RRB SSE 2014 GREEN SHIFT]

7. Which of the following phenomenon is related to the formation of clouds?

(a) Condensation   (b) Evaporation

(c) Sublimation   (d) Vulcanization

[RRB SSE 2014 GREEN SHIFT]

8. El Nino effect is:

(a) Development of low pressure areas in south east Asian region

(b) Reduction in ice caps resulting in variation in in solation absorption

(c) Prolonged warming in the Pacific Ocean surface area

(d) Sustained tornados in the eastern coast of North America

[RRB SSE 2014 GREEN SHIFT]

9. River Damoder is called the 'Sorrow of ' .

(a) Assam (b) Bengal

(c) Orissa (d) Uttar Pradesh

[RRB SSE 2014 GREEN SHIFT]

10. Woollen clothes keep the body warm in winter because-

(a) Wool is a bad conductor of heat

(b) Wool is a good conductor of heat

(c) Wool increases body temperature

(d) Wool decreases body temperature

[RRB SSE 2014 GREEN SHIFT]

11. Age of a Tree may be ascertained by :

(a) Radius of its Stem

(b) Number of Annual Rings

(c) Number of Branches

(d) Circumference of its Stem

[RRB SSE 2014 RED SHIFT]

12. The ozone layer is useful for living beings because:

(a) It serves as the source of oxygen

(b) It maintains the temperature of the earth

(c) It maintains the Nitrogen cycle of the earth

(d) It protects them from harmful ultraviolet rays of the sun

[RRB SSE 2014 RED SHIFT]

13. Identify the cyclone which caused large scale destructions in Vishakhapatnam this year in October ?

(a) Phailin (b) Katrina

(c) Hudhud (d) Nilofar

[RRB SSE 2014 RED SHIFT]

14. Which one of the following is renewable resource?

(a) Coal (b) Petroleum

(c) Natural Gas (d) Wind

[RRB SSE 2014 RED SHIFT]

15. Which of these will not he oxidised by Ozone ?

(a) KI (b) $FeSO_4$

(c) $KMnO_4$ (d) K_2MnO_4

[RRB SSE 2014 RED SHIFT]

16. Jarawas and Shompens Tribal Groups live in :

(a) Andaman and Nicobar Islands

(b) Chhattisgarh

(c) Jharkhand

(d) Madhya Pradesh

[RRB SSE 2014 RED SHIFT]

17. Which one of the following problems is not created by Noise Pollution ?

(a) Diarrhoea (b) Hypertension

(c) Deafness (d) Irritation

[RRB SSE 2014 RED SHIFT]

18. Dew is caused when

(a) humid air condenses on cool surface

(b) the sky is overcast at night

(c) the air is colder than the earth s surface

(d) the wind is too dry to cause rainfall

[RRB SSE 2014 YELLOW SHIFT]

19. Corbett National Park is in

(a) Bihar (b) Madhya Pradesh

(c) Uttarakhand (d) Himachal Pradesh

[RRB SSE 2014 YELLOW SHIFT]

20. Which crop requires water-logging for its cultivation ?

(a) Tea (b) Coffee

(c) Rice (d) Mustard

[RRB SSE 2014 YELLOW SHIFT]

21. EBOLA is a

(a) virus disease confirmed in West Africa

(b) name of Tsunami

(c) Name of anti-terrorist operation in Arab Country

(d) volcano in African Hills

[RRB SSE 2014 YELLOW SHIFT]

22. "The "Helmand Province" of Afghanistan is famous for cultivation of

(a) Tobacco (b) Wheat

(c) Cotton (d) Opium

[RRB SSE 2014 YELLOW SHIFT]

23. Where in the course of the river are Gorges, plunge pools, rapids, interlocking spurs found?

(a) Upper course

(b) Middle course

(c) Lower Middle course

(d) Lower course.

[RRB SSE 2015 1ˢᵗ SEP 1ˢᵗ SHIFT]

24. 'Usually before the onset of monsoons though the frequency of cyclones is low their intensity is high ? For which one of the following is this statement true

(a) Indian Ocean

(b) Bay of Bengal

(c) Arabian sea

(d) South China Sea

[RRB SSE 2015 1ˢᵗ SEP 1ˢᵗ SHIFT]

25. Which measure is likely to make India the world's largest green energy producer by 2022?

  (a) Making solar energy producers create systems to provide solar power to areas not covered by the grid

  (b) Introducing roof top and grid connected solar production units on build, own, operate and transfer basis.

  (c) Increase investment in solar panels, and batteries so that home owners can set up own power supply

  (d) Give private companies rights to use rooftops and fields for generating private electricity for industry.

[RRB SSE 2015 1st SEP 1st SHIFT]

26. When a gorge is formed in which direction will hard rock be eroded by the river?

  (a) Down

  (b) Backward

  (c) Along faults

  (d) Away from soft rock

[RRB SSE 2015 1st SEP 2nd SHIFT]

27. Which is the special feature which distinguishes the cyclones of the Arabian sea from those of the Bay of Bengal?

  (a) Low intensity cyclones

  (b) Occurrence of cyclones before monsoons

  (c) Absence of frequent cyclones.

  (d) Cyclones moving away from the west coast

[RRB SSE 2015 1st SEP 2nd SHIFT]

28. What will happen to the hard rock when the softer rock below is eroded?

  (a) Hard rocks will collapse and the path of the river will deepen

  (b) Broken Hard rock will form an obstruction the waterfall

  (c) A plunge pool will be formed by hydraulic action

  (d) Waterfall will slowly give way to the valley of the river.

[RRB SSE 2015 1st SEP 3rd SHIFT]

29. Which region of India does the intensity of arabian sea cyclones affect most ?

  (a) Rann of Kutch   (b) Gulf of Khambhat

  (c) Indus Delta   (d) Narmada Estuary

[RRB SSE 2015 1st SEP 3rd SHIFT]

30. What is the main problem faced in the use of solar panels for the production of power ?

  (a) Not enough sunshine

  (b) Poor storage batteries

  (c) High cost

  (d) Keeping fragile panels safe.

[RRB SSE 2015 1st SEP 3rd SHIFT]

31. What is the minimum distance at which an echo can be heard?

  (a) 25 metres   (b) 17 metres

  (c) 60 meters   (d) 30 meters

[RRB SSE 2015 1st SEP 3rd SHIFT]

32. The working of a jet engine is based on

  (a) Laws of Air pressure

  (b) Principle of Archimedes

  (c) Theory of Relativity

  (d) Newton's law of action and reaction

[RRB SSE 2015 1st SEP 3rd SHIFT]

33. What effect does the rotation of the Earth have on the wind system ?

  (a) Winds do not rise above 100 kms near the Equator

  (b) Ocean currents carry the wind in the direction they flow in

  (c) Winds are deflected to the right of their course in the northern Hemisphere

  (d) Ocean currents are faster flowing east ward.

[RRB SSE 2015 1st SEP 3rd SHIFT]

34. What is the major component of Honey?

  (a) Fructose   (b) Sucrose

  (c) Maltose   (d) Glucose

[RRB SSE 2015 1st SEP 3rd SHIFT]

35. Which of one of these features are found only in the upper course of the river?

  (a) Meander   (b) Channel bar

  (c) Waterfall   (d) Alluvial fan

[RRB SSE 2015 2nd SEP 1st SHIFT]

36. Why does coasts Pakistan and the Oman coast not get cyclones?

  (a) The track of the cyclone is land ward

  (b) Cyclones dissipate over the ocean itself

  (c) Warm oceans prevent the cyclone from moving

  (d) Off shore trade wind blows away the cyclones.

[RRB SSE 2015 2nd SEP 1st SHIFT]

37. If a layer of soft rock like sandstone underlies granite or basalt, which feature will be formed ?

  (a) Rock Face   (b) Waterfall

  (c) Gorge   (d) Valley

[RRB SSE 2015 2nd SEP 2nd SHIFT]

38. What will be the likely effect on rains in India if a cyclonic depression develops into a storm in the Arabian Sea?

(a) Monsoon weakens

(b) SW monsoon changes direction

(c) Rainfall increases on Gujarat coast

(d) Monsoon come sooner.

[RRB SSE 2015 2nd SEP 2nd SHIFT]

39. Which of the following areas has the largest number of sunny days which is an ideal condition for solar power generation ?

(a) West Coast   (b) East Coast

(c) Northern India   (d) Himalaya

[RRB SSE 2015 2nd SEP 2nd SHIFT]

40. Along the course of the river where will a plunge pool form?

(a) Areas where there are more hard rocks

(b) Along the course of the river where boulders fall

(c) Where hydraulic action is more

(d) In a flood prone area of the river.

[RRB SSE 2015 2nd SEP 3rd SHIFT]

41. Off the coast of India where would there be high intensity, but infrequent cyclones?

(a) Indian Ocean   (b) Bay of Bengal

(c) South China Sea   (d) Arabian sea

[RRB SSE 2015 2nd SEP 3rd SHIFT]

42. What is the use of the information from the Geostationary satellites and Low Earth Orbiting Satellites put to in India?

(a) Remote sensing maps of land use and water resources.

(b) Thematic mapping for E - governance

(c) Timely decision making regarding disaster management.

(d) Planning for the layout of smart cities .

[RRB SSE 2015 2nd SEP 3rd SHIFT]

43. Which one of the given process increases the length of the river?

(a) Deepening of the gorge and excess water flow in .

(b) Headward erosion in a waterfall when the cap rock falls off.

(c) Hard rocks fall into the channel and the river course changes

(d) River water gets diverted by another iver near the source

[RRB SSE 2015 3rd SEP 1st SHIFT]

44. When the cyclones develop into storms they take away the energy of the monsoon depression. What is the effect of this on the India?

(a) Weak monsoon over West Coast

(b) Se Surges in the Narmada

(c) Stormy weather in the Arabian Sea

(d) Upwelling of sea water and high tide.

[RRB SSE 2015 3rd SEP 1st SHIFT]

45. Why have the Solar Panels been located over water canals in Gujarat ?

(a) Increase the temperature of the canal water

(b) To reduce evaporation and generate electricity

(c) Reduce the heating of the panels by cool water

(d) Keeping the panels clean and dry.

[RRB SSE 2015 3rd SEP 1st SHIFT]

46. Which island will now on be the centre for immigration check of luxury cruises to India?

(a) Kerala   (b) Andan Islands

(c) Minicoy   (d) Lakshwadweep Islands

[RRB SSE 2015 3rd SEP 1st SHIFT]

47. What is the effect of the elliptical path of the Earth around the Sun?

(a) The rotation of the earth changes speed in January.

(b) The earth moves slower in January than in July.

(c) The earth has a longer summer than Spring season.

(d) The earth moves faster in January and slower in July.

[RRB SSE 2015 3rd SEP 2nd SHIFT]

48. What is the main problem faced for power generation in India?

(a) Poor quality of electricity generation power stations and dependence on coal

(b) Higher demand from industrial areas and no facilities in rural areas

(c) Low transmission capacity compared to production and land acquisition

(d) Inaccessible areas where there is difficulty in putting up transmission towers

[RRB SSE 2015 3rd SEP 2nd SHIFT]

49. Why do stars appear to be twinkling in the sky?

(a) Scattering of Light

(b) Emission of Light

(c) Absorption of Light

(d) Reflection of Light

[RRB SSE 2015 3rd SEP 2nd SHIFT]

50. What level of noise is considered permissible in and near residential colonies?

(a) Up to 30 decibels (b) Up to 50 decibels

(c) Up to 20 decibels (d) Up to 40 decibels

[RRB SSE 2015 3ⁿᵈ SEP 2ⁿᵈ SHIFT]

51. Why is Television transmission from towers restricted to a limited area?

(a) The atmosphere absorbs the signals

(b) There is interference from other signals

(c) The curvature of the Earth stops signals

(d) The signals become weak with distance

[RRB SSE 2015 3ⁿᵈ SEP 2ⁿᵈ SHIFT]

52. Which is the metal mainly used for galvanizing iron buckets for our daily use?

(a) Mercury   (b) Cadmium

(c) Tin   (d) Zinc

[RRB SSE 2015 3ⁿᵈ SEP 2ⁿᵈ SHIFT]

53. What is the common name for sodium bicarbonate?

(a) Baking soda   (b) Salt

(c) Bleaching powder (d) Soda ash

[RRB SSE 2015 3ⁿᵈ SEP 2ⁿᵈ SHIFT]

54. In which zone will the sun never be overhead but present all the year?

(a) Arctic Zone   (b) Tropical zone

(c) Temperate zone   (d) Antarctic zone

[RRB SSE 2015 3ⁿᵈ SEP 3ʳᵈ SHIFT]

55. Which form of heating in our home is similar to that of the Sun ?

(a) Sound wave   (b) Light wave

(c) Microwave   (d) Radio wave

[RRB SSE 2015 3ⁿᵈ SEP 3ʳᵈ SHIFT]

56. Why are metals good conductors of heat?

(a) Electrons are free

(b) Atoms are tightly packed

(c) Melting point is high

(d) Particles are separate

[RRB SSE 2015 3ⁿᵈ SEP 3ʳᵈ SHIFT]

57. Which one of the following has ' reflection as its constructional basics?

(a) Periscope   (b) Telescope

(c) Microscope   (d) Binocular Microscope

[RRB SSE 2015 3ⁿᵈ SEP 3ʳᵈ SHIFT]

58. Which gas is used for artificial ripening of green fruit?

(a) Calcium Carbide (b) Carbon Dioxide

(c) Ethylene   (d) Acetylene

[RRB SSE 2015 3ⁿᵈ SEP 3ʳᵈ SHIFT]

59. Which of the following gases is used for removing impurities in water?

(a) Hydrogen   (b) Oxygen

(c) Chlorine   (d) Carbon Dioxide

[RRB SSE 2015 3ⁿᵈ SEP 3ʳᵈ SHIFT]

ANSWER KEY

RRB JUNIOR ENGINEER

1. (b)	**2.** (b)	**3.** (b)	**4.** (c)	**5.** (c)	**6.** (b)	**7.** (d)	**8.** (d)	**9.** (c)	**10.** (d)
11. (a)	**12.** (b)	**13.** (c)	**14.** (a)	**15.** (c)	**16.** (a)	**17.** (a)	**18.** (a)	**19.** (b)	**20.** (b)
21. (d)	**22.** (c)	**23.** (b)	**24.** (c)	**25.** (a)	**26.** (c)	**27.** (a)	**28.** (c)	**29.** (c)	**30.** (a)
31. (d)	**32.** (b)	**33.** (d)	**34.** (c)	**35.** (c)	**36.** (a)	**37.** (b)	**38.** (c)	**39.** (a)	**40.** (c)
41. (b)	**42.** (b)	**43.** (c)	**44.** (b)	**45.** (d)	**46.** (a)	**47.** (a)	**48.** (b)	**49.** (a)	**50.** (c)
51. (c)	**52.** (a)	**53.** (c)	**54.** (c)	**55.** (d)	**56.** (a)	**57.** (c)	**58.** (c)	**59.** (c)	**60.** (a)
61. (d)	**62.** (c)	**63.** (b)	**64.** (d)	**65.** (a)	**66.** (b)	**67.** (b)	**68.** (b)	**69.** (d)	**70.** (b)
71. (c)	**72.** (c)	**73.** (b)	**74.** (d)	**75.** (a)	**76.** (d)	**77.** (d)	**78.** (b)	**79.** (a)	**80.** (a)
81. (c)	**82.** (a)	**83.** (a)	**84.** (a)	**85.** (a)	**86.** (a)	**87.** (b)	**88.** (a)		

RRB SENIOR SECTION ENGINEER

1. (d)	**2.** (c)	**3.** (b)	**4.** (d)	**5.** (a)	**6.** (b)	**7.** (b)	**8.** (c)	**9.** (b)	**10.** (a)
11. (b)	**12.** (d)	**13.** (c)	**14.** (d)	**15.** (c)	**16.** (a)	**17.** (a)	**18.** (a)	**19.** (c)	**20.** (c)
21. (a)	**22.** (d)	**23.** (a)	**24.** (b)	**25.** (b)	**26.** (b)	**27.** (c)	**28.** (c)	**29.** (b)	**30.** (d)
31. (b)	**32.** (d)	**33.** (c)	**34.** (a)	**35.** (c)	**36.** (b)	**37.** (b)	**38.** (a)	**39.** (b)	**40.** (c)
41. (d)	**42.** (c)	**43.** (b)	**44.** (a)	**45.** (b)	**46.** (d)	**47.** (d)	**48.** (c)	**49.** (a)	**50.** (b)
51. (c)	**52.** (d)	**53.** (a)	**54.** (c)	**55.** (c)	**56.** (a)	**57.** (c)	**58.** (c)	**59.** (b)	

EXPLANATIONS

RRB JUNIOR ENGINEER

1. Hirakud Dam is built across the Mahanadi River, about 15 kilometres (9.3 mi) from Sambalpur in the state of Odisha in India. Behind the dam extends a lake, Hirakud Reservoir, 55 km (34 mi) long. It is one of the first major multipurpose river valley projects started after India's independence.

2. Biochemical Oxygen Demand (BOD, also called Biological Oxygen Demand) is the amount of dissolved oxygen needed (i.e. demanded) by aerobic biological organisms to break down organic material present in a given water sample at certain temperature over a specific time period. The BOD value is most commonly expressed in milligrams of oxygen consumed per litre of sample during 5 days of incubation at 20 °C.

3. Approximate percentage of oxygen in the Earth's atmosphere is 21%. According to NASA, the gases in Earth's atmosphere include: Nitrogen is about 78 percent. Oxygen is about 21 percent. Argon is about 0.93 percent.

4. A lunar eclipse occurs when the Moon passes directly behind Earth and into its shadow. This can occur only when the Sun, Earth, and Moon are exactly or very closely aligned (in syzygy), with Earth between the other two. A lunar eclipse can occur only on the night of a full moon.

5. Mirages generally occur in deserts.Desert mirages occur because light bends to move through warmer, less dense air. In the desert, refraction-caused illusions are known as inferior mirages.

6. In October 2014 a cyclone hit Vishakhapatnam. The name of the cyclone was hudhud. Extremely Severe Cyclonic Storm Hudhud was a strong tropical cyclone that caused extensive damage and loss of life in eastern India and Nepal during October 2014. Hudhud originated from a low pressure system that formed under the influence of an upper-air cyclonic circulation in the Andaman Sea on October 6.

7. Gir National Park is a wildlife sanctuary in Gujarat, western India. It was established to protect Asiatic lions, which frequent the fenced-off Devalia Safari Park, along with leopards and antelopes. It is known for the 'Asiatic Lions'.

8. The Indian Standard Time (I.S.T.) is ahead of Greenwich Mean Time (G.M.T.) by 5 hours 30 minutes.Indian Standard Time (IST) is the time observed throughout India, with a time offset of UTC+05:30.

9. The sugarcane plant is subject to many diseases. Red rot (important in Indonesia and South Asia) is characterized by interrupted red and white patches within the cane along with a sour alcoholic odour when the cane is split open. Caused by the fungus Colletotrichum falcatum (Glomerella tucumanensis), red rot first attracts attention by a yellowing and withering of the leaf, and eventually the entire plant dies.

10. Mars is often called the 'Red Planet' because it appears in the sky as an orange-red star. The colour caused the ancient Greeks and Romans to name it after their god of war. Today, thanks to visiting spacecraft, we know that the planet's appearance is due to rust in the Martian rocks.

11. Galena, also called lead glance, is the natural mineral form of lead(II) sulfide. It is the most important ore of lead and an important source of silver. Galena is one of the most abundant and widely distributed sulfide minerals. It crystallizes in the cubic crystal system often showing octahedral forms.

12. In October 2014 a cyclone hit Vishakhapatnam. The name of the cyclone was hudhud. Extremely Severe Cyclonic Storm Hudhud was a strong tropical cyclone that caused extensive damage and loss of life in eastern India and Nepal during October 2014. Hudhud originated from a low pressure system that formed under the influence of an upper-air cyclonic circulation in the Andaman Sea on October 6.

13. The most effective farming method for returning minerals to the soil is crop rotation.

14. Winter rains in North-Western India are caused by Western Disturbances. A Western Disturbance is an extratropical storm originating in the Mediterranean region that brings sudden winter rain to the northwestern parts of the Indian subcontinent. It is a non-monsoonal precipitation pattern driven by the westerlies.

15. Kaziranga National Park is a protected area in the northeast Indian state of Assam. Spread across the floodplains of the Brahmaputra River, its forests, wetlands and grasslands are home to tigers, elephants and the world's largest population of Indian one-horned rhinoceroses.

16. The United Nations Development Programme is the United Nations' global development network. Headquartered in New York City, UNDP advocates for change and connects countries to knowledge, experience and resources to help people build a better life. UNDP has aim to provide technical assistance to stimulate economic and social development.

17. From the given options the plate tectonics are movement of plates supporting the continents.There are nine major plates, according to World Atlas. These plates are named after the landforms found on them. The nine major plates are North American, Pacific, Eurasian, African, Indo-Australian, Australian, Indian, South American and Antarctic

18. Saraswati river is to the Triveni Sangam or confluence of rivers at Allahabad.

19. If the supply of coffee goes up then the price of coffee goes down.

20. Beetle is not a 'social insect'.Beetles are a group of insects that form the order Coleoptera, in the superorder Endopterygota. Their front pair of wings is hardened into wing-cases, elytra, distinguishing them from most other insects.

21. Herbert Spencer is best known for the expression "survival of the fittest", which he coined in Principles of Biology (1864), after reading Charles Darwin's On the Origin of *Species*.This term strongly suggests natural selection, yet as Spencer extended evolution into realms of sociology and ethics, he also made use of Lamarckism.

22. The major cause of top soil being lost due to soil erosion is deforestation.

23. Virus is not living being, because it does not possess the machinery to duplicate itself.

24. Green plants make food in the form of carbohydrates by combining carbon dioxide and water using energy from sunlight. Glucose may be converted into other carbohydrates such as starch (a storage carbohydrate), cellulose or lignin (structural carbohydrates).

25. Thalassemia is in all cases a hereditary disorder.Thalassemia is an inherited blood disorder in which the body makes an abnormal form of hemoglobin. Hemoglobin is the protein molecule in red blood cells that carries oxygen.

26. In the geography class students were confused regarding the difference between climate and weather. Climate is the sum total of weather conditions over a large area for a long period of time and weather is the state of atmosphere over an area at any point of time.

27. A gel is a suspension of a solid in a liquid.

28. Calcium dihydrogen phosphate is used in the food industry as a leavening agent, i.e., to cause baked goods to rise. Because it is acidic, when combined with an alkali ingredient, commonly sodium bicarbonate (baking soda) or potassium bicarbonate, it reacts to produce carbon dioxide and a salt.

29. When mother was heating the oven to a certain temperature for baking a cake, the daughter wanted to know the difference between heat and temperature. In mother's response Heat and temperature both flow between temperatures is not the correct statement in the given options.

30. Plants will always grow, wind will always blow, solar cells will give electrical energy Waves forever will make energy. Child wrote in the poem about Renewable energy resources.

31. The colour of an object is the colour it reflects. Red in green light when there is no red light wrong statement.

32. The Brahmaputra is one of the major rivers of Asia, The Brahmaputra River, also called Yarlung Tsangpo in Tibetan language, originates on the Angsi Glacier located on the northern side of the Himalayas in Burang County of Tibet.The Brahmaputra enters India in the state of Arunachal Pradesh, where it is called Siang.

33. The father of our nation Mahatma Gandhi said 'Earth has enough for man's need but not enough for man's greed'.

34. The artificial satellites cannot be used for Monitoring atmospheric pollution.

35. Filtration method used to separate yoghurt (Curd) from water contained in it.

36. Out of two bottles of pickle, one old and one freshly made, the old one can be detected by its smell and taste caused by oxidation of oil in the pickle making it rancid.

37. Hair dyes contain the base Ammonium Hydroxide.

38. Water is available in sinduates and streams which are always there even without rainfall not true regarding the Thar Desert.

39. Hotspot is a region of high endemic biodiversity. A biodiversity hotspot is a biogeographic region that is both a significant reservoir of biodiversity and is threatened with destruction.

40. Decibel is the unit of Intensity of sound. sound intensity is the power per square meter. The common unit of power is the watt. The unit of SL is called the decibel (abbreviated dB). I is the intensity of the sound expressed in watts per meter and Io is the reference intensity defined to be 10-12 w/m2.

41. One early morning, with no traffic on roads, Rahul while cycling down from Red Fort to his residence noted the distance covered and the total time taken to reach home. What can he calculate speed from this data.

42. Radium was discovered by Marie Sklodowska Curie, a Polish chemist, and Pierre Curie, a French chemist, in 1898. Marie Curie obtained radium from pitchblende, a material that contains uranium, after noticing that unrefined pitchblende was more radioactive than the uranium that was separated from it. Radium & Uranium pair out of the following are radioactive and available abundantly.

43. Sun's energy does not get converted into nuclear energy.The Sun is the star at the center of the Solar System. It is a nearly perfect sphere of hot plasma,with internal convective motion that generates a magnetic field via a dynamo process.It is by far the most important source of energy for life on Earth.

44. The unit for measurement of energy is joule.

45. Energy experts predict that many countries will face severe electricity blackouts very soon because Greater demand for energy and extreme depletion of oil and natural gas.

46. Among the given options, the correct difference between topography and landscape is Topography is natural, landscape is the handiwork of humans.

47. Wires in our homes are made of metal because metals are good conductors of electricity

48. The summer solstice (or estival solstice), also known as midsummer, occurs when one of the Earth's poles has its maximum tilt toward the Sun. It happens twice yearly, once in each hemisphere (Northern and Southern). For that hemisphere, the summer solstice is when the Sun reaches its highest position in the sky and is the day with the longest period of daylight. At the pole, there is continuous daylight around the summer solstice.

49. Through Africa continent, do the equator, the tropic of cancer and the tropic of capricorn pass through.

50. Shiva Sundaram Falls are located in the course of the river Kaveri.

51. Tripura is a state in Northeast India. The third-smallest state in the country, and is bordered by Bangladesh to the north,south, and west, and the Indian states of Assam and Mizoram to the east.

52. The torque on a rectangular coil placed in uniform magnetic field is large when the number of turns is large.

53. The Eastern and Western Ghats meet at the Nilgiri Hills. The Nilgiri Mountains literally blue hills form part of the Western Ghats in western Tamil Nadu of Southern India. At least 24 of the Nilgiri Mountains' peaks are above 2,000 metres, the highest peak being Doddabetta, at 2,637 metres.

54. Zoji La is a high mountain pass in the Indian state of Jammu and Kashmir, Bara-lacha la also known as Bara-lacha Pass, or Bara aLa, is a high mountain pass in Zanskar range, connecting Lahaul district in Himachal Pradesh. Jelep La or Jelep Pass, elevation 4,267 m or 13,999 ft, is a high mountain pass between East Sikkim District, Sikkim, India and Tibet Autonomous Region, China. Niti Pass is an international high mountain *pass* at an elevation of 5.070m (16,633ft) connecting Uttarakhand.

55. The Karakoram highway connects China-Pakistan countries. The highway, connecting the Gilgit–Baltistan region to the ancient Silk Road, runs approximately 1,300 km (810 mi) from Kashgar, a city in the Xinjiang region of China, to Abbottabad, of Pakistan.

56. On raising the temperature of the medium, velocity of light increases.

57. Among the given options, chromium is a paramagnetic.

58. If the length of a simple pendulum increases by 4%, then it's time period will be increased by 2%.

59. The Tungabhadra Dam also known as Pampa Sagar is constructed across the Tungabhadra River, a tributary of the Krishna River. The dam is in Munirabad, Koppal district of Karnataka.The Idukki Dam is a double curvature Arch dam constructed across the Periyar River in a narrow gorge between two granite hills locally known as Kuravan and Kurathi in Kerala, India. Nagarjuna Sagar Dam, one of the world's largest and tallest Masonry dam built across the Krishna river at Nagarjuna Sagar which is in Nalgonda District, Telangana State, before 2014, it was in Andhra Pradesh.

60. Among the given states, the latitudes that pass through Sikkim also pass through Rajasthan.

61. River Indus originates from Kailash Range. Indus River is one of the longest rivers in Asia. Originating in the Tibetan Plateau in the vicinity of Lake Manasarovar, the river runs a course through the Ladakh region of Jammu and Kashmir, towards Gilgit-Baltistan and the Hindukush ranges, and then flows in a southerly direction along the entire length of Pakistan to merge into the Arabian Sea near the port city of Karachi in Sindh. It is the longest river and national river of Pakistan

62. If a ship moves from fresh water into sea water, it will rise a little higher.

63. The focal length of a convex lens is shorter for blue light than for red.

64. Celcius is a common misspelling of Celsius, a scale and unit of measurement for temperature.

65. If a small raindrop falls through air, its velocity goes on decreasing.

66. Neap tides occur during first and third quarter phases of moon. Neap tides are especially weak tides. They occur when the gravitational forces of the Moon and the Sun are perpendicular to one another (with respect to the Earth).

67. If a moving body doubles its velocity, then its kinetic energy becomes four times.

68. The blackboard seems black because it does not reflect any colour.

69. The magnetic lines of force produced through a bar magnet does not cross anywhere in the magnet.

70. Because of low humidity clouds do not precipitate in deserts.

71. The atmospheric layer which reflects radio waves is called ionosphere. The ionosphere is defined as the layer of the Earth's atmosphere that is ionized by solar and cosmic radiation.

72. In the interior of Earth, temperature rises with increasing depth. Geothermal gradient is the rate of increasing temperature with respect to increasing depth in the Earth's interior. Away from tectonic plate boundaries, it is about 25–30 °C/km (72-87 °F/mi) of depth near the surface in most of the world.

73. If an object is placed at the centre of curvature of a concave mirror, the position of image is between the principal focus and the centre of curvature.

74. Among the given options, the speed of sound is maximum in the wood.

75. Microwave oven consumes less power due to small frequency of radiation.

76. The difference in the duration of day and night increases as one moves from Equator to Poles.

77. An endoscope, used by doctors for examine the inside of patient's stomach, works on the principle of Total internal reflection of fight.

78. The coil in a heater is made up of Nichrome. Nichrome 80/20 is an ideal material, because it has relatively high resistance and forms an adherent layer of chromium oxide when it is heated for the first time. Material beneath this layer will not oxidize, preventing the wire from breaking or burning out.

79. When a body moves in a simple harmonic motion, then the phase difference (in degrees) between velocity and acceleration is 90.

80. Among the given options, the correct matching regarding town and rivers is Jabalpur-Narmada, Paris-Seine, London-Thames, Lahore-Ravi.

81. The the percentage of given salt in sea water in decreasing order Sodium Chloride-Magnesium Chloride- Magnesium Sulphate-Calcium Sulphate

82. The large states of India in order of area are Rajasthan, Madhya Pradesh, Maharashtra.

83. The best and poorest conductor of heat are respectively silver and lead.

84. The ratio of transverse deformation to longitudinal deformation is called poisson ratio. Poisson's ratio, denoted by the Greek letter 'nu', and named after Siméon Poisson, is the negative of the ratio of transverse strain to axial strain. For small values of these changes, is the amount of transversal expansion divided by the amount of axial compression.

85. Burning of dry leaves is not permitted because it produces Carbon dioxide which is a greenhouse gas and causes global warming.

86. Concept of Zero was given by India to the world.

87. The Thar Desert, also known as the Great Indian Desert, is a large arid region in the northwestern part of the Indian subcontinent that covers an area of 200,000 km^2 (77,000 sq mi) and forms a natural boundary between India and Pakistan. It is the world's 18th largest desert, and the world's 9th largest subtropical desert. More than 60% of the desert lies in the state of Rajasthan, and extends into Gujarat, Punjab, and Haryana.

88. Development that meets the needs of the present without compromising ability of future generations to meet their own needs is sustainable development.

RRB SENIOR SECTION ENGINEER

1. As of 2013, the concentration of carbon dioxide in Earth' s atmosphere is 400 parts per million. For every 1,000,000 gas molecules in our atmosphere, about 400 are carbon dioxide molecules (see the special note about water vapor below).

2. Average terrestrial albedo at the top of the atmosphere is 30 to 35% (estimated around 0.30) because of cloud cover, but widely varies locally across the surface because of different geological and environmental features such as illumination, insolation effects, climate and weather, snow, solar photovoltaic effects, trees, water, clouds, aerosol effects, black carbon emissions and human activities.

3. The illumination of a beam of light due to scattering on collision with particles suspended in a fluid, is called tyndall effect. Tyndall in 1869, observed that if a strong beam of light is passed through a colloidal solution then the path of light is illuminated. This phenomenon is called Tyndall Effect. This happens due to the scattering of light by particles of dust in the air.

4. Intensity of earthquake is measured in Richter scale. There are a number of ways to measure the magnitude of an earthquake. The first widely-used method, the Richter scale, was developed by Charles F. Richter in 1934. It used a formula based on amplitude of the largest wave recorded on a specific type of seismometer and the distance between the earthquake and the seismometer.

5. Several nations are following a Kyoto protocol which binds them to reduce emission targets. This protocol was adopted in Kyoto, Japan

6. Major constituent of Argillaceous rock is Clay or Alumina. Argillaceous minerals may appear silvery upon optical reflection and are minerals containing substantial amounts of clay-like components. Argillaceous components are fine-grained (less than 2 μm) aluminosilicates.

7. Vulcanization (or vulcanisation) is a chemical process for converting natural rubber or related polymers into more durable materials via the addition of sulfur or other equivalent curatives or accelerators. Condensation is the phenomenon related to the formation of clouds.Waterspouts do not suck up water; the water seen in the main funnel cloud is actually water droplets formed by condensation. Water vapor or water vapour (see spelling differences), also aqueous vapor, is the gas phase of water. It is one state of water within the hydrosphere.

8. El Nino effect is prolonged warming in the Pacific Ocean surface area. El Nino Southern Oscillation refers to the cycle of warm and cold temperatures, as measured by sea surface temperature, SST, of the tropical central and eastern Pacific Ocean. El Nino is accompanied by high air pressure in the western Pacific and low air pressure in the eastern Pacific.

9. River Damoder is called the 'Sorrow of ' West Bengal because of its ravaging floods in the plains of West Bengal.

10. Woolen clothes keep the body warm because Wool is a poor conductor of heat because it traps a large amount of air between its fibres.

11. Age of a Tree may be ascertained by number of Annual Rings. Annual rings can be counted using two different methods. You can extract an increment core from the tree using an increment borer.

12. The ozone layer is useful for living beings because it protects them from harmful ultraviolet rays of the sun.

13. Extremely Severe Cyclonic Storm Hudhud was a strong tropical cyclone that caused extensive damage and loss of life in eastern India and Nepal during October 2014. Hudhud originated from a low pressure system that formed under the influence of an upper-air cyclonic circulation in the Andaman Sea on October 6.

14. A renewable resource is a resource which can be used repeatedly and replaced naturally. Examples include oxygen, fresh water, wind, solar energy and biomass. Gasoline, coal, natural gas, diesel, plastics and other fossil fuels are not renewable.

15. Among the given options, $KMnO_4$ will not be oxidised by Ozone.

16. The Andaman Islands are home to four 'Negrito' tribes – the Great Andamanese, Onge, Jarawa and Sentinelese. The Nicobar Islands are home to two 'Mongoloid' tribes – the Shompen and Nicobarese. Jarawas and Shompens Tribal Groups live in Andaman and Nicobar Islands.

17. Among the given options, Diarrhoea problems is not created by Noise Pollution. Diarrhea or Diarrhoea, is the condition of having at least three loose or liquid bowel movements each day. It often lasts for a few days and can result in dehydration due to fluid loss.

18. Dew is water in the form of droplets that appears on thin, exposed objects in the morning or evening due to condensation. As the exposed surface cools by radiating its heat, atmospheric moisture condenses at a rate greater than that at which it can evaporate, resulting in the formation of water droplets.

19. Jim Corbett National Park is the oldest national park *in India* and was established in 1936 as Hailey National Park to protect the endangered *Bengal* tiger. It is located in Nainital district of Uttarakhand and was named after Jim Corbett who played a key role in its establishment.

20. A crop's demand for freedom from waterlogging may vary between seasons of the year, as with the growing of rice (Oryza sativa). In irrigated agricultural land, waterlogging is often accompanied by soil salinity as waterlogged soils prevent leaching of the salts imported by the irrigation water.

21. EBOLA is a virus disease confirmed in West Africa. Ebola is a deadly disease caused by a virus. There are five strains, and four of them can make people sick. After entering the body, it kills cells, making some of them explode. It wrecks the immune system, causes heavy bleeding inside the body, and damages almost every organ. The virus is scary, but it's also rare.

22. Helmand is believed to be one of the world's largest opium-producing regions, responsible for around 42% of the world's total production.

23. In the upper course of the river are Gorges, plunge pools, rapids, interlocking spurs found. In the upper course of a river gradients are steep and river channels are narrow. Vertical erosion is greatest in the upper course of a river. As the result of this typical features include steep valley sides, interlocking spurs, rapids, gorges and waterfalls.

24. 'Usually before the onset of monsoons though the frequency of cyclones is low their intensity is high because of Bay of Bengal.

25. By introducing roof top and grid connected solar production units on build, own, operate and transfer basis measures will make India the world's largest green energy producer by 2022.

26. When a gorge is formed in backward direction, then hard rocks will be eroded by the river.

27. Absence of frequent cyclones is the special feature which distinguishes the cyclones of the Arabian sea from those of the Bay of Bengal.

28. A waterfall happens when there is a band of hard rock overlying soft rock. Soft rock erodes more quickly than hard rock which is called differential erosion. As a result of this differential erosion the soft rock erodes away to leave an area of hard rock overhanging a plunge pool which is created by hydraulic action. As the overhang is unsupported it eventually collapses.

29. Among the given options, the region of India does the intensity of arabian sea cyclones affect most is Gulf of Khambhat.

30. Keeping fragile panels saf is the main problem faced in the use of solar panels for the production of power.

31. 17 metres is the minimum distance at which an echo can be heard.

32. The working of a jet engine is based on Newton's law of action and reaction.

33. Winds are deflected to the right of their course in the northern Hemisphere due to the rotation of the Earth have on the wind system.

34. Fructose is the major component of Honey. honey is mainly fructose (about 38%) and glucose (about 32%) with remaining sugars including maltose, sucrose, and other complex carbohydrates.

35. In the upper course of a river gradients are steep and river channels are narrow. Vertical erosion is greatest in the upper course of a river. As the result of this typical features include steep valley sides, interlocking spurs, rapids, gorges and waterfalls.

36. Pakistan and the Oman coast do not get cyclones because cyclones dissipate over the ocean itself.

37. If a layer of soft rock like sandstone underlies granite or basalt, then waterfall will be formed.

38. The likely effect on rains in India if a cyclonic depression develops into a storm in the Arabian Sea is monsoon weakens.

39. East Coast has the largest number of sunny days which is an ideal condition for solar power generation.

40. A plunge pool (or plunge basin or waterfall lake) is a deep depression in a stream bed at the base of a waterfall; it is created by the erosional forces of falling water on the rocks at fall's base where the water impacts. The term may refer to the water occupying the depression, or the depression itself.

41. Off the coast of Arabian sea, there would be high intensity, but infrequent cyclones.

42. The use of the information from the Geostationary satellites and Low Earth Orbiting Satellites put to in India is that timely decision making regarding disaster management.

43. Headward erosion in a waterfall when the cap rock falls off increases the length of the river.

44. When the cyclones develop into storms they take away the energy of the monsoon depression. Weak monsoon over West Coast is the effect of this on the India.

45. Solar Panels been located over water canals in Gujarat to reduce evaporation and generate electricity.

46. Lakshadweep Islands will now on be the centre for immigration check of luxury cruises to India.

47. The effect of the elliptical path of the Earth around the Sun is that earth moves faster in January and slower in July.

48. Low transmission capacity compared to production and land acquisition is the main problem faced for power generation in India.

49. Due to scattering of Light, stars appear to be twinkling in the sky. Stars do not really twinkle, they just appear to twinkle when seen from the surface of Earth. The stars twinkle in the night sky because of the effects of our atmosphere. When starlight enters our atmosphere it is affected by winds in the atmosphere and by areas with different temperatures and densities.

50. Up to 50 decibels of noise is considered permissible in and near residential colonies.

51. Television transmission from towers restricted to a limited area due to the curvature of the Earth stops signals.

52. Zinc is the metal mainly used for galvanizing iron buckets for our daily use.

53. Baking soda is the common name for sodium bicarbonate. Sodium bicarbonate, commonly known as baking soda, is a chemical compound with the formula $NaHCOf$. It is a salt composed of sodium ions and bicarbonate ions. Sodium bicarbonate is a white solid that is crystalline, but often appears as a fine powder.

54. In Temperate zone, the sun never be overhead but present all the year.Temperate Zone. Either of two regions of the Earth of intermediate latitude, the North Temperate Zone, between the Arctic Circle and the Tropic of Cancer, or the South Temperate Zone, between the Antarctic Circle and the Tropic of Capricorn.

55. Microwave form of heating in our home is similar to that of the Sun.

56. The metals good conductors of heat because they are Electrons free.

57. Microscope has ' reflection as its constructional basics. Microscope is an instrument used to see objects that are too small to be seen by the naked eye. Microscopy is the science of investigating small objects and structures using such an instrument.

58. Ethylene gas is used for artificial ripening of green fruit.Calcium carbide is also used in some countries for artificially ripening fruit. When calcium carbide comes in contact with moisture, it produces acetylene gas, which is quite similar in its effects to the natural ripening agent, ethylene. Acetylene acts like ethylene and accelerates the ripening process.

59. Oxygen is used for removing impurities in water.

SPORTS AND AWARDS

RRB JUNIOR ENGINEER

1. Who received the first Nobel prize in Physics in India?
(a) Dr. C.V. Raman
(b) Dr. Hargobind Khurana
(c) Prof. C.N.R. Rao
(d) Prof. Narlikar
[RRB JE 2014 GREEN SHIFT]

2. Which country won the FIFA world cup, 2014 in Football ?
(a) Germany　　　(b) Argentina
(c) Brazil　　　(d) France
[RRB JE 2014 RED SHIFT]

3. Who is the winner of Mens Singles Title in Tennis in US open, 2014 ?
(a) Roger Federer　　　(b) Kei Nishikori
(c) Marin Cilic　　　(d) Rafael Nadal
[RRB JE 2014 RED SHIFT]

4. Who is the winner of Nobel Prize, 2014 in the field of Economics ?
(a) Patrick Modiano　　　(b) Malala Yousafzai
(c) Jean Tirole　　　(d) Kailash Satyarthi
[RRB JE 2014 RED SHIFT]

5. UBER Cup is related to
(a) International Badminton (Men)
(b) International Volleyball (Men)
(c) International Volleyball (Women)
(d) International Badminton (Women)
[RRB JE 2014 YELLOW SHIFT]

6. First Sportsperson to be conferred with Award "Bhart Ratna"
(a) Sachin Tendulkar　(b) Dhyan Chand
(c) Balbir Singh　　　(d) Vijay Amritraj
[RRB JE 2014 YELLOW SHIFT]

7. Next Asian Games in2018 shall be held in
(a) Seoul　　　(b) Bangkok
(c) Kualalumpur　　　(d) Jakarta
[RRB JE 2014 YELLOW SHIFT]

8. Who among the following did not win a medal in Asian Games 2014 ?
(a) Yogeshwar Dutt　(b) Sushil Kumar
(c) Abhinav Bindra　(d) Jitu Rai
[RRB JE 2014 YELLOW SHIFT]

9. What is common amongst Mahesh Bhupathi, Ivan Lendl, Roger Federer ?
(a) They are all Arjun Award winners
(b) They all International Tennis players
(c) They are all Social Activists
(d) They are all Asian Games medal winners
[RRB JE 2014 YELLOW SHIFT]

10. Which of the following pairs was announced recently as Joint Noble Peace Prize winner.
(a) Kailash Satyarthi and Malala
(b) Amartya Sen and Benazir
(c) Morkel and Hosni Mubarak
(d) Anwar Sadat and Begin
[RRB JE 2014 YELLOW SHIFT]

11. The UN Public service award 2015 for eliminating open defecation has been given to
(a) Surat in Gujarat
(b) Gorakhpur in Uttar Pradesh
(c) Nadia in West Bengal
(d) Mahabaleshwar in Maharashtra
[RRB JE 2015 26ᵗʰ AUG 1ˢᵗ SHIFT]

12. The Champion's League Trophy is given for
(a) the best club in Soccer
(b) best player of team in Basket ball
(c) maximum goal maker in Hockey
(d) man of the match in Cricket
[RRB JE 2015 26ᵗʰ AUG 1ˢᵗ SHIFT]

13. Cricket batsman has to leave the field for "hit wicket" when
(a) Ball hits leg before bat
(b) Keeper removes the bail
(c) Bat hits any fielder
(d) Wicket is touched by bat or body of the batsman
[RRB JE 2015 26ᵗʰ AUG 1ˢᵗ SHIFT]

14. The latest Nobel Peace Prize was awarded to two people, a man and a woman. To which countries do they belong?
(a) China
(b) India and Pakistan
(c) US and Greece
(d) India and Indonesia
[RRB JE 2015 26ᵗʰ AUG 2ⁿᵈ SHIFT]

15. The tournament that takes place in Roland Garros in Paris is associated with
(a) Lawn tennis   (b) Table tennis
(c) Basketball   (d) Bowling
[RRB JE 2015 26ᵗʰ AUG 2ⁿᵈ SHIFT]

16. Which is the national sport of India?
(a) Cricket   (b) Football
(c) Hockey   (d) Kabaddi
[RRB JE 2015 26ᵗʰ AUG 2ⁿᵈ SHIFT]

17. The football player has to leave the field if the referee shows him
(a) Green card once
(b) Yellow card once
(c) Green card twice
(d) Yellow card twice or Red card once
[RRB JE 2015 26ᵗʰ AUG 3ʳᵈ SHIFT]

18. The first Indian to win an Olympic gold medal in an individual capacity was
(a) Abhinav Bindra   (b) Milkha Singh
(c) PT Usha   (d) Vijender Kumar
[RRB JE 2015 26ᵗʰ AUG 3ʳᵈ SHIFT]

19. Which statement is not true for a game of Badminton?
(a) Total points to be scored are 21
(b) If both sides score upto game point, the winner ne ds two clear u points in a row
(c) The game never ends in a draw
(d) Total points to be scored are 15
[RRB JE 2015 27ᵗʰ AUG 1ˢᵗ SHIFT]

20. Paralympics is a multisport even involving those athletes who are
(a) only visually challenged
(b) only hearing impaired
(c) just mentally challenged
(d) with a range of physical disability
[RRB JE 2015 27ᵗʰ AUG 1ˢᵗ SHIFT]

21. With which game is the Ranji Trophy associated?
(a) Football   (b) Hockey
(c) Cricket   (d) Basket ball
[RRB JE 2015 27ᵗʰ AUG 2ⁿᵈ SHIFT]

22. In woman tennis records, which of the following is an unmatched pair of champion and championship Trophy won by her
(a) Li Na : Wimbledon
(b) Serene Williams : Australian Open
(c) Maria Sharapova : French Open
(d) Samantha Stosur : US Open
[RRB JE 2015 27ᵗʰ AUG 2ⁿᵈ SHIFT]

23. In a game of cricket, when the ball bounces more than once before reaching batsman's side, it is called
(a) Bouncer   (b) Yorker
(c) Short ball   (d) Dead ball
[RRB JE 2015 27ᵗʰ AUG 3ʳᵈ SHIFT]

24. How many points are awarded for one normal baske in a game of basketball?
(a) 1   (b) 2
(c) 3   (d) 2 or 3
[RRB JE 2015 27ᵗʰ AUG 3ʳᵈ SHIFT]

25. In Baseball, how many players are there in each side
(a) 5   (b) 7
(c) 9   (d) 11
[RRB JE 2015 28ᵗʰ AUG 1ˢᵗ SHIFT]

26. Which nation won the Azlan shah cup Hockey in april 2015
(a) India   (b) South korea
(c) Australia   (d) New Zealand
[RRB JE 2015 28ᵗʰ AUG 1ˢᵗ SHIFT]

27. Who has been bestowed with the 46th Dada Saheb Phalke Award for 2014?
(a) Rishi kapoor   (b) Shashi kapoor
(c) Pran   (d) Gulzar
[RRB JE 2015 28ᵗʰ AUG 1ˢᵗ SHIFT]

28. Which film was adjusted as the Best Motion pictures at the 87th Academy awards (oscars) on February 22, 2015?
(a) The theory of everything
(b) The Grand- budapest Hotel
(c) Birdman
(d) still Alice
[RRB JE 2015 28ᵗʰ AUG 1ˢᵗ SHIFT]

29. The first Commonwealth Games were held in the year 1930 at
(a) London (UK)
(b) Sydney (Australia)
(c) Hamilton (Canada)
(d) Auckland (New Zealand)
[RRB JE 2015 28ᵗʰ AUG 2ⁿᵈ SHIFT]

30. Which of the following is currently matched
(a) Nehru trophy   - Table tennis
(b) Holkar tropliy   - Bridge
(c) Ruia trophy   - Kabaddi
(d) B. C. Roy Trophy   - Lawn Tennis
[RRB JE 2015 28ᵗʰ AUG 2ⁿᵈ SHIFT]

31. A renewed hindi poet who received the sahitya Akedemi award for his work 'Hawa mein hastakshar' passed away on april 1, 2015 is

(a) Ajit Kumar

(b) Kailash Vajpayi

(c) Harisliankar Parsai

(d) Ravindra Kalia

[RRB JE 2015 28ᵗʰ AUG 2ⁿᵈ SHIFT]

32. Who has been declared the best actor and the best actress at the 62nd national film awards announced on march 24, 2014 in new delhi?

(a) Sanjari Yijay & kangana Ranaut

(b) Sanjari Yijay & Baljinder kaur

(c) Bobby simhaa & Kangana ranaut

(d) Bobby simhaa & Baljinder kaur

[RRB JE 2015 28ᵗʰ AUG 2ⁿᵈ SHIFT]

33. Ryder cup is related with which sport

(a) Football   (b) Golf

(c) Badminton   (d) Cricket

[RRB JE 2015 28ᵗʰ AUG 3ʳᵈ SHIFT]

34. The Badminton player who won the Malaysian open on April 5, is

(a) Chen Long   (b) Lin Dan

(c) Carolina Marin   (d) Li-xuerui

[RRB JE 2015 28ᵗʰ AUG 3ʳᵈ SHIFT]

35. Merdeka cup is associated with

(a) Cricket   (b) Football

(c) Rugby   (d) Hockey

[RRB JE 2015 29ᵗʰ AUG 1ˢᵗ SHIFT]

36. The five intertwined rings or circles on the Olympic flag made of which colours (from left to right)

(a) Blue, yellow, black green and red

(b) Yellow, red, green, black and blue

(c) Red, green, black, yellow and blue

(d) Yellow, green, black, blue and red

[RRB JE 2015 29ᵗʰ AUG 1ˢᵗ SHIFT]

37. Who was presented the Man Booker international Prize for 2015 in London on May 20, 2015?

(a) George Szirtes

(b) Lesley Nneka Arimah

(c) Laszlo Krasznahorkai

(d) Kevin Jared Hosein

[RRB JE 2015 29ᵗʰ AUG 1ˢᵗ SHIFT]

38. French director Jacques Audiard won the Palme d'or, the top honour of the 68th Cannes film festival on May 24, 2015 for which film?

(a) Son of soul   (b) Dheepan

(c) The Lobster   (d) The Measure of a Man

[RRB JE 2015 29ᵗʰ AUG 1ˢᵗ SHIFT]

39. Which one of the following is the oldest Grand Slam of the World

(a) Wimbledon   (b) French Open

(c) Australian Open   (d) US Open

[RRB JE 2015 29ᵗʰ AUG 2ⁿᵈ SHIFT]

40. The Dronacharya award for sports coaches was instituted in the year

(a) 1984   (b) 1985

(c) 1987   (d) 1988

[RRB JE 2015 29ᵗʰ AUG 2ⁿᵈ SHIFT]

41. The Olympics Games in 2016 will be held in

(a) London   (b) Russia

(c) Germany   (d) Brazil

[RRB JE 2015 29ᵗʰ AUG 3ʳᵈ SHIFT]

42. Which of the following pairs is not correct

(a) Rangaswamy cup   - hockey

(b) Federation cup   - badminton

(c) Deodhar trophy   - cricket

(d) Rovers cup   - Football

[RRB JE 2015 29ᵗʰ AUG 3ʳᵈ SHIFT]

43. An athlete driving off a high spring board can perform a variety of exercises in the air before entering the water below. Which of the following parameter of the athlete will remain constant during the fall

(a) The athlete's linear momentum

(b) The athlete's moment of inertia

(c) The athlete's kinetic energy

(d) The athlete's angular momentum

[RRB JE 2015 30ᵗʰ AUG 3ʳᵈ SHIFT]

44. The term "bogey" is associated with

(a) Tennis   (b) Golf

(c) Baseball   (d) Chess

[RRB JE 2015 30ᵗʰ AUG 3ʳᵈ SHIFT]

45. The ancient Olympic continued till about

(a) Robert Dover

(b) Pierre de Coubertin

(c) Theodosius I

(d) Ernest Curtis

[RRB JE 2015 30ᵗʰ AUG 3ʳᵈ SHIFT]

46. Which pair won the Wimbledon 2015 mixed double championship?

(a) Leander Paes & Sania Mirza

(b) Leander Paes & Martina Hingis

(c) Leander Paes & Serena Williams

(d) Leander Paes & Venus Williams

[RRB JE 2015 16th SEP 3rd SHIFT]

47. Iii which game is the term 'maiden over' used?

(a) Hockey   (b) Football

(c) Cricket   (d) Golf

[RRB JE 2015 16th SEP 3rd SHIFT]

48. The country which hosted the first Asian games was

(a) India   (b) China

(c) Indonesia   (d) Japan

[RRB JE 2015 16th SEP 3rd SHIFT]

RRB SENIOR SECTION ENGINEER

1. Who is the Winner of Pro Kabaddi league in 2014?

(a) U Mumba

(b) Jaipur Pink Panthers

(c) Patna Pirates

(d) Bengaluru Bulls

[RRB SSE 2014 RED SHIFT]

2. Who is the winner of Nobel Prize, 2014 in the field of Literature ?

(a) Philip Roth

(b) Patrick Modiano

(c) Haruki Murakami

(d) Ngugi Wa Thiong'o

[RRB SSE 2014 RED SHIFT]

3. Jitu Rai won Gold Medal in the recent Asian Games in the following field :

(a) Archery   (b) Wrestling

(c) Boxing   (d) Shooting

[RRB SSE 2014 RED SHIFT]

4. Shanti Swarup Bhatnagar Award is given for outstanding contribution in the following field:

(a) Science   (b) Literature

(c) Economy   (d) Performing Arts

[RRB SSE 2014 RED SHIFT]

5. Who is the winner of Men's Singles Title in Wimbledon, 2014 in Tennis ?

(a) Roger Federer   (b) Rafael Nadal

(c) Marin Cilic   (d) Novak Djokovic

[RRB SSE 2014 RED SHIFT]

6. Merdeka Cup is associated with

(a) International Table Tennis

(b) Badminton

(c) Hockey

(d) International Football

[RRB SSE 2014 YELLOW SHIFT]

7. Match Col. X (Sportsperson) and Col. Y (Sports):

Col. X	Col. Y
P. Jitu Rai	1. Badminton
Q. Heena Sidhu	2. Wrestling
R. Jwala Gutta	3. Shooting
S. Yogeshwar Dutt	

(a) P-3; Q-3, R-1, S-2

(b) P-2. Q-3, R-1, S-2

(c) P-2. Q-2. R-1. S-3

(d) P-3, Q-1. R-1. S-2

[RRB SSE 2014 YELLOW SHIFT]

8. The slogan of Asian Games Incheon 2014 was

(a) Green, Clean and Friendship

(b) We Cheer, We Share, We Win

(c) Diversity Shines here

(d) The Games of Your Life

[RRB SSE 2014 YELLOW SHIFT]

9. What are the three values cherished by the Commonwealth Games?

(a) Get Set, Go, and Play .

(b) Faster, Higher, Stronger.

(c) Diversity Shines here.

(d) Humanity, Equality, Destiny.

[RRB SSE 2015 1st SEP 1st SHIFT]

10. For participation in which international games event has the Men's Indian Hockey team qualified after the World Hockey League?

(a) Common wealth Games

(b) Olympics

(c) Asian Games

(d) Winter Olympics

[RRB SSE 2015 1st SEP 1st SHIFT]

11. Where will Commonwealth Games 2018 be held?

(a) Glasgow, Scotland

(b) Inchon, South Korea

(c) Gold Coast, Queensland ,Australia

(d) Abuja, Nigeria

[RRB SSE 2015 1st SEP 2nd SHIFT]

12. To participate in the Olympics at Rio de Janeiro in 2016 which game did Indian team qualify in?

   (a) Men's Hockey   (b) Swimming

   (c) Archery   (d) Boxing

[RRB SSE 2015 1st SEP 2nd SHIFT]

13. What was the mascot for the Commonwealth Games held in India in 2010?

   (a) Bison   (b) Peacock

   (c) Deer   (d) Tiger

[RRB SSE 2015 1st SEP 3rd SHIFT]

14. For the 2016 Olympics, which team defeated the Men's Indian Hockey team to secure the place?

   (a) France   (b) Germany

   (c) England   (d) Italy

[RRB SSE 2015 1st SEP 3rd SHIFT]

15. Which international sports event will be held in Gold Coast, Queensland, Australia in 2018?

   (a) Asian Games

   (b) Common wealth Games

   (c) Asia Pacific Games

   (d) Winter Olympics.

[RRB SSE 2015 2nd SEP 1st SHIFT]

16. For which project in 2015 was the Space Pioneer award presented to ISRO by the National Space Agency U.S.A?

   (a) Lunar Probe Mission

   (b) Remote Sensing maps of land use

   (c) Indian Monsoon study Satellite

   (d) Mars Orhiter Mission Options :

[RRB SSE 2015 2nd SEP 1st SHIFT]

17. Who is the present captain of the Men's Indian Hockey team at present?

   (a) Dilip Tirkey

   (b) Balbir Singh

   (c) Sardar Singh

   (d) Pangat Singh

[RRB SSE 2015 2nd SEP 2nd SHIFT]

18. Which is the distinguishing feature of the Commonwealth Games ?

   (a) It is held once in 5 years

   (b) All countries participate.

   (c) United Kingdom leads procession

   (d) English is the language of communication

[RRB SSE 2015 2nd SEP 2nd SHIFT]

19. In which position does the present Indian Men's Hockey team captain play in matches?

   (a) Defender   (b) Centre half

   (c) Goalkeeper   (d) Sweeper

[RRB SSE 2015 2nd SEP 3rd SHIFT]

20. How many countries will be invited to participate in the Commomwealth Games 2018 to be held in Gold Coast, Queensland Australia?

   (a) 100   (b) 60

   (c) 65   (d) 71

[RRB SSE 2015 2nd SEP 3rd SHIFT]

21. What is special about the way the Commonwealth Games are inaugurated?

   (a) The Queen of England sends a baton which travels.

   (b) A fire is lit in London and then in the city of the Games.

   (c) All athletes carry the flags of their country and the British flag.

   (d) The mascot for each game is decided by the Queen of England.

[RRB SSE 2015 3rd SEP 1st SHIFT]

22. Who is the captain of the women's hockey team of India?

   (a) Mamta Kharab   (b) Suraj Lata Devi

   (c) Ritu Rani   (d) Chanchana Devi

[RRB SSE 2015 3rd SEP 1st SHIFT]

ANSWER KEY

RRB JUNIOR ENGINEER

1. (a)	**2.** (a)	**3.** (c)	**4.** (c)	**5.** (d)	**6.** (a)	**7.** (d)	**8.** (b)	**9.** (b)	**10.** (a)
11. (c)	**12.** (a)	**13.** (d)	**14.** (b)	**15.** (a)	**16.** (c)	**17.** (d)	**18.** (a)	**19.** (d)	**20.** (d)
21. (c)	**22.** (a)	**23.** (d)	**24.** (d)	**25.** (c)	**26.** (d)	**27.** (b)	**28.** (c)	**29.** (c)	**30.** (b)
31. (b)	**32.** (a)	**33.** (b)	**34.** (a)	**35.** (b)	**36.** (a)	**37.** (c)	**38.** (b)	**39.** (a)	**40.** (b)
41. (d)	**42.** (b)	**43.** (d)	**44.** (b)	**45.** (c)	**46.** (b)	**47.** (c)	**48.** (a)		

RRB SENIOR SECTION ENGINEER

1. (b)	**2.** (b)	**3.** (d)	**4.** (a)	**5.** (d)	**6.** (d)	**7.** (c)	**8.** (c)	**9.** (d)	**10.** (b)
11. (c)	**12.** (a)	**13.** (d)	**14.** (c)	**15.** (b)	**16.** (d)	**17.** (c)	**18.** (d)	**19.** (b)	**20.** (d)
21. (a)	**22.** (c)								

EXPLANATIONS

RRB JUNIOR ENGINEER

1. Sir C.V Raman won the 1930 Nobel Prize in Physics for his work on the scattering of light and for the discovery of the Raman effect.He was the first Asian and first non-white to receive any Nobel Prize in the sciences. Before him Rabindranath Tagore(also Indian) had received the Nobel Prize for Literature in 1913.

2. The 2014 FIFA World Cup Final was a football match that took place on 13 July 2014 at the Maracanã Stadium in Rio de Janeiro, Brazil to determine the 2014 FIFA World Cup champion. Germany defeated Argentina 1–0 in extra time to win the 2014 FIFA World Cup.

3. Marin Cilic is the winner of Men's Singles Title in Tennis in US open, 2014

4. The Royal Swedish Academy of Sciences has decided to award The Sveriges Riksbank Prize in Economic Sciences in Memory of Alfred Nobel for 2014 to Jean Tirole "for his analysis of market power and regulation".

5. The Uber Cup, sometimes called the World Team Championships for Women, is a major international badminton competition contested by women's national badminton teams.

6. Bharat Ratna is the highest civilian award in the country and Tendulkar is the first sportsperson to get it.

7. Asian Games in 2018 was held in Jakarta, Indonesia.

8. Among the given options, Sushil Kumar did not win a medal in Asian Games 2014.

9. The common amongst the Mahesh Bhupathi, Ivan Lendl, and Roger Federer are all International Tennis players.

10. Pakistani child education activist Malala Yousafzai and Kailash Satyarthi, an Indian child rights campaigner, have jointly won the Nobel Peace Prize. At the age of just 17, Malala is the youngest ever recipient of the prize.

11. The UN Public service award 2015 for eliminating open defecation has been given to Nadia in West Bengal.

12. The Champions League Trophy is given for the best club in Soccer.Association football, more commonly known as football or soccer, is a team sport played between two teams of eleven players with a spherical ball

13. Cricket batsman has to leave the field for "hit wicket" when wicket is touched by bator body of the batsman.

14. Pakistani child education activist Malala Yousafzai and Kailash Satyarthi, an Indian child rights campaigner, have jointly won the Nobel Peace Prize. At the age of just 17, Malala is the youngest ever recipient of the prize.

15. The tournament that takes place in Roland Garros in Paris is associated with Lawn tennis.

16. For a long time, hockey was considered the national sport of India owing to its stellar performances in the Olympic Games. But in August 2012, the Union ministry of Youth Affairs declared that India does not have a game that has been officially designated as its National game.

17. The football player has to leave the field if the referee shows him yellow card twice or red card once.

18. Abhinav Bindra is an Indian businessman and retired professional shooter who is a former World and Olympic champion in the 10 metre Air Rifle event.By winning the gold in the 10 metre Air Rifle event at the 2008 Beijing Olympic Games, he became the first Indian to win an individual gold medal at the Olympic Games.

19. Every time you win a rally, you get a point. Starting from zero, the first person to reach 21 points wins the game. In club badminton, this is usually where you stop and choose players for the next game.Total 15 points to be scored in Badminton is not true.

20. Paralympic Games is a major international multi-sport event involving athletes with a range of disabilities, including impaired muscle power , impaired passive range of movement, limb deficiency , leg length difference, short stature, hypertonia, ataxia, athetosis, vision impairment and intellectual impairment. All Paralympic Games are governed by the International Paralympic Committee (IPC).

21. The Ranji Trophy is a domestic first-class cricket championship played in India between teams representing regional and state cricket associations. The competition is named after first Indian cricketer who played international cricket, Ranjitsinhji, who was also known as "Ranji".

22. In women's tennis records, Li Na : Wimbledon is an unmatched pair of champion and championship Trophy won by her.

23. In a game of cricket, when the ball bounces more than once before reaching batsman's side, it is called Dead ball.

24. 2 or 3 points are awarded for one normal baske in a game of basketball.

25. A baseball game is played between two teams, each composed of nine players.

26. New Zealand won the Azlan shah cup Hockey in april 2015.

27. Shashi kapoor was bestowed with the 46th Dada Saheb Phalke Award for 2014. The Dadasaheb Phalke Award is India's highest award in cinema. It is presented annually at the National Film Awards ceremony by the Directorate of Film Festivals, an organisation set up by the Ministry of Information and Broadcasting.

28. Birdman was adjusted as the Best Motion pictures at the 87th Academy awards (oscars) on February 22, 2015.

29. The first Commonwealth Games were held in the year 1930 at Hamilton (Canada).

30. Jaggy Shivdasani is one of India's most successful bridge players. Having burst onto the India's national scene in 1976 by winning the premier Holkar Trophy he went on to win all national titles, usually multiple times.

31. A renewed hindi poet, Kailash Vajpeyi received the sahitya Akademi award for his work 'Hawa mein hastakshar' passed away on april 1, 2015.

32. Sanjari Vijay & kangana Ranaut have been declared the best actor and the best actress at the 62nd national film awards announced on march 24, 2014 in new delhi.

33. The Ryder Cup is a biennial men's golf competition between teams from Europe and the United States. The competition is contested every two years with the venue alternating between courses in the United States and Europe. The Ryder Cup is named after the English businessman Samuel Ryder who donated the trophy.

34. The Badminton player, Chen Long won the Malaysian open on April 5. Chen Long, is a Chinese professional badminton player. He is the reigning Olympic champion and two-time World champion and All England champion.

35. Merdeka cup is associated with Football. Pestabola Merdeka or Merdeka Tournament is a football friendly tournament held in Malaysia to honour the Independence Day. The competition is named after the Malay word for independence.

36. The five intertwined rings or circles on the Olympic flag made of Blue, yellow, black green and red colours.

37. Laszlo Krasznahorkai was presented the Man Booker international Prize for 2015 in London on May 20, 2015.

38. French director Jacques Audiard won the Palme d'or, the top honour of the 68th Cannes film festival on May 24, 2015 for the film Dheepan.

39. The Championships, Wimbledon, commonly known simply as Wimbledon, is the oldest tennis tournament in the world. It has been held at the All England Club in Wimbledon, London, since 1877 and is played on outdoor grass courts.Wimbledon is one of the four Grand Slam tennis tournaments, the others being the Australian Open, the French Open and the US Open. Since the Australian Open shifted to hardcourt in 1988, Wimbledon is the only major still played on grass.

40. The Dronacharya Award, officially known as Dronacharya Award for Outstanding Coaches in Sports and Games. It was Instituted in 1985, the award is given only to the disciplines included in the events like Olympic Games, Paralympic Games, Asian Games, Commonwealth Games, World Championship and World Cup along with Cricket, Indigenous Games, and Parasports.

41. The 2016 Summer Olympics officially known as the Games of the XXXI Olympiad and commonly known as Rio 2016 was an international multi-sport event that was held from 5 to 21 August 2016 in Rio de Janeiro, Brazil.

42. Among the given options, Federation cup - badminton is not correct. Fed Cup is the premier international team competition in women's tennis, launched in 1963 to celebrate the 50th Anniversary of the International Tennis Federation (ITF).

43. An athlete driving off a high spring board can perform a variety of exercises in the air before entering the water below. The angular momentum of the athlete's will remain constant during the fall.

44. The term "bogey" is associated with Golf.

45. The ancient Olympic continued till about Theodosius I.

46. Leander Paes & Martina Hingis won the Wimbledon 2015 mixed double championship.

47. A maiden over is one in which no runs are scored. Leg byes and byes scored in the over are not counted against the bowler in a maiden over. A wicket maiden is one in which no runs are scored and a wicket is taken: double and triple wicket maidens have also been recorded. Bowling a maiden over in ODI and T20 forms of cricket is very important and difficult.

48. The Asian Games, also known as Asiad is a continental multi-sport event held every four years among athletes from all over Asia. The Games were regulated by the Asian Games Federation (AGF) from the first Games in New Delhi, India, until the 1978 Games. Since the 1982 Games, they have been organized by the Olympic Council of Asia (OCA).

RRB SENIOR SECTION ENGINEER

1. The Pro Kabaddi League currently known as Vivo Pro Kabaddi League for sponsorship purpose is a professional-level Kabaddi league in India. It was launched in 2014 and is broadcast on Star Sports. Jaipur Pink Panthers beat U Mumba by 35-24 to win the inaugural Pro Kabaddi League.

2. The Nobel Prize in Literature 2014 was awarded to Patrick Modiano "for the art of memory with which he has evoked the most ungraspable human destinies and uncovered the life-world of the occupation".

3. In the 2014 Asian Games held at Incheon in South Korea, Jitu Rai won the gold medal in the 50 m pistol category. He also won a bronze in the men's 10m air pistol team event.

4. The Shanti Swarup Bhatnagar Prize for Science and Technology is a science award in India given annually by the Council of Scientific and Industrial Research for notable and outstanding research, applied or fundamental, in biology, chemistry, environmental science, engineering, mathematics, medicine and Physics.

5. Novak Djokovic is the winner of Men's Singles Title in Wimbledon, 2014 in Tennis.

6. Pestabola Merdeka or Merdeka Tournament is a football friendly tournament held in Malaysia to honour the Independence Day. The competition is named after the Malay word for independence.

7. Jitu Rai is an Indian shooter of Nepali origin who competes in the 10 metre air pistol and 50 metre pistol events. Heena Sidhu is an Indian sport shooter. On 7 April 2014, Sidhu became the first Indian pistol shooter to reach number one in world rankings by the International Shooting Sport Federation. Jwala Gutta is a retired left-handed Indian badminton player. Yogeshwar Dutt is an Indian freestyle wrestler. At the 2012 Summer Olympics, he won the bronze medal in the 60 kg category.

8. The slogan of Asian Games Incheon 2014 was *"Diversity Shines Here"* It represents and highlights the significance of Asia's wonderful diversity in history, cultures, and religions.

9. Humanity, Equality, Destiny are the three values cherished by the Commonwealth Games.

10. For participation in Olympics games event has the Men's Indian Hockey team qualified after the World Hockey League.

11. The 2018 Commonwealth Games, officially known as the XXI Commonwealth Games and commonly known as Gold Coast 2018, were an international multi-sport event for members of the Commonwealth that were held on the Gold Coast, Queensland, Australia, between 4 and 15 April 2018.

12. To participate in the Olympics at Rio de Janeiro in 2016, Indian men's hockey team qualified for knock-outs for the first time since Moscow Games in 1980. Even though they lost their match 2-1 against Netherlands earlier in the day, it was a 4-4 draw between Germany and Argentina that propelled them into the quarter-final.

13. Tiger was the mascot for the Commonwealth Games held in India in 2010.Shera, mascot of the XIX Commonwealth Games 2010 Delhi, is the most visible face of the XIX Commonwealth Games 2010 Delhi. His name comes from the Hindi word Sher – meaning tiger. Shera truly represents the modern Indian.

14. For the 2016 Olympics, England team defeated the Men's Indian Hockey team to secure the place.

15. Commonwealth Games was held in Gold Coast, Queensland, Australia in 2018.

16. Mars Orbiter Mission Options was the Space Pioneer award 2015 presented to ISRO by the National Space Agency U.S.A.

17. Sardara Singh sometimes referred as Sardar Singh, is an Indian professional field hockey player and captain of the Indian national team.

18. English is the language of communication, one of the distinguishing feature of the Commonwealth Games.

19. Centre half position does the present Indian Men's Hockey team captain play in matches.

20. 71 countries was invited to participate in the Commonwealth Games 2018 to be held in Gold Coast, Queensland Australia.

21. The special about the way the Commonwealth Games inaugurated was the Queen of England sent a baton which travels.

22. Ritu Rani is the captain of the women's hockey team of India.Ritu Rani is an Indian field hockey player and former captain of the national team. She plays as a halfback. Rani has led the team to medal winning performances most notably the bronze at the 2014 Asian Games.

ECONOMY, BANKING & FINANCE

RRB JUNIOR ENGINEER

1. Who among the following can accept the deposits of money from the public, as a business in financial transactions?

(a) Individuals

(b) Firms

(c) Unincorporated Associations

(d) None of the above

[RRB JE 2014 GREEN SHIFT]

2. NEFT and RTGS are the means for

(a) Money transfer

(b) Fiscal control policy

(c) Monitoring tax collection

(d) Implementing GST

[RRB JE 2014 GREEN SHIFT]

3. The concept of joint sector implies cooperation between

(a) Public Sector and Private Sector Industries

(b) State Government and Central Government Enterprises

(c) Domestic and Foreign Industries

(d) Cooperation between two Government Departments

[RRB JE 2014 YELLOW SHIFT]

4. Which of the following is an apex financing agency for the institutions providing investment and production credit for promoting the various developmental activities in rural areas ?

(a) RBI   (b) NABARD

(c) SIDBI   (d) IMPEX

[RRB JE 2014 YELLOW SHIFT]

5. India's First Bank exclusively for Women is

(a) Mahila Kalyan Bank

(b) Bhartiya Mahila Bank

(c) Bharti Bank

(d) SIDBI

[RRB JE 2014 YELLOW SHIFT]

6. What is PPP (Purchasing Power Parity)?

(a) Method of measuring relative purchasing power of currencies of different countries

(b) Ability to purchase commodities by citizens of different states of a country

(c) A measure of socioeconomic development of a nation

(d) An index for purchasing power of citizens of neighbouring countries

[RRB JE 2015 26th AUG 1st SHIFT]

7. Which nationalized bank presently has a Woman as its CEO?

(a) Indian Overseas Bank

(b) State Bank of India

(c) Punjab National Bar

(d) Central Bank on India

[RRB JE 2015 26th AUG 1st SHIFT]

8. The record of a country's transaction in goods and assets with the rest of the world is its

(a) Capital amount

(b) Current amount

(c) Balance of payment

(d) Balance of trade

[RRB JE 2015 26th AUG 1st SHIFT]

9. Which of the following statements regarding international trade is true?

(a) Higher change rate makes country's exports cheaper

(b) Higher exchange rate makes country's imports cheaper

(c) Lower exchange rate makes country's imports cheaper in domestic markets

(d) Lower exchange rate makes country's exports cheaper

[RRB JE 2015 26th AUG 2nd SHIFT]

10. The main cause of balance of payments (BoP) deficit in developed free market economies is

(a) Less demand for country's exports

(b) Less demand for country's imports

(c) Rising demand for country's exports

(d) Recurring Political instability in the country

[RRB JE 2015 26th AUG 2nd SHIFT]

11. If the Gross Domestic Product (GDP) of a country is higher than Gross National Product (GNP), then

(a) The total production by national and foreign individuals within the geographical boundaries of a country is lower than produced by its citizens on its land or foreign soil

(b) Net payment outflow to foreign assets is greater than net income inflow from assets abroad

(c) The strength of the country's basal economy is less than economic strength of the nationals of the country

(d) Net payments outflow is lower than incoming inflow

[RRB JE 2015 26th AUG 2nd SHIFT]

12. The relationship between quantity, revenue and price is

(a) Quantity times Price = Revenue

(b) Revenue times Price = Quantity

(c) Quantity times Revenue = Price

(d) Price times Quantity = Current price

[RRB JE 2015 26th AUG 3rd SHIFT]

13. One of the following is not an objective of the Mid-day Meal scheme in school launched by the government. Select from options given below

(a) Provide full nutritional support to children at the Primary stage of education

(b) Encourage disadvantaged section of the society to attend school regularly and concentrate on studies

(c) Improve the nutritional status of children in the primary section

(d) Bridge the gender and social category gaps in schools at the primary level itself

[RRB JE 2015 27th AUG 1st SHIFT]

14. Give the term for 'Price of one currency in terms of another'.

(a) Effective exchange rate

(b) Nominal exchange rate

(c) Spot rate

(d) Purchasing Power Parity

[RRB JE 2015 27th AUG 1st SHIFT]

15. The labour or workforce of a country does not include one of the following.

(a) Employees of Government

(b) Self employed

(c) Unemployed

(d) Those of age less than 14 years

[RRB JE 2015 27th AUG 1st SHIFT]

16. The terms of trade measure

(a) Ratio of export prices and import prices

(b) Sum of export prices and import prices

(c) Difference of export price and import price

(d) Product of export price and import price

[RRB JE 2015 27th AUG 1st SHIFT]

17. Which of the following statement is not true regarding the second five year plan of India?

(a) The plan was based on the Mahalanobis model of economic development, the architect of which was the Indian statistician PC Mahalanobis

(b) The second five year plan was operational from 1956-1961

(c) The plan assumed a closed economy in which the main trading activity would be centered around importing capital goods

(d) The plan also focused on agriculture, that being the main sector on which the largest chunk of our population depended

[RRB JE 2015 27th AUG 2nd SHIFT]

18. What is 'The Euro?'

(a) The single European currency

(b) The citizens of Europe

(c) Name of a European T.V company

(d) Abbreviation for 'European Union'

[RRB JE 2015 27th AUG 2nd SHIFT]

19. What is not true about the Jan Dhan Yojana of PM Narendra Modi?

(a) It is a scheme aiming to accomplishing the objective of providing banking accounts with a debit card

(b) Scheme of opening ATM banking for all accounts new and old

(c) It has the facility of overdraft upto Rs. 5000/- for Aadhar Card linked accounts

(d) It has inbuilt accident insurance

[RRB JE 2015 27th AUG 2nd SHIFT]

20. What is meant by 'Wholesale Price'?

(a) Price of goods at factor gate

(b) Price of a basket of good and services

(c) Minimum price fixed for import of a commodity

(d) Maximum price fixed tor export of a commodity

[RRB JE 2015 27th AUG 2nd SHIFT]

21. Comparative advantage and absolute advantage are terms related to

(a) International trade

(b) E-commerce

(c) Commercial vehicular exchange

(d) Movement of commodities within a country

[RRB JE 2015 27ᵗʰ AUG 3ʳᵈ SHIFT]

22. The terms of trade measures

(a) the ratio of export prices to import prices

(b) extent of international competitiveness

(c) effective exchange rates

(d) Nominal exchange rates

[RRB JE 2015 27ᵗʰ AUG 3ʳᵈ SHIFT]

23. Depreciation is equal to

(a) Gross National Product – Net National Product

(b) Net National Product – Gross National Product

(c) Gross National Product – Personal Income

(d) Personal Income – Personal Taxes

[RRB JE 2015 28ᵗʰ AUG 1ˢᵗ SHIFT]

24. The slogan 'Garibi Unmulan' (Poverty eradication) was given n which Five year plan

(a) Second plan   (b) Fourth plan

(c) Fifth plan   (d) Sixth plan

[RRB JE 2015 28ᵗʰ AUG 1ˢᵗ SHIFT]

25. Which one of the following was the Chairman of the Committee on Pricing and Taxation of Petroleum Products?

(a) Raja j. Chelliah   (b) C. Rangrajan

(c) Y.V.Reddy   (d) Abid Hussain

[RRB JE 2015 28ᵗʰ AUG 2ⁿᵈ SHIFT]

26. Twenty Point Programme' (Bees-sutri Karyakrama) was first launched in the Year

(a) 1969   (b) 1975

(c) 1977   (d) 1982

[RRB JE 2015 28ᵗʰ AUG 3ʳᵈ SHIFT]

27. Among other things, which one of the following was the purpose for which the Deepak Parekh Committee was constituted

(a) To study the current socio-economic conditions of certain minority communities

(b) To suggest measures for financing the development of infrastructure

(c) To frame a policy on the production of genetically modified organisms

(d) To suggest measures to reduce the fiscal deficit in the Union Budget

[RRB JE 2015 28ᵗʰ AUG 3ʳᵈ SHIFT]

28. When was the Jawahar Rojgar Yojana launched?

(a) 1985   (b) 1987

(c) 1989   (d) 1991

[RRB JE 2015 29ᵗʰ AUG 1ˢᵗ SHIFT]

29. National Agricultural Insurance Scheme replacing Comprehensive Corp Insurance Scheme was introduced in the year?

(a) 1997   (b) 1998

(c) 1999   (d) 2000

[RRB JE 2015 29ᵗʰ AUG 1ˢᵗ SHIFT]

30. Which of the following pairs are correctly matched

Enterprise	Industrial Group
1. VSNL	Bharati Group
2. Mundra SEZ	Adani Group
3. CMC Ltd	Tata Group
4. IPCL	Reliance Group

Select the correct answer using the codes given below

(a) 1, 2 and 3   (b) 1, 2 and 4

(c) 3 and 4   (d) 2, 3 and 4

[RRB JE 2015 29ᵗʰ AUG 1ˢᵗ SHIFT]

31. The state, which signed $400 million loan pact with WTO on June 4, 2015 is ......

(a) Andhra pradesh   (b) Telangana

(c) Kerala   (d) Tamil nadu

[RRB JE 2015 29ᵗʰ AUG 2ⁿᵈ SHIFT]

32. Which one of the following pairs is NOT correctly matched

Scheme	Commencement Year
(a) TRYSEM	August, 1979
(b) NREP	October, 1980
(c) JRY	April, 1995
(d) SGSY	April, 1999

[RRB JE 2015 29ᵗʰ AUG 3ʳᵈ SHIFT]

33. Commercial paper is a source of credit for which one of the following

(a) Corporate Industry

(b) Small Scale Industries

(c) Commercial Banks

(d) Foreign Banks

[RRB JE 2015 29ᵗʰ AUG 3ʳᵈ SHIFT]

34. Who amongst the following has decided to withdraw its nominee directors from the boards of the private sector banks

(a) Registrar of Companies

(b) Reserve Bank of India

(c) Registrar of Co-operative Societies

(d) State Governments

[RRB JE 2015 29ᵗʰ AUG 3ʳᵈ SHIFT]

35. Which public enterprise got the status of miniratna (Category-I) in June, 2015

(a) EIL   (b) IREDA

(c) NHPC   (d) Bridge & Roof

[RRB JE 2015 29ᵗʰ AUG 3ʳᵈ SHIFT]

36. When was the concept of the Human Development Index (HDI) introduced by the United Nations Development Programme?

(a) 1990   (b) 1991

(c) 1993   (d) 1995

[RRB JE 2015 30ᵗʰ AUG 3ʳᵈ SHIFT]

37. Tarapore Committee was associated with which one of the following

(a) Special Economic Zone

(b) Fully capital Account Convertibility

(c) Effect of oil-price on the Indian Economy

(d) Foreign Exchange Reserve

[RRB JE 2015 30ᵗʰ AUG 3ʳᵈ SHIFT]

38. MODVAT is related to

(a) Sales Tax   (b) Wealth Tax

(c) Income Tax   (d) Excise Duty

[RRB JE 2015 30ᵗʰ AUG 3ʳᵈ SHIFT]

39. The Total national income divided by the number of people in the nation is

(a) GDP

(b) National Income

(c) Per Capita Income

(d) Human Development Index

[RRB JE 2015 16ᵗʰ SEP 3ʳᵈ SHIFT]

RRB SENIOR SECTION ENGINEER

1. Air India's losses in previous financial year were to the tune of (in crores of rupees):

(a) 4   (b) 40

(c) 400   (d) 4000

[RRB SSE 2014 GREEN SHIFT]

2. Cash-reserve ratio of a commercial bank is fixed by-

(a) Ministry of Finance

(b) Ministry of Commerce

(c) RBI

(d) Management of the commercial bank

[RRB SSE 2014 GREEN SHIFT]

3. Currently which 5 year plan is under execution in India?

(a) 12th   (b) 13th

(c) 14th   (d) 15th

[RRB SSE 2014 GREEN SHIFT]

4. As per Census, 2011. What is the Sex Ratio (i.e. No. of Females per 1000 Males) of India ?

(a) 914   (b) 923

(c) 940   (d) 956

[RRB SSE 2014 RED SHIFT]

5. One can open a Savings Account in India except in

(a) A Nationalised Bank

(b) A Cooperative Bank

(c) a Private Bank

(d) Reserve Bank of India

[RRB SSE 2014 YELLOW SHIFT]

6. The Term "Inside Trading" is related to

(a) Share Market   (b) Horse racing

(c) Taxation   (d) Public expenditure

[RRB SSE 2014 YELLOW SHIFT]

7. Main objective of newly announced "Pradhanmantri Jan-Dhan Yojna" is_____ ?

(a) to provide a bank account to every poor

(b) to provide a interest free loan to farmers

(c) to provide financial assistance to tribal communication

(d) to provide free medical facility to minority people

[RRB SSE 2014 YELLOW SHIFT]

8. What is the difference between Economic growth and Economic Development?

(a) Economic growth is the increase in the prosperity of a region whereas economic development is a result of policy of the Government

(b) Economic growth leads to greater employment, economic development increases national income

(c) Economic growth is the Increase in production of goods and services over the previous year, economic development is the impact it has on income of an area.

(d) Economic growth is quantifiable whereas development can only be described or felt.

[RRB SSE 2015 1ˢᵗ SEP 1ˢᵗ SHIFT]

9. What is the advantage of E -commerce?

(a) Is Private, secure, and fast, and allows worldwide competition.,

(b) Encourages production based on natural resources.

(c) Permits international trade without too many regulations.

(d) Protects both the supplier and consumer.

[RRB SSE 2015 1ˢᵗ SEP 1ˢᵗ SHIFT]

10. What is the likely change that Foreign Direct Investment will bring about in Indian Horticulture?

(a) Increased use of fertilizer and hybrid seeds.

(b) Slowing down of organic farming .

(c) More investment in floriculture in hill reas.

(d) Expansion of area under plantation

[RRB SSE 2015 1ˢᵗ SEP 2ⁿᵈ SHIFT]

11. What information does the Gross Domestic Product not show?

(a) Contribution of industry towards the national Income

(b) Expenditure on goods and services by the government

(c) Income distribution across different sections of the population.

(d) Purchasing power of the people in a country.

[RRB SSE 2015 1ˢᵗ SEP 3ʳᵈ SHIFT]

12. How do e- commerce ventures build up trust of the buyers in their goods?

(a) Cash on deliveryfacility

(b) Ensure a flexible return policy

(c) Better advertising

(d) Prompt delivery

[RRB SSE 2015 1ˢᵗ SEP 3ʳᵈ SHIFT]

13. Which new policy in India today allows the expansion of cold storages, inc eased production of organic manure, research into hybrid seeds and employment ?

(a) Foreign direct investment in Horticulture.

(b) Direct subsidy to farmers for orchards.

(c) State farms to act as models for farmers.

(d) Increased education in farming techniques

[RRB SSE 2015 2ⁿᵈ SEP 1ˢᵗ SHIFT]

14. What indicator is more suitable for finding the economic development of a country?

(a) Human Development Index

(b) Gross Domestic Product

(c) Consumption Level

(d) Income Level

[RRB SSE 2015 2ⁿᵈ SEP 1ˢᵗ SHIFT]

15. Which traditional communication agency in India is now looking forward to providing e-commerce facilities ?

(a) Radio Broadcast   (b) Television Broadcast

(c) Courier   (d) Post offices

[RRB SSE 2015 2ⁿᵈ SEP 1ˢᵗ SHIFT]

16. Which is the only plantation crop in which foreign direct investment is permitted so far?

(a) Coconut   (b) Tea

(c) Rubber   (d) Jute

[RRB SSE 2015 2ⁿᵈ SEP 2ⁿᵈ SHIFT]

17. What is the term used to describe the moneylender, support groups, cooperatives in the rural economy?

(a) Social Capital   (b) Financial Capital

(c) Human capital   (d) Physical capital

[RRB SSE 2015 2ⁿᵈ SEP 2ⁿᵈ SHIFT]

18. In which sector in India is E-commerce has grown the fastest in India ?

(a) Luxury goods

(b) Farm goods

(c) Groceries

(d) Travel Booking

[RRB SSE 2015 2ⁿᵈ SEP 2ⁿᵈ SHIFT]

19. What new practices have been introduced in horticulture due to Foreign Direct Investment?

(a) Use of poly houses and production of hybrid seeds

(b) Drip irrigation and regulated water use

(c) Use of new plant materials for cultivation of hybrid vegetables

(d) Improvement in organic farming techniques

[RRB SSE 2015 2ⁿᵈ SEP 3ʳᵈ SHIFT]

20. Which form of business allows for private and secure, fast business and allows worldwide competition?

(a) Commerce   (b) Retail Stores

(c) Industries   (d) Private enterprises.

[RRB SSE 2015 2ⁿᵈ SEP 3ʳᵈ SHIFT]

21. Which denomination of currency notes of the year 2005 are proposed to be withdrawn because they do not have the safety features of the present currency notes ?

(a) Rs 50 and 100

(b) Rs 5 and 10

(c) Rs 500 and 1000

(d) Rs 1000 and 5000

[RRB SSE 2015 2ⁿᵈ SEP 3ʳᵈ SHIFT]

22. Which of the following is not a positive effect of Foreign Direct Investment on the Indian Market?

(a) Stimulates economic activity

(b) Increase in prices

(c) Cheaper goods for consumers

(d) Increased employment

[RRB SSE 2015 3ⁿᵈ SEP 1ˢᵗ SHIFT]

23. Why has the government excluded some wealthy groups from availing benefits related their status as backward classes?

(a) Increase opportunity to be employed

(b) Bring more backward groups for benefits

(c) To ensure that there is equality

(d) Increase the right of the poorest.

[RRB SSE 2015 3ⁿᵈ SEP 1ˢᵗ SHIFT]

24. What will be the special e-commerce facility offered by the Indian Postal Services ?

(a) Rural artisans can sell goods online.

(b) Farmers can buy seeds and fertilisers easily.

(c) Health services in rural areas can be provided promptly

(d) Same day delivery of letters to villages.

[RRB SSE 2015 3ⁿᵈ SEP 1ˢᵗ SHIFT]

25. What are the components of the natural components of development ?

(a) Institutions, political structure, rights

(b) Roads, electricity, banks,

(c) Savings, Insurance, Salaries.

(d) Resources, environment, Food, health

[RRB SSE 2015 3ⁿᵈ SEP 1ˢᵗ SHIFT]

26. What were the major changes in feudal period agriculture which led to the rise of surplus production?

(a) Food shortages in different areas allowing trach from surplus.

(b) Renting out of land to smaller peasants.

(c) New inventions like the iron plough and horse drawn ploughs.

(d) Cultivation of more than one crop at given time in different fields.

[RRB SSE 2015 3ⁿᵈ SEP 2ⁿᵈ SHIFT]

27. What has been the trend of growth of al population and urban population in the 2011 Census?

(a) Rural population has increased but urban population decreased

(b) Rural population has increased but urban population increased further.

(c) There is increased migration from urban to rural areas

(d) Urban areas have increased and included rural population.

[RRB SSE 2015 3ⁿᵈ SEP 2ⁿᵈ SHIFT]

28. Which sector of the Indian economy has 95% of the workforce and contributes 57% of the national domestic product

(a) Industrial workers

(b) Unorganised sector

(c) Service sector

(d) Transport workers

[RRB SSE 2015 3ⁿᵈ SEP 2ⁿᵈ SHIFT]

29. The development of which industries does the Make in India effort which will increase GDP from the current 15 % to 25 % focuses on ?

(a) Electronics, Automobile and shipbuilding

(b) Consumer appliances, sports goods and robots

(c) Engineering goods, electrical goods and chemicals

(d) Paper, Textiles and Sugar

[RRB SSE 2015 3ⁿᵈ SEP 3ʳᵈ SHIFT]

30. In which sector are most farm workers leaving overcrowded farms moving ito?

(a) Large manufacturing

(b) Government employment

(c) Small scale industries

(d) Informal sector

[RRB SSE 2015 3ⁿᵈ SEP 3ʳᵈ SHIFT]

ANSWER KEY

RRB JUNIOR ENGINEER

1. (d)	**2.** (a)	**3.** (a)	**4.** (b)	**5.** (b)	**6.** (a)	**7.** (b)	**8.** (c)	**9.** (a)	**10.** (a)
11. (b)	**12.** (a)	**13.** (d)	**14.** (b)	**15.** (d)	**16.** (a)	**17.** (d)	**18.** (a)	**19.** (b)	**20.** (a)
21. (d)	**22.** (a)	**23.** (a)	**24.** (c)	**25.** (b)	**26.** (b)	**27.** (b)	**28.** (c)	**29.** (c)	**30.** (d)
31. (d)	**32.** (c)	**33.** (a)	**34.** (b)	**35.** (b)	**36.** (a)	**37.** (b)	**38.** (d)	**39.** (c)	

RRB SENIOR SECTION ENGINEER

1. (d)	**2.** (c)	**3.** (a)	**4.** (c)	**5.** (d)	**6.** (a)	**7.** (a)	**8.** (c)	**9.** (a)	**10.** (a)
11. (c)	**12.** (b)	**13.** (a)	**14.** (a)	**15.** (d)	**16.** (d)	**17.** (a)	**18.** (d)	**19.** (b)	**20.** (a)
21. (c)	**22.** (b)	**23.** (c)	**24.** (a)	**25.** (d)	**26.** (d)	**27.** (b)	**28.** (b)	**29.** (a)	**30.** (d)

EXPLANATIONS

RRB JUNIOR ENGINEER

1. Among the given options, No one can accept the deposits of money from the public, as a business in financial transactions.

2. NEFT or National Electronic Funds Transfer, RTGS or Real Time Gross Settlement and IMPS or Immediate Payment Service are three platforms that enable instant money transfers. NEFT is a payment system that enables electronic transfer of funds from one bank to another bank account.

3. The concept of joint sector implies cooperation Between Public Sector and Private Sector Industries.

4. NABARD is an apex financing agency for the institutions providing investment and production credit for promoting the various developmental activities in rural areas.

5. India's First Bank exclusively for Women is Bhartiya Mahila Bank. Inaugurating the first branch of the Bharatiya Mahila Bank in the financial city of Mumbai, Prime Minister Manmohan Singh told dignitaries that despite great successes made by some women in India, many continued to face financial exclusion.

6. PPP (Purchasing Power Parity) method of measuring the relative purchasing power of currencies of different countries.

7. As on 2016, State Bank of India has a woman as its CEO. Arundhati Bhattacharya is a retired Indian banker and former Chairman of the State Bank of India. She is the first woman to be the Chairman of State Bank of India . In 2016, she was listed as the 25th most powerful woman in the world by Forbes. She is the only Indian listed on Fortune's world's greatest leaders list ranked at 26.

8. The balance of payments, also known as balance of international payments and abbreviated B.O.P. or BoP, of a country is the record of all economic transactions between the residents of the country and the rest of world in a particular period of time. The balance of payments is a summary of all monetary transactions between a country and rest of the world. These transactions are made by individuals, firms and government bodies.

9. Higher change rate makes country's exports cheaper, statement is true regarding international trade.

10. The main cause of balance of payments (BoP) deficit in developed free market economies is less demand for country's exports.

11. If the Gross Domestic Product (GDP) of a country is higher than Gross National Product (GNP), then Net payment outflow to foreign assets is greater than net income inflow from assets abroad.

12. The relationship between quantity, revenue and price is Quantity times Price = Revenue

13. Bridge the gender and social category gaps in schools at the primary level itself is not an objective of the Mid-day Meal scheme in school launched by the government.

14. The nominal exchange rate E is defined as the number of units of the domestic currency that can purchase a unit of a given foreign currency. A decrease in this variable is termed nominal appreciation of the currency.

15. The labour or workforce of a country does not include those of age less than 14 years.

16. The terms of trade is the relative price of imports in terms of exports and is defined as the ratio of export prices to import prices. It can be interpreted as the amount of import goods an economy can purchase per unit of export goods.

17. Among the given options, The plan also focused on agriculture, that being the main sector on which the largest chunk of our population depended is not true regarding the second five year plan of India.

18. The euro is the official currency of the European Union and its territories. Currently, 19 of 28 member states use the euro; this group of states is known as the eurozone or euro area. It is the second largest and second most traded currency in the foreign exchange market after the United States dollar. The euro is subdivided into 100 cents.

19. Among the given options, Scheme of opening ATM banking for all accounts new and old is not true about the Jan Dhan Yojana of PM Narendra Modi.

20. The Price of goods at factory gate is called as wholesale price.

21. Comparative advantage and absolute advantage are terms related to movement of commodities within a country.

22. The terms of trade measures the ratio of export prices to import prices.

23. Depreciation is equal to Gross National Product – Net National Product.

24. The slogan 'Garibi Unmulan' (Poverty eradication) was given in fifth five year plan. The Fifth Five-Year Plan laid stress on employment, poverty alleviation (Garibi Hatao), and justice. The plan also focused on self-reliance in agricultural production and defence

25. C. Rangarajan was the Chairman of the Committee on Pricing and Taxation of Petroleum Products.

26. The Twenty Point Programme (TPP) was launched by the Government of India in 1975. The Programme was first revised in 1982 and again in 1986.

27. The purpose for which the Deepak Parekh Committee was constituted to suggest measures for financing the development of infrastructure.

28. In the year 1989 the Jawahar Rozgar Yojana was launched. The main target of this plan was the people below poverty line. This plan which works towards its main aim of providing 90 to 100 days of employment to people residing in the rural and most backward areas is the biggest employment generating programmes in the country.

29. National Agricultural Insurance Scheme replacing Comprehensive Crop Insurance Scheme was introduced in the year 1999. The Government then introduced in 1999-2000, a new scheme titled "National Agricultural Insurance Scheme" (NAIS) or "Rashtriya Krishi Bima Yojana" (RKBY). NAIS envisages coverage of all food crops (cereals and pulses), oilseeds, horticultural and commercial crops.

30. From the given options, Mundra SEZ -Adani Group, CMC Ltd -Tata Group, IPCL -Reliance Group are correctly matched.

31. The World Bank and the government of Tamil Nadu signed a loan and project agreement that would enable the international bank to provide $400 million to the government for its Sustainable Urban Development Project.

32. Among the given options, JRY April, 1995 is not correct. JRY launched on April 1 1989.

33. Commercial paper is a source of credit for corporate industry.

34. Reserve Bank of India has decided to withdraw its nominee directors from the boards of the private sector banks.

35. Indian Renewable Energy Development Agency Limited (IREDA) is a Mini Ratna (Category – I) Government of India Enterprise under the administrative control of Ministry of New and Renewable Energy (MNRE).

36. The concept of the Human Development Index (HDI) introduced by the United Nations Development Programme in the year 1990.

37. Tarapore Committee was associated with fully capital account convertibility. Committee on Capital Account Convertibility. Committee on Capital Account Convertibility, commonly known as the Tarapore Committee, was an experts' committee formed by the Reserve Bank of India to study the feasibility of capital account convertibility in India. It submitted its report in 1997.

38. MODVAT is related to excise duty. MODVAT (Modified Value Added Tax) is a unique system under Central Excise Rules that permits manufacturers of excisable goods to avail credit of duty paid on the notified inputs received and used in or in relation to the manufacture of final products and to utilise such credit towards the duty liability on removal of final goods.

39. The Total national income divided by the number of people in the nation is Per Capita Income.

RRB SENIOR SECTION ENGINEER

1. The national carrier expected to post losses in the region of Rs 3,900 crore for 2013-14, senior company executives estimate, despite a projected 18% jump in revenues to Rs 19,500 crore. Among the given options 4000 crores is the closest one.

2. Cash-reserve ratio of a commercial bank is fixed by RBI.

3. 12th Five Year Plan of the Government of India (2012–17) was India's last Five Year Plan.

4. As per Census, 2011. 940 is the Sex Ratio (i.e.No. of Females per 1000 Males) of India.

5. One can open a Savings Account in India except in Reserve Bank of India.

6. The Term "Inside Trading" is related to share Market. Insider trading is the trading of a public company's stock or other securities (such as bonds or stock options) by individuals with access to nonpublic information about the company. In various countries, some kinds of trading based on insider information are illegal.

7. Pradhan Mantri Jan-Dhan Yojana, a major socio-economic initiative of the National Democratic Alliance government, was announced by the Prime Minister in his Independence Day speech. It is an ambitious attempt at extending formal financial services in a country where only 58.7 per cent of an estimated 24.67 crore households avail themselves of banking services.

8. The difference between Economic growth and Economic Development is that Economic growth is the Increase in production of goods and services over the previous year, economic development is the impact it has on income of an area.

9. The advantage of E -commerce is Private, secure, and fast, and allows worldwide competition.E-marketing may be defined as using email to market your message, products and services to potential and current customers.

10. Increased use of fertilizer and hybrid seeds is the likely change that Foreign Direct Investment will bring about in Indian Horticulture.

11. Information regarding the income distribution across different sections of the population does not show by Gross Domestic Product.

12. e- commerce ventures build up trust of the buyers in their goods is by ensuring a flexible return policy.

13. Foreign direct investment in Horticulture allows the expansion of cold storages; increased production of organic manure, research into hybrid seeds and employment.

14. Human Development Index is more suitable for finding the economic development of a country. Human Development Index (HDI) is a statistic (composite index) of life expectancy, education, and per capita income indicators, which are used to rank countries into four tiers of human development.

15. Post offices agency in India is now looking forward to providing e-commerce facilities.India Post is re-inventing itself to cater to the burgeoning e-commerce services industry in the country by setting up data centres, arming the postman with hand-held devices and implementing softwares for facilities like cash on delivery (CoD).

16. Jute is the only plantation crop in which foreign direct investment is permitted so far.

17. Social Capital is the term used to describe the moneylender, support groups, cooperatives in the rural economy.

18. Travel Booking sector in India is E-commerce has grown the fastest in India.

19. Drip irrigation and regulated water use have been introduced in horticulture due to Foreign Direct Investment.

20. Commerce form of business allows for private and secure, fast business and allows worldwide competition.

21. Rs 500 and 1000 denomination of currency notes of the year 2005 are proposed to be withdrawn because they do not have the safety features of the present currency notes.

22. Increase in prices is not a positive effect of Foreign Direct Investment on the Indian Market.

23. To ensure that there is equality the government excluded some wealthy groups from availing benefits related their status as backward classes.

24. Rural artisans can sell goods online will be the special e-commerce facility offered by the Indian Postal Services.

25. Resources, environment, Food, health are the components of the natural components of development.

26. The major changes in feudal period agriculture which led to the rise of surplus production were cultivation of more than one crop at given time in different fields.

27. The trend of growth of al population and urban population in the 2011 Census was that Rural population has increased but urban population increased further.

28. Unorganised sector sector of the Indian economy has 95% of the workforce and contributes 57% of the national domestic product.

29. The development of Electronics, Automobile and shipbuilding the Make in India effort which will increase GDP from the current 15% to 25%.

30. The most farm workers leaving overcrowded farms moving into the informal sector.

6 CHAPTER

INDIA AND WORLD CURRENT AFFAIRS

RRB JUNIOR ENGINEER

1. Which of the following books was banned by all Muslim countries and India?
   (a) The Shame Within
   (b) Discovery of India
   (c) Satanic Verses
   (d) Beyond Expanse
   [RRB JE 2014 GREEN SHIFT]

2. IGMDP, in Indian context, is a
   (a) Management Development Programme
   (b) Monetary Policy
   (c) Missile Programme
   (d) Marketing Policy in Management Studies
   [RRB JE 2014 GREEN SHIFT]

3. Who is the Secretary General of United Nations?
   (a) David Cameron   (b) Stephen Harper
   (c) Jung Hong-Won   (d) Ban Ki-Moon
   [RRB JE 2014 GREEN SHIFT]

4. The human population of globe is approximately
   (a) 500 million   (b) 600 million
   (c) 6 billion   (d) 7 billion
   [RRB JE 2014 GREEN SHIFT]

5. The Hindustan Shipyard Limited is located at
   (a) Goa   (b) Cochin
   (c) Mumbai   (d) Visakhapatnam
   [RRB JE 2014 GREEN SHIFT]

6. Which state is known for its sandalwood carvings?
   (a) Maharashtra   (b) Madhya Pradesh
   (c) Kerala   (d) Karnataka
   [RRB JE 2014 GREEN SHIFT]

7. IPC stands for
   (a) International Peace Code
   (b) Indian Peace Code
   (c) Indian Penal Code
   (d) International Punishment Code
   [RRB JE 2014 GREEN SHIFT]

8. In Sept. 2014 ISRO achieved success in which project?
   (a) Launched Heavy payload vehicle
   (b) Launched geo-stationery satellite
   (c) Launched rocket to mars
   (d) Mars Orbiter successfully entered mars orbit
   [RRB JE 2014 GREEN SHIFT]

9. SAARC countries are from which part of the world?
   (a) South America   (b) South Asia
   (c) South Africa   (d) None of the above
   [RRB JE 2014 GREEN SHIFT]

10. When we open an internet site, we see 'www' ? What is the full form of www ?
    (a) World Wide Web   (b) World Wide Word
    (c) Words Wise Web   (d) None of these
    [RRB JE 2014 RED SHIFT]

11. Who wrote the book "Not Just An Accountant" published recently ?
    (a) P.C. Parakh   (b) Sanjay Baru
    (c) Vinod Rai   (d) Natwar Singh
    [RRB JE 2014 RED SHIFT]

12. Who is the President of China ? (As on 01.11.2014)
    (a) Li Keqiang   (b) Xi Jinping
    (c) Shinzo Abe   (d) Hu Jintao
    [RRB JE 2014 RED SHIFT]

13. Who is the Chief Minister of Tamil Nadu ? (As on 01.11.2014)
    (a) Mr. O. Panneerselvam
    (b) Ms. J. jayalalitha
    (c) Mr. Karunanidhi
    (d) Mr. Dayanidhi Maran
    [RRB JE 2014 RED SHIFT]

14. Who is the Chairperson of National Commission for Women in India ? (As on 01.11.2014)
    (a) Jayanti Patnaik
    (b) Girija Vyas
    (c) Mamta Sharma
    (d) Lalitha Kumaramangalam
    [RRB JE 2014 RED SHIFT]

15. The Headquarters of West Central Railway is located at :
    (a) Jabalpur   (b) Jaipur
    (c) Allahabad   (d) Ahmedabad
    [RRB JE 2014 RED SHIFT]

16. The United Nations Day (U.N.Day) is celebrated every year on :

(a) Dec 26   (b) Nov 14

(c) Sept 5   (d) Oct 24

[RRB JE 2014 RED SHIFT]

17. With the formation of Telangana, how many States are there in our country now ?

(a) 30   (b) 29

(c) 28   (d) 31

[RRB JE 2014 RED SHIFT]

18. Lokpriya Gopinath Bardoloi International Airport is located at :

(a) Jaipur   (b) Bangalore

(c) Guwahati   (d) Hyderabad

[RRB JE 2014 RED SHIFT]

19. The Radcliffe Commission was appointed to

(a) Solve the problem of minorities in India

(b) Give effect to the Independence Bill

(c) Delimit the boundaries between India and Pakistan

(d) Enquire into the riots in East Bengal

[RRB JE 2014 YELLOW SHIFT]

20. Which Country of Africa which was highly affected by disease Ebola has been declared Ebola-free by WHO ?

(a) Sierre Leone   (b) Liberia

(c) Nigeria   (d) Guinea

[RRB JE 2014 YELLOW SHIFT]

21. Who was recently sworn in as President of Afghanistan ?

(a) Abdullah Abdullah

(b) Hamid Karzai

(c) Ashraf Ghani

(d) B. Rabbani

[RRB JE 2014 YELLOW SHIFT]

22. What among the following is planned to be developed under "Sansad Adarsh Gram Yojana" of Central Government.

(a) Village   (b) Smart Cities

(c) River Cleaning   (d) Roads

[RRB JE 2014 YELLOW SHIFT]

23. Popular TV programme "Satyamev Jyate" is anchored by

(a) Salman Khan   (b) Akshay Kumar

(c) Amitabh Bachchan   (d) Aamir Khan

[RRB JE 2014 YELLOW SHIFT]

24. Who is called the Father of Hindi Theatre of India?

(a) Raja Harish Chandra

(b) Dada Sahib Phalke

(c) Bhartendu Harishchandra

(d) Prithvi Raj Kapoor

[RRB JE 2014 YELLOW SHIFT]

25. One region of India with high railway density is from Chhattisgarh to Jharkhand because of

(a) Industrialization

(b) Agricultural produce

(c) Mineral deposits

(d) Large population

[RRB JE 2015 26ᵗʰ AUG 1ˢᵗ SHIFT]

26. In PM Narendra Modi's recent visit to Korea, one important issue of discussion with their president was

(a) building a variety of skills in the youth

(b) building bridges across rivers

(c) developing international understanding

(d) exploring natural resources

[RRB JE 2015 26ᵗʰ AUG 1ˢᵗ SHIFT]

27. About 30% of the 'Great wall of China' has recently been found to have disappeared due to

(a) Just Natural causes

(b) Global Warming

(c) Natural disasters

(d) Natural causes and theft of bricks for building houses

[RRB JE 2015 26ᵗʰ AUG 2ⁿᵈ SHIFT]

28. Who is Dalai Lama and where does he live?

(a) Tibetan Spiritual leader living in Dharamshala, Himachal Pradesh

(b) Buddhist monk living in Tibet

(c) Tibetan rebel fighting the Chinese

(d) Religious leader from Tibet living in Kushalnagar, Coorg

[RRB JE 2015 26ᵗʰ AUG 2ⁿᵈ SHIFT]

29. A maximum of how many partners can a trading business firm have according to Indian Partnership Act?

(a) 20   (b) 15

(c) 10   (d) 5

[RRB JE 2015 26ᵗʰ AUG 3ʳᵈ SHIFT]

30. The latest country to give up its national currency and adopt "euro" as its currency is

(a) Latvia   (b) Lebanon

(c) Brazil   (d) Italy

[RRB JE 2015 26ᵗʰ AUG 3ʳᵈ SHIFT]

31. BCMI project connects Bangladesh, China and India with

(a) Manila   (b) Myanmar

(c) Malaysia   (d) Morocco

[RRB JE 2015 26th AUG 3rd SHIFT]

32. The making of 'maps' is called

(a) Calligraphy   (b) Numismatics

(c) Cartography   (d) Philately

[RRB JE 2015 26th AUG 3rd SHIFT]

33. Which of the following statements is not true?

(a) Amartya Sen is the only economist from India/ of Indian origin to have won the Nobel Prize for Economics

(b) Amartya Sen is also credited with developing the input output method with C.V. Raman

(c) Amartya Sen received the Nobel Prize in 1998 for his contribution to welfare economics

(d) Amartya Sen is also known as a champion of nationalism, secularism

[RRB JE 2015 26th AUG 3rd SHIFT]

34. The country called 'Land of the Rising Sun' is

(a) China   (b) Norway

(c) Japan   (d) Sweden

[RRB JE 2015 27th AUG 1st SHIFT]

35. How many states does India have, and which is the last one to get statehood?

(a) 29 : Telengana

(b) 24 : Delhi

(c) 22 : Lakshadweep

(d) 30 : Uttaranchal

[RRB JE 2015 27th AUG 2nd SHIFT]

36. Select the appropriate information about cartels.

(a) Cartels are group of nations getting together to decide on price & quantity of a commodity.

(b) Every country has many cartels.

(c) Group of individuals can also form cartels.

(d) Cartels can also be formed by a group of industries

[RRB JE 2015 27th AUG 2nd SHIFT]

37. The state capital of Haryana and Punjab is

(a) Ambala

(b) Chandigarh

(c) Chandigarh and Ludhiana respectively

(d) Rohtak and Amritsar respectively

[RRB JE 2015 27th AUG 3rd SHIFT]

38. The economic group called "group of seven" (G7) does not include

(a) Canada   (b) Germany

(c) Japan   (d) Netherlands

[RRB JE 2015 27th AUG 3rd SHIFT]

39. Scientists of which country have invented a new super powerful electron microscope-super STEM 3 That can examine objects a million times smaller than a human hair?

(a) Australia   (b) France

(c) Britain   (d) USA

[RRB JE 2015 28th AUG 1st SHIFT]

40. Currently half of the world's population lives in just six countries. Identify them from the following

(a) India, China, Bangladesh, Pakistan, Brazil, Indonesia

(b) India, China, Bangladesh, South Africa, Pakistan, Indonesia

(c) China, India, United States, Indonesia, Brazil, Pakistan

(d) China, India, Bangladesh, United States, Pakistan, Indonesia

[RRB JE 2015 28th AUG 3rd SHIFT]

41. Who among the following developed the concept of Human Development Index

(a) Amartya Sen   (b) (a)S.Kadir

(c) Alva Myrdal   (d) Mehboob-ul-Haq

[RRB JE 2015 28th AUG 3rd SHIFT]

42. The country, which has decided to lift ban on rice import from india in may 2015, is

(a) USA   (b) China

(c) Brazil   (d) Iran

[RRB JE 2015 28th AUG 3rd SHIFT]

43. Who has been nominated by India to be the first president of $100 billion BRICS bank being set up by the five big emerging economies in may 2015

(a) M.V. Tanksale   (b) K.V. Kamath

(c) O.P. Bhatt   (d) Shikha Sharma

[RRB JE 2015 28th AUG 3rd SHIFT]

44. Which of the following is not correctly matched?

(Country)	**- Capital)**
(a) Indonesia	- Jakarta
(b) Maldive	- Mali
(c) North Korea	- Seoul
(d) Zimbabwe	- Harare

[RRB JE 2015 29th AUG 1st SHIFT]

45. Maharashtra's first Indian Institute of Information Technology (IIIT) will be setup in which city?

(a) Nagpur   (b) Aurangabad

(c) Navi Mumbai   (d) Pune

For the above question, User had specified 'ignore' during keys upload.

[RRB JE 2015 29ᵗʰ AUG 1ˢᵗ SHIFT]

46. Which of the following is the name of the organisation, created to provide full employment and self-reliance to the women folk in India

(a) OECD   (b) ROSCA

(c) USO   (d) SEWA

[RRB JE 2015 29ᵗʰ AUG 2ⁿᵈ SHIFT]

47. Which one of the following committees recommended the abolition of reservation of items for small scale sector in industry

(a) Abid Hussain Committee

(b) Narasimhan Committee

(c) Nayak Committee

(d) Rakesh Mohan Committee

[RRB JE 2015 29ᵗʰ AUG 2ⁿᵈ SHIFT]

48. Shilling is the currency of

(a) Kenya   (b) South Korea

(c) Israel   (d) Ghana

[RRB JE 2015 29ᵗʰ AUG 2ⁿᵈ SHIFT]

49. Which three districts have been included into the national capital Region on June 09, 2015?

(a) Jind, Karnal, Muzaffarnagar

(b) Jind, Karnal, Rohtak

(c) Palwal, Karnal, Muzaffarnagar

(d) Bhiwani, Rohtak, Karnal

[RRB JE 2015 29ᵗʰ AUG 2ⁿᵈ SHIFT]

50. The sixth Petersberg climate dialogue to decide on a negotiation draft for the UN Climate change conference in Paris held in which city on may 18-19, 2015

(a) Tokyo   (b) Shanghai

(c) Kyoto   (d) Berlin

[RRB JE 2015 29ᵗʰ AUG 2ⁿᵈ SHIFT]

51. Which of the following is called 'Gateway of Pacific'

(a) Suez Canal   (b) Panama Canal

(c) Bering Sea   (d) Gulf of Alaska

[RRB JE 2015 29ᵗʰ AUG 3ʳᵈ SHIFT]

52. Match List 1 with List 2 and select the correct answer from the codes given below in the list

List 1 (Steel Plants)

A. Bhilai

B. Rourkela

C. Durgapur

D. Burnpur

List 2 (Countries/Co. Associated)

1. Indian Iron and Steel Co.

2. Russia

3. Germany

4. Great Britain

(a) A-3 B-1 C-4 D-2

(b) A-4 B-3 C-2 D-1

(c) A-2 B-3 C-4 D-1

(d) A-2 B-4 C-1 D-3

[RRB JE 2015 29ᵗʰ AUG 3ʳᵈ SHIFT]

53. Pawan Hans launched helicopter services in June 2015 in

(a) Jammu & Kashmir

(b) Nagaland

(c) Arunachal Pradesh

(d) Sikkim

[RRB JE 2015 29ᵗʰ AUG 3ʳᵈ SHIFT]

54. On 15 June 2015 India signed a motor vehicle agreement with three SAARC nations named

(a) Bangladesh, Srilanka, Maldives

(b) Bangladesh, Nepal, Bhutan

(c) Bangladesh, Pakistan, Srilanka

(d) Nepal, Srilanka, Maldives

[RRB JE 2015 29ᵗʰ AUG 3ʳᵈ SHIFT]

55. The government has approved setting up of how many ITBP outposts along the china border in Arunachala Pradesh and Sikkim?

(a) 30   (b) 35

(c) 42   (d) 45

[RRB JE 2015 30ᵗʰ AUG 3ʳᵈ SHIFT]

56. Mark Rutte, who visited in India in June 2015, is prime minister of

(a) Sweden   (b) Norway

(c) Netherlands   (d) Belarus

[RRB JE 2015 30ᵗʰ AUG 3ʳᵈ SHIFT]

57. Union Cabinet on June 17, 2015 approved housing for all scheme by

(a) 2025   (b) 2022

(c) 2018   (d) 2030

[RRB JE 2015 30ᵗʰ AUG 3ʳᵈ SHIFT]

58. Which city of our country is called Pink city?

(a) Jaipur   (b) Udaipur

(c) Bilaspur   (d) Kanpur

[RRB JE 2015 16ᵗʰ SEP 3ʳᵈ SHIFT]

59. Our national anthem Jana Gana Mana is written by

(a) Iqbal

(b) Rabindra Nath Tagore

(c) Gulzar

(d) Subhadra Kumari Chauhan

[RRB JE 2015 16ᵗʰ SEP 3ʳᵈ SHIFT]

60. Indian flag is called 'Tiranga' as it has three colours. Which colour stands for prosperity and life?

(a) Orange   (b) White

(c) Green   (d) Blue

[RRB JE 2015 16ᵗʰ SEP 3ʳᵈ SHIFT]

61. Out of the following, which day is not declared as a 'National Holiday'?

(a) Republic Day

(b) Netaji Subhash Chandra Bose's birthday

(c) Independence Day

(d) Mahatma Gandhi's birthday

[RRB JE 2015 16ᵗʰ SEP 3ʳᵈ SHIFT]

62. What does National Literacy Mission or NLM aim at

(a) Making all children of the country literate

(b) Imparting functional literacy to adult no - literates

(c) Educating the semi-literates

(d) Giving vocational training to the educated

[RRB JE 2015 16ᵗʰ SEP 3ʳᵈ SHIFT]

RRB SENIOR SECTION ENGINEER

1. Which of the following is NOT an NGO?

(a) Amnesty International

(b) World Watch

(c) PUCL

(d) NHRC

[RRB SSE 2014 GREEN SHIFT]

2. Lufthansa Airlines is from which country'?

(a) USA   (b) Malaysia

(c) Germany   (d) Russia

[RRB SSE 2014 GREEN SHIFT]

3. Raja Ravi Varma was famous for:

(a) His struggle against the British

(b) Music & Singing

(c) Paintings

(d) Hindu reforms

[RRB SSE 2014 GREEN SHIFT]

4. In September 2014, which state was affected by flood?

(a) Karnataka   (b) Madhya Pradesh

(c) Gujarat   (d) Jammu & Kashmir

[RRB SSE 2014 GREEN SHIFT]

5. Who is the Chief Minister of Haryana ? (As on 01.11.2014)

(a) Manohar LaL Khattar

(b) Sushma Swaraj

(c) Om Prakash Chautala

(d) Bhupendra Singh Hooda

[RRB SSE 2014 RED SHIFT]

6. The United Nations Day (U.N. Day) is celebrated every year on :

(a) Oct. 24   (b) Nov. 6

(c) Dec. 26   (d) March 1

[RRB SSE 2014 RED SHIFT]

7. At present, who is the Chief Justice of India ?

(As on 01.11.2014)

(a) Justice H.L. Dattu

(b) Justice R.M. Lodha

(c) Justice P. Sathashivam

(d) Justice A. Kabir

[RRB SSE 2014 RED SHIFT]

8. Identify the Country which was successful in putting a space craft into the Martian Orbit on its maiden attempt ?

(a) Russia   (b) China

(c) India   (d) USA

[RRB SSE 2014 RED SHIFT]

9. Sardar Patel was born on October 31, 1875. His birth anniversary on October 31, this year was observed as :

(a) Rashtriya Ekta Diwas (National Unity Day)

(b) Anti-Corruption Day

(c) Anti Communal Day

(d) Swachh Bharat Day (Clean India Day)

[RRB SSE 2014 RED SHIFT]

10. The Headquarters of South East Central Railway is Located at:

(a) Kolkata   (b) Nagpur

(c) Secunderabad   (d) Bilaspur

[RRB SSE 2014 RED SHIFT]

11. The term MOM was in news in relation to

(a) CAG report   (b) Asian Games

(c) Mangalyaan   (d) Election Commission

[RRB SSE 2014 YELLOW SHIFT]

12. Recently, referendum for independence was held in

(a) Hongkong   (b) Ireland

(c) Scotland   (d) Germany

[RRB SSE 2014 YELLOW SHIFT]

13. Which of the following celebrities was recently appointed as "Brand Ambassador" of Telengana?

(a) Deepika Pallikal   (b) WS Laxman

(c) Saina Nehwal   (d) Sania Mirza

[RRB SSE 2014 YELLOW SHIFT]

14. BKS Iyengar, who died recently, was a world renowned

(a) Yoga Guru   (b) Artist

(c) Folk Singer   (d) Film Director

[RRB SSE 2014 YELLOW SHIFT]

15. Which Country has recently launched "Gandhi Inspired Tourist Attraction Project" ?

(a) England   (b) South Africa

(c) USA   (d) Japan

[RRB SSE 2014 YELLOW SHIFT]

16. Who among the following has designed the logo and slogan of the "Swachch Bharat Abhiyan"

(a) Neelam Bhattacharjee

(b) Anant and Bhagyashree

(c) Uday Kumar

(d) Virman Kohli

[RRB SSE 2014 YELLOW SHIFT]

17. What new feature has been focussed on in the National Horticulture Mission 2005-2006?

(a) Production of vegetable, cultivation seed, integrated Nutrient management, integrated pest management and organic farming.

(b) Insurance for crops like coconut and cashew plantations in Kerala and Northeast for additional income to farmers.

(c) Provision drip irrigation, cold chains and allocating seed production incentives for farmers.

(d) Expansion of area under cultivation of fruits, spices, flowers, medicinal and aromatic plants, cashew and cocoa

[RRB SSE 2015 1st SEP 1st SHIFT]

18. Which countries would benefit from the Kunming to Kolkata high speed rail corridor?

(a) Bangladesh, China, Myanmar, India.

(b) China, Myanmar, Bhutan , India.

(c) India , Vietnam, Myanmar, Bangladesh.

(d) Myanmar, China, Nepal and India.

[RRB SSE 2015 1st SEP 1st SHIFT]

19. What are the main features of the Smart city which has been proposed to meet the needs of the 843 million urban population India by the year 2050,?

(a) More roads, and high speed trains to connect the cities and towns

(b) Support to small towns to modernise and improve their civic amenities

(c) Eco Friendly, satellite cities, efficient quality of urban life.

(d) Improved garbage disposal and urban sanitation measures.

[RRB SSE 2015 1st SEP 1st SHIFT]

20. What is SAKAAR?

(a) Latest technology to track satellites from Earth

(b) An application to view the space images.

(c) An Application to find location of stars

(d) A device to receive data about space probes.

[RRB SSE 2015 1st SEP 1st SHIFT]

21. Which latest development in the area of transport would help enhance trade between Bangladesh, China, Myanmar, India?

(a) Waterway linkage across rivers

(b) Opening of high altitude passes

(c) High speed rail corridor

(d) Rebuilding of the Stillwell road.

[RRB SSE 2015 1st SEP 2nd SHIFT]

22. For the development of which two cities as Smart cities will French collaboration be received ?

(a) Chennai and Chandernagore

(b) Puducheri and Nagpur

(c) Mahe and Puducheri

(d) Diu and Daman.

[RRB SSE 2015 1ˢᵗ SEP 2ⁿᵈ SHIFT]

23. What is the Acronym of the application to view the space images developed by ISRO.

(a) GAG AN   (b) DEEP

(c) VAYUYAN   (d) SAKAAR

[RRB SSE 2015 1ˢᵗ SEP 3ʳᵈ SHIFT]

24. What is the main consideration of China in reviving the New Silk Route?

(a) Countering the IMF policies .

(b) Being equal to the U.S.A as an economic power,

(c) Constitution of an Asian Trade bloc.

(d) Helping neighboring countries develop

[RRB SSE 2015 1ˢᵗ SEP 3ʳᵈ SHIFT]

25. Which of the following issues is a priority for Smart Cities to address?

(a) Removal of old buildings and improvement of areas.

(b) Increase in office space and inclusion of industries.

(c) Increasing ICT connectivity and use for work.

(d) Reduction in traffic congestion and lean energy.

[RRB SSE 2015 1ˢᵗ SEP 3ʳᵈ SHIFT]

26. In which city of India is the Agency for Remote sensing located?

(a) Sriharikota   (b) Hyderabad

(c) Bengaluru   (d) Thiruvananthapuram

[RRB SSE 2015 1ˢᵗ SEP 3ʳᵈ SHIFT]

27. In which four States are there mega solar power generation facilities proposed to be developed?

(a) Manipur, Meghalaya, Jammu & Kashmir, and Bihar

(b) Punjab, Haryana , Delhi, Tamilnadu

(c) Jammu & Kashmir, Gujarat, Tamilnadu, Rajasthan

(d) Nagaland, Mizoram, Manipur, Assam

[RRB SSE 2015 2ⁿᵈ SEP 1ˢᵗ SHIFT]

28. What are the two towns across the Line of Control in Jammu and Kashmir across which trade was opened after 60 years in 2004?

(a) Islamabad and Muzaffarabad

(b) Chakothi and Srinagar

(c) Srinagar and Islamabad

(d) Isalamabad to Chakothi

[RRB SSE 2015 2ⁿᵈ SEP 1ˢᵗ SHIFT]

29. What is the main a m of developing Smart cities?

(a) Increase internet connectivity, make work places near homes, use real time data for supply of goods.

(b) To build satellite towns near existing urban areas, upgrade existing mid-sized cities, and to build settlements along industrial corridors.

(c) Increase the number of industries in cities, widen the employment opportunities.

(d) Decongest the metropolitan cities, develop large city regions with rail connectivity.

[RRB SSE 2015 2ⁿᵈ SEP 1ˢᵗ SHIFT]

30. Along which of the deep sea routes has there been a decline in trade 2005- 2015?

(a) Intra Asian Routes.

(b) Trans Pacific route.

(c) Asia Europ routes

(d) Asia Africa Routes

[RRB SSE 2015 2ⁿᵈ SEP 2ⁿᵈ SHIFT]

31. Which three countries are collaborating with India to build Smart cities ?

(a) France, Singapore and Japan

(b) China, Singapore and Japan

(c) Japan, Russia and France

(d) France, Germany and USA.

[RRB SSE 2015 2ⁿᵈ SEP 2ⁿᵈ SHIFT]

32. Which is the latest area in which ISRO has developed expertise in ?

(a) Flazard Prediction

(b) Distance Education

(c) Radio telecasting

(d) Tele medicine

[RRB SSE 2015 2ⁿᵈ SEP 2ⁿᵈ SHIFT]

33. In which area would there be reduction due the increase in the number of factories, cities and roads and infrastructure?

  (a) Finance   (b) Environment

  (c) Quality of life   (d) Community growth

[RRB SSE 2015 2nd SEP 3rd SHIFT]

34. What does the term BOOT in Solar Energy Production stand for?

  (a) Buy-Own- Operate-Transfer

  (b) Build - Output - Operate- Trade

  (c) Buy-Own - Organise-Transfer

  (d) Build-Own-Output-Transfer

[RRB SSE 2015 2nd SEP 3rd SHIFT]

35. In Which State are the French collaborating to develop smart cities which will resist earthquakes, allow tourism, and build ropeways and metro cable cars ?

  (a) Karnataka

  (b) Himachal Pradesh

  (c) Assam

  (d) Jammu and Kashmir.

[RRB SSE 2015 2nd SEP 3rd SHIFT]

36. Which type of collaboration is India getting from Singapore in building smart cities?

  (a) Expansion of tourism, building fast metros and railways and water purification

  (b) Information Technology management of cities, and efficient sewerage treatment.

  (c) Cleaning the rivers, converting sea water to potable water and expanding facilities of ports.

  (d) Building the broad roads, and increasing the living areas for the urban poor.

[RRB SSE 2015 3rd SEP 1st SHIFT]

37. Which award was given to ISRO for the Lunar Proh Mission in 2009?

  (a) Sir Arthur Clarke Award

  (b) NASA award

  (c) Space Pioneer Award

  (d) IAF World Space Award

[RRB SSE 2015 3rd SEP 1st SHIFT]

38. Which is the main area in which Bihar is likely to grow most in the coming decade?

  (a) Food processing and food products

  (b) Iron and steel Production

  (c) Cotton textile and readymade clothes

  (d) Horticulture and fruit farming

[RRB SSE 2015 3rd SEP 2nd SHIFT]

39. Which setor consumes the least amount of coal today?

  (a) Medium scale industries

  (b) Railways

  (c) Large industries

  (d) Electricity production

[RRB SSE 2015 3rd SEP 2nd SHIFT]

40. Which of these States has shown a higher increase of urban population compared to the National level?

  (a) West Bengal   (b) Uttarpradesh

  (c) Tamilnadu   (d) Maharashtra

[RRB SSE 2015 3rd SEP 3rd SHIFT]

41. Which two cities of Madhya Pradesh have been included in the Delhi Mumbai Industrial Corridor?

  (a) Ujjain and Gwalior

  (b) Bina and Indore

  (c) Neemuch and Shajapur

  (d) Rewa and Bina

[RRB SSE 2015 3rd SEP 3rd SHIFT]

42. What is the main focus of the Prakash Path' policy?

  (a) Use of LED and reduction in energy need in homes

  (b) Switch to renewable energy sources in rural areas

  (c) Diversion of energy needs from industry to agriculture

  (d) Increased use of natural gas for electricity production .

[RRB SSE 2015 3rd SEP 3rd SHIFT]

ANSWER KEY

RRB JUNIOR ENGINEER

1. (c)	**2.** (c)	**3.** (d)	**4.** (d)	**5.** (d)	**6.** (d)	**7.** (c)	**8.** (d)	**9.** (b)	**10.** (a)
11. (c)	**12.** (b)	**13.** (a)	**14.** (d)	**15.** (a)	**16.** (d)	**17.** (b)	**18.** (c)	**19.** (c)	**20.** (c)
21. (c)	**22.** (a)	**23.** (d)	**24.** (a)	**25.** (c)	**26.** (a)	**27.** (d)	**28.** (a)	**29.** (a)	**30.** (a)
31. (b)	**32.** (c)	**33.** (b)	**34.** (c)	**35.** (a)	**36.** (a)	**37.** (b)	**38.** (d)	**39.** (c)	**40.** (c)
41. (d)	**42.** (d)	**43.** (b)	**44.** (c)	**45.** (a)	**46.** (d)	**47.** (a)	**48.** (a)	**49.** (a)	**50.** (d)
51. (b)	**52.** (c)	**53.** (b)	**54.** (b)	**55.** (c)	**56.** (c)	**57.** (b)	**58.** (a)	**59.** (b)	**60.** (c)
61. (b)	**62.** (b)								

RRB SENIOR SECTION ENGINEER

1. (a)	**2.** (c)	**3.** (c)	**4.** (d)	**5.** (a)	**6.** (a)	**7.** (a)	**8.** (c)	**9.** (a)	**10.** (d)
11. (c)	**12.** (c)	**13.** (d)	**14.** (a)	**15.** (b)	**16.** (b)	**17.** (c)	**18.** (a)	**19.** (c)	**20.** (b)
21. (c)	**22.** (b)	**23.** (d)	**24.** (c)	**25.** (d)	**26.** (b)	**27.** (c)	**28.** (a)	**29.** (b)	**30.** (b)
31. (a)	**32.** (d)	**33.** (c)	**34.** (a)	**35.** (b)	**36.** (b)	**37.** (c)	**38.** (a)	**39.** (b)	**40.** (d)
41. (c)	**42.** (a)								

EXPLANATIONS

RRB JUNIOR ENGINEER

1. The Satanic Verses is Salman Rushdie's fourth novel, first published in 1988 and inspired in part by the life of Muhammad, the prophet of Islam. The title refers to the satanic verses, a group of Quranic verses that refer to three Pagan Meccan goddesses Allat, Uzza, and Manat. It was banned by all Muslim countries and India.

2. The Integrated Guided Missile Development Programme was an Indian Ministry of Defence programme for the research and development of the comprehensive range of missiles.

3. Ban Ki-moon is a South Korean politician and diplomat who was the eighth Secretary-General of the United Nations from January 2007 to December 2016. Before becoming Secretary-General, Ban was a career diplomat in South Korea's Ministry of Foreign Affairs and in the United Nations.

4. According to the United Nations, world population reached 7 Billion on October 31, 2011.

5. Hindustan Shipyard Limited (HSL) is a shipyard located in Visakhapatnam on the east coast of India.

6. Karnataka state is known for its sandalwood carvings.

7. The Indian Penal Code is the main criminal code of India. It is a comprehensive code intended to cover all substantive aspects of criminal law.

8. India created history by successfully placing its spacecraft in orbit around Mars, becoming the first country in the world to succeed in such an interplanetary mission in the maiden attempt itself. With the success of "Mangalyaan", India has become the first country in the world to go to Mars in the very first try. European, American and Russian probes have managed to orbit or land on the planet, but after several attempts.

9. The South Asian Association for Regional Cooperation (SAARC) is the regional intergovernmental organization and geopolitical union of nations in South Asia. Its member states include Afghanistan, Bangladesh, Bhutan, India, Nepal, the Maldives, Pakistan and Sri Lanka.

10. The World Wide Web (abbreviated WWW or the Web) is an information space where documents and other web resources are identified by Uniform Resource Locators (URLs), interlinked by hypertext links, and can be accessed via the Internet. English scientist Tim Berners-Lee invented the World Wide Web in 1989.

11. Not just an accountant is an incisive, no-holds-barred account of India's eleventh comptroller and auditor general and a symbol of the anti-corruption movement written by Vinod Rai.

12. As on 01.11.2014, Xi Jinping is the President of China. Xi Jinping is currently serving as General Secretary of the Communist Party of China, President of the People's Republic of China

13. As on 01.11.2014, O. Panneerselvam served as the Chief Minister of Tamil Nadu from 29 September 2014 – 22 May 2015.

14. As on 01.11.2014, Lalitha Kumaramangalam is the Chairperson of National Commission for Women in India.Rekha Sharma has been appointed as the chairperson of the National Commission for Women in 2018.

15. The West Central Railway, one of the 16 zones of the Indian Railways, came into existence on 1 April 2003. It is headquartered at Jabalpur.

16. The UN was officially created when a UN charter was ratified on October 24 that year. United Nations Day was first observed on October 24, 1948. The UN recommended that United Nations Day should be a public holiday in member states since 1971.

17. On 2 June 2014, Telangana area was separated from the northwestern part of Andhra Pradesh as the newly formed 29th state with Hyderabad as its historic permanent capital.

18. Lokpriya Gopinath Bordoloi International Airport (IATA: GAU, ICAO: VEGT), also known as Guwahati International Airport and formerly as 'Borjhar Airport', is the primary international airport of the North-Eastern States of India.

19. The Radcliffe Commission was appointed to delimit the boundaries between India and Pakistan.It was named after its architect, Sir Cyril Radcliffe, who, as the joint chairman of the two boundary commissions for the two provinces.

20. Nigeria was highly affected by disease Ebola, which has been declared Ebola-free by WHO.

21. Ashraf Ghani was recently sworn in as President of Afghanistan.Mohammad Ashraf Ghanî Ahmadzai is the current President of Afghanistan, elected on 21 September 2014.

22. Village is planned to be developed under "Sansad Adarsh Gram Yojana" of Central Government. Sansad Adarsh Gram Yojana is a rural development programme broadly focusing upon the development in the villages which includes social development, cultural development and spread motivation among the people on social mobilization of the village community.

23. Satyamev Jayate (English: Truth Alone Triumphs) is an Indian *television* talk *show* aired on various channels within Star Network along with Doordarshan DD National. Popular TV programme "Satyamev Jayate" is anchored by Aamir Khan.

24. Raja Harish Chandra is called the Father of Hindi Theatre of India. Raja Harishchandra is a 1913 Indian silent film, directed and produced by Dadasaheb Phalke. It is often considered the first full-length Indian feature film.

25. One region of India with high railway density is from Chhattisgarh to Jharkhand because of Mineral deposits

26. In PM Narendra Modi's recent visit to Korea, one important issue of discussion with their president was building a variety of skills in the youth.

27. About 30% of the 'Great wall of China' has recently been found to have disappeared due to Natural causes and theft of bricks for building houses.

28. Dalai Lama is Tibetan Spiritual leader living in Dharamshala, Himachal Pradesh.

29. A maximum of 20 partners can trading business firm according to Indian Partnership Act.

30. The latest country to give up its national currency and adopt "euro" as its currency is Latvia.

31. The Bangladesh–China–India–Myanmar Forum for Regional Cooperation (BCIM) is a sub-regional organisation of Asian nations aimed at greater integration of trade and investment between the four countries.

32. Cartography is the study and practice of making maps. Combining science, aesthetics, and technique, cartography builds on the premise that reality can be modeled in ways that communicate spatial information effectively.

33. Among the given options, Amartya Sen is also credited with developing the input output method with C.V. Raman is not true.

34. Japan is an island country in East Asia. Located in the Pacific Ocean, it lies off the eastern coast of the Asian mainland and stretches from the Sea of Okhotsk in the north to the East China Sea and China in the southwest. The kanji that make up Japan's name mean "sun origin", and it is often called the "Land of the Rising Sun".

35. India is a federal union comprising 29 states and 7 union territories, for a total of 36 entities.Telangana is a state in the south of India.On 2 June 2014, the area was separated from the northwestern part of Andhra Pradesh as the newly formed 29th state with Hyderabad as its historic permanent capital.

36. Among the given options,the are group of nations getting together to decide on price & quantity of a commodity is the appropriate information about cartels.

37. Chandigarh is a city and a union territory in India that serves as the capital of the two neighbouring states of Haryana and Punjab. The city is unique as it is not a part of either of the two states but is governed directly by the Union Government, which administers all such territories in the country.

38. Among the given options, Netherlands was not a member of G7. The Group of Seven (G7) is a group consisting of Canada, France, Germany, Italy, Japan, the United Kingdom, and the United States.

39. Scientists from Britain have invented a new super powerful electron microscope-super STEM 3 that can examine objects a million times smaller than a human hair.

40. Currently half of the world's population lives in just six countries. They are China, India, United States, Indonesia, Brazil, Pakistan

41. Mehboob-ul-Haq developed the concept of Human Development Index. Mahbub ul Haq was the pioneer in developing the concept of human development. He not only articulated the human development philosophy for making economic development plans but he also provided the world with a statistical measure to quantify the indicators of economic growth with human development.

42. Among the given options, Iran has decided to lift ban on rice import from india in may 2015.

43. K.V. Kamath has been nominated by India to be the first president of $100 billion BRICS bank being set up by the five big emerging economies in may 2015.

44. North Korea-Seoul is not correctly matched. The capital of North Korea is Pyongyang.

45. Maharashtra's first Indian Institute of Information Technology (IIIT) will be setup in the city Nagpur.

46. SEWA is a trade union registered in 1972. SEWA main goals are to organise women workers for full employment. It is an organisation of poor, self-employed women workers. These are women who earn a living through their own labour or small businesses. They do not obtain regular salaried employment with welfare benefits like workers in the organised sector. They are the unprotected labour force of our country.

47. Abid Hussain Committee recommended the abolition of reservation of items for small scale sector in industry.

48. Shilling is the currency of Kenya

49. Jind, Karnal, Muzaffarnagar districts have been included into the national capital Region on June 09, 2015.

50. The Sixth Petersberg climate dialogue has decided on a negotiation draft for the UN Climate change conference in Paris held in Berlin city on may 18-19, 2015.

51. The Panama Canal is an artificial 82 km waterway in Panama that connects the Atlantic Ocean with the Pacific Ocean. The canal cuts across the Isthmus of Panama and is a conduit for maritime trade.

52. Among the given options, correct matching is Bhilai-Russia, Rourkela-Germany, Durgapur-Great Britain, Burnpur-Indian Iron and Steel Co.

53. Pawan Hans launched helicopter services in June 2015 in Nagaland.

54. On 15 June 2015 India signed a motor vehicle agreement with three SAARC nations named Bangladesh, Nepal, Bhutan.

55. The government has approved setting up of 42 ITBP outposts along the china border in Arunachal Pradesh and Sikkim.

56. Mark Rutte, who visited in India in June 2015, is prime minister of Netherlands.

57. Union Cabinet on June 17, 2015 approved housing for all scheme by 2022. The Union Cabinet chaired by the Prime Minister, Shri Narendra Modi gave its approval for launch of "Housing for All by 2022" aimed for urban areas with following components/options to States/Union Territories and cities

58. Jaipur is also known as the Pink City, due to the dominant color scheme of its buildings.

59. Our national anthem Jana Gana Mana is written by Rabindranath Tagore.

60. Indian flag is called 'Tiranga' as it has three colours. Green colour stands for prosperity and Life.

61. Among the given options, Netaji Subhash Chandra Bose's birthday is not declared as a National Holiday.

62. National Literacy Mission (NLM) was set up by the Indian government on 5 May, 1988. NLM initially had two flagship programs - "Total Literacy" and "Post literacy". The initiative was revitalized on 30 September, 1999, when they were combined as a single program: Literacy Campaigns and Operation Restoration.

RRB SENIOR SECTION ENGINEER

1. National Human Rights Commission of India (NHRC) is an autonomous public body constituted on 12 October 1993 under the Protection of Human Rights Ordinance of 28 September 1993. It was given a statutory basis by the Protection of Human Rights Act, 1993. Among the given options. NHRC is not a NGO.

2. Deutsche Lufthansa AG, commonly known as Lufthansa, is the largest German airline and, when combined with its subsidiaries, also the largest airline in Europe both in terms of fleet size and passengers carried.

3. Raja Ravi Varma was a celebrated Malayali Indian painter and artist. He is considered among the greatest painters in the history of Indian art for a number of aesthetic and broader social reasons.

4. In September 2014, the Kashmir region suffered disastrous floods across many of its districts caused by torrential rainfall. The Indian state of Jammu and Kashmir, as well as Pakistan occupied Kashmir, Gilgit-Baltistan and Punjab were affected by these floods.

5. Manohar Lal Khattar is the Chief Minister of Haryana. was sworn-in as Chief Minister of Haryana after BJP's win in the Haryana Legislative Assembly election, 2014.

6. The UN was officially created when a UN charter was ratified on October 24 that year. United Nations Day was first observed on October 24, 1948. The UN recommended that United Nations Day should be a public holiday in member states since 1971.

7. As on 01.11.2014, Justice H.L. Dattu is the Chief Justice of India.

8. India was successful in putting a spacecraft into the Martian Orbit on its maiden attempt.

9. Rashtriya Ekta Diwas was introduced by the Government of India and inaugurated by Indian Prime Minister Narendra Modi in 2014. The intent is to pay tribute to Vallabhbhai Patel, who was instrumental in keeping India united.Sardar Patel was born on October 31, 1875. His birth anniversary on October 31 was observed as Rashtriya Ekta Diwas.

10. The South East Central Railway is one of the seventeen railway zones in India. The Headquarters of South East Central Railway is located at Bilaspur.

11. The term MOM was in news in relation to Mangalyaan. Mars Orbiter Mission (MOM) also called Mangalyaan is a space probe orbiting Mars since 24 September 2014. It was launched on 5 November 2013 by the Indian Space Research Organisation (ISRO). It is India's first interplanetary mission.

12. A referendum on Scottish independence from the United Kingdom took place on Thursday 18 September 2014. The referendum question, which voters answered with "Yes" or "No", was "Should Scotland be an independent country?" The "No" side won, with 2,001,926 voting against independence and 1,617,989 voting in favour.

13. Indian tennis star Sania Mirza was appointed 'Brand Ambassador' of Telangana.

14. Bellur Krishnamachar Sundararaja Iyengar, better known as B.K.S. Iyengar, was the founder of the style of yoga known as "Iyengar Yoga" and was considered one of the foremost yoga teachers in the world.

15. South African Tourism has launched a new "Gandhi– Inspired Tourist Attraction" project that identifies 13 places that were seminal in Mohandas Karamchand Gandhi's tenure in the country.

16. Anant Khasbardar of Kolhapur in Maharashtra won the logo design contest while Bhagyasri Sheth of Rajkot in Gujarat emerged successful in the contest for tagline for the logo. Khasbardar was awarded with a cash prize of Rs 50,000 while Bhagyasri got Rs 25,000.

17. Provision drip irrigation, cold chains and allocating seed production incentives for farmers have been focussed on in the National Horticulture Mission 2005-2006.

18. Bangladesh, China, Myanmar, India would benefit from the Kunming to Kolkata high speed rail corridor.

19. Support to small towns to modernise and improve their civic amenities are the main features of the Smart city which has been proposed to meet the needs of the 843 million urban population India by the year 2050.

20. SAKAAR is an application to view the space images.Sakaar is Indian Space Research Organisation (ISRO) Augmented Reality (AR) application designed for Android devices. This AR application shows live camera view on your device to represent physical world and virtual objects/video clips are superimposed on live camera view upon pointing the device's camera at a Trigger Card.

21. High speed rail corridor is the latest development in the area of transport would help enhance trade between Bangladesh, China, Myanmar, India.

22. Chandigarh, Puducherry and Nagpur will be developed as 'Smart Cities' with the help of France which affirmed its commitment to India's ambitious plans for clean and sustainable development.

23. SAKAAR is the Acronym of the application to view the space images developed by ISRO.

24. Constitution of an Asian Trade bloc is the main consideration of China in reviving the New Silk Route. New Silk Route ("NSR" or New Silk Route Partners LLC) is a $1.4-billion private equity firm that invests in private companies in India, Asia, and the Middle East.

25. Reduction in traffic congestion and lean energy is a priority issue for smart cities to address.

26. National Remote Sensing Centre or NRSC, located at Hyderabad is one of the centres of the Indian Space Research Organisation (ISRO), striving to realise the Indian Space Vision, as a key player in Earth Observation Programme and Disaster Management Support programme.

27. Jammu & Kashmir, Gujarat, Tamil Nadu, Rajasthan four States are there mega solar power generation facilities proposed to be developed.

28. Islamabad and Muzaffarabad are the two towns across the Line of Control in Jammu and Kashmir across which trade was opened after 60 years in 2004.

29. The main aim of developing Smart cities is to build satellite towns near existing urban areas, upgrade existing mid-sized cities, and to build settlements along industrial corridors.

30. Along Trans Pacific deep sea route has there been a decline in trade 2005- 2015.

31. France, Singapore and Japan three countries are collaborating with India to build Smart cities.

32. Telemedicine is the latest area in which ISRO has developed expertise in.

33. In the area of quality of life there would be reduction due to the increase in the number of factories, cities and roads and infrastructure.

34. The term BOOT in Solar Energy Production stands for Buy-Own- Operate-Transfer.

35. French collaborating to develop smart cities which will resist earthquakes, allow tourism, and build ropeways and metro cable cars Himachal Pradesh.

36. Information Technology management of cities, and efficient sewerage treatment are getting from Singapore in building smart cities in India.

37. Space Pioneer Award award was given to ISRO for the Lunar Probe Mission in 2009.

38. Food processing and food products are the main area in which Bihar is likely to grow most in the coming decade.

39. Railways sector consumes the least amount of coal today.

40. Maharashtra has shown a higher increase of urban population compared to the National level.

41. Neemuch and Shajapur two cities of Madhya Pradesh have been included in the Delhi Mumbai Industrial Corridor.

42. Use of LED and reduction in energy need in homes is the main focus of the prakash path policy. Prime Minister Narendra Modi described the LED bulb as a "Prakash Path" – "way to light," as he launched a scheme for LED bulb distribution under the domestic efficient lighting programme in Delhi; and a National Programme for LED-based Home and Street Lighting.

Environment & Pollution Control

ENVIRONMENT & POLLUTION CONTROL

RRB JUNIOR ENGINEER

1. What is carbon footprint?
   (a) measure of radioactivity from a fossil
   (b) environmental impact because of used cells and batteries
   (c) total sets of green house gas emissions by organization, individual etc.
   (d) amount of carbon content in the organic compounds
[RRB JE 2014 GREEN SHIFT]

2. Thermochemical decomposition of organic materials at high temperatures, in the absence of oxygen is called
   (a) Pyrolysis   (b) Thermolysis
   (c) Caramelization   (d) Catagenesis
[RRB JE 2014 GREEN SHIFT]

3. Acid rain is caused by presence of which of the following gases in the atmosphere
   (a) Nitrogen and oxygen
   (b) Sulfur dioxide and Nitrogen oxide
   (c) Carbon dioxide and Carbon-mono-oxide
   (d) Ozone and argon
[RRB JE 2014 GREEN SHIFT]

4. One of the main reason for depletion of ozone layer in the Earth's atmosphere is
   (a) Green house gases
   (b) Colloidal impurities
   (c) CFC and halons
   (d) Rockets and satellite launching vehicles
[RRB JE 2014 GREEN SHIFT]

5. What is the value of total hardness acceptable in potable water as per Indian Standards?
   (a) 0.3   (b) 3
   (c) 30   (d) 300
[RRB JE 2014 GREEN SHIFT]

6. Preventing rain water to run-off and its accumulation and deposition for re-use on site is called
   (a) rain water collection
   (b) micro-dams
   (c) micro-accumulation
   (d) rain water harvesting
[RRB JE 2014 GREEN SHIFT]

7. Which of the following is biodegradable pollutant?
   (a) DDT   (b) BHC
   (c) Cotton cloth   (d) Mercury
[RRB JE 2014 RED SHIFT]

8. BOD (Bio Chemical Oxygen Demand) of safe drinking water must be :
   (a) 0   (b) 50 ppm
   (c) 100 ppm   (d) 200 ppm
[RRB JE 2014 RED SHIFT]

9. Large scale deforestation decreases :
   (a) Soil Erosion   (b) Rain fall
   (c) Drought   (d) Global warming
[RRB JE 2014 RED SHIFT]

10. The prescribed per capita water demand for small cities and towns is
   (a) 135 litres per capita per day
   (b) 200 litres per capita per day
   (c) 150 litres per capita per day
   (d) 180 litres per capita per day
[RRB JE 2015 26th AUG 1st SHIFT]

11. In small water supplies such as army troops, private plants and swimming pools, the most common disinfectants used are
   (a) chlorine dioxide and potassium permanganate
   (b) ozone and uv rays
   (c) iodine and bromine
   (d) chlorine and bromine
[RRB JE 2015 26th AUG 1st SHIFT]

12. The air pollution control device, cyclone is used for the removal of
   (a) 100 μm particles
   (b) 10 μm particles
   (c) 50 μm particles
   (d) 2.5 μm particles
[RRB JE 2015 26th AUG 1st SHIFT]

13. The 20 dBA noise level is how many times more powerful than 1 dBA noise level?

(a) 10 times　　(b) 20 times

(c) 100 times　　(d) 200 times

[RRB JE 2015 26ᵗʰ AUG 1ˢᵗ SHIFT]

14. The percentage contribution of CO_2 to green house effect is

(a) 50　　(b) 30

(c) 18　　(d) 10

[RRB JE 2015 26ᵗʰ AUG 1ˢᵗ SHIFT]

15. Per capita water demand is

(a) average amount of daily water required by one person

(b) monthly average amount of daily water required by one person

(c) annual average amount of daily water required by one person

(d) weekly average amount of daily water required by one person

[RRB JE 2015 26ᵗʰ AUG 3ʳᵈ SHIFT]

16. The permissible/desirable drinking water standard for total hardness is

(a) 200 mg/l　　(b) 300 mg/l

(c) 250 mg/l　　(d) 500 mg/l

[RRB JE 2015 26ᵗʰ AUG 3ʳᵈ SHIFT]

17. In BOD_5 determination of sewage, the initial dissolved oxygen is measured to be 8.3 mg/l. However, after 5 day incubation at 20 °C temperature, the dissolved oxygen is found to be 2.3 mg/l. If the dilution factor is 1:60, the BOD_5 of the sewage would be

(a) 360 mg/l

(b) 260 mg/l

(c) cannot be determined

(d) 6.0 mg/l

[RRB JE 2015 26ᵗʰ AUG 3ʳᵈ SHIFT]

18. The suspended solids present in surface water can be determined by

(a) gravimetric test

(b) colourimetric test

(c) titrimetric test

(d) spectrophotometric test

[RRB JE 2015 27ᵗʰ AUG 1ˢᵗ SHIFT]

19. Length to width ratio of rectangular sedimentation tank should be

(a) 3 : 4　　(b) 3 : 1

(c) 4 : 1　　(d) 1 : 5

[RRB JE 2015 27ᵗʰ AUG 1ˢᵗ SHIFT]

20. In PERT analysis, event means

(a) Start or finish of a task

(b) Time taken for a task

(c) End of an activity

(d) Work involved in the project

[RRB JE 2015 27ᵗʰ AUG 2ⁿᵈ SHIFT]

21. The prescribed permissible limit of chloride in drinking water is

(a) 150 mg/l　　(b) 200 mg/l

(c) 250 mg/l　　(d) 300 mg/l

[RRB JE 2015 27ᵗʰ AUG 2ⁿᵈ SHIFT]

22. The water treatment plants are generally designed for a period of

(a) 50 years　　(b) 30 years

(c) 40 years　　(d) 25 years

[RRB JE 2015 27ᵗʰ AUG 2ⁿᵈ SHIFT]

23. The oxides of nitrogen at higher concentration levels affect a fabric resulting its colour to change from

(a) white to black　　(b) white to grey

(c) white to yellow　　(d) white to pink

[RRB JE 2015 27ᵗʰ AUG 2ⁿᵈ SHIFT]

24. Two machines are working in a noisy environment. Machines are jointly producing 75 dBA noise level, however, the background noise level is also 75 dBA. The summation of these two noise levels is

(a) 150 dBA　　(b) 75 dBA

(c) 78 dBA　　(d) 81 dBA

[RRB JE 2015 27ᵗʰ AUG 2ⁿᵈ SHIFT]

25. The unit of sound pressure level. dBA is defined as

(a) summation of measured and reference sound pressure level

(b) ratio of measured to reference sound pressure levels

(c) ratio of measured to reference sound pressure levels in logarithmic scale

(d) product of measured to reference sound pressure levels

[RRB JE 2015 27ᵗʰ AUG 3ʳᵈ SHIFT]

26. The presence of ozone is considered to be boon for humanity in

(a) troposphere　　(b) stratosphere

(c) mesosphere　　(d) ionosphere

[RRB JE 2015 27ᵗʰ AUG 3ʳᵈ SHIFT]

27. The average water consumption for government offices ranges from
    (a) 45 - 90 It per capita per day
    (b) 30 - 60 litres per capita per day
    (c) 75 - 100 litres per capita per day
    (d) 25 - 50 litres per capita per day
    [RRB JE 2015 28th AUG 1st SHIFT]

28. In water treatment, the manual screens are kept inclined at an angle of
    (a) 30 - 50° with the horizontal
    (b) 45 - 60° with the horizontal
    (c) 50 - 70° with the horizontal
    (d) 45 - 80° with the horizontal
    [RRB JE 2015 28th AUG 1st SHIFT]

29. The water distribution networks are normally designed for a period of
    (a) 40 years   (b) 30 years
    (c) 25 years   (d) 50 years
    [RRB JE 2015 28th AUG 1st SHIFT]

30. The summation of 50 dBA noise level with another 50 dBA noise level is equal to
    (a) 100 dBA   (b) 50 dBA
    (c) 53 dBA   (d) 56 dBA
    [RRB JE 2015 28th AUG 1st SHIFT]

31. The source of lead in urban atmosphere is
    (a) bursting of cracker in festive season
    (b) road traffic
    (c) construction works
    (d) small scale industries
    [RRB JE 2015 28th AUG 2nd SHIFT]

32. The noise level decreases with distance following
    (a) inverse square law
    (b) power law
    (c) directly proportional to intensity square
    (d) inversely proportional to intensity
    [RRB JE 2015 28th AUG 2nd SHIFT]

33. The major pollutant that may cause damage to prestigious monument Taj Mahal is
    (a) RSPM along with humidity
    (b) NOx with HC+Ozone
    (c) SOx with humidity
    (d) Organic vapours released from Mathura refinery
    [RRB JE 2015 28th AUG 2nd SHIFT]

34. The ultrafine particles present in surface water are removed through
    (a) coagulation and flocculation
    (b) filtration
    (c) sedimentation
    (d) reverse osmosis
    [RRB JE 2015 28th AUG 3rd SHIFT]

35. The pollutant lead present in the atmosphere may cause
    (a) respiratory disease
    (b) asthmatic disease
    (c) cardiovascular disease
    (d) pulmonary edema
    [RRB JE 2015 28th AUG 3rd SHIFT]

36. A continuous exposure of intense noise for longer duration may cause irreversible damage to the nerves and the inner ear resulting loss of sensitivity at higher frequencies which is called
    (a) acoustic trauma
    (b) annoyance
    (c) temporary threshold shift
    (d) permanent threshold shift
    [RRB JE 2015 28th AUG 3rd SHIFT]

37. The presence of CO_2 may reduce the pH of rain water up to
    (a) 5.6   (b) 4.0
    (c) 6.5   (d) 6.0
    [RRB JE 2015 28th AUG 3rd SHIFT]

38. In BOD_3 determination of sewage, the initial dissolved oxygen is measured to be 8.9 mg/l. however, after 3 day incubation at 27°C temperature, the dissolved oxygen is found to be 1.9 mg/l. If the dilution factor is 1 : 50, the BOD_5 of the sewage would be
    (a) 350 mg/l
    (b) 35 mg/l
    (c) cannot be determined
    (d) 7.0 mg/l
    [RRB JE 2015 29th AUG 1st SHIFT]

39. The continuous exposure of pollutant benzo (a) pyrene may cause
    (a) damage of trachea
    (b) swelling in bronchus
    (c) respiratory system failure
    (d) lung cancer
    [RRB JE 2015 29th AUG 1st SHIFT]

40. The noise level of 10 dB is how many times more powerful than the noise level of 1 dB

(a) 100 times   (b) 10 times

(c) 1000 times   (d) 10000 times

[RRB JE 2015 29ᵗʰ AUG 1ˢᵗ SHIFT]

41. The green house gases as per their decreasing order of effectiveness are

(a) CFC, N_2O, CO_2, CH_4

(b) CO_2, CH_4, N_2O and CFC

(c) CH_4, CO_2, N_2O and CFC

(d) CFC, CH_4, CO_2, and N_2O

[RRB JE 2015 29ᵗʰ AUG 1ˢᵗ SHIFT]

42. In villages, to disinfect the well water, the most common disinfectant used is

(a) silver and bromine

(b) potassium permanganate

(c) iodine solution

(d) chlorine and bromine

[RRB JE 2015 29ᵗʰ AUG 2ⁿᵈ SHIFT]

43. The carbon monoxide causes

(a) coughing and choking problem in respiratory system

(b) broncho-constriction

(c) headache, vomiting, slurring of speech convulsions, coma and death

(d) chronic bronchitis followed by asthma

[RRB JE 2015 29ᵗʰ AUG 2ⁿᵈ SHIFT]

44. An octave band is a frequency band with upper and lower cut-off frequencies having a ratio of

(a) 3   (b) 4

(c) 2   (d) 5

[RRB JE 2015 29ᵗʰ AUG 2ⁿᵈ SHIFT]

45. The CO_2 concentration in the atmosphere was 355 ppm in 1990 that is increasing at a rate of

(a) 1.00 ppm   (b) 1.5 ppm

(c) 0.50 ppm   (d) 0.20 ppm

[RRB JE 2015 29ᵗʰ AUG 2ⁿᵈ SHIFT]

46. The amount of oxygen required to decompose the organics under strong acidic conditions is called

(a) chemical oxygen demand

(b) biochemical oxygen demand

(c) biological oxygen demand

(d) theoretical oxygen demand

[RRB JE 2015 29ᵗʰ AUG 3ʳᵈ SHIFT]

47. The photochemical smog is

(a) criteria pollutant

(b) primary pollutant

(c) secondary pollutant

(d) carcinogenic pollutant

[RRB JE 2015 29ᵗʰ AUG 3ʳᵈ SHIFT]

48. The A - weight scale covers sounds of frequencies from

(a) 800 to 3000 HZ

(b) 500 to 2000 HZ

(c) 1000 to 3000 HZ

(d) 1200 to 4000 HZ

[RRB JE 2015 29ᵗʰ AUG 3ʳᵈ SHIFT]

49. The rain water turned acidic when its pH falls below

(a) 7.0   (b) 6.5

(c) 5.6   (d) 5.2

[RRB JE 2015 29ᵗʰ AUG 3ʳᵈ SHIFT]

50. The hardness that is equivalent to alkalinity is known as

(a) total hardness

(b) carbonate hardness

(c) non carbonate hardness

(d) pseudo hardness

[RRB JE 2015 30ᵗʰ AUG 3ʳᵈ SHIFT]

51. In case of air pollution, the most affected part of vegetation is

(a) stems of vegetation

(b) roots of vegetation

(c) leaves of vegetation

(d) fruits of vegetation

[RRB JE 2015 30ᵗʰ AUG 3ʳᵈ SHIFT]

52. The cut off frequencies of 707 HZ and 1414 HZ define an octave band, whose band centre frequency is

(a) 1050 HZ and would be referred to as the 1050 HZ octave band annoyance

(b) 1000 HZ and would be referred to as the 1000 HZ octave band

(c) 1060.5 HZ and would be referred to as the 1060.5 HZ octave band

(d) 900 HZ and would be referred to as the 900 HZ octave band

[RRB JE 2015 30ᵗʰ AUG 3ʳᵈ SHIFT]

53. In natural rainwater, the formation of carbonic acid takes place due to dissolution of CO_2 in water which causes reduction of pH

(a) 5.6 at 20 °C temperature

(b) 5.6 at 25 °C temperature

(c) 6.5 at 20 °C temperature

(d) 6.6 at 20 °C temperature

[RRB JE 2015 30ᵗʰ AUG 3ʳᵈ SHIFT]

54. The right time of deforestation from plain areas is

(a) summer season

(b) winter season

(c) rainy season

(d) spring season

[RRB JE 2015 16ᵗʰ SEP 3ʳᵈ SHIFT]

55. The taste and odour in surface water may be controlled by

(a) Disinfection of water

(b) Reverse osmosis

(c) Coagulation and flocculation

(d) Aeration

[RRB JE 2015 16ᵗʰ SEP 3ʳᵈ SHIFT]

56. The exposure of high concentration of nitrogen dioxide may cause

(a) coughing, choking and breathing problems

(b) acute bronchitis

(c) irritation to nasal cavity

(d) suffocation and headache

[RRB JE 2015 16ᵗʰ SEP 3ʳᵈ SHIFT]

57. Identify the incorrect statement/option: The psychological effect of noise pollution is

(a) Insomnia as a result of lack of undisturbed and refreshing sleep

(b) emotional disturbance

(c) decrease in heart output and pain in heart

(d) depression and fatigue

[RRB JE 2015 16ᵗʰ SEP 3ʳᵈ SHIFT]

58. Identify the incorrect statement/option: The ill-effect of depletion of the ozone layer is

(a) skin melanoma

(b) damage to the immune system

(c) eye ailment such as cataract

(d) to make the aquatic ecosystem sterile

[RRB JE 2015 16ᵗʰ SEP 3ʳᵈ SHIFT]

RRB SENIOR SECTION ENGINEER

1. In potable water, the dissolved oxygen is stipulated as-

(a) $<6\mu g/l$ (b) $>6\mu g/l$

(c) $<6mg/l$ (d) $>6mg/l$

[RRB SSE 2014 GREEN SHIFT]

2. In reference to Acid rain, what is correct statement

(a) The pH value is below 5.6

(b) It occurs due to presence of sulphuric acid or nitric acid in the atmosphere

(c) Maximum acid is due to strong Carbonic Acid

(d) Acid rain affects ecosystem

[RRB SSE 2014 YELLOW SHIFT]

3. The working principle of turbidimeter is based on

(a) reflection of light

(b) refraction of light

(c) scattering of light

(d) adsorption of light

[RRB SSE 2015 1ˢᵗ SEP 1ˢᵗ SHIFT]

4. The major source of carcinogenic hydrocarbon, benzo (α) pyrene present in urban atmosphere is

(a) construction activities

(b) road traffic

(c) bursting of crackers

(d) domestic burning

[RRB SSE 2015 1ˢᵗ SEP 1ˢᵗ SHIFT]

5. The prescribed permissible noise level, Leq for commercial area at day time is

(a) 75 dBA   (b) 50 dBA

(c) 55 dBA   (d) 65 dBA

[RRB SSE 2015 1ˢᵗ SEP 1ˢᵗ SHIFT]

6. The global warming is caused by green house gases, which are

(a) CO, N_2O, CH_4 and CFC

(b) CO_2, NO_2, CH_4 and H_2O

(c) CO_2, N_2O, CH_4 and H_2O

(d) CO_2, NO_2, CH_4 and CFC

[RRB SSE 2015 1ˢᵗ SEP 1ˢᵗ SHIFT]

7. Which of the following roles fly ash does not play in concrete

(a) Improving the workability

(b) Accelerating the strength gain

(c) Delaying the setting time of concrete

(d) Helps in long-term strength gain

[RRB SSE 2015 1ˢᵗ SEP 2ⁿᵈ SHIFT]

8. One turbidity unit NTU is equal to

   (a) 1.0 mg/l farmazin   (b) 1.0 meq/l SiO_2

   (c) 1.0 mg/l SiO_2 (d) 1.0 meq/l kaolin

                    [RRB SSE 2015 1ˢᵗ SEP 2ⁿᵈ SHIFT]

9. The prescribed permissible noise level, Leq for residential area at day time is

   (a) 65 dBA   (b) 45 dBA

   (c) 50 dBA   (d) 55 dBA

                    [RRB SSE 2015 1ˢᵗ SEP 2ⁿᵈ SHIFT]

10. Which of the following is not used as a supplementary cementations material?

   (a) Fly ash   (b) Gypsum

   (c) Rice husk ash   (d) Silica fume

                    [RRB SSE 2015 1ˢᵗ SEP 3ʳᵈ SHIFT]

11. According to IS 456, if the maximum aggregate size is increased from 20 mm to 40 mm, the minimum cement content requirement changes (in kg/cum) by

   (a) –20   (b) 20

   (c) –30   (d) 30

                    [RRB SSE 2015 1ˢᵗ SEP 3ʳᵈ SHIFT]

12. The turbidity in surface water is due to presence of

   (a) dissolved organics

   (b) colloidal material

   (c) dissolved in organics

   (d) dissolved colors

                    [RRB SSE 2015 1ˢᵗ SEP 3ʳᵈ SHIFT]

13. The prescribed permissible noise level, for residential area at night time is

   (a) 45 dBA   (b) 50 dBA

   (c) 40 dBA   (d) 55 dBA

                    [RRB SSE 2015 1ˢᵗ SEP 3ʳᵈ SHIFT]

14. The continuous exposure of high concentration of reparable suspended particulate matter may cause

   (a) eye irritation

   (b) kidney damage

   (c) failure of respiratory system

   (d) cardiac disease

                    [RRB SSE 2015 2ⁿᵈ SEP 1ˢᵗ SHIFT]

15. The prescribed permissible noise level, Leq for commercial area at night time is

   (a) 45 dBA   (b) 65 dBA

   (c) 50 dBA   (d) 55 dBA

                    [RRB SSE 2015 2ⁿᵈ SEP 1ˢᵗ SHIFT]

16. The pH of acid rain should always be less than

   (a) 5.6 even after precipitation

   (b) 7.0 after precipitation

   (c) 6.5 after precipitation

   (d) 4.2 after precipitation

                    [RRB SSE 2015 2ⁿᵈ SEP 1ˢᵗ SHIFT]

17. The exposure of gaseous pollutant sulphur dioxide may cause

   (a) bronchitis and pulmonary emphysema

   (b) lungs failure and kidney damage

   (c) gastrointestinal problem

   (d) the irritation in alveoli of the lungs

                    [RRB SSE 2015 2ⁿᵈ SEP 2ⁿᵈ SHIFT]

18. The machine 'A' and machine 'B' produce equal noise levels, i.e., 60 dBA each. The summation of these two noise levels is

   (a) 100 dBA   (b) 66 dBA

   (c) 63 dBA   (d) 55 dBA

                    [RRB SSE 2015 2ⁿᵈ SEP 2ⁿᵈ SHIFT]

19. In stratosphere, the temperature increases with altitude due to presence of

   (a) radicals   (b) chlorofluorocarbons

   (c) HCFCs   (d) Ozone

                    [RRB SSE 2015 2ⁿᵈ SEP 2ⁿᵈ SHIFT]

20. Nuclear density guage can be used for all the following purposes, except

   (a) Moisture content

   (b) Wet density

   (c) Dry density

   (d) Standard penetration reading

                    [RRB SSE 2015 2ⁿᵈ SEP 3ʳᵈ SHIFT]

21. A water borne disease poliomyelitis is caused by

   (a) viruses   (b) protozoa

   (c) bacteria   (d) helminthes

                    [RRB SSE 2015 2ⁿᵈ SEP 3ʳᵈ SHIFT]

22. In potable water, the permissible limit of nitrate nitrogen is

   (a) 10 mg/l   (b) 25 mg/l

   (c) 40 mg/l   (d) 15 mg/l

                    [RRB SSE 2015 2ⁿᵈ SEP 3ʳᵈ SHIFT]

23. Carbon monoxide forms carboxyhemoglobin in human blood that may cause

   (a) increased oxygen carrying capacity

   (b) decreased oxygen carrying capacity

   (c) damage in central nervous system

   (d) damage in circulatory system

                    [RRB SSE 2015 2ⁿᵈ SEP 3ʳᵈ SHIFT]

24. Two machines are working in a noisy environment and jointly product 55 dBA noise level. If the environmental noise level is also 55 dBA, the summation of noise levels is
(a) 110 dBA   (b) 56 dBA
(c) 55 dBA   (d) 58 dBA
[RRB SSE 2015 2nd SEP 3rd SHIFT]

25. The average concentration of ozone present in the stratosphere is approximately
(a) 5 ppm   (b) 0.05 ppm
(c) 10 ppm   (d) 15 ppm
[RRB SSE 2015 2nd SEP 3rd SHIFT]

26. The total coliform bacteria are reported as most probable number (MPN) per
(a) 10 ml of water   (b) 1000 ml of water
(c) 100 ml of water   (d) 1ml of water
[RRB SSE 2015 3rd SEP 1st SHIFT]

27. The anthropogenic sources of air pollution in well planned city is
(a) construction activities, road traffics, rail traffic, fugitive emissions
(b) construction activities, road traffic, domestic burning
(c) construction activities, road traffics, bursting of crackers, dust storms
(d) construction activities, road traffics, domestic burning, industrial emissions
[RRB SSE 2015 3rd SEP 1st SHIFT]

28. When the measured and standard reference pressure level becomes equal, the sound pressure level (SPL) is equivalent to
(a) 1 dBA   (b) 10 dBA
(c) 0 dBA   (d) 1.012 dBA
[RRB SSE 2015 3rd SEP 1st SHIFT]

29. The major green house gases contributing in global warming are
(a) carbon dioxide, nitrous oxide, methane and water vapours
(b) carbon dioxide, sulphur dioxide, water vapours and chlorofluorocarbons
(c) carbon monoxide, nitrous oxide, methane and, hydro-chlorofluorocarbons
(d) carbon dioxide, nitrogen dioxide, water vapours , methane and ozone
[RRB SSE 2015 3rd SEP 1st SHIFT]

30. The desirable amount of fluoride ions in potable waters for optimal dental health is:
(a) 1.5 mg/l   (b) 1.0 mg/l
(c) 0.5 mg/l   (d) 0.05 mg/l
[RRB SSE 2015 3rd SEP 2nd SHIFT]

31. Which of the following is not considered as secondary pollutant?
(a) Photochemical smog
(b) Peroxy acetyl nitrate
(c) Acid mist
(d) Carbon monoxide
[RRB SSE 2015 3rd SEP 2nd SHIFT]

32. In the statistical distribution of noise levels, the back ground noise level is represented by:
(a) L_{90} (b) L_{50}
(c) L_{10} (d) L_1
[RRB SSE 2015 3rd SEP 2nd SHIFT]

33. Acid rain is caused due to formation of:
(a) sulphuric acid and carbonic acid in the atmosphere
(b) sulphuric acid and nitric acid in the atmosphere
(c) nitric acid and carbonic acid in the atmosphere
(d) sulphuric acid, nitric acid and carbonic acid in the atmosphere
[RRB SSE 2015 3rd SEP 2nd SHIFT]

34. Chlorofluorocarbons are
(a) bad absorber of infrared radiations
(b) good reflector of ultraviolet radiations
(c) good absorber of ultraviolet radiations
(d) good absorber of infrared radiations
[RRB SSE 2015 3rd SEP 3rd SHIFT]

35. If the statistical distribution of noise levels in terms of $L_1, L_{10}, L_{50}, L_{90}$ are given , the equivalent noise levels, Leq can be estimated as
(a) $L_{eq} = L_{90} + (L_{10} - L_{60})^2/60$
(b) $L_{eq} = L_{50} + (L_{10} - L_{90})^2/60$
(c) $L_{eq} - L_{10} + (L_{10} - L_{90})^2/60$
(d) $L_{eq} = L_{60} + (L_{10} - L_{90})^2/60$
[RRB SSE 2015 3rd SEP 3rd SHIFT]

36. The glasses of artificial green houses are
(a) transparent to incoming solar radiation but opaque to outgoing infrared radiation
(b) opaque to incoming infrared radiation but transparent to outgoing infrared radiation
(c) opaque to incoming solar radiation as well as outgoing infrared radiation
(d) opaque to incoming solar radiation but transparent to outgoing infrared radiation
[RRB SSE 2015 3rd SEP 3rd SHIFT]

ANSWER KEY

RRB JUNIOR ENGINEER

1. (c)	**2.** (a)	**3.** (b)	**4.** (c)	**5.** (d)	**6.** (d)	**7.** (c)	**8.** (a)	**9.** (b)	**10.** (a)
11. (c)	**12.** (b)	**13.** (c)	**14.** (a)	**15.** (c)	**16.** (b)	**17.** (c)	**18.** (a)	**19.** (b)	**20.** (a)
21. (c)	**22.** (b)	**23.** (c)	**24.** (c)	**25.** (c)	**26.** (b)	**27.** (a)	**28.** (b)	**29.** (b)	**30.** (c)
31. (b)	**32.** (a)	**33.** (c)	**34.** (b)	**35.** (c)	**36.** (d)	**37.** (a)	**38.** (c)	**39.** (d)	**40.** (b)
41. (a)	**42.** (b)	**43.** (c)	**44.** (c)	**45.** (b)	**46.** (a)	**47.** (c)	**48.** (a)	**49.** (c)	**50.** (*)
51. (c)	**52.** (a)	**53.** (a)	**54.** (b)	**55.** (d)	**56.** (b)	**57.** (c)	**58.** (a)		

RRB SENIOR SECTION ENGINEER

1. (a)	**2.** (b)	**3.** (c)	**4.** (b)	**5.** (d)	**6.** (c)	**7.** (b)	**8.** (c)	**9.** (d)	**10.** (b)
11. (c)	**12.** (b)	**13.** (a)	**14.** (c)	**15.** (d)	**16.** (a)	**17.** (a)	**18.** (c)	**19.** (d)	**20.** (d)
21. (a)	**22.** (a)	**23.** (b)	**24.** (d)	**25.** (c)	**26.** (c)	**27.** (b)	**28.** (c)	**29.** (a)	**30.** (b)
31. (d)	**32.** (a)	**33.** (b)	**34.** (c)	**35.** (b)	**36.** (a)				

EXPLANATIONS

RRB JUNIOR ENGINEER

1. A carbon footprint is historically defined as the total emissions caused by an individual, event, organisation, or product, expressed as carbon dioxide equivalent.

2. Pyrolysis is the thermal decomposition of materials at elevated temperatures in an inert atmosphere. It involves the change of chemical composition and is irreversible. The word is coined from the Greek-derived elements pyro "fire" and lysis "separating".

3. Sox and NOx are responsible for acid rain.

4. Chlorofluorocarbons (CFCs) and other halogenated **ozone depleting** substances (ODS) are mainly responsible for man-made chemical **ozone depletion**. The total amount of effective halogens (chlorine and bromine) in the stratosphere can be calculated and are known as the equivalent effective stratospheric chlorine (EESC).

5. 300 mg/l is the acceptable standard.

6. **Rainwater** harvesting is **the accumulation** and storage of **rainwater** for **reuse** on-**site**, rather than allowing it to **run off**.

7. Biodegradable pollutants: Those pollutants which can be broken down into simpler, harmless, substances in nature in due course of time (by the action of micro-organisms like certain bacteria) are called biodegradable pollutants. Cotton cloth is biodegradable pollutant.

8. A **water** supply with a **BOD** level of 1-2 ppm is considered to be very clean.

   A **water** supply with a **BOD** level of 3-5 ppm is considered moderately **clean**. In **water** with a **BOD** level of 6-9 ppm, the **water** is considered somewhat polluted because there is usually organic matter present and bacteria are decomposing this waste.

9. Large scale deforestation decreases rain fall. **Drop in rainfall** occurs because **deforestation reduces** the natural recycling of moisture from soils, through vegetation, and into the atmosphere, from where it returns as **rainfall**.

10. The prescribed per capita water demand for small cities and towns is 135 litres per capita per day.

11. The most common disinfectants are iodine and bromine. **Bromine** does not oxidize ammonia or other nitrogen substances. Hypobromous acid reacts with sunlight. When the pH value is between 7 and 8,5 dibromoamine is **the most common** form of **bromine**. Dibromoamine is almost as effective as free chlorine in killing microorganisms.

12. The most frequently used **Air Pollution Control Devices** for controlling **air pollution** emissions are Fabric filters (also called bag houses),**Cyclones** (or Multi **cyclones**), Wet scrubbers, Electrostatic Precipitator. Cyclone removes 10 mm particles.

13. On the **decibel** scale, the smallest audible **sound** (near total silence) is 1 dB. A **sound** 10 **times more powerful** is 10 dB. A **sound** 100 **times more powerful than** near total silence is **20** dB. A **sound** 1,000 **times more powerful than** near total silence is 30 dB.

14. They estimated that water vapor accounts for about 50% of Earth's greenhouse effect, with clouds contributing 25%, carbon dioxide 20%, and the minor greenhouse gases and aerosols accounting for the remaining 5%. In the study, the reference **model** atmosphere is for 1980 conditions.

15. Generally, it **means** the average amount of **water** each person in a particular area uses on a daily basis, expressed as "gallons **per capita per** day."

16. 300 mg/l is the permissible limit of the hardness.

17. Cannot be determined.

18. **Gravimetric analysis** is a technique through which the amount of an analyte (the ion being analyzed) can be determined through the measurement of mass. **Gravimetric** analyses depend on comparing the masses of two compounds containing the analyte.

19. A typical long **rectangular** tank have **length** ranging from 2 to 4 times their **width**.

20. *PERT event*: a point that marks the start or completion of one or more activities. It consumes no time and uses no resources. When it marks the completion of one or more activities, it is not "reached" (does not occur) until *all* of the activities leading to that event have been completed.

21. The prescribed permissible limit of chloride in drinking water is 250 mg/l.

22. Water treatment plants are generally designed for 30 years.

23. Fabric color changes from white to yellow.

24. How do you add noise levels?

    Sound pressure levels are expressed in decibels, which is a logarithmic scale. Therefore we cannot simply arithmetically add noise levels.

    For example, 35 dB plus 35 dB does not equal 70 dB.

    To add two or more noise levels, if the difference between the highest and next highest noise level is:

    0–1 dB then add 3 dB to the higher level to give the total noise level

    2–3 dB then add 2 dB to the higher level to give the total noise level

    4–9 dB then add 1 dB to the higher level to give the total noise level

    10 dB and over, then the noise level is unchanged (i.e. the higher level is the total level)

    So, 75 dB plus 75 dB equals 78 dB.

25. A-weighted decibels, abbreviated **dBA**, or **dBa**, or dB(a), are an expression of the relative loudness of sounds in air as perceived by the human ear. In the A-weighted system, the decibel values of sounds at low frequencies are reduced, compared with unweighted decibels, in which no correction is made for audio frequency.

26. The presence of ozone is considered to be boon for humanity in stratosphere.

28. The manual screens are kept inclined at an angle of 45-60 degrees with the horizontal.

29. The water distribution networks are normally designed for a period of 30 years.

30. The summation of 50 dBA noise level with another 50 dBA noise level is equal to 53 dBA.

31. Source of lead is traffic. Lead is a pollutant which comes out of vehicle emissions.

32. Inverse Square law:-

    For a spherical wave of a point source we get: The **sound** pressure **level** (SPL) **decreases** with doubling of **distance** by (")6 **dB**. The **sound** pressure **level** (SPL) **decreases** with doubling of **distance** only by (")3 **dB**.

33. The major pollutant that may cause damage to prestigious monument Taj Mahal is S)x with humidity.

34. The ultrafine particles present in surface water are removed through filtration.

35. High amounts of lead can be dangerous for small children and can lead to lower IQs and kidney problems. For adults, exposure to lead can increase the chance of having heart attacks or strokes.

36. A **permanent threshold shift** is a **permanent shift** in the auditory **threshold**. It may occur suddenly or develop gradually over time. A **permanent threshold shift** results in **permanent** hearing loss.

37. The presence of CO_2 may reduce the pH of rain water up to 5.6.

38. can not be determined.

39. BaP is stable and **can** remain (and travel) in the environment for a long period of time - it is a **Persistent** Organic **Pollutant** (POP). Releases of BaP therefore **cause** concern at a global environmental level as well as on a local scale. Inhalation of **benzo(a)pyrene may cause** respiratory tract irritation.

40. 10 times

41. $CFC < N_2O < CO_2 < CH_4$

42. In villages, to disinfect the well water, the most common disinfectant used is potassium permanganate

45. Increasing at the rate of 1.5 ppm.

46. Chemical oxygen demand (COD) is a measure of the capacity of water to consume **oxygen** during the decomposition of organic matter and the oxidation of inorganic **chemicals** such as Ammonia and nitrite.

47. Products like ozone, aldehydes, and peroxyacetyl nitrates are called **secondary** pollutants. The mixture of these primary and **secondary** pollutants forms **photochemical smog**. Both the primary and **secondary** pollutants in **photochemical smog** are highly reactive.

48. The 'A' weighting filter **covers** the full **frequency** range of 20 Hz to 20 kHz.

49. Normal, clean rain has a pH value of **between 5.0 and 5.5**, which is slightly acidic. However, when rain combines with sulfur dioxide or nitrogen oxides—produced from power plants and automobiles—the rain becomes much more acidic. Typical acid rain has a pH value of 4.0.

51. Leaves of vegetation are most affected by air pollution.

54. Winter season is the right time for deforestation.

55. Aeration is a practical solution for taste and odor control when the problem is caused by volatile compounds, such as hydrogen sulfide.

56. Higher levels can cause trouble breathing, collapse and even death. Repeated exposure to high levels may lead to permanent lung damage. Nitrogen Dioxide is a **dark** brown to yellowish liquid or reddish-brown gas with a strong odor.

57. There is no effect of noise pollution on heart output. Change in heart output is not psychological effect of noise pollution.

58. Effects of **ozone layer depletion**:

Skin Cancer: exposure to UV rays from sun can lead to increased risk for developing of several types of skin cancers. Malignant melanoma, basal and squamous cell carcinoma are the most common cancers caused by exposure to UV rays. Eye Damage: UV rays are **harmful** for our eyes too.

RRB SENIOR SECTION ENGINEER

1. $<6 \mu g/l$

2. pH value is generally less than 4 and it occurs due to presence of sulphuric and nitric acid.

3. The Turbidity meter uses the principle of Nephelometry. As light of a known intensity is passed through a sample some of the light will be scattered by particles in the sample. A detector is placed at 90° to the sample to collect the scattered light. The intensity of the scattered light is compared to that of the source. This value is reported as a Nephelometric Turbidity Unit, or NTU. The meter is calibrated with Formazine standards of a known NTU.

4. Road traffic is the major source of carcinogenic hydrocarbon present in urban atmosphere.

5. The prescribed permissible noise level, Leq for commercial area at day time is 65 dBA.

According to Central Pollution Control Board,

Area Code	Category of Area	Limits in dB(A), Leq	
		Day time	Night time
A	Industrial area	75	70
B	Commercial area	65	55
C	Residential area	55	45
D	Silence Zone	50	40

6. Green house gases are the gas mixed in the atmosphere that <u>absorbs the infrared radiation emitted by the earth's surface</u>.

We are not accustomed to these gases because neither nitrogen nor oxygen, the two most abundant gases of the atmosphere (78% and 21%, respectively), that many of us have heard of, have this ability to intercept infrared radiation.

7. Fly ash never improves strength of concrete.

The advantages of using fly ash far outweigh the disadvantages. The most important benefit is reduced permeability to water and aggressive chemicals. Properly cured concrete made with fly ash creates a denser product because the size of the pores are reduced.

8. One turbidity unit NTU is equal to 1.0 mg/l SiO2.

9. The prescribed permissible noise level, Leq is 55 dBA.

According to Central Pollution Control Board,

Area Code	Category of Area	Limits in dB(A), Leq	
		Day time	Night time
A	Industrial area	75	70
B	Commercial area	65	55
C	Residential area	55	45
D	Silence Zone	50	40

10. Gypsum is not used as a supplementary cementations material.

12. Turbidity in surface water is due to colloidal material.

13. The prescribed permissible noise level, Leq is 45 dBA.

According to Central Pollution Control Board,

Area Code	Category of Area	Limits in dB(A), Leq	
		Day time	Night time
A	Industrial area	75	70
B	Commercial area	65	55
C	Residential area	55	45
D	Silence Zone	50	40

14. Continuous exposure to suspended particles are harmful to the lungs and can cause failure of respiratory system.

15. The prescribed permissible noise level, Leq for commercial area at night time is 55 dBA.

According to Central Pollution Control Board,

Area Code	Category of Area	Limits in dB(A), Leq	
		Day time	Night time
A	Industrial area	75	70
B	Commercial area	65	55
C	Residential area	55	45
D	Silence Zone	50	40

16. pH of acid rain should always be less than 5.6 even after precipitation.

17. The exposure of gaseous pollutant sulphur dioxide may cause bronchitis and pulmonary emphysema.

19. In the stratosphere, temperature increases with altitude. The reason is that the direct heat source for the stratosphere is the Sun. A layer of ozone molecules absorbs solar radiation, which heats the stratosphere. The amount of ozone present in the ozone layer is tiny, only a few molecules per million air molecules.

20. Nuclear density gauge can be used for all the following purposes except standard penetration reading.

21. A virus that may cause paralysis and is easily preventable by the polio vaccine.

22. The permissible limit of nitrate nitrogen in potable water is 10 mg/l .

25. The average concentration of ozone present in the stratosphere is approximately 10 ppm.

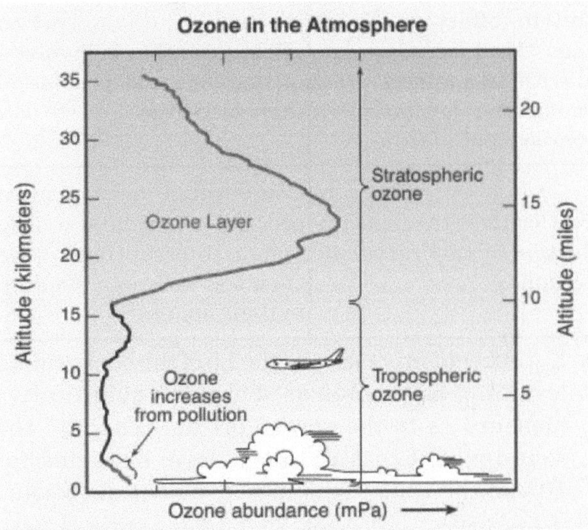

26. Total or fecal coliform bacteria are reported as most probable number per 100 mL

27. Anthropogenic sources of air pollution in well planned city are construction activities, road traffics, and domestic burning

28. When the measured and standard reference pressure level becomes equal, the sound pressure level (SPL) is equivalent to 0 dBA

29. The major green house gases contributing in global warming are carbon dioxide , nitrous oxide,methane and water vapor.

30. The desirable amount of flue le ions in potable waters for optimal dental health is 1.0 mg/l

31. **Primary Pollutants**

Versus

Secondary Pollutants

Air pollutant emitted direclty from a source into the atmosphere.	Air pollutant formed in the atmosphere as a result of the chemical or physical interactions between the primary pollutants themselves or between the primary pollutants and other atmospheric components.

Sulfure dioxide (SO_2) carbon monoxide (CO_2),nitrogen oxides (No_x), and particulate matter (PM).	Photochemical oxidants (ozone, nitrogen dioxide, sulfur trioxide) and secondary particular matter.
Chemical reactants characterized with a direct pollution effect on living beings and ecosystems, and with an indirect effect through the formation of secondary pollutants.	Chemical products, highly reactive when photoactivation is involved in the chemical process of their formation
Direct control through the reduction of anthropogenic emissions.	Complicated control process: understanding and interrupting the chemical reactions leading to their generation.

32. L_{90} is frequently taken as the Lp of the background level. L_{10}-L_{90} is often used to give a quantitative measure as to the spread or "how choppy" the sound was. L_{10} is the noise level exceeded for 10% of the time of the measurement duration.

33. Scientists have discovered that air pollution from burning of fossil fuels is the major cause of acid rain. The main chemicals in air pollution that create acid rain are sulfur dioxide (SO_2) and nitrogen (NOx). Acid rain usually forms high in the clouds where sulfur dioxide and nitrogen oxides react with water, oxygen, and oxidants. this mixture forms a mild solution of sulfuric acid and nitric acid. Sunlight increases the rate of most of these reactions. Rainwater, snow, fog, and other forms of precipitation containing those mild solutions of sulfuric and nitric acids fall to earth as acid rain.

34. CFCs are highly stable, essentially inert chemicals in the troposphere, with correspondingly long residence times. For example, CFC-11 has an atmospheric lifetime of 60 years, CFC-12 120 years, CFC-113 90 years, and CFC-114 200 years. CFC are good absorber of UV Radiation which in turn are harmful for the environment.

35. Noise from roadways changes from moment to moment, but it is possible to describe the noise energy over time in terms of its "equivalent level". The Leq is a single level that has the same sound energy as the fluctuating level over a stated time period. $Leq = L_{50} + [(L_{10} - L_{90})^2/60]$

36. The glasses of artificial green houses are transparent to incoming solar radiation but opaque to outgoing infrared radiation. Due to which , temperature increases due to green house effect.

BASICS OF COMPUTERS AND APPLICATIONS

RRB JUNIOR ENGINEER

1. In the context of Information Technology, OCR means
(a) Optical Character Recognition
(b) Octagonal Cyclic Recharge
(c) Octadecimal Cyclic Regeneration
(d) Optical Character Regeneration
[RRB JE 2014 GREEN SHIFT]

2. In Boolean algebra $\left(\overline{1+1\cdot\overline{0+0}}\right) = ?$
(a) 0   (b) 1
(c) 2   (d) –1
[RRB JE 2014 GREEN SHIFT]

3. Which of the following is not an I/O device of the computer?
(a) Keyboard   (b) Joy stick
(c) ALU   (d) Printer
[RRB JE 2014 GREEN SHIFT]

4. What is floating point with reference to computers?
(a) It is a software subroutine around which other subroutines are built
(b) It is a representation of real numbers to facilitate computing
(c) It is the main algebraic formula of the software
(d) It is the voltage point given to various operating units of the computer
[RRB JE 2014 GREEN SHIFT]

5. A system of digital rules for exchange and processing of data between various devices is called
(a) software programme
(b) algorithm
(c) protocol
(d) information processing
[RRB JE 2014 GREEN SHIFT]

6. A theoretical computer with infinite type and memory, used in analysis of problems of computation, is called
(a) Tape calculator   (b) Babbage machine
(c) Turing machine   (d) Theoretical machine
[RRB JE 2014 GREEN SHIFT]

7. ASCII coding allocated binary codes to English alphabets and symbols for computer use. More recently a new standard has been adopted which allocates code to almost all the languages of the world and also to symbols covering more than a lakh characters. The new standard is called
(a) CCS
(b) Unicode
(c) Standard CCS code
(d) Universal CCS code
[RRB JE 2014 GREEN SHIFT]

8. For using passwords on the Internet a software is used so that the password is not intercepted easily. It is called
(a) Coding   (b) Malware
(c) Virus   (d) Encryption
[RRB JE 2014 GREEN SHIFT]

9. A software, coding of which is available freely on Internet and is open for users for further use and improvement and which is generally developed in a collaborative manner is called
(a) open source software
(b) unlicensed software
(c) free software
(d) community software
[RRB JE 2014 GREEN SHIFT]

10. Which of the following are machine level languages?
(a) C++   (b) Java
(c) Python   (d) None of these
[RRB JE 2014 GREEN SHIFT]

11. Which of the following statements is incorrect?
(a) Microsoft windows is GUI
(b) Linux is GUI
(c) More than 5000 kB data can be stored in a DVD
(d) A 1 TB flash drive can store 2 million files each of size 1 MB
[RRB JE 2014 GREEN SHIFT]

12. The terms ALU, CPU, I/O devices pertain to
 (a) computers
 (b) environmental engineering
 (c) diesel engine
 (d) engineering drawing and orthogonal projections
[RRB JE 2014 GREEN SHIFT]

13. In a computing device 'MHz' is mentioned in the specifications. It refers to
 (a) size of memory
 (b) speed of computation
 (c) clock speed
 (d) none of the above
[RRB JE 2014 GREEN SHIFT]

14. The value of binary 1111 is :
 (a) 2^3
 (b) $2^3 - 1$
 (c) 24
 (d) $2^4 - 1$
[RRB JE 2014 RED SHIFT]

15. The term 'Operating System' means :
 (a) A set of programmes which controls computer working
 (b) The way a computer operator works
 (c) Conversion of high level language into machine level language
 (d) None of these
[RRB JE 2014 RED SHIFT]

16. The language which a computer can understand is:
 (a) High Level Language
 (b) Machine Language
 (c) Assembly Language
 (d) All of these
[RRB JE 2014 RED SHIFT]

17. Primary storage in computer terminology refers to :
 (a) Hard Disc Drive
 (b) Random Access Memory (RAM)
 (c) Read Only Memory(ROM)
 (d) The storage device where the operating system is stored
[RRB JE 2014 RED SHIFT]

18. A byte is group of:
 (a) 2 bits
 (b) 4 bits
 (c) 8 bits
 (d) 16 bits
[RRB JE 2014 RED SHIFT]

19. ______will translate the complete programme at once from a high level language to the machine language.
 (a) Compiler
 (b) Assembler
 (c) Joystick
 (d) Bus
[RRB JE 2014 RED SHIFT]

20. A file which contains transient data to be processed in combination with a master file is called :
 (a) Sequential file
 (b) Master file
 (c) Random organization file
 (d) Transmission file
[RRB JE 2014 RED SHIFT]

21. Which of the following is a presentation graphics software ?
 (a) MS Windows
 (b) MS Word
 (c) MS Excel
 (d) MS PowerPoint
[RRB JE 2014 RED SHIFT]

22. Compiler and interpreters are examples of :
 (a) System software
 (b) Application software
 (c) Both (a) and (b)
 (d) None of these
[RRB JE 2014 RED SHIFT]

23. In a computer, a compiler is
 (a) a program that places programs into memory and prepares them for execution
 (b) a program that automate the translation of assembly language into machine language
 (c) a program that accepts a program written in a high level languag and produces an object program
 (d) a program that appears to execute a source program if it were machine language
[RRB JE 2014 YELLOW SHIFT]

24. The operating system of a computer serves as a software interface between the user and
 (a) hardware
 (b) peripheral
 (c) memory
 (d) Screen
[RRB JE 2014 YELLOW SHIFT]

25. Which of the following hardware components is the most important to the operation of database management system ?
 (a) High-resolution video display
 (b) Printer
 (c) High-speed large-capacity disk
 (d) Plotter
[RRB JE 2014 YELLOW SHIFT]

26. MS Word is an example of

(a) An operating system

(b) Processing device

(c) Application software

(d) System software

[RRB JE 2014 YELLOW SHIFT]

27. A computer virus is a

(a) Hardware   (b) Software

(c) Bacteria   (d) Freeware

[RRB JE 2014 YELLOW SHIFT]

28. Shortcut key to "Centre Align" the selected text in MS Word is

(a) Ctrl + C   (b) Ctrl + E

(c) Ctrl + F   (d) Ctrl + X

[RRB JE 2014 YELLOW SHIFT]

29. The software in computer that transfers the object program from secondary memory to the main memory is called

(a) Assembler   (b) Loader

(c) Linker   (d) Task builder

[RRB JE 2014 YELLOW SHIFT]

30. In a computer, the system identifies a file by its

(a) Name   (b) Absolute Path

(c) File owner   (d) Inode number

[RRB JE 2014 YELLOW SHIFT]

31. In a computer, Virtual Memory is

(a) an extremely large main memory

(b) an extremely large secondary memory

(c) an illusion of an extremely large memory

(d) a type of memory used in super computers

[RRB JE 2014 YELLOW SHIFT]

32. In a computer, Disk scheduling involves deciding

(a) which disk should be accessed next

(b) the order in which disk access requests must be serviced

(c) the physical location where files should be accessed in the disk

(d) None of these

[RRB JE 2014 YELLOW SHIFT]

33. Which of the following is not a valid category of impact printers?

(a) Dot-matrix printers

(b) Line printers

(c) Drum printers

(d) Ink-jet printers

[RRB JE 2015 26ᵗʰ AUG 1ˢᵗ SHIFT]

34. Which of the following is not true about RAM?

(a) Random access memory

(b) Read write memory

(c) Volatile memory

(d) Sequential access memory

[RRB JE 2015 26ᵗʰ AUG 1ˢᵗ SHIFT]

35. Which of the following is not a component of Central Processing Unit (CPU)?

(a) Arithmetic and Logic Unit (ALU)

(b) Control Unit (CU)

(c) Registers

(d) Random Access Memory (RAM)

[RRB JE 2015 26ᵗʰ AUG 1ˢᵗ SHIFT]

36. ASCII stands for ____

(a) American Standard Code for Immediate Interchange

(b) American Standard Code for Immediate Information

(c) American Standard Code for Information Interchange

(d) Australian Standard Code for Information Interchange

[RRB JE 2015 26ᵗʰ AUG 1ˢᵗ SHIFT]

37. The binary representation of 99.25 is ______

(a) $(110001110)_2$ (b) $(1100011.0)_2$

(c) $(1101011.10)_2$ (d) $(1000011.11)_2$

[RRB JE 2015 26ᵗʰ AUG 1ˢᵗ SHIFT]

38. Considering X as a binary variable, the Boolean expression X + 1 is equivalent to

(a) X   (b) 1

(c) 0   (d) X'

[RRB JE 2015 26ᵗʰ AUG 1ˢᵗ SHIFT]

39. The 2's compliment of the binary number $(11001001)_2$ is

(a) $(00110110)_2$ (b) $(00111111)_2$

(c) $(00110111)_2$ (d) $(10110111)_2$

[RRB JE 2015 26ᵗʰ AUG 1ˢᵗ SHIFT]

40. Which of the following is a real-time operating system?

(a) Mac OS X   (b) Linux

(c) Windows   (d) Windows CE

[RRB JE 2015 26ᵗʰ AUG 1ˢᵗ SHIFT]

41. Class 'A' IP addresses use ______ bits for Network ID.

(a) 8   (b) 16

(c) 24   (d) 32

[RRB JE 2015 26ᵗʰ AUG 1ˢᵗ SHIFT]

42. Which of the following is not a Web browser?

(a) Chrome   (b) Internet Explorer

(c) Opera   (d) Hadoop

[RRB JE 2015 26ᵗʰ AUG 1ˢᵗ SHIFT]

43. Which of the following is not a valid category of impact printers?

(a) Daisy-wheel printers

(b) Line printers

(c) Drum printers

(d) Laser printers

[RRB JE 2015 26ᵗʰ AUG 2ⁿᵈ SHIFT]

44. Which of the following is not true about ROM?

(a) Random access memory

(b) Read only memory

(c) Non-volatile memory

(d) Sequential access memory

[RRB JE 2015 26ᵗʰ AUG 2ⁿᵈ SHIFT]

45. Which of the following is a component of Central Processing Unit (CPU)?

(a) Hard Disk

(b) Keyboard

(c) Registers

(d) Random Access Memory (RAM)

[RRB JE 2015 26ᵗʰ AUG 2ⁿᵈ SHIFT]

46. Original ASCII coding scheme uses _______ bits for coding 128 different characters.

(a) 6   (b) 7

(c) 8   (d) 16

[RRB JE 2015 26ᵗʰ AUG 2ⁿᵈ SHIFT]

47. The binary representation of 129.25 is ____.

(a) $(10000001.01)_2$ (b) $(11000001.01)_2$

(c) $(10000011.10)_2$ (d) $(10000001.11)_2$

[RRB JE 2015 26ᵗʰ AUG 2ⁿᵈ SHIFT]

48. Considering X as a binary variable, the Boolean expression $X + 0$ is equivalent to

(a) X   (b) 1

(c) 0   (d) X'

[RRB JE 2015 26ᵗʰ AUG 2ⁿᵈ SHIFT]

49. The 2's compliment of the binary number $(10001100)_2$ is

(a) $(01001000)_2$ (b) $(01110100)_2$

(c) $(00100111)_2$ (d) $(11110111)_2$

[RRB JE 2015 26ᵗʰ AUG 2ⁿᵈ SHIFT]

50. Windows 7 is a _____

(a) Real-time operating system

(b) Multi-user operating system

(c) Multi-tasking operating system

(d) Distributed operating system

[RRB JE 2015 26ᵗʰ AUG 2ⁿᵈ SHIFT]

51. Class 'A' IP addresses use ____ bits for Host ID.

(a) 8   (b) 16

(c) 24   (d) 32

[RRB JE 2015 26ᵗʰ AUG 2ⁿᵈ SHIFT]

52. Which of the following is not a Web browser?

(a) Opera   (b) NetSurf

(c) WWW   (d) Chrome

[RRB JE 2015 26ᵗʰ AUG 2ⁿᵈ SHIFT]

53. Printer is a(an) ____

(a) Input device

(b) Output device

(c) Storage device

(d) Both input and output device

[RRB JE 2015 26ᵗʰ AUG 3ʳᵈ SHIFT]

54. Which of the following is not true about EPROM?

(a) Random access memory

(b) Erasable programmable read only memory

(c) Non-volatile memory

(d) Sequential access memory

[RRB JE 2015 26ᵗʰ AUG 3ʳᵈ SHIFT]

55. Which of the following components of CPU temporarily stores data for ALU operations?

(a) Arithmetic and Logic Unit (ALU)

(b) Control Unit (CU)

(c) Registers

(d) Random Access Memory (RAM)

[RRB JE 2015 26ᵗʰ AUG 3ʳᵈ SHIFT]

56. BCD coding scheme uses ____________ bits to code decimal digits.

(a) 4   (b) 8

(c) 16   (d) 32

[RRB JE 2015 26ᵗʰ AUG 3ʳᵈ SHIFT]

57. The binary representation of 195.5 is ______

(a) $(11000001.01)_2$ (b) $(11000001.11)_2$

(c) $(11000011.01)_2$ (d) $(11000011.10)_2$

[RRB JE 2015 26ᵗʰ AUG 3ʳᵈ SHIFT]

58. Considering X as a binary variable, the Boolean expression X.1 is equivalent to

(a) X   (b) 1

(c) 0   (d) X'

[RRB JE 2015 26ᵗʰ AUG 3ʳᵈ SHIFT]

59. The 2's compliment of the binary number $(00000000)_2$ is

(a) $(11111111)_2$ (b) $(00000000)_2$

(c) $(10101010)_2$ (d) $(01010101)_2$

[RRB JE 2015 26ᵗʰ AUG 3ʳᵈ SHIFT]

60. A proprietary technology developed by Microsoft that allows embedding and linking to documents and other objects is

(a) DOM   (b) MODEM

(c) OLE   (d) OpenDoc

[RRB JE 2015 26ᵗʰ AUG 3ʳᵈ SHIFT]

61. Class 'B' IP addresses use _______ bits for Network ID.

(a) 8   (b) 16

(c) 24   (d) 32

[RRB JE 2015 26ᵗʰ AUG 3ʳᵈ SHIFT]

62. Which of the following is not a Web browser?

(a) Netscape Navigator

(b) NetSurf

(c) XML

(d) Opera

[RRB JE 2015 26ᵗʰ AUG 3ʳᵈ SHIFT]

53. Which of the following is not a valid category of impact printers?

(a) Chain printers   (b) Line printers

(c) Band printers   (d) Ink-jet printers

[RRB JE 2015 27ᵗʰ AUG 1ˢᵗ SHIFT]

64. Which of the following is not true about PROM?

(a) Random access memory

(b) Programmable read only memory

(c) Non-volatile memory

(d) Sequential access memory

[RRB JE 2015 27ᵗʰ AUG 1ˢᵗ SHIFT]

65. Which of the following components of CPU is responsible to direct the system to execute instructions?

(a) Arithmetic and logic Unit (ALU)

(b) Control Unit (CU)

(c) Registers

(d) Random Access Memory (RAM)

[RRB JE 2015 27ᵗʰ AUG 1ˢᵗ SHIFT]

66. BCD stands for ____

(a) Binary Coded Decimal

(b) Binary Code Display

(c) Bidirectional Coded Data

(d) Binary Coded Data

[RRB JE 2015 27ᵗʰ AUG 1ˢᵗ SHIFT]

67. The binary representation of 144.5 is _____

(a) $(0010000.01)_2$ (b) $(10010001.11)_2$

(c) $(10010000.10)_2$ (d) $(10011001.11)_2$

[RRB JE 2015 27ᵗʰ AUG 1ˢᵗ SHIFT]

68. Considering X as a binary variable, the Boolean expression X.0 is equivalent to

(a) X   (b) 1

(c) 0   (d) X'

[RRB JE 2015 27ᵗʰ AUG 1ˢᵗ SHIFT]

69. The 2's compliment of the binary number $(1000000)_2$ is

(a) $(01111111)_2$ (b) $(10101010)_2$

(c) $(10000000)_2$ (d) $(01010101)_2$

[RRB JE 2015 27ᵗʰ AUG 1ˢᵗ SHIFT]

70. Linux is a/an ____

(a) Application software

(b) Word processor

(c) Database management system

(d) System software

[RRB JE 2015 27ᵗʰ AUG 1ˢᵗ SHIFT]

71. Class 'B' IP addresses use ____ bits for Host ID.

(a) 8   (b) 16

(c) 24   (d) 32

[RRB JE 2015 27ᵗʰ AUG 1ˢᵗ SHIFT]

72. Which of the following is not a Web browser?

(a) Netscape Navigator

(b) Safari

(c) HTML

(d) Chrome

[RRB JE 2015 27ᵗʰ AUG 1ˢᵗ SHIFT]

73. Mouse is a (an)______________________

(a) Input device

(b) Output device

(c) Storage device

(d) Both input and output device

[RRB JE 2015 27ᵗʰ AUG 2ⁿᵈ SHIFT]

74. Which of the following is not true about EEPROM?

(a) Random access memory

(b) Electrically erasable programmable read only memory

(d) Non-volatile memory

(d) Sequential access memory

[RRB JE 2015 27th AUG 2nd SHIFT]

75. Which of the following is not a valid category of "system bus" in a computer system?

(a) Data bus

(b) Control bus

(c) Address bus

(d) Memory bus

[RRB JE 2015 27th AUG 2nd SHIFT]

76. EBCDIC stands for _____

(a) Extended Binary Coded Data Intechange Code

(b) Expanded Binary Coded Decimal Interchange Code

(c) Extended Binary Coded Decimal Interchange Code

(d) Expanded Binary Coded Data Interchange Code

[RRB JE 2015 27th AUG 2nd SHIFT]

77. The octal representation of 195.25 is ____

(a) $(303.20)_8$ (b) $(303.02)_8$

(c) $(313.20)_8$ (d) $(323.20)_8$

[RRB JE 2015 27th AUG 2nd SHIFT]

78. Considering X as a binary variable, the Boolean expression X + X' is equivalent to

(a) X   (b) 1

(c) 0   (d) X'

[RRB JE 2015 27th AUG 2nd SHIFT]

79. The 2's compliment of the binary number $(11111111)_2$ is

(a) $(10000000)_2$ (b) $(00000000)_2$

(c) $(00000001)_2$ (d) $(01010101)_2$

[RRB JE 2015 27th AUG 2nd SHIFT]

80. Which of the following operating systems is case sensitive?

(a) Unix   (b) MS-DOS

(c) MS-Windows   (d) Mac OS X

[RRB JE 2015 27th AUG 2nd SHIFT]

81. Class 'C' IP addresses use _____ bits for Host ID.

(a) 8   (b) 16

(c) 24   (d) 32

[RRB JE 2015 27th AUG 2nd SHIFT]

82. Which of the following is not an e-mail protocol?

(a) POP   (b) IMAP

(c) SMTP   (d) FTP

[RRB JE 2015 27th AUG 2nd SHIFT]

83. Joystick is a(an) ____

(a) input device

(b) Output device

(c) Storage device

(d) Both input and output device

[RRB JE 2015 27th AUG 3rd SHIFT]

84. Which of the following is not true about Cache memory?

(a) Faster memory than RAM

(b) Volatile memory

(c) Smaller in size than RAM

(d) Sequential access memory

[RRB JE 2015 27th AUG 3rd SHIFT]

85. Which of the following statement is not true?

(a) Data bus is bidirectional

(b) Address bus is bidirectional

(c) Address bus is unidirectional

(d) Same data bus is used for both read and write operations

[RRB JE 2015 27th AUG 3rd SHIFT]

86. EBCDIC coding scheme uses _____ bits to code different characters.

(a) 4   (b) 8

(c) 16   (d) 32

[RRB JE 2015 27th AUG 3rd SHIFT]

87. The hexadecimal representation of 125.25 is _____

(a) $(7D.40)_{16}$ (b) $(7D.04)_{16}$

(c) $(D7.40)_{16}$ (d) $(D7.04)_{16}$

[RRB JE 2015 27th AUG 3rd SHIFT]

88. Considering X as a binary variable, the Boolean expression X.X' is equivalent to

(a) X   (b) 1

(c) 0   (d) X'

[RRB JE 2015 27th AUG 3rd SHIFT]

89. The 2's compliment of the binary number $(10101010)_2$ is

(a) $(10000000)_2$ (b) $(00000000)_2$

(c) $(01010110)_2$ (d) $(10101010)_2$

[RRB JE 2015 27ᵗʰ AUG 3ʳᵈ SHIFT]

90. A programming language which enables a programmer to write programs that are more or less independent of a particular type of computer is called __________

(a) Assembly language

(b) Machine language

(c) Low-level language

(d) High-level language

[RRB JE 2015 27ᵗʰ AUG 3ʳᵈ SHIFT]

91. Class 'C' IP addresses use bits for Network ID.

(a) 8   (b) 16

(c) 24   (d) 32

[RRB JE 2015 27ᵗʰ AUG 3ʳᵈ SHIFT]

92. W3C stands for ______

(a) World Wide Web Consortium

(b) World Wide Web Community

(c) World Wide Website Consortium

(d) World Wide Websites Community

[RRB JE 2015 27ᵗʰ AUG 3ʳᵈ SHIFT]

93. Monitor (VDU) is a(an) _____

(a) Output device

(b) Input device

(c) Storage device

(d) Both input and output device

[RRB JE 2015 28ᵗʰ AUG 1ˢᵗ SHIFT]

94. Which of the following memories is directly accessible by the CPU?

(a) RAM   (b) Hard Disk

(c) Magnetic Tape   (d) DVD

[RRB JE 2015 28ᵗʰ AUG 1ˢᵗ SHIFT]

95. Static RAM (SRAM) is faster than Dynamic RAM (DRAM) because __________

(a) SRAM uses capacitors

(b) SRAM is costlier

(c) SRAM does not require refreshing

(d) SRAM is cheaper

[RRB JE 2015 28ᵗʰ AUG 1ˢᵗ SHIFT]

96. UTF-8 is a(an) ______

(a) 8-bit fixed-width encoding

(b) 8-bit variable-width encoding

(c) 16-bit variable-width encoding

(c) 16-bit fixed-width encoding

[RRB JE 2015 28ᵗʰ AUG 1ˢᵗ SHIFT]

97. The hexadecimal representation of 225.5 is ___

(a) $(E1.08)_{16}$ (b) $(E1.80)_{16}$

(c) $(lE.SO)_{16}$ (d) $(1E.08)_{16}$

[RRB JE 2015 28ᵗʰ AUG 1ˢᵗ SHIFT]

98. Considering X and Y as binary variables, the Boolean expression X + XY' is equivalent to

(a) X   (b) 1

(c) 0   (d) Y

[RRB JE 2015 28ᵗʰ AUG 1ˢᵗ SHIFT]

99. The 2's compliment of the binary number $(01010101)_2$ is

(a) $(10000000)_2$ (c) $(01010110)_2$

(c) $(01010110)_2$ (d) $(10101011)_2$

[RRB JE 2015 28ᵗʰ AUG 1ˢᵗ SHIFT]

100. Compiler is used to convert

(a) High-level language programs into machine codes

(b) Low-level language programs into machine codes

(c) Assembly language programs into machine codes

(d) High-level language programs into assembly codes

[RRB JE 2015 28ᵗʰ AUG 1ˢᵗ SHIFT]

101. In class 'A' IP addresses, number of network ID bits used to identify the class is

(a) 0   (b) 1

(c) 2   (d) 3

[RRB JE 2015 28ᵗʰ AUG 1ˢᵗ SHIFT]

102. Which of the following categories of networks has smallest geographic area?

(a) MAN   (b) PAN

(c) LAN   (d) WAN

[RRB JE 2015 28ᵗʰ AUG 1ˢᵗ SHIFT]

103. Which of the following is a volatile memory?

(a) Cache memory   (b) Hard Disk

(c) DVD   (d) CD

[RRB JE 2015 28ᵗʰ AUG 2ⁿᵈ SHIFT]

104. Dynamic RAM (DRAM) is slower than Static RAM (SRAM) because _______

(a) DRAM uses flip-flops

(b) DRAM is costlier

(c) DRAM requires refreshing

(d) DRAM is cheaper

[RRB JE 2015 28ᵗʰ AUG 2ⁿᵈ SHIFT]

105. UTF-16 is a(an) ______

(a) 8-bit fixed-width encoding

(b) 8-bit variable-width encoding

(c) 16-bit variable-width encoding

(d) 16-bit fixed-width encoding

[RRB JE 2015 28th AUG 2nd SHIFT]

106. The hexadecimal representation of $(407)_8$ is ______

(a) $(107)_{16}$ (b) $(701)_{16}$

(c) $(017)_{16}$ (d) $(710)_{16}$

[RRB JE 2015 28th AUG 2nd SHIFT]

107. Considering X and Y as binary variables, the Boolean expression Y + XY is equivalent to

(a) X   (b) 1

(c) 0   (d) Y

[RRB JE 2015 28th AUG 2nd SHIFT]

108. The 2's compliment of the binary number $(11110000)_2$ is

(a) $(00001111)_2$ (c) $(00010000)_2$

(b) $(11110000)_2$ (d) $(10101010)_2$

[RRB JE 2015 28th AUG 2nd SHIFT]

109. Which of the following category of viruses does not replicate themselves?

(a) Worms

(b) Trojan horses

(c) Boot sector viruses

(d) Macro viruses

[RRB JE 2015 28th AUG 2nd SHIFT]

110. In class 'B' IP addresses, number of network ID bits used to identify the class is ______

(a) 0   (b) 1

(c) 2   (d) 3

[RRB JE 2015 28th AUG 2nd SHIFT]

111. Which of the following categories of networks has largest geographic area?

(a) WAN   (b) PAN

(c) LAN   (d) MAN

[RRB JE 2015 28th AUG 2nd SHIFT]

112. DVD stands for ______

(a) Digital Video Disk

(b) Digital Variable Disk

(c) Digital Versatile Disk

(d) Digital Versatile Data

[RRB JE 2015 28th AUG 3rd SHIFT]

113. Which of the following can be treated as both input as well as output device?

(a) Mouse   (b) Printer

(c) Memory   (d) Plotter

[RRB JE 2015 28th AUG 3rd SHIFT]

114. UTF-32 is a(an) ______

(a) 16-bit fixed-width encoding

(b) 16-bit variable-width encoding

(c) 32-bit variable-width encoding

(d) 32-bit fixed-width encoding

[RRB JE 2015 28th AUG 3rd SHIFT]

115. The octal representation of $(AOE)_{16}$ is ______

(a) $(5016)_8$

(b) $(5061)_8$

(c) $(1650)_8$

(d) $(5610)_8$

[RRB JE 2015 28th AUG 3rd SHIFT]

116. Considering X and Y as binary variables, the Boolean expression X(X + Y') is equivalent to

(a) X   (b) 1

(c) 0   (d) Y

[RRB JE 2015 28th AUG 3rd SHIFT]

117. The 2's compliment of the binary number $(00001111)_2$ is

(a) $(00001111)_2$

(b) $(11110000)_2$

(c) $(10101010)_2$

(d) $(11110001)_2$

[RRB JE 2015 28th AUG 3rd SHIFT]

118. Which of the following categories of viruses normally infect executable code, such as .com and .exe files?

(a) File infector viruses

(b) Boot sector viruses

(c) Master boot record viruses

(d) Macro viruses

[RRB JE 2015 28th AUG 3rd SHIFT]

119. In class 'C' IP addresses, number of network ID bits used to identify the class is

(a) 0   (b) 1

(c) 2   (d) 3

[RRB JE 2015 28th AUG 3rd SHIFT]

120. Which of the following is a general-purpose network?

(a) Storage Area Network (SAN)

(b) Enterprise Private Network (EPN)

(c) Enterprise Private Network (EPN)

(d) Virtual Private Network (VPN)

[RRB JE 2015 28th AUG 3rd SHIFT]

121. Which of the following is not a pointing device?

(a) Mouse   (b) Trackball

(c) Joystick   (d) Keyboard

[RRB JE 2015 29th AUG 1st SHIFT]

122. Which of the following is not a valid property to characterize storage unit

(a) Storage capacity (b) Size

(c) Access time   (d) Cost per bit of storage

[RRB JE 2015 29th AUG 1st SHIFT]

123. The time elapsed between the submission of a job and obtaining the results is known as

(a) Seek time   (b) Latency

(c) Turnaround time (d) Execution time

[RRB JE 2015 29th AUG 1st SHIFT]

124. The binary representation of the decimal number 45.25 is

(a) $(101101.01)_2$ (b) $(101101.10)_2$

(c) $(101010.01)_2$ (d) $(101010.10)_2$

[RRB JE 2015 29th AUG 1st SHIFT]

125. Considering X and Y as binary variables, the Boolean expression $X + Y + 1$ is equivalent to

(a) X   (b) 1

(c) 0   (d) Y

[RRB JE 2015 29th AUG 1st SHIFT]

126. In assembly language ______ are used to represent operation codes.

(a) Alphabets   (b) Pseudo codes

(c) Mnemonics   (d) Symbols

[RRB JE 2015 29th AUG 1st SHIFT]

127. Which of the following is not a word processor?

(a) MS-Word   (b) Notepad

(c) Wordpad   (d) Wordpress

[RRB JE 2015 29th AUG 1st SHIFT]

128. The length of an IPv4 address is

(a) 8 bits   (b) 16 bits

(c) 32 bits   (d) 64 bits

[RRB JE 2015 29th AUG 1st SHIFT]

129. Internet Explorer is a

(a) Web browser

(b) Web search engine

(c) Hypertext transfer protocol

(d) Web data store

[RRB JE 2015 29th AUG 1st SHIFT]

130. Which of the following is the most simple, intuitive, and easiest to use of all input devices?

(a) Mouse   (b) Trackball

(c) Keyboard   (d) Touch screen

[RRB JE 2015 29th AUG 2nd SHIFT]

131. Both RAM and ROM are

(a) Random access memory

(b) Sequential access memory

(c) Read and write memory

(d) Read only memory

[RRB JE 2015 29th AUG 2nd SHIFT]

132. Unix is a ______ operating system.

(a) Single-user and time-sharing

(b) Multi-user and time-sharing

(c) Multi-user and distributed

(d) Real-time

[RRB JE 2015 29th AUG 2nd SHIFT]

133. The decimal representation of the binary number $(101010.011)_2$ is

(a) 42.25   (b) 24.25

(c) 24.375   (d) 42.375

[RRB JE 2015 29th AUG 2nd SHIFT]

134. Considering X and Y as binary variables, the Boolean expression $X.Y.0$ is equivalent to

(a) X   (b) 1

(c) 0   (d) Y

[RRB JE 2015 29th AUG 2nd SHIFT]

135. Assembly language is a

(a) Machine independent language

(b) Machine dependent language

(c) High-level language

(d) Language which requires interpreter

[RRB JE 2015 29th AUG 2nd SHIFT]

136. Mail-merge is a component of

(a) MS-Word   (b) WordPress

(c) MS-Excel   (d) MS-Access

[RRB JE 2015 29th AUG 2nd SHIFT]

137. Internet is a

(a) Local Area Network (LAN)

(b) Metropolitan Area Network (LAN)

(c) Wide Area Network (WAN)

(d) Storage Area Network (SAN)

[RRB JE 2015 29th AUG 2nd SHIFT]

138. Google Chrome is a

(a) Application layer protocol

(b) Web search engine

(c) Web browser

(d) Web data store

[RRB JE 2015 29th AUG 2nd SHIFT]

139. Which of the following device is used to recognize a pre specified type of mark made by pencil or pen?

(a) Bar-Code Reader (b) OCR

(c) Scanner (d) OMR

[RRB JE 2015 29th AUG 3rd SHIFT]

140. Both EPROM and EEPROM are

(a) Sequential access memory

(b) Random accurs memory

(c) Volatile memory

(d) Destructive memory

[RRB JE 2015 29th AUG 3rd SHIFT]

141. The Unix operating system is written in

(a) C (b) C++

(c) Pascal (d) Fortran

[RRB JE 2015 29th AUG 3rd SHIFT]

142. The octal representation of the binary number $(1101010.01)_2$ is

(a) $(152.2)_8$ (b) $(152.1)_8$

(c) $(650.2)_8$ (d) $(650.1)_8$

[RRB JE 2015 29th AUG 3rd SHIFT]

143. Considering X and Y as binary variables, the Boolean expression XY + X'Y is equivalent to

(a) X (b) 1

(c) 0 (d) Y

[RRB JE 2015 29th AUG 3rd SHIFT]

144. Which of the following takes one statement of a high-level language program at a time and translate it into machine instruction, which is immediately executed?

(a) Assembler (b) Compiler

(c) Interpreter (d) Loader

[RRB JE 2015 29th AUG 3rd SHIFT]

145. Which of the following is a database management system?

(a) MS-Word (b) MS-Excel

(c) MS-PowerPoint (d) MS-Access

[RRB JE 2015 29th AUG 3rd SHIFT]

146. Which of the following is not an application layer protocol?

(a) HTTP (b) IP

(c) TELNET (d) FTP

[RRB JE 2015 29th AUG 3rd SHIFT]

147. Netscape Navigator is a

(a) Network layer protocol

(b) Presentation layer protocol

(c) Web browser

(d) Web search engine

[RRB JE 2015 29th AUG 3rd SHIFT]

148. Which of the following is used by banking industry for faster processing of large volume of cheques?

(a) Bar-Code Reader

(b) OCR

(c) MICR

(d) OMR

[RRB JE 2015 30th AUG 3rd SHIFT]

149. EEPROM stands for

(a) Electrically Erasable Programmable ROM

(b) Electronically Erasable Programmable ROM

(c) Electrically Engineered Programmable ROM

(d) Electrically Erasable Persistent ROM

[RRB JE 2015 30th AUG 3rd SHIFT]

150. The primary objective of a time-sharing operating system is to

(a) Avoid thrashing

(b) Provide fast response to each user of the computer

(c) Provide fast execution of processes

(d) Optimize computer memory usage

[RRB JE 2015 30th AUG 3rd SHIFT]

151. The hexadecimal representation of the binary number $(1101010.01)_2$ is

(a) (6A.4)16 (b) (6A.1)16

(c) (D2.4)16 (d) (D2.1)16

[RRB JE 2015 30th AUG 3rd SHIFT]

152. Considering X and Y as binary variables, the Boolean expression X'Y + X'Y' is equivalent to

(a) X
(b) Y
(c) X'
(d) Y'

[RRB JE 2015 30th AUG 3rd SHIFT]

153. Which of the following programming languages is mainly popular for business data processing?

(a) C
(b) Pascal
(c) FORTRAN
(d) COBOL

[RRB JE 2015 30th AUG 3rd SHIFT]

154. In cut-paste operation of MS-Word

(a) A text can be cut, and paste exactly once
(b) A text can be cut, and paste multiple times
(c) A text can't be cut if a background color is set
(d) A text can't be cut if it length is more than 128 characters

[RRB JE 2015 30th AUG 3rd SHIFT]

155. Which of the following is a Class-A IP address?

(a) 130.10.10.10
(b) 125.250.250.250
(c) 165.255.255.255
(d) 200.128.128.128

[RRB JE 2015 30th AUG 3rd SHIFT]

156. Safari is a

(a) Transport layer protocol
(b) Application layer protocol
(c) Web search engine
(d) Web browser

[RRB JE 2015 30th AUG 3rd SHIFT]

157. Which of the following characteristics of computers makes them free from monotony, tiredness, and lack of concentration?

(a) Speed
(b) Accuracy
(c) Diligence
(d) Versatility

[RRB JE 2015 16th SEP 3rd SHIFT]

158. Which of the following input device converts bitmap images of characters to equivalent ASCII codes?

(a) OCR
(b) OMR
(c) Scanner
(d) Touch Screen

[RRB JE 2015 16th SEP 3rd SHIFT]

159. Which of the following is a non-impact printer?

(a) Dot-Matrix printer
(b) Inkjet printer
(c) Drum printer
(d) Chain/Band printer

[RRB JE 2015 16th SEP 3rd SHIFT]

160. Which of the following categories of systems uses multiple CPUs to process either instructions from different and independent programs or different instructions from the same program simultaneously?

(a) Multiprogramming system
(b) Multitasking system
(c) Multiprocessing system
(d) Multithreading system

[RRB JE 2015 16th SEP 3rd SHIFT]

161. If $(101)n = 65$, where n represents the base of the respective number system, then the value of n is

(a) 2
(b) 4
(c) 8
(d) 16

[RRB JE 2015 16th SEP 3rd SHIFT]

162. Considering X and Y as binary variables, the Boolean expression XY' + X'Y' is equivalent to

(a) X
(b) X'
(c) Y
(d) Y'

[RRB JE 2015 16th SEP 3rd SHIFT]

163. In Binary Coded Decimal (BCD) systems, the decimal number 81 is represented as

(a) 10000001
(b) 10100010
(c) 01010001
(d) 00011000

[RRB JE 2015 16th SEP 3rd SHIFT]

164. Which of the following tasks can't be performed using MS-Word?

(a) Charts creation
(b) Nested tables creation
(c) Review
(d) Matrix inverse calculation

[RRB JE 2015 16th SEP 3rd SHIFT]

165. In Class-B IP addresses, number of bits used to identify class is

(a) 1
(b) 2
(c) 3
(d) 4

[RRB JE 2015 16th SEP 3rd SHIFT]

166. Which of the following is not an antivirus software?

(a) iOS
(b) Kaspersky
(c) AVG
(d) McAfee

[RRB JE 2015 16th SEP 3rd SHIFT]

RRB SENIOR SECTION ENGINEER

1. Which of these is NOT an Operating System?

  (a) Android   (b) iOS

  (c) Linux   (d) Power point

                       [RRB SSE 2014 YELLOW SHIFT]

2. A software user interface feature that allows the user to view something very similar to the end result while the document is being created is called-

  (a) Format creator   (b) Format fidelity

  (c) WYSIWYG   (d) WYGIWYS

                       [RRB SSE 2014 YELLOW SHIFT]

3. In a computer system there are softwares and languages at various levels, like High level Language (HL), Machine Language (ML), Compiler (C). Which of the following is the correct indicative representation from user (U) to the computer (COMP)?

  (a) U $\rightleftharpoons$ HL $\rightleftharpoons$ C $\rightleftharpoons$ ML $\rightleftharpoons$ Comp

  (b) U $\rightleftharpoons$ C $\rightleftharpoons$ ML $\rightleftharpoons$ HL $\rightleftharpoons$ Comp

  (c) U $\rightleftharpoons$ C $\rightleftharpoons$ HL $\rightleftharpoons$ ML $\rightleftharpoons$ Comp

  (d) U $\rightleftharpoons$ ML $\rightleftharpoons$ HL $\rightleftharpoons$ C $\rightleftharpoons$ Comp

                       [RRB SSE 2014 YELLOW SHIFT]

4. Which of these devices performs the function of both input device and output device for a computer?

  (a) Joy Stick   (b) Mouse

  (c) Modem   (d) Printer

                       [RRB SSE 2014 YELLOW SHIFT]

5. Who wrote/invented the Linux software?

  (a) Microsoft   (b) Apple INC

  (c) IBM   (d) None of these

                       [RRB SSE 2014 YELLOW SHIFT]

6. A technique of anonymous communication over a computer network using encryption of messages and splitting between the nodes, is called-

  (a) Spice routing   (b) Onion routing

  (c) Cabbage routing   (d) Flower routing

                       [RRB SSE 2014 YELLOW SHIFT]

7. Processing speed of computer is measured in-

  (a) MIPS(Million Instruction Per Second)

  (b) MHz of clock

  (c) Both (a) and (b)

  (d) None of these   **[RRB SSE 2014 YELLOW SHIFT]**

8. To close a presentation and quit PowerPoint, one must click the close button on the :

  (a) menu bar   (b) title bar

  (c) standard tool bar   (d) common tasks toolbar

                       [RRB SSE 2014 RED SHIFT]

9. Expression + + i is equivalent in 'C' to :

  (a) i = i + 1   (b) i = i + 2

  (c) i = 2i   (d) None of these

                       [RRB SSE 2014 RED SHIFT]

10. Which of the following rational relation operations in 'C means "not equal to" ?

  (a) #   (b) ==

  (c) ! =   (d) < =

                       [RRB SSE 2014 RED SHIFT]

11. Microsoft Windows is a/an :

  (a) Word-processing program

  (b) Database program

  (c) Operating system

  (d) Graphics program

                       [RRB SSE 2014 RED SHIFT]

12. __________will translate the complete program at once from a High Level Language to the Machine Language.

  (a) Compiler   (b) Joy stick

  (c) Ports   (d) Light pen

                       [RRB SSE 2014 RED SHIFT]

13. The word function that corrects text as we type is referred to as :

  (a) Auto insert   (b) Auto correct

  (c) Auto summarize   (d) Track changes

                       [RRB SSE 2014 RED SHIFT]

14. Primary Storage, in computer terminology, refers to :

  (a) Hard Disc Drive

  (b) Random Access Memory (RAM)

  (c) Read Only Memory (ROM)

  (d) The storage device where the operating system is stored

                       [RRB SSE 2014 RED SHIFT]

15. What does an electronic spreadsheet consist of ?

  (a) Rows   (b) Columns

  (c) Cells   (d) All of the above

                       [RRB SSE 2014 RED SHIFT]

16. Which extention is given to word document by default ?

  (a) DOC   (b) COM

  (c) EXT   (d) None of these

                       [RRB SSE 2014 RED SHIFT]

17. Which Network protocol is used to send e-mail?

  (a) FTP   (b) SSH

  (c) POP3   (d) SMTP

                       [RRB SSE 2014 YELLOW SHIFT]

18. The use of a cache in Computer system increases the

(a) available memory space for the program

(b) available memory space for the data

(c) available speed of memory access

(d) addressing range of CPU

[RRB SSE 2014 YELLOW SHIFT]

19. In a microprocessor when a CPU is interrupted, it

(a) Stops execution of instructions

(b) Acknowledges interrupt and branches off subroutine

(c) Acknowledges interrupt and continues

(d) Acknowledges interrupt and waits for the next instruction from the interrupting device

[RRB SSE 2014 YELLOW SHIFT]

20. The MODEM is used with a personal computer to do which of the following ?

(a) Convert from serial to parallel and vice versa

(b) Convert signals between TTL and RS232 C standard and vice versa

(c) Convert from digital to analog signals and vice versa

(d) To convert the computer to a long distance communication link

[RRB SSE 2014 YELLOW SHIFT]

21. The term digitization refers to

(a) conversion of analogue into digital

(b) conversion of digital into analogue

(c) use of analogue form of electricity

(d) a form of cringing physical quantities

[RRB SSE 2014 YELLOW SHIFT]

22. What is the process of utilizing one data link for transmission of a group of variables known as ?

(a) Encoding   (b) Decoding

(c) Demultiplexing   (d) Multiplexing

[RRB SSE 2014 YELLOW SHIFT]

23. Part of the Computer where data and instructions are held is

(a) Register Unit   (b) Accumulator

(c) Memory Unit   (d) CPU

[RRB SSE 2014 YELLOW SHIFT]

24. In a Computer. Assembler is

(a) a program that places programs into memory and prepares them for execution

(b) a program that automates the translation of assembly language into machine language

(c) a program that accepts a program written in a high level language and produces an object program

(d) is a program that appears to execute a source program as if it were machine language

[RRB SSE 2014 YELLOW SHIFT]

25. Which of the following is NOT a register in Computer ?

(a) Accumulator   (b) Stack Pointer

(c) Program Counter   (d) Buffer

[RRB SSE 2014 YELLOW SHIFT]

26. Which of the following is an integral component of CPU?

(a) Hard Disk   (b) RAM

(c) NIC   (d) Registers

[RRB SSE 2015 3ʳᵈ SEP 1ˢᵗ SHIFT]

27. Which of the following is not an operating system?

(a) iOS   (b) Android

(c) Mac OSX   (d) Hadoop

[RRB SSE 2015 3ʳᵈ SEP 1ˢᵗ SHIFT]

28. Considering 2's complement representation for negative numbers, -128 will be stored into an 8-bit memory space as

(a) 11111111   (b) 10000000

(c) 11111110   (d) 0000001

[RRB SSE 2015 3ʳᵈ SEP 1ˢᵗ SHIFT]

29. Considering X and Y as binary variables, the equivalent Boolean expression for $(X + Y)'$ is

(a) $X'.Y$ (b) $X.Y'$

(c) $X'.Y'$ (d) $X' + Y'$

[RRB SSE 2015 3ʳᵈ SEP 1ˢᵗ SHIFT]

30. 'Java' is a_______________

(a) Low-level programming language

(b) High-level programming language

(c) Assembly language

(d) Machine language

[RRB SSE 2015 3ʳᵈ SEP 1ˢᵗ SHIFT]

31. Which of the following statements about Machine language is correct?

(a) Machine language is machine dependent

(b) Machine language is machine independent

(c) Machine language is easier than high-level language to write programs

(d) Machine language programs require assembler

[RRB SSE 2015 3ʳᵈ SEP 1ˢᵗ SHIFT]

32. HTTP stands for
(a) Hyper Text Transmission Protocol
(b) Hyper Text Transfer Program
(c) Hyper Text Transfer Protocol
(d) Hyper Text Transmission Program
[RRB SSE 2015 3rd SEP 1st SHIFT]

33. A Virus can not______________________
(a) Steal hard disk space
(b) Steal CPU time
(c) Log keystrokes
(d) Increase/decrease the word length of CPU
[RRB SSE 2015 3rd SEP 1st SHIFT]

34. Which of the following is not a valid category of Read Only Memory (ROM)?
(a) PROM   (b) EPROM
(c) EE PROM   (d) EEEPROM
[RRB SSE 2015 3rd SEP 1st SHIFT]

35. The 16's compliment of the hexadecimal number $(A10)_{16}$ is
(a) $(5FO)_{16}$ (b) $(5EO)_{16}$
(c) $(5EF)_{16}$ (d) $(6FO)_{16}$
[RRB SSE 2015 3rd SEP 1st SHIFT]

36. Which of the following works on the principle of 'locality of reference'?
(a) RAM   (b) ROM
(c) Cache memory (d) Associative memory
[RRB SSE 2015 1st SEP 2nd SHIFT]

37. Which of the following is a real time operating system?
(a) MS-Windows   (b) Linux
(c) Unix   (d) QNX
[RRB SSE 2015 1st SEP 2nd SHIFT]

38. Considering 1's complement representation for negative numbers, -126 will be stored into an 8 bit memory space as
(a) 10000001   (b) 11111111
(c) 10111110   (d) 11100001
[RRB SSE 2015 1st SEP 2nd SHIFT]

39. Considering X and Y as binary variables, the equivalent Boolean expression for (X.Y)' is
(a) X'+Y   (b) X + Y'
(c) X' + Y'   (d) X'.Y'
[RRB SSE 2015 1st SEP 2nd SHIFT]

40. 'C' is a________________
(a) Low-level programming language
(b) High-level programming language
(c) Assembly language
(d) Machine language
[RRB SSE 2015 1st SEP 2nd SHIFT]

41. Which of the following statements about Assembly language is correct?
(a) Assembly language is machine dependent
(b) Assembly language is machine independent
(c) Assembly language is easier than high-level language to write programs
(d) Assembly language programs require interpreter
[RRB SSE 2015 1st SEP 2nd SHIFT]

42. HTTPS stands for
(a) HyperText Transmission Protocol Secure
(b) Hyper Text Transfer Program Secure
(c) HyperText Transfer Protocol Secure
(d) Hyper Text Transmission Program Secure
[RRB SSE 2015 1st SEP 2nd SHIFT]

43. Which of the following is not a valid category of computer viruses?
(a) Macro viruses
(b) Trojans
(c) Memory resident viruse
(d) Interrupts
[RRB SSE 2015 1st SEP 2nd SHIFT]

44. Which of the following is a sequential access memory?
(a) RAM   (b) ROM
(c) Hard Disk   (d) Magnetic Tape
[RRB SSE 2015 1st SEP 2nd SHIFT]

45. The 2's complement of the binary number $(11001100)_2$ is
(a) $(00110100)_2$ (b) $(00110011)_2$
(c) $(00110000)_2$ (d) $(11110100)_2$
[RRB SSE 2015 1st SEP 2nd SHIFT]

46. Wi-Fi stands for
(a) Wireless Fidelity   (b) Wired Fidelity
(c) Wireless Field   (d) Wireless Finite
[RRB SSE 2015 1st SEP 3rd SHIFT]

47. UNIX is a________________
(a) Real-time operating system
(b) Single-user operating system
(c) Multi-tasking operating system
(d) Distributed operating system
[RRB SSE 2015 1st SEP 3rd SHIFT]

48. Considering 2's complement representation for negative numbers, -86 will be stored into an 8-bit memory space as
(a) 10101010   (b) 11000111
(c) 10111000   (d) 11101101
[RRB SSE 2015 1st SEP 3rd SHIFT]

49. Considering X and Y as binary variables, the equivalent Boolean expression for X(X + Y) is

(a) X   (b) Y

(c) XY   (d) X + Y

[RRB SSE 2015 1ˢᵗ SEP 3ʳᵈ SHIFT]

50. 'C++' is a

(a) Low-level programming language

(b) High-level programming language

(c) Assembly language

(d) Machine language

[RRB SSE 2015 1ˢᵗ SEP 3ʳᵈ SHIFT]

51. Which of the following statements about High-Level language is correct?

(a) High-Level language is machine dependent

(b) High-Level language is machine independent

(c) High-Level language is difficult than Assembly language to write programs

(d) High-level language programs require Assembler

[RRB SSE 2015 1ˢᵗ SEP 3ʳᵈ SHIFT]

52. World Wide Web (WWW) was invented by

(a) Bill Gates   (b) Steve Jobs

(c) Tim Berners-Lee   (d) Alan Turing

[RRB SSE 2015 1ˢᵗ SEP 3ʳᵈ SHIFT]

53. Which of the following is not an 'overwrite' virus?

(a) Trj.Reboot   (b) Meve

(c) Way   (d) Trivial.88.D

[RRB SSE 2015 1ˢᵗ SEP 3ʳᵈ SHIFT]

54. Which of the following is not a valid unit to represent the speed of CPU?

(a) Hertz (Hz)   (b) MIPS

(c) MFLOPS   (d) Byte

[RRB SSE 2015 1ˢᵗ SEP 3ʳᵈ SHIFT]

55. The 2's compliment of the binary number $(00111100)_2$ is

(a) $(11000100)_2$ (b) $(11000011)_2$

(c) $(00110000)_2$ (d) $(11110100)_2$

[RRB SSE 2015 1ˢᵗ SEP 3ʳᵈ SHIFT]

56. MODEM stands for

(a) Modulator Demodulator

(b) Modular Demography

(c) Model Demodulation

(d) Modulation Demodulation

[RRB SSE 2015 2ⁿᵈ SEP 1ˢᵗ SHIFT]

57. Unix is a/an _______________________

(a) Application software

(b) Word processor

(c) Database management system

(d) System software

[RRB SSE 2015 2ⁿᵈ SEP 1ˢᵗ SHIFT]

58. Considering 1's complement representation for negative number -85 will be stored into an 8-bit memory space as

(a) 10101010   (b) 10111111

(c) 10100110   (d) 11101001

[RRB SSE 2015 2ⁿᵈ SEP 1ˢᵗ SHIFT]

59. Considering X and Y as binary variables the equivalent Boolean expression for X + XY is

(a) X   (b) Y

(c) XY   (d) X + Y

[RRB SSE 2015 2ⁿᵈ SEP 1ˢᵗ SHIFT]

60. 'FORTRAN' is a _______________________

(a) Low-level programming language

(b) High-level programming language

(c) Assembly language

(d) Machine language

[RRB SSE 2015 2ⁿᵈ SEP 1ˢᵗ SHIFT]

61. Which of the following statements about High-Level language is not correct?

(a) High-Level language is machine dependent

(b) High-Level language programs use interpreter

(c) High-Level language programs use compiler

(d) High-Level language is machine independent

[RRB SSE 2015 2ⁿᵈ SEP 1ˢᵗ SHIFT]

62. HTML stands for

(a) HyperText Markup Language

(b) HyperText Manipulation Language

(c) HyperText Management Language

(d) HyperText Maintenance Language

[RRB SSE 2015 2ⁿᵈ SEP 1ˢᵗ SHIFT]

63. Which of the following viruses is generally found in the hard disk's root directory, but it keeps on changing location?

(a) Trj.Reboot   (b) Vienna

(c) Way   (d) Trivial.88.D

[RRB SSE 2015 2ⁿᵈ SEP 1ˢᵗ SHIFT]

64. Which of the following memory has highest access speed?

(a) Hard Disk   (b) RAM

(c) ROM   (d) Cache memory

[RRB SSE 2015 2ⁿᵈ SEP 1ˢᵗ SHIFT]

65. The 8's complement of the octal number $(4060)_8$ is

(a) $(3720)_8$ (b) $(3717)_8$

(c) $(4020)_8$ (d) $(4720)_8$

[RRB SSE 2015 2ⁿᵈ SEP 1ˢᵗ SHIFT]

66. ROM is a_____________________
(a) Random access memory
(b) Sequential access memory
(c) Read and write memory
(d) Volatile memory
[RRB SSE 2015 2nd SEP 2nd SHIFT]

67. Virtual memory is a ________________
(a) Volatile memory of unlimited capacity
(b) Non-volatile memory of unlimited capacity
(c) A technique to execute smaller programs into larger memory
(d) A technique to execute larger programs into smaller memory
[RRB SSE 2015 2nd SEP 2nd SHIFT]

68. Considering signed-magnitude representation for negative numbers, -42 will be stored into an 8-bit memory space as
(a) 10101010
(b) 10110111
(c) 10110010
(d) 10100001
[RRB SSE 2015 2nd SEP 2nd SHIFT]

69. Considering X and Y as binary variables, the equivalent Boolean expression for Y(X + Y) is
(a) X
(b) Y
(c) XY
(d) X + Y
[RRB SSE 2015 2nd SEP 2nd SHIFT]

70. 'COBOL' is a_________________________
(a) Low-level programming language
(b) High-level programming language
(c) Assembly language
(d) Machine language
[RRB SSE 2015 2nd SEP 2nd SHIFT]

71. Which of the following statements is not correct?
(a) Interpreter is used to execute (interpret) high-level language programs
(b) Compiler is used to translate high-level language programs into machine codes
(c) Assembler is used to translate assembly language programs into machine codes
(d) Interpreter is used to execute (interpret) assembly language programs
[RRB SSE 2015 2nd SEP 2nd SHIFT]

72. Which of the following is not an Internet Service Provider (ISP) in India?
(a) BSNL
(b) Tata Consultancy Services (TCS)
(c) Reliance
(d) Airtel
[RRB SSE 2015 2nd SEP 2nd SHIFT]

73. Which of the following viruse spreads via malicious emails?
(a) Trj.Reboot
(b) Vienna
(c) JS.Fortnight
(d) Trivial.88.D
[RRB SSE 2015 2nd SEP 2nd SHIFT]

74. A microprocessor with 8-bit word length can process____________ bits data simultaneously.
(a) 4
(b) 8
(c) 16
(d) 32
[RRB SSE 2015 2nd SEP 2nd SHIFT]

75. The 15's complement of the hexadecimal number $(B0210)_{16}$ is
(a) $(4FDEF)_{16}$
(b) $(4FDF0)_{16}$
(c) $(50EF0)_{16}$
(d) $(40DE0)_{16}$
[RRB SSE 2015 2nd SEP 2nd SHIFT]

76. Which of the following CPU registers stores the address of the next instruction to be executed?
(a) Program Counter register
(b) Accumulator register
(c) Instruction register
(d) Memory Address register
[RRB SSE 2015 2nd SEP 3rd SHIFT]

77. An instruction consisting of an operation code and operand address(es) is called
(a) Mnemonics
(b) Pseudo code
(c) Assembly language instruction
(d) Machine language instruction
[RRB SSE 2015 2nd SEP 3rd SHIFT]

78. BIOS, which is a part of operating systems of PCs, stands for
(a) Binary Input Output System
(b) Basic Input Output System
(c) Basic Input Output Synchronization
(d) Binary Input Output Synchronization
[RRB SSE 2015 2nd SEP 3rd SHIFT]

79. For a memory of size 64K words with each word storing 8 bits, the size of Memory Address Register (MAR) is
(a) 8 bits
(b) 16 bits
(c) 32 bits
(d) 64 bits
[RRB SSE 2015 2nd SEP 3rd SHIFT]

80. Which of the following statements is not true about an MS-Word document?
(a) Different portions of texts may have different fonts
(b) Different portions of texts may have different font size
(c) Copy-paste texts can't be deleted
(d) A table can have only one row and column
[RRB SSE 2015 2nd SEP 3rd SHIFT]

81. Procedural language is also knwn as
(a) Functional language
(b) Imperative language
(c) Rule-based language
(d) Logic programing language
[RRB SSE 2015 2nd SEP 3rd SHIFT]

82. ASCII is a________bit code.
(a) 8 (b) 12
(c) 16 (d) 32
[RRB SSE 2015 2nd SEP 3rd SHIFT]

83. In Boolean Algebra, A + AA′ is equivalent to
(a) 0 (b) 1
(c) A (d) A'
[RRB SSE 2015 2nd SEP 3rd SHIFT]

84. The IP addresses are ________ bytes long.
(a) 2 (b) 4
(c) 8 (d) 16
[RRB SSE 2015 2nd SEP 3rd SHIFT]

85. The main reason behind the popularity of the World Wide Web is the use of the concept called
(a) PageRank
(b) Hypertext
(c) Information indexing
(d) Information retrieval
[RRB SSE 2015 2nd SEP 3rd SHIFT]

86. Program Counter (PC) register stores the
(a) Address of the first memory block
(b) Address of the last memory block
(c) Address of the next instruction to be executed
(d) Size of the primary memory
[RRB SSE 2015 3rd SEP 1st SHIFT]

87. Number of bits needed to code 64 operations is
(a) 4 (b) 6
(c) 8 (d) 16
[RRB SSE 2015 3rd SEP 1st SHIFT]

88. BIOS, which is a part of operating systems of PCs, is stored in
(a) RAM (b) Hard Disk
(c) Cache memory (d) ROM
[RRB SSE 2015 3rd SEP 1st SHIFT]

89. For a memory of size 64K words with each word storing 8 bits, the size of Memory Data Register (MDR) is
(a) 8 bits (b) 16 bits
(c) 32 bits (d) 64 bits
[RRB SSE 2015 3rd SEP 1st SHIFT]

90. Which of the following doesn't support WYSIWYG (what you see is what you get) display facility for documents?
(a) MS-Word (b) Latex Editor
(c) NotePad (d) WordPad
[RRB SSE 2015 3rd SEP 1st SHIFT]

91. Logic programming language is also known as
(a) Procedural language
(b) Low-level language
(c) Imperative language
(d) Non-procedural language
[RRB SSE 2015 3rd SEP 1st SHIFT]

92. Unicode uses ________bits to code a large number of character including various special characters.
(a) 8 (b) 16
(c) 24 (d) 32
[RRB SSE 2015 3rd SEP 1st SHIFT]

93. In Boolean Algebra, AB + AB' is equivalent to
(a) 0 (b) 1
(c) A (d) B
[RRB SSE 2015 3rd SEP 1st SHIFT]

94. In decimal-dotted notation of an IP address, the maximum value of each component can be
(a) 255 (b) 256
(c) 512 (d) 1024
[RRB SSE 2015 3rd SEP 1st SHIFT]

95. Uniform Resource Locator (URL) is a(an) __________ scheme, which WWW browsers use to locate sites on the internet.
(a) Addressing
(b) Paging
(c) Data management
(d) Ranking
[RRB SSE 2015 3rd SEP 1st SHIFT]

96. Program Counter (PC) register is an integral part of:
(a) Hard Disk (b) RAM
(c) Cache memory (d) CPU
[RRB SSE 2015 3rd SEP 2nd SHIFT]

97. Number of bits needed to code 256 operations is:
(a) 4 (b) 6
(c) 8 (d) 16
[RRB SSE 2015 3rd SEP 2nd SHIFT]

98. When power is turned on ________ takes control and does power-on-self-test.
(a) BIOS (b) ALU
(c) CU (d) RAM
[RRB SSE 2015 3rd SEP 2nd SHIFT]

99. The time interval between the time at which a read/write command is given to the memory and the time when next such instruction can be issued to the memory is called:

   (a) Access time   (b) Cycle time

   (c) Write time   (d) Seek time

[RRB SSE 2015 3rd SEP 2nd SHIFT]

100. The default alignment of texts in MS-Excel is:

   (a) Left   (b) Right

   (c) Centre   (d) Justify

[RRB SSE 2015 3rd SEP 2nd SHIFT]

101. Functional language is also known as

   (a) Procedural language

   (b) Non-procedural language

   (c) Imperative language

   (d) Low-level language

[RRB SSE 2015 3rd SEP 2nd SHIFT]

102. In a binary number, the leftmost bit is called:

   (a) Most significant bit

   (b) Least significant bit

   (c) Carry bit

   (d) Extra bit

[RRB SSE 2015 3rd SEP 2nd SHIFT]

103. In Boolean Algebra, A (A + B') is equivalent to:

   (a) 0   (b) 1

   (c) A   (d) B

[RRB SSE 2015 3rd SEP 2nd SHIFT]

104. Telnet service enables an internet user for:

   (a) File transfer

   (b) Booting remote computer

   (c) Remote login

   (d) User account creation on remote computer

[RRB SSE 2015 3rd SEP 2nd SHIFT]

105. Which of the following is not a Web browser?

   (a) Chrome   (b) FireFox

   (c) MacWeb   (d) FTP

[RRB SSE 2015 3rd SEP 2nd SHIFT]

106. Accumulator is an integral component of

   (a) CPU   (b) Hard Disk

   (c) RAM   (d) Cache memory

[RRB SSE 2015 3rd SEP 3rd SHIFT]

107. Number of bits needed to code 512 operations is

   (a) 4   (b) 7

   (c) 8   (d) 9

[RRB SSE 2015 3rd SEP 3rd SHIFT]

108. Booting the computer system is a process which

   (a) Brings operating system from hard disk to main memory

   (b) Brings operating system from main memory to hard disk

   (c) Brings all users data from hard disk to main memory

   (d) Brings all users data from main memory to hard disk

[RRB SSE 2015 3rd SEP 3rd SHIFT]

109. A variant of __________ is called flash memory.

   (a) Virtual memory   (b) Cache memory

   (c) EEPROM   (d) RAM

[RRB SSE 2015 3rd SEP 3rd SHIFT]

110. The default alignment of numeric values in MS-Excel is

   (a) Left   (b) Right

   (c) Centre   (d) Justify

[RRB SSE 2015 3rd SEP 3rd SHIFT]

111. PROLOG is a

   (a) Procedural language

   (b) Logic programming language

   (c) Imperative language

   (d) Functional language

[RRB SSE 2015 3rd SEP 3rd SHIFT]

112. In a binary number, the rightmost bit called

   (a) Most significant bit

   (b) Least significant bit

   (c) Carry bit

   (d) Extra bit

[RRB SSE 2015 3rd SEP 3rd SHIFT]

113. In Boolean Algebra, A′ (A + B′) is equivalent to

   (a) A′B   (b) AB"

   (c) AB   (d) A′B′

[RRB SSE 2015 3rd SEP 3rd SHIFT]

114. Usenet service enables a group of internet users

   (a) For remote login

   (b) For file transfer

   (c) To exchange views/information on some common topic of interest

   (d) To boot remote computer

[RRB SSE 2015 3rd SEP 3rd SHIFT]

115. Which of the following is not a Web browser?

   (a) XHTML   (b) FireFox

   (c) MacWeb   (d) Net Scape

[RRB SSE 2015 3rd SEP 3rd SHIFT]

ANSWER KEY

RRB JUNIOR ENGINEER

1. (a)	**2.** (a)	**3.** (c)	**4.** (b)	**5.** (c)	**6.** (c)	**7.** (b)	**8.** (d)	**9.** (a)	**10.** (d)
11. (d)	**12.** (a)	**13.** (c)	**14.** (d)	**15.** (a)	**16.** (b)	**17.** (b)	**18.** (c)	**19.** (a)	**20.** (d)
21. (d)	**22.** (a)	**23.** (c)	**24.** (a)	**25.** (c)	**26.** (c)	**27.** (b)	**28.** (b)	**29.** (b)	**30.** (d)
31. (c)	**32.** (b)	**33.** (d)	**34.** (d)	**35.** (d)	**36.** (c)	**37.** (b)	**38.** (b)	**39.** (c)	**40.** (d)
41. (a)	**42.** (d)	**43.** (d)	**44.** (d)	**45.** (c)	**46.** (b)	**47.** (a)	**48.** (a)	**49.** (b)	**50.** (c)
51. (c)	**52.** (c)	**53.** (b)	**54.** (d)	**55.** (c)	**56.** (a)	**57.** (d)	**58.** (a)	**59.** (b)	**60.** (c)
61. (b)	**62.** (c)	**63.** (d)	**64.** (d)	**65.** (b)	**66.** (a)	**67.** (c)	**68.** (c)	**69.** (c)	**70.** (d)
71. (b)	**72.** (c)	**73.** (a)	**74.** (d)	**75.** (d)	**76.** (c)	**77.** (a)	**78.** (b)	**79.** (c)	**80.** (a)
81. (a)	**82.** (d)	**83.** (a)	**84.** ((d)	**85.** (b)	**86.** (b)	**87.** (a)	**88.** (c)	**89.** (c)	**90.** (d)
91. (c)	**92.** (a)	**93.** (a)	**94.** (a)	**95.** (c)	**96.** (b)	**97.** (b)	**98.** (a)	**99.** (d)	**100.** (a)
101. (b)	**102.** (b)	**103.** (a)	**104.** (c)	**105.** (c)	**106.** (a)	**107.** (d)	**108.** (c)	**109.** (b)	**110.** (c)
111. (a)	**112.** (c)	**113.** (c)	**114.** (d)	**115.** (a)	**116.** (a)	**117.** (d)	**118.** (a)	**119.** (d)	**120.** (b)
121. (d)	**122.** (b)	**123.** (c)	**124.** (a)	**125.** (b)	**126.** (c)	**127.** (d)	**128.** (c)	**129.** (a)	**130.** (d)
131. (a)	**132.** (b)	**133.** (d)	**134.** (c)	**135.** (b)	**136.** (a)	**137.** (c)	**138.** (c)	**139.** (d)	**140.** (b)
141. (a)	**142.** (a)	**143.** (d)	**144.** (c)	**145.** (d)	**146.** (b)	**147.** (c)	**148.** (c)	**149.** (a)	**150.** (b)
151. (a)	**152.** (c)	**153.** (d)	**154.** (b)	**155.** (b)	**156.** (d)	**157.** (c)	**158.** (a)	**159.** (b)	**160.** (c)
161. (c)	**162.** (d)	**163.** (c)	**164.** (d)	**165.** (b)	**166.** (a)				

RRB SENIOR SECTION ENGINEER

1. (d)	**2.** (c)	**3.** (a)	**4.** (c)	**5.** (d)	**6.** (c)	**7.** (b)	**8.** (b)	**9.** (b)	**10.** (c)
11. (c)	**12.** (a)	**13.** (b)	**14.** (b)	**15.** (d)	**16.** (a)	**17.** (d)	**18.** (c)	**19.** (b)	**20.** (d)
21. (a)	**22.** (d)	**23.** (c)	**24.** (b)	**25.** (d)	**26.** (d)	**27.** (d)	**28.** (b)	**29.** (c)	**30.** (b)
31. (a)	**32.** (c)	**33.** (d)	**34.** (d)	**35.** (a)	**36.** (c)	**37.** (d)	**38.** (a)	**39.** (c)	**40.** (b)
41. (a)	**42.** (c)	**43.** (d)	**44.** (d)	**45.** (a)	**46.** (a)	**47.** (c)	**48.** (a)	**49.** (a)	**50.** (b)
51. (b)	**52.** (c)	**53.** (b)	**54.** (d)	**55.** (a)	**56.** (a)	**57.** (d)	**58.** (a)	**59.** (a)	**60.** (b)
61. (a)	**62.** (a)	**63.** (b)	**64.** (d)	**65.** (a)	**66.** (a)	**67.** (a)	**68.** (a)	**69.** (b)	**70.** (b)
71. (d)	**72.** (b)	**73.** (c)	**74.** (b)	**75.** (a)	**76.** (a)	**77.** (d)	**78.** (b)	**79.** (b)	**80.** (d)
81. (b)	**82.** (a)	**83.** (c)	**84.** (b)	**85.** (b)	**86.** (c)	**87.** (b)	**88.** (d)	**89.** (a)	**90.** (b)
91. (d)	**92.** (b)	**93.** (c)	**94.** (a)	**95.** (a)	**96.** (d)	**97.** (c)	**98.** (a)	**99.** (b)	**100.** (a)
101. (b)	**102.** (a)	**103.** (c)	**104.** (c)	**105.** (d)	**106.** (a)	**107.** (d)	**108.** (a)	**109.** (c)	**110.** (b)
111. (b)	**112.** (b)	**113.** (d)	**114.** (c)	**115.** (a)					

EXPLANATIONS

RRB JUNIOR ENGINEER

1. Optical Character Reader is full form of OCR, which can read a character and convert its bitmap image to equivalent ASCII codes.

2. It is equivalent to $0.1 = 0$

3. Arithmetic Logical Unit is not an Input device while all the other three are.

4. Floating point numbers are used in computers to represent real numbers. Since real numbers can not be accurately represented in computers through binary numbers.

5. Protocols are rules developed for exchanging and processing of data between various devices. Examples include HTTP, IP, FTTP etc.

6. Turing machine is a mathematical model of a hypothetical computing machine which can use a predefined set of rules to determine a result from a set of input variables.

7. The new standard which allocates codes to almost all languages and symbols, totaling more than a lakh is called Unicode. It makes transfer and reuse of translated data etc. very easy. Also it represents each character with 16 bits.

8. To protect passwords etc. Encryption is used which is coding each data point in a particular pattern which is not easy to decode.

9. Open source softwares like Unix have their source code freely available and these are developed through collaboration of coders from across the world. Many developers as a principle use only open source softwares.

10. All the languages mentioned here are high level languages, in which it is easier to write code.

11. 1 TB flash drive can store approximately 1 million file sizes each of 1 MB.

12. All these devices are related to computers. CPU is Central Processing Unit, while ALU is Arithmetic and Logical unit, while I/O is Input Output devices.

13. MHz is used to measure the number of operations that can be done by the CPU in 1 second. So it refers to clock speed.

14. 1111 of binary is $2^4 - 1$. It is $2^3 + 2^2 + 2^1 + 2^0$

15. An operating system (OS) is system software that manages computer hardware and software resources and provides common services for computer programs.

16. Computers understand machine language, which is written in binary or bits. So all language programs need to be converted to machine language to be executed.

17. RAM of a computer is its primary storage. It is a type of computer memory that can be accessed randomly; that is, any byte of memory can be accessed without touching the preceding bytes. RAM is found in servers, PCs, tablets, smartphones and other devices, such as printers

18. A byte is group of 8 bits. This is basically an 8-bit word.

19. Compilers translate the high level language program to machine language at once, before it is to be executed.

20. Transmission files contain transient data to be processed.

21. MS Power Point is one of the most popular presentation softwares, which helps to create attractive and structured slides. It is used in almost all offices across the world.

22. Compilers and Interpreters are System software just like Operating System. System software serves as the interface between the hardware and the end users.

23. Compilers convert high level language programs into machine language at once for execution. It basically produces and object program.

24. Operating system basically runs a computer. It is system software, meaning it acts as interface between user and hardware.

25. Database management systems need both high storage and high speed. Therefore high speed large capacity disk is ideal and most important.

26. MS word is a simple software compared to operating systems etc. It helps in particular tasks of a user, which here is creating text documents. Such softwares are called Application software.

27. Computer viruses are softwares, however they are malignant softwares which are aimed to harm the computers they reach.

28. To centre align the text is MS word, Ctrl + E command is used. Ctrl + F helps find some words in the document. Ctrl + C helps copy text while Ctrl + X helps cut text.

29. Loaders are softwares used before running programs. They load the object program from secondary memory to main memory from where it would be executed.

30. Inodes are data structures that contain information about files that are created when a file system is created. Each file has an inode and is identified by an inode number in the file system where it resides and helps the system identify the files.

31. Virtual memory is a memory management capability of an OS that uses hardware and software to allow a computer to compensate for physical memory shortages by temporarily transferring data from random access memory (RAM) to disk storage. Thus it gives the illusion of an extremely large memory.

32. Just as it appears by the words, disk scheduling means the order in which disk access requests must be served by the system.

33. Ink-jet printers are not impact printers since a jet of ink is release which sticks to paper for printing and there is not a direct contact between printer hardware and paper.

34. RAM is random access memory, so it is not sequential access.

35. RAM is not inside the CPU while all other 3 units are.

36. ASCII was developed in America and so is named accordingly. The 255 codes of ASCII represent all alphanumeric and special symbols.

37. Options A and B both represent 99. However 0.25 is represented when 2nd bit after the decimal is 1, since it's magnitude would be ¼.

38. Any Boolean variable added to 1, will always result in 1.

39. To find 2's complement an easy way would be to invert the digits and finally add 1.

40. Windows Embedded Compact, formerly Windows Embedded CE and Windows CE, is an operating system subfamily developed by Microsoft as part of its Windows Embedded family of products, esp. for mobiles. It is real-time OS.

41. Class A IP addresses use only 8 bits for Network ID and 24 bits for hosts. It is used for large networks.

42. Hadoop is an open source distributed processing framework that manages data processing and storage for big data applications running in clustered systems. It is not a web browser.

43. In laser printer a laser beam scan back and forth across a drum inside the printer, building up a pattern of static electricity. The static electricity attracts onto the page a kind of powdered ink called toner. Finally, as in a photocopier, a fuser unit bonds the toner to the paper. Thus it is not impact printer.

44. ROM is a Random access memory and not sequential.

45. Register is one of a small set of data holding places that are part of the computer processor. A register may hold an instruction, a storage address, or any kind of data. Thus it is inside the CPU, while other components are not.

46. To code 128 characters, only 7 bits are needed. Now ASCII codes have 8 bits, unlike the original ASCII code which had 7.

47. Option A and D correctly represent 129. However only option A represents 0.25, because its 2nd bit after decimal is 1 meaning its magnitude is ¼

48. Any Boolean variable added to 0, would be the same variable.

49. The number represents 140. When subtracted from 256, it gives 116. That is represented by option B. 64+32+16+4

50. Windows 7 is a multi-tasking operating system where multiple programs can be run at the same time.

51. Class A IP addresses have 1st bit as 0, and encompass the range of 0.0.0.0 to 127.255.255.255. This class is for large networks and has 8 bits for network and 24 bits for hosts.

52. www is acronym of World wide web. All others are browsers.

53. Printer is an output device where we get the result of whatever instruction we gave to the computer to print.

54. EPROM is Erasable Programmable Read Only Memory. And like all ROMs, it is Random Access Memory.

55. Registers are used to temporarily store data for ALU operations.

56. To BCD-encode a decimal number using the common encoding, each decimal digit is stored in a four-bit nibble; two digits are stored in each byte. Unlike binary encoded numbers, BCD encoded numbers can easily be displayed by mapping each of the nibbles to a different character.

57. 195.5 is represented by option D. 128+64+2+1 = 195. And 0.5 is represented by the first digit after decimal, which has a magnitude of ½.

58. Any Boolean variable multiplied by 1 will result in same value.

59. To find 2's complement an easy way would be to invert the digits and finally add 1. But the result here can't be represented in 8 bits. In 9 bits it would be 100000000. So in 8 bits it is represented by 00000000.

60. Object Linking and Embedding is a component document technology from Microsoft that allows you to dynamically link files and applications together. For instance, an Excel spreadsheet can be embedded within a Microsoft Word document using OLE.

61. An IP address which belongs to class B has the first two bits in the first octet set to 10, i.e. Class B IP Addresses range from 128.0.x.x to 191.255.x.x. So 16 bits are used for network ID.

62. XML is not a browser by extensible markup language.

63. Inkjet printer releases small jets of ink to print each character and hence there is no direct contact of printer hardware with paper, so called non-impact printer.

64. PROM is Programmable Read Only Memory. And like all ROMs, it is Random Access Memory.

65. The control unit (CU) is a component of a computer's central processing unit (CPU) that directs the operation of the processor. It tells the computer's memory, arithmetic/logic unit and input and output devices how to respond to the instructions that have been sent to the processor.

66. Binary Coded Decimal utilizes 4 bits to code decimal numbers.

67. 144 is represented as 128+16. 0.5 is represented by the first digit after the decimal point.

68. Any Boolean variable multiplied by 0 would always give value 0.

69. To find 2's complement an easy way would be to invert the digits and finally add 1.

70. Linus is an Operating system, hence system software. System softwares connect user to the computer hardware.

71. An IP address which belongs to class B has the first two bits in the first octet set to 10, i.e. Class B IP Addresses range from 128.0.x.x to 191.255.x.x. So 16 bits are used for host ID.

72. HTML is Hyper Text Markup Language, so is not a web browser.

73. Mouse is an input device which users use to click, scroll etc.

74. EEPROM is Electrically Erasable Programmable Read Only Memory. And like all ROMs, it is Random Access Memory.

75. The internal bus, also known as internal data bus, memory bus, system bus or Front-Side-Bus, connects all the internal components of a computer, such as CPU and memory, to the motherboard. The memory bus is usually in the form of a set of wires or conductors which connects electrical components and allow transfers of data and addresses from the main memory to the central processing unit (CPU) or a memory controller. It is thus not a system bus. Control bus, data bus and address bus are part of system bus.

76. EBCDIC (Extended Binary Coded Decimal Interchange Code) is a binary code for alphabetic and numeric characters that IBM developed for its larger operating systems.

77. 303.20 in Octal is equivalent to decimal number 3*8^2+3 + 2*1/8 = 195.25

78. X + X' will always be equal to 1. When X = 0, X' =1 and vice versa.

79. To find 2's complement an easy way would be to invert the digits and finally add 1. SO here all 1's get inverted to 0's . And then 1 is added to rightmost bit. So answer is 00000001.

80. When interacting with the Unix operating system, one of the first things you need to know is that, unlike other computer systems, everything in Unix is case-sensitive. So one has to be careful when typing in commands.

81. The first octet of Class C IP address has its first 3 bits set to 110, that is: Class C IP addresses range from 192.0.0.x to 223.255.255.x . So only 8 bits are needed for Host ID.

82. FTP is file transfer protocol and not an email protocol.

83. A joystick is an input device consisting of a stick that pivots on a base and reports its angle or direction to the device it is controlling.

84. Cache memory has been created to be random access and not sequential access.

85. Address bus is Unidirectional because the microprocessor is addressing a specific memory location. Outside devices can not write into Microprocessor. (Please change answer key to B here)

86. EBCDIC (Extended Binary Coded Decimal Interchange Code) is a binary code for alphabetic and numeric characters that IBM developed for its larger operating systems. It uses 8 bits to code different characters.

87. 7D. 40 in hexadecimal is equal to 7*16+13 + 4*1/16 in decimal = 125.25

88. X.X' is always 0, because when X = 1, X' = 0 and vice versa.

89. To find 2's complement an easy way would be to invert the digits and finally add 1. So here all 1's get inverted to 0's . And then 1 is added to rightmost bit.

90. High level languages are independent of the type of computer and also they are easy to write code in. eg. Java, C, C++ etc.

91. The first octet of Class C IP address has its first 3 bits set to 110, that is: Class C IP addresses range from 192.0.0.x to 223.255.255.x . So only 8 bits are needed for Host ID. Mean 24 bits for Network ID.

92. W3C is World Wide Web Consortium. It is the main international standards organization for the World Wide Web.

93. Monitor is an Output device which displays results according to the user's instructions to the computer.

94. RAM is the primary storage and it is directly accessible by the CPU for its functioning.

95. Static RAM holds data which is not refreshed regularly unlike Dynamic RAM. Therefore its speed is faster.

96. UTF-8 is a variable width character encoding capable of encoding all 1,112,064 valid code points in Unicode using one to four 8-bit bytes. The encoding is defined by the Unicode standard, and was originally designed by Ken Thompson and Rob Pike.

97. E1.80 in hexadecimal = $14*16+1+8*1/16$ in decimal = 225.5

98. $X+XY' = X(1+Y') = X.1 = X$

99. To find 2's complement an easy way would be to invert the digits and finally add 1. So here all 1's get inverted to 0's . And then 1 is added to rightmost bit.

100. Compilers convert High level programs written by users into machine codes, which then become standard to execute on a computer.

101. Class A IP addresses, where the 1st bit is 0, encompass the range of 0.0.0.0 to 127.255.255.255. This class is for large networks and has 8 bits for network and 24 bits for hosts. Thus only the first bit is used to identify class. So 1 bit.

102. A personal area network (PAN) is a computer network for interconnecting devices centered on an individual person's workspace. A PAN provides data transmission amongst devices such as computers, smartphones, tablets and personal digital assistants. Thus it occupies the smallest geographical area.

103. Cache memory is volatile since it is only needed for small periods during program executions.

104. Static RAM holds data which is not refreshed regularly unlike Dynamic RAM. Therefore DRM is slower.

105. UTF-16 (16-bit Unicode Transformation Format) is a character encoding capable of encoding all 1,112,064 valid code points of Unicode. The encoding is variable-length, as code points are encoded with one or two 16-bit code units

106. 407 in Octal = $4*8^2+7 = 16^2 + 7 = 107$ in Hexadecimal.

107. $Y+ XY = Y(1+X) = Y.1 = Y$

108. To find 2's complement an easy way would be to invert the digits and finally add 1. So here all 1's get inverted to 0's . And then 1 is added to rightmost bit.

109. A Trojan horse or Trojan is a type of malware that is often disguised as legitimate software. Trojans can be employed by cyber-thieves and hackers trying to gain information. However it does not self-replicate.

110. In class B IP addresses Class is 10, so 2 bits are needed to identify the class.

111. A wide area network is a telecommunications network or computer network that extends over a large geographical distance/place. Wide area networks are often established with leased telecommunication circuits.

112. DVD (an abbreviation of digital versatile disk) is a digital optical disk storage format invented and developed by Philips and Sony in 1995.

113. Memory can be treated as both input and output device because instructions can be taken from the memory and the output or result can be written and stored in the memory.

114. UTF-32 stands for Unicode Transformation Format in 32 bits. It is a protocol to encode Unicode code points that uses exactly 32 bits per Unicode code point. SO it is fixed width.

115. A0E in hexadecimal = $10*16^2+14 = 5*16^2 + 8+6 = 5* 8^3 + 8 + 6 = 5016$ in Octadecimal.

116. $X(X+Y') = X + XY' = X(1+Y') = X.1 = X$

117. To find 2's complement an easy way would be to invert the digits and finally add 1. So here all 1's get inverted to 0's . And then 1 is added to rightmost bit.

118. A file-infecting virus is a type of malware that infects executable files with the intent to cause permanent damage or make them unusable. A file-infecting virus overwrites code or inserts infected code into a executable file.

119. In class C IP addresses Class is 110, so 3 bits are needed to identify the class.

120. A local area network is a set of physically interconnected computers and computer equipment within a limited area. This area may be one building or a limited number of buildings. LAN's are connected together to create WAN. Thus LAN is a general purpose network as it is most commonly used network especially within organizations.

121. Keyboard is an input device but it can't be pointed, it can be typed on.

122. Size is a physical feature, which is not valid when characterizing storage as across the years size has been decreasing significantly for same storage capacity.

123. Turnaround time is a standard term used in computer and all everyday projects to denote the time elapsed between submission of a job and getting the results.

124. options A and B both represent 45 correctly. However, 0.25 is ¼ which is represented correctly by option A, since the significance of the 2nd bit after the decimal point is ¼.

125. Any variable when added to 1 will always result in the value of 1.

126. MNEMONIC is a pattern of letters, ideas, or associations that assists in remembering something. So, it is usually used by assembly language programmers to remember the "OPERATIONS" a machine can do, like "ADD" and "MUL" and "MOV" etc.

127. Wordpress is an application to create Blogs and Web pages, and is not a Word Processor unlike others.

128. IPv4 address is 32 bits. There are four numbers to be stored and all are represented by 8 bits.

129. Internet Explorer is one of the earliest Web browsers and one of the most popular because it is bundled with Microsoft Windows.

130. As is the practical experience of users, touch screen is the simplest to use and most intuitive input device.

131. RAM and ROM are both Random access. You don't have to go sequentially to access data. That is a major requirement as well to be able to access the data fast.

132. Unix is multi-user and time-sharing operating system, where multiple users can operate their own programs simultaneously or multitask as well.

133. 101010.011 The whole number part totals to be 42. The fractional part totals to be 0.25+0.125 = 0.375.

134. Any variable multiplied by 0 would always result in 0.

135. Assembly language is a machine-dependent, low-level language that uses words instead of binary code to program a specific computer system. Programmers use an assembler to create the machine code for a particular computer system.

136. Mail merge is a component of MS-word where it is used to create a standard mail template to send to individuals.

137. Internet is a Wide area network since it connects computer systems across the world.

138. Google Chrome is one of the most popular web browsers currently.

139. Optical Mark Readers reads pencil or pen marks made in pre-defined positions on paper forms as responses to questions or tick list prompts.

140. EPROM and EEPROM are Erasable Programmable Read-Only Memory and is a type of non-volatile memory used in computers. EEPROM is integrated in microcontrollers for smart cards and remote keyless system etc. They are Random Access Memories.

141. Unix operating system is written in C language. Its history dates back to 1969.

142. the binary number represents 106.25 . So the Octal number will have 2 after the decimal. The whole number part of option A totals to 106. So it is the answer.

143. XY+X'Y = (X+X')Y = 1.Y = Y

144. Interpreters are used to translate high level language code into machine language, one instruction at a time and execute those instructions.

145. MS-Access is a project management application, which can also manage databases.

146. Internet Protocol is not application layer protocol, but the principal communications protocol in the Internet protocol suite for relaying datagrams across network boundaries. Its routing function enables internetworking, and essentially establishes the Internet.

147. Netscape is one of the earliest browsers which was quite popular in 1990s and competed with Microsoft's Internet Explorer.

148. MICR (magnetic ink character recognition) is a technology used to verify the legitimacy or originality of paper documents, especially cheques. Special ink, which is sensitive to magnetic fields, is used in the printing of certain characters on the original documents. Thus banks use it.

149. EEPROM is Electrically Erasable Programmable Read Only Memory. And like all ROMs, it is Random Access Memory.

150. Time-sharing is done by operating systems to provide fast response to each user sharing the system, instead of making them wait for turn sequentially.

151. To convert binary number to hexadecimal, take 4 bits from left together and convert t hexadecimal. So 1101010 gets converted to 6 and 10 or basically 6A. .01 in binary is 0.25 which is .4 in Hexadecimal.

152. X'Y + X'Y' = X' (Y+Y') = X' .1 = X'

153. COBOL language is quite popular in business data processing.

154. In cut-paste operation, just like copy paste, once a text piece is cut it can be pasted multiple times.

155. Class A IP addresses encompass the range of 0.0.0.0 to 127.255.255.255. So only B can be correct.

156. Safari web browser has been developed by Apple for its computers.

157. Computers are diligent in their operations means they are highly accurate and always give out the required output if the input is correct.

158. Optical Character Reader can read a character and convert its bitmap image to equivalent ASCII codes.

159. Inkjet printer releases small jets of ink to print each character and hence there is no direct contact of printer hardware with paper, so called non-impact printer.

160. Multiprocessing system uses multiple CPUs to process different instructions from same program or independent programs simultaneously.

161. $n^2 + 1 = 65$. Therefore $n^2 = 64$ or n=8.

162. XY'+X'Y' = (X+X')Y' = 1.Y' = Y'

163. 81 = 64+16+1 = 01010001 (Please change answer key to C)

164. MS-word can't be used to calculate. Other functions mentioned in the question can be done in MS-word.

165. An IP address which belongs to class B has the first two bits in the first octet set to 10, i.e. Class B IP Addresses range from 128.0.x.x to 191.255.x.x. The default subnet mask for Class B is 255.255.x.x. Hence only 2 bytes or 16 bits are required to identify class.

166. iOS is an operating system and not an antivirus software.

RRB SENIOR SECTION ENGINEER

1. Powerpoint is not an operating system but an application to make presentation slides.

2. When users can see something very similar to end result while document creation, it is called WYSIWYG.

3. It is the correct representation where user gives input in high level language, it is then compiled and becomes machine language which is computed and the output is similarly provided to the user.

4. The modem is an input and an output device. It is used for sending and receiving information and data over telephone lines.

5. LINUX software was invented by Linus Torvalds while studying computer science at University of Helsinki in 1991.

7. Processing speed is measured in MHz. Nowadays it is even measured in GHz i.e. Giga Hertz. Basically it represents how many operations can be processed in 1 second.

8. To close applications such as Powerpoint, MS-word etc. one must click the close button on the title bar which is at the top right hand corner.

9. ++I in C means i = i + 2. This was a way developed to write smaller lines in code.

10. != means not equal to in C.

11. Microsoft Windows is the world's most popular commercial operating system for PCs.

12. Compilers are used to translate entire programs from High level language to machine language, so that computer can understand and execute it.

13. When we type text, Auto correct feature corrects the word's spelling or any other portion of the text.

14. Primary storage, also known as main storage or memory, is the area in a computer in which data is stored for quick access by the computer's processor. The terms random access memory (RAM) and memory are often used as synonyms for primary or main storage.

15. An electronic spreadsheet like MS-Excel consists of Cells which are arranged in Rows and Columns. So all are present.

16. Word document gets an extension .Doc by default.

17. SMTP, simple mail transfer protocol, is used for sending e-mails.

18. Use of a cache where the frequently needed data is stored increases the available speed of memory access.

19. CPU when interrupted acknowledges the interrupt and branches off subroutine for other processes.

20. MODEM helps the computer in long distance communication and become a communication link, since it can receive and send signals.

21. Digitization means converting Analog signals to Digital signals.

22. Multiplexing is a method by which multiple analog or digital signals are combined into one signal over a shared medium. The aim is to share a scarce resource. For example, in telecommunications, several telephone calls may be carried using one wire.

23. Memory unit holds data and instructions for processing.

24. Assembly language is in codes which needs to be changed into machine language for execution. This is function of Assembler.

25. Buffer is a location where temporary data can be saved.

26. A CPU needs Registers to help it work, while it can work without RAM or Hard Disk

27. Hadoop is a big data software and not an Operating System.

28. -128 in 2's complement will be 128 represented in Base 2. So 10000000

29. As shown below $(X+Y)' = X'.Y'$

X	Y	X + Y	(X+Y)'	X'	Y'	X'.Y'
0	0	0	1	1	1	1
0	1	1	0	1	0	0
1	0	1	0	0	1	0
1	1	1	0	0	0	0

30. Java is a High Level programming Language which has evolved through other stages and is easier to write programs in

31. Machine Language depends on the type of machine it is written for, therefore machine dependent and it is tougher to write programs in compared to Higher Level languages

32. Hyper Text Transfer protocol was established so that two computers connected on a network can talk to each other without any understanding or transmission loss. It is used in the beginning of Network URLs.

33. Viruses can steal hard disk space or CPU time and even log keystrokes. However they cannot increase or decrease word length of CPU, which is an in-built parameter.

34. All others are examples of Read Only memory, while EEEPROM does not exist

35. $(A10)_{16} = 10 \times 16^2 + 16 + 0 = 2576$. In 16's complement it's value would be 4096-2576 = 1280

1280 is represented as $5 \times 16^2 + 15 \times 16 + 0 = 5F0$

36. Cache Memory works on the locality of reference principle because it locally stores content in faster memory which is referred more.

37. QNX is a real time operating system aimed at the embedded systems market.

38. 126 is written as 01111110. 1's complement means every bit needs to be reversed. 0 to be changed to 1 and 1 to 0. So it would be 10000001.

39. As we can see from table, $(X.Y)' = X' + Y'$

X	Y	X'	Y'	(X.Y)	(X.Y)'	X'+Y'
0	0	1	1	0	1	1
0	1	1	0	0	1	1
1	0	0	1	0	1	1
1	1	0	0	1	0	0

40. C is a high level programming language which has evolved through other stages and is easier to write programs in

41. Assembly Language depends on the type of machine it is written for, therefore machine dependent and it is tougher to write programs in compared to Higher Level languages

42. Hyper Text Transfer protocol was established so that two computers connected on a network can talk to each other without any understanding or transmission loss. It is used in the beginning of Network URLs. It's secure version is called HTTPS

43. Interrupts are not viruses because they are not malignant softwares but internal problems

44. In Magnetic tape we can move from one data point to other in a sequence and not directly. While in other storages we can. So it is Sequential Access memory.

45. To find 2's complement an easy way would be to invert the digits and finally add 1.

46. Wi Fi stands for Wireless Fidelity

47. UNIX is not real time or distributed but it is a multitasking operating system.

48. To find 2's complement an easy way would be to invert the digits and finally add 1.

49. X.(X+Y) = X + X.Y = X (1 + Y) = X .1 = X

50. C++ is a high level programming language which has evolved through other stages and is easier to write programs in

51. High level programming language is machine independent since it can run on any machine after compilation.

52. Tim Berners-Lee invented world wide web for use in his college network, which later got adopted by organizations and nations.

53. Meve virus does not overwrite or corrupt programs, but it corrupts files and documents which are used in any way.

54. Byte represents 8 bits and it is not a unit to measure CPU speed of processing, but just the length of a data point.

55. 00111100 represents 60. Its 2's complement would be 256-60 = 196. It is written as 11000100

56. MODEM is short for Modulator Demodulator, which represents the frequency it modulates and then demodulates to receive and emit signal

57. Unix is an Operating system, so basically a system software.

58. 85 is represented as 01010101, so it's 1's complement would be reverse of each bit. So it is 10101010

59. X + XY = X (1+Y) = X .1 = X

60. FORTRAN was the world's first high level programming language.

61. High level programming languages are not dependent on machine, since they can run on all machines after compilation.

62. HTML is used to write on Web pages and this standard was developed and named Hyper Text Markup Language

63. Vienna virus is found in Root Directory but keeps changing location

64. CACHE memory being localized has highest access speed and hence is used to store data that is used most frequently.

65. 4060 = 4×8^3 + 6×8 = 2096. It's complement would be 4096-2096 = 2000, which is represented as 3×8^3 + 7×8^2 + 2×8

66. ROM can be accessed Randomly from any point. Unlike Magnetic Tape, it is not sequential.

67. Virtual memory is a memory management capability of an OS that uses hardware and software to allow a computer to compensate for physical memory shortages by temporarily transferring data from random access memory (RAM) to disk storage. So it is volatile and of unlimited storage.

68. In signed magnitude representation, left most bit is kept 1 for negative numbers and 0 for positive numbers. Rest of the bits represent the magnitude of the number. Here leftmost bit would be 1, and then write 42 in binary in 7 bits. So answer is 10101010

69. Y(X+Y) = YX + Y = Y (X+1) = Y.1 = Y

70. COBOL is a high level programming language which has evolved through other stages and is easier to write programs in

71. Interpreter executes high level language programs and not machine level language programs. It is done by assembler.

72. TCS does not provide Internet Service in India, while BSNL, Airtel and Reliance do.

73. JS Fortnight spreads by mail but other viruses attack the computers they are in and don't spread by mail.

74. 8 bit microprocessor can process 8 bits simultaneously. Similarly for other bits.

75. 15's complement of Hexadecimal number is simply reversing the digits, that is changing them so that sum of original and new digits is 15. So 4 becomes B or F becomes 0.

76. Program counter register is used to store the next instruction to be executed in a program to make it run faster. All the three registers mentioned here are for different functions as their names also suggest.

77. Machine language programs are run directly by computers. (They don't need compiler or interpreter). So a machine language instruction must contain operation code and operand address.

78. BIOS stands for Basic Input Output System. The BIOS helps set the computer's input output devices and their functions whenever a PC is started.

79. MAR holds the memory location of data that needs to be accessed. When reading from memory, data addressed by MAR is fed into the MDR (memory data register) and then used by the CPU. For memory of 64K with with each word storing 8 bits, MAR should be of 16 bits to be able to hold two words simultaneously.

80. In MS Word, a table can have any number of rows and columns. All other statements are true.

81. A procedural language is a type of computer programming language that contains a systematic order of statements, functions and commands to complete a computational task or program. Procedural language is also known as imperative language.

82. ASCII is a 8 bit code. It contains 255 different alphanumeric and special symbols.

83. AA' is always zero. Since when A is 1, A' is 0 and vice versa. So A+AA' = A.

84. IP addresses are 4 bytes long. That is they are made of 4 different number separated by dots. Example 192.168.1.15

85. World wide web is popular because of Hypertext and its transfer protocol as well as its markup language. HTTP and HTML.

86. Program Counter Register always stores address of the next instruction to be executed. It is quite evident from its name also. This makes the program execution process fast.

87. To code 64 operations number of bits needed = 6, because $2^6 = 64$. If we have less than 6 bits we can code maximum of 32 operations.

88. BIOS is always stored in ROM, because it should be rewritten or deleted by the computer operator. It can be Read or Accessed only.

89. When reading from memory, data addressed by Memory Access Register is fed into the MDR (memory data register) and then used by the CPU. For memory of 64K with each word storing 8 bits, MDR should be of 8 bits to be able to hold one word.

90. Latex Editor does not support WYSIWYG because its structure of data arrangement is codeable unlike MS-word, Notepad etc. Therefore it is often used by Mathematicians and other high level Science content creators.

91. Logic programming is a type of programming paradigm which is largely based on formal logic. Any program written in a logic programming language is a set of sentences in logical form, expressing facts and rules about some problem domain. Hence it is called non-procedural language

92. Unicode uses two bytes (16 bits) for each character but can only encode the first 65,536 code points, the so-called Basic Multilingual Plane (BMP). The first 128 codes are same as ASCII.

93. AB + AB' = A (B + B') = A.1 = A

94. In decimal-dotted notation, maximum value of each component can be 255 because it is coded using 8 bits.

95. URL helps world wide web find the address of a website or webpage, hence it is an addressing scheme.

96. Program Counter Register is used to store information regards next instruction to be executed. Hence it is located in the CPU and an integral part.

97. 256 operations would need 8 bits, because $2^8 = 256$

98. BIOS (Basic Input Output System) takes control and does power-on-self-test when Power is turned on in a PC.

99. Cycle time is the time between execution of one command and the next. It shows the speed of the CPU.

100. By default text in MS-word is left aligned just like a normal handwritten document or a standard typed document.

101. A functional language is a programming language built over and around logical functions or procedures within its programming structure. It is based on and is similar to mathematical functions in its program flow. Hence it is called non-procedural language.

102. Leftmost bit is the highest magnitude bit in binary. Hence it is called the most significant bit.

103. A(A+B') = A + AB' = A(1+B') = A.1 = A

104. Telnet is a protocol that allows you to connect to remote computers (called hosts) over a TCP/IP network (such as the internet). Using telnet client software on your computer, you can make a connection to a telnet server, which is the remote host.

105. FTP is not a web browser but used to transfer data on locally connected systems.

106. An accumulator is a register for short-term, intermediate storage of arithmetic and logic data in a computer's CPU (central processing unit). In modern computers, any register can function as an accumulator.

107. $512 = 2^9$. Hence 9 bits are needed to code 512 operations.

108. When a computer is booted, it basically means started for operations, the operating system is brought to the main memory from the hard disk where it is always stored.

109. Flash memory is basically a version of EEPROM. It is a read-only memory whose contents can be erased and reprogrammed using a pulsed voltage: Electrically Erasable Programmable Read-Only Memory

110. When you write numbers in MS-Excel, they are right aligned by default and can be changed by user as per need.

111. Prolog is a general-purpose logic programming language associated with artificial intelligence and computational linguistics.

112. In a binary number, the rightmost bit represents the base to the power 0. And just like a decimal number, it is the least magnitude bit, hence called least significant bit.

113. $A'(A+B') = A'A + A'B' = 0 + A'B' = A'B'$

114. Usenet is a worldwide distributed discussion system available on computers. It was developed from the general-purpose UUCP dial-up network architecture. Hence it enables a group of internet users to exchange information/views on a common topic of interest or any other discussion.

115. XHTML is not a Web browser but Extensible Hypertext Markup Language (XHTML), which is part of the family of XML markup languages.

Printed by Libri Plureos GmbH in Hamburg,
Germany